Internet Effectively:

A Beginner's Guide to the World Wide Web

Internet Effectively:
A Beginner's Guide to the World Wide Web

First Edition

Tyrone Adams
University of Louisiana, Lafayette

Sharon Scollard
Mohawk College of Applied Arts and Technology

Norman Clark
Appalachian State University

PEARSON

Addison
Wesley

Boston San Francisco New York
London Toronto Sydney Tokyo Singapore Madrid
Mexico City Munich Paris Cape Town Hong Kong Montreal

Senior Acquisitions Editor: Michael Hirsch
Project Editor: Maite Suarez-Rivas
Production Supervisor: Marilyn Lloyd
Marketing Manager: Michelle Brown
Marketing Coordinator: Jake Zavracky
Project Management: Elizabeth Hopwood/Dartmouth Publishing, Inc.
Composition: Gillian Hall/The Aardvark Group
Copyeditor: Jay Donahue
Technical Art: Dartmouth Publishing, Inc.
Proofreader: Kathy Cantwell
Text Design: Alisa Andreola/Dartmouth Publishing, Inc.
Cover Design: Joyce Cosentino Wells
Cover Image: ©2005 Photodisc
Prepress and Manufacturing: Caroline Fell

Access the latest information about Addison-Wesley titles from our World Wide Web site: http://www.aw-bc.com/computing

Many of the designations used by manufacturers and sellers to distinguish their products are claimed as trademarks. Where those designations appear in this book, and Addison-Wesley was aware of a trademark claim, the designations have been printed in initial caps or all caps.

The programs and applications presented in this book have been included for their instructional value. They have been tested with care, but are not guaranteed for any particular purpose. The publisher does not offer any warranties or representations, nor does it accept any liabilities with respect to the programs or applications.

Library of Congress Cataloging-in-Publication Data

Adams, Tyrone.
   Internet effectively : a beginner's guide to the World Wide Web / Tyrone Adams, Sharon Scollard.-- 1st ed.
       p. cm.
   Includes bibliographical references and index.
   ISBN 0-321-30429-2
   1. Internet. 2. World Wide Web. I. Scollard, Sharon. II. Title.

 TK5105.875.I57A33423 2006
 004.67'8--dc22

                                                        2004060169

ISBN 0-321-30429-2
3 4 5 6 7 8 9 10-CRK-08070605

To my loving wife Brenda and two children,
Alexander and Cecilia
—Ty Adams

To my children, Angela, Robyn, and Andrew
—Sharon Scollard

Preface

Wow! Some 10 or 15 years ago, most people had not even heard about the Internet. Today, not only have most folks heard about the Internet, they can't imagine a world without it. There's no doubt about it either, we're living in the "Digital Age." Keeping in touch with your friends and family? Send them email, digital pictures, or chat online. Going on a vacation or trip? Get directions on the Web, reserve your airline ticket and hotel on the Web, and look at a live Webcam to see the beach you're heading to. Want to work from home? Not a problem, because now you can connect to your workstation over the Internet, and send that important document as an email attachment. What once took days, weeks, or even months to deliver can now be done in a matter of seconds. Of course, this has totally revolutionized how people, businesses, and institutions *communicate* and *interact* with one another.

It has probably become increasingly clear to you, given that you have likely had some experience "surfing the 'Net," that not everyone out there knows what they are doing. There's a vast difference between simply being online, and effectively using the Internet—and, moreover, understanding the profound impact it has on our world. And, that's precisely why we have written *Internet Effectively: A Beginner's Guide to the World Wide Web*. We want to take you on something of a journey. We will show you what the Internet and World Wide Web is, how it works, how you can maximize your time and efforts online, and how it continues to affect society. We want to be your personal guides to effectively using the Internet.

Expanding the Internet and Web Skills of Novice Users

Today, becoming literate entails more than simply learning how to read and write. Nowadays, it also means possessing a fluency in online technologies. Becoming literate now includes learning to send email, successfully searching online resources, and understanding Web technologies. We wrote this book for many reasons. But, the main reason is because our students told us that they wanted to know more than just *how* to do something online; they also wanted to know *why* they were doing it. So, this book is primarily dedicated to all those students in our classes who dared to ask the humble question: "But why?"

This book is a guide to both using and understanding the Internet. Each chapter provides not only step-by-step guidelines, but also useful background information to help you become proficient with many Internet skills. There are also ideas and exercises to reinforce what you're learning, and push you a little further. By reading this book and doing the exercises at the end of each chapter, your Internet experiences and proficiencies will multiply.

Understanding How the Internet Impacts Our World

In addition to the obvious changes that the Internet has brought to our daily lives, it also has brought with it interesting social, communication, ethical, and legal issues. Have you ever downloaded music or a movie using a peer-to-peer sharing program? Should you be doing that? Did you know that IM chat programs have introduced a new way to communicate with acronyms? LOL!!! It used to be the case that living in a remote part of the world was isolating. Not any more. You can take courses at major universities around the world, purchase products, and catch up on news, all via the Internet. How is this changing society? Are lawmakers able to keep up with all these changes? Does freedom of speech exist on the Internet? Is my privacy protected on the Internet? These ideas will become clear as you read this book.

Who Should Read This Book?

Internet Effectively provides a useful resource, whether you are new to the Internet or a veteran hacker. If you're new, you will be guided step-by-step. If you're proficient, you will find background information, helpful tips, and services and resources you may not be aware of. There are no prerequisites for using this book. It is appropriate for any standalone course that introduces the Internet and the World Wide Web. It is also designed to be used in a computer literacy or computer fluency course that has extensive coverage of Internet topics. There is substantial coverage of Web design and HTML coding, allowing *Internet Effectively* to be used in a beginning Web design course.

Even if you aren't taking a course, this book has a lot to offer. The breadth of topics we cover makes this a useful information resource to increase what you are able to accomplish with the Internet and World Wide Web.

Organization of the Book

This book consists of 15 chapters, divided into 5 parts.

> **Part 1** **"Welcome to the Internet"** provides readers with basic information on the history of the Internet, and gives them an opportunity to get online and get hands-on experience early on.
>
> **Part 2** **"Utilizing the Internet and the World Wide Web"** focuses on the skills needed for everyday use of the World Wide Web. This includes detailed chapters on conducting effective searches, maximizing the use of email, and the growing area of E-Commerce.
>
> **Part 3** **"Designing Information for the World Wide Web"** covers the skills and concepts needed for the basic design of Web sites. This part includes chapters covering basic HTML, more advanced Web design using Cascading Style Sheets and XHTML, HTML editors, and images and multimedia.

Part 4 **"Communication on the Internet"** discusses the way that communication has evolved as a result of the Internet. It includes chapters on mass communication via mailing lists and newsgroups, real-time communication by way of chat clients and teleconferencing, and online entertainment and education.

Part 5 **"The Impact of the Internet"** covers how the world has been affected by the development of the Internet. It includes a chapter on how traditional media has been impacted, a chapter on legal issues surrounding the Internet, and a look at the future innovations that will continue to shape the Internet.

Covers Core Material from Curriculum 2001's Recommendation for Net-Centric Computing

In December 2001, a joint task force of the IEEE Computer Society and the Association for Computing Machinery released *Computing Curricula 2001* (http://www.computer.org/organization/cc2001/final). The report recommends that every undergraduate computer science degree program incorporates 15 hours of instruction related to net-centric computing issues. *Internet Effectively* covers all the major topics outlined in the model syllabus for CS 130, Introduction to the World Wide Web. The table below shows the mapping between the units of CS 130 and the chapters of this book.

Unit	Name	Chapter(s)
NC1	Introduction to net-centric computing	1, 2
NC2	Communication and networking	2
NC3	Network security	2, 4, 5, 10, 11, 12
NC4	The Web as an example of client-server computing	1, 2, 3, 7
NC5	Building Web applications	6, 7, 8, 9
NC6	Network management	2
NC7	Compression and decompression	4, 9
NC8	Multimedia data technologies	9
HC5	Graphical user interface design	6, 7, 8, 9
HC7	HCI aspects of multimedia systems	3, 6, 7, 8, 9
SE3	Software tools and environments	1, 3, 6, 7, 8, 9
SP6	Intellectual property	9, 10, 14
SP7	Privacy and civil liberties	4, 5, 13, 14

Supplements

The following supplements are available to all readers of this book at `http://www.aw-bc.com/adams_scollard`

- An organized list linking to the Web sites mentioned in the book.
- The HTML pages created in the Web programming chapters.
- Images used in chapters and exercises.
- Links to the most current technical news and legal information about the Internet.

The following supplements are available to qualified instructors only. Please contact your local Addison-Wesley representative, or send an email to `aw.cse@aw.com`, for information about how to access them.

- All code and image examples from the book.
- Solutions to end-of-chapter exercises and projects.
- PowerPoint lecture slides outlining the material in each chapter.
- A test bank with more than 300 multiple-choice, short answer, and true/false questions.

All material is also available in CourseCompass™, WebCT, and BlackBoard versions. CourseCompass is a nationally hosted, dynamic, interactive online course management system powered by BlackBoard, leaders in the development of Internet-based learning tools. This easy-to-use and customizable program enables professors to tailor content and functionality to meet individual course needs. To see a demo, visit `http://www.coursecompass.com`. Please contact your local Addison-Wesley representative for more information on obtaining Web content in these various formats.

Acknowledgments

We would like to thank the following people for their content and accuracy reviews. We consider you an important part of our book team, and this is a better book because of your participation. Thanks to:

Carlene Woodside, Southeastern Community College

Jennifer L. Gregg, University of Louisville

Joanne Pinkston-McDuffie, Daytona Beach Community College

Kenny Atkins, Cabrillo College

Lucia Oxendale, West Virginia University Institute of Technology

P. J. Teel, Victor Valley College

Victoria Staifer, University of Toledo

Elizabeth Haynes, University of Southern Mississippi

The people at Addison-Wesley are a top-notch team. The following deserve our thanks and praise for their hard work and various contributions: Maite Suarez-Rivas, Marilyn Lloyd, Michelle Brown, Joyce Cosentino Wells, Bethany Tidd, and Caroline Fell.

Tyrone L. Adams: First, I must thank my wife, Brenda Adams, who has been a guiding light in my life. Next, to my children, Alexander and Cecilia, you are my pride and joy! Thanks to my mother and father, Betty and Fred Adams. To my disciplinary mentor Steve Smith, from the University of Arkansas: thanks for teaching me how to think freely. To my mentor at Florida State University, Marilyn J. Young: thanks for teaching me how to write. And, to my supervisors at the University of Louisiana at Lafayette, Michael Maher and David Barry: thanks for your patience. Another big thanks goes to my research assistants: Leah Dishong (who worked on the bibliography) and Amy Fowdy (who did some great proofreading). There are many others that I would like to thank: The Becker 3, Violeta Antorveza, Phil Auter, Kathleen S. Kelly, Phillip LaFleur, Jo Ann Mendoza, and Bob Schrag. Most importantly, however, I would like to thank our editor at Addison-Wesley, Michael Hirsch, for taking on this project with focus and grace. And to my co-author "Prolific" Sharon Scollard: *you go girl!*

Sharon Scollard: We all have special people in our lives from whom we draw strength. I believe I am more fortunate than most in that regard. I certainly drew on their strength during this project. Thanks to my children, Angela, Robyn, and Andrew, who found a very distracted mom sitting in front of her computer, saying "just a minute," while she wrote one more paragraph. Thanks also to Richard Aron, for your technical input and tremendous personal support. A big thanks to friends and family; your support is always treasured. Thanks Ty, for the late-night chat meetings and perseverance. And finally, a big "thank you" goes to our editor Michael Hirsch, for your gentle guidance and vision, which allowed this project to evolve.

Brief Contents

Part 1	*Welcome to the Internet!*	1
Chapter 1	Let's Get Online, Already! 3	
Chapter 2	The Development of the Internet 29	

Part 2	*Utilizing the Internet and World Wide Web*	51
Chapter 3	Finding Resources on the World Wide Web 53	
Chapter 4	Email 85	
Chapter 5	Doing Business on the Web 137	

Part 3	*Designing Information for the World Wide Web*	157
Chapter 6	An Introduction to HTML 159	
Chapter 7	An Introduction to CSS, XHTML, and Advanced Web Development Concepts 201	
Chapter 8	HTML Editors 227	
Chapter 9	Graphics and Multimedia on the World Wide Web 277	

Part 4	*Communication on the Internet*	307
Chapter 10	Mass Communication Tools 309	
Chapter 11	Real-Time Communication 341	
Chapter 12	Entertainment and Education 365	

Part 5	*The Impact of the Internet*	385
Chapter 13	The Internet's Impact on Traditional Media 387	
Chapter 14	The Internet and the Law 407	
Chapter 15	Keeping Pace with Innovations 437	

Glossary		455

References and Readings		469

Index		479

Contents

Part 1   Welcome to the Internet!   **1**

Chapter 1   Let's Get Online, Already!   **3**

What Do People Do Online?   4

Connecting to the Internet   5
    What Does Internet Service Include?   6

Dial-up Services   6
    Traditional Dial-up Services   6
    Broadband Services   7
    Wi-Fi   8

ISPs for Travelers   9

Connecting to Work   10
    Local Area Networks   10
    Intranets   10
    Virtual Private Networks   11

Acceptable Use Policies and Privacy Policies   11

Hand-Held and Other Devices   12

Internet Software   12
    URLs   13
    Web Browser Basics   13
    Advertisements on the Web   20
    Email Clients   22

Security Risks   22
    Virus   22
    Trojan Horse   22
    Worm   22
    Adware   22
    Spyware   23
    Browser Hijacker   23
    Web Bug   23
    Mini Distributed Denial of Service Attacks (mDDoS)   23

Security Measures   23

Providing Credit Card and Other Sensitive Information   24

Downloading Software   24
    Commercial Software   25
    Shareware   25
    Freeware   25
    Open Source   25

What Happens When You Connect?   25
   IP Addresses   25
   Domain Name System   26
   Troubleshooting   26
Summary   27
Review Questions and Hands-on Exercises   27

Chapter 2 The Development of the Internet   29

Welcome to the Internet   29
Development of the Internet: from the 1940s to the Present   30
   RAND Engineers Envision a "Galactic Network"   30
   ARPANET   33
   A Reliable Protocol in NCP   33
Communications Tools   33
   The Personalization of Email   34
TCP/IP and Internetworking   35
Request For Comment (RFC) Documents   36
ARPANET Goes Public   38
U.S. National Science Foundation to the Rescue   38
Internet2   38
Internet History Timeline   38
Internet Development around the World   40
   Canada   40
   Mexico   41
   Europe   42
Convergence of Efforts in the U.S.   43
Domain Names   43
The World Wide Web   44
Who Is in Charge of the Internet?   45
Summary   48
Review Questions and Hands-on Exercises   48

Part 2   *Utilizing the Internet and the World Wide Web*   51

Chapter 3 Finding Resources on the World Wide Web   53

Browser Plug-ins   53
What's Available on the Web?   54
Online Research Tools   55
   Search Engines   56
   Directory Outlines   60
   Bibliographic Databases   61

Site-Specific Search Engines and Site-Maps   63
Subject-Specific Search Engines and Directory Outlines   64
Metasearch Engines   65
Topic Rings   66
Frequently Asked Question Pages   67
Expert Inquiries   68
General References   68
Searching for Jobs   70
Searching for People   70

Searching Strategies   72
Initiating a Search   72
Refining a Search   73
Boolean Operators and Wildcard Characters   73

Understanding Evaluation Criteria   74
Accuracy   75
Authority   76
Audience and Objectivity   76
Purpose   77
Current Information   77
Depth of Coverage   78

Citing Internet Resources   78
Finding Software   78
Open Source Licensing   79
File Compression   80

Summary   81
Review Questions and Hands-on Exercises   81

Chapter 4 Email   85

Brief History of Email   85
Getting an Email Account   86
Email Basics   87
Using Webmail   87
Setting Up an Email Client for POP or IMAP   88
Userid   88
Password   88
Incoming Mail Server   89
Outgoing Mail Server   89
Microsoft Exchange Server   89
Mail Setup in Outlook Express   89
Sending a Message   92
Sending to Multiple Recipients   96
Binary Files and MIME   96
File Attachments   96
Smileys and Other Emoticons   100
Netiquette   101
Return Receipts   102
Importance Indicator   103

Address Book Feature   105
  Creating a Contact in Microsoft Outlook Express   105
  Creating an Address Book Entry in Eudora   109

Receiving, Reading, and Managing Email   110
  Receiving and Setting Automatic Receive Settings in Outlook Express   111
  Receiving and Setting Automatic Receive Settings in Eudora   111
  Receiving Messages Using Webmail   112

Bounced Mail   114

Email Header Information   114

Replying to an Email Message   117

Reply All, Forward, and Redirect   120

Deleting Email Messages   120

Managing Email Using Folders   121
  Managing Email Using Outlook Express   122
  Managing Email Using Eudora   124

Additional Email Features   125

SPAM   126

Spam Blockers   127

Email Trackers   127

Web Bugs   127

To Email, or Not to Email?   128

Email and Personal Information Security   129
  Viruses and Worms   129
  Hoaxes and Chain Letters   130
  Phishing   131

Encrypting Email   132

Summary   133

Review Questions and Hands-on Exercises   133

Chapter 5 Doing Business on the Web   **137**

E-Business and E-Commerce   138
  E-Commerce   138
  E-Business   138
  EDI   138

Classifications of E-Commerce   138
  Business-to-Business (B2B)   138
  Business-to-Consumer (B2C)   139
  Business-to-Business-to-Consumer (B2B2C)   139
  Consumer-to-Business (C2B)   140
  Consumer-to-Consumer (C2C)   140
  Mobile Commerce (M-Commerce)   141

E-Commerce Business Models   141
  Online Direct Marketing   141
  Product and Service Customization   142
  Consumer Online Auctions   142
  Electronic Tendering   143
  Find the Best Price   143

Affiliate Marketing   143
Viral Marketing   143
Group Purchasing   144
B2B Electronic Marketplaces, Exchanges, and Auctions   144
Supply Chain Management   145
EDI and XML   146
Putting a Small Business Online   147
Selecting and Buying a Domain Name   147
Determining the Goals for Your Web Presence   148
Marketing   148
Retail and Online Services   148
Information Delivery   149
Customer Support   149
Developing and Promoting Your Web Site   149
Other Considerations   149
E-Commerce Options for the Consumer   150
Business and Consumer Research   150
Online Shopping   150
Cookies   151
Online Banking   152
Online Stock Trading   152
Summary   154
Review Questions and Hands-on Exercises   154

Part 3   *Designing Information for the World Wide Web*   **157**

Chapter 6   An Introduction to HTML   **159**
Definition and Evolution of HTML   159
What is HTML?   159
The Evolution of HTML and Web Browsers   160
HTML Innovations   161
Creating Web Pages with HTML   162
Basic Web Page Structure   162
Heading Tags   166
Formatting Tags   167
Tag Attributes   169
Font Tag <font>   169
Font Color   170
Font Face   172
Align Attribute   174
Hypertext Links   175
Page Properties   179
Images   180
Image Alignment   181
Image As a Link   188
Lists   188
Comment Tag   191

Browser-Specific Issues   192

Optimizing for Search Engines   192

    Do   193

    Don't   194

Uploading Your Web Site to a Web Server (FTP)   194

Summary   196

Review Questions and Hands-on Exercises   196

Chapter 7 An Introduction to CSS, XHTML, and Advanced Web Development Concepts   201

Cascading Style Sheets   201

    Style Rules   202

    Using Multiple Selectors   207

    Style Classes   207

    Deprecated Tags   208

Java Applets   215

XML and XHTML   215

    XML   215

    XHTML   216

    Backwards and Forward Compatibility   216

    XHTML Rules   217

    XHTML Validation   221

Database Driven Web Applications   222

Summary   225

Review Questions and Hands-on Exercises   225

Chapter 8 HTML Editors   227

Text Editors   227

    Programming Editors   228

    CoffeeCup HTML Editor   228

WYSIWYG Editors   245

    Word Processing Applications   246

    Netscape Composer   246

    Macromedia Dreamweaver   258

    Microsoft FrontPage   270

Summary   273

Review Questions and Hands-on Exercises   273

Chapter 9 Graphics and Multimedia on the World Wide Web   277

Basic Design Principles: CRAP   278

    Contrast   278

    Repetition   278

    Alignment   278

    Proximity   278

Image File Types   279
  Images or Graphics?   279
  Raster and Vector Graphics   279
  Graphics Formats   279
Creating Rollover Images Using Macromedia Fireworks   282
  Creating Buttons   282
  Adding Rollover Images Using Dreamweaver   286
Creating a Transparent Image   287
  Copying Part of an Image   288
Techniques for Working with Larger Images   293
  Interlaced Images   293
  Sliced Images   293
Animation   293
  Animated GIFs   294
  JavaScript Animation   294
  Java Applets   294
  Flash and Shockwave Animation   295
Audio and Video   295
  Downloading   295
  Streaming   295
  Audio   295
  Internet Radio   296
  Video   296
  Adding Sound to a Web Page   297
Webcasts   299
  How to Run a Successful Webinar   299
Other Media   300
  Word Processing and Spreadsheet Documents   300
  Portable Document Format (PDF) Files   300
  Other Document Formats   301
Web Page Usability and Accessibility   301
  Section 508 and the Americans with Disabilities Act (ADA)   301
Summary   303
Review Questions and Hands-on Exercises   304

Part 4   *Communication on the Internet*   **307**

Chapter 10 Mass Communication Tools   **309**
Mailing Lists   310
  How Do Mailing Lists Work?   310
  Moderated or Unmoderated?   310
  Restricted or Open?   311
  What is the Difference between a Mailing List and a Newsletter?   311
  Finding a Listserv List   311
  Subscribing to a Listserv Mailing List   312
  Subscribing to a Discussion Mailing List   314

Sending a Message to a Mailing List   316
Mailing List Commands   318
Digest Mode   319
Unsubscribing from a Mailing List   319
Listserv, Majordomo, Listproc, and Other Mailing List Software   320
Discussion Lists with Web Access   320
Finding Mailing Lists   321
Some Discussion List Etiquette and Tips You Need to Know   321

Newsgroups   322
Understanding How Newsgroups Are Organized   323
Accessing Newsgroups Using the Web   323
FAQs   324
Searching Usenet   325
Using Your ISP Newsfeed   325
Subscription-Based Newsfeeds   329
Some Newsgroup Etiquette You Need to Know   329

Web-Based Discussion Boards   330
Start Your Own Discussion Board   330

Blogs   330
Searching for Blogs   332

RSS (Rich Site Summary, Really Simple Syndication)   332
Searching for RSS Feeds   333
RSS Desktop Headline Viewer—FeedReader   333
Atom   336
Other RSS and Atom Feed Readers   336

Summary   337
Review Questions and Hands-on Exercises   337

Chapter 11 Real-Time Communication   341

Instant Messaging   342
America Online Instant Messenger (AIM)   342
AIM Features   344
Security and Sending Files   346
Audio Chat   346
Videoconferencing   348
MSN Messenger   350
Yahoo! Messenger   351
ICQ   351
Trillian   352

Effective Chatting   353
A Brief History of Text Chat   353
Chat Etiquette and Culture   354

Effective Videoconferencing   354
A Brief History of Videoconferencing   354
Videoconferencing Etiquette   356

IM in the Workplace   359
Summary   361
Review Questions and Hands-on Exercises   361

Chapter 12 Entertainment and Education **365**

Gaming 366
  History of Video Gaming   366
  History of Computer Gaming   367
  Gaming Today   368
  Types of Games   368
  How Games Are Played on the Internet   369

Gambling 372
  Casinos   373
  Sports Betting   374

Casual Gambling 374
  Tips for Choosing an Online Gambling Site   374
  Gambling as an Addiction   375

Distance Education 375
  Distance Education Defined   375
  Distance Education Delivery Tools   375
  Popular Web Courseware Tools   376
  Compressed Interactive Video Networks   378

Telemedicine and Remote Surgery   380

Summary   382

Review Questions and Hands-on Exercises   382

Part 5   *The Impact of the Internet*   **385**

Chapter 13 The Internet's Impact on Traditional Media **387**

Trends in New Media   387
  Depiction as Satan or Savior   388
  Commercialization   388
  Concentration   389

Media Interaction   391
  Books   391
  Newspapers and Magazines   393
  Radio, Video, and Recordings   396
  Film   397
  Television   398

Peer-to-Peer Networking (P2P)   400
  What is Peer-to-Peer Networking?   400
  How Does a P2P File Sharing Network Work?   400
  Social Issues with P2P Networking   401

Summary   403

Review Questions and Hands-on Exercises   403

Chapter 14 The Internet and the Law   407

Intellectual Property Law   407
   Copyright Law   408
   Trademark Law   412
   Patent Law   415

First Amendment Issues   415
   Free Speech Law   416
   Unpopular, Controversial, and Offensive Communications   416
   "Indecent" and "Obscene" Communications   417
   Controversies over Filtering Devices   426

Tort Liability   427
   What Is Tort Law?   427
   Privacy Law   428
   Libel, Slander, and Defamation   432

Summary   435
Review Questions and Hands-on Exercises   435

Chapter 15 Keeping Pace with Innovations   437

Adopting a Medium   438
   Phase One: Elites   438
   Phase Two: Popularization   439
   Phase Three: Specialization   439

The Role of Change Agents in the Diffusion of Innovations   440
Decentralizing Our World   441
   Decentralizing Government   442
   Decentralizing Education   443
   Decentralizing the Economy   445
   Decentralizing the Community   447
   Decentralizing the Individual   448

Resources: Keeping Pace with the Internet   449
   Mailing Lists, Discussion Groups, and Online Journals   449
   News Alerts   450
   Bookmark Web Sites   450
   Magazines   450
   Books   450

Summary   451
Review Questions and Hands-on Exercises   451

Glossary   455

References and Readings   469

Index   479

WELCOME TO THE INTERNET!

part 1

Chapter

Let's Get Online, Already!   1

The Development of the Internet   2

Let's Get Online, Already!

chapter 1

Are you ready to get online? It seems as if everyone is talking about sending email, surfing the Web, or buying something online. Have you been online, but feel a bit overwhelmed or lost? Do you feel like there's so much more to see and do online, if you only knew what was available and where to find things? Do you find yourself asking any of the following questions?

- ☐ Can I really meet people from all over the world?
- ☐ Can I find reliable information on any topic, without having to go to a library?
- ☐ I came across a really great Web site a few weeks ago, but I can't remember where it is. How can I find it again?
- ☐ What are the real issues with viruses?
- ☐ What about privacy? Is Big Brother watching?
- ☐ Is it safe to trade stocks or send my credit card information over the Internet?
- ☐ Is there an easy way to sell things over the Internet?
- ☐ How can I connect to the Internet from home?
- ☐ Can I use teleconferencing so I can see video of the person I'm talking to?
- ☐ Can I make my own Web page, or should I pay someone to do it?

The Internet is a robust communication tool and information resource. It is so powerful that it has literally transformed our society, and the way that we do business. Of course, any tool that transforms a society always presents new issues and challenges to that society. In this book, we will address these concerns and many more.

Chapter Objectives

This chapter helps you understand

- things people do when they are online.
- how to select an Internet Service Provider (ISP).
- how to connect to the Internet.
- common policies ISPs use to govern online activity.
- the growing importance of hand-held and other Internet-ready devices.
- how to effectively use a Web browser.
- security risks inherent to using the Internet.
- security measures you can take to protect your system.
- the risks inherent to providing credit card or other personal information online.
- how to download software from the Internet.
- the IP addressing and domain name system (DNS) that makes the Internet and World Wide Web work.

What Do People Do Online?

With so much information available, and so many activities to choose from, how do people spend their time online?

Here are the most popular activities. Over the years, this list has remained fairly consistent.

- Sending or receiving email (67%)
- Doing research for work or school (45%)
- Finding information about products and services (41%)
- Checking news and weather (40%)
- Finding information about hobbies or special interests (36%)
- Surfing the Web to explore new and different sites (32%)
- Shopping online (22%)
- Finding information about local amusements and activities (19%)
- Paying bills (18%)
- Downloading or playing games (18%)
- Investing and financial management (15%)
- Making travel plans or arrangements (15%)
- Finding information about health or disease (15%) (Harris Interactive, 2004)

As you can see, after email, the next four popular activities all involve seeking information. In this chapter, we will start by getting online and viewing Web pages. So . . . let's get online, already!

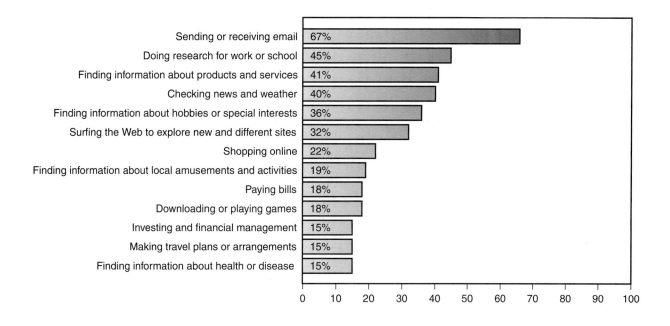

Sending or receiving email	67%
Doing research for work or school	45%
Finding information about products and services	41%
Checking news and weather	40%
Finding information about hobbies or special interests	36%
Surfing the Web to explore new and different sites	32%
Shopping online	22%
Finding information about local amusements and activities	19%
Paying bills	18%
Downloading or playing games	18%
Investing and financial management	15%
Making travel plans or arrangements	15%
Finding information about health or disease	15%

Connecting to the Internet

There are a variety of methods available for connecting to the Internet. If you're connecting from home, you'll need a computer and an account with an **Internet Service Provider (ISP)**. There are some free online options, as well as a wide variety of paid subscription options, including dial-up through a telephone provider, cable, and satellite. Your options will depend on what is available where you live.

You don't need a new, fast computer to connect to the Internet. Any computer built in the last four or five years will be adequate for doing basic tasks, including using email and surfing the Web. As we discuss each of the Internet connection options, we'll mention any specific hardware that may be required. If you're using an older computer and need an upgrade, you'll get the most performance increase by adding **Random Access Memory (RAM)**, and by upgrading the hard drive.

In most cases, a **modem** (**mod**ulator/**dem**odulator) is required in order to connect to the Internet. A modem translates the data from electrical signals in your computer to a signal that can be accepted by the carrier—such as a telephone or cable signal—and then translates back again when it receives the signal. Your computer may come with a telephone modem, but if a specialized modem is required, you can arrange to rent or purchase one through your ISP or local computer store.

If you're connecting at your workplace, a cyber café, or public library, there are a variety of options. Your workplace likely has a **local area network (LAN)**, which is a collection of computers, printers, and shared network drives. If the LAN spans a large geographic area, such as several buildings, or connections between cities, it is called a **wide area network (WAN)**. Generally, a corporation will connect their local area network (LAN) directly to a leased Internet line. You may hear the terms T1 and T3 to describe types of telecommunications lines, and the terms OC3, OC12, OC48, and so on, to describe

≈ tip

∴ Keep the phone number for your ISP's technical support line handy, written near your computer. If you have trouble with your Internet connection, you may not be able to go online to find the number!

fiber optic lines. They are part of the backbone of the Internet; the main routes on the *information highway*. Smaller corporations, and places such as a small library or cyber café, may purchase a business subscription package from an ISP.

What Does Internet Service Include?

Regardless of the type of commercial Internet service to which you subscribe, you should expect to receive an email address, be able to surf the Web, and use the other services available on the Internet. Also expect some storage space on the ISP's Web server, which you can use to store Web pages and other files. In addition, the ISP should provide 24/7 (24 hours per day, 7 days per week) technical support. This is important, because regardless of your technical expertise, there will be times when you find yourself calling technical support to check to see if their service is having problems, or to walk you through a complicated set-up of some sort. Some ISPs provide additional service such as anti-virus protection, and a spam filter. **Spam** is unsolicited email and it has become quite a problem in recent years.

When shopping for an ISP, it is valuable to understand how data transfer speed is measured. Data travels in two directions. **Downloading** refers to data transmission received by your computer from another computer over the Internet. **Uploading** refers to data transmission sent from your computer to another computer on the Internet. Data transmission rate is referred to as **bandwidth.** Download transmission speeds are much higher than upload transmission speeds. The idea is that most of the traffic will be download traffic, as you retrieve email, and download Web pages and other documents. Data transfers are measured in **Kbps** (kilobits per second, one-thousand bits per second, or roughly 125 characters per second), **Mbps** (megabits per second, one-million bits per second, or roughly 1250 characters per second), or **Gbps** (gigabits per second, one-billion bits per second, or roughly 12,500 characters per second). So, ISPs will advertise the bandwidth they provide in terms of download and upload speeds. For connectivity to leased lines and over LAN connections, where the bandwidth is much higher, the speed will be measured in Gbps.

Dial-up Services

Traditional Dial-up Services

Telephone companies and other Internet Service providers offer traditional dial-up services for which you will need a modem and a telephone line. They offer economical packages, and packages for a variety of different amounts of connection hours per month. This is a slower service, usually 56 Kbps, and while you are connected to your ISP, your phone line is in use. Some ISPs also incorporate download acceleration software in order to boost the speed higher than 56 Kbps. As there are a wide variety of operating systems, and technical issues sometimes associated with connecting to an ISP, ask your provider's technical support to walk you through the connection setup. Don't be shy about calling technical support. They're there to provide this service.

There are some free dial-up services available. They will ordinarily require you to keep an advertising window open, as banner ads will be displayed while you are connected. They have restrictions on hours and length of time for connections, and if they offer technical support at all, charge a hefty per-minute fee.

In the early 1990s, as the Internet emerged as an important communications medium, community concerns regarding Internet access gave birth to volunteer-based *Freenets*. There are long-established Freenets in many large communities, which are still largely volunteer organizations and often based at the local public library. Some are still able to offer free Internet access through grants and funding, but many charge a nominal fee in order to continue operating. Freenets normally have community discussion boards, volunteer technical support help, and information about the community.

Broadband Services

Broadband services are fast, direct connections to an ISP, and you can be connected 24 hours per day. There are a variety of options including DSL/ADSL, cable, and satellite.

Your local telephone company and other ISPs may offer **DSL** (Digital Subscriber Line) or **ADSL** (Asymmetrical Digital Subscriber Line) as a broadband option. This is a connection through your telephone line that allows you to make phone calls while you're online. ADSL is one type of DSL, but often the ISPs refer to the connection as simply DSL. Basically, ADSL technology makes use of the fact that the telephone line will carry a high range of frequencies, and the frequencies used for voice transmission are in a very small range. ADSL transmits data over the unused frequencies. The transmission speed ranges from 128 Kbps to 4 Mbps download and 64 Kbps to 800 Kbps upload. Some ISPs have a graduated pricing scale for increased speeds. You will require a DSL modem, which you will be able to rent or purchase from your ISP or one of the large, chain computer stores. ADSL is not available in all areas, as it requires upgraded telephone lines. Some local telephone companies will also have package pricing that includes telephone services and Internet access. Generally, the ADSL modem connects directly to the computer through a Universal Serial Bus (USB) port, which is a standard connection available on most computers.

Many local cable companies also offer Internet access. Some cable companies offer two types of access: a light access and a high speed access. The light access will be comparable in speed to a low-end DSL connection, offering speeds such as 128 Kbps download and 64 Kbps upload. The high speed access will offer speeds such as 3–5 Mbps download and 128 Kbps to 1 Mbps upload. Many cable companies will also have package pricing that includes television signal service. You will require a cable modem and an Ethernet Network Interface Card (NIC). The NIC is often included with newer computers and you may see a port on the back of your computer that looks like a telephone jack, but a little larger. The computer connects via the network cable from the NIC to the cable modem and the cable modem connects directly into the cable outlet via coaxial cable (the same cable you use to connect your television to the cable outlet).

Satellite Internet access may be an option for you if you have a clear, unobstructed view of the southern sky. Essentially, you will require installation of a satellite dish, and a specialized modem. Like the cable modem, the satellite modem connects to the NIC in your computer. Download speeds are 500 Kbps to 1 Mbps, and upload speeds are 50 Kbps to 100 Kbps, placing satellite access between DSL and cable, in general. This may be a good option if you have no other broadband option available. Early versions of satellite Internet service was one-way, in that data was downloaded from satellite, but upload was accomplished with dial-up access. Many satellite service providers now offer two-way (bi-directional) service via satellite.

How Communications Satellites and Satellite Internet Access Works

Satellites were once used primarily by the intelligence community to track military actions. Today, communications satellites are an everyday part of our existence. We may be listening to satellite radio in our cars, watching television (either satellite or cable), or reading a newspaper that has been digitized and delivered to a publishing house via satellite. There are many types of satellites, each with a specific purpose: weather, scientific, broadcast, navigational, rescue, Earth observation, military, and communications. **Satellites** circle the Earth in a fixed orbit. Communications satellites, interestingly, need to be in a **geosynchronous orbit**, or fixed over a geographic position to function. So, they don't actually orbit the Earth, they *hover* over a particular geography with the assistance of rocket power.

Communications satellites dispatch voice transmissions (telephone) and they also exchange data between computers via the Internet. They are a critical component of the Internet because they allow for the global transmission of data via radio signals. Inside every satellite are hundreds, if not thousands, of transponders. The job of a **transponder** is to receive a radio signal (in this case, data transmission) on one radio frequency, and to amplify it with power (generated from solar panels and rechargeable batteries) while it is being retransmitted back to Earth on another radio frequency. That way signals don't get **crossed**.

With satellite Internet connection, your computer relays your requests through your dish, to the satellite in orbit. The satellite in orbit, in turn, relays the signal to the ISP's network operations center (NOC), or satellite ground station. The NOC relays the requested information back to the satellite, which, in turn, broadcasts it back to your computer.

Wi-Fi

Wireless Internet access is becoming popular in public places such as coffee shops, airports, libraries, and hotels. This technology, called **Wi-Fi** (pronounced W-eye F-eye) is an acronym for *wireless fidelity* and refers to a high-frequency wireless local area network (WLAN). You may also see this term written as *WiFi*. A computer is said to be *Wi-Fi enabled* if it has a wireless network card installed. If a Wi-Fi enabled computer is not already connected to a network via a NIC, it will constantly look for **hotspots**, much like your cell phone will search for a signal. This signal is sent from a *wireless access point*, which is connected to a computer, and often connected to a network as well. Download speeds can range from 11 Mbps–54 Mbps, much faster than cable connections. Wi-Fi

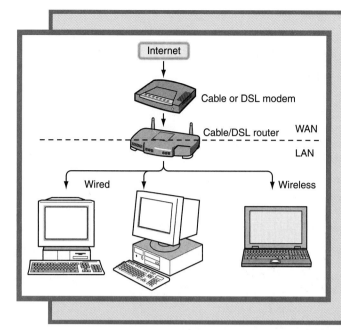

How a Wireless Home Network Works

In order to create a wireless home network, you will require a cable or DSL connection, and a cable/DSL router. The DSL or cable modem is connected to the cable/DSL router, and the router is connected to your computer via network cable. Each computer connecting to the network will require a wireless card.

technology is a good solution for a home network and would enable all computers connected to share the Internet connection and resources such as a printer, scanner, and files. It eliminates the need to run wires through the house and is powerful enough to provide fast connections over small distances.

Wi-Fi signals present some security problems. The range of the signal from a wireless access point varies depending on obstacles, signal strength, and other factors. It could be detected from as far as 200 feet away, but corporations using a wireless access point with a high-powered antenna could transmit a signal 1500 feet or further. The security issue lies with limiting access to the network over the wireless signal. If the signal is completely open, any computer with a Wi-Fi card can connect to it. It is possible that someone sitting in a car in front of your house would be able to access your Wi-Fi network using his or her notebook computer. In the corporate world, this has become a huge security issue as IT departments scramble to find all the wireless access points in their organizations and secure them. **Wardriving** is the technique of driving around a city in a vehicle, with a notebook computer and an antenna, detecting open WLANs (Wireless Local Area Network), often with exploitation in mind. If you are setting up a home network with a wireless access point, you can quickly secure it using an encryption system called **WEP** (Wired Equivalent Privacy). The software that comes with the wireless access point will allow you to specify a WEP key. Once you specify a WEP key, you also have to include it in the software that comes with the Wi-Fi card in each of the computers that will be attaching to the network. If a computer does not have the correct WEP key, it will not be able to connect to the network. This will prevent that person in the car from connecting, and using your Internet connection or compromising your files.

ISPs for Travelers

When shopping for an ISP, you will find that there are local ISPs with service restricted to a smaller geographic area, and national or even international ISPs with service available across a country—or spanning international borders. A good resource for finding ISPs is The List at `http://www.thelist.com`. If you travel frequently, an inexpensive national ISP might be worth considering, and the best, and possibly only option is a dial-up service. Although this is slower than broadband, it is widely available, and avoids the frustration of bringing specialized equipment with you. Cable and DSL are not available everywhere, but you can almost always connect to a telephone line. Some ISPs have lists of dial-up access numbers available. These lists can be downloaded and stored in Palm Pilots so that you can have the list handy when you travel. If you're traveling, make sure you have the phone number of the technical support line for your ISP, as well as a list of dial-up access numbers.

You will find that many hotels include Internet connection in the price of your room, or for a nominal fee. This is typically a network connection, and you will require a network card in your laptop or notebook computer. Be sure to have network cable with you and a security cable as well, so that you can secure your computer to a piece of furniture while you are not in the room. If you consider connecting instead via telephone to a national provider, be aware that most hotels charge for local phone calls and some charge by the minute, so this could become costly. Some hotels also offer wireless service for a modest fee. Other options for travelers include cyber cafés, local libraries, and some coffee shops and bookstores.

Connecting to Work

If you're traveling, or you would like to work from home, you may be wondering if it's possible to connect to your computer workstation or another computer system at work. It all depends on the exact setup at your workplace, but we can provide you with some general information to point you in the right direction.

Local Area Networks

Your computer workstation at your workplace is probably connected to a local area network (LAN). As previously mentioned, a LAN is a collection of computers, printers, and other devices connected so that resources can be shared. Your workstation is definitely connected to some sort of LAN if you share a printer with others and have access to a network drive to store files. Usually, the LAN, or the series of LANs you are somehow connected to, has Internet access through a special purpose computer called a **gateway**, which connects to a powerful leased Internet line such as a T3 or OC48. LAN transmission speeds are fast. Most LANs use a technology called **Ethernet**, which is essentially the method of connecting the computers and devices and the protocols used to transmit data. A **protocol** is a system of communicating data from one location to another. In our discussion of transmission speeds and ISPs, we were using figures such as 56 Kbps and 5 Mbps. Ethernet speeds are measured as 10 Mbps, 100 Mbps, or 100 Gbps. This explains why you're getting super-fast Internet access at work, and wondering why the service at home is so much slower.

Intranets

When you're using your workstation at work, you may find that you have access to several types of systems and networks. Your company may have an **intranet**. An intranet is a network for internal use only. Your corporate intranet may contain information such as the corporate telephone directory, forms for requesting office supplies, human resources documents, and the like. You may need a userid and password to access it, or you may only be able to access it from your workstation.

If you work for a medium- or large-sized company, you will likely find that you cannot simply connect to your workstation from a remote location over the Internet.

Virtual Private Networks

One method that you may be able to use to connect to the systems at your workplace is through a **Virtual Private Network (VPN)**. A VPN is a LAN or series of LANs that are secure and have restrictions for user connections. Security is a huge issue, because there will be some important files and systems available through a VPN. Ordinarily, if your workplace has a VPN, you can connect directly to it through a **VPN Dial-up Network (VPDN)**. In this case, your technicians may provide you with software called **desktop client software**, which may connect to a **Network Access Server (NAS)**, which, in turn, connects to the VPN. An NAS will ensure that only people who are authorized can connect to the VPN. Some people refer to this method of connection as **tunneling**. You might say that you are "tunneling into the network." With this system the data will be encrypted. The trade-off is that you are using a telephone line connection, so the data transfer will be slower. The benefit for you is that you can access important information at work, from virtually anywhere in the world. This is invaluable for individuals such as salespeople and trainers, who must travel.

Acceptable Use Policies and Privacy Policies

ISPs are communications carriers, just like telephone companies, and are not responsible for the information that is transmitted; just as your telephone company is not responsible for the telephone conversations you have. An ISP typically outlines its terms of service, in the form of an Acceptable Use Policy. An **Acceptable Use Policy (AUP)** is a legal document, written to protect the ISP from unlawful use of its service, and outlines prohibited uses of the service and possible consequences of misuse. As a rule, the AUP will specify that unacceptable use includes downloading illegal material, storing illegal material on the ISP's server, sending email or messages that are threatening, defamatory, or otherwise illegal, hacking into other computer systems, distributing your userid and password for others to use your account, mass emailing, and any other activity that might be misuse. You may have to physically sign an AUP, or click an accept button before you are allowed to use the service.

It is very common to be presented with some form of AUP when you are using a public Internet service such as at a cyber café, school, or hotel. Many elementary and high schools insist that parents are required to sign an AUP in addition to a consent form, and children may be required to sign them as well, prior to being allowed Internet access.

The ISP, school, or other entity providing Internet service, usually reserves the right to suspend or cancel Internet access if an abuse of the service is found. ISPs do not routinely check the material on their servers, monitor email, or monitor downloading of material. But, if an abuse is brought to their attention, they will generally investigate and take appropriate action.

tip

∴ If you think that someone else has your userid and password, contact your technical support department as soon as possible so that your password can be reset. It's better to be safe than sorry!

Along with the AUP, some ISPs and many corporations also make available their **Privacy Policy**. This document outlines their policy for protecting your personal information. If a corporation or ISP makes their membership or customer list available, it should be outlined in their Privacy Policy. This document will specify the type of information that is gathered and how it is safeguarded.

Hand-Held and Other Devices

When we think of being online, we normally think of using a computer. There are a wide variety of other devices that also use the Internet, however. Cell phones and PDAs (Personal Digital Assistant) such as RIM's Blackberry have features that enable them to send and receive email and do some limited Web surfing. Typically the ISP is the carrier of the cell phone service, or pager service. Home appliances, such as a refrigerator with a touch screen, can also be connected to the home network and access email and the Web.

Internet Software

Now that we've discussed how to connect to the Internet, let's look at the software required in order to effectively utilize the vast resources available!

In order to **surf the Web**, you will require a **Web browser**. A Web browser is the software you use to download and view Web pages. Some people refer to downloading and viewing Web pages as "surfing the Web." If you are using Windows, you already have Internet Explorer installed, and the vast majority of people use Internet Explorer to view Web pages. It's handy. There are a variety of other Web browsers available as well, including Mozilla, Netscape, and Opera. If you are using a Macintosh computer, you are probably using Safari. All of the Web browsers have the same basic functionality. They will allow you to download and view Web pages, navigate through pages previously visited, and bookmark favorite pages to revisit.

Once your computer is connected to the Internet, you will be able to use your Web browser to surf the Web. If your computer is not connected to the Internet, you will see an error message in the browser window when you try to view Web pages.

Let's do some hands-on exercises to go through some basic browsing techniques. Hands-on tasks will be denoted by an arrow symbol ().

➤ Make sure your computer is connected to the Internet.
➤ Open Internet Explorer, or Safari if you are using a Macintosh computer. You should see an icon on your desktop or on the task bar, or click Start to see one in the listing as well.

You may find that the Web browser automatically loads a page. The page that loads when the Web browser is first launched is called the *home page* and you can specify a different one, or none at all, within the browser preferences.

URLs

As each dwelling has an address, every Web page on the Internet has a distinct address. A Web page can be requested by entering the address in the Web browser, or by selecting a link from another Web page. A Web page address is called the **URL (Uniform Resource Locator**, or **Universal Resource Locator)**. A typical URL might be `http://www.yahoo.com` or something a lot longer such as `http://dir.yahoo.com/computers_and_internet/ internet/world_wide_web/`. The structure of the URL is essentially as follows:

```
transfer-type://name-of-computer/directory/file
```

The transfer-type is a protocol that is the method of data transfer. Web pages are created using the **HyperText Markup Language (HTML)**, and typically the transfer type is **http (HyperText Transfer Protocol)**. You may also see **https (HyperText Transfer Protocol Secure)** if the Web page is part of a site where the data must be encrypted. Other protocols you may see include **mailto:** for sending mail, and **ftp:// (File Transfer Protocol)** for sending files. It is important to note that, in general, URLs are case-sensitive so the URL must be entered exactly as specified.

Web Browser Basics

Let's do some quick surfing to get a feel for how this works. Refer to Figure 1.1 for the parts of the Web browser.

➤ In the address bar, type: `http://www.aw.com`
➤ Press the *Enter* key. This will request the Web page and it will load into the browser window.

Let's have a look at the browser window. Regardless of the Web browser you are using, you will find similar buttons and functionality, as shown in Figure 1.1.

Any Web page may contain hypertext links. Hypertext links, or hyperlinks, are typically text colored blue and underlined. An image could be a hyperlink as well. When you click these links, another Web page will be requested and loaded.

➤ Move the mouse pointer over the Web page slowly, and notice that as it passes over a hypertext link, the mouse pointer changes to a hand.
➤ Click one of the links to load a new Web page.

One of the most frequently visited pages on the Internet is Yahoo! (`http:// www.yahoo.com`). Yahoo! is a search page, and you can also browse pages by category. This is a good place to start, if you'd like to get a feel for the type of information that is available in general.

➤ Click in the address bar to activate it.
➤ Drag to highlight the URL if it is not already highlighted.
➤ Press the *Delete* key to delete the URL.
➤ Type: `http://www.yahoo.com`

tip

You can open a Web page by typing the URL in the address bar, using the File, Open option from the menu, or clicking on a hypertext link.

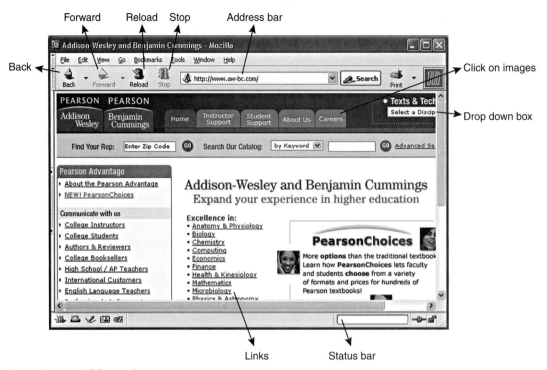

Figure 1.1 Web browser basics; see: `http://www.aw-bc.com/`

➤ Press the *Enter* key to load the Yahoo! page.

➤ Click in the search box, which is on the Yahoo! page, to activate it.

➤ Type a search term for any topic that interests you.

➤ Press the *Enter* key or click the *Search* button in order to load the listing of pages that satisfy your search criteria. Effective searching techniques will be discussed in a later chapter.

➤ Feel free to click links to browse through different pages.

The *Back* and *Forward* buttons will allow you to navigate through pages you have previously viewed.

➤ If there are images on the Web page, feel free to click where indicated to load another page.

➤ Click the *Back* button to view the page most recently visited.

➤ Click the *Forward* button to view the next Web page in the sequence of viewed pages.

You may see items on Web pages such as drop-down boxes, which reveal choices when clicked, text boxes to enter information such as search terms, menus that fold out items when your mouse pointer hovers over them, and animation that includes spots where you can click to select choices. The mouse pointer does not always change to a hand when there is a clickable area.

tip

∴ You do not have to type `http://` In fact, most sites do not require you to type `www.` either. For instance, you can type `yahoo.com` in the address bar rather than `http://www.yahoo.com`

If a Web page is taking a particularly long time to load, you can click the *Stop* button to stop the transmission. When a Web page is loading, you should notice that the browser icon in the upper right hand corner is animated, and there may be a progress bar on the status bar as well. There are lots of reasons for a page not to load the first time, and it happens from time to time. When a page is taking a long time to load, click the *Stop* button, and then click the *Refresh* button. The *Refresh* button will reload the Web page.

Temporary Files (Cache) Each Web page you open, and all the images, are stored on your hard drive temporarily. The temporary file storage may also be referred to as the **cache**. This is important to know because the *Refresh* button may reload a temporary file if it exists. If you find yourself looking at a page that has old information on it, you can force a reload from the original source by holding down the *Shift* key while you click the *Refresh* button.

Clearing the Cache The Web browser is configured to use a small percentage of the hard drive for the cache, and as the cache fills, older files will be deleted and newer files will be stored. You may wish to clear the cache manually. Usually, you will find the cache setting in the options or preferences settings in the Web browser. Internet Explorer uses the term **Temporary Files** to describe the files in the cache. If you are using Internet Explorer, take a moment to clear the cache as follows.

➤ Click the menu options *Tools, Internet Options*. The Internet Options dialog box will display, as shown in Figure 1.2.

➤ Click the *Delete Files* button to delete the cache files.

Figure 1.2 Internet Options dialog box.

➤ A dialog box will appear, confirming the file deletion. Click the *OK* button to delete the files.

Missing Page Errors The World Wide Web has been described as the world's largest pile of books, where anyone can throw a book on a pile, take one away, remove pages from a book, add them, and no one keeps track of this. Basically, anyone can store a Web page on a Web server, and it can be accessible to the world. Web pages can also disappear as quickly as they appear, and this creates a dynamic environment. You will frequently come across an error message indicating that a Web page does not exist. Often, in the error page, you will see a reference to "HTTP 404 - File not found." You may hear some technical people refer to a "404 error" when discussing missing pages, and this is the error they are referring to.

Bookmarks and Favorites Rather than keeping lists of pages you would like to revisit, you can store the URL of a Web page as a bookmark or favorite. Internet Explorer uses the term *favorite* and Mozilla, Netscape, and other browsers use the term *bookmark*. Let's look at an example using Internet Explorer.

➤ As you are surfing, select a page you would like to revisit.

➤ Click the menu items, *Favorites, Add to Favorites,* as shown in Figure 1.3.

Figure 1.3   Internet Explorer *Favorites, Add to Favorites.*

You should see the *Add Favorite* dialog box, as shown in Figure 1.4.

Figure 1.4   Internet Explorer Favorites folders.

➤ Type an appropriate name for the favorite entry in the Name box (*Dogs* was chosen in the example above).

You can start to organize your favorites into folders, or you can create an entry that will appear in the favorites drop-down listing. If you wish to have an entry in the drop-down listing, do not add it to a folder.

Let's store this new entry in a folder so that it appears inside the folder menu.

➤ Click on a folder in the listing to store the favorite entry in a particular folder.
➤ Click the *OK* button to complete the favorite entry.

Now the new entry has been added to the list of favorites inside the folder. You can verify this.

➤ Click the *Favorite* menu item.
➤ Click the name of the Folder where you stored the favorite entry.

You should see your new entry in the list.

The method to create bookmark entries in other browsers is virtually identical to creating favorite entries in Internet Explorer.

History While you are surfing, your Web browser is keeping a history list of all of the pages you have visited. The browser options will allow you to delete the history list, or specify how many days to keep the list. If you've visited a site you'd like to revisit but have forgotten the URL and did not add it to the favorites list, the history list can be particularly useful.

Notice that there is a down arrow on the *Back* button. When you Click the down arrow, you will see the session history list, as shown in Figure 1.5. This list will expire when you close the Web browser.

Figure 1.5   Internet Explorer History.

You will also notice a *History* menu item.

Let's revisit a page:

➤   Click the down arrow beside the *Back* button to reveal the history list.
➤   Click one of the menu items on the history list to revisit a previous Web page.

Let's look at the history list:

➤   Click the down arrow beside the *Back* button to reveal the history list.
➤   Click the *History* menu item.

You will see a history list open in the new pane on the left side of the browser window, as shown in Figure 1.6. Note that you can see a listing from today or several days ago. You can click the name of any of the sites listed to revisit it.

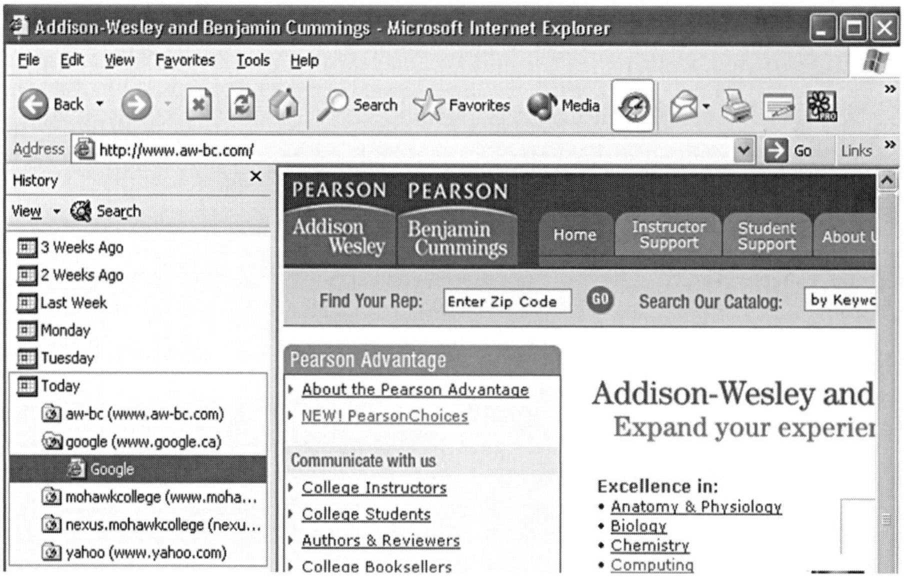

Figure 1.6   Internet Explorer History pane.

➤   When you have finished viewing the history pane, close the pane by clicking on the close (**x**) symbol in the upper right corner of the pane.

In the *View* menu, you will find options for navigating, such as *Stop, Refresh,* and *Go To.*

∴ Did you find a useful Web page a few days ago but forgot to book-mark it? No problem, check the history!

Clearing the Browser History You may find an occasion to wish to clear the history list maintained by the Web browser. Let's clear the history list in Internet Explorer.

➤ Click the menu options *Tools, Internet Options*. The Internet Options dialog box will appear, as shown in Figure 1.2. We saw this dialog box previously when clearing the cache.

➤ Click the *Clear History* button to clear the history list.

➤ A confirmation dialog box will appear. Click the *Yes* button to confirm the deletion of the history list.

Notice that there is also an input box indicating the number of days to keep the history list entries. You can increase and decrease this number, as well.

➤ Click the *OK* button to accept the changes and close the dialog box.

Browser Options and Features There are many options in the Web browser that can be configured by the user. Here are a few options you may find helpful:

Task	How to
Save a Web page and its images	Use the *File, Save* menu options
Print a Web page	Use the *File, Print* options or click the *Print* button
Clear the history list	Use the *Tools, Internet Options* menu items and the *Clear History* button
Change the default colors, and override Web page text and link colors	Use *Tools, Internet Options* and click the *Colors* button
Increase or decrease the text size—note this may not always affect the text size, as the Web page designer may have specified a point size for the text, or the text may be in an image	Use *View, Text Size, Largest* or use *View, Text Size, Smallest*

Setting the Home Page Let's set the home page. When you click the *Home* button, the home page will load.

➤ Make sure the new home page is displayed in the browser window.

➤ Select the menu options *Tools, Internet Options*. A dialog box will appear, as shown in Figure 1.7.

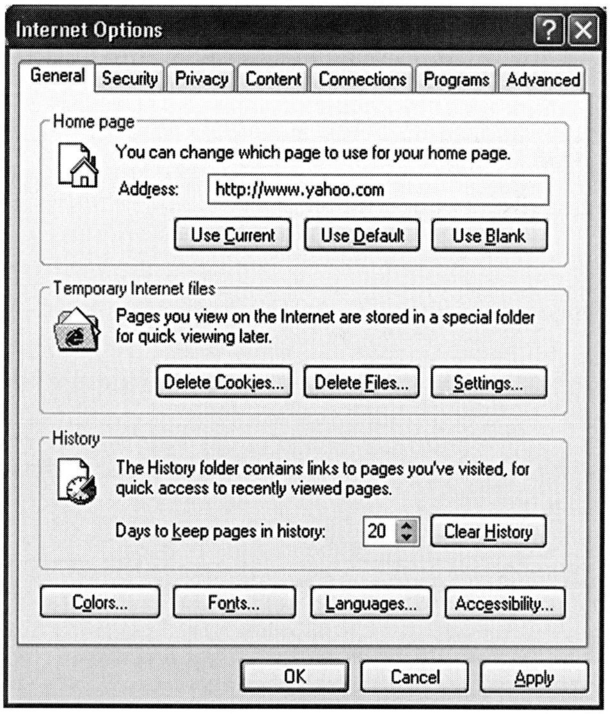

Figure 1.7   Internet Explorer Internet Options dialog box.

➤ Click the *Use Current* button to set the current page as the new home page.

➤ Click the *OK* button to save the changes. Now, you can use the *Home* button as a shortcut to load this Web page.

Although Internet Explorer is definitely the most widely used Web browser, there are other free Web browsers available. As with any software, each has some useful and unique features, and lacks others.

Notice, as shown in Figure 1.8, that in Mozilla, the *Back, Forward, Refresh,* and *Stop* buttons and address bar are in the same relative positions as they are in Internet Explorer.

Again, notice, as shown in Figure 1.9, that in Netscape, the navigation buttons and address bar are in the same relative locations as they are in Internet Explorer.

Netscape and Mozilla also have many of the options listed earlier, and you will find them in the *Edit, Preferences* menus. Other Web browsers include Opera, Firefox, and Safari for the Apple Macintosh computer.

Advertisements on the Web

Advertising is everywhere. You will find images and banner ads on many Web pages you visit, and advertisers hope you will click the image or ad and visit their sites. Typically,

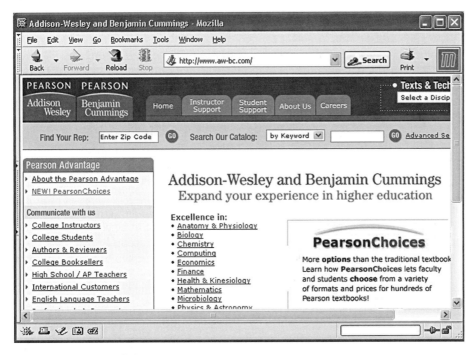

Figure 1.8   The Mozilla browser.

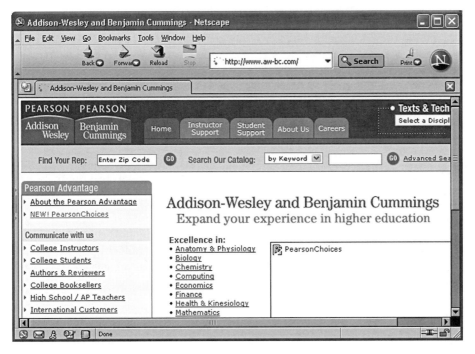

Figure 1.9   The Netscape browser.

advertisers will pay a *click-through* fee to the host of a page if someone clicks on the banner and visits their sites.

In order to better get your attention, advertisers are now promoting their services and products through pop-ups or pop-unders. These are instances of the browser window that pop up on top of your window, or pop underneath your window. Often, people will close a pop-up window before it fully loads, so pop-unders have become more common, as you will not see this window until after it loads and you close or move your other windows. Some Web browsers, such as Mozilla and Netscape include a pop-up blocker as a feature. You can also install third party pop-up and ad blocker software such as the Google toolbar, available at `http://www.google.com`.

Email Clients

In addition to a Web browser, you will also require software to be able to read, send, and manage email messages. If you are using Windows, you probably have Microsoft's Outlook Express installed. Mozilla and Netscape also include email software. The term *client* refers to software that works in conjunction with a server. In the case of email, the server would be an email server and the client software would be able to receive and send email through the server when connected to the Internet. Techniques for using email and issues associated with email are discussed in detail in Chapter 4, Email.

Security Risks

As soon as you connect to the Internet, your computer is vulnerable to security risks. The malicious hazards include viruses, Trojan horses, worms, adware, spyware, browser hijackers, Web bugs, and mini distributed denial of service (mDDoS) attacks.

Virus

A virus is a small computer program and the level of destruction it could cause can range from simple annoyance and use of computer processing time, to erasing files on your hard drive and rendering your computer inoperable.

Trojan Horse

A Trojan horse is a small program designed to gather information such as userids and passwords, and send those to the person who wrote the program.

Worm

A worm is a program designed to copy itself and send itself to other computers on the network. Worms may also contain viruses, and we will revisit this concept in Chapter 4, Email.

Adware

Adware is simply advertising and could be in the form of rolling banners, or in a pop-up or pop-under window. Adware is advertising-supported software and may be necessary for generating revenue in order for that software to be freely available. Adware may install components on your system in order to gather marketing information, and if this practice is in place, a disclosure will be displayed. It is not a security risk *per se*, but may be associated with spyware.

Spyware

Spyware is often associated with adware, and is any computer program that takes advantage of your Internet connection and reports the list of Web sites you have visited, or tracks your Internet usage in some other way. Components installed with adware that are not identified by a disclosure, and are installed without the knowledge of the user, are considered to be spyware. It is not uncommon for spyware components to be combined with other software as well.

Browser Hijacker

A browser hijacker is a program that is designed to change the settings on your Web browser. A *home page hijacker* changes the home page in order for you to see advertising or increase the hit count for their page. A browser hijacker can also install *browser helper objects (BHOs)* which are designed to capture the list of URLs you've typed, forms you've completed, including credit card numbers, and send this information to the originator of the programs. Unfortunately browser hijackers have also been known to produce pop-up ads for pornography, add bookmarks for pornography sites, and redirect users to pornographic Web sites when they mistype a URL. A browser hijacker is a specialized form of spyware.

Web Bug

A Web bug is a small invisible image on a Web page and it is designed to track the Web pages you view as you surf to other pages that also contain Web bugs. This technique is also used to track email messages.

Mini Distributed Denial of Service Attacks (mDDoS)

A distributed denial of service (DDoS) attack occurs when a group of compromised computer systems simultaneously send messages to the computer system under attack. Effectively, the computer system under attack is overwhelmed and cannot accept messages from other systems while the attack is happening. Typically this has been aimed at larger corporations. Individuals can also be the targets of mini DDoS attacks (mDDoS). This is emerging in the gaming community as a particular individual is targeted and individuals launch a program that sends repeated messages to the target, effectively overwhelming the system to the point where it is paralyzed. The mDDoS attack is relatively new; however it is something to be aware of.

Security Measures

The security risks may be enough to make you want to put your computer back in the box and forget about connecting to the Internet, but there are a few simple measures you can take to protect yourself well.

1. Choose an ISP that is using spam blocking and anti-virus software. This prevents most virus-infected files from delivery to your email address.

2. Make sure your computer's operating system is up to date with the current patches installed. Many viruses take advantage of vulnerabilities that are well-documented, and preventable with current software patches.

3. Install anti-virus software and make sure that the signature or data files are current. You can purchase anti-virus software for a modest fee, and this generally includes a year or more of updates to the data or signature files. These files are updated through your Internet connection. Anti-virus software will detect and remove viruses, worms, and Trojan horses. Some anti-virus software also detects spyware.

4. Use spyware removal software such as Ad-Aware (`http://www.download.com`), to check your system for spyware and eliminate it. Again, make sure the current updates are used. Spyware removal software will remove spyware and Web browser hijackers. This software will not detect viruses.

5. Install firewall software, or use a router, which contains a firewall for your protection. Firewall software will stop intruders and may be effective against mDDoS attacks. Basically, any Internet communication must go through the firewall and you can determine the level of security. There are software packages available that are combination firewall, anti-virus, and anti-spam as well. A router is a physical piece of hardware that is commonly used to connect two or more computers, or to set up a wireless network. Most routers also come with firewall software.

Providing Credit Card and Other Sensitive Information

In general, it is wise to be wary of providing your credit card number to anyone. Never send your credit card number or other sensitive information via email. Email is not encrypted and it is too easily misrouted or bounced. Most reputable E-Commerce sites will use a secure server, with encryption. Always look for the encryption symbol, which is a picture of a little lock in the lower right corner of the browser window, as shown in Figure 1.10.

Figure 1.10   Internet Explorer Secure Server symbol.

When you see the encryption symbol, the data is encrypted when it is sent, and this provides some protection against someone who might be able to sniff the data from the transmission.

tip

∴ If you receive an email asking for your credit card number or bankcard number, call the credit card company or bank instead to verify whether the request is legitimate!

Downloading Software

There is a wide variety of useful and fun software available on the Internet to download, legitimately. The software falls into the general categories of commercial software, shareware, freeware, and open source. There are many sources available for downloading software including Download.com (`http://www.download.com`) and Tucows (`http://www.tucows.com`)

Commercial Software

As bandwidth increases, vendors are moving more and more toward selling software on their Web sites, and allowing the customer to download the software immediately. This is fully functional software and may include technical support as well. Usually, they will have a purchase form available, and you will be asked for your credit card number. Ensure that you are using a secure site before you provide your credit card information.

Shareware

This software may be freely distributed and it is essentially on a "try before you buy" basis. Most shareware is limited either as partially functional, time limited such as a 30-day trial, or perhaps includes a logo in a final product. Generally, you will be prompted to purchase each time the software is loaded, or reminded that your trial period is coming to an end. If you choose to purchase, you may be provided with a registration key, which unlocks the rest of the software features, or provided with instructions for downloading a new fully functional copy.

Freeware

This software is completely free and may be freely distributed. Often, it has been created by a Good Samaritan, with the understanding that credit will be given to the programmer, and the program will not be altered in any way.

Open Source

Open Source software is a special type of freeware or shareware. Open Source means that the source code, or original program, is made available and others are invited to help with the development and submit improvements, becoming part of the group who is developing it. Open Source can also mean that the software use requires a paid license, and the source code is available. Linux is a good example of Open Source software, and you will find more information about open source in general at Source Forge (`http://www.sourceforge.net`).

What Happens When You Connect?

Now that we've looked at how to connect to the Internet, the basics of browsing, and security issues, let's have a quick look at the technology behind viewing Web pages.

IP Addresses

Regardless of whether a network is the Internet, or a corporate LAN, each computer connected to a network is assigned an **Internet Protocol (IP) address**. An example of an IP address would be 127.324.0.89. When your computer connects to your ISP's service, it becomes part of a network (which happens to be the Internet), and your computer is assigned an IP address. Your ISP maintains a table of the IP addresses assigned, and the users they are assigned to. All traffic is logged by the IP address, but of course, once the IP address is known, the IP address table can determine the identity of the user. Usually, an ISP has a large block of IP addresses, which are distributed to users on a rotational basis as they become free. If you are using a broadband connection, your IP address may change as your ISP decides to rotate addresses, and you may not be aware of it. If you are connecting using a dial-up connection, you will be assigned a new IP address each time you connect.

Domain Name System

A **host** is a computer connected directly to the Internet. Your home computer is not a host, but the ISP you connect to has at least one host, which is connected directly to the Internet. Every computer and every host connected to the Internet also has an IP address. In the case of hosts, IP addresses are assigned a permanent address or static IP address. Host IP addresses are often assigned a name as well. For instance, www.yahoo.com has a permanent IP address associated with it. A permanent IP address is referred to as a static IP address. When we type a URL in the browser address bar, the Domain Name System (DNS) translates the name to an IP address and sends the request to the IP address. DNS is a complicated system, but suffice it to say that you can purchase a domain name, and have your Web site hosted at an ISP, who will ensure that your domain name is registered and assigned a static IP address.

Troubleshooting

Given that data must travel from one computer to another, through a series of other computers, problems can occur in a number of places and troubleshooting can be a bit of a challenge. If you have typed a Web page address in the address bar and it doesn't seem to be loading, there are a few things you can check:

1. Make sure you've paid attention to each character in the URL, particularly with respect to case sensitivity.

2. Click the *Stop* button in the browser window, then the *Reload* button, and see if that forces the page to load.

3. Try loading a different page. If you try several pages, and none seems to be loading, the problem is likely with your Internet connection. If this is the case, try powering off the broadband modem if you have one. Don't hesitate to call your ISP's technical support line. They will be able to tell you if there are problems with the ISP, and may be able to walk you through a problem from your end as well.

SUMMARY

Now that you've read through the chapter, you are prepared to:

- Identify the types of activities that people participate in when online.
- Connect your computer to the Internet and discriminate between dial-up, broadband, Wi-Fi, and other Internet Service Provider (ISP) alternatives.
- Understand the differences between a Local Area Network (LAN), Intranet, and Virtual Private Network (VPN).
- Recognize the importance of an Acceptable Use Policy (AUP) and a Privacy Policy.
- Appreciate how hand-held and other Internet-ready devices connect to the Internet.
- Demonstrate your literacy with basic Internet software, understanding URLs, Web browser basics, temporary files (cache), missing page errors, history, browser options and features, advertisements on the Web, and various email clients.
- Identify several security risks inherent to using the Internet including: viruses, Trojan horses, worms, adware, spyware, browser hijackers, Web bugs, and mini distributed denial of service attacks (mDDoS).
- Take security measures to protect your system.
- Identify the pitfalls inherent to providing credit card or other sensitive information.
- Recognize and download various types of software (commercial, shareware, freeware, and open source).
- Understand what happens when you connect to the Internet via the IP addressing and domain name system.

Review Questions and Hands-on Exercises

Review Questions

1. What is the activity performed most often when using the Internet?
2. What is an ISP?
3. Name two different options for a broadband connection to the Internet.
4. What is a Wi-Fi hotspot?
5. What type of Internet service would be suitable for someone who travels a lot?
6. You want to work from home, but you discover that your workplace has a VPN. Is it possible to connect over the Internet?
7. What types of software are required in order to be able to surf the Web and use email?
8. If you're using a public machine such as at a cyber café or open access area in a school, what should you consider if you want to do your banking online?

9. What types of software should you consider running for security purposes when you're connecting to the Internet?

10. What's the difference between spyware and a virus?

11. Is it safe to provide your credit card number on a form on a Web page?

12. Describe the differences between shareware, freeware, and open source software.

13. When you are connected to the Internet, why does your computer require an IP address?

14. You've typed a URL into the address bar of your Web browser, but the page does not seem to be loading. Describe the steps you can take to troubleshoot this.

Hands-on Exercises

1. Open a Web browser and go to your ISP's page. If you do not subscribe to an ISP, go to `http://www.thelist.com` and choose one. Look for the information on the site to answer the following questions.

   a. What is the technical support phone number?

   b. What are the technical support service hours?

   c. Are there broadband connections available, and if so, what are the upload and download speeds?

   d. Is there a page available that announces the current status of the network?

   e. Does your ISP offer extra services such as classes, incentives for recommending customers, links to community organizations or events, or any other value added extras?

2. Open a Web browser and go to `http://securityresponse.symantec.com/` to see the latest virus threats. What are the three top virus threats currently?

3. Open a Web browser and go to Download.com (`http://www.download.com`). What are the three most popular software downloads?

The Development of the Internet

chapter 2

Chapter Objectives

This chapter helps you understand

- the development of the Internet from the 1940s to the present.
- how nuclear threats and the space age ushered in the idea of the Internet.
- how RAND engineers developed the idea of a "Galactic Network."
- the evolution of ARPANET and the National Control Protocol (NCP).
- how email contributed to the rise of Internet communication.
- the importance of TCP/IP to internetworking.
- the importance of Request for Comments (RFC) documents.
- how the U.S. National Science Foundation played an integral role in the development of the Internet.
- what Internet2 is, and who uses it.
- how the Internet is developing around the world.
- what domain names are, and how to get one.
- what the World Wide Web is, and how to use it.

Welcome to the Internet

In William Gibson's 1984 science fiction novel *Neuromancer*, we were introduced to the concept of "Cyberspace." Per Gibson's account, people could literally "jack" into a three-dimensional interactive computer network by plugging a cable into their heads, allowing them to mentally "see" a rich virtual reality. He described it this way, "Cyberspace: a graphic representation of data abstracted from the banks of every computer in the human system." Although you can't quite plug your brain into Cyberspace (yet), you can access a worldwide network of computers through your keyboard and mouse.

And, accessing these computers (and the information stored on them) has caused a significant amount of excitement among its users. But a lot of users out there still don't know, exactly, what Cyberspace is. Some people think that the Internet and the World Wide Web are the same thing, but they're not. The World Wide Web is a collection of files including Web pages, pictures, audio, video, and other files, stored on computers all over the world. The Internet is the collection of computer networks all over the world, and these networks include the computers that store the files we access when we use the World Wide Web. The World Wide Web is part of the Internet, but the Internet also includes email, videoconferencing, peer-to-peer file sharing, gaming, and other features that are separate from the World Wide Web. So, let's take a look behind the scenes at how the Internet developed.

Development of the Internet: from the 1940s to the Present

RAND Engineers Envision a "Galactic Network"

With the advent of the Space Age and threat of nuclear war during the late-1950s, scientists at the Research and Development (RAND) Corporation (a private think-tank based in Santa Monica, California), were given the task of developing a communications network that could withstand a nuclear attack. The challenge was to create a network that could withstand losing one or more communications links should they be eliminated by an attack, and automatically route messages through areas that were still connected.

Traditional communication networks used a central hub, and messages were broadcast from that hub to other computers or communications installations. At first, RAND's "galactic network" was considered highly unconventional. RAND's strategy was to create a supercomputer network that was organized so that there were many hubs scattered throughout the country and messages could travel from any hub through a variety of different routes. RAND's strategy was a distributed network as opposed to the traditional centralized network. Figure 2.1 illustrates a centralized network and a distributed network.

RAND designed its network idea (Figure 2.2), based on the assumption that no single computer or communication line was critical. Communication could be accomplished using several different routes. Each computer would routinely look for all the other computers on the network. If a computer or line went out, the remaining computers would collectively bypass the system malfunction. Likewise, if a computer or communication line came back up, the other computers would immediately recognize it.

Let's look at Figure 2.2 for a moment to see how this works. If you wanted to transmit a message from, say, Chicago to Atlanta, the network could route the message from Chicago to Indianapolis to Atlanta. The message could also be routed from Chicago to New York to Washington to Atlanta. Depending upon which point or line went down, a message from Chicago to Atlanta could be routed via several other combinations.

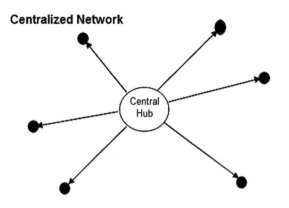

Centralized Network

Distributed Network

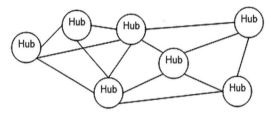

Figure 2.1   Centralized and Distributed Networks.

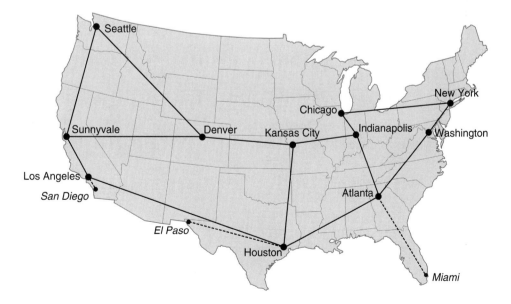

Figure 2.2   An example of ARPANET's connectivity.

Nuclear Threats and the Space Age

Hiroshima and Nagasaki

To understand the interrelationship between the Internet and the Web, we must revisit the end of World War II in 1945 when the U.S. dropped atomic bombs on Hiroshima and Nagasaki (Walker, 2003; Hogan 1996). While Harry S Truman's decision to use these weapons may have ultimately produced Japan's unconditional surrender, it also made the threat of having another atomic exchange seem imminent. Several nations began developing their own atomic and nuclear arsenals: USSR (confirmed in 1949), Great Britain (1952), France (1960), China (1964), and India (1974). Today, the tactical nuclear landscape is much more widespread and sophisticated.

Sputnik I, ARPA, Explorer I, and EMPs

Still, nothing was as troubling to U.S. scientists and politicians as the launching of Earth's first artificial satellite on October 4, 1957: **U.S.S.R. Sputnik I.** This event heightened the Cold War to an entirely new level (Siddiqi, 2003; Divine 1993). Given the invention of satellites, nuclear payloads could now be deployed in, and from, space. Alarmed, the **U.S. Advanced Research Projects Agency (ARPA)** was formed to consider the strategic issues made possible by new scientific

discoveries, and to seek out counter-measures to preexisting technological problems. In 1958, the National Aeronautics and Space Administration (NASA) was also formed to organize U.S. efforts to establish strategic satellites and explore space. Wasting no time, NASA launched its first satellite, **U.S. Explorer I** on January 31, 1958, rivaling the Soviet accomplishment.

Now that the U.S. had secured the same advantage as the Soviets in space, ARPA began examining new evidence that made the "satellite attack" scenario even more disturbing. In 1959, physicists investigating the effects of test blasts in Los Alamos, New Mexico found that the electromagnetic pulse (EMP) surging from a nuclear explosion rendered much of their electronic equipment inoperative. As testing continued, pulses were detected hundreds of miles away from the epicenters of the test blasts (O'Neil, 1995). These EMPs neutralized any equipment using electricity—lights, battery-powered radios, spark plugs inside combustible engines, telephones, and even computer equipment. This was made quite apparent when a 1.4-megaton test blast, approximately 250 miles in the atmosphere above Johnston Island in the Pacific, produced an EMP strong enough to cause unexpected electrical failures throughout Hawaii (over 800 miles away).

ARPANET

In 1968, the Advanced Research Project Agency (ARPA), of the U.S. Department of Defense, began to develop an **internetwork** on the West Coast of the U.S. An internetwork is a collection of computer networks, joined so that a computer on one network can send a message to a computer on another network. ARPA's network was called ARPANET. Each network connected to an internetwork has at least one computer that connects directly to the internetwork. A computer connected directly to the internetwork is called a host. For example, if a user at UCLA wanted to send a message to a user at Stanford, this is what would happen. The user at UCLA sends the message and it goes to the host computer at UCLA. The host computer at UCLA sends the message to the host computer at Stanford. The host computer at Stanford then delivers the message to the specific computer at Stanford. How the message gets from the host at UCLA to the host at Stanford is a function of the internetwork, and ARPANET could route the package a variety of different ways.

On September 2, 1969, UCLA became the first **host** connected to ARPANET. The Stanford Research Institute, the University of California at Santa Barbara (UCSB), and the University of Utah were connected within the following two months.

In its infancy, the hosts at UCLA, Stanford, UCSB, and Utah would periodically crash. Despite this, the system provided some extraordinary benefits for researchers: (1) it could transfer sizable amounts of data from one network to the other; (2) it allowed them to make use of remote computers at other select institutions, which was especially important since "access time" was scarce; (3) it allowed for the writing or installation of programs on remote computers; and (4) it increased interpersonal communication between the people at these institutions. While ARPA wanted to see all four of these benefits materialize, they did not anticipate the growth in interpersonal communication.

A Reliable Protocol in NCP

To improve ARPANET, ARPA requested that the four test institutions develop a more capable and reliable protocol for transferring packets of information. A protocol is basically a set of rules governing information transfer from one computer to another and **packets** are small packages of information. **National Control Protocol (NCP)** was the new protocol developed in 1970. The release of NCP allowed ARPANET to begin its first expansion phase. Figure 2.3 shows the increase in the number of hosts connected to ARPANET during the 1970s.

Communications Tools

People who had access to ARPANET and its resources were researchers at major research institutions and private firms on the cutting edge of science and technology research and development. It was not a publicly accessible internetwork.

In 1972, Ray Tomlinson invented the first email program that could deliver messages across ARPANET. In 1973, vocal patterns were coded into transmittable signals, and history recorded the first multi-party conference call using ARPANET. Building upon Tomlinson's invention of email, in 1975 Steve Walker created a way to

Packets and Protocols

The Birth of Communication Protocols

RAND worked in conjunction with the Massachusetts Institute of Technology (MIT) and the University of California at Los Angeles (UCLA) during the 1960s to build a set of communication protocols that would direct information around broken or clogged points on the network. A **protocol** is basically a set of rules governing information transfer from one computer to another. Today there are a wide variety of protocols available. The principal theorists who developed these protocols in the 1960s were Americans Paul Baran (RAND) and Lawrence Roberts (MIT). But their ideas were merely notions in articles, and had not yet been tested by the rigors of programming.

NPL Net and Packets

Interestingly, it would be the British who would first put these American theories into action. At the National

Physical Laboratory in 1967, Donald W. Davies developed the **NPL Network** using the first **packets** to transfer data. Based upon the American hypotheses, the British team agreed with Baran and Roberts that any data traveling on such a dispersed system would have to emulate the structure of the network (Metcalfe et al., 1996). In other words, if the network were going to function on a distributed model, then so too should the data. As a result, they designed a system that would allocate data streams into **packets**, smaller bundles that made traffic more manageable across the Internet. This way, if a few packets of the whole transmission got lost, at least the general message would probably make it through the network. And, if a piece or segment of the transmission were somehow intercepted, it would make little sense without the remainder of the data. This system was the first attempt to design a formal network protocol.

send one email to many people using one address. But perhaps the most important invention of this era was the 1975 debut of a durable new network protocol called the **Transmission Control Protocol (TCP)**. It was initially tested during the first satellite link-up of ARPANET between Hawaii and Great Britain (Zakon, 2004).

The Personalization of Email

As the Department of Defense continued to finance ARPANET, network administrators suddenly found themselves in an interesting predicament. As early as 1973, ARPA's internal audits confirmed that email alone was totaling nearly 75% of all network activ-

INTERNET GROWTH

Date	Hosts	Date	Hosts	Networks	Domains
12/69	4	07/89	130,000	650	3,900
06/70	9	10/89	159,000	837	
10/70	11	10/90	313,000	2,063	9,300
12/70	13	01/91	376,000	2,338	
04/71	23	07/91	535,000	3,086	16,000
10/72	31	10/91	617,000	3,556	18,000
01/73	35	01/92	727,000	4,526	
06/74	62	04/92	890,000	5,291	20,000
03/77	111	07/92	992,000	6,569	16,300
12/79	188	10/92	1,136,000	7,505	18,100
08/81	213	01/93	1,313,000	8,258	21,000
05/82	235	04/93	1,486,000	9,722	22,000
08/83	562	07/93	1,776,000	13,767	26,000
10/84	1,024	10/93	2,056,000	16,533	28,000
10/85	1,961	01/94	2,217,000	20,539	30,000
02/86	2,308	07/94	3,212,000	25,210	46,000
11/86	5,089	10/94	3,864,000	37,022	56,000
12/87	28,174	01/95	4,852,000	39,410	71,000
07/88	33,000	07/95	6,642,000	61,538	120,000
10/88	56,000	01/96	9,472,000	93,671	240,000
01/89	80,000	07/96	12,881,000	134,365	488,000
		01/97	16,146,000		828,000
		07/97	19,540,000		1,301,000

Figure 2.3   Internet growth.

ity. Users were establishing individual ARPANET accounts, and were spending a substantial portion of their workday chatting via email with their colleagues. They were not, as had been anticipated, spending their time analyzing data. Instead, they were all *communicating through computers*—about their projects, about their friends and families, and about themselves.

TCP/IP and Internetworking

During the late-1970s, many corporations and state agencies had invested a considerable amount of money and energy into building their own *private* computer networks. These networks enabled each organization to consolidate their resources and provided electronic communication, but the networks of one company could not communicate with the networks of another. A few of the private networks had adopted TCP/IP but very few of the private networks had access to one another. The problems remained: How could accountants for the U.S. Department of State access billing records at Honeywell? How could officials working for the State of Florida interact with Sperry-Rand on an upcoming project? In 1983 when ARPA announced that it would be switching from the National Control Protocol (NCP) to **TCP/IP (Transmission Control Protocol/Internet Protocol)** on its network hosts, most others jumped on the bandwagon as well.

tip

∴ According to the W3C Manual of Style (http://www.w3 .org/2001/06/manual/) the words *Internet* and *Web* always begin with a capital letter.

A large number of previously private and new networks began adopting TCP/IP, too. As TCP/IP was installed on each new network and connected directly to ARPANET, it was connecting at least one of its main computers as a host to the larger Internetwork. This extended ARPANET as a communication vehicle to all the networks and the resources connected to them. This encompassed the lines running to the computers, the host system; the machines (if any existed) networked from that host, and most certainly the people using those machines. Throughout the 1980s, this Internetwork continued to grow and incorporate new systems until it took on its own social meaning as a formal place: the **Internet.**

Request For Comment (RFC) Documents

The definitive documents, detailing all the protocols, and other technical information regarding standards and how the Internet works, can be found in a collection of documents called RFCs (Request for Comments). Initially, as a new Internet feature was developed, the researcher would write an RFC document and distribute it among the other researchers hoping for feedback, and adding it to the bank of other RFCs. Collectively, they would form the technical specifications of the Internet protocols and standards, and then perhaps one day when it was fully developed, create the final document. However, the development has continued at a very rapid pace, and the RFCs have become the final documents themselves. The RFCs can be found at the Internet RFC archive (`http://www.faqs.org/rfcs/`). Thousands of these documents have been developed.

If you were to browse through these documents, you may find that a few of them look particularly odd. Researchers do have a sense of humor, and there are many April Fool's RFCs that have been developed over the years on April 1st, as a prank. They look very serious when you first read them. Here are some examples:

RFC 2324—Hyper Text Coffee Pot Control Protocol (HTCPCP/1.0) (April 1, 1998)

> Describes a protocol for monitoring coffee pots connected to the Internet.

RFC 1149—A Standard for the Transmission of IP Datagrams on Avian Carriers (April 1, 1990)

> Describes in detail, the process for using duct tape to secure a message to the leg of a carrier pigeon, and using a fleet of carrier pigeons for transporting messages.

RFC 2795—The Infinite Monkey Protocol Suite (April 1, 2000)

> "This memo describes a protocol suite which supports an infinite number of monkeys that sit at an infinite number of typewriters in order to determine when they have either produced the entire works of William Shakespeare or a good television show. The suite includes communications and control protocols for monkeys and the organizations that interact with them." (RFC 2795, 2004).

RFC 3751—Omniscience Protocol Requirements (April 1, 2004)

> Describes a protocol that can install itself without detection, monitor activity, determine the intent of someone to commit an illegal act, such as copyright infringement, and report the doings of the "evil doers" to the "good guys."

tip

∴ If you are looking for information on Internet specifications, you can search for keywords on the Internet RFC archive site (`http://www.faqs.org/rfcs/`) rather than trying to guess which RFC may have the information you are looking for.

The TCP/IP Stack

TCP/IP is actually a family of protocols, in which TCP and IP are only two of the protocols in the suite. When network analysts and other computer professionals talk about network protocols, they often talk about the **stack**. The stack refers to the concept that the protocols are organized into layers. The stack divides the protocols into layers of types of communication. The TCP/IP stack is composed of four layers: Link, Network, Transport, and Application. Their basic functions are outlined in the table below:

Application

Protocols: Telnet, FTP, RPC, email, chat, WWW clients

Function: Users interact with the network

Transport

Protocol: TCP (Transmission Control Protocol)

Function: Ensures that packets are received in the order sent and retransmits if there is an error

Network

Protocol: IP (Internet Protocol)

Function: Determines, based on the destination IP address, how to get the data to its destination

Link

Devices: Network card, device driver

Function: Communicates with the hardware, strips header information when received and adds header information to send

This is a very simplified view and many protocols and details have been omitted, but it is useful for a brief overview.

Let's look at a quick example. When an application such as email sends a message to another email address, several steps happen very quickly.

1. The destination name is converted to an IP address, via the Domain Name System.

2. Email sends the message to the transport layer.

3. Transmission Control Protocol (TCP) breaks the message up into packets, and adds header information such as destination IP address, and originating IP address.

4. The transport layer sends the packets to the network layer.

5. Internet Protocol (IP) takes over at the network layer and determines which router the packets should be sent to, in order to head toward their destination. The packets are handed to the link layer.

6. The network card sends the packets out through the network, where they head to the router, on their way to the destination.

Again this is very simplified, but HTTP, email, and other clients and protocols interact with TCP/IP at the application layer, working together to send and receive packets of information. And all of this is happening in the blink of an eye, or faster.

ARPANET Goes Public

While ARPA wanted expansion to happen, they were shocked at the rate of network expansion. Given that most of the network traffic was email and other communication, ARPA took measures to protect the research and development community from being overwhelmed by "online noise" and developed a dedicated access-only network in 1983 called MILNET. They relocated all critical ARPA staff to MILNET, and left ARPANET to the public. In the end, ARPANET simply became a victim of its own success. With its rapid popularity, it accidentally grew beyond the scope and mission of its designers. As ARPANET rapidly evolved, the "network" as it once existed is no longer in operation. On its 20th Anniversary, the first supercomputer ever connected to ARPANET was symbolically disconnected at UCLA in 1989.

U.S. National Science Foundation to the Rescue

In 1984, one year after ARPA retreated from ARPANET, the U.S. National Science Foundation (NSF) emerged to continue to spearhead Internet development. Through their Office of Advanced Scientific Computing, and with the financial backing of both Congress and the White House, plans were made to build a massive new information superstructure named **NSFNET**. NSF introduced five supercomputing facilities in 1986 that would provide the nation's major research institutions with high-speed computing access (Zakon, 2004). In 1988, NSFNET upgraded the dedicated lines running between these systems to T1 fiber-optics. This allowed data-transfer rates of nearly 1.5 Mbps (millions of **bits** of data per second). A **byte** of data is 8 bits, or a single ASCII character. This was quite an upgrade, considering that ARPANET's cross-country network only allowed for throughput of 56 Kbps (thousands of bits per second). And in 1991, NSFNET once again upgraded the network to T3 fiber-optics, allowing for nearly 25 times the flow of data over its T1 predecessor (44.7 Mbps). In less than a decade, NSFNET had constructed an enormous data pipeline stretching across the U.S. It became known as the **U.S. backbone.**

Internet2

Today, development is focused on Internet2, or the Abilene network. A consortium of universities, corporations, and government agencies has created partnerships to advance Internet technology further. As it is today, the Internet will not sustain unlimited growth. Internet2 development focuses on increasing bandwidth, and advanced technologies such as digital laboratories and digital video. You will find more information about the Internet2 initiative at http://www.internet2.edu.

tip

∴ The National Science Foundation is an active organization and more information can be found at http://www.nsf.gov/.

Internet History Timeline

Here is a quick thumbnail history of some of the important events that led to the development of the Internet.

1945	The U.S. dropped atomic bombs on Hiroshima and Nagasaki ushering in the Atomic Age.
1957	The Soviets launched the world's first artificial satellite, U.S.S.R. Sputnik I.
1958	The Americans rivaled the launch of Sputnik I with Explorer I.
1958	The National Aeronautics and Space Administration (NASA) was formed.
1958	Scientists at the Research and Development (RAND) Corporation (a private think tank based in Santa Monica, California), were given the task of developing a communications network that could withstand a nuclear attack.
1959	Physicists investigating the effects of atomic test blasts in Los Alamos, New Mexico found that the electromagnetic pulse (EMP) surging from a nuclear explosion rendered much of their electronic equipment inoperative.
The 1960s	RAND worked in conjunction with the Massachusetts Institute of Technology (MIT) and the University of California at Los Angeles (UCLA) to build a set of communication protocols that would direct information around broken or clogged points on a network.
1967	At the National Physical Laboratory, Donald W. Davies developed the NPL Network using the first packets to transfer data.
1968	The Advanced Research Project Agency (ARPA) began to develop an internetwork on the West Coast of the U.S.
1969	UCLA became the first host connected to ARPANET.
1970	The National Control Protocol (NCP) was developed in 1970. The release of NCP allowed ARPANET to begin its first expansion phase.
1972	Ray Tomlinson invented the first email program that could deliver messages across ARPANET.
1975	Debut of a durable new network protocol called the Transmission Control Protocol (TCP).
Late 1970s	Many corporations and state agencies invested a considerable amount of money and energy into building their own private computer networks.
1983	When ARPA announced that it would be switching from the National Control Protocol (NCP) to TCP/IP (Transmission Control Protocol/Internet Protocol) on its network hosts, many others jumped on the bandwagon as well.

(continues)

(continued)

1984	One year after ARPA retreated from ARPANET, the U.S. National Science Foundation (NSF) emerged to continue to spearhead Internet development.
1986	NSF introduced five supercomputing facilities in 1986 that would provide the nation's major research institutions with high-speed computing access.
1988	NSFNET upgraded its dedicated lines to T1 fiber-optics.
1991	NSFNET upgraded its network to T3 fiber-optics, allowing for nearly 25 times the flow of data over its T1 predecessor
1991	Commercial ISPs were allowed to join in.
1991	Tim Berners-Lee invented the World Wide Web
1992	The National Science Foundation awarded a five-year contract for managing domain name registration to Network Solutions, Inc.
1993	Students at the University of Illinois wrote a Web browser called Mosaic.
1995	Web traffic surpassed all other forms of online data flow to become the primary information transferred on the Internet.

Internet Development around the World

Canada, Mexico, countries in Europe, and many others were also developing their own infrastructure in the 1980s and 1990s.

Canada

Canada, in particular, began its drive to network its universities via bitnet in 1984 with its first link between Ithaca, NY, and Toronto, Ontario. **Bitnet** is an acronym that stands for **B**ecause **I**t's **T**ime **NET**work, and was a vast wide-area network (WAN) that maintained its own set of operating protocols apart from TCP/IP. In 1985, all Canadian universities were connected to **NetNorth**, the Canadian university network. In 1988, Canada connected to NSFNET and began the switch to TCP/IP. In 1990, as Canadian network traffic increased, **CA*Net** was launched using primarily 56 Kbps lines. Network traffic growth continued to explode and in 1997 the Canadian government launched **CA*Net II**, using a core fiber-optic network. The trend of higher traffic and more required bandwidth continued and in 1998 **CA*Net 3**, the first full-scale national optical Internet, was implemented (see Figure 2.4). These lines operate at 40 Gbps, or nearly 750,000 times the previous rate of the original CA*Net. Canada is currently in the deployment stage of **CA*Net 4**, as shown in Figure 2.4, which will yield four to eight times the information capacity of CA*Net 3.

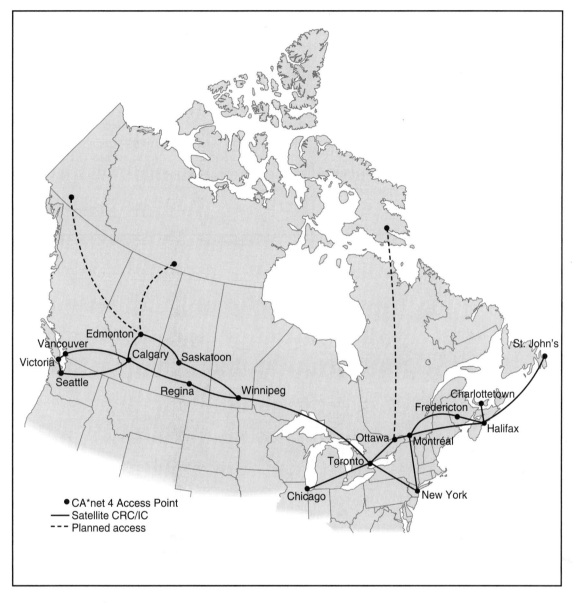

Figure 2.4   Canada's CA*Net 4.

Mexico

In Mexico, the Monterrey Institute of Superior Technology Studies established the first Mexican connection to the Internet in 1989. Between 1989 and 1994, other schools followed suit, connecting their regional networks to the Internet via the newly formed National Technology Network (NTN). In 1995, the Government of Mexico began constructing its own national backbone. In 1996, at the request of the Mexican government, Mexico's telephone company opened the academic research network for commercial applications. As a result, from 1996 to 1998, TelMex operated as an ISP monopoly in Mexico. In 1999, governmental deregulations opened the NTN network to free market reform, allowing for other ISPs to provide Internet connectivity (Thomasson, Foster, and Press, 2004). The competition bred excellence in service, reduced public costs to connect and, as an added benefit, also opened the door to direct foreign investments to build competing backbones. In 2001, Mexico announced the **e-Mexico initiative**: "a $400 million project designed to provide Internet access to all of Mexico's population" (p. 26). Today, Mexico has numerous international connections, including lines running to the prestigious **U.S. Abilene Network** (known as Internet2) ranging from 46 Mbps to 10 Gbps, as shown in Figure 2.5.

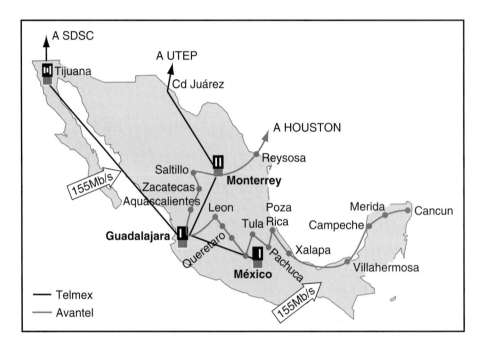

Figure 2.5 Mexico's backbone.

Europe

National borders, languages, and cultures complicated the development of the Internet infrastructure in Europe. There was some early resistance in the 1980s and 1990s to adopt TCP/IP. The majority of countries in Europe preferred to use their own private data lines and protocols. The European Union has since emerged and today these independent networks are internetworked.

The first pan-European attempt to interlink these independent networks began with the founding of **RARE** (Réseaux Associés pour la Recherche Européenne/European Association of Research Networks) in 1986. A serious attempt to define long-term objectives for Europe's academic research and development network was RARE's **COSINE**

Project (Cooperation for Open Systems Interconnection in Europe) who advocated the use of the OSI protocol suite. However, OSI was not compatible with TCP/IP, so a better answer was required: **the DANTE Project**. DANTE began on July 6, 1993 at St. John's College in Cambridge University. The project's charge was: "to rationalize the management of otherwise fragmented, uncoordinated, expensive and inefficient transnational services and operational facilities" (Dante, 2005).

DANTE began to develop the first pan-European network in 1993. From 1993 to 1997 its main project was **EuropaNET**, connecting 18 nations running 2 Mbps data lines. Yet, the most important switch during this time was that the service implemented TCP/IP. As was the case in Canada, network capacity was reached, requiring more bandwidth, and from 1997 to 1998 a new network was born: **TEN-34** emerged, connecting the same 18 countries, but now at speeds of 34 Mbps. Between 1998 and 2001, **TEN-155** was deployed, connecting 19 countries at speeds of 155 Mbps to 622 Mbps. And at the time of this publication, the **GÉANT** network connects 32 countries at speeds of between 2.5 Gbps and 10 Gbps. The GÉANT network, as shown in Figure 2.6, is one of the most advanced telecommunications structures designed for distributed networking in the world today.

Convergence of Efforts in the U.S.

Almost every U.S. government agency with a need for a distributed network helped fund the effort: the National Institutes of Health, NASA, the Department of Energy, the Department of Education, the Department of Commerce, and many more, regularly provided grants to organizations in need of connecting to the Internet.

Before 1991, only educational and governmental institutions could use the Internet. But in 1991, that restriction was lifted, opening up the way for commercial institutions to join in. The number of computers and hosts connected, and the amount of information available, began to mushroom rapidly. Internet service providers (ISPs) provided a means for the general population to use the vast resources of the Internet from their home computers. The Internet quickly became a full-fledged mass medium.

Domain Names

As discussed in Chapter 1, every computer and every host connected to the Internet is assigned an IP address. Most hosts are also assigned a domain name so that the user does not have to remember IP addresses. In the early days, the list of hosts and IP addresses was maintained in a small text file. By 1984 the Domain Name System was established. This is a system of computers with lists of domain names and IP addresses. No single system stores all the domain names and IP addresses.

You may have encountered many of the original six **Top Level Domains (TLDs)**, which comprise com (commerce), edu (education), org (organization—for non-profit organizations), net (network), gov (government), and mil (military). Very quickly, regional codes also emerged including country, state, and province codes (for Canada). You might see a domain name that includes hostname.k12.ut.us (K–12 school, Utah, U.S.) or hostname.gov.on.ca (government, Ontario, Canada). You will find that domain names are part of an email address or World Wide Web page address (URL—Uniform Resource Locator).

⁖ If you are trying to think of your own domain name, you can put words together or add a hyphen such as *my-site.com* or *MyCompany.com*.

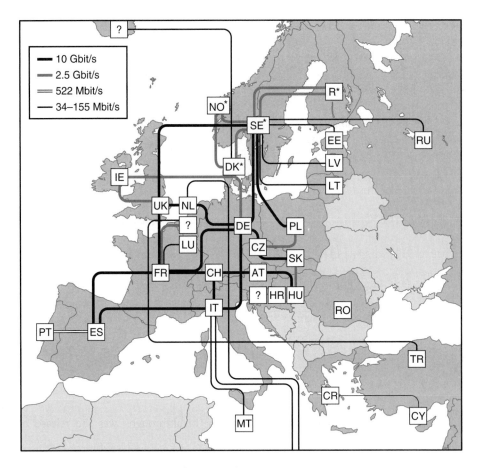

Figure 2.6 GEANT's Distributed Academic Network.

In 1992, the National Science Foundation awarded a five-year contract for managing domain name registration to Network Solutions Inc. (NSI). When the contract began, there were 7500 domain names registered. At the end of the contract there were over 2 million. NSI managed domain name registration for non-military top-level domain names including com, gov, edu, org, and net. When the NSI contract expired, the NSF struck an agreement with the non-profit organization Internet Corporation for Assigned Numbers and Names (ICANN) to manage top-level domain registration. Today, ICANN accredits registrars to register domain names and virtually anyone can buy a domain name.

The World Wide Web

Of all the innovations that have contributed to the development of the Internet, perhaps the most powerful contribution was made in 1991 (that crucial year, again!) by programmer Tim Berners-Lee, who was working for the European Particle Physics

Laboratory (CERN) in Geneva. Berners-Lee is credited with developing the World Wide Web (WWW). The WWW is a network of hypertext documents created by millions of people throughout the world. A **hypertext document** is a document containing links, and when the user clicks on a link, another document is displayed. The hypertext transfer protocol (HTTP) is a protocol used for retrieving Web pages and it works with TCP/IP. The URL specifies the protocol, host, and domain name in the form of *protocol://host-name.domain*. For example, the URL `http://www.w3.org/` specifies the protocol as HTTP, the hostname is *www* and the domain name is *w3.org*.

Before the Web and HTTP, users used a text-based resource known as Gopher (named after the Golden Gophers at the University of Minnesota where the device was invented). **Gopher** was a simple system of text menus that users had to "dig" (pun intended) their way through to get to the information they wanted. Berners-Lee made this process more user-friendly by designing a simple markup language called Hypertext Markup Language (HTML). The most revolutionary feature of HTML is the ability to create hypertext links, which point to other documents on the WWW, including Web pages. When the user clicks on a hypertext link, the document is requested from the host computer, and sent back to the user's computer.

When Berners-Lee engineered the Web, NSFNET traffic was at 1 trillion bits per month. In 1993, students at the University of Illinois wrote a program called Mosaic. This revolutionized the Web. This was the first graphical Web browser, which allowed people to point and click links, view graphic images, and much more. By 1995, the Web surpassed all other forms of online data flow to become the primary information transferred on the Internet.

Much of the explosion in Web use comes from a convergence of four major events preceding and during 1995. The first of these breakthroughs was the release of Windows 95. This popular product made using the Internet accessible to the masses because it provided a turnkey means of accessing the Internet through a simple telephone line. The next breakthrough came when Netscape released its Web browser designed for Windows 95. The third important event was the rise of private Internet service providers like America Online, Prodigy, CompuServe, and independent ISPs. But perhaps one of the most important reasons of all is that technology prices began to drop, as the speed and efficiency of the technology continued to increase.

Figure 2.7 indicates the growth *of information* on the Web. This chart tells us how many millions of Web sites (not pages) have been placed on servers since the summer of 1993. What is interesting about this chart is that it demonstrates the explosion of information occurring just after 1995. Another reason for this explosion is that in 1995 ownership of the Internet backbone lines was transferred from the government to private institutions, like MCI. The growth of information available is exponential, and has continued to grow at a rapid rate, with no signs of slowing down.

Who Is in Charge of the Internet?

As you've seen, the Internet is a truly global medium, and it does require some organizing infrastructure in order for it to work and expand. There are a few key organizations you should know about, indicated in the table on page 46.

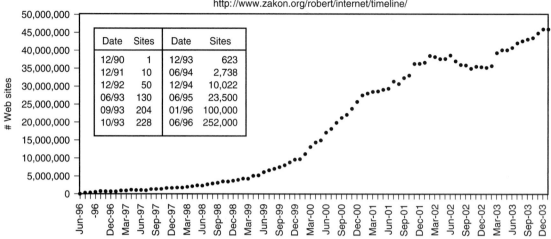

Figure 2.7   Growth of information on the WWW, as measured by the number of Web sites.

The Internet Society (ISOC)

http://www.isoc.org/

Membership:	An international organization composed of more than 150 organizations and 16,000 members in 180 countries.
Oversees:	A global clearinghouse of Internet information and education; coordinates Internet activities around the world.

The Internet Engineering Task Force (IETF)

http://www.ietf.org/

Membership:	A large international community of network engineers, vendors and any other interested individuals, and members of ISOC.
Oversees:	Technical working groups of the IETF oversee growth and change in the Internet architecture.

Internet Corporation for Assigned Names and Numbers (ICANN)

http://www.icann.org/

Membership:	An internationally organized non-profit corporation.
Oversees:	Responsible for assignment of generic Top Level Domain names (gTLD) and country code Top Level Domain names (ccTLD).

(continues)

The Internet Architecture Board (IAB)

http://www.iab.org/

Membership:	A committee of the IETF and advisory board to ISOC.
Oversees:	Internet architectural standards, appoints the RFC editor, administration for IANA.

Internet Assigned Numbers Authority (IANA)

http://www.iana.org/

Membership:	Based at ICANN.
Oversees:	In charge of assignment of unique parameters including IP addresses. Awarded domain name registration to ICANN.

SUMMARY

Now that you've read through the chapter, you are prepared to:

- Explain the development of the Internet from the 1940s to the present.
- Describe how the nuclear threat and Space Age forced U.S. scientists at the RAND Corporation to envision a "Galactic Network" for computer-based communications.
- Discuss the importance of packets and protocols.
- Recount the development of ARPANET, and understand the importance of the National Control Protocol (NCP) in its early formation.
- Assess the impact that some of the early communication tools, like email, had on the proliferation of the Internet.
- Explain the importance of TCP/IP, and describe how it relates to the concept of inter-networking.
- Detail some of the Request for Comments (RFC) documents available online, and understand why RFCs are important.
- Describe how ARPANET went public, and how the U.S. National Science Foundation funded the production of the early Internet.
- Briefly discuss Internet2, and its importance to major research and development institutions.
- Illustrate how the Internet has blossomed in other parts of the world, like Canada, Mexico, and Europe.
- Describe the convergence of technologies that contributed to the Internet development.
- Understand the domain name system and search for your own domain name.
- Discuss the importance of the World Wide Web and the success of the Internet.

Review Questions and Hands-on Exercises

Review Questions

1. What was the significance of nuclear testing in the development of the Internet?

2. What is the difference between a network and an internetwork?

3. What is a host computer?

4. What is the significance of ARPANET in relation to the development of the Internet?

5. What is an RFC document?

6. What is bandwidth, and how is it measured?

7. What is a packet?

8. What is the significance of the Domain Name System in the evolution of the Internet?

9. Describe two additional large-scale networking initiatives that were occurring around the world in addition to ARPANET?

10. What major contribution did Tim Berners-Lee make toward the development of the Internet?

11. What is the IETF and why is it important in the development of the Internet?

Hands-on Exercises

1. Open a Web browser and open the Hobbes' Internet Timeline at (`http://www.zakon.org/robert/internet/timeline/`).
   a. What is the earliest event in the timeline?
   b. In 1969 the first nodes were established. Where were they?
   c. In 1986 NSFNET was established. Which supercomputer sites were established?

2. The Yahoo! search directory is rich with resources including links to Internet statistics and demographics. Explore the Yahoo! Internet Statistics and Demographics links at `http://dir.yahoo.com/Computers_and_Internet/Internet/Statistics_and_Demographics/`. Look for information to try to determine answers to the following questions. You may not find the exact answer, but you will find some helpful information for each topic area below.
   a. How many people are online worldwide?
   b. What are the top five host names?
   c. Browse through the links for maps. What types of maps are available? Can you find a recent map for the backbone in the U.S, Canada, and Europe?

3. The Living Internet is rich in resources with excellent explanations of the history and current usage of Internet features. Explore the Living Internet at `http://livinginternet.com` and try to determine the answers to the following questions.
   a. In the History section, there are several names of people who have contributed to the development of the Internet. Choose one of the developers and summarize his contribution to the Internet in one or two sentences.
   b. What is the Internet Society?
   c. What is the Internet Engineering Task Force?

    d. Internet Myths and Legends describes the Internet Coke machine. Is this a myth or a legend? Feel free to also explore Yahoo's Devices Connected to the Internet for some interesting reading

    `http://dir.yahoo.com/Computers_and_Internet/`
    `Internet/Devices_Connected_to_the_Internet/`

4. As you surf the Web, you may wonder who owns some of the domain names, or you may be considering purchasing your own and wonder if it's been purchased already. A valuable resource to explore domain name ownership is a *whois* database. The InterNIC Whois search will allow you to explore top-level domains. Open the InterNIC Whois page at `http://www.internic.net/whois.html`. There are many other *whois* databases. Also have a look at Allwhois at `http://www.allwhois.com` to find this information.

    a. Search for the domain of your local college or university, if you know the domain. Also search for the following:

        i. mit.edu

        ii. umaine.edu

        iii. unr.edu

        iv. unt.edu

    b. Does anyone own *yourlastname.com*? Also check for *yourlastname.net* and *yourlastname.org*.

    c. Search for the domains of some of your favorite sites.

UTILIZING THE INTERNET AND WORLD WIDE WEB

part 2

	Chapter
Finding Resources on the World Wide Web	3
Email	4
Doing Business on the Web	5

Finding Resources on the World Wide Web

chapter 3

Chapter Objectives

This chapter helps you understand

- ☐ what's available on the World Wide Web.
- ☐ various online research tools at your disposal.
- ☐ several advanced searching strategies.
- ☐ how to evaluate any information you find online.
- ☐ how to reference and cite information that you find online.
- ☐ how to find and download software from the Internet.

Now that you have your computer configured and know how the Internet is structured, you want to get straight to the Web—right? Well, you aren't alone. The CIA World Fact Book reported in 2003 that there are over 604 million Internet users worldwide, and growing. One of the most popular search engines, Google (http://www.google.com) *was searching well over 4 billion Web pages in 2004 and is growing daily. That's where this chapter comes in. We want to familiarize you with some of the resources available on the Web, and help you develop your online search strategies.*

Browser Plug-ins

In Chapter 1, we looked at a variety of different Web browsers available. Be aware that **plug-in components** may be necessary to view the value-added features in some Web pages. You may be prompted to download and install a plug-in on occasion. Plug-in components are small programs that provide an environment in your browser for a specialized software program to run, or for viewing a specialized file, such as video or animation. There are hundreds of plug-ins available (usually free), which have been written for a variety of applications. If it's not clear to you why a plug-in is required, don't install it. Don't go to the trouble of finding and installing plug-ins manually. When you attempt to download a program or file that requires a plug-in, you will be prompted and can download at that time. The box below contains a list of several popular plug-ins (ranked by their popularity).

Plug-ins and Features

Plug-in Name	Quick Details
Adobe Acrobat Reader	Adobe .pdf files are widely used because they will print exactly the same on any printer. This overcomes issues like pagination—page lengths may be slightly different, throwing off page numbers and formatting. In order to print and view .pdf files, you need Adobe Acrobat Reader. In order to create .pdf files, you would have to purchase Adobe Acrobat.
QuickTime	This is a popular video player, supporting a wide variety of video formats. QuickTime movies themselves (.mov extension) have always been supported, but the QuickTime player also supports a long list of image, audio, and video formats.
RealPlayer	RealPlayer is a plug-in that supports streaming video. Streaming video plays as it is being downloaded, as opposed to having to download an entire video before playing it.
Flash Player	The Flash Player enables your browser to play animations created with Macromedia's Flash. These animations may also include action scripting. This allows interactivity with the user, including clicking buttons, completing forms, and even pulling information from a database for a user to view. This may be the most popular plug-in, but most newer browsers have incorporated the Flash Player into the browser software so you may never be prompted to install it.

What's Available on the Web?

There is a wealth of data available on the Web, but it boils down to three types: (1) hypertext documents, (2) data files, and (3) media files. Hypertext documents (Web pages) can include text, hypertext links, graphics, movie files, Java Applets, etc. A great example of a hypertext document might be a news site that converges text and graphics into an interactive site. An example of a news site is shown in Figure 3.1.

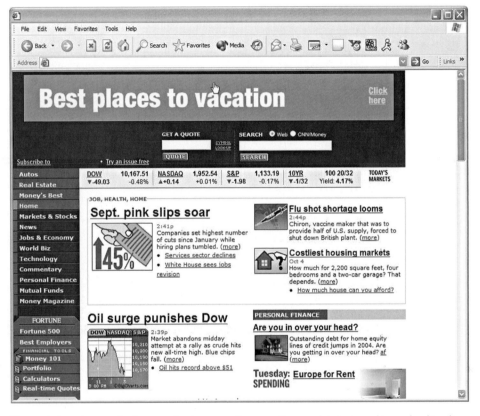

Figure 3.1   An example of a news site that uses a "converged" approach to text, graphics, and multimedia.

A **data file** can be a spreadsheet, word processing document, or another file you might deal with on a daily basis. These files can be downloaded via a hypertext link on a Web page. Depending on the Web browser you are using, you may be prompted to open the file or save it. Figure 3.2 shows a spreadsheet data file open in Internet Explorer.

A **media file** is a specialized data file that contains audio or video data. Basically, your browser will handle it and either launch a plug-in, or prompt you to save the file. Real Audio and Video media are streamed and require a specialized player.

Online Research Tools

The goal of online research is to provide you with the information you need, so you need to know how to use the tools available on the Web. We'll cover 12 different research

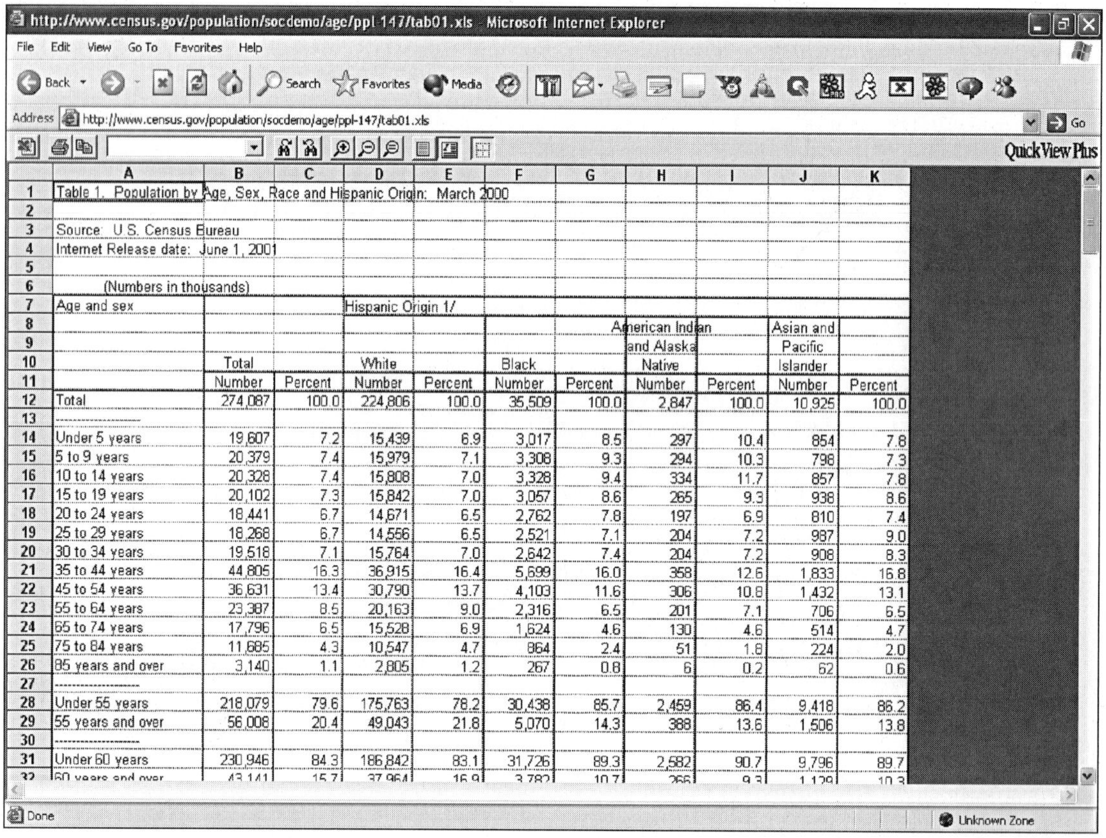

	A	B	C	D	E	F	G	H	I	J	K
1	Table 1. Population by Age, Sex, Race and Hispanic Origin: March 2000										
2											
3	Source: U.S. Census Bureau										
4	Internet Release date: June 1, 2001										
5											
6	(Numbers in thousands)										
7	Age and sex			Hispanic Origin 1/							
8								American Indian		Asian and	
9								and Alaska		Pacific	
10		Total		White		Black		Native		Islander	
11		Number	Percent	Number	Percent	Number	Percent	Number	Percent	Number	Percent
12	Total	274,087	100.0	224,806	100.0	35,509	100.0	2,847	100.0	10,925	100.0
13	-------------------										
14	Under 5 years	19,607	7.2	15,439	6.9	3,017	8.5	297	10.4	854	7.8
15	5 to 9 years	20,379	7.4	15,979	7.1	3,308	9.3	294	10.3	798	7.3
16	10 to 14 years	20,328	7.4	15,808	7.0	3,328	9.4	334	11.7	857	7.8
17	15 to 19 years	20,102	7.3	15,842	7.0	3,057	8.6	265	9.3	938	8.6
18	20 to 24 years	18,441	6.7	14,671	6.5	2,762	7.8	197	6.9	810	7.4
19	25 to 29 years	18,268	6.7	14,556	6.5	2,521	7.1	204	7.2	987	9.0
20	30 to 34 years	19,518	7.1	15,764	7.0	2,642	7.4	204	7.2	908	8.3
21	35 to 44 years	44,805	16.3	36,915	16.4	5,699	16.0	358	12.6	1,833	16.8
22	45 to 54 years	36,631	13.4	30,790	13.7	4,103	11.6	306	10.8	1,432	13.1
23	55 to 64 years	23,387	8.5	20,163	9.0	2,316	6.5	201	7.1	706	6.5
24	65 to 74 years	17,796	6.5	15,528	6.9	1,624	4.6	130	4.6	514	4.7
25	75 to 84 years	11,685	4.3	10,547	4.7	864	2.4	51	1.8	224	2.0
26	85 years and over	3,140	1.1	2,805	1.2	267	0.8	6	0.2	62	0.6
27	-------------------										
28	Under 55 years	218,079	79.6	175,763	78.2	30,438	85.7	2,459	86.4	9,418	86.2
29	55 years and over	56,008	20.4	49,043	21.8	5,070	14.3	388	13.6	1,506	13.8
30	-------------------										
31	Under 60 years	230,946	84.3	186,842	83.1	31,726	89.3	2,582	90.7	9,796	89.7
32	60 years and over	43,141	15.7	37,964	16.9	3,782	10.7	266	9.3	1,129	10.3

Figure 3.2 The Census Report on Population Trends in the U.S. An example of an Excel spreadsheet opening in a Web browser.

tools. For each, we'll talk about what it is, how to use it, and what its inherent advantages and disadvantages are.

Search Engines

A **search engine** is a Web-based program that allows users to submit key term requests to an online database. You have probably heard of some of these search engines before:

- Altavista.com (`http://www.av.com`)
- AskJeeves.com (`http://www.ask.com`)
- Excite.com (`http://www.excite.com`)
- Google.com (`http://www.google.com`)
- HotBot.com (`http://www.hotbot.com`)
- Infoseek.com (`http://www.infoseek.com`)
- LookSmart.com (`http://www.looksmart.com`)
- Lycos.com (`http://www.lycos.com`)
- Microsoft Search (`http://www.msn.com`)
- Yahoo.com (`http://www.yahoo.com`)

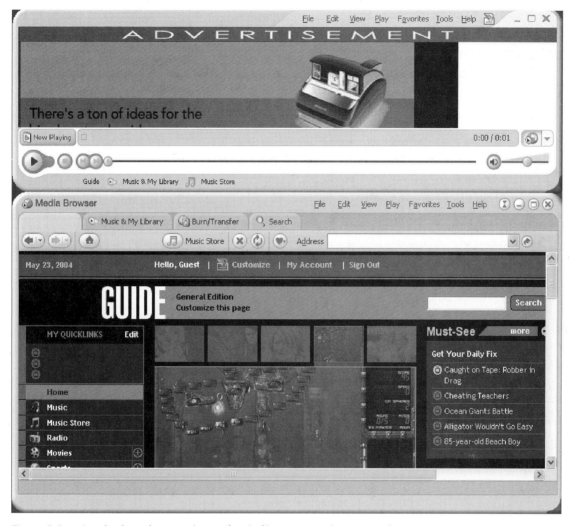

Figure 3.3   A media player plays several types of media files, integrating them into an all-in-one media client.

Search engine pages will contain an input box with a button next to it marked *Search* or *Submit*. Type the search term in the input box and press the *Enter* key on your keyboard (or click the button next to the input box).

The search engine scans its database to locate matches containing your key terms and provides a results page containing links to the resulting Web pages (Thurow, 2002). The results are usually listed in order of decreasing relevance. If you happen to have misspelled your search, as we did purposely in Figure 3.4 (*Atlana* rather than *Atlanta*), the search engine may list Web pages with that misspelling. The search engine, as is the case with most software, does only what you tell it to do. Some search engines, such as Google.com, will offer an alternative to a misspelled word.

Choosing Keywords   Be sure to use double quotes (") around phrases, especially if the keyword is three characters or less, or if your search term contains a number. Most

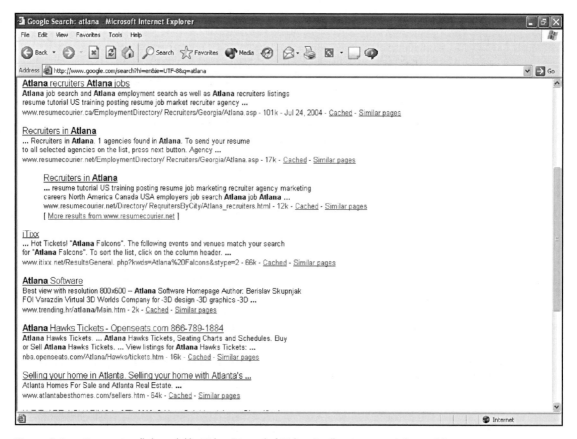

Figure 3.4 Even a misspelled search like "Atlana" instead of "Atlanta" will retrieve several thousand documents.

search engines do not search for words that are three characters or less, so if your search term is a short word, include it in a phrase. Here are examples of phrases that will be more effective encased in quotes:

"Windows XP"

"123 Main Street East"

"Jane R. Doe"

You can combine multiple keywords to refine your search. Simply type all the keywords, separating each by a space, and the search engine will look for Web pages containing all your keywords. Your keywords can also include phrases encased in quotes. Here are some examples of keyword searches:

nutrition bagel carbohydrate

dog barking "city bylaw"

➣ Open one of the search engine Web sites in a browser window.

➣ Choose one search term such as "dog" and note the number of results.

➣ Add another keyword to your search, such as "barking" and notice that the number of results has changed.

Advanced Search Features Many search engines include an advanced search page that helps to refine your search. Advanced features include searching for file type, Boolean operators (which we will discuss in detail later), file creation date, where terms occur in a page, and restricting the search to a particular domain for an *ad hoc* site search.

➤ Open the Google search page (`http://www.google.com`) in your Web browser.

➤ Click the *Advanced Search* link to see the options for advanced searching.

➤ Feel free to test it out with some keywords of your choice, and the date features to narrow down the search. Note that you can also select file types as well. This is useful if you're looking for images, video, or other file types.

➤ Open the Altavista search page (`http://www.av.com`) in your Web browser.

➤ Again, click the *Advanced Search* link to see the page of options for advanced searching and feel free to test it out with some keywords of your choice.

Search engines first appeared in 1994, as an effort to bring order to the upsurge of data being placed online (Berry and Browne, 1999). They are vital tools, which have become so popular that many have evolved into **portals,** or customizable entry-points to the Internet. Billed as something of a one-stop-shop for everyone's e-needs, portals offer services, which may include an email account, Web page space, and software. These are provided free to the user in an effort to ensure that the company's Web site is visited frequently and the appropriate advertising banners will be seen. A really good example of a portal is the My Yahoo! portal at `http://my.yahoo.com`. You can customize your My Yahoo! page to include news, weather, stock portfolio, mail, search, horoscope, comics, and other features on your page.

It is important to know that a search engine is not actually searching the entire Web, but only the Web pages it has found. Web pages are found in one of two ways: (1) knowbots, or (2) site notification. **Knowbots** are computer programs designed to crawl from one Web page to another through the links on each Web page, gathering keywords or whole pages as they go. They may also be referred to as "robots," "'bots," "spiders," or "crawlers," and they gather the majority of data provided by search sites.

The second method, **site notification**, is initiated by a person wishing to place a Web site URL in the search engine's database, using the search engine's submit procedure. A fast way to submit your URL to search engines is to use an online Web site registration services that sends out notifications to multiple search engines, for a modest fee.

Pros and Cons The main advantage of using a search engine is that it *searches* a large number of Web pages for your keywords. One disadvantage, however, is that a large search engine can give you more "hits," or search results, than you need. If you were to type in the word *toy*, for example, you would get back millions of Web page results.

Another issue with search engines is that you are relying on the Web page designer to identify his or her own data. When knowbots find a page on the Web, they use complicated algorithms to rank the importance of that data. For example, most databases will pay the most attention to the words in the title of the page, and in other key areas. Some Web pages also contain a **keywords meta-tag,** which identifies keywords for a search engine to index. Unscrupulous Web page designers use this knowledge to their advantage, placing frequently searched terms in the key section of the code, even if the page has nothing to do with the subject. Conversely, novice designers may not be aware of ranking methods, and fail to either properly identify the Web pages in the title or use other search engine optimization techniques.

For these reasons, search engine results can be very long, including Web pages that have nothing to do with your subject, and will be incomplete because no search engine contains an index of all Web pages.

Directory Outlines

What Are They? The second most familiar search tool is the **directory outline.** These contain a list of topics that can be browsed and searched, ranging from general to specific lists of subtopics and Web sites. A good example of a directory outline is Yahoo! (`http://www.yahoo.com`). Directory outlines evolved from the early days of the Web (circa 1995), when ambitious individuals began trying to categorize everything online (Angel, 2002). Moving from general to more specific sets of categorization, directory outlines provide structured option sets such that the user can choose categories of data containing links to topic areas or Web sites, as shown in Figure 3.5. If you wanted to search for a fan page for your favorite musician, for instance, you would work your way down through categories such as entertainment, music, classic rock, artist, and fan groups.

In the latter half of the 1990s, search engines and directory outlines began to converge, and the two formats became something of an integrated platform (Miller, 2000). Today, some search engines that were exclusively key term driven now also offer directory outlines and vice versa.

tip

Remember to use quotes around keywords that include numbers, and around phrases or titles. Examples include "John Doe," "2010 Olympic Games," and "Windows XP."

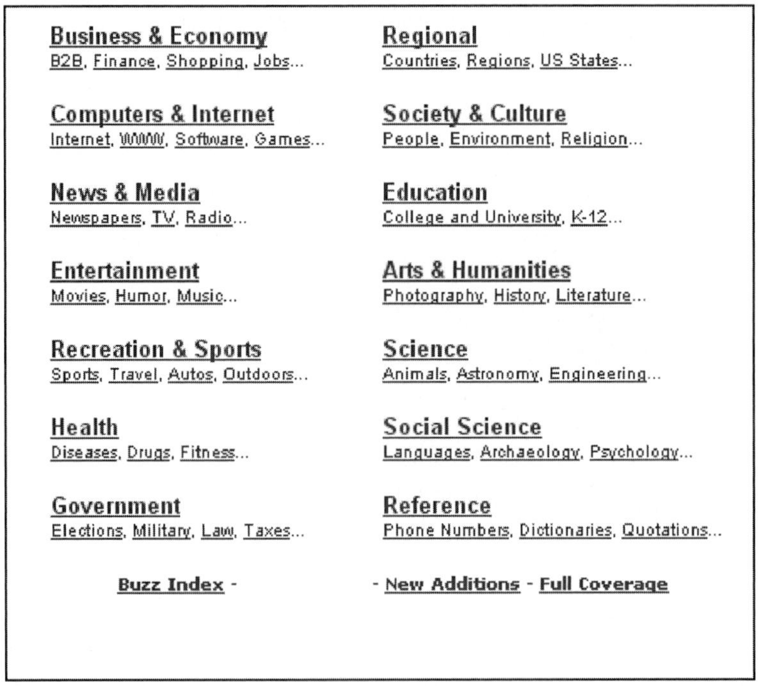
Business & Economy
B2B, Finance, Shopping, Jobs...
Regional
Countries, Regions, US States...
Computers & Internet
Internet, WWW, Software, Games...
Society & Culture
People, Environment, Religion...
News & Media
Newspapers, TV, Radio...
Education
College and University, K-12...
Entertainment
Movies, Humor, Music...
Arts & Humanities
Photography, History, Literature...
Recreation & Sports
Sports, Travel, Autos, Outdoors...
Science
Animals, Astronomy, Engineering...
Health
Diseases, Drugs, Fitness...
Social Science
Languages, Archaeology, Psychology...
Government
Elections, Military, Law, Taxes...
Reference
Phone Numbers, Dictionaries, Quotations...
Buzz Index -
- New Additions - Full Coverage

Figure 3.5 An example of a directory outline.

Pros and Cons The major advantage, which can also be a disadvantage, to the directory outline is that directories do not use knowbots for data retrieval and indexing. Web pages are indexed by humans. From its inception, Yahoo! has always adhered to this model, hiring employee topic managers to classify links. The advantage is that sites are categorized properly, and you will be much less likely to find irrelevant sites in the result list. About.com (`http://www.about.com`) has taken this approach one step further and provided people called *topic guides* who search for the most useful sites for a wide variety of topics.

The smaller volume of indexed Web pages in a directory outline may be a disadvantage if you are looking for something very specific and perhaps unusual.

Bibliographic Databases

What Are They? **Bibliographic databases** are reference collections to research materials such as journals and books. These databases are assembled by professionals, indexed according to keywords, and often have abstracts or even the complete text of the article/book. Because of the massive amount of work that goes into creating these databases, there is often a fee to access them. However, most college libraries subscribe to several databases, which you can access from computers in the library, and sometimes from any computer on your campus. For example, EBSCO shown in Figure 3.6, allows you to

≋*tip*

∴ If you are searching for a topic that is fairly common, start with a small directory such as Yahoo!. This will yield a smaller, but generally higher quality number of results.

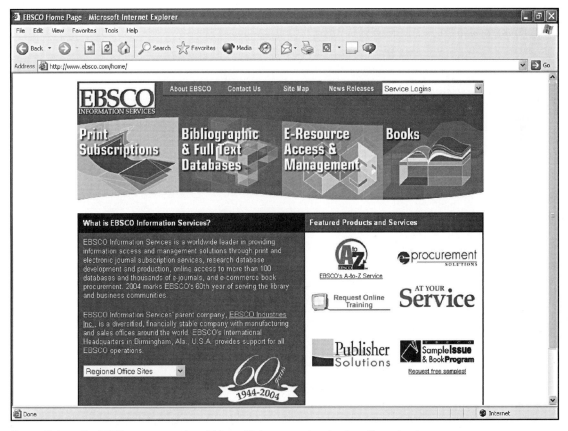

Figure 3.6   The EBSCO gateway provides a bibliographic bonanza to its subscribers. Your university library is likely a subscriber.

search through periodicals, research journals, ERIC documents, and much more, and often includes the full text. And, of course, most libraries today provide a Web interface to the database of books held in their collection, as shown in Figure 3.7.

Pros and Cons If you're doing academic research, your best bet for quality, reliable resources is the bibliographic database. In general, the Web pages resulting from general search engines and directories can be published by anyone. A bibliographic database contains academic research, which has been reviewed and edited by experts.

Bibliographic databases may contain an electronic form of the printed material, but most often will contain a reference to it. For example, the library database will return the call number of a book, but you will have to go through the book stacks to find it. Some databases provide the full text of recent periodical articles, but often you'll have to go to your library's collection of journals to find what you need. This may seem like a disadvantage, but online bibliographic databases are much easier to use than printed catalogs.

One drawback of these databases is that they rely heavily upon human effort. Because of this, they are likely to be slightly out of date. It is difficult for a periodical index, for example, to stay on top of thousands of publications that come out monthly, or weekly. But with advances in automation, these databases are doing an increasingly better job of staying current.

≋tip

∴ You will find bibliographic databases at library sites and you may require a userid and password to access them.

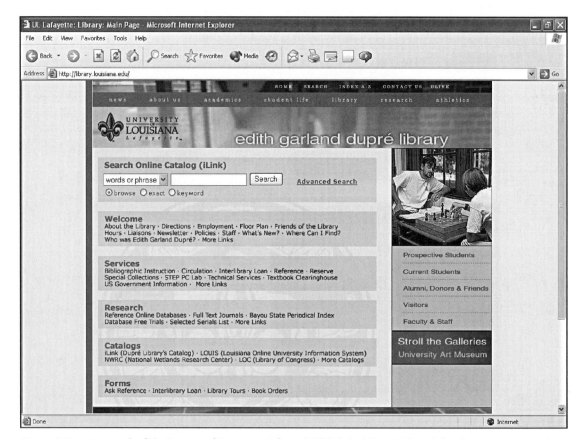

Figure 3.7   An example of The University of Louisiana at Lafayette's Edith Garland Dupré's Library Index. Most universities now have online indexes available for their book collections and online services.

Site-Specific Search Engines and Site Maps

What Are They? Site-specific search engines search only the data on a Web site, as shown in Figure 3.8. **Site maps** are outlines of a site's layout, which can be used as a navigational guide, as shown in Figure 3.9. Often, when you visit the site of a company that sells products online, you will notice that they have a key term input-box on the Web page for customer searching.

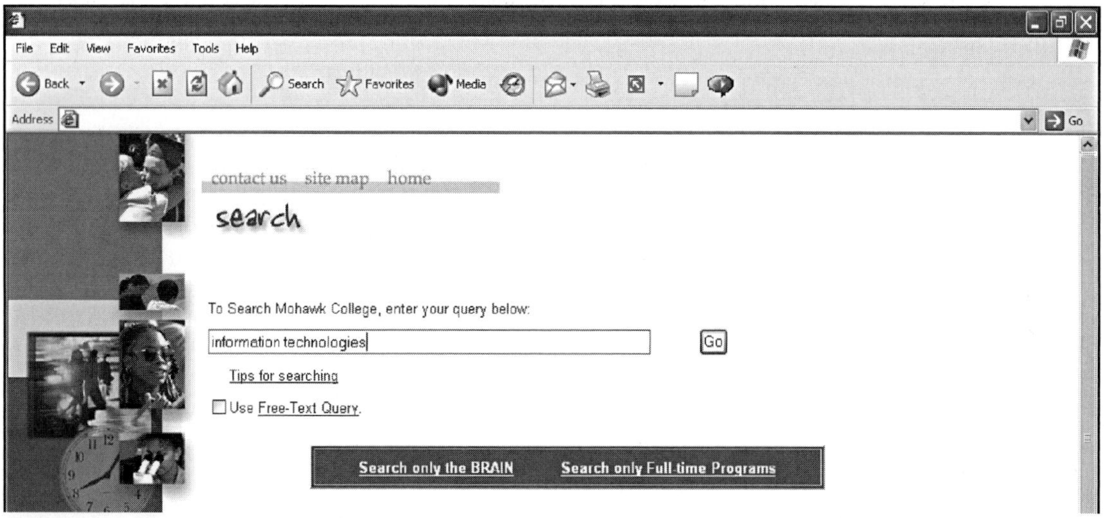

Figure 3.8   An example of a site-specific search engine.

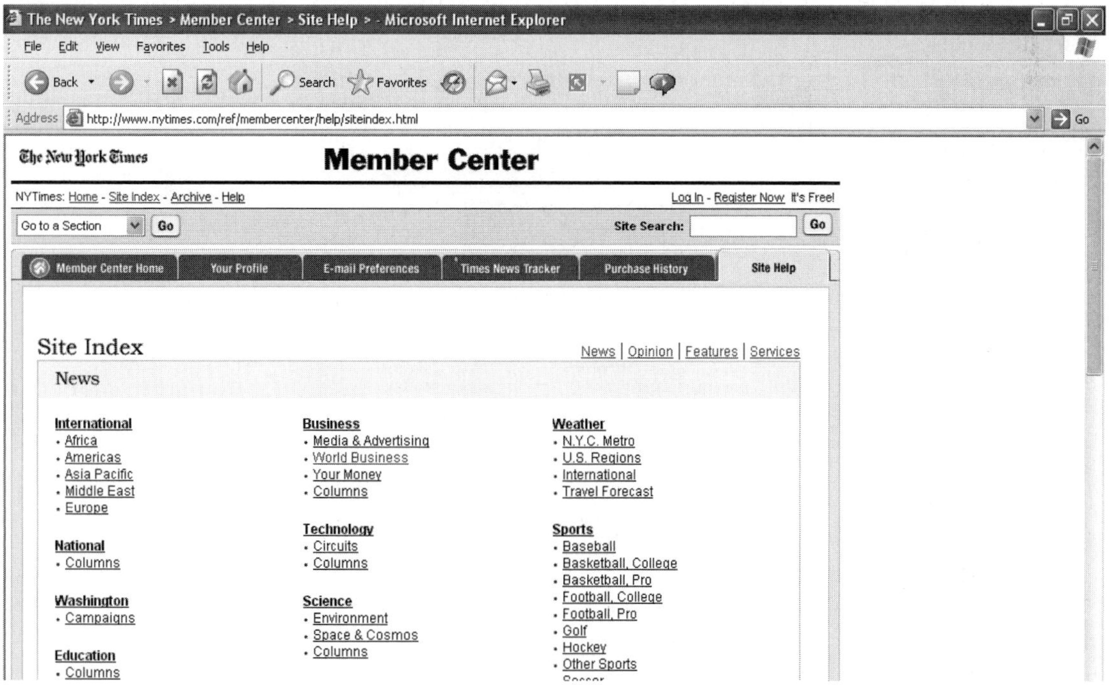

Figure 3.9   An example of NYTimes.com's site map. From here, you can find all the information you need by category.

When using these tools, treat them just as you would a major search engine or directory outline.

Pros and Cons Since site-specific engines only search the site to which they are attached, they are far more limited than general search engines, but the results will be very specific without a lot of unrelated results. If, for example, you're looking for information about the types of engines in the latest line of Toyota pickup trucks, you could use a general search engine to find this information but it is more efficient to first try the Toyota site (http://www.toyota.com) and use the site-specific search tool.

Typically the approach that researchers take is to find a good site using a general search engine, then search that site with its own site-specific tool.

Subject-Specific Search Engines and Directory Outlines

What Are They? Once programmers figured out how to direct knowbots to read specific files and directories across the Internet, the introduction of a new type of search interface emerged around 1996: the **subject-specific search engine**. These, and directory outlines, seek out the data stored on many different Web sites about a particular topic or theme. For instance, if you would like some information about Captain James T. Kirk, pregnancy and parenting, or boating, it is quite likely that a search engine dedicated to that data exists. ImOutdoors is a good example of a site-specific search engine, as shown in Figure 3.10.

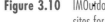

tip

⸪ Google will allow you to search a site using the *site* keyword. For instance, you can use the search term: *site:www.sony.com* to search the Sony site.

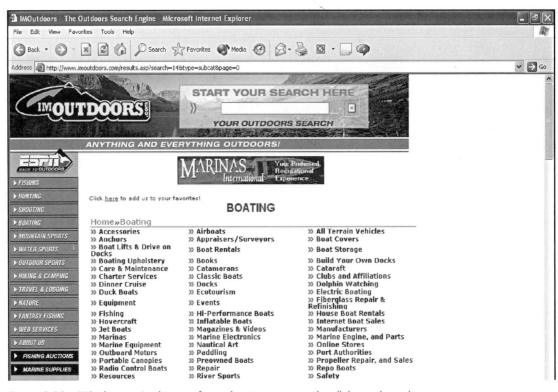

Figure 3.10   IMOutdoors.com's subject-specific search engine groups together all the popular outdoors sites for you, in one easy reference.

Pros and Cons Subject-specific tools may seem limited because they only search for a very specific type of data, but if you want that type of data, they can be invaluable. You can find many subject-specific search engines at Search.com (`http://www.search.com`).

One thing you should be wary of is that the subject-specific search engines and directory outlines are being created by topic enthusiasts who may advertise them to be comprehensive, when, in fact, they are not.

Metasearch Engines

What Are They? **Metasearch engines** (or **meta-engines**) are search engines that submit a key-term to several search engines, consolidating the results. An example of a metasearch engine is Dogpile (`http://www.dogpile.com`).

Metasearch engines are not search databases; each is a portal, or interface to many other search engines. The metasearch engine's usefulness is in the content-comparison formula that each site creates as a means for sorting through the various results (Michael and Salter, 2003, p. 12). The meta-engine gives higher importance to sites that rank high on several of the engines that it searched. Metasearch engines also often include features such as removing duplicate hits, and ranking or sorting results. An example of a meta-engine is shown in Figure 3.11.

Pros and Cons Meta-engines can make it easier for you to search several engines at once, but one shortcoming is that when it comes to more complex search requests, some metasearch engines do not adapt the search request for specific search engines. For instance, your search request might be *dogs OR cats* to yield results containing either

∴ Since you will be using a search engine frequently, set your home page as your favorite search engine Web page, or install the search engine toolbar if available!

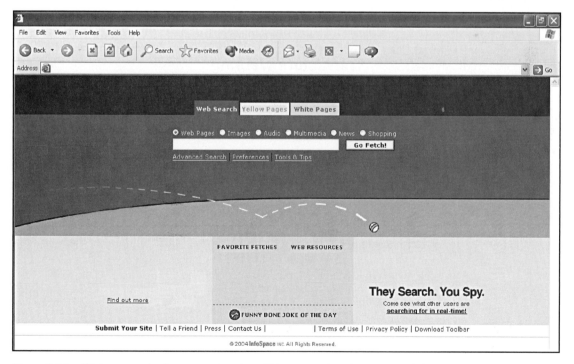

Figure 3.11 This is an example of a metasearch engine, which scans search engines to retrieve links to high-relevance Web sites.

dogs or *cats*. Some search engines will require the word *OR* to be capitalized and others won't. The meta-engine may not capitalize the word automatically so the search results may be inaccurate. Simple searches are effective, however.

Two other problems: A metasearch engine cannot possibly go deep enough into each database to get accurate results. Because it queries several search engines, only about 5% to 15% of the data on every responding search engine is successfully queried before the meta-engine moves on to the next search tool. Otherwise, a query might take several minutes instead of several seconds. Finally, meta-engines are often a bit behind the times. Major developments in search technology occur on the general search engines far before they do on the metasearch engines (Kahaner, 1998; Burwell, et al., 1998).

For a preliminary search, metasearches are one of the best tools, because you get a snapshot sample of a specific topic. Another benefit of the metasearch engine is that it can search through more documentation than Web pages alone. Some meta-engines scan Usenet newsgroup postings, file transfer protocol (FTP) sites, and inter-company subscription databases. For instance, Dogpile (`http://www.dogpile.com`) has the ability to scan Career Builder's employment database (`http://www.careerbuilder.com`) for listings.

Topic Rings

What Are They? A Web site that is part of a **topic ring** (also called a **WebRing**) is one in a series of Web sites with a common theme. Web sites in the topic ring will contain links to the next and previous Web sites in the series, as shown in Figure 3.12. These rings are like a community of data, a virtual neighborhood of similar sites.

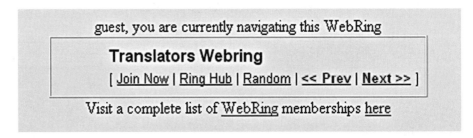

Figure 3.12　An example of a WebRing navigation bar.

Ordinarily, topic rings are managed from a remote site where the "ring leader" often recruits sites about the topic into the ring via email, and enters their locations onto an enumerated list which is used by the ring program to govern which site is next or back, which link will be the random site, etc.

Pros and Cons Topic rings are generally not searchable, but if you're interested in browsing, the advantage to a topic ring is that it allows you to quickly reach related sites. These groups often serve an editorial function, ensuring that the Web sites on the ring are active, and to some extent, reliable sources. Some topic rings have as many as 2000 participant Web sites, while some are merely 10–15 Web sites small.

Frequently Asked Question Pages

What Are They? **Frequently Asked Question** (or **FAQ**) **Pages** are compilations of the most frequently asked questions and their answers, pertaining to a given topic, usually assembled on a single Web page. FAQ documents are usually very thorough and well-organized, evolving over time as a result of much online dialogue in special interest groups. If the same question is repeatedly asked someone will post it to a page where people can read the answer at any time. You will find many FAQ pages at the Internet FAQ Archives (http://www.faqs.org). Figure 3.13 is an example of a FAQ page for Rottweiler dogs.

There seems to be a FAQ page available for almost every topic imaginable: lawnmower engine repair, bass fishing, personal finance, chemotherapy, and so on. The

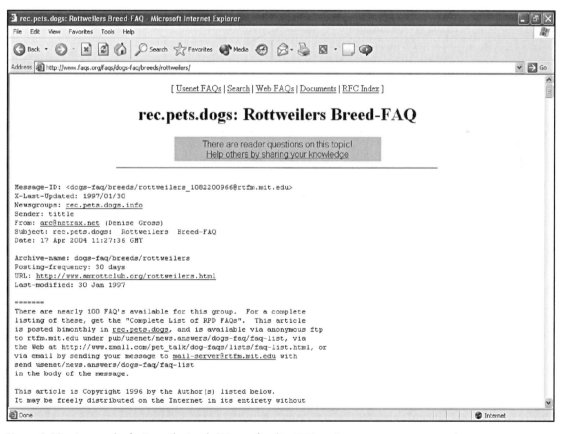

Figure 3.13 An example of a Rottweiler Breeds FAQ page found on FAQS.org (http://www.faqs.org).
FAQs can be very helpful instruments if you are looking for questions and answers that may have already surfaced.

authors of these documents do not charge for their topic-oriented research, even though some of them are professionals in their respective fields.

Pros and Cons FAQ libraries such as the Internet FAQ Archives (`http://www.faqs.org`) attempt to authenticate FAQ documents. However, some FAQs are quite out of date, and contain bias and possibly, misinformation. Always verify information found in a FAQ document with a reliable source.

Expert Inquiries

What Are They? **Expert inquiries** are direct requests for data from a recognized expert, or body of experts. If you have thoroughly exhausted the online searching process and still cannot find the data that you need, it may be time to contact an expert. Searching the Web will result in many Web sites advertising consultants who are more than willing to help for a fee. But if you cannot afford these, knowing where to look for friendly experts and how to ask for data may be extremely beneficial (Lane and Burwell, 1996).

Your best bet is to search for the email addresses of experts at sites dedicated to public research and service; including hospitals, colleges and universities, research think-tanks, and professional or academic organizations. Colleges and universities are an excellent choice, because their mission is to help distribute knowledge, and they commonly house a wide range of experts. If you contact an expert at a local institution, chances are you could set up a face-to-face meeting to get even more information. When you have such a powerful collection of intellectual resources at your disposal, it only makes sense to use them (Androit, 1999; Notess, 1998; Berinstein and Berjorner, 1998).

If you can find a mailing list or newsgroup related to your topic, one of those people probably knows the answer to the question you have. For example, one of the authors of this text once had a quotation from Bertrand Russell, and he needed to find the source. He could have searched through everything Russell wrote. Instead, he went to a site that indexes listserv mailing lists (`http://www.tile.net`), searched for "Bertrand Russell," and found a listserv mailing list dedicated to studying Russell's work. He subscribed to the listserv, sent a message with the quoted text, and asked the group for the source of the quotation. Within 15 minutes, he received a reply telling him the book and page number of the quotation.

If you can't get in touch with an expert, you might want to try reaching a whole group of them. You can reach these groups by using a mailing list or a newsgroup. Many newsgroups are archived, and can be searched at Google (`groups.google.com`). You may find a group where it would be suitable to post your question, or even find the answer itself.

Pros and Cons The advantages and disadvantages of using expert inquiries can be summed up in two words: human nature. Some are, by nature, extremely giving of their time and helpful; others, frankly, are not. If you contact an expert who is unhelpful, do not give up. Instead, seek out another one. You may find someone who is willing to take a minute or two to send you a quick answer to your question.

General References

What Are They? **General references** online are similar to what you would find if you were looking at a traditional almanac, dictionary, encyclopedia, or other resource. Online versions are searchable, hyperlinked, and more easily retrievable via the Web. An example of a general reference is shown in Figure 3.14.

➤ **Reference.com** (http://www.reference.com) is a portal to an online almanac, atlas, business directory, dictionary, encyclopedia, legal resource library, literature library, medical library, thesaurus, and Web directory, sponsored by Lexico Publishing Group, LLC. It is one of the most comprehensive collections of online reference materials on the Web.

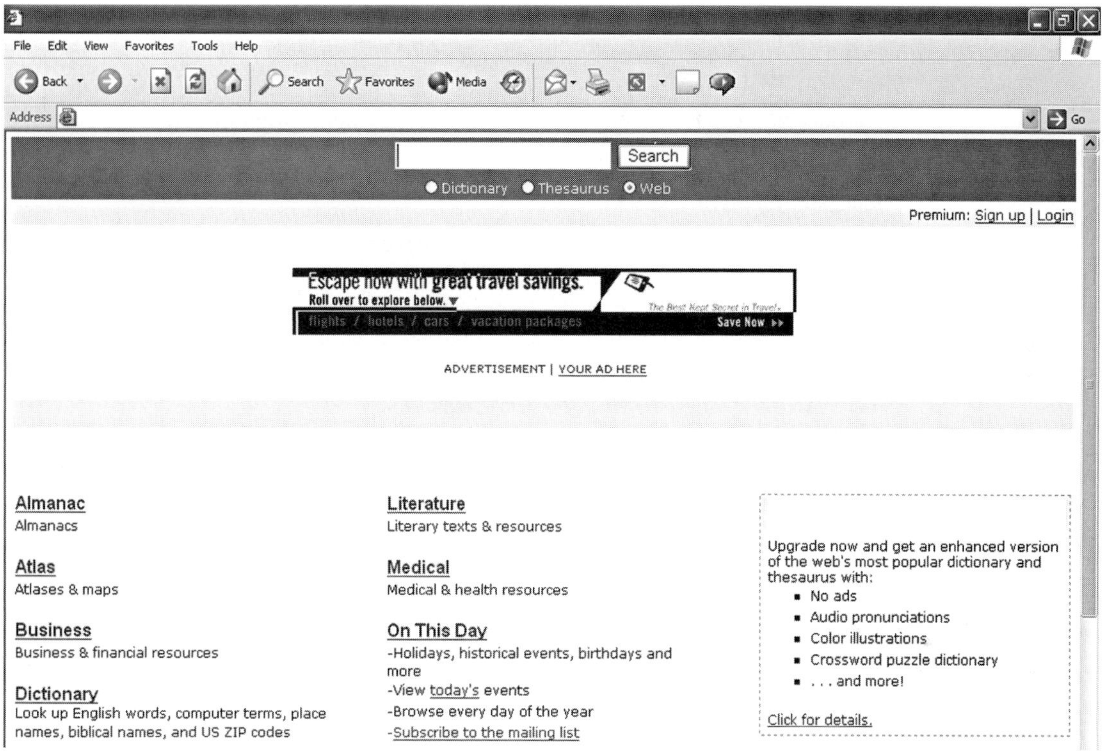

Figure 3.14 An example of a general reference Web site.

➤ **Dictionary.com** (http://www.dictionary.com) is the online dictionary hosted by Reference.com. In addition to reading the text, you can actually hear the word spoken via your computer speakers, and know that you are pronouncing it correctly. This site is a meta-search that will display results from many dictionaries.

➤ **Encyclopedias** are also available online. There are many types of encyclopedias that can be found online including general encyclopedias and those dedicated to particular subjects. Some of the most popular general encyclopedias are: Encyclopedia Britannica (http://www.britannica.com), Encylopedia.com (http://www.encyclopedia.com), Information Please (http://www.infoplease.com), MS Encarta Online (msn.encarta.com), and Wikipedia (http://www.wikipedia.com).

➤ **Interactive maps and driving instructions** are also freely available through a variety of sources. Whether you are driving to a specific location, or even

⅍tip

∴ Bookmark some of your favorite reference pages for quick access!

through a string of locations, interactive maps and driving instructions can be of great assistance. Mapquest (http://www.mapquest.com), Yahoo! Maps (maps.yahoo.com), and Rand McNally (http://www.randmcnally.com) all offer online maps, which will allow you to select the quickest path from A to Z with a simple search. You can also select maps according to scale, whether you want to see a macro or micro-route. This is something you cannot do easily with traditional maps.

Pros and Cons With regard to general reference material, there are clearly more advantages than disadvantages since these resources are generally free, or a fraction of the cost of traditional resources. The main advantage to these resources, of course, is that once you become familiar with them, they are quite easy to use.

Searching for Jobs

One of the most powerful resources made available since the Internet revolution is the online job search. There are thousands of job boards and job search engines available on the Internet (Dikel, 2004, p. 3–5). Some of the most popular of these general boards are: America's Job Bank (http://www.ajb.org), Careerjournal.com (http://www.careerjournal.com), Jobs.com (http://www.jobs.com), Monster.com (http://www.monster.com), Yahoo! HotJobs (hotjobs.yahoo.com), and Workopolis (http://www.workopolis.com). A good example of a specialized job site in the Information Technology sector, is Dice.com (http://www.dice.com). Don't hesitate to use a search site to find job sites.

Searching for People

The experience of looking for people's email addresses, mailing addresses, and public data can range from scary, when you see how much is out there, to frustrating, when you discover you can't find any information at all.

➤ **Finding an email address** can be next to impossible. Some people say that the easiest way to find someone's email address is to ask them for it. First, we suggest that you attempt to look up your friend's name on the Internet using a general search engine. If the name is common, the search is likely to yield far too many results. Some helpful email search sites include 411locate.com (http://www.411locate.com), Bigfoot.com (http://www.bigfoot.com), Email-lookup.com (http://email-lookup.com), FreshAddress.com (http://www.freshaddress.com), and Yahoo's People Online (http://people.yahoo.com). If you know where someone works, you may be able find his or her email address on the corporate Web site using the site's search feature.

➤ **Searching for mailing addresses** (or snail mail addresses) is a bit easier because there are telephone white pages online. Many search sites are available for North America, but fewer for other regions of the world. We'd like to suggest any one of the following online services to find someone's physical mailing address: 411.com (http://www.411.com), or for Canada: 411.ca (http://www.411.ca), Addresses.com (http://www.addresses.com), AnyWho.com (http://www.anywho.com), SmartPages.com (http://www.smartpages.com), WhitePages.com (http://www.whitepages.com), and WhoWhere.com (http://www.whowhere.com).

➤ **Finding personal information** is also hit and miss on the Web. There are some pay services that may be able to provide information such as what's in someone's FBI file, credit report information, criminal records, cell phone numbers, unlisted telephone numbers, driver's license information, marriage and divorce records, personal interest profiles, military records, and social security records. These include: FindSomeone.com (`http://find-someone.com`), InteliUS (`http://find.intelius.com`), KnowX (`http://www.knowx.com`), PeopleData (`http://www.peopledata.com`), and USSearch (`http://www.ussearch.com`). Again, have your credit card ready, because these Web sites charge to access the publicly available information and deliver it to you in a tidy report. An example of one of the "sleuthing" sites is shown in Figure 3.15.

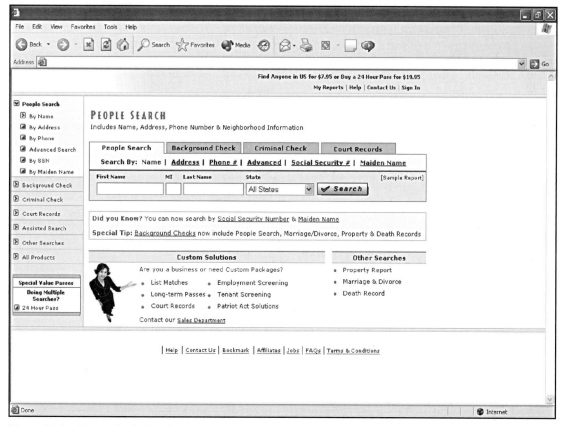

Figure 3.15 An example of a "sleuthing" site.

➤ **Reverse telephone number lookup** can be accomplished by visiting The Reverse Telephone Directory (`http://www.reversephonedirectory.com`), which is a portal for major reverse telephone number search engines. Simply enter the telephone number and if the number is listed in the white pages, it will appear. You should be aware that some telephone directory services also allow people to opt out of the listing but this is on an individual directory basis. You should also be aware that changing your phone number from listed to unlisted will not erase it from these directories, as older directories are archived.

Here's a summary of the search resources covered:

Search Resource	Example	Strength
Search Engine	Google (http://www.google.com)	General search
Directory Outline	Yahoo! (http://www.yahoo.com)	Hand-indexed, general search of popular topics
Bibliographic Database	Found at a library site	Current and specialized searches
Site-Specific Search Engines	Found as a search	Searching an individual Web site resource box on a Web site.
Subject-Specific Search Engines	Many found at http://www.search.com	More detailed searches of a specific topic area
Metasearch Engine	Metacrawler (http://www.metacrawler.com)	Broad searches of detailed topics
Topic Rings	Many found at http://www.webring.org	General information of specific topics
Frequently Asked Questions	Many found at http://www.faqs.org	Detailed information including pointers to other resources about specific topics
Expert Inquiries	Search for experts, may be found in FAQ documents or college and university Web pages	Communication with an expert
General References	http://www.reference.com	Dictionary, thesaurus, calculators, encyclopedia, and other reference material

Searching Strategies

In this next section, we'll talk about ways to define your online research at three stages in the process: (1) initiating a search, (2) refining a search, and (3) completing a search.

Initiating a Search

An old saying goes, "Well begun is half done." Starting your search well is probably the best way to save yourself the most time.

> ➤ **Pick the right tool for the job:** With 12 different choices, you need to think about which one is the most appropriate for your task. Think back on the various pros and cons we discussed. If you have specific content that you're look-

ing for, a site- or subject-specific search engine is probably your best bet. For example, if you are looking for a news story, go to a news source such as CNN (`http://www.cnn.com`) and use their search engine. If you are looking for a friend's email address and you know what school they attend, go to that school's Web site and use their site-search.

➤ **Pick good keywords:** When creating a search engine query, it is best to use specific search terms. The more specific you can be, the more likely you'll get relevant results. Try to use multiple keywords; think of synonyms and related people, events, or places. For example, if you are looking for information comparing Intel and AMD chips, simply entering the word *Intel* will pull up thousands of pages. Instead, enter in a series of terms: *Intel AMD chips compare speed processor.* Also think about alternate spellings of words, and even misspellings. Some search engines will automatically search for variants of a word: for example, if you enter the word *house*, they will also look for *housing, houses, housed,* and others.

➤ **Don't be lazy:** Chances are good that no matter how unique you think your question is, someone else has probably already asked it. Rather than asking the question again, search through FAQs and newsgroups first. While experts, generally, are more than willing to help people find their way, they typically don't tolerate laziness. These experts are bombarded with questions on a daily basis. That is *why* the FAQ page was created in the first place.

➤ **Phrase your questions to experts precisely:** Whether you are asking a search engine or a group of experts, the more specific your question is, the better response you will get. If you sent an email message to a newsgroup of Web designers asking them how to design a Web page, you may get a reply telling you to go take a course, or no reply at all. If, however, you ask them how to remove the border from a table using Macromedia Dreamweaver MX, you are more likely to get the answer you need. Many times you'll get better replies if you tell the group what you already know. That way, they will better understand what you are looking for, and you will be less likely to get data that you already have.

Refining a Search

Many search engines will yield thousands of results for searches of single words or terms. Luckily, most search engines accommodate **Boolean operators** and **wildcard characters.** Boolean operators are terms used to manage the logical operations of the search engine (Schneider, et al., 2003). Search engines are not standardized, therefore they write their own rules when it comes to which advanced features they support. Not all search engines support Boolean operators, and when they do, they also choose whether to use the operator words or symbols.

Boolean Operators and Wildcard Characters

AND   This Boolean operator forces the search engine to find results that contain all of the keywords entered. Say that you wanted to locate data about horse ranches in Mexico. You could simply type: *horse ranch Mexico.* When you enter individual words separated by spaces, the search engine will return results that contain all the words, then continue searching for documents that

tip

∴ Most search engines will not require you to use the keyword "and" for the search. Simply listing the keywords separated by a space will perform an "and" search.

tip

∴ When you list two or more search terms, the search engine will list the Web resources that contain all the words at the top of the results list. It will continue to list Web resources that contain some of the search terms, then only one search term.

contain any of the words, so the return list is much larger than it needs to be. To ensure that only documents containing all three of these words would appear in your results pages, you would enter each word separated by the Boolean operator *and*. For instance, if you were looking for documents containing the words *horse, ranch, and Mexico*, you would enter the search query: *horse* **and** *ranch* **and** *Mexico*. On some search engines, **and** can also be expressed by using the (**&**) or (**+**) characters.

OR   This operator expands the search to include pages that contain at least one of the keywords entered. For instance, if you were doing research on *dogs* and *cats* you could use the search query: *dog OR cat*. In our daily terminology we would say "I'm researching dogs and cats" and it would be understood that you are collecting information about both animals. In computing terminology, if we use the word *and* in a search, then a document has to contain *both* dogs and cats. In order to form the search query properly, we need to use the operator "or" to mean that the document must contain either the term *dog* OR the term *cat*. Some search engines require you to enter the operator, such as *OR*, using upper case characters. Some search engines will also support using the symbolic character (|) for **or**.

NOT   This operator excludes pages that have a particular term in them. For example, to search for information about countries in Europe, but not France, you can use the query: *travel* **and** *Europe* **not** *France*. The search engine would disallow any documents containing the term *France*. Again, you may need to capitalize the Boolean operator *NOT*. Some search engines will also support using the characters for **not** include (!) and (-) instead of the word *not*.

NEAR   This operator will result in hits that have keywords located close to each other. For example, you might be looking for data on making a good seafood gumbo. You could use the query: *gumbo* **near** *shrimp*. In this case, the keyword *shrimp* would have to be within ten words of the keyword *gumbo*. Most search engines are automatically programmed to use a ten-word separator count, though some will use more or less. Some search engines will support using a tilde (~) instead of the word **near**.

*   The asterisk wildcard character searches for the root-word either preceding or following the asterisk. For example, if you are looking for documents about litigation, litigant, or litigator, you could use the query: *litiga**. The search engine will return results that contain any word that begins with the letters "litiga."

Understanding Evaluation Criteria

As you are aware, anyone can publish a Web page about anything. The information may or may not be accurate, reliable or useful, so it is critical to evaluate the information you find. Basically, you need to ask yourself the following questions:

1. Is the information accurate?
2. Is the person or organization publishing this information credible?
3. Who is the intended audience?
4. What was the purpose for publishing this information?

tip

∴ Don't believe everything you read! Question the accuracy, purpose, and authorship of the information you have found before you rely on it.

5. How recent is this information?

6. Is the information covered in sufficient depth?

Accuracy

One of the most common criticisms of the Internet is that it is full of unchecked, unverified rumors. In evaluating accuracy, three important methods of verification are editorial checks, multiple sources, and personal experience. Snopes.com (`http://www.snopes.com`), as shown in Figure 3.16, is one of many Web sites with some good information about urban legends and hoaxes.

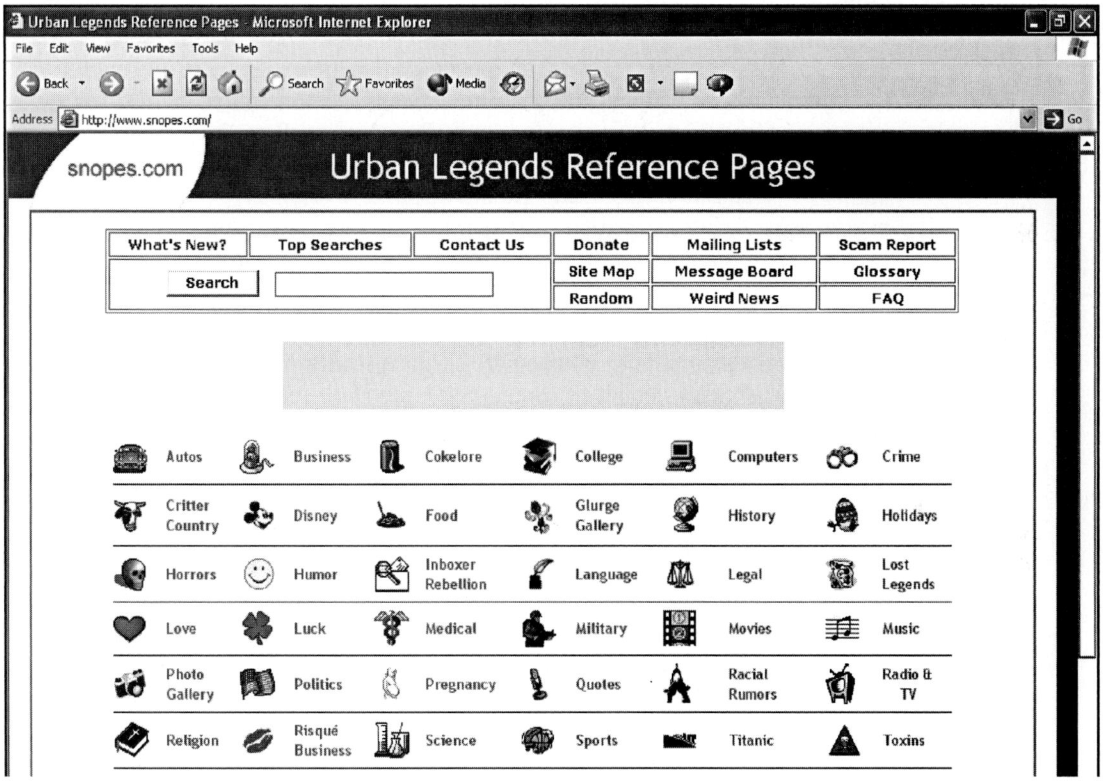

Figure 3.16 Snopes.com and other such sites, hold a wealth of information on urban legends—especially where computing is concerned. Before you buy into a social myth, you should always check an urban legends site.

Editorial Checks In the case of traditional book and newspaper publication, information has to be scrutinized by one or more editors who are charged with the task of checking that the information is as detailed and accurate as possible. However, the Internet has radically changed these dynamics of publication, and anyone with a computer and an Internet connection can publish their information for the rest of the world to read. Some would argue that this is free speech at its finest; however it also means that the reader should be even more critical of material published on the Internet. If the Web site you've found is a traditional media site such as a television network or newspaper site, you can be sure there has been an editorial check.

Multiple Sources A fundamental procedure used by journalists to verify information is to search for more than one source. If they cannot find at least two sources, they will not publish that information. This slows down the publication of news, but improves its accuracy. An advantage of the World Wide Web is that you can quickly seek out multiple sources, but be sure to question whether the secondary sources you are relying on are also accurate.

Personal Experience One of the most basic tests of reliability is your own experience and instinct. If your instinct tells you that the information doesn't sound quite right, follow your hunch and look for other sources.

Authority

Determining the source of information helps to determine if the information is credible. Some sources are more credible than others. For example, if you are looking for medical information, you might be more inclined to rely on the information from the world-renowned *Mayo Clinic* Web site than from *Bob's Medical Page* Web site, even though both may contain accurate information. It is important to question the credentials of the author or organization publishing the information. Additionally, we look at the source to determine if the information is biased. For instance, research about the benefits of smoking sponsored by a tobacco company may be biased in favor of the consumer purchasing the product.

You will find that many Web pages do not contain authorship information, making it difficult to figure out who published the information. You will also encounter instances of information out of context. Here are some techniques that may give you some clues to the author.

- **Check the page for an email address:** Most pages will have some means of providing feedback to either the author or administrator of the page. If the email address is not the name of the author, you can use this address to send a message and inquire about the authorship.
- **Go home:** If the page you've found is in the middle of a site, look for a link back to "home." This should lead you to the site's top-level page and often you will find the information you need there.
- **Backtrack the URL:** Look at the URL and try deleting the characters at the end of the URL to the next slash character (/). For example, let's suppose the URL is http://www1.appstate.edu/~clarkne/emailnet.htm. Delete emailnet.htm and use the URL http://www1.appstate.edu/~clarkne/. If that doesn't result in a Web page, try deleting again and use the URL http://www1.appstate.edu.

In the end, if you're not sure who the author is, don't rely on the information.

Audience and Objectivity

When considering a message, you ought to ask the question: "for whom did they make this information?" The information you find may be tailored to a particular audience. For example, a book about cancer would be written differently for doctors than it would be written for children, or parents of children with cancer, or adults with cancer. If you are providing the Web page reference for other people, you will need to determine if it is suitable for them.

Here are some features to examine which will indicate the intended audience:

- **Identity statements that say who "we" are:** For example, the intended audience for the Sting fan club page *Sting etc.* (`http://stingetc.com/`) should be blatantly obvious.
- **Language level:** Pages intended for children obviously will use a more limited vocabulary and simpler syntax.
- **Jargon level:** Pages intended for professionals in a particular field will include more specialized terms and acronyms.

Purpose

Whether we are writing a letter, talking on the phone, or sending email, we should have a goal, a purpose, in mind. For example, when *Consumer Reports* prints an article comparing the safety features of that year's new pickup trucks, their primary purpose is to *inform* you. When Toyota airs an advertisement for a new truck, their primary purpose is to *persuade* you to buy one. When Greenpeace sends you a brochure detailing the negative impacts of oil spills, their primary purpose is to *advocate* social change, and possibly even get you to contribute to their campaign. And when film directors shoot a pickup truck jumping across a canyon, their primary purpose is to *entertain* you. The purpose of information is typically some combination of informing, persuading, advocating, and entertaining.

As you evaluate Web pages, keep the following tips in mind to help you to determine the varying purpose(s) and motive(s) of the information you read.

- **Domain analysis:** Keep in mind that a .com address indicates a commercial site and its primary purpose is probably to persuade you to buy a product. The .gov domain indicates a government site and its purpose is probably to inform. The .org domain indicates a non-profit organization site and its purpose is probably to inform or advocate for a cause.
- **Balance and bias:** Are both sides of an issue given equal treatment, or is only one side discussed? If you sense an imbalance, the purpose of the site is probably either to persuade or advocate, and not to simply inform.
- **Is that a fact?:** Pay attention to the presentation of facts and opinions. If you see many statements beginning with phrases such as "I think," or "in my opinion," be aware of the intended persuasion behind such statements. Look for the author of this information. Is their opinion a valuable one? If you're searching for valuable information, you ought to be looking for facts and not opinions. After all, everyone has an opinion, including you.

Current Information

Many fields, especially within the area of new communication technologies, are changing so rapidly that it is difficult to stay current. A major advantage of using the Internet for research is that you can get extremely current information. While books can take years to be published, Web sites can be posted in an afternoon. So if you are doing research in a rapidly changing field, such as new technologies, you will often find the most recent developments posted online.

Web pages can also be out of date, though, and they may not have a date posted on them at all. Even when you see a date posted, question its meaning. Is this the date the Web page was first written? Or is this the date that the document was first placed online? Or is this the date the page was last revised? If it was last updated on that date, was the content updated or did the author simply change the color scheme?

Depth of Coverage

Once you have found a site that has a credible author, is recent, objective, and accurate, the final question you will probably ask is: "is the topic covered in sufficient depth?" With traditional media outlets, the depth of coverage is directly related to the time it takes to produce the message. Nightly news broadcasts and newspaper staffs, for example, have a little less than 24 hours to develop their content. Weekly news programs such as *60 Minutes* and *20/20* are allotted more time, and therefore usually provide better in-depth coverage of their stories. Magazines and academic journals are often released in either monthly or quarterly periods, depending upon their circulation. And books can take months, or in some cases, years, to write. Thus, we have come to expect that a book about the Internet will go into more depth and offer more complete coverage than, say, a newspaper article or news broadcast on the same topic.

As publication on the Internet can be very fast, you will find that many sites do not cover topics in depth, particularly if the topic is rapidly evolving. Regardless, the advantage of the Internet is that if you can't find the depth you need at one Web site, chances are pretty good that you can find several additional Web sites with more information. In fact, most news Web sites take advantage of their ability to archive old stories, and will include at the bottom of a current page, a list of links to older, related stories. By making use of these sources, you should be able to increase the quantity and quality of information that you gather about your topic.

Citing Internet Resources

If you are going to use any information you've found on the World Wide Web in a publication, presentation, report, or other document you are distributing, you have to cite it to give credit to the original source. Citing sources is necessary for two important reasons. First, if you do not cite the sources you use, you could be accused of **plagiarism.** Plagiarism is defined as presenting someone else's ideas as your own. At the college level, plagiarism is an extremely serious offense, and often results in penalties as severe as expulsion from school. Second, citing your sources is necessary so that your reader can find the same information you found, and where you found it. This is standard academic and professional protocol, which you will be required to follow no matter what career you select.

We will be showing you how to cite and reference Web resources according to the: *Publication Manual of the American Psychological Association*, 5th ed. (Washington: APA, 2001). While there are several quality publication manuals in circulation, the widely popular *APA Publication Manual* offers detailed information about how to cite online sources.

Finding Software

Another one of the cool things about the Internet is the abundance of software available. Of course, there are hundreds of **software review sites** out there detailing how specific software functions. If you are looking to add some software to your computer via **freeware**

≈ *tip*

∴ If you refer to a Web page, you *must* acknowledge the authorship with a citation to avoid accusations of plagiarism!

Citing and Referencing Web Materials

The American Psychological Association (APA)

Web Document

Whenever citing a Web document, be sure to try to include as many of these elements as possible:

Author's name (where listed)

Date of publication (if there is no date, use "n.d.")

Title of document (in italics)

Date you accessed the source

The name of the source and the URL

Example:

Obie, D. (2004). *Determine the goals for your small business Web site.* Retrieved July 27, 2004, from SCORE Web site: http://www.score.org/eb_6.html

See:

http://www.dianahacker.com/resdoc/

In-Text References

It has been suggested that the U.S. is in the midst of a great postmodern renaissance (Schrag, 2004).

Schrag suggested that the U.S. is in the midst of a great postmodern renaissance (2004).

(free software programs) or **shareware** (titles that allow you limited usage or usability until you purchase the full version), there are several excellent sites you can visit. May we suggest: C|Net's Download.com (http://www.download.com), PC World's download site (http://www.pcworld.com/downloads/), TUCOWS.com (http://www.tucows.com), and the download portal for ZDNet.com (http://www.zdnet.com/). You'll find that these sites rank the software according to ease of use, speed, download popularity, and other rankings. Regardless of where you acquire the software, be sure to scan it with anti-virus software before you execute or install it.

Open Source Licensing

When computer programmers write software such as word processing programs and spreadsheet programs, they use a powerful language such as C++ or Java. The original code, readable commands written in a programming language, is referred to as the source code. Once the program has been tested and completed, the C++ or Java commands are transformed into files called executable files, which can be installed on the user's computer. You cannot read the original commands in the executable code, as the executable code is a translation of the original, closer to a machine language of 1s and 0s. Most commercial software vendors do not want you to be able to read the commands, as this is their trade secret, much like a chef does not want you to have his detailed recipes, so they provide only the executable code to the customer.

The **Open Source** movement is founded on the idea that software programs can be developed much more quickly if many programmers are volunteering their time to work on them, and the source code is readily available. If software is *Open Source* it means that the source code is available and can be modified and improved. This movement has been steadily growing since the 1980s. The Linux operating system is a good example of open source software, as it has sprung from a grass roots effort initiated by Linus Torvalds, when he was a student in Finland in 1991, and has evolved to become a viable competitor to the Windows operating system. In general, Open Source software is free; however the term is evolving to mean that the source code is available, but not necessarily free. Some commercial software vendors call their products *Open Source* referring to the fact that the source code is available, although they charge a licensing fee for their product (Rosenberg, 2000).

Interestingly, many corporations have chosen not to use free software in general, whether it is Open Source or other free software. The rationale is that if the software is free, there is no accountability if the software should fail and business is adversely affected. Some corporations use Open Source and other free software widely.

You will find lots of information about the Open Source Initiative at their Web site (http://www.opensource.org) and also take a few moments to browse Source-Forge.net (http://www.sourceforge.net), which is the largest Open Source software development site.

File Compression

File compression is a method used for reducing the size of a file, but also for combining several files into one. When you download software, you will often find that you are downloading a single file that is a compressed file composed of multiple files. The compressed file will generally have a file extension of *.zip* or *.exe*. Your anti-virus software should be able to scan zipped files, so be sure to scan the file before you use it.

:: If you need to send several files to someone, particularly if they are large files, consider compressing them first to save download time!

If you are using Windows XP, you will find that you can open a compressed .zip file and extract the individual files. If you are not using Windows XP, there are products available such as Winzip (http://www.winzip.com), which you can use to create compressed files and unzip compressed files.

Compressed files with an .exe extension are referred to as self-extracting files, and they do not require file compression software in order to extract the files. You can execute these files by double-clicking on them.

SUMMARY

Now that you've read through the chapter, you are prepared to:

▣ Identify and use some of the advanced browser plug-in features.

▣ Discuss the variety of content available on the World Wide Web.

▣ Identify the strengths of specific online research tools, such as: (1) search engines, (2) directory outlines, (3) bibliographic databases, (4) site-specific search engines and site maps, (5) subject-specific search engines and directory outlines, (6) metasearch engines, (7) topic rings, (8) frequently asked questions (FAQ) pages, (9) expert inquiries, (10) general reference tools, (11) job search engines, and (12) people search engines.

▣ Utilize efficient searching strategies, including initiating a search and refining a search with Boolean operators and wildcard characters.

▣ Implement the evaluation criteria of: accuracy, authority, audience and objectivity, purpose, timeliness of information, information, and depth of information coverage.

▣ Cite Web sites that you find online according to the American Psychological Association's Style Manual.

▣ Find and use shareware, freeware, and open source software.

▣ Recognize file compression and manage compressed files.

Review Questions and Hands-on Exercises
Review Questions

1. What is a browser plug-in?

2. Suggest some appropriate search keywords that would result in Web pages containing information that would answer the following questions. Keep in mind that you can use double quotes around phrases and multiple word terms, and separate individual words with a space for multiple keyword searches.

   a. When was Mozart born and where did he live?

   b. Which minerals are found in a glacier?

   c. How many calories are in a scoop of ice cream?

   d. How many songs did Elvis write?

   e. What is the population of Detroit?

3. What is the difference between a directory and a search engine?

4. What is the difference between a search engine and a metasearch engine?

5.   What is the difference between a site-specific search engine and a general search engine?

6.   Using a search engine that accepts Boolean operators, the following searches are entered. Describe the resulting list of Web pages.

    a.   dog OR cat

    b.   dog AND cat

    c.   dog cat

    d.   dog AND cat NOT beagle

    e.   "jack russell" NEAR terrier

    f.   custom* AND "paint job" NEAR car

    g.   "kansas city" NOT missouri

7.   You've found a Web page that looks like a great resource, but you notice the following things about it. Should you use or refer to this site, and if so, what special considerations should you be concerned about?

    a.   There is no author or date listed.

    b.   It is part of a well-respected educational institution site.

    c.   It's written in very technical, highly detailed language that will not be easily understood by most of the population.

8.   You would like to use facts and quotes from the following Web sites in a document you are creating. Specify how each Web site should be cited in your document.

    a.   An article entitled *Internet for Beginners* by Paul Gil, found at `http://netforbeginners.about.com/`, downloaded today.

    b.   A newspaper article entitled *Internet Trends and Tips* written today by Jonathan Lew from the *New York Times*, downloaded today from `http://www.nytimes.com/articles/internet`

    c.   The city of Seattle at `http://www.cityofseattle.net/` downloaded today.

9.   You download some software and the file ends in .zip. What type of file is this, and what will you need to do to be able to use this software?

10.   What is the difference between shareware, freeware, and open source software?

1. Suggest one or more appropriate search sites for each of the following searches. Be sure to suggest specialized search resources if they are available.

   a. General information on grass fertilizer.

   b. Information on the nesting habits of bald eagles in Maine.

   c. Official rules for North American professional soccer.

   d. The definition of the word "etymology."

   e. Driving instructions to travel from Toronto, Ontario to Miami, Florida.

   f. The owner of the telephone number (705) 555-1212.

   g. A word to use instead of "exciting."

   h. A software upgrade for a digital camera your friend purchased from Kodak.

   i. The mailing address for your friend Bob Smith, who lives in Denver, Colorado.

   j. The mailing address for your friend John Doe, who lives in Calgary, Alberta, Canada.

   k. Locations of all of the branches of the public library in Portland, Oregon.

   l. Download a new screen saver.

2. Compare search engines by performing the following searches using Yahoo! (`http://www.yahoo.com`), Google (`http://www.google.com`), and Lycos (`http://www.lycos.com`), and write down the number of results for each search using each engine. Notice that more search terms narrows the search and fewer results for each engine will be found.

   a. camp

   b. camping

   c. camp*

   d. camp wisconsin

   e. camp wisconsin hiking swimming OR swim

3. Create search queries for the following searches. Use the Yahoo! search directory, or another search site that uses Boolean operators and perform the following searches:

   a. Fertilizers for grass.

   b. Dog training for a beagle.

     c. Recipe containing chicken, red peppers, and chili powder.

     d. Music festivals in North America in the summer months.

     e. Colleges and universities in British Columbia, Canada.

     f. Current video games, but not Nintendo video games.

4. Choose several of the sites found in any of the searches in the above question. Use the evaluation criteria to determine whether the sites you have found contain information you could rely on.

5. Open the Download.com (`http://www.download.com`) site in your Web browser and search for the following:

     a. What are the five most popular software downloads?

     b. Find at least three different file compression programs.

     c. Find some games. Notice which files are shareware, freeware, or open source, and which are compressed.

Email

chapter 4

Chapter Objectives

This chapter helps you understand

- how email was developed.
- the variety of email accounts available.
- how email messages are sent and received.
- address book features and email management.
- what spam is, and how it can be avoided.
- how to add personality to your email with smileys and emoticons.
- the Internet rules of etiquette (netiquette).
- the issues surrounding viruses and hoaxes, and how to protect yourself.

Email is one of the oldest forms of online communication. Using it has become an essential office skill, and on a personal level, it has brought back traditional letter writing in a new electronic form. The Internet culture developed some interesting **netiquette** *guidelines in the days when only text could be sent via email. First, let's put email in historical perspective, then we'll look at the range of options available today.*

Brief History of Email

Email was first used in the 1960s, but messages could only be sent to users who had accounts on the same mainframe computer. Essentially, a text message was sent from one user's account to another user's account. So, an email address, as we know it today was not required.

In the late 1960s, Ray Tomlinson, a networking specialist at BBN Consulting, set out to convert this single-computer utility into a multi-computer messaging system. He combined the intra-computer email system used on mainframes with an ARPANET file transfer application (known as CPYNET) and designated remote computers with "locator addresses." To do so, he used the "at" symbol, @, to separate the user name from the computer name. Tomlinson's first email message to a remote computer read: "QWERTYUIOP" (the top row of characters on a keyboard). While not as poetic as "Watson, come here, I need you . . . " it highlights the alphanumeric symbolism inherent to email communications (Baron, 2000).

Tomlinson released two programs in 1972 that worked together on ARPANET. They were READMAIL and SNDMSG. Early ARPANET adopters quickly used the applications, even though they were rather primitive (Johnson, 1999). READMAIL had one major design flaw in that the program would download all email messages into a single lengthy text file. Later that year, Lawrence Roberts and Steve Crocker improved upon Tomlinson's concept by installing an email management device named RD. RD allowed ARPANET users to view an email menu by sender, subject line, and date-stamp. And, it retrieved a specific email file from the menu, rather than having to go through the list item-by-item (Stewart, 2000). As we shall see, the method of using separate programs for sending email and receiving email still exists today.

Throughout the early-1970s, ARPANET developers expanded the functionality of email. For instance, in 1973, Barry Wessler improved the RD email-reading program by adding the ability to delete messages from the mainframe, calling this version NRD. In 1974, Marty Yonke revamped the NRD email reader to include a simplistic "help file" system that would tell the user exactly how to use the interface, renaming this software BANANARD (Stewart, 2000). In 1975, John Vittal developed an all-in-one release, named MSG, adding features such as automatic addressing for email replies and email forwarding (Stewart, 2000). Many consider MSG to be the first fully developed email utility.

In the late 1980s, companies began providing Internet and email access to the public. For instance, Compuserve and MCI Mail emerged in 1989, providing email service within their systems, to the public for the first time. The early successes of Compuserve and MCI Mail inspired Internet pioneer Steve Case to design a business plan and secure venture capital during the early-1990s. His idea was to provide phone-based Internet service with email access to every home in the U.S. His plan was quite successful. Steve Case became the Founder and CEO of AOL (America OnLine) (Swisher, 1999).

Getting an Email Account

Today there are a variety of options for accessing email. Most ISPs provide a Web interface and **POP** (Post Office Protocol) email access. A **Webmail interface** is just a Web page provided by your ISP that allows you to log in and see your email messages via the Web. This is great because you can check your email from anywhere in the world, using a computer that has an Internet connection and a Web browser. POP email access requires you to use an email client. An **email client** is a computer program designed to send, receive, and manage email. Examples of email clients include Microsoft's Outlook Express, Netscape Communicator's Mail, Pegasus, and Eudora. In this chapter, we will use Microsoft's Outlook Express and Eudora to illustrate POP email setup and features.

If you don't subscribe to an ISP, an alternative is to obtain an email account from one of the free services such as hotmail.com or yahoo.com. There are hundreds of choices for Webmail accounts. Many colleges and universities also provide email accounts for free to students and alumni. These accounts generally have a restriction for the amount of space available for file attachments and require the user to log in occasionally or the account expires. The provider stores email messages and address books. For instance, if you have a Hotmail account, and have stored addresses in the address book, they are not stored on your computer. They are all stored on the Hotmail site. This is convenient; however you should be aware that although this information is not publicly available, there are no guarantees that the information is secure. Be sure to copy and paste any important messages to your personal computer.

Email Basics

Whether you're using Webmail or an email address assigned by your ISP, you will be able to send email messages to multiple recipients, with file attachments, receive email, store addresses in an address book, and file email messages into folders.

All email addresses have the form *userid@host.domain*. The **userid** is the login id that you use for logging into the Webmail service, or your ISP service. You may want to give some thought to the userid you choose. If you anticipate using the email account for business purposes, or to send messages to a teacher or client, consider that they will see your userid and choose something a bit professional. A good choice is first initial and last name or some combination of your first and last name. Choosing a userid that makes a politically incorrect or offensive statement may be something you choose for personal correspondence with people who know you, but can mean the difference between getting a job or not, or getting a reply or not, if you use it for business or other more formal purposes.

Using Webmail

There are dozens of Webmail sites available these days, and they offer basic service for free. Obtaining an account is as simple as completing a few forms and choosing your userid. Some of the sites have been around for a number of years, including Hotmail and Yahoo! and you may not be able to get the userid you like from the more popular sites. In that case, most people get really creative by using underscores for "spaces" or adding numbers to the end of the userid.

Most of the Webmail sites will limit the size of file attachments, and amount of storage available. Some offer an optional service where you can pay for more storage. Some also offer notification features where you can specify that an email message be sent to another account, pager, or cell phone when you receive email. Other possible features include blocking senders, filtering junk mail, marking messages as important, using a calendar, and searching mail.

An example of a Webmail interface is shown in Figure 4.1. You can check for new messages by clicking on a link or button on the page, or reloading the inbox page. Messages can be viewed by clicking on the sender name or subject of the message, and deleted by clicking the checkbox and then the delete button or delete menu item. You will also have to empty the trash to complete the delete procedure. Using a Webmail interface is very intuitive.

If you are using a public computer, be sure to log out or close the browser window to end your email session, otherwise the next person to use the computer may have access to your Webmail account.

tip

∴ Choose a password that is easy for you to remember but difficult for others to guess. Combining familiar numbers with other information is a useful way to do this. For instance if your street address is 1423 Main St. and you live in Toledo, your password could be 1423Toledo.

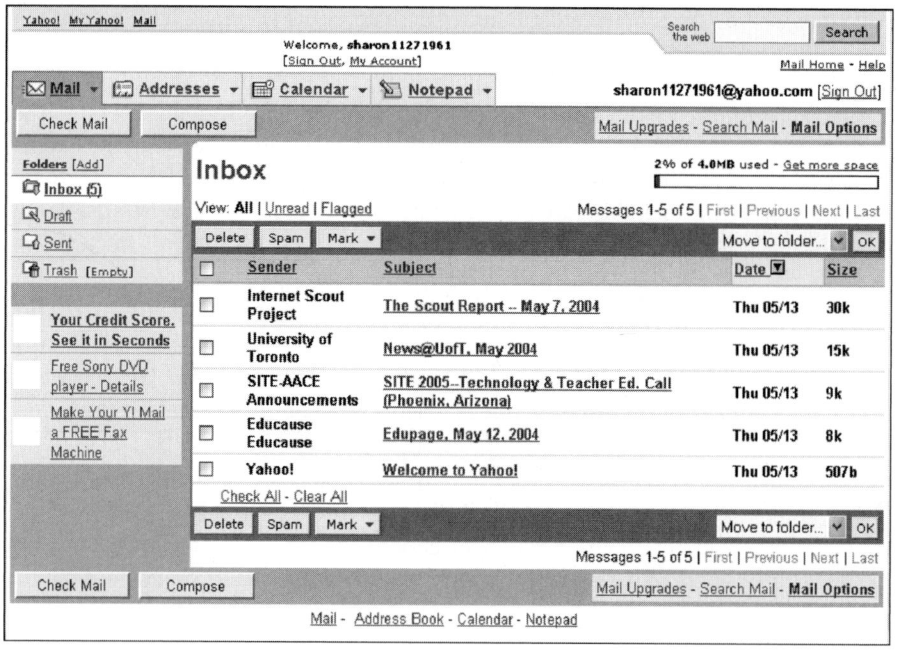

Figure 4.1   An example of Webmail.

Typically, Webmail is sponsored, so you can expect to see advertising in your window, and a few lines advertising the Webmail service on each outgoing message. Webmail providers also have a link somewhere on their site outlining their privacy policy.

Setting Up an Email Client for POP or IMAP

Regardless of the email client you may choose to use, there are a few key items you will need to know if you are going to be setting up your email manually. Some ISPs provide a setup disk, which sets up your email in a client such as Eudora, Pegasus, or Outlook Express. Most ISPs do not provide this, and it's up to you to set up your email, or to call the ISP's technical support to walk you through it.

Userid

This is your login id if you use dial-up and log into your connection. If you are using a broadband connection such as cable or DSL, be sure to write down your userid when the technician sets up your account.

Password

This is the password used with the userid for connecting to your ISP's service. Again, if you are using a broadband connection such as cable or DSL, be sure to write down your password when your account is set up and also ask what the procedure is to change your password.

Incoming Mail Server

This is the name of the server you will be connecting to in order to receive incoming mail. There are two major types of connections: POP and IMAP.

POP (Post Office Protocol) is generally used by ISPs and some corporate servers. If you're not sure, choose POP because that's the most likely. Some people refer to picking up your mail as "Popping it off the server." POP connections download your email messages from the server to your local computer, then disconnect. This protocol is ideal for supporting offline mail usage. Once you've downloaded your mail, you can disconnect from the Internet, read your messages, compose replies, organize your mail, and then reconnect to send. If you're paying for your Internet connection by the hour, you can save some money by reading and composing offline. The email client will have options allowing you to specify how often to check automatically for mail and whether to leave the mail on the server. Don't leave the mail on the server unless you are checking mail from a computer where you do not usually store your email. Your ISP will have a limit for the amount of email storage available, and if you never download the mail, you will exceed the limit and your email account will bounce any mail received after you have reached your quota. Ordinarily, the name of the server is something like *pop.domain* or *mail.domain* (i.e., *pop.xyzisp.com*).

IMAP (Internet Message Access Protocol) was originally developed in 1986 at Stanford University, but really didn't become popular until a decade later. Generally, ISPs do not support IMAP for subscribers, but if you are connecting to your email at work, you may find that you require an IMAP setup. IMAP connections access email messages directly on the server and do not download them locally. You can manage mailboxes directly on the server, and outgoing messages are sent from there as well, not through your ISP's outgoing mail.

Outgoing Mail Server

If you are using an ISP with POP mail, you will need to know the name of the outgoing mail server. The outgoing mail protocol is typically SMTP (Simple Mail Transfer Protocol). You will often find that the name of the outgoing mail server is *smtp.domain*, or in some cases the name of the POP server and the SMTP server are the same.

Microsoft Exchange Server

Microsoft's Exchange server is a special case. If you need to connect to an exchange server, you also need to use Microsoft Outlook or Outlook Express. The Exchange server provides multi-user Outlook features in addition to email, which include calendar scheduling, access to mailing group lists, and sharing documents.

Mail Setup in Outlook Express

Most email clients will have a similar method available for setting up an email account. Let's look at a sample setup procedure using Microsoft's Outlook Express. Outlook Express has the same basic features as Outlook but does not include some of the advanced features.

➤ Select the menu items *Tools, Email Accounts.*

➤ Select the option *Add a new email account,* as shown in Figure 4.2.

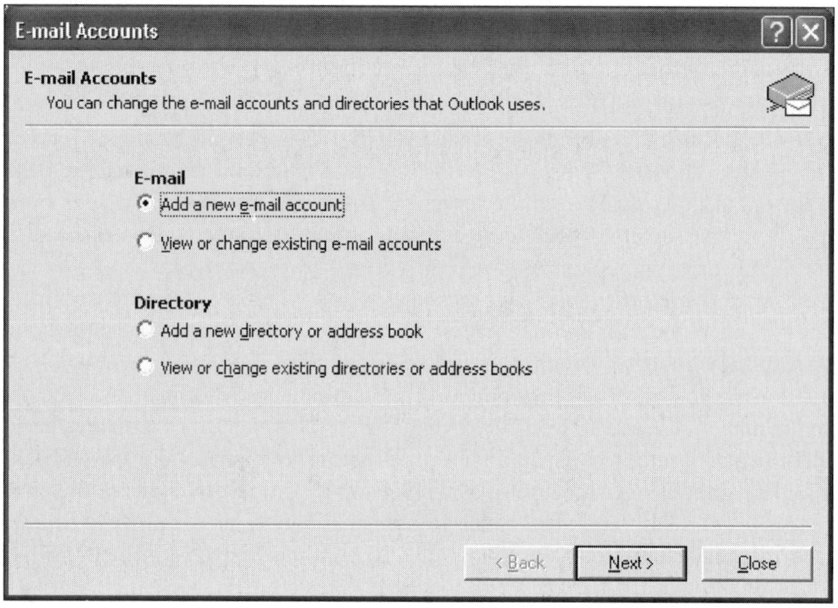

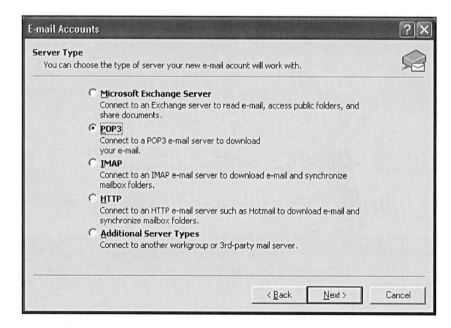

Figure 4.2   Microsoft Outlook new email account dialog.

➣   Click the *Next* button.

The email accounts dialog box containing server types should appear, as shown in Figure 4.3.

Figure 4.3   Microsoft Outlook email server type.

Setting up Email in Eudora for Windows or Macintosh

Microsoft Outlook Express is a popular email client, however there are many other high-quality free or sponsor ware email clients. Eudora is a good example of a robust, free email client. Let's set up POP email using Eudora, and note that many of the tasks are similar. Eudora is available in both Windows and Apple Macintosh versions.

➤ Open a Web browser and point to the Eudora site at
   http://www.eudora.com

➤ Download the latest version of Eudora and install it.

➤ When the dialog box appears prompting you to select Eudora as the default mail program, click on the *No* button.

➤ When the setup wizard appears, click on the *Cancel* button to cancel out of the wizard. We will set up an email account manually.

➤ Select the menu items *Tools, Options* to reveal the setup dialog box, as shown in Figure 4.4.

➤ Enter the information for Real Name, Return Address, Mail Server (incoming), Login Name, and SMTP Server (outgoing). Figure 4.5 shows a sample of information.

Figure 4.4   Options dialog box in Eudora 6.2.

Figure 4.5   Options dialog box in Eudora 6.2 showing sample information.

➤ Select the *POP3* option and click the *Next* button. The "3" refers to the version number.

The dialog box in Figure 4.6 lists some fictitious information for a POP3 email setup. Notice that there are fields for incoming and outgoing mail servers.

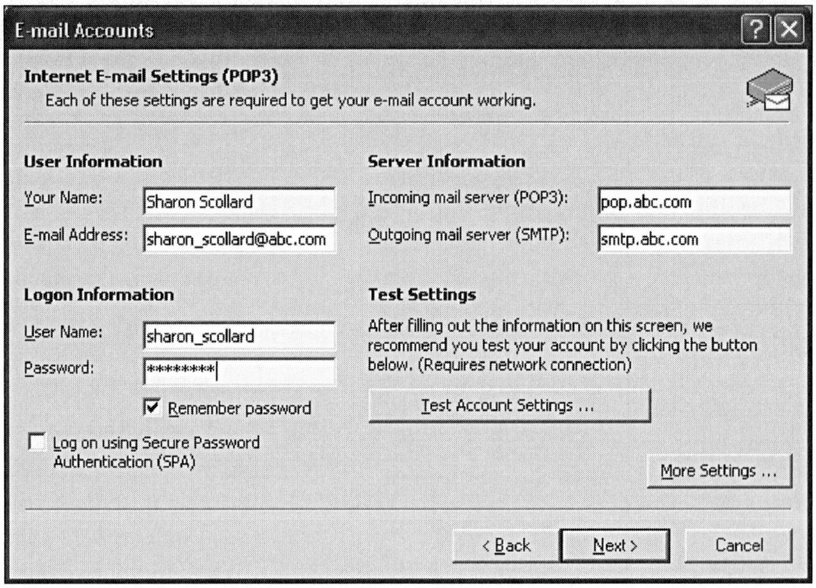

E-mail Accounts

Internet E-mail Settings (POP3)
Each of these settings are required to get your e-mail account working.

User Information
Your Name: Sharon Scollard
E-mail Address: sharon_scollard@abc.com

Logon Information
User Name: sharon_scollard
Password: ********
☑ Remember password
☐ Log on using Secure Password Authentication (SPA)

Server Information
Incoming mail server (POP3): pop.abc.com
Outgoing mail server (SMTP): smtp.abc.com

Test Settings
After filling out the information on this screen, we recommend you test your account by clicking the button below. (Requires network connection)

Test Account Settings ...

More Settings ...

< Back   Next >   Cancel

Figure 4.6   Microsoft Outlook POP3 settings.

➤ Complete the name and server information for your account.
➤ Click the *Next* button.
➤ You should see a dialog box indicating that your email setup has been completed. Click the *Finish* button.

ISPs may have customized settings that are required, so after you have set up your email package, test it by sending yourself a message. If the email is not sending or receiving properly, it is wise to call your ISP's technical support and ask them to help you to check your configuration settings.

Sending a Message

Let's send an email message to multiple recipients.

➤ Open an email composition window. In Eudora you can use the commands *Message, New*. If you are using Webmail, you should see a link labeled *compose*, or *new mail message*. Typically this is in the upper left corner. If you are using Microsoft Outlook Express, click *New, Mail Message*.

A mail composition window, which looks similar to Figure 4.7, will open.

Notice that the input boxes available are *To:*, *Cc:, Bcc:, Subject:* and a large area at the bottom for the actual message. If the Bcc: field is not displayed in Microsoft

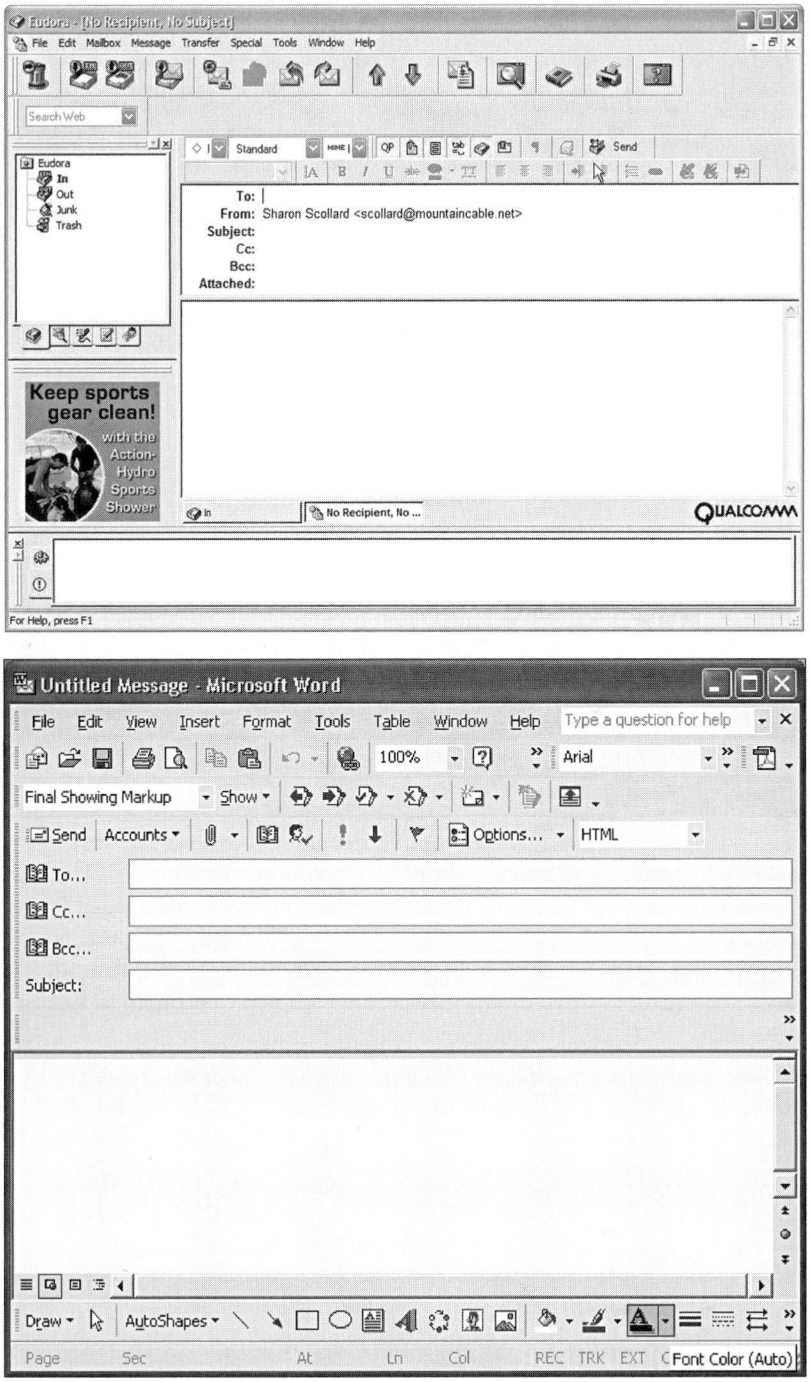

Figure 4.7   Top: A Eudora email composition window. Bottom: A Microsoft Outlook Express composition window. Note the similarities.

Outlook Express, click *Options, Bcc Field,* as shown in Figure 4.8. The Bcc field is displayed in Eudora and may be displayed in the Webmail interface.

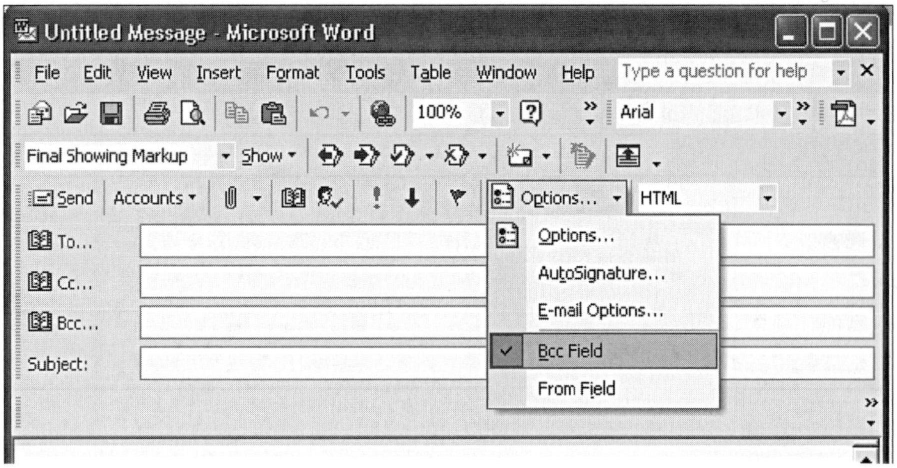

Figure 4.8   Microsoft Outlook email—selecting the Bcc field.

The *To:, Cc:,* and *Bcc:* fields are for email addresses for the recipient(s). The term Cc has been used for years, and would appear at the bottom of a traditional letter or memo to refer to "carbon copy," indicating that someone had been sent a copy of the correspondence. These days, people also refer to *Cc* as "computer copy." The term *Bcc* refers to *blind carbon copy* (or *blind computer copy).* When you add a Bcc recipient, the recipients in the Cc and To fields will not see the Bcc recipients in the header of the email message. The Bccc recipients will see the To and Cc recipients in the header of the email message, but will not see the other Bcc recipients.

You can send to multiple recipients by separating email addresses with a comma. The *To:* and *Cc:* fields are a matter of business protocol. Typically the email message is sent *To* someone for their direct information or action, and the email is *Cc'd* to someone for their information, but not action. The email may be Bcc'd to someone for his or her information as well. Perhaps you are writing a sensitive email to a colleague, and wish to keep your boss in the loop, but do not wish your colleague to realize you are sending the message to your boss. In that case, you would Bcc your boss.

➤ As a quick example, compose a message placing email addresses of two friends in the To: field (separated by a comma), another in the Cc field, and Bcc to yourself. Use email addresses of people you know. The message window might look as shown in Figure 4.9.

You'll find that you can use your word processing skills when composing the message. Copy, paste, delete, backspace, work as expected, and some clients like Microsoft Outlook Express even allow you to specify fonts, add images, and use other word processing features. Some email clients also do a spell check before the message is sent.

➤ When you're ready to send the message, click the *Send* button or link.

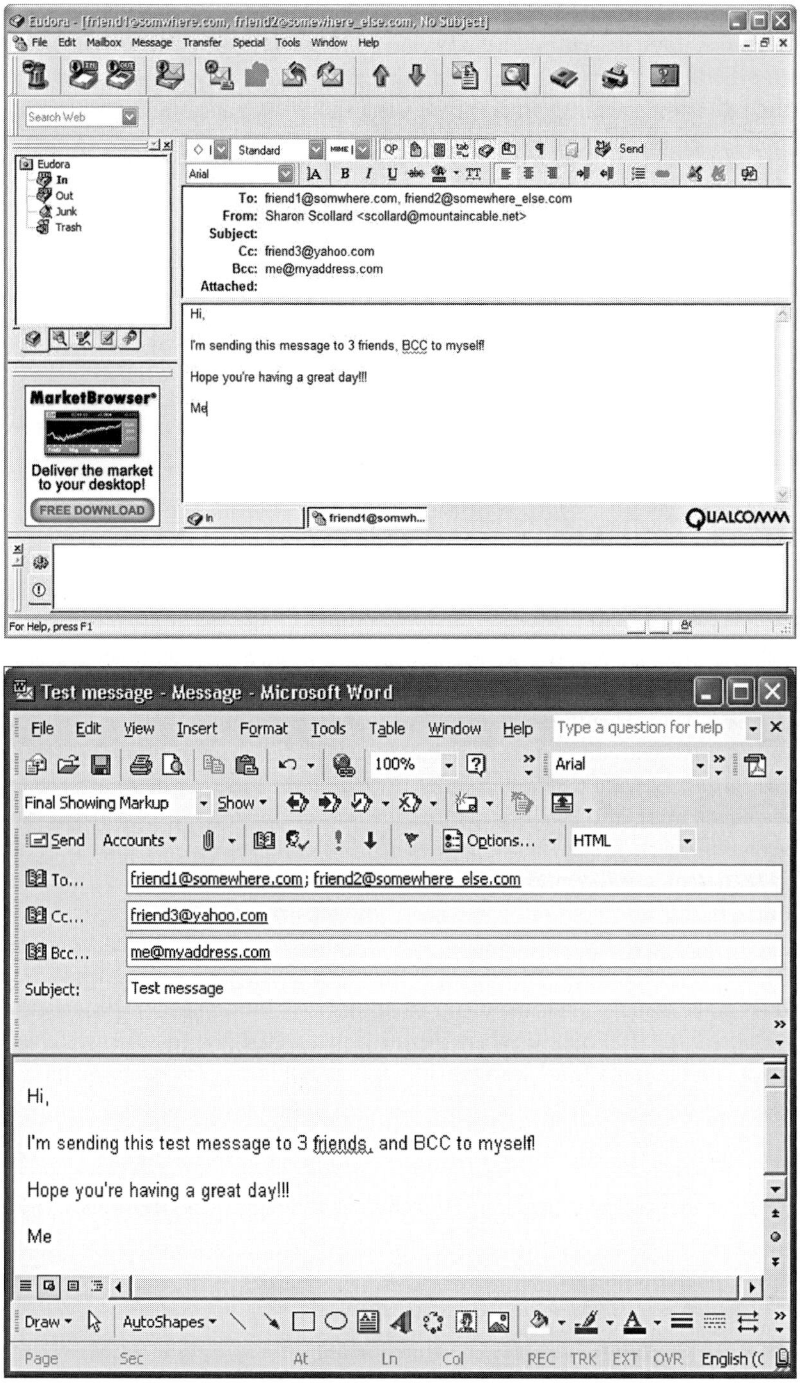

Figure 4.9   Top: Eudora email composition window—composing a message.
Bottom: Microsoft Outlook email composition window—composing a message.

The message will be sent to its destination and typically arrive within seconds or a few minutes. If you've composed a message and change your mind about sending it, you can close the window before you send it. If the email client is configured to send immediately then once you click "send" the message will be delivered. Email clients can also be configured to delay sending for a period of time, or diverted to a draft folder until the user sends the drafts at a later time. An alert message may appear asking you if you're sure you want to cancel, or if the message should be saved for later retrieval, depending on the email client you are using.

The *subject* should be short and to the point, reflecting the content of the message. The recipient will scan subjects when looking for messages.

Sending to Multiple Recipients

You can send email to multiple recipients by separating each email address with a comma or semicolon. Be very careful when sending to multiple recipients, as people will tend to assume that someone else will answer the email or take action. Try to send the email message directly to very few recipients, but perhaps Cc the message to others for their information only.

Binary Files and MIME

If the information you would like to send is simple, plain text, this is suitable for the body of the email message. If the text does not have any formatting at all, it is referred to as **ASCII text** (American Standard Code for Information Interchange) and dates back to the mainframe days. However, we often need to send other types of files such as Word documents, images, videos, and many other files that are not plain ASCII text. All these files, except for ASCII text, are binary files. Binary files are encoded files, and generally require some sort of software package in order to read or view them. The issue of sending them via email arose, and in 1991 the solution was developed. The **Multi-Purpose Internet Mail Extension (MIME) protocol** was developed; this protocol takes care of the encoding required to send a binary file, and the decoding required to read it once it has been received. Email clients and Web interfaces have now incorporated MIME types, so the end user does not have to even think about this. It's all happening in the background. You may also see references to MIME types in other software. For instance, Web browsers often have options that allow you to specify which application packages to associate with specific MIME types. When files are downloaded, the browser will check the MIME types and automatically load the appropriate application to open the file.

File Attachments

Let's send another message to illustrate file attachment and some other features.

➢ Open an email composition window.

Let's attach a file to the message. File attachments are appropriate when sending a file that is not text or is perhaps a word processing document you wish to share with someone else. You can attach any type of file, and any size of file.

➢ Type your friend's email address in the *To:* field. You can use your own email address, if you like.

➢ If you are using a Webmail interface, click the attachment link. If you are using Microsoft Outlook Express, click the drop-down arrow beside the paper clip and select *File*, as shown in Figure 4.10. If you are using Eudora, click the *Attach File* button or use the *Message, Attach File* commands, as shown in Figure 4.10.

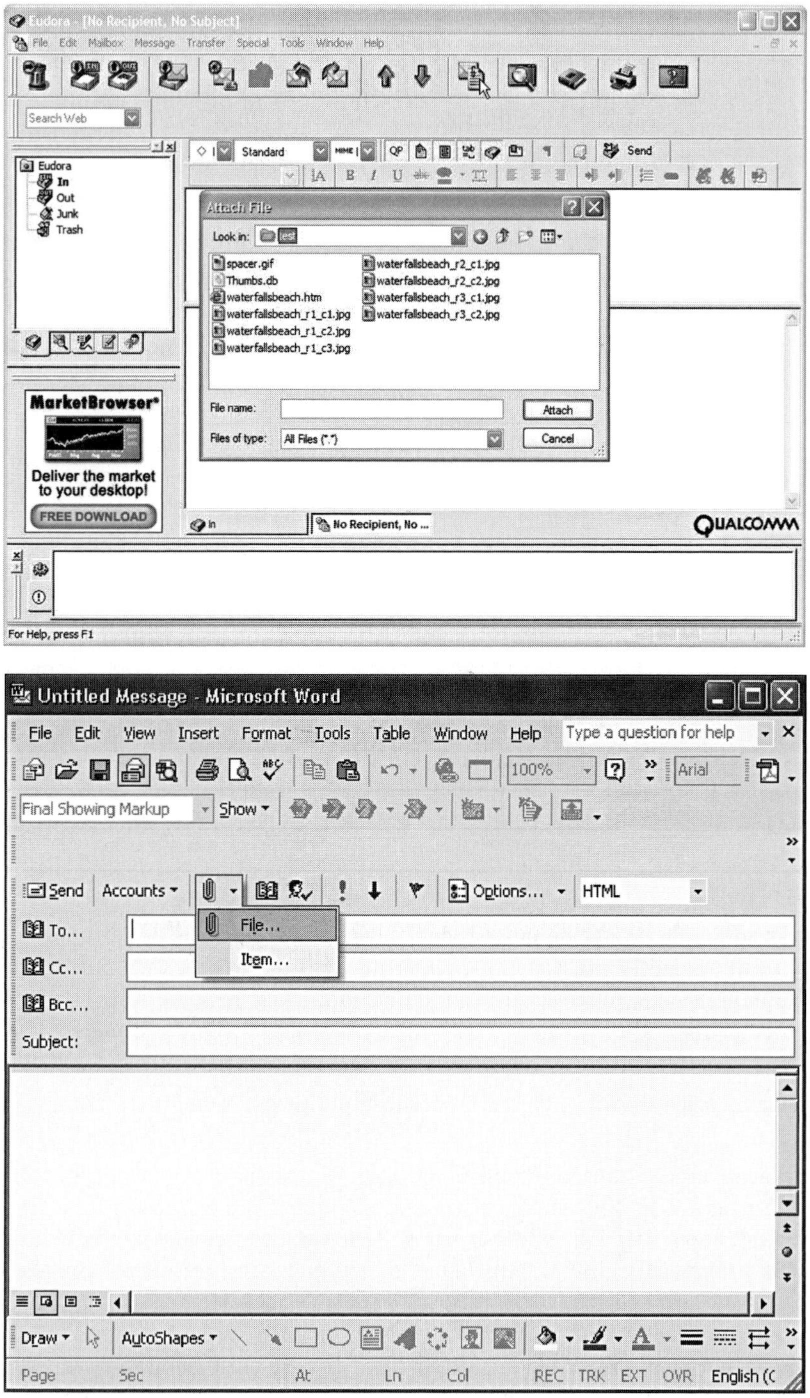

Figure 4.10 Top: Eudora email composition window—file attachment.
Bottom: Microsoft Outlook email composition window—file attachment.

A browse window will open, and you will be able to browse your hard drive for a file.

➤ Choose a file that you have recently created; perhaps a word-processing file, or picture.

➤ In Microsoft Outlook Express, click the *Insert button*. In Eudora, click the *Attach* button. If you are using Webmail, the button might be labeled *save, Okay,* or *attach*. The name of the file should appear in the attach field. The window might look as shown in Figure 4.11.

To:	friend1@hotmail.com
From:	Sharon Scollard <scollard@mountaincable.net>
Subject:	
Cc:	
Bcc:	
Attached:	C:\Data\wildernesscamping\images\hikers.jpg;

📖 To...	friend1@hotmail.com
📖 Cc...	
📖 Bcc...	
Subject:	
Attach...	📎 gray_lines.jpg (4 KB)

Figure 4.11   Top: Eudora email composition window—file attachment.
Bottom: Microsoft Outlook email composition window—file attachment.

You can add multiple attachments to email messages, and files can be any type and any size. If the file is quite large, (over 300 K), you might want to check with the recipient to determine if their email service can handle large files. In some cases, such as most free Webmail services, file transfer size and storage space is severely limited.

➤ Type the message shown in Figure 4.12, substituting your name.

There are several features in this email message. Notice that after you've typed the URL, it appears as a link. Most email clients, and Web interfaces will recognize a URL that begins with *http://* and will code it as a link. This way, the recipient will be able to click the link to browse to the site. The *http://* is important, as many clients and Web interfaces will not recognize the URL without it. By default, most email clients and Web interfaces send messages in HTML format. You can generally override that and send messages in plain text. In Microsoft Outlook Express, you can click the drop-down box, which has the HTML option, and you can choose plain text, as shown in Figure 4.13. In Eudora, you will find the HTML (stylized) and plain text options in the *Tools, Options* dialog box in the *Stylized Text* feature, as shown in Figure 4.13.

tip

∴ When you receive a file attached to an email message, always scan it for viruses. Even if you know the person who sent it, it's still possible that the file contains a virus. Definitely scan it before you execute it if it is a program file!

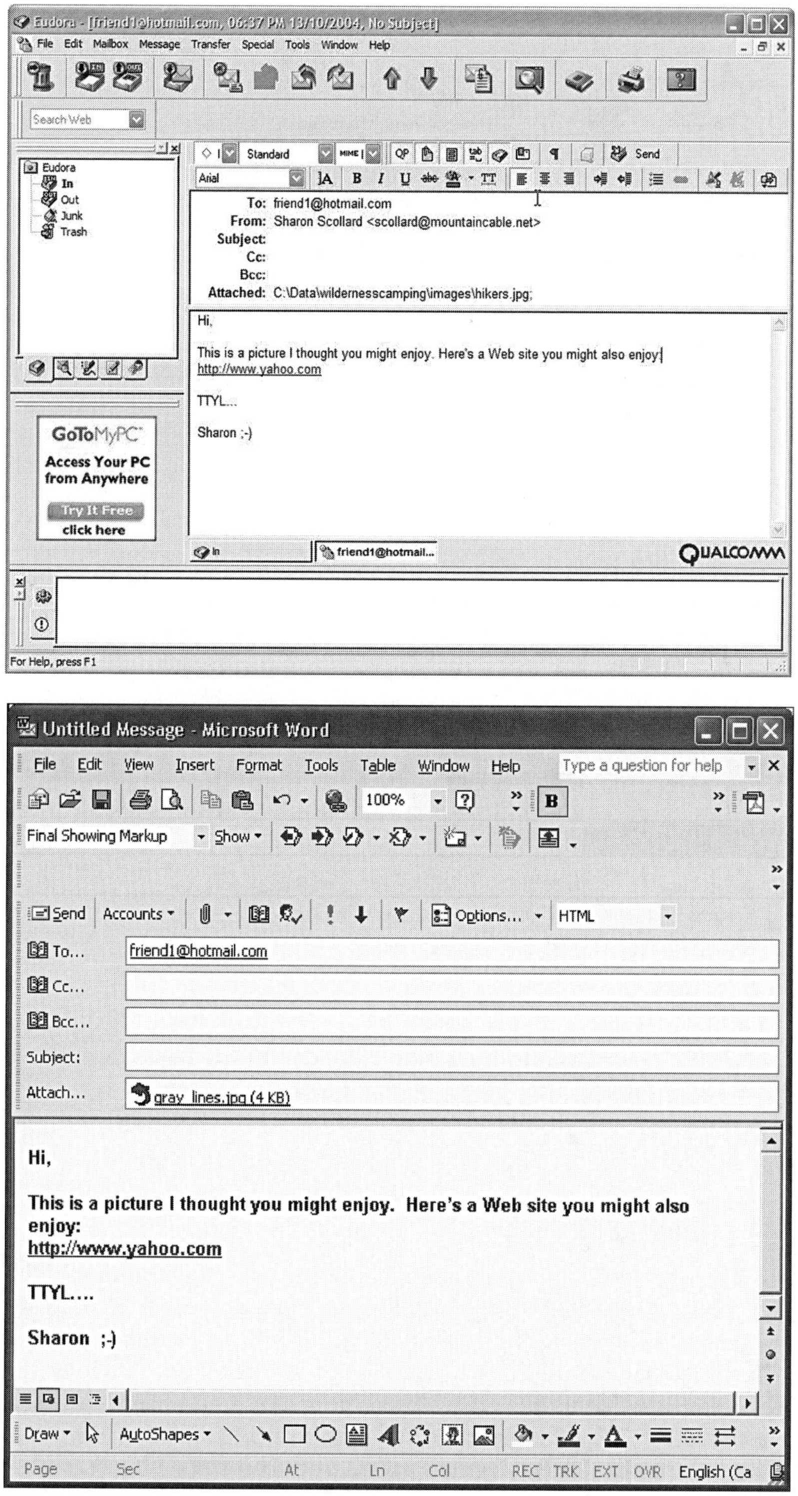

Figure 4.12 Top: Eudora email composition window—message with URL, acronym, and smiley emoticon. Bottom: Microsoft Outlook email composition window—message with URL, acronym, and smiley emoticon.

Figure 4.13   Top: Eudora Options dialog box with both stylized and plain text selected.
Bottom: Microsoft Outlook email composition window—HTML drop-down with plain text option.

Once this option is selected, the message will be converted to plain text, without any formatting. Other packages may have this selection in the options, or as a link or button in the window.

Smileys and Other Emoticons

This message may look a little cryptic as you read it. Notice there is a short form, *TTYL* and a smiley ;-) at the end of the message. As discussed previously, email began as text only communication, however, text by itself can be very formal, and as senders created more casual emails, some conventions to show some emotions, and acronyms for common expressions evolved in every day usage. The smiley is also referred to as an *emoticon* (emotional icon). To see the smiley ;-) tilt your head to the left to see two eyes, a nose and a smile. This one is winking. In fact, the original smile, :-) has become so common that some of the word processing packages automatically replace :-) with ☺. There are literally hundreds of smileys. Feel free to search for "smiley" in your favorite search engine. Some of the most common are:

:-) smile

:) smile—no nose

:-/ hmmm

:-(sad face

:(sad face—no nose

8-) smile with glasses

Similarly, short forms evolved for common phrases. Here are a few of the more popular ones:

BBL—be back later	PLZ—please
BTW—by the way	ROTFL—rolling on the floor laughing
IMO—in my opinion	TTYL—talk to you later
IMHO—in my humble opinion	TY—thank you
LOL—laughing out loud	*S*—smile

A search for "emoticon" will result in sites with both smileys and acronyms. These acronyms are frequently used in chat programs.

Netiquette

Etiquette, in its broadest sense, is proper social behavior as prescribed by some authority. Each culture, classes within cultures, and geographic regions, has its own rules of etiquette. The Internet has its own culture and its own etiquette. Internet etiquette is called netiquette (Internet and etiquette). There are some general guidelines for communicating on the Internet. RFC 1855—Netiquette Guidelines describes some general rules of Netiquette. Although it was written in 1995, many of the guidelines still hold true.

First and foremost, be sensitive to other people's feelings and be cautious with the words that you use about them. Remember that at the other end of every message is another human being—a fact that is all too easy to forget when all you see in front of you is a computer screen. Ask yourself, "Would I say this to them in person?" If not, reconsider your message.

Here are a few basic rules for email, and they also apply to communication in news groups and mailing lists. In general, the rule is "be considerate."

- **DON'T SHOUT.** Using all uppercase characters is considered shouting.
- **Use a meaningful subject line.** Keep it short, and to the point.
- **Be careful what you say.** If you're talking about someone, assume that the email you're writing will be forwarded to the person you're talking about.
- **Be cognizant of ownership.** If you are using corporate email, do not send personal messages. The corporation owns your email messages. Be aware that corporations keep backups of their mail server files and your emails have a very long life span.
- **Be relevant.** When replying to a long email message, delete long passages that are not relevant to your conversation.
- **Be concise.** Do not include a long email message with a reply such as "I agree" or something similar.

◾ **Email is not chat.** When corresponding for business purposes do not use chat acronyms such as "plz," "l8r," or "ty." Similarly, correspondence to a teacher or client is a more formal correspondence than a message you would send to a friend.

◾ **Keep the message short.** Get right to the point. In business, people don't have time to read long, rambling messages. You can be more flexible with personal correspondences.

◾ **Consider bandwidth.** Don't send a large file attachment to someone who is using a dial-up connection or to someone using a free Webmail service such as Hotmail.

◾ **Do not send heated messages.** These are called flames. If you're angry or stressed, compose the message offline, and then walk away. Re-read it a day later, and then decide whether or not it is reasonable. Flames will often come back to burn you.

◾ **Remember that the recipient may be from another culture, and another part of the world.** Use regional expressions sparingly, and be clear in your wording. Do not use sarcasm. It rarely comes across successfully and almost always looks bad.

◾ **Make yourself look good online.** Check spelling and grammar, and present yourself well. Your email will be treated much more seriously.

◾ **Remember that you are not anonymous.** This is true even if you're using a free Webmail service and have not identified yourself. Your IP address is always in the long headers, and if you choose to send email that is controversial or illegal, it can be traced.

Return Receipts

Perhaps you decide that the message you are sending is important enough that you would like to know when the recipient receives it. One method is to request a return receipt. The recipient will have the option of notifying you automatically. Typically, Web interfaces do not have this option, and not all email clients have this option.

➤ In Microsoft Outlook Express select the *Options drop-down* and select *Options* from the drop-down menu, as shown in Figure 4.14.

The dialog box shown in Figure 4.15 will appear.

➤ Select the checkbox for *Request a delivery receipt for this message*.
➤ Click the *Close* button.
➤ Similarly, in Eudora you can click the *Return Receipt* button, as shown in Figure 4.16.

When the message is sent, the request is sent along with it. When the recipient views the message in the inbox, a dialog box will pop up and ask the recipient to acknowledge receipt of the message. If the user selects *yes*, an email will be sent back to the sender, indicating that the message was received. It is important to note that the recipient can choose not to acknowledge delivery. A return receipt is an acknowledgement that the email was received. If you do not receive a return receipt it could be because the message was not received, but it could also be that the recipient chose not to return the receipt.

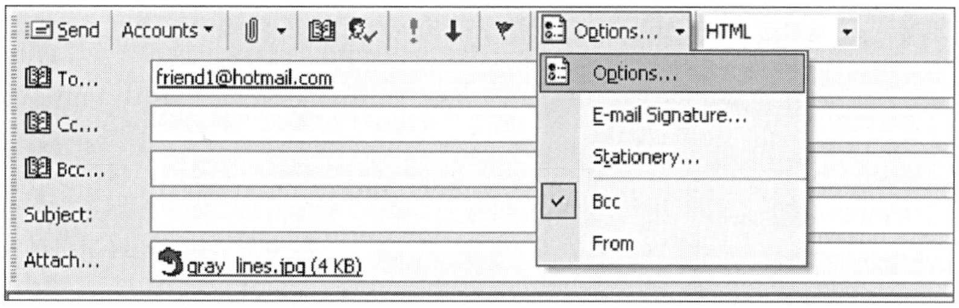

Figure 4.14　Microsoft Outlook email composition window: Options drop-down menu.

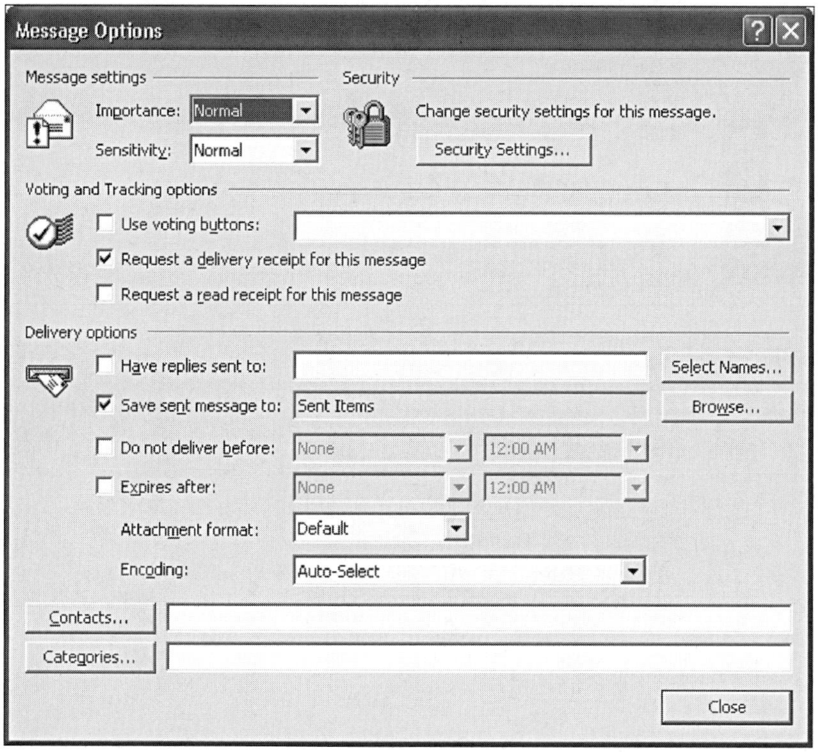

Figure 4.15　Microsoft Outlook Message Options dialog box.

Importance Indicator

You can also set the importance indicator of the message as high or low. In Microsoft Outlook Express, the red exclamation is high importance and the blue down arrow is low importance, as shown in Figure 4.17. In Eudora, the priority is a drop-down list with options ranging from highest to lowest, as shown in Figure 4.17.

Web interfaces typically do not have this feature. Some of the other email clients have degrees of importance such as highest, high, normal, lower, lowest.

➤ In Outlook Express, click the *blue arrow* to set the importance to low for this message. In Eudora, click the importance drop-down and set the priority to *lowest*.

≋ *tip*

∴ Not all email clients have a return receipt feature. If you are concerned about the recipient receiving an important email message, ask the recipient to reply to you, confirming that the message has been received.

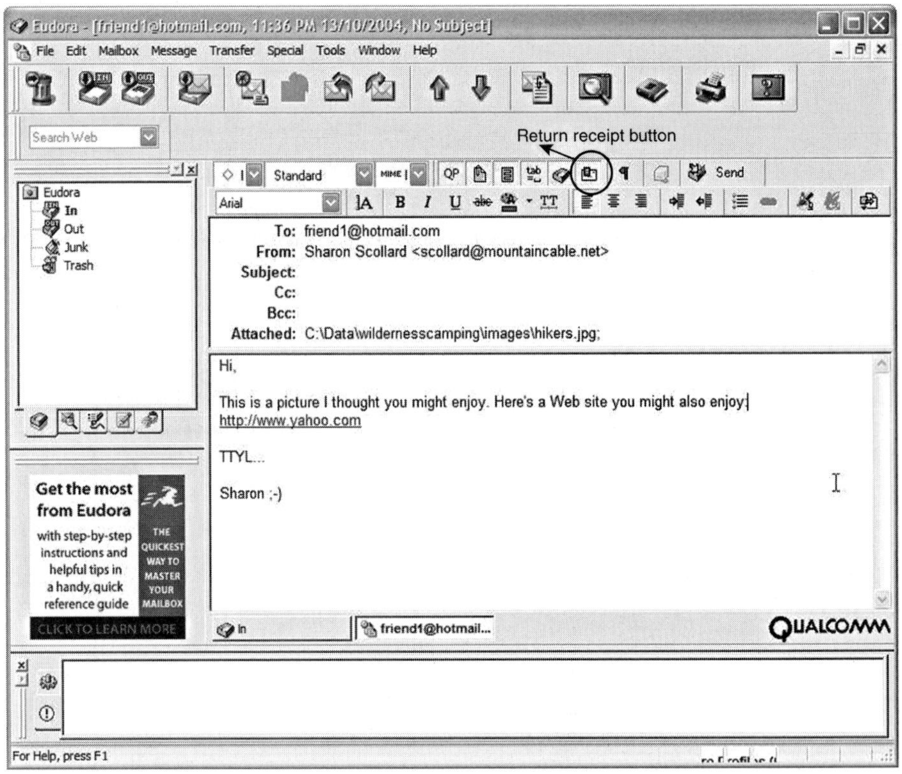

Figure 4.16   Return Receipt button in Eudora.

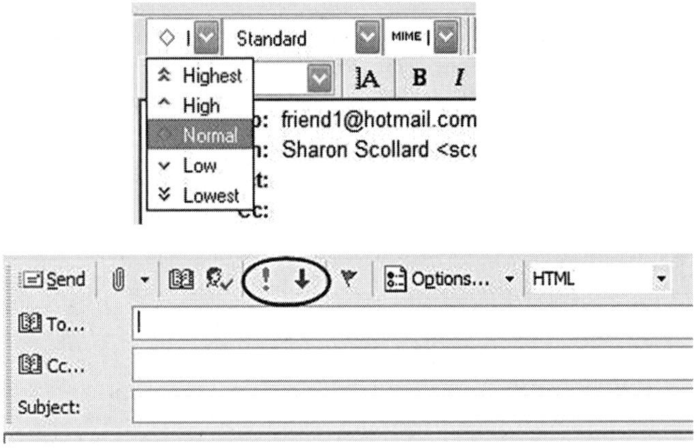

Figure 4.17   Top: Eudora email composition window—importance indicator.
Bottom: Microsoft Outlook email composition window—importance indicator.

Most messages you send should be normal priority. Be sure to use highest priority sparingly. Like the boy who cried wolf, if you use highest priority routinely, it will be largely ignored. Do use lower priority when the message is informative but not urgent. Most people will appreciate knowing that they can read the message at their leisure.

➤   Feel free to send the message, or close if you wish to exit without sending.

Address Book Feature

Generally, both Web interfaces and email clients have some sort of address book feature for managing email addresses. This will allow you to store individual email addresses, and quickly access them for *To:, Cc:,* and *Bcc:* fields. Each method is slightly different, but the similarities include adding at least an email and name to an address book entry, and referring to the address book to add the email address into the field.

Creating a Contact in Microsoft Outlook Express

Let's look at an example in Microsoft Outlook Express, and then in Eudora.

➤ In Microsoft Outlook Express click the *Contacts* button in the main Outlook Express window, as shown in Figure 4.18.

Figure 4.18 Microsoft Outlook *Contacts* button.

First we will have to add a contact to the contact list.

If you don't have any contacts on file, you may see a blank window with instructions to double-click to add contacts, as shown in Figure 4.19.

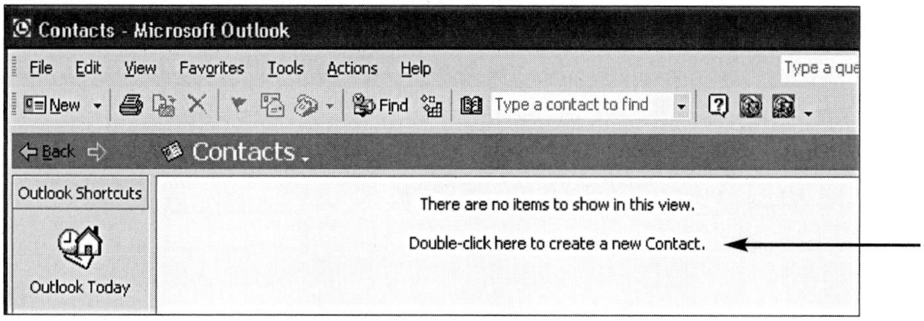

Figure 4.19 Microsoft Outlook contact window.

➤ *Double-click* the instructions pointed out in Figure 4.19.

An untitled Contact window similar to that shown in Figure 4.20 will appear.

Microsoft Outlook Express is a powerful program that will handle large contact lists with detailed information. Web interfaces manage much less information, and you may have fields for name and email address only.

➤ Add information for name and email address for one of your friends or colleagues.

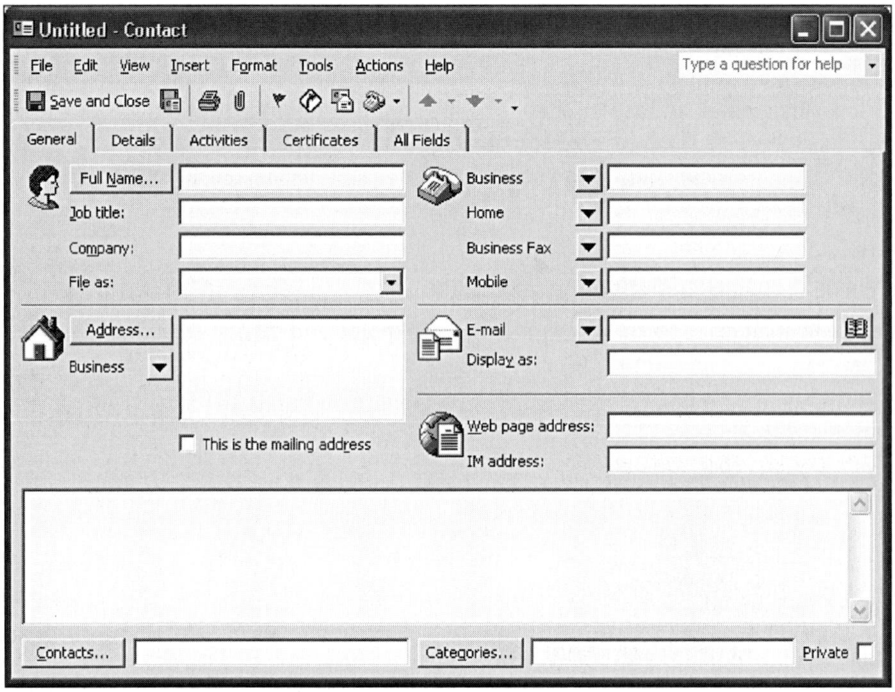

Figure 4.20 Microsoft Outlook untitled Contact window.

Here's some fictitious information, and yours might look similar, as shown in Figure 4.21.

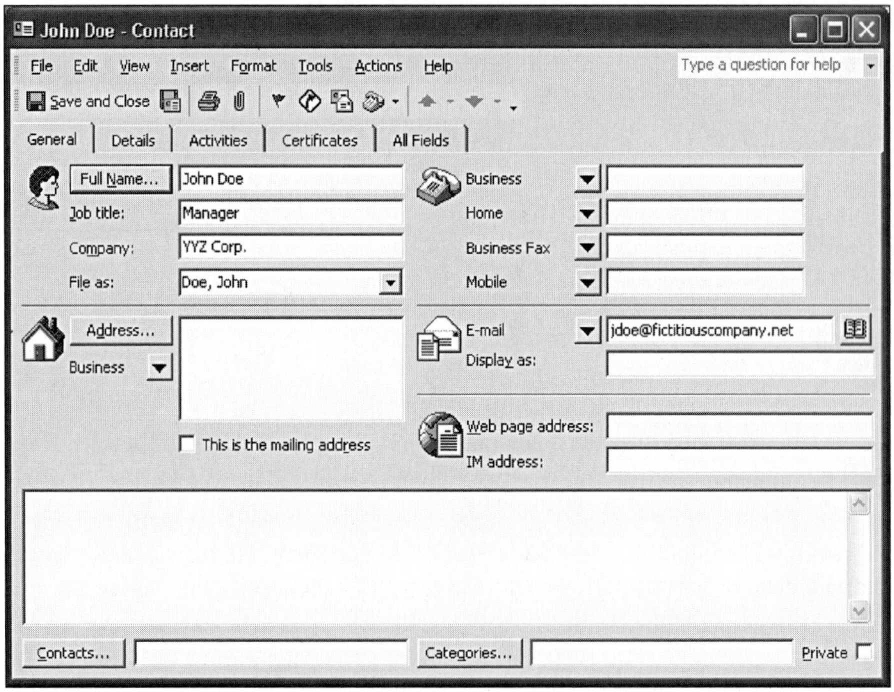

Figure 4.21 Microsoft Outlook contact details completed.

➤ Click *Save and Close*.

You should see the new contact appear in the contacts window, as shown in Figure 4.22.

Future new contacts can be added using the *New, Contact* menu items, as shown in Figure 4.23.

Figure 4.22 Microsoft Outlook new contact added.

Figure 4.23 Microsoft Outlook New, Contact menu item

If this is the first contact you have added you may have to close Outlook Express and open it again to make sure the contact is saved and will be recognized by the mail window.

Let's create an email message using our new contact.

➤ Open Outlook Express and select *File, New, Mail Message* from the menu.
➤ Click the address book icon in the *To* field, as shown in Figure 4.24, to open the address book.

The address book window will open. Notice the drop-down box in the upper-right corner. It specifies the address book in use. In our case, we are using the contacts as the address book, as shown in Figure 4.25.

➤ Click *John Doe* to select the name and click the *To ->* button to copy the address into the To: box. Similarly, once other contacts are added, you can select other names for the *To:, Cc:,* and *Bcc:* boxes.
➤ Click the *OK* button to add the address to the field in the new message.

Typically, another advantage of address books is that you can simply type the name of the contact into the field, and the email address will be automatically substituted when you move to another name or field.

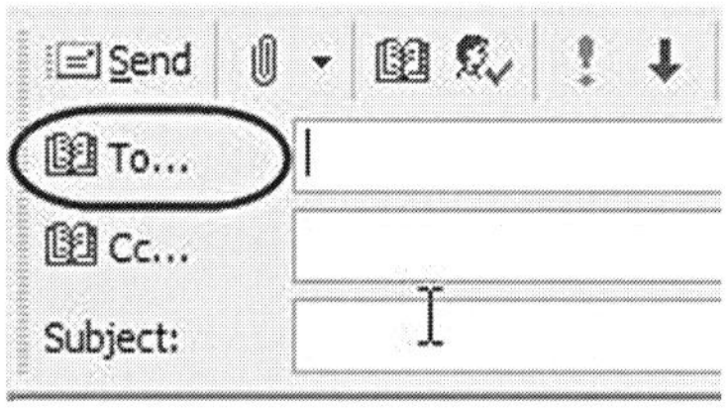

Figure 4.24 Microsoft Outlook: To: address book icon.

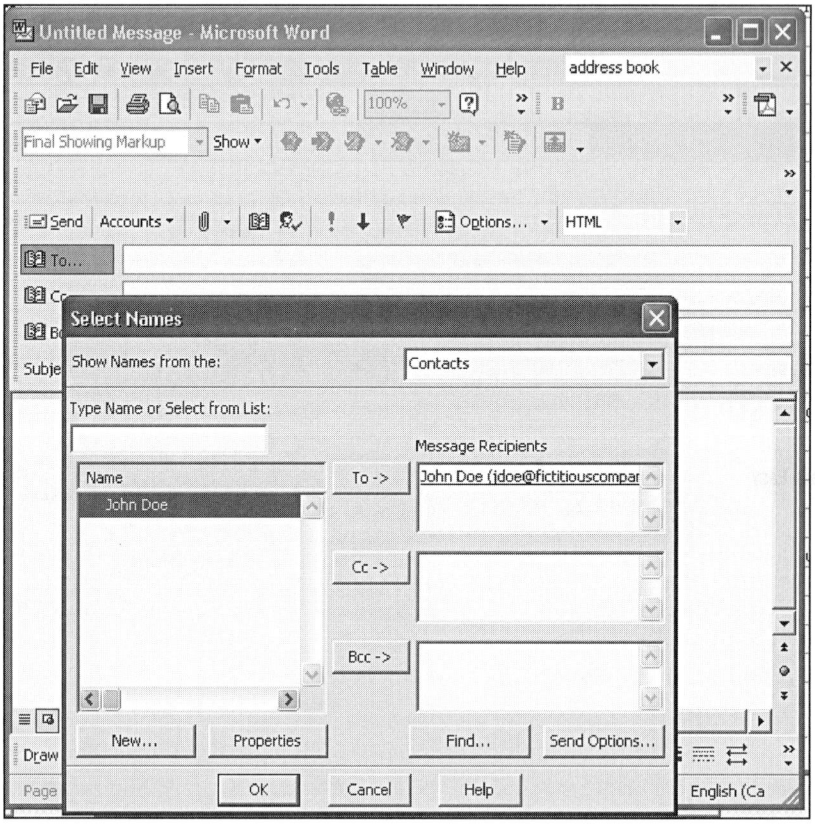

Figure 4.25 Microsoft Outlook address book.

> Try typing *John Doe* or one of your contacts' names in the Cc: field. Click the message body and you should see the name converted to the email address. Some email packages do not substitute the email address for the nickname.

> Feel free to complete the message and send it, or close the window to cancel.

Although these examples have been provided using Outlook Express, you will find the same or similar features in any email client or Web interface. Let's create an address book entry using Eudora to illustrate this as well.

Creating an Address Book Entry in Eudora

➤ Click the *Address Book* button to open the address book dialog box, as shown in Figure 4.26.

➤ Click the *New button* button to start a new address book, as shown in Figure 4.26.

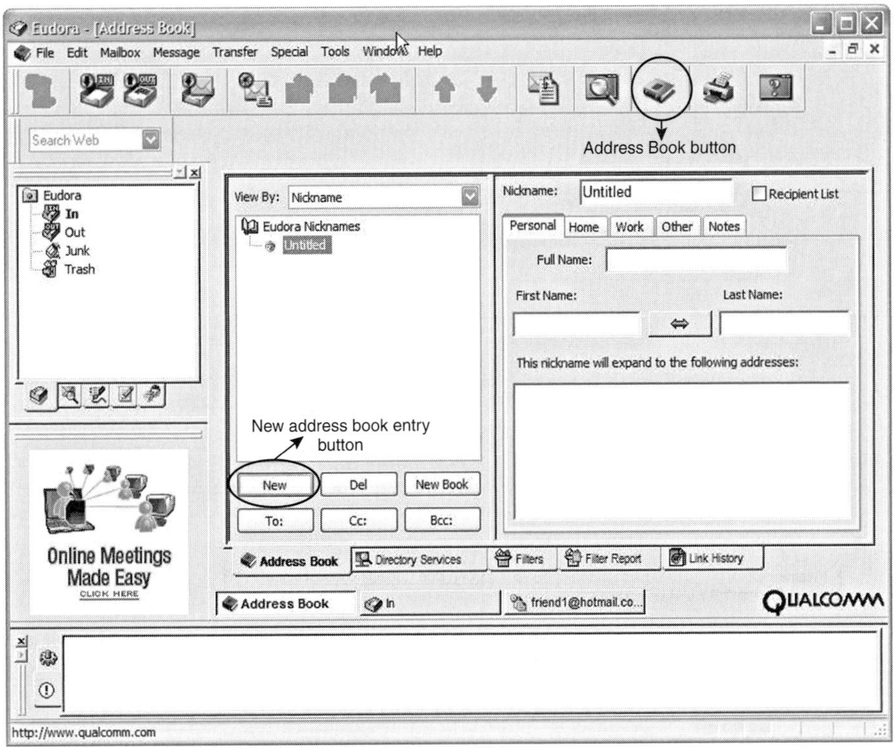

Figure 4.26 Address book dialog box in Eudora.

Let's set up an address book entry for one of your friends or work colleagues. This example, shown in Figure 4.27, uses "John Doe", but you can substitute your own information.

➤ In the *Nickname box* type: John
➤ In the *Full Name* box type: John Doe
➤ In the *First Name* box type: John
➤ In the *Last Name* box type: Doe
➤ In the *Address area* type: jdoe@abc.com
➤ Click the *File, Save* menu commands to save this new address book entry.

Notice that there are tabs in the address book dialog box for contact information for Home, Work, Other, and Notes. Feel free to add more information for each of the address book entries you create.

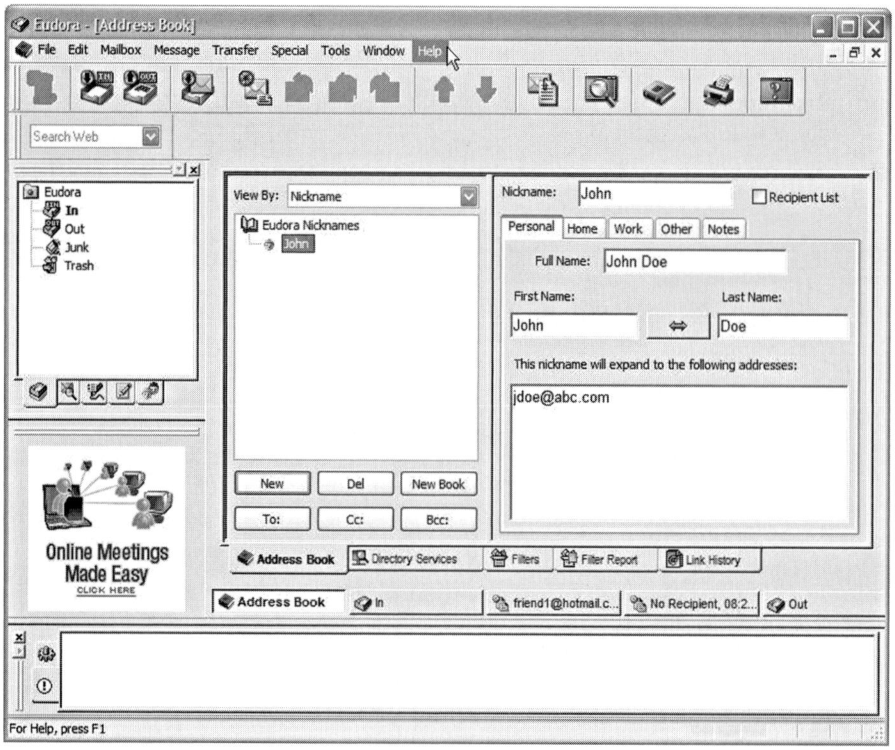

Figure 4.27 Address book dialog box with information for a contact in Eudora.

As with Microsoft Outlook Express, we can use the nickname in place of the address in any of the address inputs, To:, Cc:, and Bcc:.

➤ Click the *New Message* button to open an email composition window, as shown in Figure 4.28.

Figure 4.28 *New Message* button in Eudora.

➤ In the *To:* field type: John (or the nickname you chose for your address book entry).

➤ Feel free to type a quick message and send it. You will find that Eudora will substitute the email address for the nickname.

≋tip

∴ If you are using an address book, be sure to keep a copy of the addresses in some other location as well. Occasionally, print the email addresses and other contact information. This will come in handy if your computer is inaccessible or you lose your data!

Receiving, Reading, and Managing Email

Receiving and reading email is fairly intuitive. Basically, your email client, or Web interface, connects to your provider's email server, and provides a listing of the email messages in your inbox. Email clients will have options to specify how often to automatically check for new email messages and download them.

Receiving and Setting Automatic Receive Settings in Outlook Express

➤ Click the *Send/Receive* button to both send and receive email messages.

Make sure that the inbox is selected in the panel on the left. You can click a message to read it in the Preview pane underneath the email listing, or double-click it to open the message in a new window. Feel free to click one of the messages in your inbox.

➤ Click the *Tools, Options* menu commands to open the email Options dialog box.
➤ Click the *Mail Setup* tab and the *Send/Receive* button, as shown in Figure 4.29.

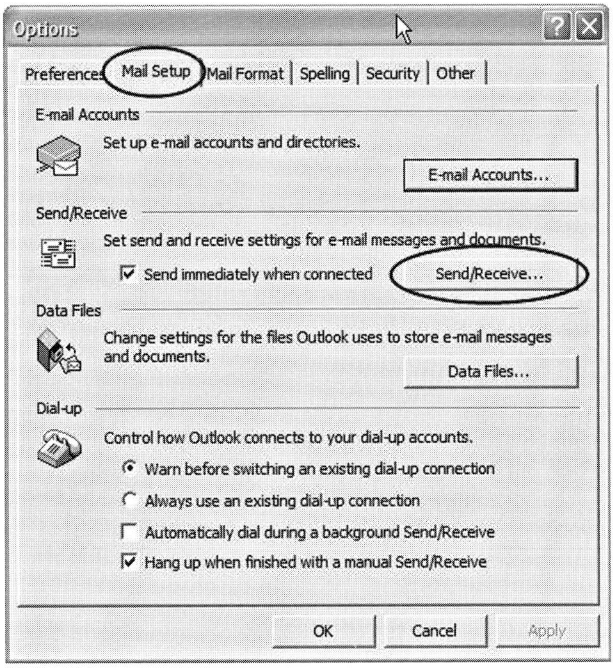

Figure 4.29   Email Options dialog box in Microsoft Outlook Express.

➤ Click the checkbox to schedule an automatic send and receive, and select the time to be every 1 minute, as shown in Figure 4.30.
➤ Click the *Close* button to accept the changes for the email settings.
➤ Click the *OK* button to accept the changes for options.

Receiving and Setting Automatic Receive Settings in Eudora

➤ Click the *Check Mail* button, shown in Figure 4.31, to download any new email messages.
➤ Be sure that the inbox has been selected so that you can see the listing of email in the inbox, as shown in Figure 4.32. If the inbox has not been selected, then double-click *In* or click the *Inbox* button, as indicated in Figure 4.32.

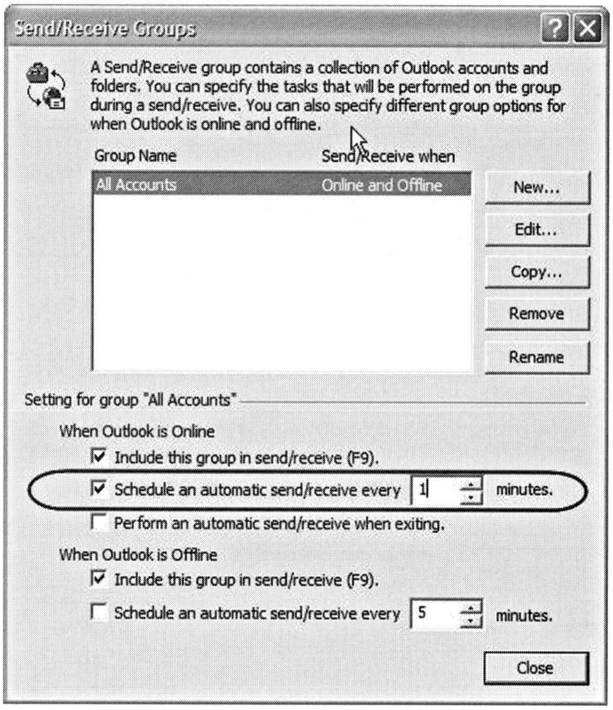

Figure 4.30   Setting the automatic send/receive for email in Microsoft Outlook Express.

Figure 4.31   *Check Mail* button in Eudora.

Let's set up the automatic checking feature.

➤ Click the *Tools, Options* menu commands and click the *Checking Mail* button, as shown in Figure 4.33.

➤ Edit the number of minutes to check for email as 1 minute, as shown in Figure 4.33.

➤ Click the *OK* button to select the checking email options.

Receiving Messages Using Webmail

Some Webmail interfaces may provide an alert box when new email messages are received, or you may have to click the *Refresh* button on the Web browser in order to update the inbox listing. You can click an email message subject in a Webmail email listing in order to view the message.

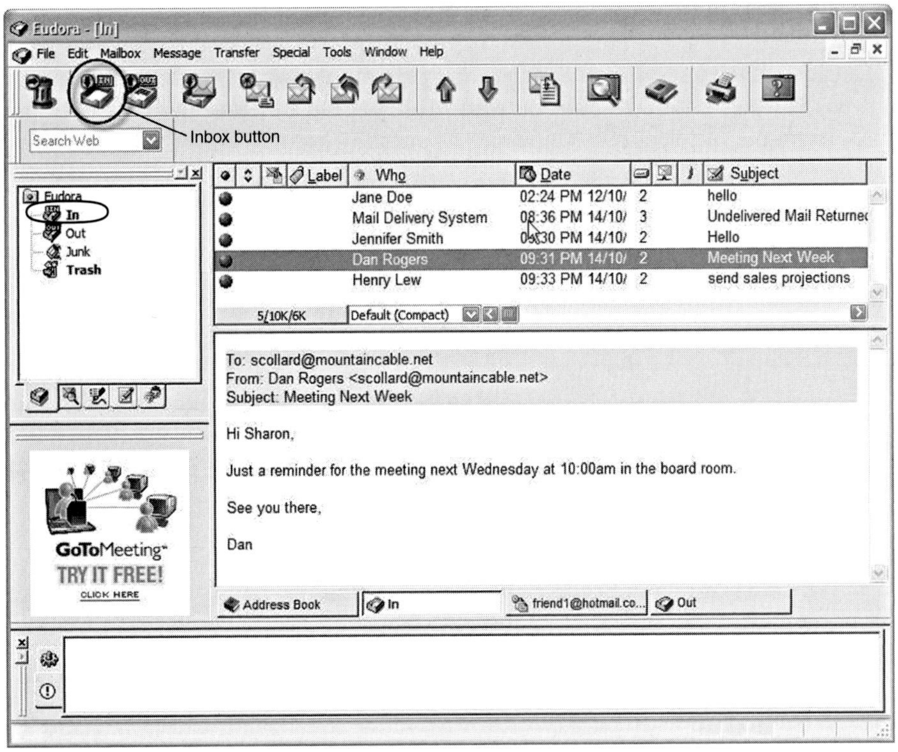

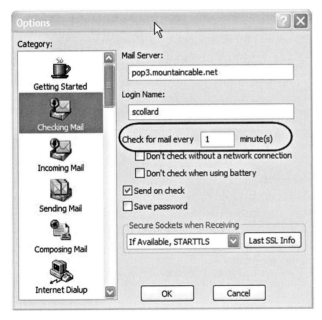

Figure 4.32 Inbox and email messages in Eudora.

Figure 4.33 Setting the checking email options in Eudora.

Bounced Mail

There are a few interesting issues surrounding incoming email, though. First, if there is a typo in an email address when you send email, you may receive a message telling you that the host or recipient does not exist. The message shown in Figure 4.34 is an example of a bounced email message.

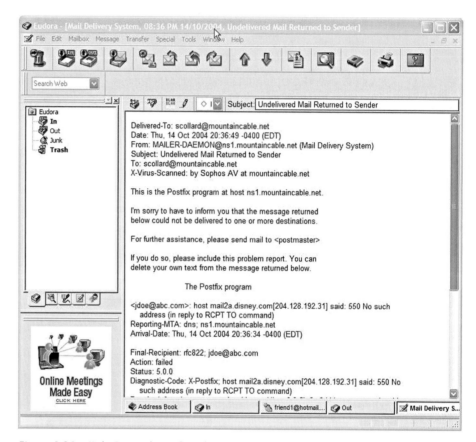

Figure 4.34   Mailer Daemon bounced email message.

Some email clients do not show bounced messages; so if you need to know that a message has been received, do not depend on "no news is good news." A bounced message tells you that a message has not been delivered yet. Sometimes these messages are not sent until hours after a message has been originally sent. If you need to depend on the recipient receiving a message, you can add a return receipt, or ask the recipient to confirm with you via email or even phone.

Email Header Information

Email messages come packed with information about the route taken between the sender and recipient. This information can be useful in several different scenarios. For instance, let's say you receive an email message and the sender's name is Judy Garland.

Did she really send it? Not likely, as she passed away in 1969. So, where did this message come from, and how might you find out if it's "real"? Or, let's say you receive a message and the date stamp is more than a week old. Is it late? Was it really sent more than a week ago?

Let's look at an email message to see what information is included.

➤ Using Outlook Express, *open an email message* in the inbox by *double-clicking it.*

➤ From the menu, select *View, Options.*

You should see a window similar to the one shown in Figure 4.35.

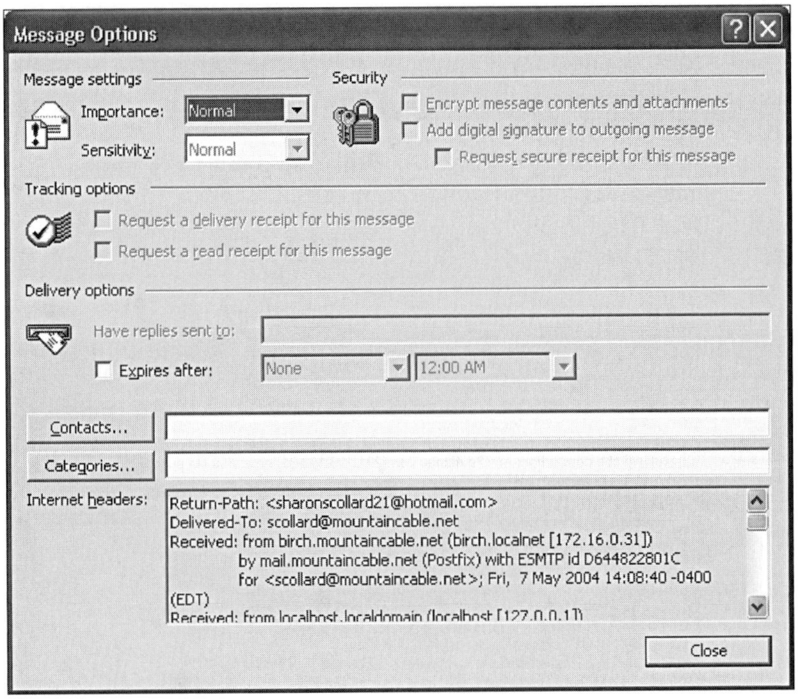

Figure 4.35 Microsoft Outlook Internet Headers.

➤ Similarly, in Eudora, double-click a message to view it in the message pane, and click the *Show Long Headers* button, as shown in Figure 4.36.

Notice the Internet headers at the bottom of the window in Microsoft Outlook Express, or the headers displaying in Eudora. It might look something like this:

Return-Path: <sharonscollard21@hotmail.com>
Delivered-To: scollard@mountaincable.net
Received: from birch.mountaincable.net (birch.localnet [172.16.0.31])
by mail.mountaincable.net (Postfix) with ESMTP id D644822801C
for <scollard@mountaincable.net>; Fri,   7 May 2004 14:08:40 -0400 (EDT)
Received: from localhost.localdomain (localhost [127.0.0.1])
by birch.mountaincable.net (Postfix) with ESMTP id 4FBCC769FC

for <scollard@mountaincable.net>; Fri,   7 May 2004 14:08:40 -0400 (EDT)
Received: from hotmail.com (bay8-f90.bay8.hotmail.com [64.4.27.90])
by birch.mountaincable.net (Prefix); Fri, 7 May 2004 14:8:40 -0400
Received: from mail pickup service by hotmail.com with Microsoft SMTPSVC;
Fri, 7 May 2004 11:08:39 -0700
Received: from 24.215.58.207 by by8fd.bay8.hotmail.msn.com with HTTP;
Fri, 07 May 2004 18:08:39 GMT
X-Originating-IP: [24.215.58.207]
X-Originating-Email: [sharonscollard21@hotmail.com]
X-Sender: sharonscollard21@hotmail.com
From: "Sharon Scollard" <sharonscollard21@hotmail.com>
To: scollard@mountaincable.net
Subject: test for headers
Date: Fri, 07 May 2004 18:08:39 +0000
Mime-Version: 1.0
Content-Type: text/plain; format=flowed
Message-ID: <BAY8-F90Pt4hgB0UWGA0000a024@hotmail.com>
X-OriginalArrivalTime: 07 May 2004 18:08:39.0355 (UTC)
FILETIME=[52C6D8B0:01C4345E]
X-UIDL: nRo"!`$o"!XnT"!3RC"!

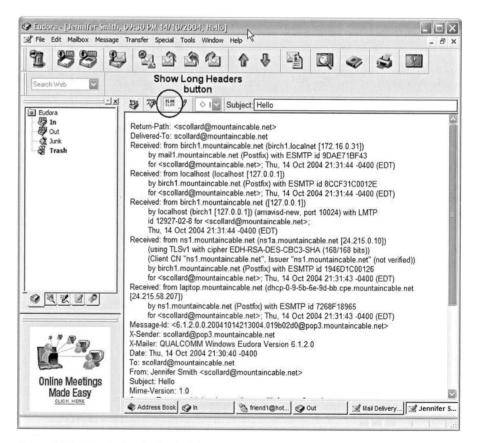

Figure 4.36 Showing long headers in Eudora.

It's all very cryptic. But as you scan through it, you will see a series of dates and times. Routers and servers add these when the message is passed along the line. These dates and times will tell you if the message was sent a week ago, or today. Notice the progression of dates/times from top to bottom. Beside each of the dates you will see a reference such as +0400 or -0700. These are referring to the time relative to Greenwich Mean Time (GMT). For instance, one of the time stamps is 14:08:40 +0400. This indicates hh:mm:ss for hours, minutes, and seconds using the 24-hour clock. This message was stamped at 2:08 P.M. (and 20 seconds) and is four hours later than GMT. This eliminates any confusion that time zones might cause.

Now we know when it was really sent, but how do we know who sent it? Well, even at the best of times, the most we can know for sure is the IP address and/or domain where the message originated. In the headers above, this information is close to the top:

Received: from birch.mountaincable.net (birch.localnet [172.16.0.31])
        by mail.mountaincable.net (Postfix) with ESMTP id D644822801C
        for <scollard@mountaincable.net>; Fri, 7 May 2004 14:08:40 -0400 (EDT)

This message came from a server named *birch.mountaincable.net* from the IP address 172.16.0.31. The sender's name does not appear in the headers because this information cannot be verified. As you saw, in setting up an email account, you can choose any name for the sender name, so I can send a message with the sender name "Judy Garland" by selecting this name as the sender in my email client or Web interface setup. ISPs assign an IP address to each computer connecting to their service, but IP addresses are assigned on a rotational basis, and you will have a different IP address each time you connect. The ISP will have a list of IP addresses and the accounts they were assigned in a given time period, but due to privacy laws, you will not likely be able to get that information without assistance from a lawyer or the police.

Replying to an Email Message

Whether you're using a Web interface or an email client, you will be able to reply to email messages. Let's look at this feature.

You will receive your messages automatically, or will be able to click a button such as *check mail*, *send/receive* or in the case of a Web interface, reload the Web page. Your email messages will be delivered to your inbox, and from there you can read them, reply to them, and file them into folders.

Figure 4.37 shows an example of inboxes in Eudora and Outlook Express, which contain some email messages. The body of the top message is displayed in the larger pane, as shown in Figure 4.37.

Notice that for each email message, the received date/time, and size are indicated. As previously mentioned, the received date/time may be the sender's date/time and if the sender is in a different time zone, or the clock on their computer is set incorrectly, could indicate a misleading date/time.

Replying to email is fairly intuitive. Regardless of the email package you are using the same basic steps apply:

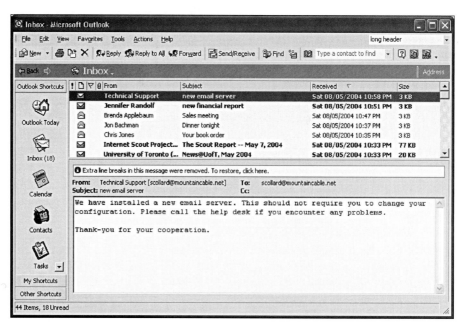

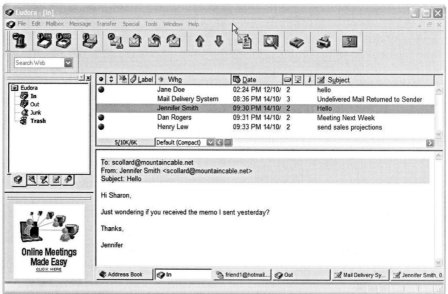

Figure 4.37   Top: Microsoft Outlook Express inbox. Bottom: Eudora inbox.

➢ Select the email message you wish to reply by clicking on it once.

➢ Click the *Reply* button, or use the menu items, looking for options such as *Message, Reply* in some packages. You can hover your mouse pointer over each button and a small tip should appear labeling the button so that you can determine which is the *Reply* button.

Once you have selected the reply feature, a new message composition window will open, and depending on the options set, you should see the old message, and a

flashing insertion point above or below the original message. The old message will have some header information about the sender, a symbol on the left of each line such as |
or > to denote that it is the original message. An example of a reply message is shown in Figure 4.38, with my reply at the top of the message.

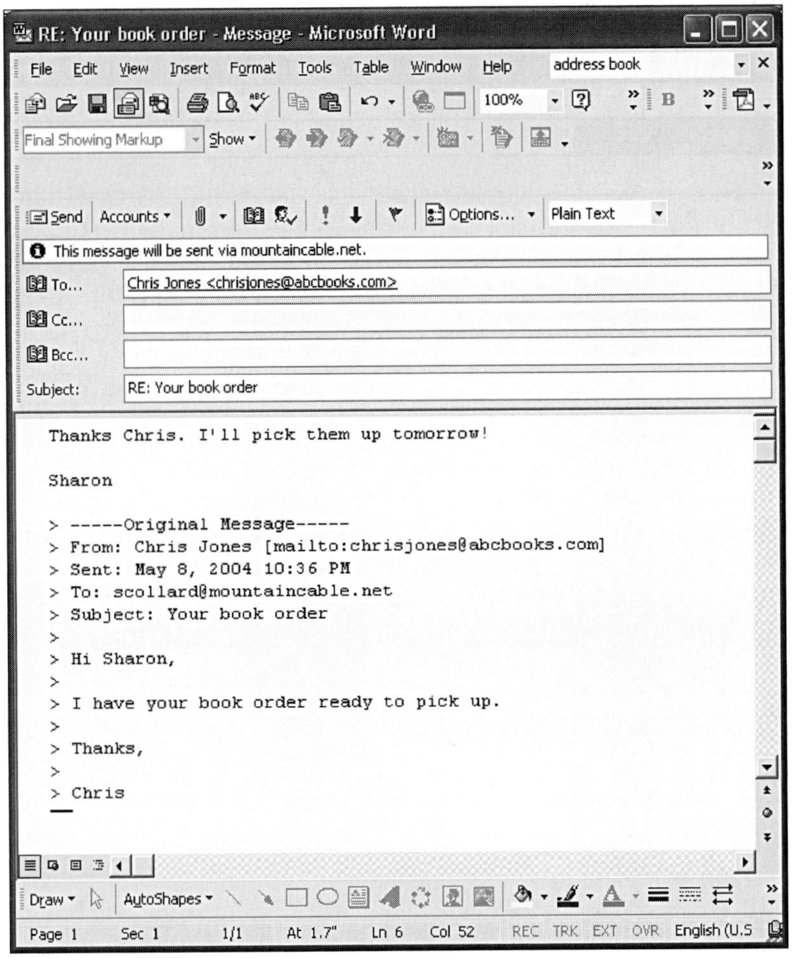

Figure 4.38 Microsoft Outlook reply to an email message.

Typically, you should leave in the message, the relevant parts to which you are replying. Some people reply to each portion of the message, some reply above the message and some reply below. It's your call, but typically it's easier for the reader if the reply is above the message. If your reply is throughout the message, more like a conversation, indicate this to the recipient. If you are replying to a long message, with "I agree" or some other short response, then delete all or most of the original message.

➢ Once editing is complete, you can send the message as usual.

If the message includes an attachment, there will be a link at the bottom of the message, or in the header, for you to click to save or open the file. Do not open an attachment unless you are running antivirus software. The risk of viruses will be discussed later in this chapter. For now, suffice it to say, that you should not open an attachment, unless you are expecting it from a friend or colleague and you are sure that it does not contain a virus. Anti-virus software can scan email attachments before you open them.

Reply All, Forward, and Redirect

There are a few other reply and sending options available in most email clients and Web interfaces. They are:

Reply All: All the To: and Cc: recipients are automatically included in the reply message. You can edit, attach files, and enter additional recipients in the To:, Cc:, and Bcc: fields as usual. If you wish to reply only to the sender, use the *Reply* feature. Be very careful when you select *Reply All* as all recipients will receive your email.

Forward: Send the complete message, with attachments. You can edit, attach files, and enter recipients in the To:, Cc:, and Bcc: fields as usual.

Redirect: Send the complete message, with attachments, but retain the original sender. Typically, the redirect will append "(by way of John Doe)" to the end of the subject so that the recipient knows that the message came via John Doe, although it is originally from someone else. The advantage of this type of send is that when the recipient replies, the reply address will be the original sender's and not yours. This is typically used if you receive a message from someone, but want to forward it to someone else who will be replying to it. Figure 4.39 shows an email message listing that includes three messages at the bottom that have been redirected, as indicated by the addendum *(by way of . . .)*.

!	□	▽	ⓘ	From	Subject	Received ▽	Size
				Chris Jones	Your book order	Sat 08/05/2004 10:...	3 KB
				Internet Scout Project (by way of Sharon Scollard <sharon@golden.net>)	The Scout Report -- May 7, 2004	Sat 08/05/2004 10:...	77 KB
				University of Toronto (by way of Sharon Scollard <sharon@golden.net>)	**News@UofT, May 2004**	**Sat 08/05/2004 1...**	**20 KB**
				Educause Educause (by way of Sharon Scollard <sharon@golden.net>)	Edupage, May 07, 2004	Sat 08/05/2004 10:...	18 KB

Figure 4.39 Outlook inbox showing redirected messages.

Deleting Email Messages

tip

∴ Be careful when using the Reply feature versus the Reply All feature. If you mean to reply only to the person who sent the message, use the Reply feature. If you mean to reply to everyone who received the original message, use the Reply All feature. And double-check before you click send! It's too easy to write a message that others shouldn't see, and then accidentally send it to them!

Regardless of whether you are using a Web interface or email client, you will be able to delete unwanted email messages. Deleting messages is generally a two-step process as follows.

➤ Click a message you wish to delete.

➤ Click the *Delete* button, or look for a link or menu item such as *delete message* or *Message, Delete*. The message will be sent to the trash. Some Web interfaces may prompt you to permanently delete it at this point if there isn't a separate trash folder available.

➤ Empty the trash. Some email clients and Web interfaces automatically empty the trash on exit, so it is not necessary for you to do it manually. You should be aware that a trash option exists in most packages, so don't assume that the message is gone after you've deleted it. Look for a menu item such as *File, empty trash*, or a trash folder. Microsoft Outlook Express has a deleted items folder and you can right-click it and select the menu item *Empty "Deleted Items" Folder*, as shown in Figure 4.40.

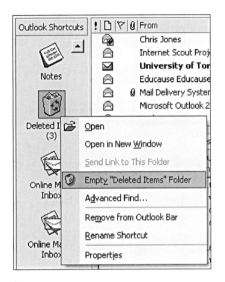

Figure 4.40   Microsoft Outlook "empty deleted items folder" menu option.

➤ In Eudora you can empty the trash using the menu commands *Special, Empty Trash*, as shown in Figure 4.41.

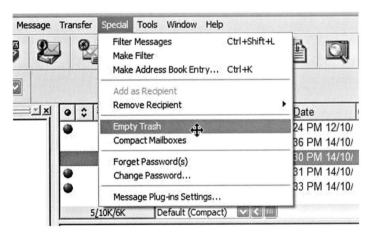

Figure 4.41   Special, Empty Trash menu items in Eudora.

Managing Email Using Folders

Regardless of whether you are using a Web interface or email client, there is typically an email management system available where you can organize messages into folders. The

≋ tip

∴ If you accidentally delete an email message, it may be in the trash folder. You can open the trash folder and transfer the message back to the inbox or another folder if it hasn't been permanently deleted.

method used to do this varies depending on the email client or Web interface you are using, but generally you can create folders, delete them, and copy and/or move messages into them.

Managing Email Using Outlook Express

Here's a quick example using Outlook Express.

➤ Select the menu options *File, Folder, New Folder,* as shown in Figure 4.42.

Figure 4.42   Microsoft Outlook menu File, Folder, New Folder.

➤ Type `Personal` in the *Name:* field to create a new folder called *Personal,* as shown in Figure 4.43.

➤ Outlook Express will prompt you, asking if you would like a shortcut added to your shortcut bar. Click *OK*.

➤ Click the *Inbox* label above the message listing to view the folder listing, as shown in Figure 4.44.

➤ If you wish, you can click the Personal folder to view the contents of the folder (which is currently empty). You can click the Personal folder label to view the folder listing again, and click the inbox to return to the inbox listing.

Let's move a message to the Personal folder.

➤ Choose a message in your inbox, and *right-click* it to reveal the menu, as shown in Figure 4.45.

➤ Select the item *move to folder*. A folder-listing box will appear.

➤ Select the *Personal folder* from the list.

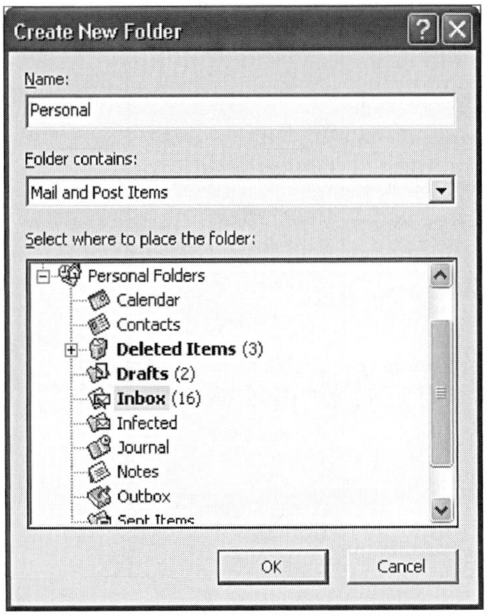

Figure 4.43 Outlook—creating a new folder.

Figure 4.44 Outlook—folders listing.

➤ Click the *OK* button to move the message to the folder.

➤ Click the *Inbox* label as before, to reveal the folder listings.

➤ Click the *Personal folder* to display the Personal folder listing. You should see that your message is in the Personal folder.

➤ Click the *Personal folder label* and select the *Inbox folder* to return to the inbox listing. You should notice that the message moved to the Personal folder, has been deleted from the inbox.

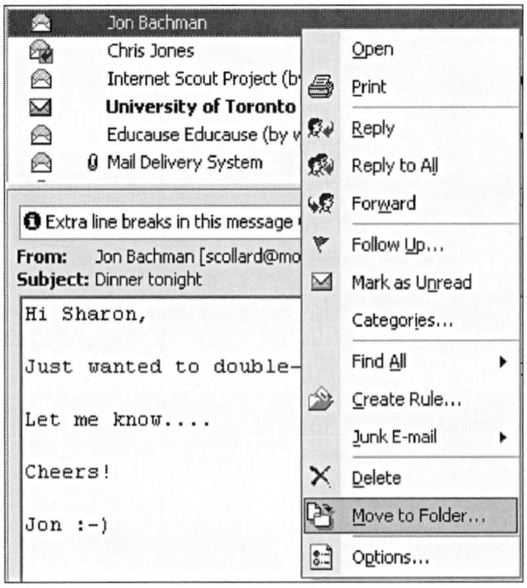

Figure 4.45   Outlook—right-click on a message.

There are often other methods available to move and copy messages, which include dragging the message to the folder icon. You will find that in Outlook Express, for instance, you can display the shortcut bar, and drag the message into the folder. This transfers a copy of the message into the folder. You can right-drag the message to the folder and a shortcut menu will display options for moving or copying. These methods vary from one email client to another.

Managing Email Using Eudora

➢   Click the menu options *Mailbox, New*. The new mailbox dialog box will appear.

➢   In the mailbox name input box, type: Personal, as shown in Figure 4.46.

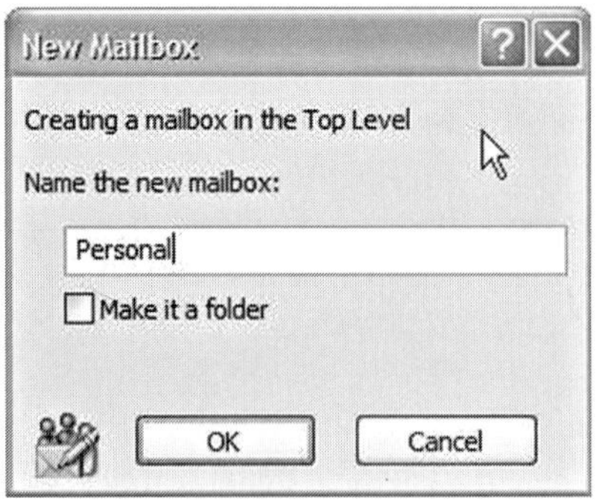

Figure 4.46   Eudora new mailbox dialog box.

➢   Click the *OK* button to create the new mailbox.

➤ Select the message you would like to move and drag it to the new mailbox, as shown in Figure 4.47.

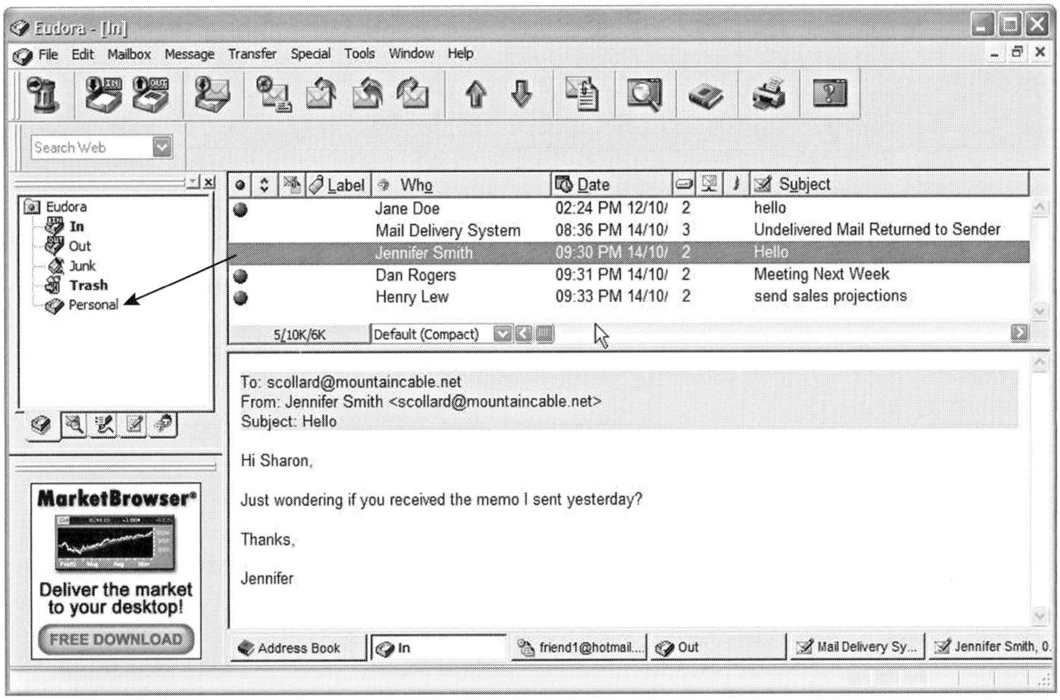

Figure 4.47 Dragging a message to the new mailbox in Eudora.

➤ You can double-click the new *Personal* mailbox to see the listing of email messages available in it. Feel free to double-click the *In* mailbox to return to the listing in the inbox.

Additional Email Features

Email clients have many features, which may include some or all of the following.

Filters: Filters (some clients refer to them as rules) automatically file messages into folders depending on the criteria selected. For instance, you may want to file messages from your mother automatically into your Personal folder, or messages from a mailing list into a Mailing List folder. Criteria can include keywords in the subject, body, and a particular sender's email address.

Signature: You may wish to add your contact information or a message to the bottom of each email message you send. This can be done with a signature. Most email clients will also accommodate multiple signatures.

Sorting: Typically you can sort email messages by clicking on the heading at the top of the listing. For instance, to sort by Subject, you can click the Subject heading at the top of the column. Some Web interfaces will also allow this feature. You can click the heading at the top of the column, and the page will reload with the list sorted on that column.

Printing: Usually there is a print button, and/or menu such as *File, Print*. Using a Web interface, you would print the Web page, using your browser features.

Multiple email accounts: Many email clients, and even some Webmail accounts will facilitate access to multiple email accounts. Generally, an email client will not be able to access Web client mail, but some of the Webmail sites offer an option to pay for conversion to POP mail. Email clients can be configured, as you have seen, to access POP email connections. Webmail that is not available through a POP connection cannot be accessed using an email client. When you use an email client to download mail from other accounts, it is important to note that you will use only the SMTP server for the account you are directly connected to. ISPs generally prohibit sending email messages through their SMTP servers if the user is not connected directly to their service. This restriction prevents unauthorized users from sending mail through their SMTP server.

SPAM

There's no question that unsolicited email has reached epidemic proportions. Although this may seem like a relatively new thing, its history dates back to May 3, 1978 when a Digital Equipment Corporation executive sent an email message to all the users on ARPANET, advertising his wares (BBC, 2003). At the time, it created a huge controversy as it broke an unwritten rule that messages were to be non-commercial. Unsolicited email has grown in volume from 8% of email traffic in 2001 to approximately 83% today.

On March 31, 1993, a Usenet system administrator, Richard Depew, accidentally posted a message to over 200 Usenet news groups, enraging the Usenet community (BBC, 2003). The history and evolution of Usenet news groups will be explained in the Mass Communication chapter. The Usenet community used the term spam in its gaming groups, to refer to annoyances, and applied the term to mean *unsolicited email*. Spam ("**Sp**iced h**am**") is a canned, spiced luncheon meat, produced by Hormel Foods. The term *spam* in reference to email comes from a comedy sketch, by the British comedy show, *Monty Python's Flying Circus*. The sketch "spam, spam, spam" in which every dish is served with spam, much to the patron's annoyance, and through the attempt to order a meal a chorus of Vikings sing, "SPAM, SPAM, SPAM . . . " at progressively higher volumes. As *spam* in the comedy skit was an annoyance, the term has been used to refer to unsolicited email, which is pervasive and annoying.

One of the most infamous cases of spam was in 1994 when the Arizona law firm Canter and Seigel posted a message to thousands of Usenet news groups advertising their services for an upcoming green card lottery. The Internet can be somewhat self-policing, and the Usenet news community retaliated with email replies to the lawyers' email address, causing server crashes for their ISP, Internet Direct. Internet Direct cancelled their account, despite threats of lawsuits (Electronic Frontier Foundation, 1994).

Spam Blockers

There are a few methods available to block spam so that it does not appear in your inbox.

Spam blockers, or **anti-spam software** as it is often called, can be installed as an add-on to automatically route unwanted email into a separate folder or go directly to the trash. These tools literally read your messages using predefined terms and syntax, and move the message to a place where you can view it when you have more time (if at all). Most anti-spam software will allow you to set the level of filtering required, some to the point where you specify which email addresses are permitted to send mail to you, and messages from other email addresses will be trashed. The better software will allow you to set your own spam rules, and save all incoming messages into a folder where you can manually view them. This is important because you may find that your filtering was a bit too aggressive and some important mail was filtered. Some anti-spam software packages also have additional features such as blocking pop-up and pop-under windows. For reviews of the most up-to-date anti-spam software, perform a search using your favorite search engine, using the terms "anti-spam reviews."

Before you install a spam blocker, check with your ISP to see if they are already running anti-spam software. Some ISPs run anti-spam and anti-virus software on their mail servers and provide a Web interface for users to view the blocked mail, deliver it or delete it, and set filtering levels.

Email Trackers

In the early days of email, it was possible to determine whether or not the recipient had opened the message you sent. Due to privacy and security concerns, this feature has largely been disabled. In recent years, **email trackers** have emerged. These email add-ins trace the path of your email as it is received and forwarded from one person to the next. Some would argue that these devices are an invasion of privacy, and it is something you should definitely be aware of. If you use the term "email tracker" in your favorite search engine, you will quickly see a list of current trackers available. Some provide a basic free service, and more detailed tracking information for a subscription fee.

Web Bugs

Although the companies developing email trackers do not disclose their exact technology, a very common technique used to track visitors to Web sites, and through email, is to place a Web bug in an email message or on a Web page. A **Web bug** is an image, one pixel in size, and transparent, so that it blends in with the background and does not appear visible to the user. The code used to place the image in the page or email, requests the image from the email tracking site or Web site. The image is requested when the email is opened, or when the Web page is viewed.

When the email message or Web page you are viewing requests the image, a lot of information about your technology is sent along with it. This information includes your IP address, the date/time of the request (that is, when you opened the email or

⁂ tip

∴ If you are testing out several different email clients to find the one you like, be sure to use the appropriate settings to leave the email messages on the server. If the messages are still on the server when you've settled on an email client, you can download them all at that time.

viewed the Web page), the type of Web browser or email client you are using, and any previously set cookie value. In the case of an email tracker, the tracker software may insert the image into the outgoing email, and assign a tracking number in its database in order to be able to provide you with statistics. The technique of using Web bugs for tracking and gathering information is widely used in spam, and many Web sites. In fact, some companies work together to consolidate tracking information as the user is surfing.

To illustrate how your surfing might be tracked, imagine the following scenario: You've surfed to Company A's site, and the Web bug on this site, actually comes from Company Z and it recorded your 'hit.' You surf to Company B's site, and the Web bug on this site, also comes from Company Z. Company Z recorded your IP address when you loaded the page from Company A, and has traced the fact that you have moved on to Company B. You surf to Company C, which also has a Web bug from Company Z, and you fill out a customer request form, which includes your email address and other information. Now, Company C has both your IP address and your email address, and if there's an agreement to share this data, Company Z now has your email address, and a record associating that with the other Web pages you viewed.

Similarly, an email message that contains a Web bug will gather information from each recipient of the message and record it. When the message is forwarded, the image would be forwarded with it, as shown in Figure 4.48.

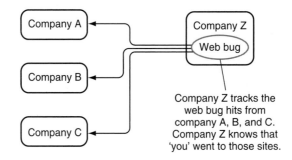

Figure 4.48 Web bugs.

There is software available that will strip Web bugs from email messages before you read them. There are also browser add-ins that will show you the Web bugs on a page. The browser add-ins do not strip the images, but they will replace the image with an icon such as a picture of a bug, to show you where they are. This is not perfect technology, however. The transparent image is also widely used as a spacer in Web design, and may not be a Web bug at all. So, knowing that it is there does not truly tell you whether it is benign or covertly tracking your path.

To Email, or Not to Email?

As you know, email communication is not the same as **face-to-face (FTF)** communication, or even the telephone, although, in some ways they are similar. When should you use email instead of other forms of communication? Dr. Jacob Palme (1995) has done extensive research on using email efficiently, and offers the following three suggestions:

- Use email instead of the telephone when you have to reach more than one person. Otherwise, you end up having to say the same thing over and over.
- Use email instead of postal mail when the message will be short. If you have to send a very long message, either use an attachment or the post. If you have to send a critical or formal document, you're better off using the postal system (legal documents which require signatures, for example).
- Use email instead of face-to-face meetings for large groups, if people have to travel, or if the meeting would be short.

Email has disadvantages as well. If your message isn't precisely worded, misunderstandings can occur. It is also difficult to make formal decisions or reach a consensus using only online communication. In sensitive situations, or when you need all your persuasive powers, you are better off using email to arrange a time and place to meet face-to-face.

In the business world, you will undoubtedly use email for completing projects. But email is not best for all stages of a project. Palme (1995) divides projects into three phases: preparation, where you gather ideas and propose solutions; the actual decision-making stage; and the execution of the plan. Email is not well suited to the decision-making phase, but it can be used very effectively for the first and last phases. Ideas and solutions can be tossed out to the group quite easily via email, and the details of how exactly things will be done can also be worked out online. Thus, for groups who need to work together, email can reduce the time spent meeting face-to-face. Each person can spend a few minutes a day (whenever it is convenient for them) getting and sharing background information through email before the meeting takes place. Once the decision has been made, simple issues and questions can quickly be resolved online instead of having to call another meeting.

Email and Personal Information Security

Viruses and Worms

Once your computer is connected to the Internet, a critical consideration is security. The most likely vulnerability is through file attachments from email messages.

File attachments can be useful documents from friends and colleagues, or they can also be viruses and worms harboring malicious code, which can range from programs that just send themselves to other people and clog email servers, to highly destructive code that infects computers, erases files, and renders computers inoperable. Technically, viruses are pieces of code embedded in otherwise benign files. Generally, they require some action on the part of the user to execute. The file must be opened or run. Worms are designed to replicate themselves across networks to other computers. Worms can also contain viruses. The code contained in a virus or worm is called the **payload**. Some viruses contain a payload that is not malicious and perhaps displays a political message or slowly draws a Christmas card on the screen. The damage caused by these viruses is loss of productivity and loss of resources while the virus is transmitted through the email systems.

John Shoch at the Xerox Palo Alto Research Center developed the first worm in 1979. He developed a program designed to look for idle processors and facilitate testing, and would replicate itself over the network. The unintended effect was the security threat it posed by replicating itself. He coined the term "worm" from a science fiction book *Shockwave Rider* by John Brunning in which a "tapeworm program" wreaks havoc traveling through a computer network (*Computer History Museum*, 2004).

On November 2, 1988, long before the Web was developed, the Internet community had an eye-opening experience, as the first worm was unleashed. It quickly infected 10% of the hosts before it could be stopped. Robert T. Morris, a graduate student at Cornell University, created a worm that was not malicious, for the purposes of proving that it could propagate through the Internet, and released it through MIT to disguise its origin at Cornell. The Morris worm crippled dozens of systems due to the network load from replicating itself, and cleanup costs ranged from $200–$53,000 per site. Today's costs would be astronomical. Robert Morris was tried and convicted of violating the 1986 Computer Fraud and Abuse Act. He was fined $10,000, given three years probation, and required to do 400 hours of community service. As a response to the Morris worm, the Computer Emergency Response Team (CERT) was created (*The Free Dictionary*, 2004).

Viruses and worms are cleverly disguised as screen savers, games, greeting cards, and even text files. One of the most famous viruses is the *I LOVE YOU* or *Lovebug* virus. In May 2000, this virus appeared in mailboxes all over the world. Preying on human weakness, the body of the email message said, "kindly check the attached LOVELETTER coming from me" (F-Secure, 2004). This sneaky virus was a file attachment disguised as a text file, but in fact it was a Visual Basic file (LOVE-LETTER-FOR-YOU.TXT.vbs). Thousands of people opened the file attachment, and if they also had Microsoft Outlook installed, the worm sent itself to everyone in their address book. Large sites such as the U.S. Navy, U.S. Senate, Ford, and even Microsoft were forced to shut down all or part of their email systems and it is estimated that the damage costs were approximately $1 billion (*E-commerce News*, 2004).

So what are the lessons learned here? An important thing to remember is that an email attachment virus or worm will not unleash itself or infect your computer unless you open it.

Lesson 1: Do not open file attachments unless you are expecting them. If you receive a file attachment and do not know the sender, do not open it. There are viruses sent under the guise of Microsoft Support, or your ISP technical support, and they could be sent from someone you know who has been infected, as was the case with the Lovebug virus.

Lesson 2: Install anti-virus software and use it. Make sure that the anti-virus signature files are up-to-date, and if possible, enable the email-scanning feature. Some ISPs and corporations run anti-virus software on their email servers and do not automatically send emails that have infected file attachments. Check with your ISP technical support to determine what level of virus protection is available.

≋ tip

∴ If you email someone who doesn't seem to respond, ask which method of communication would be best. Some people prefer voice mail to email.

Hoaxes and Chain Letters

Hoaxes and chain letters are an annoyance, cost us time, and can crash email servers with the volume of email sent, as they are sent to multiple recipients. Some corporations and institutions completely forbid users to send chain letters. Your best protection against falling into the trap for forwarding a chain email message or propagating a hoax, is information. So, here's some helpful information to dispel some of the myths, and enable you to recognize a hoax when you see one.

Hoaxes are fake warnings of impending doom, warning about fake viruses, instructing you to delete files (which are not viruses), playing on your sympathy for situations that do not exist or have long since been resolved, offering prizes from well-known corporations for forwarding the message to as many people as possible, and other similar scenarios. Chain letters implore you to pass the message to as many people as possible to avoid bad luck, or in order to receive good luck, or money.

Here are some telltale signs of hoaxes and chain letters:

- **"Pass this message to everyone you know."** This is the hidden purpose of the message—to bring down email servers with volume.

- **ALL CAPS.** A real virus warning will be written in a more formal, technical manner.

- **Dire warnings of impending doom such as wiping out your entire hard drive.** Although there certainly are malicious viruses around that will do just that, a legitimate warning will have plenty of technical description and possibly a remedy as well. A legitimate warning will typically inform you not to open email attachments, or take some other reasonable precaution.

- **A sum of money or prize will be won after this email is forwarded to some number of people.** This is a common chain letter theme.

- **Forward this message to some number of people and a video clip, or animation will appear.** This is not going to happen, as the email message will not have any special coding to detect the number of people it is forwarded to, and will not contain the video clip or animation.

- **Forwarding this email can save a dying child, or will send money to other victims.** Playing upon your sympathies in order to coerce you into forwarding the email is a common theme in chain letters.

If you receive suspicious email warning of dire consequences, do a little online sleuthing. Check a reputable site such as the Hoax Encyclopedia (`http://antivirus.about.com/library/blenhoax.htm`) or the Virus Encyclopedia (`http://antivirus.about.com/library/blency.htm`). The reputable anti-virus software companies also have extensive virus information available on their sites, and you can check those as well to determine the likelihood that the information you've received is a hoax or legitimate.

Phishing

Phishing is the use of a spoofed email and/or fraudulent Web site designed to trick the reader into divulging personal or financial information. A spoofed email is an email message created to look like it came from someone else rather than the true sender.

For instance, one example of a clever phishing attack is a spoofed email apparently from Citibank, as shown in Figure 4.49.

Notice that the URL contains an IP address. This is a telltale sign that there is something amiss. The Web site will look as if it is a Citibank site, but a company or individual not associated with Citibank will own the IP address.

```
Dear Customer:

Recently there have been a large number of cyber attacks pointing our database servers. In order to
safeguard your account, we require you to sign on immediately.

This personal check is requested of you as a precautionary measure and to ensure yourselves that
everything is normal with your balance and personal information.

This process is mandatory, and if you did not sign on within the nearest time your account may be
subject to temporary suspension.

Please make sure you have your Citibank(R) debit card number and your User ID and Password at hand.

Please use our secure counter server to indicate that you have signed on, please click the link bellow:

http://221.4.199.31/verification/

!! Note that we have no particular indications that your details have been compromised in any way.

Thank you for your prompt attention to this matter and thank you for using Citibank(R)

Regards,

Citibank(R) Card Department
```

Figure 4.49   Phishing attack email message.

The Anti-Phishing Working Group (`http://www.antiphishing.org`) is an organization dedicated to tracking trends in phishing attacks and providing good information on the latest scams and protecting yourself.

Encrypting Email

Email transmission is a **clear text** transmission. This means that it is unencrypted. Someone with packet-sniffing software might be able to collect the packets and effectively read the information contained within them. For this reason, it is important not to send information such as your credit card number via an email message. Sometimes important information must be sent via email, though, and if this is the case, there is email encryption software available that will encrypt the message before it is sent, and allow the recipient to decipher the message.

One of the most popular email encryption software packages is PGP (Pretty Good Privacy). It works using public keys and private keys. An over-simplified explanation is that the message you send will be encrypted using your public key, as well as the private key of the recipient. You will ensure that your recipient has received the private key by another means. When the email has been received, the recipient will provide the private key to decipher the message.

SUMMARY

Now that you've read through the chapter, you are prepared to:

- Use a variety of email clients and interfaces including Microsoft Outlook Express, Eudora, and Webmail to send, receive, and manage email messages.
- Understand the difference between reply, reply all, forward, and redirect.
- Send email messages using different levels of importance, and with return receipts.
- Send email messages with file attachments and understand the danger in opening a file attachment with regard to viruses.
- Use the rules of netiquette, smileys, and emoticons to add personality to your email messages.
- Manage contacts in an address book.
- Understand some methods that you can use to protect your personal information and computer security from spam, phishing attacks, email trackers, viruses, and hoaxes.

Review Questions and Hands-on Exercises

Review Questions

1. What is the difference between POP email access and Webmail email access?

2. What are the advantages and disadvantages of using POP email versus Webmail email access?

3. What is an email client?

4. Which email client will you be using if you are connecting to a Microsoft Exchange server?

5. You receive a message from your friend, but your email address is not in the To or Cc field in the header. What feature has your friend used?

6. What is the difference between Cc and Bcc?

7. What is a binary file?

8. You receive an email message with the symbols :-) in it. What does this mean?

9. You have sent a message to a work colleague and requested a return receipt. The message was sent five days ago and you have not received the return receipt. Has the recipient received your message and ignored it?

10. You have a list of contacts in your email address book. Describe at least three different shortcuts available to send a message to someone in your address book.

11. You receive a message from your boss, but the content of the message is completely out of character. How can you tell if your boss really sent this message?

12. What is spam and how can you reduce the amount of spam you receive?

13. You receive a message from a friend who tells you that they will be able to track the mail and will know if you forward it to anyone else. Is this possible, and if so, how?

14. What is netiquette?

15. You receive an email message from a good friend. The subject heading is "for your approval" and it contains a file attachment, but no message. You weren't expecting the file, but you're curious. What should you do?

16. You receive an email message that describes a contest and if you forward this email message to everyone you know, you could win $10,000. Should you forward the email, after all, what have you got to lose?

17. You are considering sending your credit card number to someone using email, but you've heard that it isn't secure. Is there a method you can use to email your credit card number, so that it is secure?

18. What is phishing and how can you find out more information about it?

Hands-on Exercises

1. Open a Web browser and load your ISP's web site. If you do not have an ISP, choose one from The List at http://www.thelist.com. Find the technical support page and answer the following questions.
   a. What are the names of the SMTP and POP email servers?
   b. Is your ISP running any spam blocking software or anti-virus software for email file attachments?
   c. Does your ISP offer a Webmail service so you can send and receive mail?

2. Open your email client or Webmail page. Gather email addresses from several friends or colleagues. If you do not have email addresses, you can go to some of the free Webmail sites and fill out the applications to get more email addresses for yourself. Perform the following tasks.
   a. Create and send an email message as follows.
      i. Compose a message To one email address and Cc to yourself.
      ii. Include the subject "test message."
      iii. In the body of the message, write a friendly *hello* message.
      iv. If the Return Receipt feature is available in the package you are using, then apply it to this message.
      v. Set the message importance to *high*.
      iv. Refresh the page, or go to the inbox to receive your message.

b. Compose a message to yourself including a file attachment of a small image file from your hard drive. In the body of the message, type `http://www.yahoo.com`. Refresh the page, or go to the inbox to receive your message. When you receive your message, notice that the URL appears as a link.

c. Use the address book feature to store the email addresses of at least two friends or colleagues, or the email addresses you have acquired for yourself.

d. Use the address book feature to send a message To one of the email addresses in the address book. Use the address book feature to Cc this email message to yourself. Include the subject *friendly hello*. In the body of the message, include a friendly *hello* message.

e. Select one of the messages you have received and view the long headers, if possible. You may have to check the Help menu for directions for viewing long headers if you are using a package other than Microsoft Outlook Express.

f. Create a folder for personal email. Move one of the email messages in your inbox into the personal email folder.

g. Select one of the messages in your inbox and delete it. You may have to empty the trash as well, to permanently delete the message.

3. Investigate the features of the email package you are using. You can explore menus, or explore the Help menu available. Answer the following questions. Which of the following features does your email package have?

a. Filters (these may be called *rules*)

b. Signature

c. Multiple email account management

4. Investigate spam-blocking software available. Open your favorite search engine and use the keywords *spam blocking software*. Explore some of the links and find at least three products that would allow the user to specify options within the software to allow the user to receive email from specified email addresses.

5. Investigate anti-virus software. Open your favorite search engine and use the keywords *anti-virus software*. Explore some of the links and find at least three products that have Web sites that provide detailed information about current virus threats. Determine how long the license permits updates for signature files.

6. Investigate latest trends in phishing at `http://www.antiphishing.org`. What are the trends in the last six months, and what are two of the most recent phishing attacks?

Doing Business on the Web

chapter 5

Chapter Objectives

This chapter helps you understand

- [ ] the distinction between E-Business and E-Commerce.
- [ ] the classes of E-Commerce models.
- [ ] numerous E-Commerce "business" models.
- [ ] the concept of supply chain management.
- [ ] how to put a small business online.
- [ ] the types of E-Commerce options available to the consumer.

In 1992, U.S. Rep. Frederick Boucher proposed an amendment to the National Science Foundation Act of 1950, to allow commerce on the Internet (Nerds 2.0, 2004). Prior to that, NSF was permitted only to support a research network. In 1994, shopping malls arrived on the Internet (Zakon, 2004). Many people think of retail transactions when they hear the term *E-Commerce*, but this is a very small component of E-Business and the business functions performed utilizing the Internet, as we shall see.

Many businesses and organizations provide a Web portal for customers and employees. A Web portal is a site designed to provide access to features such as a catalogue, search page, email, chat forums, news, and the like. It is primarily a marketing tool, but many companies use an internal Web portal for employees to consolidate email, company news, and intranet pages. A good example of a Web portal is the U.S. government portal, Firstgov.gov (http://www.firstgov.gov), which consolidates a wide variety of government service and information Web sites. A good example of a personal Web portal is My Yahoo! (http://my.yahoo.com).

Let's look at a simplified overview of the Internet with respect to business and commercial applications.

E-Business and E-Commerce

The development and popularity of the Internet forced many people to rethink how business was conducted, and how this new medium could be utilized in a business plan.

E-Commerce

A common definition of **Electronic Commerce** or **E-Commerce** entails electronic transactions, the buying and selling of goods and services, between business partners.

E-Business

Electronic Business or **E-Business** is broader in scope. E-Business includes electronic transactions between business partners, but also includes transactions within the organization, servicing customers, and collaboration with business partners. This implies employing electronics in the buying and selling of goods and services, in addition to customer relations management, communication with business partners, inventory control, purchasing, and many other business functions.

EDI

E-Business is not a new concept. In the 1960s, Electronic Funds Transfer (EFT) was used. **Electronic Data Interchange (EDI)** was emerging as a method of transmitting data in a standardized format from one computer system to another within an organization, but more importantly, between organizations' computer systems (Clarke, 2004). For instance, paper purchase orders were replaced with the EDI equivalent, and items could be ordered automatically from another organization using EDI as part of an inventory control system. An EDI message might include a shipping address, items to ship, and instructions to ship these items from a warehouse to a retailer. EDI messages can be customized, and the multiple parties who are communicating would negotiate agreements for standardization of messages. This would stipulate which information must be included, which information may be optional, and the required format for this information. EDI messages can be transmitted using private networks and over the Internet.

There are estimates that even today, as more and more corporations make use of Internet connectivity, as much as 95% of E-Business is still powered by EDI (Wikipedia, 2004).

Classifications of E-Commerce

E-Commerce is often classified by the nature of the transaction and the parties who are participating. Let's look at a list of the common types of transactions.

➤   As you read these explanations, view the Web sites mentioned for added clarity.

Business-to-Business (B2B)

In this case, both participants are businesses or other organizations. Most E-Commerce transactions today are **Business-to-Business (B2B)**, including EDI transactions over the Internet. An example of this might be Amazon.com (`http://www.amazon.com`) ordering office supplies from Staples (`http://www.staples.com`) using EDI or some other computer-automated method. A great resource for B2B information is B2Business.net (`http://www.b2business.net`). Figure 5.1 shows a B2B general resource and portal site.

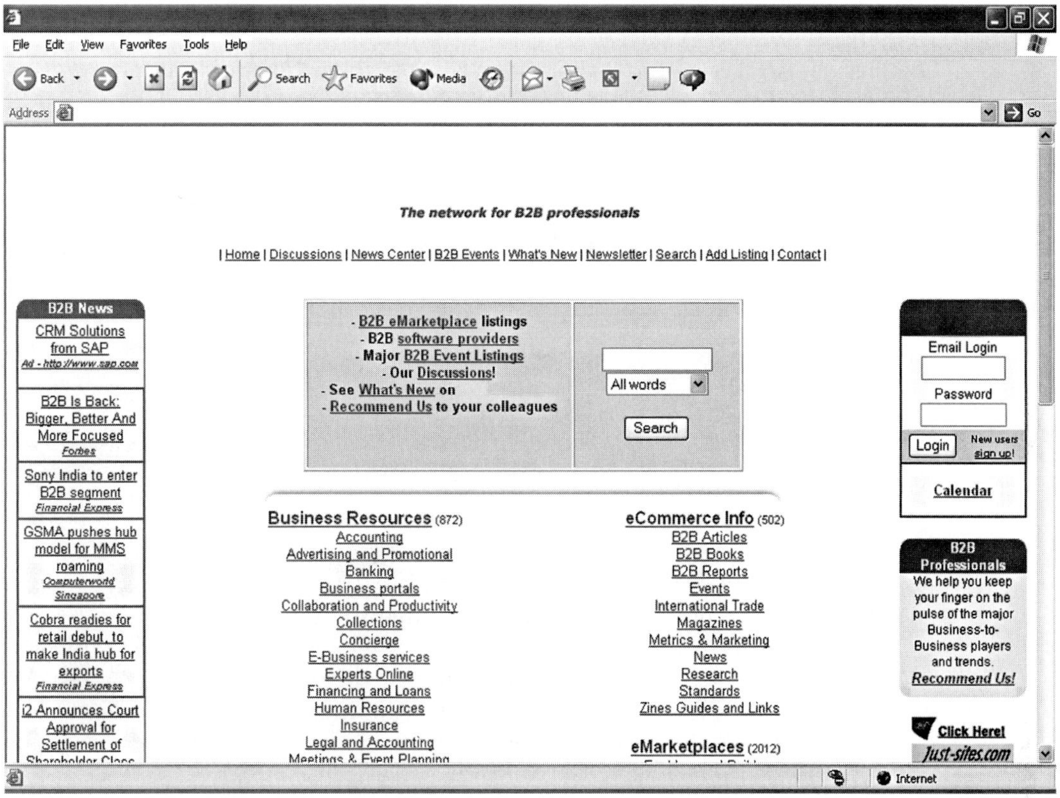

Figure 5.1 An example of a general resource and portal for B2B.

Business-to-Consumer (B2C)

These transactions include retail transactions on the Internet, and are often what people think of when they hear the term *E-Commerce*. For instance, when you purchase a book at Amazon.com (`http://www.amazon.com`), the transaction is between the business (Amazon.com) and the consumer (you). This type of business model is also referred to as **e-tailing**.

Business-to-Business-to-Consumer (B2B2C)

An example of this type of transaction is a business that provides a product to another business, which, in turn, provides a product to a consumer. Essentially this model is manufacturer-to-retailer-to-customer where, for instance, a manufacturer of saws sells saws to the hardware store, which in turn, sells the saws to the consumer. This is simple supply chain management, as the product is supplied from the manufacturer to the retailer to the consumer. Many people think of this model when they hear the term *B2B*.

🌀 *tip*

∴ When shopping online, and comparing to brick and mortar store prices, remember that shipping is often an additional cost. Some e-tailers include free shipping for larger orders, or high-priority shipping for an additional cost.

Consumer-to-Business (C2B)

An example of this type of transaction includes an individual consumer selling to a business or organization, but also includes an individual consumer who seeks sellers to bid on products or services they require. One example of this is a consumer who posts a Request For Quote (RFQ) on the Internet, hoping companies will bid on the product or service. Another example of this is a travel site such as Travelocity.com (`http://www.travelocity.com`), which is a Web portal for the consumer travel industry, allowing the consumer to find and book vacations, including hotel, flight, and car rental. Figure 5.2 shows an example of a consumer travel portal site.

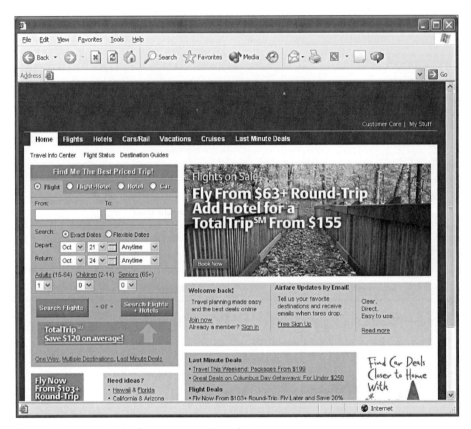

Figure 5.2　An example of a consumer travel portal site.

Consumer-to-Consumer (C2C)

C2C transactions entail consumers selling or buying directly between each other. This includes online classified ads, individual Web sites, and selling items through online auction sites. An interesting example of an online auction site is eBay.com (`http://www.ebay.com`).

Mobile Commerce (M-Commerce)

These are transactions completed in a wireless environment and may involve using a cell phone, or other hand-held device capable of sending and receiving data over a wireless connection.

Here's a quick summary of classifications of E-Commerce:

Classification	Example	Sample Web Site
Business-to-Business (B2B)	Staples sells office supplies to Sony.	Staples (http://www.staples.com) uses EDI transactions over the Internet but not through the Web site.
Business-to-Consumer (B2C)	Amazon.com sells books to individual consumers.	Amazon (http://www.amazon.com)
Business-to-Business-to-Consumer (B2B2C)	3M sells products to Staples, which in turn sells those products to individual consumers.	3M (http://www.3m.com) Staples (http://www.staples.com)
Consumer-to-Business (C2B)	An individual consumer uses a portal or comparison Web site to shop for products and services.	Travelocity (http://www.travelocity.com)
Consumer-to-Consumer (C2C)	Individual consumers sell products directly to each other using online ads or auction sites.	eBay (http://www.ebay.com)
Mobile Commerce (M-Commerce)	Transactions completed using a wireless device such as a cell phone.	Accessing Amazon (http://www.amazon.com) with a cell phone

E-Commerce Business Models

Now that we know the common types of E-Commerce business classifications, it's useful to look at some of the business models that utilize the Internet.

Online Direct Marketing

Retailers have incorporated an online presence to sell their products directly to consumers. Another less obvious model is a manufacturer selling online directly to customers. Manufacturers who use this business model are able to eliminate the intermediary. This model is used primarily for B2C and B2B E-Commerce.

Product and Service Customization

Customization of products and services is not a new idea, but the Internet lends itself to automating customization and fast manufacturing and delivery. Consumers can upload an image to be used for a logo on a T-shirt or baseball cap, upload a digital file of a poster or document for a printing company, select fabric and frame style for custom furniture, and choose computer components to be included in a new computer purchase. Dell (http://www.dell.com) is a good example of customization of a computer product, allowing the consumer to select the components, and then build and ship the computer for arrival at its destination within days. Automobile manufacturers have also incorporated customization into their Web sites, as consumers are encouraged to build their own car; specifying make, model, color, and a wide variety of other features. Dealerships can also offer on-the-spot leasing approval through a selection of lenders, incorporating credit checks and approvals through a selection of lenders within minutes. This model is used primarily for B2C E-Commerce. Figure 5.3 shows a good example of a product customization site.

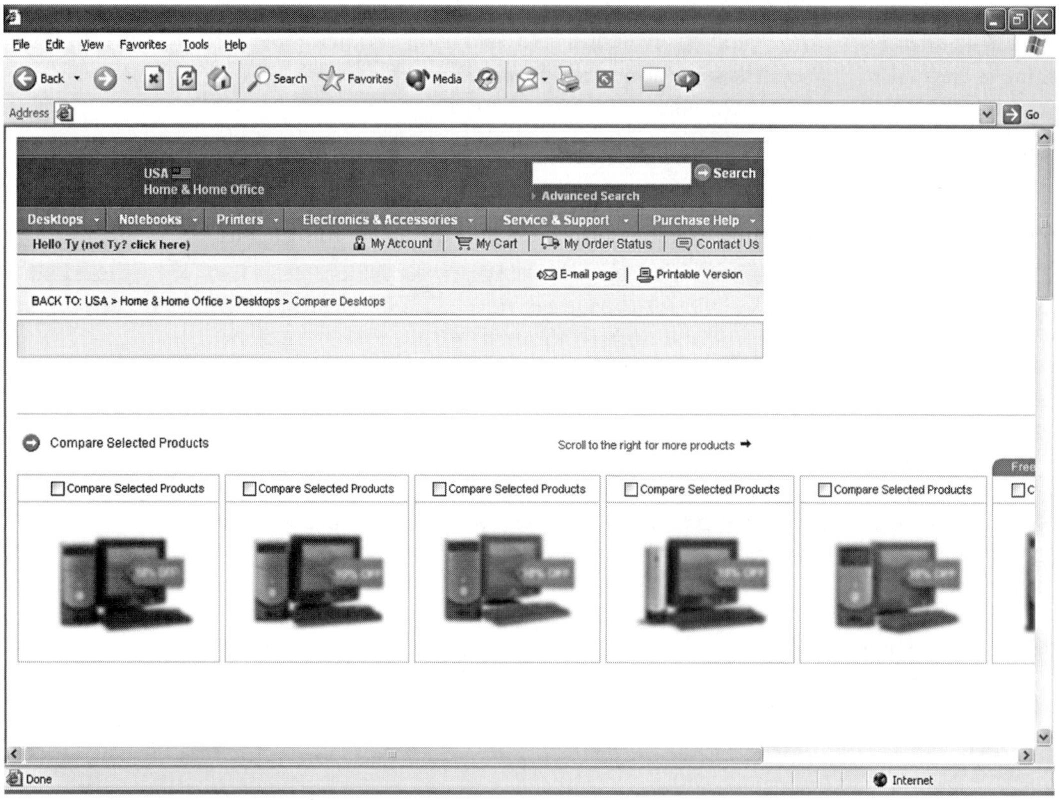

Figure 5.3   An example of a product customization site.

Consumer Online Auctions

The largest, and possibly most famous, online consumer auction is eBay (http://www.ebay.com). **Online auctions** allow consumers to bid on products and services. The highest bidder wins the purchase for the item, and the seller ships it. Financial transactions are facilitated through PayPal (http://www.paypal.com) or some other financial account manager. These sites allow users to create an account, accept payments, invoice, and pay other merchants. They handle the credit card authorization, and deposit money in your account for withdrawal later. This model is used primarily in B2C or C2C E-Commerce.

Electronic Tendering

Tendering is also not a new concept. Large organizations make their purchases through a tendering system where the buyer places an item for tender on a Request For Quote (RFQ) system. Suppliers bid on the job or product. This is also known as a **reverse auction**. The bidder with the lowest price wins the tender. This model is used primarily in B2B E-Commerce, but may also be used in business-to-government (B2G) E-Commerce.

Find the Best Price

In this model, an intermediary company or association will display a listing to the consumer with a selection of items that fall within the consumer's criteria. A good example of this in the travel industry is Travelocity (http://www.travelocity.com) for the purchase of flights, hotel rooms, and car rentals. Other examples include E-Loan (http://www.eloan.com), a loan brokering company, Insweb (http://www.insweb.com), a company that provides insurance comparison quotes for home, auto, health, and other insurance needs, and Quotesmith (http://www.quotesmith.com), which provides health insurance quotes for people with specific health issues, from a variety of insurance companies. An interesting example for real estate is the ability to search listings through the National Association of Realtors' site, Realtor.com (http://www.realtor.com) or the Canadian Real Estate Association, Multiple Listing Service (http://www.mls.ca), searching for price, location, and features. This model is used primarily in B2C E-Commerce.

Affiliate Marketing

Affiliate marketing is an arrangement between two businesses where each places a banner ad or logo of the other on their Web site, and pays a commission for sales completed as a result of the referral (Rayport and Jaworski, 2003). Companies can have many affiliate arrangements. Amazon (http://www.amazon.com) has approximately 500,000 affiliates, and as you search for books and CDs on their site, you will find that affiliates on subsequent pages are selected according to your searches. You'll find lots of useful information about affiliate marketing at Affiliate World (http://www.affiliates-world.com), as shown in Figure 5.4. This model is used primarily in B2C E-Commerce.

Viral Marketing

Viral marketing, also called **advocacy marketing**, is basically electronic word-of-mouth marketing in which consumers promote a product or service by telling other consumers about it. You will find "rate this product" reviews and recommendations by consumers on sites such as Amazon (http://www.amazon.com). A newer approach is the use of Web logs (or **Blogs**) to promote products or services in a very casual manner. Web logs were initially introduced as online journals and most serve that function, but some are used effectively as marketing tools. Viral marketing strategies can also include sending consumers email

≋ *tip*

:: Most consumer auction sites also provide customer ratings of sellers. It's a good idea to check the seller's rating to see if customers who have purchased from the seller have been satisfied with the product and shipping.

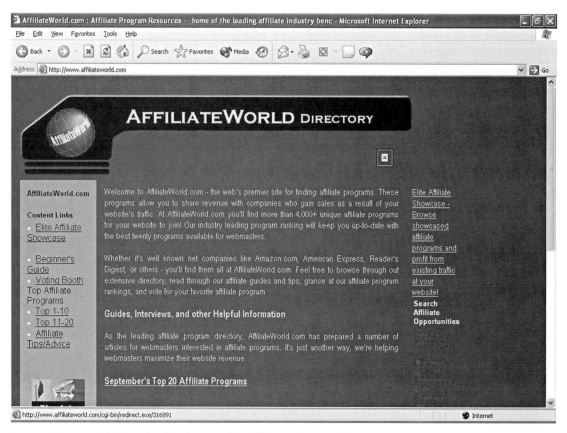

Figure 5.4   You'll find lots of useful information about affiliate marketing at Affiliate World.

with some value-added product, such as a free game, which carries the business logo. Hotmail (`http://www.hotmail.com`) is a good example of viral marketing, where each email message sent from a Hotmail account carries with it an invitation to use Hotmail. This has been an effective strategy, as Hotmail grew from zero to 12 million subscribers in its first 18 months (Turban and King, 2003, p. 182). One of the downsides is that this method has been used to spread some email hoaxes and people have become wary. With the spread of viruses, people are not inclined to accept and open file attachments from advertisers. This model is used primarily in B2C E-Commerce.

Group Purchasing

The power of bulk purchasing is not a new concept, but the Internet has facilitated formation of larger groups, and access to purchasing as widespread group members can be offered easily online. A good example of group purchasing in the educational sector is Shop2Gether.com (`http://www.shop2gether.com`). This model is used primarily in B2B and B2C E-Commerce.

B2B Electronic Marketplaces, Exchanges, and Auctions

Electronic marketplaces (E-Marketplaces) have existed for decades as isolated applications like stock market and commodity exchanges. In 1999, E-Marketplaces emerged (Turban and King, 2003, p. 15). A special type of E-Marketplace, called a **vertical marketplace** (or vertical portal, or vortal), services only one industry. This is an online marketplace specializing in retail goods and enables transactions for members with individual vendors. A good example of a vertical marketplace is Bakery Online (`http://www.bakeryonline.com`) an E-Marketplace for the food industry.

An exchange is similar to a marketplace, but more horizontal in that there may be a variety of goods and services available. A good example of a commodity exchange is the World Wide Retail Exchange (`http://www.worldwideretailexchange.org`), which specializes in retail goods including food, non-food, textile, and drug store goods. Figure 5.5 is an example of an exchange site.

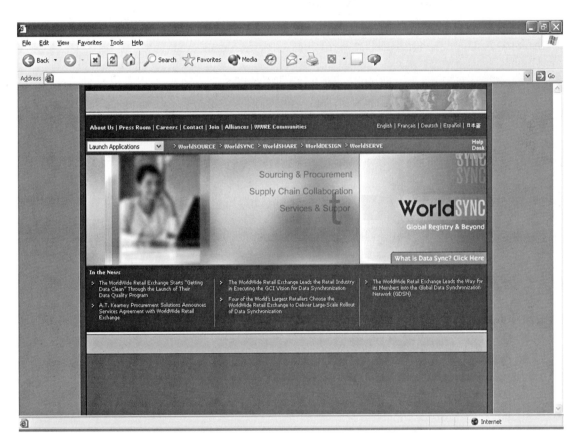

Figure 5.5   An example of an exchange site.

A B2B auction is much like the B2C auction site, eBay, but deals in commodities and goods for businesses. You will find commodities such as hydro, bulk sales in retail and manufacturing goods and equipment, and medical and scientific lab supplies. A good example of a B2B auction site is Dove Bid (`http://www.dovebid.com`).

Supply Chain Management

Supply Chain Management (SCM) is the collection and integration of business processes involved in the provision of products and services from the supplier or originator, to the customer

tip

∴ Although there are many personal blogs, there are also many marketing blogs designed to look like personal blogs. When you read a blog, read for reliability as you would any other Web page. Is the author credible? Is the blog written for the purpose of selling a product or service?

or end user. The activities involved include purchasing, materials handling, production, warehousing, inventory control, distribution, and delivery. SCM involves coordinating all these activities. Obviously, efficiency is important in every step of bringing the product or service from the supplier to the consumer.

A critical factor in efficient SCM is information sharing. For instance, it is not uncommon for the supplier to have daily inventory reports from the retailer so that stock can be automatically replenished. One of the biggest hurdles is automating this process, and coordinating communication between computer systems of the retailer and various suppliers. From the supplier's perspective, the same challenges exist, in that one supplier may have to automate inventory report and stock replenishment orders with a large variety of retailers. For example, Procter & Gamble (P&G) collects inventory information from Wal-Mart every day for every item in every store. P&G has similar arrangements with other retailers (Turban, et al., 2002, p. 643). This level of accuracy allows P&G to plan production according to need, and to automatically ship goods when inventory falls below an agreed level.

EDI and XML

The Internet has facilitated communication between computer systems in separate organizations. However, as noted previously, EDI is well-established and used for the vast majority of B2B communication. EDI messages can be sent over the Internet. EDI messages are composed according to a set of well-recognized standards, such as EDIFACT (Electronic Data Interchange for Administration, Commerce, and Transportation—or Trade). The EDIFACT standard has emerged as a multi-industry, multi-national standard, and is widely used. An example of an EDI message:

```
UNB+UNOA:1+US::US+83729::THEM+960531:0305+003829++ORDERS'
UNH+1+ORDERS:91:2:UN'
BGM+220+A761902+4:19960530:102+9'
RFF+CT:EUA01349'
RFF+AAV::C'
TXT+THIS IS A SAMPLE EDI MESSAGE….. '
NAD+BY++MY COMPANY PLC::::+++++EW4 34J'
CTA+PD'
COM+01752 382975:TE+01752 382975:FX+0:TL'
CTA+OC+:A.SURNAME'
COM+2904:EX'
CTA+TI+:J.SMITH'
COM+0:EX'
CTA+SU'
COM+0161 365 7476:TE+01752 670633:FX'
UNT+15+1'
UNZ+1+001934'
```

An alternative to EDI is **XML**. XML (eXtensible Markup Language) describes the data using standards agreed upon by the two parties who are communicating. You can think of XML as a customizable tagging system. An example of XML describing some customer information might be as follows:

```
<customer>
        <customerid>12345</customerid>
        <name>Widget Supplier Inc.</name>
        <address>123 Main St. W.</address>
        <city>Smalltown</city>
        <state>NY</state>
        <zipcode>10001</zipcode>
</customer>
```

Without a background in XML, you can see that this tagging system is quite readable. Of course, it can become much more complex and can describe any sort of data, including product inventory, shipping, purchasing, and other data. XML messages can be sent over the Internet from one computer system to another, and the two companies would decide on the tagging format to describe their data. One of the advantages of using XML is that it can be incorporated into a more secure system that includes encryption. However, it's not a case of choosing either XML or EDI. In fact, to use secure encryption, some companies have adopted a process of sending their EDI messages wrapped in XML tags, thereby taking advantage of the best of both worlds.

Putting a Small Business Online

Whether or not you make use of an Internet presence for your business is really part of an overall business plan. If you have a small business and have decided you'd like an online presence as part of your business plan and marketing approach, where do you begin? Your online presence can be as minimal as a single Web page with some contact information including an email address, or an elaborate online ordering system, or something in between. There will be a few key items that will require careful consideration, such as selecting a domain name, finding a Web hosting company, determining the goals of your Web presence, and developing and promoting a Web site. Let's have a look at each of these, as well as other tips and issues to consider.

Selecting and Buying a Domain Name

The domain name you select is an important part of your marketing strategy. You need to decide whether you would like to use your company name, product name, or just a snappy phrase.

Domain names are registered and stored in an assortment of databases. Historically, the computer command used to access the listing in the domain databases was whois, and today these databases are known still as *whois* databases. You can search the *whois* databases to see if the domain you would like is available or has already been registered. There are several good search sites, including Internic's Whois search (http://www.internic.net/whois.html) and Network Solution's WHOIS search (http://www.networksolutions.com/cgi-bin/whois/whois). There are regional *whois* databases, and some can be found at Universal Whois (http://www.uwhois.com).

➤ Choose one of the *whois* search sites and search for a domain using your company name, or your last name, to see if it has been registered.

≈*tip*

∴ When trying to come up with a domain name, show your ideas to as many people as possible. Your friends, family, and associates may be able to offer helpful suggestions!

When you find a registered domain name, you will see that the information provided includes the name of the person who registered the domain, address, contact information, and the registration company used. Because this information is readily available, some search sites such as Network Solutions, include an extra layer of security such that the user must enter a code displayed in an image before this information is provided. This is to protect the site from data-mining techniques that are designed to capture email addresses and company information. You may have to get creative with a domain name, as many of the simple ones have been registered for years. You can use the underscore (_), or hyphen (-) characters, but try to avoid numbers and letters that may be confusing to the user. For instance, zero can be confused with the letter O, and the number 1 can be confused with the letters l or I. If the .com name you'd really like has been registered, you can try your regional area (state or province domain). You can also consider contacting the individual who has registered the domain name and negotiating to purchase it.

Once you've settled on a domain name, you must pay to register it, and find a Web hosting company. A Web hosting company, typically an ISP, will provide Web space and host your domain on their Web server for a monthly fee. It is wise to shop around for an ISP, as there are a wide variety of competitive Web hosting and business packages available. Your ISP will likely be able to register your domain, or you can also search for domain registration online. There are many domain registration companies, and the prices are very competitive and inexpensive. You do not have to use your host ISP to register your domain name, so you are free to look for a competitive price.

Determining the Goals for Your Web Presence

The next step, once you have your domain name and your ISP Web hosting company determined, is to determine the goals for your Web presence. You have a variety of options, ranging from a simple Web page you could create yourself to turnkey services you can purchase, to custom work for which you could hire a Web developer to create and maintain. Define a primary goal for your Web site, and move toward that, starting with a simple Web page if necessary. You will have to balance your short- and long-term business goals with the needs of your customers and the resources you have available (Obie, 2004). Spend some time doing research on the Web looking for your competitors' sites, and making note of features and functions that you find useful on Web sites in general. Here are a few things to consider.

Marketing

If your business is primarily an off-line business, you may want to consider a Web presence as a marketing tool. Use your Web site to deliver information about your business, encourage customer contact, and build loyalty.

Retail and Online Services

If your business is primarily retail sales of goods or some type of online service, you may want to consider selling online and creating a storefront. You will have to consider how you will implement product and service ordering, payment, and customer feedback. Use your Web site to provide information about your products or services, encourage customer contact, and build brand loyalty. Consider providing value-added information about your products or services, related articles and tips for using and caring for your products, or the advantages of using your services over the alternatives.

Information Delivery

If your business is publishing information, then it lends itself to make the information available on the Web. You will need to determine how you will handle payment and make your information available and whether you'll provide samples or teasers. You can consider subscription or pay-per-use models. Consider providing other supplementary information for free to enhance your primary publications.

Customer Support

One of the useful aspects of the Internet is that it is a communications medium, and you can make use of a Web presence for customer support and service. Customer support can begin with placing an email address and contact information on a simple Web page in addition to up-to-date product information, and a frequently asked questions (FAQ) page. A FAQ page includes a list of questions that customers frequently ask, along with answers and pointers to further information or tips. Customer support can also include feedback forms, surveys, and real time online support.

Developing and Promoting Your Web Site

If you'd like to start with a simple Web page, this is something you can design and maintain yourself. In this book, we will cover Web site design, including editing tools that can be used to design a simple site. As you decide to move to a more complicated design requiring graphic design, customer feedback, shopping cart, and other interactive features, you may have to consider hiring a Web development company or a consultant to take over the design and maintenance. One thing to consider at this point is negotiating the development of a content management system so that you can easily update the content without needing programming knowledge to do it. There are also turnkey operations available for shopping carts, transaction processing, and basic site development. Your ISP may have some of these turnkey applications readily available as well.

Here are some basic Web site design and promotion considerations:

- Ensure that your Web site is optimized for search engines, users with disabilities, and users who access your site with a dial-up Internet connection.
- Make it very clear whether your product or service is global or local, as you may have visitors to your Web site from all over the world.
- Change or update your Web site often, so that there is always new content. Do not change just for the sake of change, but add value with tips, articles, contests, or something fun to give the users a reason to come back.
- Integrate your online presence with your business. Be sure to add your URL and email address to business cards, publications, brochures, *Yellow Pages* ads, and letterhead.

Other Considerations

There are a few other techniques you can implement in order to draw attention to your Web site and promote and support a customer base.

- Consider sending a monthly newsletter to all the email addresses you collect from current and potential customers, and from feedback from your Web site.
- Be sure to answer any email within 24 hours, as online customers have grown to expect prompt replies.

- Join an affiliate program, allowing an affiliate to place their logo on your site, and your logo on theirs.
- Analyze your Web site traffic. Your ISP may provide a page of statistics and analysis. Notice which pages users view the most, and how much time they spend viewing them.

E-Commerce Options for the Consumer

As a consumer, the Internet offers a wide variety of resources for business and consumer research, online shopping, and investment portfolio management of mutual funds and stocks through day trading.

Business and Consumer Research

Although many people do not yet purchase products online, those same people will often research products online. In the rankings of most popular Internet activities, consumer research was 3rd, after email and research for work or school, and shopping online was 7th. As noted, online shopping is a rapidly growing activity, but so is consumer research. Between 2000 and 2003, the number of people who responded in a survey that they utilized online consumer research often or very often, rose from 25% to 41%. Available information ranges from customer support and product manuals, to retail and pricing information, to ad hoc customer feedback and review boards. Major business and consumer research sites such as Hoovers (http://www.hoovers.com) and Consumer Reports (http://ConsumerReports.org) are also online. Both of these sites allow partial use for free and subscription use for more detailed research.

Online Shopping

Consumer online shopping is rapidly growing. Online sales in the U.S. for 2003 reached a record high of $114 billion, representing 5.3% of retail sales. Figures for 2004 are expected to climb to $144 billion, or 6.6% of retail sales. Consumers have access to 24 hour online shopping, international shopping, and specialty items. E-Commerce online shopping models include storefronts, auctions, and portals.

Storefronts are individual stores with a Web presence. Typically, storefronts do not include an entire inventory of their items, but some are quite comprehensive. Storefronts typically include a shopping cart system and options for payment and shipping. Some E-tailers will not allow customers to ship to a shipping address that is different from the credit card billing address. When providing your credit card number and shipping information, be sure that you are using a secure site so that this information is encrypted.

Auction sites, such as eBay (http://www.ebay.com) have become very popular for the individual as a purchaser and as a seller. Although eBay may be the most famous consumer auction site, there are many more sites available, such as Amazon (http://www.amazon.com) and Yahoo! Auctions (http://auctions.yahoo.com), and others are emerging as well. There are many people who have established a business by scouring auction sites for under-priced items and reselling them at their current value for a profit. Although many people will place a bid and manually check in as the auction progresses, there is also auction-bidding software available such as Auction Sentry (http://www.auction-sentry.com). This type of software will track bids on items you are interested in, alert you when there is bidding action, and set up a timed

tip

∴ Putting a business online is more than simply publishing a Web site. A Web site is a small part of an overall marketing plan. Be sure to put your Web site URL on your business cards and any correspondence to customers!

delayed bid so that you can place your bid just before closing. Setting up a timed delayed bid is referred to as **sniping**. If you are selling items, this type of software will also track bidding action on all your items, as shown in Figure 5.6.

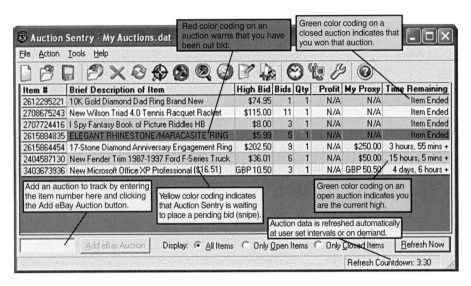

Figure 5.6   Auction Sentry will track the items you are bidding on, or selling, to see how you are performing in bid-based online shopping environments.

Portals for consumers, like portals for businesses, are Web sites offering a variety of storefronts and often some method of price comparison and search filtering. Some portals offer price comparison shopping and are essentially a gateway to storefronts. Pricing Central (http://www.pricingcentral.com) is a good example of a price comparison portal. Pricing Central lists a wide variety of E-tailers, but there are also other portals that are more industry specific, such as Travelocity (http://www .travelocity.com) for the vacation and travel industry.

Cookies

When you are shopping at an online store, the site will need some mechanism of keeping shopping cart information, or tracking your selections from one page to another. Typically, you will have to ensure that cookies are enabled in your Web browser. A **cookie** is a small text file stored on your computer system, and a Web site may write or read a cookie. There is no risk of viruses with this method because the browser ensures that only a small bit of text information is written or read, and text characters alone cannot store a virus. Generally, cookies are enabled in the Web browser default settings. Some Web sites set permanent cookies that are read each time you access the site. A good example is Mapquest (http://www.mapquest.com), which will write a cookie in order to "remember" the most recent map requests. Some sites set temporary cookies, which are used only as long as you are accessing the site, and not written to your hard drive. If you delete all cookies, no need to worry. Web sites using cookies will simply write new cookies next time you load them.

⋇ *tip*

∴ If you are concerned about cookies stored on your computer, you can remove them. In Internet Explorer you can use the menu commands *Tools*, *Options* and on the General tab, you will find a *Delete Cookies* button. In other Web browsers you can use the menu commands *Edit*, *Options* and generally in the advanced options there is a feature available for deleting cookies.

Online Banking

In 1995, online banking began modestly with the introduction of bank account statements available to Wells Fargo customers through their Web site. With a modest 300,000 Americans taking advantage of online banking features in 1995, growth has rapidly escalated to an estimated 29–33 million users in December 2003, representing 31% of American households. It is estimated that by the end of the decade, more than 50% of households will be doing their banking online (Online Banking Report, 2004). Online banking has become very popular and includes features such as bill payments, transferring funds between accounts, opening accounts, and current mortgage information and mortgage features, such as initiating extra payments. You should be aware that on average bill payments might take 1–2 business days to transfer, although the funds may be immediately debited from your account. Your bank may also allow you to manage your mutual funds and other investments, and perhaps buy and sell stocks as well. You will have to log in to your banking site using a client id number and prearranged password. If you are using a public computer, be sure to log out properly and/or close the Web browser window so that no one else will be able to access your banking information.

Online Stock Trading

When discussing online investing, the distinction must be made between **online trading** and **day trading**. Online trading refers to buying and selling stocks and mutual funds through an online brokerage, as opposed to using the telephone and a full-service brokerage. Online traders may buy and sell only a few times per year, or daily, but will keep investments overnight. Conversely, day trading is at the opposite end of the trading activity spectrum, and refers to buying and selling stocks through the course of the day, ending the day with all stocks closed and no open positions.

Many people manage their own investment portfolios and partake in online trading of stocks and mutual funds. In general, trades are done through an online brokerage. Some good examples of online brokerages are Charles Schwab (`http://www.charlesschwab.com`) and TD Waterhouse (`http://www.tdwaterhouse.com`). When comparing brokerages, it is useful to examine three main areas: (1) fees for online market orders, (2) minimum amount needed to open an account, and (3) services provided. You will find that within all these areas, there is quite a range of available options. Some offer investment advice, others don't. Some have a limit to the number of shares traded, while others are unlimited. The amount required to open an account can vary from as low as $500 or less to more than $15,000. Some charge quarterly maintenance fees, some require a minimum balance in the account, and the list goes on. Shop carefully before choosing an online brokerage, and be sure to itemize your priorities. Are you more interested in investing in mutual funds? Do you need investment advice from time to time? Are you more interested in trading stocks on a daily basis, or are you likely to buy and sell only a few times per year?

For those who are a little more serious in their daily investments. and would like immediate trades rather than waiting for the broker to buy or sell, the best option is **Direct Access Trading (DAT)**. One of the most popular software packages for real time, direct access trading is RealTick (`http://www.realtick.com`). You will require an account

⋰ tip

⋰ If you are doing your banking, stock trading, or other financial tasks online, and someone else will be using your computer, be sure to close all open Web browsers. This will clear the cache and help protect your financial Web sites.

with a direct access brokerage and be provided with account information. Then you will be able to use RealTick, as shown in Figure 5.7, or another package like it, to perform your trades directly with the exchanges for immediate results.

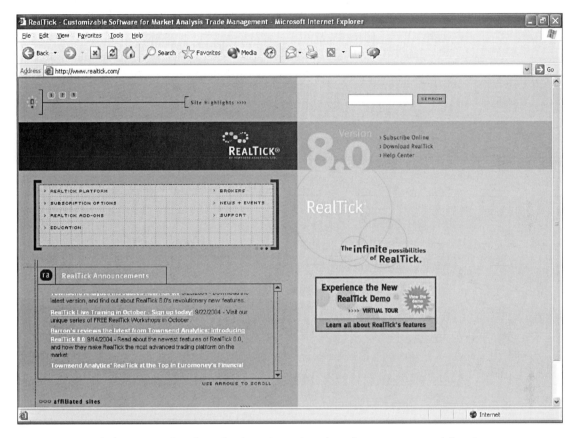

Figure 5.7   RealTick.com is a trading aficionado's dream. It provides real-time floor executions, provided you have the money to risk.

SUMMARY

Now that you've read through the chapter, you are prepared to:

- Discriminate between E-Business and E-Commerce, paying particular attention to the advent of electronic data interchange (EDI).

- Consider the many E-Commerce models in play: Business-to-Business (B2B), Business-to-Consumer (B2C), Business-to-Business-to-Consumer (B2B2C), Consumer-to-Business (C2B), Consumer-to-Consumer (C2C), and Mobile Commerce (M-Commerce).

- Weigh the differences and similarities between several E-Business models: online direct marketing, product and service customization, consumer online auctions, electronic tendering, find the best price, affiliate marketing, viral marketing, group purchasing, B2B electronic marketplaces, exchanges and auctions, and supply chain management.

- Move your small business online by: selecting and buying a domain name, determining the goals for your Web presence, and marketing your inventory. As well, you should be able to: determine whether or not you wish to implement an online strategy, how you wish to deliver information, how you want to offer customer support, and how you want to develop and promote your Web site.

- Assess some of the E-Commerce options for the consumer, such as: business and consumer research, online shopping, online banking, and online stock trading.

Review Questions and Hands-on Exercises

Review Questions

1. Explain the difference between E-Commerce and E-Business.

2. What is EDI?

3. What is XML?

4. Is XML likely to replace EDI? Why or why not?

5. Explain the difference between B2B and B2C.

6. What is a reverse auction?

7. You've decided you'd like to move toward an online presence for your small business. Describe some steps you must take before creating a Web page.

8. What sort of customer service support could your Web site provide?

9. Describe some techniques you could use to promote your Web site.

10. Are cookies a security risk? Why or why not?

11. If you are using a public computer to do your online banking, what precautions can you take so that others do not have access to your banking site?

12. What is the difference between online stock trading and day trading?

Hands-on Exercises

1. Open a Web browser and browse through the eBay site at
   `http://www.ebay.com` as an example of a consumer auction site. Answer the
   following questions:

   a. List five different types of products that are sold on eBay.

   b. Which payment methods are available?

   c. In addition to the United States, eBay has sites for use in specific countries. List five other countries where eBay is available.

2. Open a Web browser and open your favorite search engine. Use search terms
   to find at least five sites for each category listed.

   a. online auction

   b. vertical portal

   c. reverse auction

   d. B2B exchange

3. Open a Web browser and open the site for your ISP. If you do not use an ISP,
   choose one from The List at `http://www.thelist.com`.

   a. Does your ISP offer Web hosting?

   b. Does your ISP offer business packages? If so, what is the cost?

   c. Does your ISP offer domain registration?

4. You've decided that you'd like to put a small retail business, called "Writing
   Instruments" online. The retail business sells pens and pencils, which can be
   customized to add a company name or other engraved text.

   a. Check Internic's Whois search (`http://www.internic.net/whois.html`) to
   determine if a suitable domain name is available. Get a little creative and
   try variations on "Writing Instruments."

   b. What would be a suitable target market?

   c. You'd like your Web site to fit in with the competitors' and will start with
   basic information. Search for a few office supply company sites.

       i. What are the important links on the competitors' sites?
       ii. What sort of color schemes do they use?
       iii. Which page contains their contact information?
       iv. If you were going to start with three or four Web pages, what sort of
       information would they contain?

5. You've decided that you might like to try buying stocks on your own. What
   information resources are available for researching publicly traded companies?

6. Open a Web browser and open either Charles Schwab (http://www
.charlesschwab.com) or TD Waterhouse (http://www.tdwaterhouse.com).
Search these sites to find answers to the following questions.

   a. Is there a minimum amount of money required to open an account?

   b. Is investment advice available?

   c. Is there a limit to the number of shares that can be traded?

   d. Is there a minimum amount of money that must be kept in an account?

   e. Are there any other value-added services provided?

DESIGNING INFORMATION FOR THE WORLD WIDE WEB

part 3

	Chapter
An Introduction to HTML	6
An Introduction to CSS, XHTML, and Advanced Web Development Concepts	7
HTML Editors	8
Graphics and Multimedia on the World Wide Web	9

An Introduction to HTML

Chapter Objectives

This chapter helps you understand

- ☐ what Hypertext Markup Language is.
- ☐ the evolution of HTML and Web browsers.
- ☐ some of the innovations that have occurred regarding HTML.
- ☐ how to create Web pages using HTML.
- ☐ some of the browser-specific issues bearing upon HTML.
- ☐ how to optimize your work for a search engine.
- ☐ how to use File Transfer Protocol (FTP) to upload your work.

Definition and Evolution of HTML

Web pages are composed of text, images, and perhaps some multimedia content to grab your attention. When you click a link or enter a URL, the Web browser instructs your computer to request the Web page from the server on which it is located. When the Web page is received, it is rendered in the Web browser. This means that the Web browser interprets the coding in the document and places content in the browser window. You've probably noticed that when you change the size of the browser window, the content may shift around a bit, as the browser renders the page again.

What is HTML?

As you've seen, you can click text or an image in the document and another Web page will load. The item you click in order to load another Web page is called a **hypertext link** or **hyperlink**. The term hypertext basically refers to the ability to link documents together. A hypertext document is not necessarily a Web page. The help documents found in the help menu of a word processing package are typically hypertext documents. These documents often contain text links to other help documents. The coding in the Web page, which is rendered by the browser, is written in HyperText Markup Language (HTML).

A **markup language** is not a programming language. It is a language comprising tags that are used to describe content. In the case of HTML, the tags describe hypertext links, formatting such as bold, italics, underline, center titles, color text, and so forth. For example, you might see the following sentence in the browser window.

The **Web browser** is used to view <u>HTML</u> documents.

The HTML required to render the sentence above would be as follows:

```
The <b>Web browser</b> is used to view <u>HTML</u> documents.
```

Notice that the <b> tag is used for bold and the <u> tag is used for underline. Paired tags, such as these, include an opening tag and a closing tag. The opening tag for underline is <u> and the closing tag is </u>. Text contained between the paired tags <u></u> will be rendered as underlined text. In this chapter, we will explore some of these tags as an introduction to HTML.

You can view the source code of a Web page in your browser. The source code will contain HTML and other coding, such as JavaScript.

➤ Open your favorite Web browser and view a Web page.
➤ Use the command *View, Source* (or *View, Page Source*, depending on the browser you are using).

The source code should open in a new window. Some of the code looks very cryptic indeed.

➤ Close the source code window when you have finished viewing the code.

Most people who create and edit simple Web pages do not write the code manually. They use an HTML editor. You can edit Web pages in an HTML editor very much like a word processing package, and it will generate the HTML code while you edit the page. There are a wide variety of HTML editors available. We will explore a selection of HTML editors in Chapter 8.

The Evolution of HTML and Web Browsers

Hypertext, as a concept, was first discussed by academics as early as the 1940s. The essential idea is that documents are linked so that the user can easily view one related document after another. In its current form, we can click text or image links in one document to view a related document. There were a few key innovations between then and now, which are notable in the development of the World Wide Web.

At a trade show in 1960, Douglas Englebart debuted an electronic communication package featuring email and a text-based filing system called hypertext. Hypertext allowed users to select highlighted words in a document by using the keyboard to control a pointer. When the user selected the highlighted word, the computer retrieved a new document and displayed it. In 1964, as it became more cumbersome to use the keyboard with hypertext, Englebart invented the mouse (Abbate, 1999).

Bill Atkinson was a computer programmer working for Apple Computer Inc., in the late 1980s. He developed a program called *Hypercard*, which displayed filing cards on the screen containing text and images. Users could click buttons on the screen to navigate through the cards.

Tim Berners-Lee is widely recognized as the inventor of the World Wide Web. In 1988, he was working as a programmer at the European Laboratory for Particle Physics (CERN) in Geneva, Switzerland, and was responsible for distributing documents to researchers all over the world. He wanted to make the documents available so that researchers could download them to their computers. Additionally, he wanted to cross-reference them so that the researcher could click text in the document to download a related document. He developed hypertext documents and the Hypertext Transfer Protocol (HTTP) required to transfer the files from one computer to another over the network, which are the fundamental technologies of the World Wide Web. Berners-Lee went on to become the Director of the **World Wide Web Consortium** (http://www.w3c.org), a not-for-profit research organization geared toward promoting standards and innovations in Web-based communication, including HTML.

In 1992, Marc Andreessen, a multimedia specialist from the University of Illinois at Urbana-Champaign (UIUC), was introduced to Berners-Lee's text-only hypertext browser. Andreessen was involved with the National Supercomputing Agency, where he had virtually unlimited computing resources and a vision to make the supercomputers at UIUC accessible to the nation's networked institutions. He saw a need to add media components, such as images, to a hypertext browser. Andreessen and his students developed a new browser, **NCSA Mosaic,** which was user-friendly and able to handle a variety of media files (Reid, 1997). By 1993, it had been installed on over 1 million machines. Andreessen later teamed up with Jim Clark, a Silicon Valley venture capitalist who also founded industry giants Silicon Graphics and Healtheon. Together, Andreessen and Clark founded Netscape Communications, which is now owned by America Online.

HTML Innovations

So what made the development of HTML and hypertext documents such a big deal? First of all, viewing HTML documents is platform independent and therefore compatibility issues were eliminated. This means that you can view an HTML document no matter which operating system platform you're using.

Overcoming the incompatibility issue with HTML, and the development of HTTP and TCP/IP for file transfer provided the biggest innovation of all: online global communication. Web pages can be retrieved from anywhere in the world. Recall that HTTP (HyperText Transfer Protocol) is the communication protocol for transferring Web page data, and TCP/IP (Transmission Control Protocol/Internet Protocol) is the set of communication protocols for transferring data over the Internet. The combination of HTTP and TCP/IP allows Web page data to be transferred from one computer to another over the Internet.

Another exciting innovation was interactive documents incorporating media content. Web browsers can display images, movie clips, audio, animation, and other media content. HTML documents do not contain the media files themselves, but contain coding which points to these files, and they are downloaded and rendered by the browser. Media content, in addition to hypertext functionality, provides a truly interactive experience for the user, on a global scale.

Like all technologies, HTML is still evolving, and the Web publishing standard is slowly shifting toward XHTML. **XHTML** (eXtensible HyperText Markup Language) is basically HTML with a few more rules, so that it conforms to XML standards. Uses for XHTML and some of the basic rules will be discussed in further detail. First we will build some simple HTML pages, then we will edit them so that they meet XHTML standards. HTML is very forgiving, so we will be a little sloppy, but we will edit the code later to convert to the more strict XHTML standards.

Creating Web Pages with HTML

The best way to learn about HTML is to roll up your sleeves and build a small Web site. So, let's do it! Of course, this can become quite complicated if you need transaction processing, customer logins, or information from a database such as a large catalogue. But, you'll see that creating some simple pages is not complicated at all, and definitely not something you need to hire a Web page design consultant to do. All you need is **Notepad** and a Web browser.

Basic Web Page Structure

We'll create a small Web site and also a few little pages to test out some features. The purpose of this chapter is to provide a small taste of HTML and other Web page building tools. We will look at only a few basic tags and some of their attributes.

➤ Create a folder called *wildernesscamping* on your hard drive. This is where we will save the Web page files in these exercises.

➤ Open Notepad. Depending on the operating system you are using, you should find it using *Start, Programs, Accessories, Notepad*.

➤ Open Internet Explorer or another Web browser.

➤ Size the windows so you can see both on the screen. You may want to place the windows side by side.

The basic procedure is to type the HTML code in Notepad, save the file, then refresh and view the file in the Web browser.

The basic structure of an HTML document includes a head area and a body area. The head area will contain a title for the page and the body area will contain the page information that will be displayed in the browser window. Let's set up the basic structure, and we'll add to it as we go along. Let's build a Web site based on a camping theme.

➤ In Notepad, type the following code. Don't worry about uppercase or lowercase, as HTML is not case-sensitive. Notice that all the tags in this example are paired. For each opening tag, there is a corresponding closing tag such as `<html>` and its closing tag `</html>`.

```
<html>
<head>
        <title>Wilderness Camping</title>
</head>
<body>

Wilderness Camping

Enjoy a vacation in the wilderness! Our facilities include:

Camping
Hiking
Swimming
Luxury Inn Accommodations
Camp Store

</body>
</html>
```

➤ Use the commands *File, Save* to open the *Save As* dialog box. In Notepad be sure to use the *All Files* feature from the *Save as type* drop-down menu so that you save this file as .htm and not as .txt.

Notepad will automatically save files as .txt but we will need to make sure our Web pages are saved as .htm or .html. If you save your page as .txt it will not render in the browser window. The browsers will look for .htm, .html, and a few other specific file types and will render the code as a Web page. Let's save this file as *camping.htm*.

➤ From the *Save In* drop-down box, choose the *wildernesscamping* folder from your hard drive listing.

➤ Click the drop-down box for *Save as type* and select *All Files*.

➤ In the file name box, type: camping.htm, as shown in Figure 6.1.

➤ Click the *Save* button to save the file.

Let's view our new Web page in the browser window. You will notice that it displays as one paragraph. We will add HTML tags, add spacing, and format the text as we go along.

➤ In **Internet Explorer**, or the Web browser you have open, use the command *File, Open*.

➤ Click the *Browse* button to open the *File* dialog box.

➤ Click the *Look in* drop-down box and select the folder containing the *camping.htm* file.

➤ Click the *camping.htm* file and click the *Open* button to open the file, as shown in Figure 6.2.

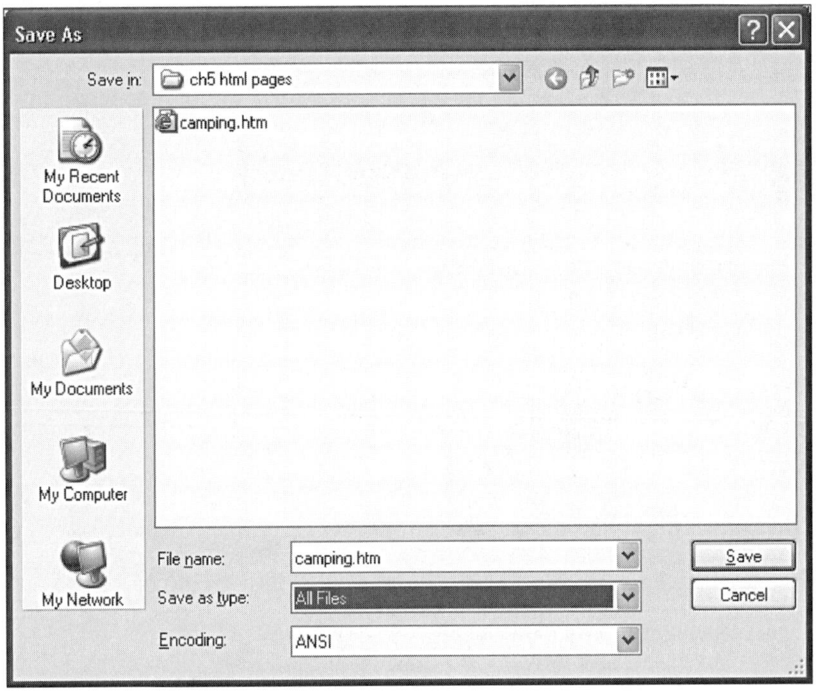

Figure 6.1   Notepad Save As dialog box.

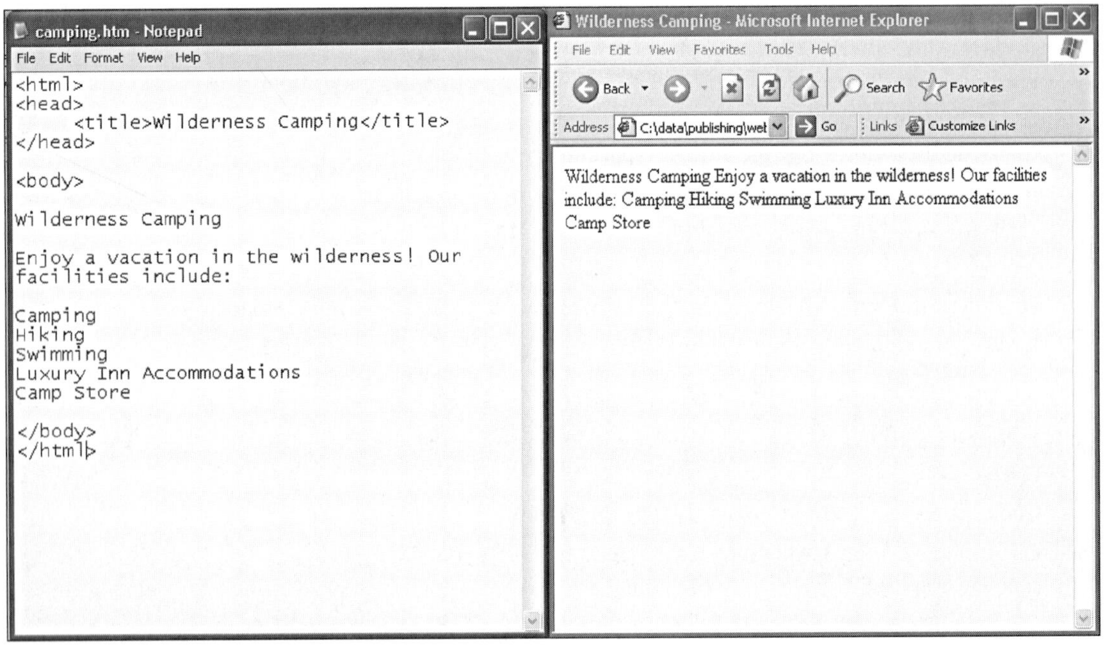

Figure 6.2   Notepad and Internet Explorer.

As you can see, the text appears in the browser window as one long paragraph. HTML ignores line breaks and multiple spaces in text. The title *Wilderness Camping* appears in the title bar, at the very top of the browser window, as shown in Figure 6.3.

Figure 6.3   Title in Internet Explorer.

The HTML code contains a head area and a body area. The head area contains the title, which appears in the browser title bar. The body area contains the information that will appear in the main browser window. The `<html>` tag defines this document as an HTML document.

Let's add some tags to format the text. The `<br>` tag will add a line break, bumping the text that follows it down to a new line. The `<br>` tag is a single tag, not paired. The `<h1>` tag is a paired tag, and will format a heading, style 1.

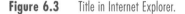   Edit the code in Notepad as follows:

```
<h1>Wilderness Camping</h1>
Enjoy a vacation in the wilderness! Our
facilities include:<br>
Camping<br>
Hiking<br>
Swimming<br>
Luxury Inn Accommodations<br>
Camp Store<br>
```

Save the file in Notepad.

Click the *Refresh* button, as shown in Figure 6.4, to refresh the page in Internet Explorer, or the Web browser you have chosen.

Figure 6.4   Internet Explorer *Refresh* button.

⚛ *tip*

∴ When designing your own Web pages, choose a title that is specific and meaningful. Most search engines place more importance on keywords that are in the title. A relevant title will elevate your page in the search result ranking!

The Notepad and Web browser windows should look similar to Figure 6.5.

```
camping2.htm - Notepad
File  Edit  Format  View  Help
<html>
<head>
    <title>Wilderness Camping</title>
</head>

<body>

<h1>Wilderness Camping</h1>

Enjoy a vacation in the wilderness! Our
facilities include:<br>

Camping<br>
Hiking<br>
Swimming<br>
Luxury Inn Accommodations<br>
Camp Store<br>

</body>
</html>
```

Wilderness Camping - Microsoft Internet Explorer
File Edit View Favorites Tools Help
Back Search Favorites
Address I pages\camping2.htm Go Links Customize Links

Wilderness Camping

Enjoy a vacation in the wilderness! Our facilities include:
Camping
Hiking
Swimming
Luxury Inn Accommodations
Camp Store

Figure 6.5   Notepad and Internet Explorer.

Heading Tags

There are six heading tag styles available. The heading styles add formatting to the text including bold, italics, and font size. They may display with slight differences in each browser (Internet Explorer, Safari, Mozilla, Netscape), but will be similar. You don't have to use <h1> for the first heading. You can choose an appropriate heading style. Think of it as a shortcut instead of using individual tags to apply the formatting. If you like, you can open another instance of Notepad and generate a test page of the headings as follows:

➤   Open another Notepad window.

➤   As this is a test page, we'll skip a head area and only use a body area. Type the following:

```
<html>
<body>

<h1>Heading style 1</h1>
<h2>Heading style 2</h2>
<h3>Heading style 3</h3>
<h4>Heading style 4</h4>
<h5>Heading style 5</h5>
```

tip

∴ When experimenting with HTML tags, creating a small test page is a great idea. You can copy and paste code from other pages into a test page and play with it!

```
<h6>Heading style 6</h6>

</body>
</html>
```

➤ Save this file as *headingtags.htm* Again, remember to use the *all files* feature from the *save as type* drop-down menu so that you save this file as .htm and not as .txt.

➤ Open another Web browser window and open the *headingtags.htm* file in the Web browser.

Your windows should look similar to Figure 6.6. Notice that the heading tags automatically add a blank line after each heading.

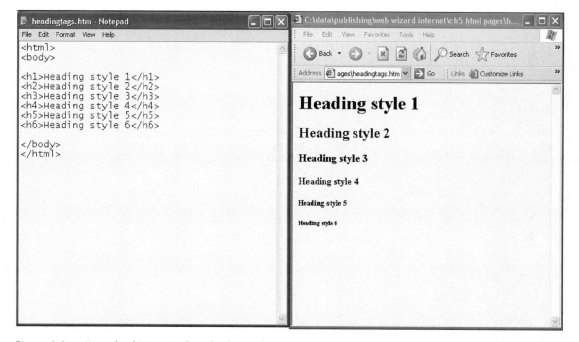

Figure 6.6   Notepad and Internet Explorer, *headingtags.htm.*

Formatting Tags

Let's get back to the camping page and add some formatting. We'll make use of the following tags:

`<p>`   new paragraph

`<i>`   italics

`<b>`   bold

`<font>` font color and size

As you will see, we can combine formatting using several tags together.

➤   In Notepad, edit the *camping.htm* document to add more content as follows:

```
<html>
<head>
        <title>Wilderness Camping</title>
</head>

<body>

<h1>Wilderness Camping</h1>

Enjoy a vacation in the wilderness! Our facilities include:<br>

Camping<br>
Hiking<br>
Swimming<br>
Luxury Inn Accommodations<br>
Camp Store<br>

<p>
If you need a <b>vacation away from the big city</b> and <i>enjoy
the great outdoors,</i> our <u>wilderness camping is the perfect
getaway!</u> You'll see lots of wildlife, spectacular scenery and
fall asleep to the sounds of nature.
<font size="+2"><b>Be sure to check out our Camp Store for
specials.</b></font>
</p>

<h2><font color="red">Important information</font></h2>

<p>
Although we maintain a safe environment, it is important for
hikers to always be on guard for wildlife and erosion on the
trails. <u><i><b>Occasionally we close hiking trails when bears
are spotted in the area.</b></i></u>
</p>

</body>
</html>
```

➤   Save the *camping.htm* file, and click the *Refresh* button in the Web browser to view the changes.

The Notepad and Web browser windows should look similar to Figure 6.7.

Notice that tags can be combined, such as <u><i><b>, to achieve the effects of underline, italics, and bold. The order of the tags does not matter, and the order in

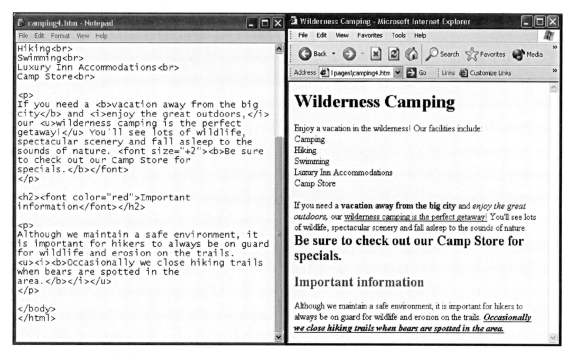

Figure 6.7   Notepad and Internet Explorer, *camping.htm.*

which they are closed also does not matter. It is good programming practice to close the tags from the inside out. For example, `<u><i><b>text</b></i></u>` closes the bold tag first because it is the innermost tag.

Tag Attributes

The `<font>` tag has a variety of options available for size, color, and font face. These options are called **attributes**. In the above example, the `<font>` tag was used with attributes for size and color. For example, `<font size="+2">` specified that the text was to be rendered two sizes larger than normal (+2). Attribute values should be encased in double quotes, but the quotes can be omitted if the attribute value does not contain any spaces. We could have used the tag `<font size=+2>` to achieve the same effect in this case. You will find that some attributes or values can be used in more than one tag. For instance, the color names can be used in the body tag.

Font Tag `<font>`

The Font tag has several options for attributes. Font size is a relative measurement. It can be measured using two different scales. Without a + or – indicator, font size is an absolute size, where 3 is the normal font. Numbers below 3 are smaller than normal and numbers above 3 are larger than normal. Absolute fonts use a scale from 1 to 7.

With a + or – indicator, font size is relative to the normal size. A font size of +2 is two sizes larger than normal and a font size of –1 is one size smaller than normal. Relative font size uses a scale from –4 to –1 and +1 to +4.

➤   Open a new instance of Notepad and enter the following, as a test of font size.

```
<html>
<body>

<h2>Absolute Font Sizes</h2>

<font size=1>size 1</font><br>
<font size=2>size 2</font><br>
<font size=3>size 3</font><br>
<font size=4>size 4</font><br>
<font size=5>size 5</font><br>
<font size=6>size 6</font><br>
<font size=7>size 7</font><br>

<h2>Relative Font Sizes</h2>

<font size=-4>size -4</font><br>
<font size=-3>size -3</font><br>
<font size=-2>size -2</font><br>
<font size=-1>size -1</font><br>

<font size=+1>size +1</font><br>
<font size=+2>size +2</font><br>
<font size=+3>size +3</font><br>
<font size=+4>size +4</font><br>

</body>
</html>
```

➤   Save this file as *fontsizetest.htm*. Again, remember to use the *All Files* feature from the *Save as type* drop-down menu so that you save this file as .htm and not as .txt.

➤   Open a new instance of Internet Explorer, or another Web browser, and open the *fontsizetest.htm* file in the Web browser.

The *fontsizetest.htm* file should look something like Figure 6.8.

➤   Feel free to close the *fontsizetest.htm* Notepad window and the Web browser window that contains the *fontsizetest.htm* page when you have finished viewing the files.

Font Color

The color attribute of the font tag was also used in the *camping.htm* example. In our example, we used the tag <font color="red">. In this instance, we used the color name. When we start to look at the issue of using colors in HTML, we quickly find that not all colors display the same in every browser. Sometimes there are subtle differences from one browser to another, but sometimes they are obvious. There are 216 colors,

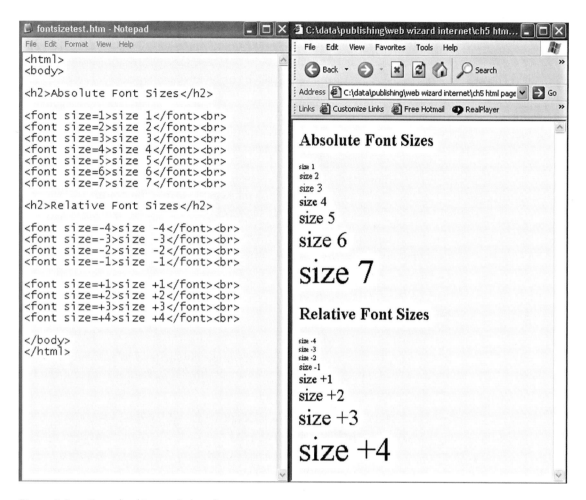

Figure 6.8   Notepad and Internet Explorer, font size test.

which display essentially the same in any browser. These are considered to be **browser safe colors**. Colors outside of these must be converted or blended on some computers and therefore do not display consistently.

Although many computers will display millions of colors, there are still many computers that will display only 256 colors. When one of those computers attempts to display a color outside of those 256, it must either convert the color to one available in its palette or mix colors together to achieve a similar effect. The technique of mixing colors is called **dithering** and will be discussed as we talk about images in depth later. Having said that there are 216 browser safe colors, and yet many computers will display 256, why aren't there 256 browser safe colors? There are 40 colors that vary on a Mac and Windows computer, and do not display identically on both. Those 40 colors have not been included in the browser safe palette.

➤   View the following Web pages, which contain palettes of colors:

Browser Safe Colors by Jennifer Kymin
`http://webdesign.about.com/library/bl_colors.htm`

Netscape Named Colors by Jennifer Kymin (not all of these are browser safe!)
`http://webdesign.about.com/library/bl_namedcolors.htm`

You can also use your favorite search engine to search for pages of "browser safe colors."

You will find that some of the Web pages refer to the colors using a six-character code of numbers and characters, and others refer to the colors with names. The six-character code represents intensity of color in Red, Green, and Blue. The characters are digits of a hexadecimal (hex) code. The first pair represents the intensity for red, the middle pair represents the intensity for green, and the last pair represents the intensity for blue. This color scale is referred to as the RGB (Red Green Blue) scale. Typically the RGB number is preceded by the # symbol but newer browsers can render the color without it. Here are some examples:

Red = #FF0000

Lime (green) = #00FF00

Blue = #00FF00

Black = #000000

White = #FFFFFF

There are 16 color names that were the originally accepted color names and older browsers will recognize them. They are part of the HTML standard. Here is the list, each with their associated RGB hex code value.

Black = #000000	Green = #008000	Silver = #C0C0C0
Gray = #808080	Olive = #808000	White = #FFFFFF
Yellow = #FFF00	Maroon = #800000	Navy = #000080
Red = #FF0000	Blue = #0000FF	Purple = #800080
Teal = #008080	Fuchsia = #FF00FF	Aqua = #00FFFF
Lime = #00FF00		

Font Face

The last attribute available for the font tag is the face attribute. The face attribute allows you to specify a font type. The most important thing to keep in mind is that each computer configuration is different, and not all fonts are available on all machines. For instance, you may want to use a font called *flat brush* but this is a custom font that is not available on most computers. The font you choose must be available on the user's computer; otherwise the page will render with the default browser fonts. There is a solution to this problem, however. In general, there are three basic types of fonts that will render reliably.

Serif   These fonts have little embellishments called *serifs* at the tips of the letters. Times and Times New Roman are serif fonts.

Sans-serif   These fonts are very plain and do not have serifs. Arial and Helvetica are good examples of sans-serif fonts.

Monospaced   Characters in these fonts are all equal widths. For instance, the letter *i* is the same width as the letter *m*. Courier and Courier New are good examples of monospaced fonts.

When specifying font face, you can specify a list of fonts, and the first font available on the user's computer will be used. To be as flexible as possible, specify a font that is available on Windows computers, another available on Apple Macintosh computers, and a generic font family. Below is a list of the three common font families listing the Windows font, the Macintosh font, and the generic font family.

Sans-serif	Arial, Helvetica, sans-serif
Serif	Times New Roman, Times, serif
Monospaced	Courier New, Courier, monospaced

Typically, browsers display text in a serif font by default, so if you use the face attribute and specify a serif font, you may not see any change at all.

Let's add some font enhancements to the *camping.htm* document. When you use attributes in an HTML tag, the order of the attributes is not important, and you can use multiple attributes.

➤   In Notepad modify the *camping.htm* document as follows. The <font> tag has been added in the headings and in the paragraphs. Changes are indicated in dark text.

```
<html>
<head>
        <title>Wilderness Camping</title>
</head>

<body>

<h1><font color=green face="arial, helvetica, sans-serif">
Wilderness Camping</font></h1>

Enjoy a vacation in the wilderness! Our facilities include:<br>

Camping<br>
Hiking<br>
Swimming<br>
Luxury Inn Accommodations<br>
Camp Store<br>

<p><font face="times new roman, times, serif">
If you need a <b>vacation away from the big city</b> and <i>enjoy
the great outdoors,</i> our <u>wilderness camping is the perfect
getaway!</u> You'll see lots of wildlife, spectacular scenery and
fall asleep to the sounds of nature.
<font size="+2"><b>Be sure to check out our Camp Store for
specials.</b></font>
</font></p>

<h2><font color="red" face="arial, helvetica, sans-serif">Important
information</font></h2>
```

```
<p><font face="courier new, courier, monospaced">
Although we maintain a safe environment, it is important for
hikers to always be on guard for wildlife and erosion on the
trails. <u><i><b>Occasionally we close hiking trails when bears
are spotted in the area.</b></i></u>
</font></p>

</body>
</html>
```

➤ Save the file and refresh the page in the Web browser window.

The Web page should look something similar to Figure 6.9.

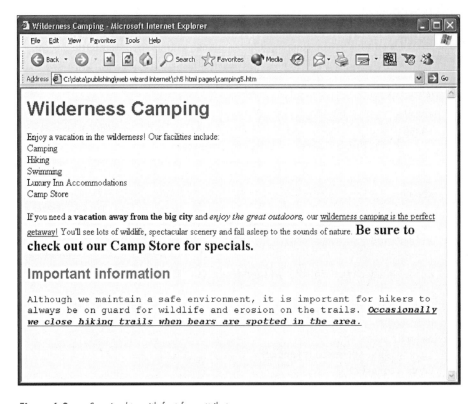

Figure 6.9   *Camping.htm* with font face attribute.

Notice that the paragraph using <font face="times new roman, times, serif"> did not change noticeably. This is because the serif font is the default font in the browser.

Align Attribute

We can change the alignment of paragraphs, headings, and other HTML elements as well. Let's center the headings.

➤ In Notepad, modify the *camping.htm* document as follows. Changes are indicated in dark text and only part of the *camping.htm* page code is displayed here.

```
<h1 align=center><font color=green face="arial, helvetica,
sans-serif">Wilderness Camping</font></h1>

Enjoy a vacation in the wilderness! Our facilities include:<br>

Camping<br>
Hiking<br>
Swimming<br>
Luxury Inn Accommodations<br>
Camp Store<br>

<p align=center><font face="times new roman, times, serif">
If you need a <b>vacation away from the big city</b> and <i>enjoy
the great outdoors,</i> our <u>wilderness camping is the perfect
getaway!</u> You'll see lots of wildlife, spectacular scenery and
fall asleep to the sounds of nature. <font size="+2"><b>Be sure to
check out our Camp Store for specials.</b></font>
</font></p>

<h2 align=center><font color="red" face="arial, helvetica,
sans-serif">Important information</font></h2>
```

➤ Save the file and refresh the page in the Web browser window.

The headings and paragraph should now be centered, as shown in Figure 6.10.

Feel free to change the size of your browser window. You will notice that the page renders again and the headings and paragraph are still centered.

Hypertext Links

Hypertext links, also known as hyperlinks, can be used to jump to topics within the same Web page, or jump to another page in the same site, or jump to a page in a completely different Web site. The tag used to create a hypertext link is the anchor tag <a>. Here is an example of a hypertext link, which will load the Yahoo! search page when the user clicks on the link.

```
<a href="http://www.yahoo.com/">Yahoo</a>
```

The *href* attribute points to the URL, which will be used when the user clicks on the link. The URL of the Web page must be encased in double quotes. It is important to be sure to include the *http* protocol in the URL when you are pointing to a Web page outside the current Web site. The text between the <a href> and </a> tags will be hyperlinked and visible to the user.

Let's add a section of *Useful Resources* to the bottom of our camping page.

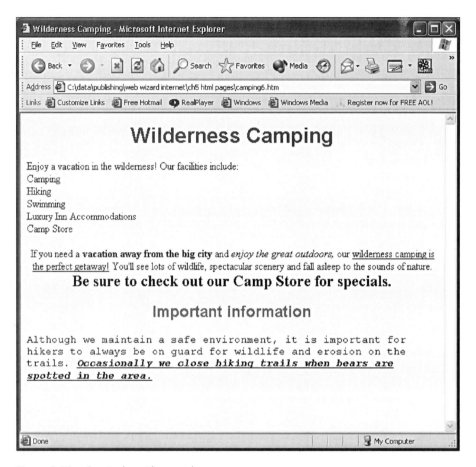

Figure 6.10   *Camping.htm* with center alignment.

➤ In Notepad, add the following to the bottom of the *camping.htm* page, before the `</body>` and `</html>` tags, and after the *Important Information* paragraph.

```
<h2>Useful Resources</h2>

<a href="http://www.hiking-trails.com/">Hiking Trails</a> - A
searchable database of hiking trails around the world.<br>
<a href="http://www.camping.com/">Camping Information</a> - For all
aspects of camping.<br>
<a href="http://www.black-bears.org/">Black Bears</a> - Information
about all aspects of black bears, including habitat, diet, and
links to many more resources.
```

➤ Save the file, and refresh the page in the Web browser window.

The page should look similar to Figure 6.11.

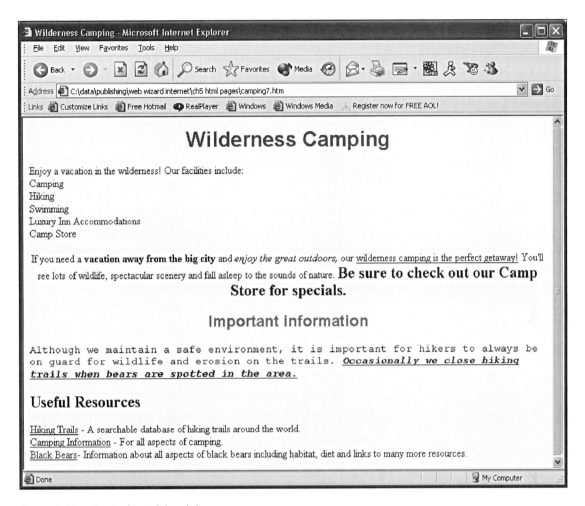

Figure 6.11 *Camping.htm* with hyperlinks.

Click the links to test them out! The links we have created are remote links, accessing pages from different Web sites not within our Wilderness Camping site. We can also create hyperlinks to pages within our site.

Let's create a page with hiking information and link to it from our main page.

➤ Open a new instance of Notepad and enter the following:

```
<html>
<head>
        <title>Hiking at Wilderness Camping</title>
</head>

<body>

<h1><font color=green>Hiking at Wilderness Camping</font></h1>
```

```
<p>At Wilderness Camping, you will find many hiking trails. Our
trails are suited for novice and experienced hikers alike. We have
short trails, which can be completed in an hour or two, and longer
trails suitable for a full day of hiking.</p>

</body>
</html>
```

➤ Save this file as *hiking.htm*. In Notepad be sure to use the *all files* feature from the *save as type* drop-down menu so that you save this file as .htm and not as .txt.

➤ Open the *hiking.htm* page in Internet Explorer, or another Web browser.

Your code and Web page should look similar to Figure 6.12.

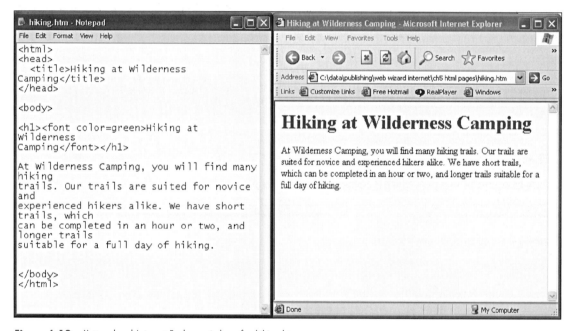

Figure 6.12   Notepad and Internet Explorer windows for *hiking.htm*.

➤ Activate the Notepad window containing the *camping.htm* file.

Instead of linking to a remote Web page, we will link to a *local* page. A local page is part of the same site as the page linking to it. Because this link is local, we will need only the name of the page in the *href* attribute. We will use the following tag:

```
<a href="hiking.htm">Hiking</a>
```

Notice that we do not use the *http://* protocol, but we do need to use the double quotes around the file name.

On the *camping.htm* page, let's add the link to the *hiking.htm* page.

➤ Activate the Notepad window containing the *camping.htm* page.
➤ Add the link to the *camping.htm* page as indicated in the darker text below:

```
Enjoy a vacation in the wilderness! Our facilities include:<br>

Camping<br>
<a href="hiking.htm">Hiking</a><br>
Swimming<br>
Luxury Inn Accommodations<br>
Camp Store<br>
```

➤ Save the *camping.htm* file in Notepad and open it in Internet Explorer or another Web browser.

You should notice that the word *Hiking* is now a link.

➤ Click the link to test it!
➤ As an exercise, activate the Notepad window containing the *hiking.htm* page, and at the bottom of the page, create a local link back to the *camping.htm* page.

The hypertext links are blue and underlined by default. The user can change this in the preferences or options settings in the Web browser, but typically the user leaves the defaults as they are. The Web page designer can also change the default link and text colors using a variety of methods. One method is to set the colors for the whole page using attributes in the body tag.

Page Properties

The body tag has attributes as follows:

text   sets the color for the text in the page.

bgcolor   sets the background color for the page.

link   sets the color for the hypertext links.

vlink   sets the color for the visited links. You will see that some links are blue and some are purple. By default, a blue link indicates that the site has not been visited and a purple link indicates that a site has been visited.

alink   sets the color for the active link. A link is active while you click it. The active link color you select will be visible when the user clicks on the link.

The colors are defined exactly as we defined them using the <font> tag. We can use either the name of the color or the RGB value. This time, let's use the RGB value. We will define the colors in the body tag as follows:

```
<body bgcolor=#ffffcc text=#663300 link=#339999 vlink=#ffcc66
alink=#66ffff>
```

➤ Activate the Notepad window containing the *camping.htm* page and edit the body tag as follows:

```
<body bgcolor=#ffffcc text=#663300 link=#339999 vlink=#ffcc66
alink=#66ffff>
```

➤ Save the file and view it in the Web browser.

The *camping.htm* page should now look similar to Figure 6.13.

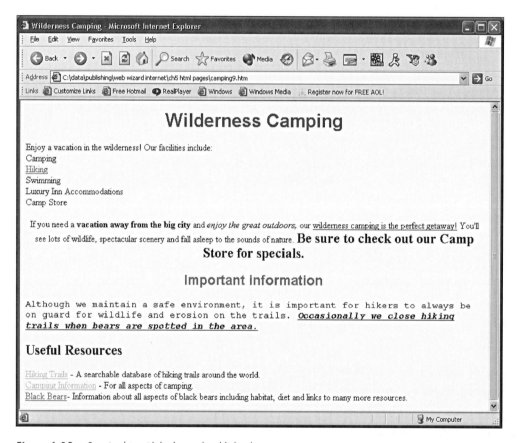

Figure 6.13 *Camping.htm* with background and link colors.

tip

∴ Although there are a large number of color names available, it's better to stick to the RGB codes when possible. It ensures backwards compatibility and may also help a future Web page designer or graphics artist to match colors.

Images

Now that we've dealt with text, formatting text, and hyperlinks, it's time to add some images. We will be discussing images in a lot more depth in Chapter 9, so suffice it to say at the moment, we will be using image formats that are suitable for Web pages because the image storage size is small.

As we begin to use more and more files in our Web site, we should organize them into folders. It makes sense at this point to place all our images in a separate folder.

➤ In the *wildernesscamping* folder, create a new folder called *images*.

➤ From the companion Web site for this book (`http://www.aw-bc.com/ adams_scollard`), download the images indicated for *the Wilderness Camping site* and store them in this new *images* folder.

An image is placed on a Web page using the `<img>` tag. The attribute *src* points to the location of the image file. In our case, the image is in the images folder, so we will have to include that information in the tag. We will use the following tag.

```
<img src="images/hikers.jpg">
```

The `src` attribute points to the images folder, and inside that, the *hikers.jpg* file. The Web page renders from top to bottom, so the placement of the image on the Web page is determined by the placement of the `<img>` tag. We'll place our tag after the facilities list and before the descriptive paragraph.

Let's add an image to the *camping.htm* page.

➤ Activate the Notepad window containing the *camping.htm* page and add the `<img>` tag after the list of facilities and before the paragraph description as follows:

```
Swimming<br>
Luxury Inn Accommodations<br>
Camp Store<br>

<img src="images/hikers.jpg">

<p align=center><font face="times new roman, times, serif"> If you
need a <b>vacation away from the big city</b>
```

➤ Save the file and view it in the Web browser.

The *camping.htm* page should now look something like Figure 6.14.

Image Alignment

The image is in the Web page, but there is wasted space around it. Let's adjust the alignment so that the rest of the text wraps to the right of the image. In this case, the image is left-aligned. Although it appears that the image is left-aligned already, by default the text is not wrapping to the right of the image.

➤ Edit the `<img>` tag to include the left-alignment as follows:

```
<img src="images/hikers.jpg" align=left>
```

➤ Save the file and view it in the Web browser.

The *camping.htm* page should now look something like Figure 6.15.

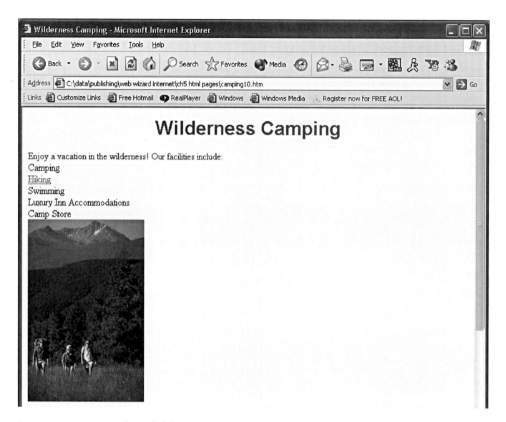

Figure 6.14   *Camping.htm* with *hikers.jpg* image.

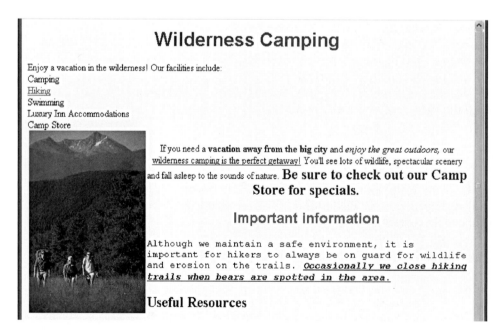

Figure 6.15   *Camping.htm* with image left-aligned.

The image position did not change, but the text is wrapping to the right of the image now.

Image alignment options may affect the image placement, but will also affect the placement of the text around the image. The alignment options are as follows:

top   This is the vertical alignment of the text with respect to the image. The image will be on the left, and the first line of the paragraph will start at the top of the image. The rest of the paragraph will continue under the image.

middle   This is the vertical alignment of the text with respect to the image. The image will be on the left, and the first line of the paragraph will start in the middle of the image. The rest of the paragraph will continue under the image.

bottom   This is the vertical alignment of the text with respect to the image. The image will be on the left, and the first line of the paragraph will start at the bottom of the image. The rest of the paragraph will continue under the image. This is the default alignment for an image.

left   This is the horizontal alignment of the image. The image will be aligned on the left margin of the Web page, and the paragraph will wrap to the right of the image.

right   This is the horizontal alignment of the image. The image will be aligned on the right margin of the Web page, and the paragraph will wrap to the left of the image.

Note that the <img> tag does not have a center alignment feature. If you wish to center an image horizontally on the page, you can use the tags. For instance, you can use <img src="images/hiker.jpg"> and the hiker image will be centered on the page.

Let's create a small test page to see the image alignment options. We will be using the same image several times.

➤   Open a new instance of Notepad and enter the following. Much of this page is a repetition of the first paragraph, with changes only to the alignment in the <img> tag and titles in the headings. Use the copy and paste features to speed up the data entry here.

```
<html>
<head>
        <title>Images test page</title>
</head>
<body>

<h3>no alignment</h3>

<img src="images/mountains.gif">This is a picture of some moun-
tains. The mountains are snow-capped and there are many trails for
hikers. There are a lot of wild animals in the mountains; includ-
ing bears, mountain lions, foxes, coyotes, and birds of prey.

<h3>align=top</h3>
```

```
<img src="images/mountains.gif" align=top>This is a picture of
some mountains. The mountains are snow-capped and there are many
trails for hikers. There are a lot of wild animals in the
mountains including bears, mountain lions, foxes, coyotes and
birds of prey.

<h3>align=middle</h3>

<img src="images/mountains.gif" align=middle>This is a picture of
some mountains. The mountains are snow-capped and there are many
trails for hikers. There are a lot of wild animals in the moun-
tains including bears, mountain lions, foxes, coyotes and birds of
prey.

<h3>align=bottom</h3>

<img src="images/mountains.gif" align=bottom>This is a picture of
some mountains. The mountains are snow-capped and there are many
trails for hikers. There are a lot of wild animals in the
mountains including bears, mountain lions, foxes, coyotes and
birds of prey.

<h3>align=left</h3>

<img src="images/mountains.gif" align=left>This is a picture of
some mountains. The mountains are snow-capped and there are many
trails for hikers. There are a lot of wild animals in the
mountains; including bears, mountain lions, foxes, coyotes, and
birds of prey.

<h3>align=right</h3>

<img src="images/mountains.gif" align=right>This is a picture of
some mountains. The mountains are snow-capped and there are many
trails for hikers. There are a lot of wild animals in the
mountains; including bears, mountain lions, foxes, coyotes, and
birds of prey.

<h3>centering an image</h3>
<center><img src="images/mountains.gif"></center>

</body>
</html>
```

➤ Save this file as *imagetest.htm* and view it in the Web browser.

The *imagetest.htm* Web page should look something like Figure 6.16.

Let's continue editing the *camping.htm* page. The image seems a bit crowded with text immediately above and close to the edge of the picture. We'll add some space around it, and also align it to the right.

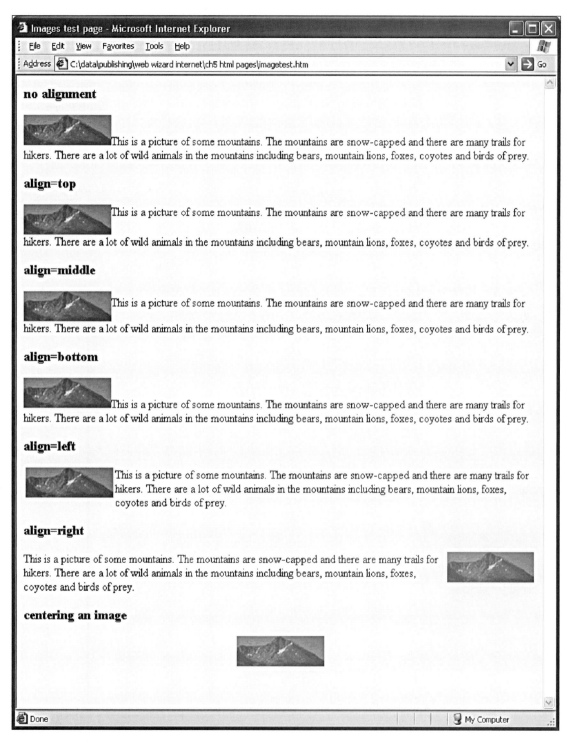

Figure 6.16 *Imagetest.htm.*

We can add "white" space around an image. White space is the area in a Web page that does not contain any content. A certain amount of white space is desirable so that the page does not appear cluttered. We can add white space around an image using the *vspace* and *hspace* attributes in the <img> tag. Vspace will provide vertical space to the areas above and below the image, and hspace will provide horizontal space to the left and right of the image. This space is measured in pixels. Let's add vertical space of 5 pixels and horizontal space of 15 pixels.

➤ In Notepad edit the <img> tag in the *camping.htm* file as follows:

```
<img src="images/hikers.jpg" align=left vspace=5 hspace=15>
```

➤ Save the file and view it in the Web browser.

The *camping.htm* page should now look something like Figure 6.17.

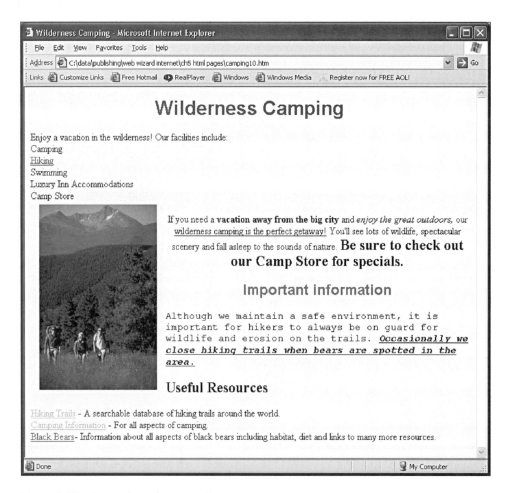

Figure 6.17 *Camping.htm* with vspace and hspace.

Notice that the image now has a margin of white space around it. There is more white space to the left and right than there is at the top and bottom.

Let's change the alignment so that the image is on the right. It still looks a little crowded where it is.

➤ In Notepad, edit the `<img>` tag in the *camping.htm* file as follows:

`<img src="images/hikers.jpg" `**`align=right`**` vspace=5 hspace=15>`

➤ Save the file and view it in the Web browser.

The *camping.htm* page should now look something like Figure 6.18.

 **≋tip**

∴ Adjusting white space is often a case of trial-and-error when manually coding HTML. Start with values for hspace and vspace that seem reasonable, and adjust them after you view the page in the Web browser.

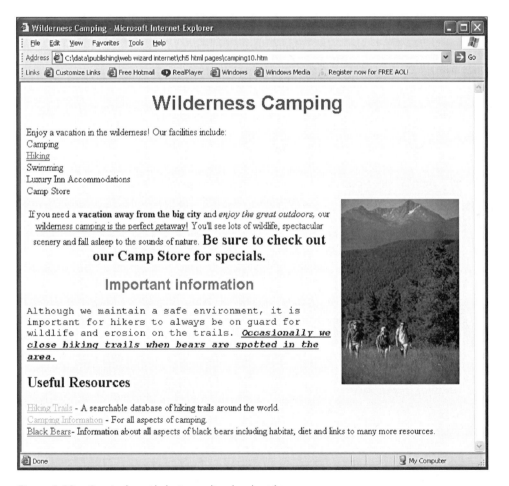

Figure 6.18   *Camping.htm* with the image aligned to the right.

Image As a Link

We can use the <a> tag to create a hyperlink around an image as well. The user will be able to click the image to load a Web page. Let's make the image a hyperlink to the *hiking.htm* page.

➤ Activate the Notepad window containing the *camping.htm* page. Edit the document to include the <a> tag around the <img> tag as follows:

```
<a href="hiking.htm">
<img src="images/hikers.jpg" align=right vspace=5 hspace=15>
</a>
```

➤ Save the file and view it in the Web browser.

You should notice a blue border around the image, and when you hover over the image with your mouse, the pointer should change to a hand. Feel free to click the image to verify that the link works.

Now, let's eliminate the border, so that it looks a little more professional. Although this is a demonstration example, when you are designing Web pages, you should make it clear to the user that an image is also a link to another page with some direction on the page telling the user to click the image, or with some text in the image that makes it obvious to the user that the image is a link.

➤ Activate the Notepad window containing the *camping.htm* page. Edit the document to include the <a> tag around the <img> tag as follows:

```
<a href="hiking.htm">
<img src="images/hikers.jpg" align=right vspace=5 hspace=15
border=0>
</a>
```

➤ Save the file and view it in the Web browser.

You should now notice that the border is removed, but the image is still a functional link.

Lists

HTML can specify formatting for numbered and bulleted lists. A numbered list is an ordered list, so we will use the ordered list <ol></ol> tags. Each list item must also be specified, and we will do this using the list item <li></li> tags.

Let's create a numbered list on the *camping.htm* page using the facilities features. Also, let's move the image up higher.

➤ In Notepad, edit the *camping.htm* file as follows. Notice that the <img> tag has been placed above the statement "Enjoy a vacation in the wilderness!" and that the <br> tags have been removed from the list items.

```
<img src="images/hikers.jpg" align=right vspace=5 hspace=15>

Enjoy a vacation in the wilderness! Our facilities include:<br>

<ol>
        <li>Camping</li>
        <li><a href="hiking.htm">Hiking</a></li>
        <li>Swimming</li>
        <li>Luxury Inn Accommodations</li>
        <li>Camp Store</li>
</ol>
```

➢ Save the file and view it in the Web browser.

The *camping.htm* page should now look something like Figure 6.19.

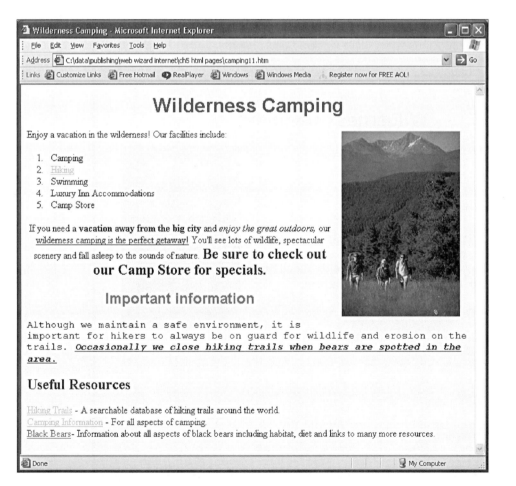

Figure 6.19   *Camping.htm* with an ordered list.

Changing the list type to a bulleted (unordered) list is easily done. The unordered list uses the <ul></ul> tags instead of the <ol></ol> tags used by the ordered list.

➤ In Notepad, edit the *camping.htm* file as follows. Simply substitute the <ol> and </ol> tags for <ul> and </ul> tags. The <li></li> tags are used with both ordered and unordered lists to identify individual list items.

```
<ul>
        <li>Camping</li>
        <li><a href="hiking.htm">Hiking</a></li>
        <li>Swimming</li>
        <li>Luxury Inn Accommodations</li>
        <li>Camp Store</li>
</ul>
```

➤ Save the file and view it in the Web browser.

The *camping.htm* page should now look something like Figure 6.20.

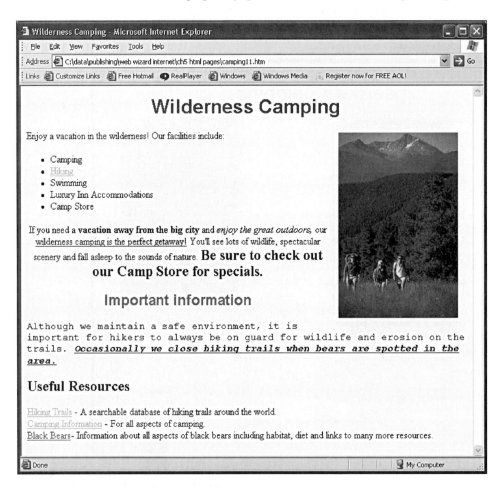

Figure 6.20 *Camping.htm* with an unordered list.

The unordered list is suitable for a list where each item is not prioritized, such as the list of facilities or a list of links. The ordered list is suitable for a prioritized list, where the items are ranked with the most important one at the top. Attributes are available for the `<ol>` tag to specify the type of numbering and start value.

Comment Tag

As the Web page designer, you may want to put your name in your work to identify it as yours, but you may also want to identify sections of a larger page, or place other comments in your page. The comment tag will be visible in the source code, but it will not be rendered in the browser. The comment tag begins with `<!--` and ends with `-->`. Let's add some comments to the *camping.htm* page.

➤ In Notepad, edit the *camping.htm* page as follows.

```
<html>
<head>
        <title>Wilderness Camping</title>
</head>

<!-- This page was created by yourname email:
yourname@youremail.com -->
<!-- Chapter 6 Exercise -->

<body bgcolor=#ffffcc text=#663300 link=#339999 vlink=#ffcc66
alink=#66ffff>
```

➤ Save the file and view it in Internet Explorer or another Web browser. You should not notice any change at all to the *camping.htm* Web page in the Web browser, but if you look at the source code, you will see that your comment has been added.

Comment tags are also useful for identifying parts of a Web page, which the designer can quickly scan. For instance, you may decide to use comment tags to identify the start and end of a long list of items, or the start and end of large sections. An example might be adding comments around our list as follows:

```
<!------ begin list of facilities ------>
<ul>
        <li>Camping</li>
        <li><a href="hiking.htm">Hiking</a></li>
        <li>Swimming</li>
        <li>Luxury Inn Accommodations</li>
        <li>Camp Store</li>
</ul>
<!------ end list of facilities ------>
```

You may add these comments to the *camping.htm* document if you wish.

Browser-Specific Issues

HTML and XHTML standards are developed and proposed by the World Wide Web Consortium (W3C). However, as software companies develop Web browsers, they have also included extra tags and attributes that are not officially part of the HTML/XHTML standards. Furthermore, older versions of browsers will support some features of HTML/XHTML but not others. If you find yourself researching more about HTML and XHTML, you will find that there are references to the tags and attributes that older versions of browsers support, and references to tags or attributes that are only supported by one particular browser or another. Web developers typically design pages that can function in browsers that are at least two years old. Some go to the trouble of including code that detects the user's browser version, and may load a different version of the Web site, which displays well in the user's browser.

In addition to browser version issues, there are a wide variety of other individual configuration settings that may affect the look of the Web pages you may create. For instance, the size of the monitor will vary as one user has a 14" monitor and another has a 19" monitor. Other configuration settings that will affect the look of a Web page include the size of the browser window (full screen, or smaller), the resolution (800 × 600, 1024 × 768, and others), and the number of colors displayed (256, 32 bit, and others). A graphic artist may carefully design a document for print media, knowing it will look exactly the same each time it is printed. A Web developer, however, must assume that the computer has a flexible configuration, and will often design for a flexible look and feel. There are some tricks, such as fixed width tables, that will ensure that a Web page looks very similar from one configuration to another, but it is a matter of some debate among designers whether to design a page so that it has flexibility and adjusts to the user's computer configuration, or design one to look "the same" on any browser.

Optimizing for Search Engines

As we have seen, there are different types of search engines. But, when any search engine is used, the result of the search will be a list of sites and resources. Optimization for search engines is the process of applying some Web design techniques to position your Web site as high as possible in the search ranking lists. One recommended technique is the use of `<meta>` tags to include a description of the page and identify keywords. The name attribute of the `<meta>` tag identifies whether the tag contains a description of the page, or keywords. There are other `<meta>` tag attributes as well, but we will limit our discussion to these two, as they are the most popular. The general form of the `<meta>` tag is as follows. As you can see, the keywords are written in a list, with a comma separating each keyword. There is no limit to the number of keywords in the list.

```
<meta name="description" content="This is your page description. You can
put a paragraph of information here.">
<meta name="keywords" content="word1, word2, word3">
```

Let's add some `<meta>` tags to the *camping.htm* page.

➤ Activate the Notepad window containing the *camping.htm* file, and edit the file to include the `<meta>` tags as follows:

```
<head>
        <title>Wilderness Camping</title>
        <meta name="description" content="Wilderness Camping is a
camping resort with facilities that include hiking, swimming and
luxury inn accommodations. Our camp store sells camping equipment,
including sleeping bags, backpacks, camp food, and tents.">
        <meta name="keywords" content="camping, camp, hiking, hike,
swim, swimming, accommodations, store, tent, wilderness">
</head>
```

➤ Save the file and view it in Internet Explorer or another Web browser. You should not notice any change to the page in the Web browser, as the `<meta>` tags are hidden, but they will be read by some search engines. Notice that the `<meta>` tags include many keywords, and the description is written to include many important keywords as well.

Although each search engine uses a different method to determine ranking, there are some techniques that will improve the ranking for your Web page with most or all search engines. Too much can be a bad thing as well, so here is a list of some simple do's and don'ts.

Do

- Include a `<title>` tag in the `<head>` area and make sure your title is short and meaningful. All search engines consider the words in the title area as important keywords.
- Create a main page that has many keywords in it. Some search engines rank a page higher that has at least 100 words in it, so ensure that your pages have at least that much. Think of the keywords users may use to find your page and try to use those words in the text of your page.
  - Place good keywords as close to the top of the page as possible.
  - Put your keywords as close together as possible. This is keyword proximity and some search engines use it in their ranking.
  - Try to use your keywords at least five to seven times for every 100 words of text. This is keyword density and some search engines use it in their ranking.
- Use a `<meta>` tag to include a description for your page. Try to limit the description to 150 characters or less.
- Use a `<meta>` tag to include keywords for your page. You can repeat the most important keywords three to seven times, but not one after another. Sprinkle them through the list randomly. Most search engines will recognize up to 1024 characters in the keywords list, so consider that to be the limit for the length of the keyword list.
- Use comment tags throughout your page and include keywords in your comments.

- ◻ **Use keywords for the filenames for your Web pages.** The filename will become part of the URL, and some search engines will consider this name to be important.

- ◻ **Choose a few important keywords and use them consistently throughout your site.** Some search engines consider these to be "themes" and will elevate your Web page in the ranking for these keywords.

- ◻ **Consider arranging for other Web sites to link to yours.** Most search engines consider link popularity as a factor in ranking. One technique you can try is to see who links to your competitors' sites and ask them to link to your site as well.

- ◻ **For more details on the criteria used by specific search engines to rank pages, do have a look at Searchengines.com** (`http://www.searchengines.com/searchEnginesRankings.html`).

Don't

- ◻ **Don't repeat a keyword in the `<title>` more than twice.** Some search engines will consider this spam and will actually penalize your site in the ranking because of it.

- ◻ **Don't repeat keywords many times in comments, `<meta>` tags, or other "invisible" text on your page to try to elevate your ranking.** This is spam. Most search engines will ignore it and some search engines will penalize you for it.

Uploading Your Web Site to a Web Server (FTP)

In order for everyone in the world to be able to see your Web pages, they must be stored on a Web server. In a nutshell, a Web server is a computer connected to the Internet that is able to accept HTTP requests, and serve the pages to the computers that request them. If you subscribe to an ISP, you probably have storage space on the ISP's Web server available for your use. There are many free sites that will host your Web pages as well.

In order to transfer your Web pages from your computer to the Web server, you will need to use File Transfer Protocol (FTP). Transferring a copy of a file from your computer to another computer on a network is called uploading and transferring a copy of a file from another computer on a network to your computer is called downloading. In the case of Web page files, the network we are using is the Internet and the computer we are transferring to and from is a Web server. Some Web development packages such as Dreamweaver and FrontPage include FTP software, and it will be seamless. You will simply click an up arrow to upload your page to the Web server, or click a down arrow to download a file from the Web server. You may not necessarily realize that the application package is logging into a Web server, using FTP to transfer the file, and disconnecting.

There are dedicated FTP packages such as WS_FTP, CuteFTP, Coffee Cup FTP, and others. You will find a good selection of FTP packages at Tucows (`http://www.tucows.com`), Download.com (`http://www.download.com`), and other software download sites.

In order to upload files to a Web server, you will need to know the name of the server, including the domain name. You will also need a userid and password for an account on the server. Your ISP will provide you with this information and the technical support team should also be able to walk you through the connection. Regard-

tip

∴ When you search for your competitors' Web sites, which search keywords do you use? Make note of those and use them in your Web site. Put them in the Web page and also in the `<meta>` tags.

less of the program you use for FTP, you should find that it has some panes, or indication of the file listing on your computer, and the file listing of the Web server you are connected to. The WS_FTP window, shown in Figure 6.21, shows the file listing of the user's computer on the left side, and the file listing of the Web server on the right side.

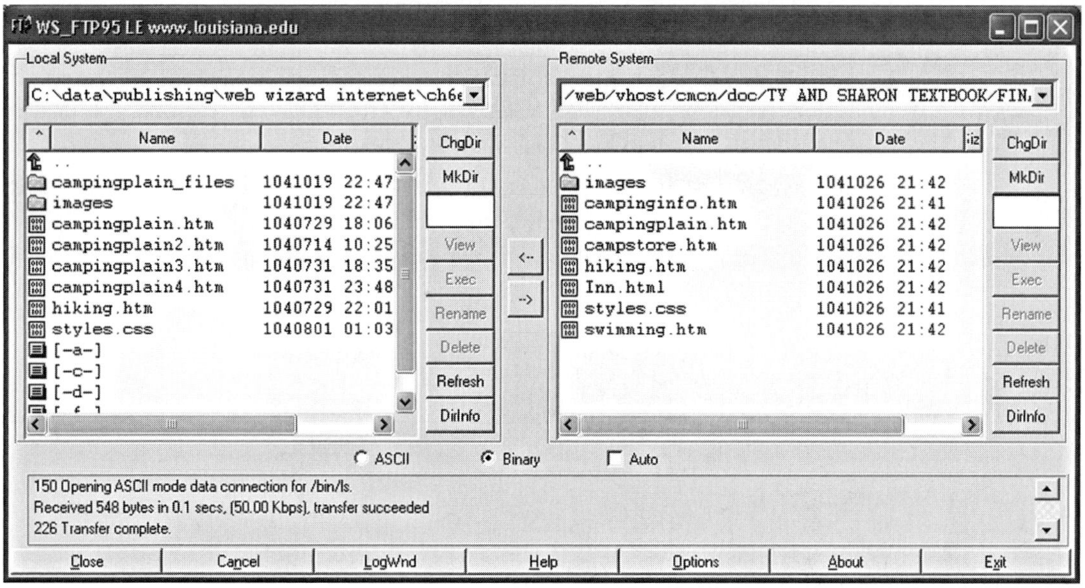

Figure 6.21   WS_FTP window.

In order to upload, you would select the file(s) on the left, and click the button with the arrow pointing from the left pane to the right pane. Most FTP packages will also allow you to drag the selected files from one pane to another, and that will initiate the transfer. Many are designed like the Windows File Explorer window and are fairly intuitive to use.

≷tip

∴ Once you've uploaded your Web pages, be sure to test them in the Web browser using the URL required to load the pages from the server! There are many reasons why a Web page may not function properly after it has been uploaded, so don't assume it will work.

SUMMARY

Now that you've read through the chapter, you are prepared to:

- Define and explain the evolution of HTML.
- Discuss the many changes that are occurring with HTML.
- Create a Web page using HTML.
- Explain basic Web page structure, including: heading tags, formatting tags, tag attributes, font tags, font color, align attributes, hypertext links, page properties, images, image alignment, image as link, lists, and comment tags.
- Handle browser-specific issues pertinent to Web page design.
- Optimize your Web page for search engine archival.
- Upload your Web site to a Web server via File Transfer Protocol (FTP).

Review Questions and Hands-on Exercises

Review Questions

1. What is HTML?

2. What is HTTP?

3. Describe the roles of the W3C and Web browser development in the evolution of HTML standards.

4. What will be the effect of using the following tags?
   a. <b>
   b. <h2>
   c. <i>
   d. <p>
   e. <font size="+3">
   f. <font size="2">
   g. <ol>

5. Why is it important to use browser safe colors?

6. What is the difference in effect when using the <br> tag versus the <p> tag?

7. When specifying a font face, why is it important to use more than one font name in the list?

8. What is the difference between a local hypertext link and a remote hypertext link?

9. In reference to the `<body>` tag attributes, what is the difference between a visited link and an active link?

10. In reference to the `<img>` tag attributes, describe the effect of the alignment attributes, left and right.

11. What is the purpose of using a `<meta>` tag?

12. Describe two different tags that can be viewed in the source code but will not render in the browser window.

13. Describe at least two placement considerations for keywords in a Web page that may influence the ranking of your page for a search engine.

14. What is FTP and when might you need to use it?

Hands-on Exercises

1. Create a *campinginfo.htm* page for our Wilderness Camping site, as shown in Figure 6.22.

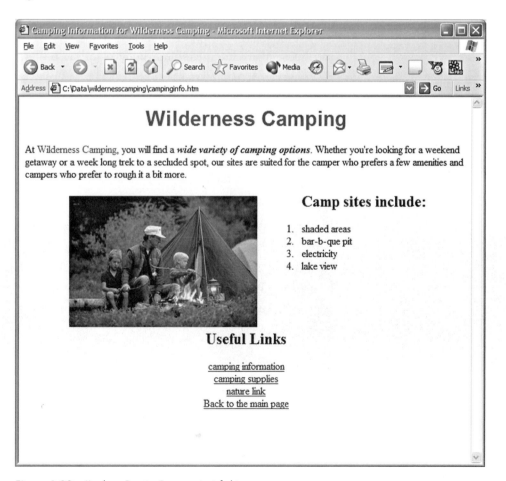

Figure 6.22   Hands-on Exercise 1—*campinginfo.htm*

Note the following:

a. The title that appears in the title bar of the browser is "Camping Information for Wilderness Camping."

b. The "Wilderness Camping" title is heading style 1, sans-serif font, centered.

c. The paragraph contains the words "Wilderness Camping" colored green, and "wide variety of options" bold and italics.

d. Use the image *tent_family.jpg* and left-align this image using hspace of 70 pixels and vspace of 5 pixels.

e. The titles "Camp sites include" and "Useful Links" are heading style 2.

f. Use an ordered list for the "Camp sites include" list.

g. Use the tag `<br clear="all">` after the ordered list so that the *Useful Links* section appears below the image. The `clear="all"` attribute breaks until the white space below the image. Values for the `clear` attribute include *left, right* and *all*. Technically we could have used `<br clear="left">` since the image is left-aligned.

h. Search for some Web pages to include in the "Useful Links" section and use the `<a href>` tag to create hyperlinks for these sites.

i. Center the list of *Useful Links*.

j. Include a link back to the main Wilderness Camping page.

k. Choose appropriate colors for the background, text, link, visited link, and active link.

2. Create a resume page for yourself. Use a format similar to Figure 6.23. Make use of the following techniques:

a. Heading tags for your name, contact information, education, and employment sections.

b. Hyperlinks for the educational institutions you've attended, and for each of your places of employment.

c. Bulleted lists for employment duties.

d. Be creative! Make use of bold, italics, font sizes, and colors to add some emphasis.

3. Create a Web page about your favorite hobby or sport, optimizing it for search engine rankings. Specify at least three techniques you have used to optimize your page. Include the following content:

a. Headings and sections for general information, specific tips, and useful links.

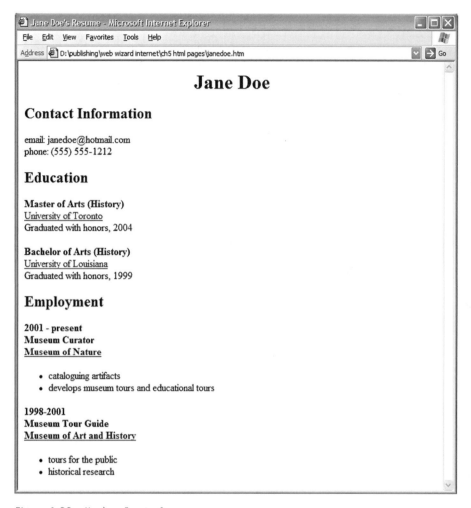

Figure 6.23 Hands-on Exercise 2—resume page.

    b. One picture centered at the top of your page.

    c. One picture aligned to the left or right of your page. Use more pictures if you wish.

    d. Use of font sizes, color, bold, and italics for emphasis.

    e. Use comments to identify yourself as the Web page author and include your email address so others may contact you.

4. Check with your ISP to determine how much storage space you have available on the ISP's Web server, and the procedure to upload pages.

An Introduction to CSS, XHTML, and Advanced Web Development Concepts

chapter **7**

Chapter Objectives

This chapter helps you understand

☐ what Cascading Style Sheets are.

☐ what JavaScript is.

☐ what Java Applets are.

☐ the differences and similarities between eXtensible Markup Language (XML), eXtensible HyperText Markup Language (XHTML) and HyperText Markup Language (HTML).

☐ what a database driven Web application is.

Cascading Style Sheets

Although the HTML standard includes many formatting tags, including `<font>`, `<b>`, `<i>`, the recommended design technique is to separate the structure and elements of the Web page from the formatting, and place the formatting in a separate Cascading Style Sheet. This is the standard for XHTML compliance, as we shall see. The structure and elements include paragraphs, headings, lists, and images. The formatting includes font color, font size, bold, underline, italic, background color, link color, and so forth. The technique is to develop a style sheet containing all of the style rules, which will describe the formatting. The style sheet is called a **Cascading Style Sheet (CSS)** because the style rules can be included in the HTML document or in a separate style sheet and will merge or cascade together, and be applied. The HTML document will be linked to the Cascading Style Sheet. In fact, you can create a single Cascading Style Sheet for many Web pages, and when you make a change to the style sheet, the change will be applied to all the Web pages that link to it.

Let's work on the *camping.htm* page. We will eliminate some of the formatting tags and replace them with style rules in a Cascading Style Sheet. Style rules can be applied three different ways. They can be embedded inside HTML tags, they can be placed in a style section in the HTML document, or they can be placed in an external style sheet. As the purpose of this chapter is only a brief overview, we will simply create an external style sheet and we will link the *camping.htm* and other Web pages to it.

Style Rules

The comment indicators for style sheets are /* and */. We will place comments in our style sheet to identify the name of the file and the author. Style sheets are often named with the extension .css (Cascading Style Sheets). Style sheets are text files, and you can use Notepad to create them. Remember to use the drop-down for *save as type: all files* so that the file is not saved with a .txt extension.

Style rules identify the name of the tag and the styles to be applied. Style rules are typically case-sensitive, so stick to lowercase letters. As we shall see, XHTML compliance requires lowercase so we will work toward that.

Let's do something fun. We will define the <a> tag so the hypertext links will not be underlined, and when the mouse pointer hovers over the link, the text will be green and the background will be white. The a:hover rule represents the <a> tag using the hover attribute.

➤ Open a new instance of Notepad and enter the following. The spacing is a convenience for you as a designer so the code does not look cluttered, and so you can easily see that brace brackets match. You will need a colon (:) separating the style property name from the value, and you will also need a semicolon (;) at the end of each rule. Also, notice that the CSS file does not contain any HTML tags such as <html> or <body>. This is a text file with style rules only.

```
/* Chapter 7 Exercise styles.css */
/* Created by: your name        */

a          { text-decoration: none; }

a:hover    { text-decoration: none;
             color: green;
             background-color: #ffffff;
           }
```

➤ Save the file as *styles.css* in the *wildernesscamping* folder. The *wildernesscamping* folder was created in the exercises in Chapter 6. If you do not have a *wildernesscamping* folder, create it on your hard drive now.

Now we will have to link the *styles.css* file to the *camping.htm* file.

➤ Activate the Notepad window containing the *camping.htm* file and edit the file as follows. We will add the style sheet link tag in the head area. This is important. The style link tag must be in the head area in order for the HTML document to recognize the link to the external style sheet.

```
<head>
    <title>Wilderness Camping</title>
    <link rel="stylesheet" type="text/css" href="styles.css">
</head>
```

➤ Use the *File, Save* menu to save the changes in the *camping.htm* file in the *wildernesscamping* folder.

➤ Open the *camping.htm* file from the *wildernesscamping* folder in a Web browser. You will need to use a Web browser that is less than two years old in order to see the styles applied. You should notice the change in the links as the style rules have been applied.

➤ Move your mouse pointer on top of a link to see the hovering effect of white background and green link color.

The <link> tag establishes a style sheet relationship between the *camping.htm* file and the *styles.css* file. The *href* attribute points to the name and location of the external style sheet. As we have saved this file in the same folder as the *camping.htm* file, we only need the file name. If the *styles.css* file were stored in a separate folder, we would also need the name of the folder in the path, as we did with the src attribute for the images.

Now, let's take out any reference to formatting in the *camping.htm* file.

➤ Activate the Notepad window containing the *camping.htm* file and edit the file as follows. All formatting tags including <b>, <u>, <i>, <font> and alignment attributes have been removed.

```
<html>
<head>
    <title>Wilderness Camping</title>
    <link rel="stylesheet" type="text/css" href="styles.css">
</head>

<!-- This page was created by yourname email:
yourname@youremail.com -->
<!-- Chapter 7 Exercise -->

<body>

<h1>Wilderness Camping</h1>

<a href="hiking.htm">
<img src="images/hikers.jpg" align=right vspace=5 hspace=15
border=0>
</a>

Enjoy a vacation in the wilderness! Our facilities include:<br>

<ol>
    <li>Camping</li>
```

tip

∴ You may find that some styles work in some Web browsers but not in others. Older Web browsers supported only a limited number of styles or none at all.

```
        <li><a href="hiking.htm">Hiking</a></li>
        <li>Swimming</li>
        <li>Luxury Inn Accommodations</li>
        <li>Camp Store</li>
    </ol>

    <p>
    If you need a vacation away from the big city and enjoy the great
    outdoors, our wilderness camping is the perfect getaway! You'll
    see lots of wildlife, spectacular scenery and fall asleep to the
    sounds of nature. Be sure to check out our Camp Store for
    specials.
    </p>

    <h2>Important information</h2>

    <p>
    Although we maintain a safe environment, it is important for
    hikers to always be on guard for wildlife and erosion on the
    trails. Occasionally we close hiking trails when bears are spotted
    in the area.
    </p>

    <h2>Useful Resources</h2>

    <a href="http://www.hiking-trails.com/">Hiking Trails</a> - A
    searchable database ofhiking trails around the world.<br>
    <a href="http://www.camping.com/">Camping Information</a> - For all
    aspects of camping.<br>
    <a href="http://www.black-bears.org/">Black Bears</a> - Information
    about all aspects of black bears, including habitat, diet, and
    links to many more resources.

    </body>
    </html>
```

➤ Save the file as *campingplain.htm* in the *wildernesscamping* folder.

➤ View the *campingplain.htm* file in a Web browser.

The *campingplain.htm* page should look very plain, something like Figure 7.1.

Move your mouse pointer over the links and notice that the link formatting is still intact. You will not see the white background hover style now since the background of the page is white. You will see it again when we change the background color. The link formatting information is coming from the *styles.css* file. We'll change the look of our page a little bit, by applying more styles.

Let's bring the background color back. The body rule has a *background-color* property. We will place the body rule as the first rule in the style sheet. We will also set the text color with the *color* property. You will find that some of the attribute names from the HTML tags are not the same names as the style properties … just in case you thought this was getting too easy.

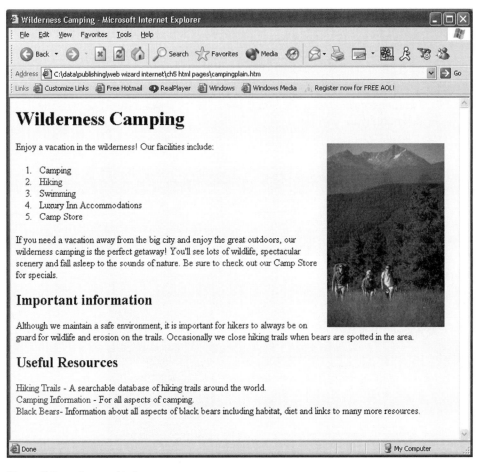

Figure 7.1   *Campingplain.htm.*

 Activate the Notepad window containing the *styles.css* file and add the body rule as follows.

```
/* Chapter 7 Exercise styles.css */
/* Created by: your name          */

body       { background-color: #ffffcc;
              color: #663300;
           }

a          { text-decoration: none; }

a:hover    { text-decoration: none;
              color: green;
              background-color: #ffffff;
           }
```

➤ Save the *styles.css* file. Activate the Web browser window and refresh the *campingplain.htm* page. Since we are now making changes to the *styles.css* file, we will have to refresh the *campingplain.htm* file because this contains the link to the *styles.css* file and will update when the HTML page is refreshed.

The *campingplain.htm* page should now have the styles formatting, something like that shown in Figure 7.2.

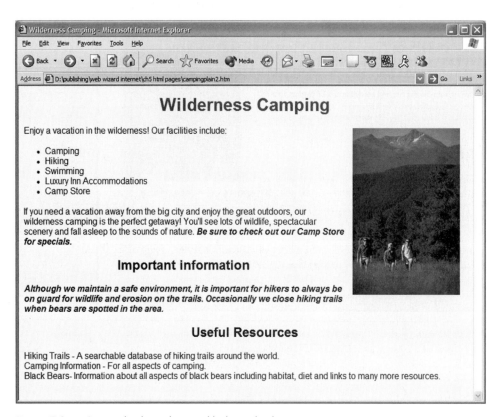

Figure 7.2   *Campingplain.htm* with text and background styles.

Notice that all the text has changed color, and the background color is also visible. As you hover your mouse pointer over the links, you should see the white background on the links visible as well.

Let's change the color of the heading defined with the <h1> tag to green. We will add a rule for the <h1> tag.

➤ Activate the Notepad window containing the *styles.css* file. Edit the file to include the h1 style rule as follows. You can add this rule to the end of the *styles.css* document, after the a: hover rule.

```
h1        { color: green; }
```

➤ Save the *styles.css* file. Activate the Web browser window and refresh the *campingplain.htm* page. You should notice that the *Wilderness Camping* heading is now green. In fact, if there were more than one `<h1>` tag in the *campingplain.htm* document, each heading would be colored green.

Using Multiple Selectors

Let's apply center alignment to all the heading tags. Even though our document contains only `<h1>` and `<h2>` tags, we'll set it up for all heading tags `<h1>` through `<h6>` in preparation for tags which may be used at a later time.

We can use multiple selectors by indicating the selectors in a list, separating each selector by a comma.

➤ Activate the Notepad window containing the *styles.css* file. Edit the file to include the heading style rule as follows. You can add this rule to the end of the *styles.css* document, after the `h1` rule.

```
h1, h2, h3, h4, h5, h6 { text-align: center; }
```

➤ Save the *styles.css* file. Activate the Web browser window and refresh the *campingplain.htm* page. You should notice that all headings are now centered.

With respect to the `<h1>` tag, we can see the effect of cascading styles. The color green is coming from the h1 rule and the centering is coming from the center alignment rule for all tags. These two styles have cascaded and been applied to the `<h1>` tag.

Style Classes

Sometimes we wish to apply different style rules to the same tag in different sections of our Web page. For instance, we may want one paragraph to be italic and bold, or we may want a section of one paragraph to be italic and bold. In this case, we would define a styles class that would render text as italic and bold, and we would apply this class to a particular tag.

Let's create a styles class, which will render text as italic and bold and apply it to the "important information" paragraph and to the sentence "Be sure to check out our Camp Store for specials."

Generic classes begin with a period and can be used with any tag. We can also create classes that can be applied only to specific tags, but we will limit our demonstration in this chapter to generic classes.

➤ Activate the Notepad window containing the *styles.css* file. Edit the file to include the heading style rule as follows. You can add this rule to the end of the *styles.css* document. Be sure to type the period before "emphasis."

```
.emphasis { font-style: italic;
            font-weight: bold;
          }
```

tip

∴ It's OK to put style rules in the CSS file even if you don't use them. You may gradually build a style sheet that you like to use for many different Web sites, as you add more rules!

Now that we've created a class, we'll have to indicate that we would like to use it in the paragraph tag in the *campingplain.htm* file. We will use the *class* attribute to indicate which style class to use.

➤ Activate the Notepad window containing the *campingplain.htm* file. Edit the <p> tag for the "Important information" paragraph as follows.

```
<h2>Important information</h2>

<p class=emphasis>

Although we maintain a safe environment, it is important for
hikers to
```

➤ Save the *campingplain.htm* file and view it in the Web browser. You should notice that the paragraph is now bold and italic.

Let's apply the new .emphasis class to a single sentence in a paragraph. In order to do this, we will have to encapsulate the sentence with the <span> </span> tags. The <span> tag has no effect on the text it contains. Its sole purpose is to be used in conjunction with a styles class to define an area and apply the style rules.

➤ Activate the Notepad window containing the *campingplain.htm* file. Edit the document to add the <span> tags as indicated below.

```
<span class=emphasis>Be sure to check out our Camp Store for
specials.</span>
```

➤ Save the *campingplain.htm* file and view it in the Web browser. You should notice that the sentence is now bold and italic, something like Figure 7.3.

Deprecated Tags

As HTML and XHTML have been evolving, some tags have been identified as deprecated. This means that although these tags are still part of the HTML standards, their use is frowned upon as "older" technology, and use of newer technology is encouraged instead. In practice, Web browsers will continue to support deprecated tags, but at some point in the future, the deprecated tags may become obsolete and dropped from the official standard.

In the *camping.htm* page, we used the <font> tag and specified attributes including size, color, and family. In the styles sheet, these attributes can be placed in the body rule, or individual tag or class rules. The <font> tag has been deprecated. Given that browsers will continue to support it, you can still use it, but the trend toward XHTML encourages the separation of elements and formatting into an HTML file for the elements and a CSS file for the styles. Since the <font> tag is a formatting tag, the effects that can be achieved with it can also be achieved through style rules. Therefore it is not necessary to use the <font> tag in the HTML document. Other deprecated tags are also formatting tags, and the effects they achieve can be achieved with style rules as well.

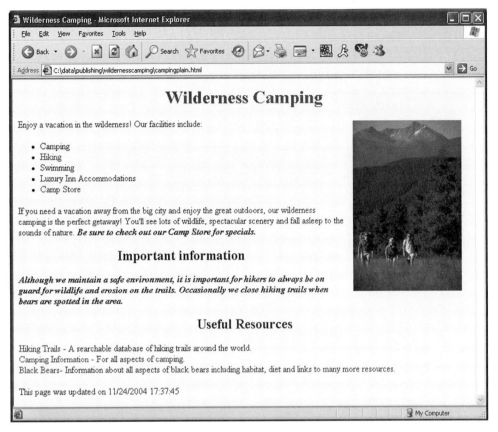

Figure 7.3 *Campingplain.htm* with paragraph styles.

Let's set the font for the whole document as *arial, helvetica, sans-serif*. In the *camping.htm* document we used the `<font>` tag and the *face* attribute. To apply the font to the whole document, we will use the *font-family* property in the body tag rule.

➤ Activate the Notepad window containing the *styles.css* file. Edit the file to include the body style rule as follows.

```
body        { background-color: #ffffcc;
              color: #663300;
              font-family: arial, helvetica, sans-serif;
            }
```

➤ Save the *styles.css* file. Activate the Web browser window and refresh the *campingplain.htm* page. You should notice that all text is now rendered as a sans-serif font.

A style sheet can be applied to more than one Web page. This is a powerful technique for changing the look of many pages in a Web site at once. Let's apply the style sheet to the *hiking.htm* page from Chapter 6.

➤   Open a new instance of Notepad and open the *hiking.htm* page from the *wildernesscamping* folder.

Let's add the `<link>` tag to link the style sheet to the *hiking.htm* page, and also add a hyperlink to the main page as well. In the section `<h1><font color=green>Hiking at Wilderness Camping</font></h1>` we won't need the `<font color=green>` tag for the `<h1>` because the style sheet will take care of setting the color.

➤   Edit the *hiking.htm* page to add the `<link>` tag and hyperlink to the *campingplain.htm* file and eliminate the `<font>` tags as follows.

```
<html>
<head>
    <title>Hiking at Wilderness Camping</title>
    <link rel="stylesheet" type="text/css" href="styles.css">
</head>

<body>

<h1>Hiking at Wilderness Camping</h1>

<p>At Wilderness Camping, you will find many hiking trails. Our
trails are suited for novice and experienced hikers alike. We have
short trails, which can be completed in an hour or two, and longer
trails suitable for a full day of hiking.</p>

<a href="campingplain.htm">Back to the main page</a>

</body>
</html>
```

➤   In the Web browser, open the *hiking.htm* page from the *wildernesscamping* folder.

You should notice that the font and other formatting matches the *campingplain.htm* page, including the hover changes for the hyperlink, as shown in Figure 7.4.

Let's make a change to the style sheet and see how it affects both the *campingplain.htm* page and the *hiking.htm* page.

Let's add a style rule for the `<p>` tag. We'll format the paragraphs to double-space, using the line-height property. This is a great feature because it's not something we can do manually. We can't guarantee the size of the browser window, and adding `<p>` or `<br>` tags will not achieve the same double-spacing effect in all browsers.

➤   Activate the Notepad window containing the *styles.css* styles sheet and edit to add the following after the last set of rules.

```
p           { line-height: 2; }
```

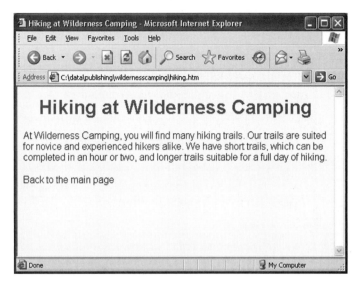

Figure 7.4 *Hiking.htm* with the *styles.css* linked.

▶ Save the *styles.css* file and refresh the *hiking.htm* page in the Web browser to see the changes.

The completed *styles.css* file should look something like Figure 7.5.

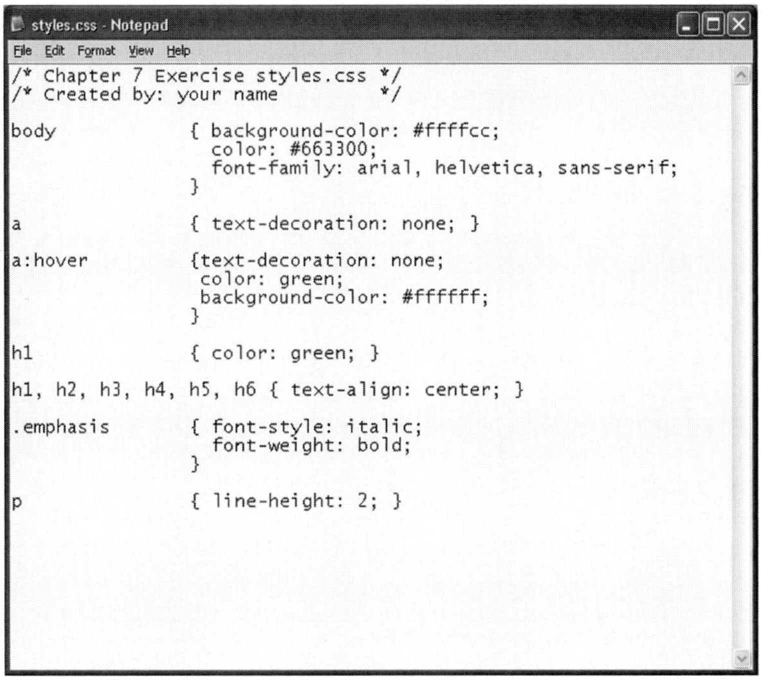

```
/* Chapter 7 Exercise styles.css */
/* Created by: your name           */

body            { background-color: #ffffcc;
                  color: #663300;
                  font-family: arial, helvetica, sans-serif;
                }

a               { text-decoration: none; }

a:hover         {text-decoration: none;
                 color: green;
                 background-color: #ffffff;
                }

h1              { color: green; }

h1, h2, h3, h4, h5, h6 { text-align: center; }

.emphasis       { font-style: italic;
                  font-weight: bold;
                }

p               { line-height: 2; }
```

Figure 7.5 *Styles.css* page.

The *hiking.htm* page should look something like Figure 7.6.

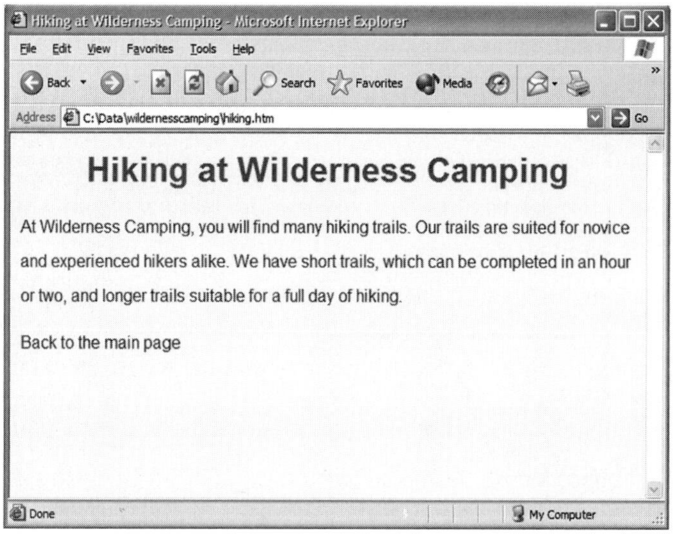

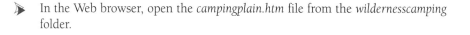

Figure 7.6   *Hiking.htm* with styles.

Notice that the text that is not contained in the paragraph tags has been aligned closer to the left and right edges of the browser window and is not double-spaced.

➤   In the Web browser, open the *campingplain.htm* file from the *wildernesscamping* folder.

Again, notice that the text in the paragraph is double-spaced. Again, the cascading effect comes into play as the `.emphasis` class rules are combined with the `<p>` rules for the important information paragraph formatting. The *campingplain.htm* page should look something like Figure 7.7.

As you can see, changing a style sheet changes the formatting of all of the pages linked to that sheet. This is a very powerful design tool for efficiently adjusting the look of a whole site at once.

JavaScript   Web pages contain text, HTML, and perhaps styles or a link to a style sheet for formatting, but they can also contain JavaScript code. JavaScript is a scripting language that provides some interactivity to the page. A scripting language is similar to a programming language. A JavaScript code segment might display an alert box containing a message for the user and require the user to click "OK" to continue. JavaScript can be used to display the date on which the file was last saved, or prevent the user from submitting a form until there is an email address in a specific text box. JavaScript can be used to create rollover image effects. You see the effect of this when you position your mouse on an image, and the image changes. We will create rollover effects in later chapters.

tip

∴ After you make changes to a style sheet, it's a good idea to view all the pages that are linked to the style sheet. Sometimes the Web page looks a little bit different from what you anticipated!

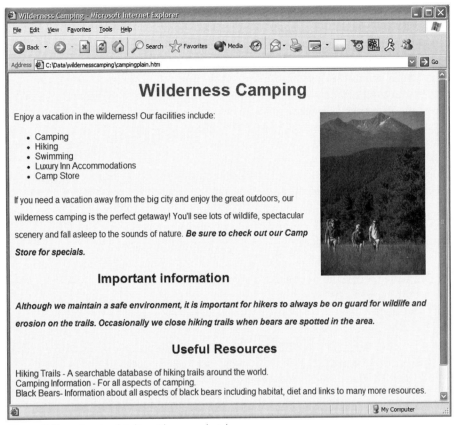

Figure 7.7 *Campingplain.htm* with paragraph styles.

JavaScript is case-sensitive, which means that commands must be entered exactly as specified, paying close attention to uppercase and lowercase characters. JavaScript commands must also end with a semicolon (;).

JavaScript commands will execute where they are found in the Web page. You will often see JavaScript contained in the <head> area, which will perform tasks as the page is loading. These tasks may include pre-loading images. When the user mouses over a rollover image, the second image is already loaded in memory, so there isn't a time lag while the browser requests and downloads the second image. Another common task for JavaScript in the <head> area is to check the version of the Web browser used, and redirect to an appropriate version of the Web site, optimized for the user's browser.

JavaScript must be contained within <script> and </script> tags. The <script> tag identifies a scripting language to be used. The default language is JavaScript, so we will use <script language="JavaScript">, but some browsers can also interpret VBScript as well. In the case of JavaScript and a Web browser, the browser interprets the JavaScript code and outputs the results to the Web browser. In the case of a programming language, rather than a scripting language, one would say that the program runs or is executed. In the case of a scripting language, the script is interpreted before it is executed. The technical difference is that a programming language typically does not require another program to interpret it first in order for it to execute, but a scripting language requires a program to interpret the code and then it is executed.

As an example, let's add a small snippet of JavaScript code to the *campingplain.htm* page, which will display the date on which the page was most recently saved. Without getting into a technical explanation of programming, suffice it to say that JavaScript can access the Web page as a document, and write to it. It can also access elements in the document including forms and images. The document has properties such as its location (URL) and the date on which it was last modified. We will make use of the date on which the document was last modified, which is accessed as the lastModified property of the document. We will write this date to the document as well. Since we would like this code to execute at the bottom of the page, let's add it near the bottom.

➤ Activate the Notepad window containing the *campingplain.htm* page from the *wildernesscamping* folder.

➤ Edit the *campingplain.htm* document to add the <p></p> tags and the JavaScript to write the last modified date to the document as follows. Be very careful to enter the JavaScript command exactly as it is written, with respect to case-sensitivity.

```
<a href="http://www.black-bears.org/">Black Bears</a> - Information
about all aspects of black bears, including habitat, diet, and
links to many more resources.
<p>
This page was updated on
<script language="JavaScript">
document.write (document.lastModified);
</script>
</p>
</body>
</html>
```

➤ Save the *campingplain.htm* file and refresh it in the Web browser.

You should notice that the date appears on the bottom of the page something like Figure 7.8.

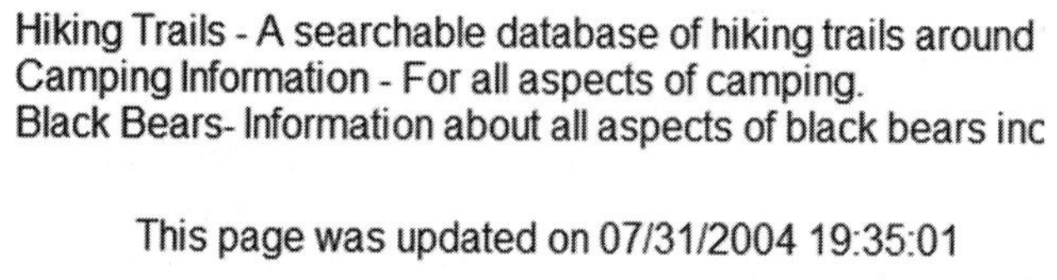

Hiking Trails - A searchable database of hiking trails around
Camping Information - For all aspects of camping.
Black Bears- Information about all aspects of black bears inc

This page was updated on 07/31/2004 19:35:01

Figure 7.8   JavaScript last modified date displayed.

The exact formatting of the date may vary from one browser to another as it adopts the default date formatting of the user's individual computer. There are a variety of other methods used for displaying the last modified date, including Web page editors and programming languages on the Web server. The advantage of using one of these methods is that you don't have to type in the date each time you edit the page. JavaScript takes care of finding the date on which the page was last modified and automatically inserts it into your document. You will find that when you save the document again, the date will automatically update.

Java Applets

There are a variety of methods used to add interactivity to a Web page. JavaScript has the advantage of being interpreted by the Web browser, contained in the Web page itself, and therefore readily available in most Web browsers.

Another method of providing interactivity is to embed a Java Applet in the Web page. This is a common method used to include a game, simulation, animated banner, or fancy animated menu in the Web page. An applet is a mini application program. An application program is a program that will perform end-user tasks. Examples of application packages include word processing packages, spreadsheet packages, and photo editing packages. An applet is not as robust as an application, so it may perform just a few small tasks. Java Applets are developed using the Java programming language. Java can be used to develop robust application packages such as fully featured word processing applications. Java is a programming language and executes directly on the computer without an additional program, as opposed to JavaScript, which is a scripting language and requires a Web browser to interpret the code before it can be executed. However, in order to view a Java Applet in a Web browser, the Web browser requires a Java plug-in. The Java plug-in is a viewer, which allows you to see the output of the Java program as it runs.

One of the best sites for free Java Applets is Java Boutique (`http://www` `.javaboutique.com`). This site includes detailed information on how to add each Java Applet to your Web page.

XML and XHTML

XML

In earlier chapters we have discussed XML (eXtensible Markup Language). XML allows us to create documents that are self-describing. For instance, we can send a database record, using XML tags to describe each of the pieces of data in the record. XML can be used to describe records from a database, and therefore transcends the problems of computer system incompatibilities. An XML document can be generated from one database, sent to another computer system over the Internet, and imported into the new database. XML documents can also describe a word processing document, spreadsheet, or inventory transaction.

tip

It is a common misconception that JavaScript is a subset of Java. It isn't. JavaScript and Java are different languages.

As technology is rapidly growing, more and more electronic devices are emerging. These devices connect to a home network and the Internet and will display documents. Now we have hand-held devices such as cell phones, PDAs, and pagers with Web access, and we also have home appliances such as refrigerators with home network and Internet access. As you know, Web browsers interpret HTML and display the resulting document, a Web page, in the browser. Some of the hand-held devices come equipped with their own mini-browser, and the appliances may run a customized browser as well. The trend for these non-computer devices is to read XML documents for the other types of applications they perform. A document is XML conforming if it follows the basic XML rules for composing a well-formed XML document. If an HTML document could be XML conforming, the same tools that read XML documents could read the HTML document, and this would be a good thing. In fact, it is happening. Standard HTML is not XML conforming, since it is a loose markup language that is very forgiving with respect to rules such as case-sensitivity and missing end tags. However, XHTML is XML conforming.

XHTML

Web pages can also be developed with an XML conforming markup language so that they can be rendered by standard Web browsers, and displayed in viewers on appliances, hand-held devices, and devices that do not have a full-featured Web browser installed. By adding a few rules to HTML, the W3C developed an XML conforming standard for HTML called XHTML (eXtensible HyperText Markup Language). The W3C recommended XHTML as the standard for Web development (rather than HTML, as they did in January 2000). But in practice, HTML isn't going to evolve into XHTML in a hurry, and today's browsers are rendering Web pages that contain deprecated tags as well as HTML documents that do not conform to XML standards. Developing Web pages using XHTML is a forward-thinking development. Using this standard, or working toward it, readies your Web site for the new devices that will require XML conformity in order for the user to be able to see documents.

Backwards and Forward Compatibility

In computing in general, **backwards compatibility** is often considered when developing new products, applications, and programs. Backwards compatibility refers to ensuring that the new product, application, or program will work with older technology. For instance, a new word processing package will generally be able to read a document created by an older package. Sometimes new devices or products are not backwards compatible. For instance, often a new video game system is not able to play the older video games from the same family of game systems. This is frustrating for the consumer.

Forward compatibility refers to developing products, applications, and programs today that will be compatible with devices and programs developed in the future. Of course, it's difficult to predict the types of developments that are coming in the future, but already XML is emerging as a portable standard for documents in general. You will find that current word processing and spreadsheet packages offer options to save documents as XML files. Using XHTML to develop your Web pages is building in forward compatibility. Hopefully this will save redevelopment work in the future, when devices are introduced requiring your site documents to conform to XML standards. Certainly, Web browsers on PCs do not require Web pages to use XHTML, and in fact, will support HTML 4 and previous standards for some time to come.

tip

∴ If you purchase a PDA, cell phone, or other appliance with Internet capability, make sure you find out how much it costs to connect. Some providers charge for each Web page request.

XHTML Rules

XHTML requires a document type tag. When developing XHTML documents, the developer can choose from three different types of XML document definitions. The developer can use the strict definition where the document cannot contain any deprecated tags, such as `<font>` and `<b>`, and must use CSS for all formatting. The developer can also use the transitional definition where the document may contain deprecated tags such as `<font>` and `<b>`. The frameset definition is required if your site uses frames. Using the transitional definition is a quick way to begin converting pages in a Web site from HTML to XHTML.

XHTML standards are built on HTML with a few more rules applied. The additional rules follow, including examples of tags that would be acceptable using HTML standards, and how they must be converted to conform to XHTML standards. We will use these rules later to manually convert our HTML pages to conform to XHTML.

- **XHTML is case sensitive.** All HTML tag names and attributes must be in lowercase, except in some cases where noted.

    HTML: `<H1 ALIGN=CENTER>`

    XHTML: `<h1 align="center">`

- **XHTML requires a document type declaration.** Choices are strict, transitional and frameset. Note the uppercase in these tags as indicated.

    HTML: no tag required

    XHTML: the three tags are as follows:

    ```
    <!DOCTYPE html
        PUBLIC "-//W3C//DTD XHTML 1.0 Strict//EN"
        "http://www.w3.org/TR/xhtml1/DTD/
        xhtml1-strict.dtd">
    <!DOCTYPE html
        PUBLIC "-//W3C//DTD XHTML 1.0 Transitional//EN"
        "http://www.w3.org/TR/xhtml1/DTD/
        xhtml1-transitional.dtd">
    <!DOCTYPE html
        PUBLIC "-//W3C//DTD XHTML 1.0 Frameset//EN"
        "http://www.w3.org/TR/xhtml1/DTD/
        xhtml1-frameset.dtd">
    ```

- **After the document type declaration, the `<html>` tag must be present**, including a reference to xml standards as follows. Pay attention to the uppercase for the language indicator.

    HTML: `<html>` tag is optional and does not have attributes.

    XHTML: `<html xmlns="http://www.w3.org/1999/xhtml"
             lang="EN">`

- **All values of attributes must be encased in double quotes.** This includes single word values as well.

    HTML: `<h1 align=center>`

    XHTML: `<h1 align="center">`

- **Hexadecimal values must be in lowercase.** The hexadecimal value is typically a color value in a tag.

  HTML: `<body bgcolor="#FFCCFF">`

  XHTML: `<body bgcolor="#ffccff">`

- **Multiple elements must be nested properly.** Proper nesting means that innermost tags must be closed first.

  HTML: `<b><i>text </b></i>`

  XHTML: `<b><i>text</i></b>`

- **End tags are required for non-empty elements.**

  HTML:
  ```
  <p>paragraph of information…
  <p>new paragraph of information.
  ```

  XHTML:
  ```
  <p>paragraph of information… </p>
  <p>new paragraph of information. </p>
  ```

- **Empty elements either have to be paired or have / terminator.**

  HTML:
  ```
  <link rel="stylesheet" type="text/css"
  href="styles.css">
  <br>
  <img src="tent.jpg">
  ```

  XHTML:
  ```
  <link rel="stylesheet" type="text/css"
  href="styles.css" />
  <br />
  <img src="tent.jpg" />
  ```

- **All attributes must have values.**

  HTML: `<input type="radio" value="5" checked>`

  XHTML: `<input type="radio" value="5" checked="checked">`

- **The `<img>` tag requires the alt attribute.** The alt attribute displays a pop-up containing the value of the alt attribute when the mouse is over the image.

  HTML: `<img src="tent.jpg">`

  XHTML: `<img src="tent.jpg" alt="picture of a tent"/>`

- **Internal JavaScript code must include the text attribute in the `<script>` tag and the XML starting and ending tags as follows.** The JavaScript comment markers // are used before XML definitions so the Web browser does not attempt to render them.

  HTML:
  ```
  <script language=:"JavaScript">
  document.write (document.lastModified);
  </script>
  ```

  XHTML:
  ```
  <script type="text/javascript"
  language="JavaScript">
  <!--
  //<![CDATA[
  document.write (document.lastModified);
  //]]>
  //-->
  </script>
  ```

This list of rules is not complete, as there are rules for tags not covered in this text, for instance. For a more complete list of rules, feel free to refer to the W3C specifications for XHTML (`http://www.w3.org/TR/xhtml1/`).

We will apply the list of rules above to manually convert the *campingplain.htm* file to an XHTML conforming document.

➤ Activate the Notepad window containing the *campingplain.htm* file.

➤ First, add the following XML definition and transitional document type declaration as the first two tags in the document. Be sure to type the uppercase and lowercase characters carefully as indicated. Be careful also not to add extra spaces. We will use an XHTML Validator, which will determine if the tags have been formed correctly. The XHTML Validator will require these tags in order to read the document.

```
<?xml version="1.0" encoding="UTF-8"?>
<!DOCTYPE html
PUBLIC "-//W3C//DTD XHTML 1.0 Transitional//EN"
"http://www.w3.org/TR/xhtml1/DTD/xhtml1-transitional.dtd">
```

➤ Replace the <html> tag with the following, again paying special attention to the use of uppercase and lowercase characters:

```
<html xmlns="http://www.w3.org/1999/xhtml" lang="EN">
```

➤ Add the alt attribute to the <img> tag and the terminator symbol / as follows. Also add the double quotes around all attribute values as indicated:

```
<img src="images/hikers.jpg" align="right" vspace="5" hspace="15"
border="0" alt='picture of hikers" />
```

➤ Look at each tag and ensure that it is typed in lowercase, with quotes around all attributes. You will have to look at each tag, as we've been purposely sloppy when entering these tags previously. Now we need to clean them up so that they conform to the XHTML standards.

➤ Add the terminator symbol to all <br> tags, and to the <link> tag.

➤ Edit the JavaScript snippet as follows:

```
<script type="text/javascript" language="javascript">
<!--
// <![CDATA[
   document.write (document.lastModified);
// ]]>
//-->
</script>
```

Here is the *campingplain.htm* page with the edited tags indicated in dark text.

```
<?xml version="1.0" encoding="UTF-8"?>
<!DOCTYPE html
PUBLIC "-//W3C//DTD XHTML 1.0 Transitional//EN"
```

```
               "http://www.w3.org/TR/xhtml1/DTD/xhtml1-transitional.dtd">

               <html xmlns="http://www.w3.org/1999/xhtml" lang="EN">

               <head>
                    <title>Wilderness Camping</title>
                    <link rel="stylesheet" type="text/css" href="styles.css" />
               </head>

               <!-- This page was created by yourname email:
               yourname@youremail.com -->
               <!-- Chapter 7 Exercise -->

               <body>

               <h1>Wilderness Camping</h1>

               <a href="hiking.htm">
               <img src="images/hikers.jpg" align="right" vspace="5" hspace="15"
               border="0" alt="picture of hikers" />
               </a>

               Enjoy a vacation in the wilderness! Our facilities include:<br/>

               <ul>
                    <li>Camping</li>
                    <li><a href="hiking.htm">Hiking</a></li>
                    <li>Swimming</li>
                    <li>Luxury Inn Accommodations</li>
                    <li>Camp Store</li>
               </ul>

               <p>
               If you need a vacation away from the big city and enjoy the great
               outdoors, our wilderness camping is the perfect getaway! You'll
               see lots of wildlife, spectacular scenery, and fall asleep to the
               sounds of nature. <span class="emphasis">Be sure to check out our
               Camp Store for specials.</span>
               </p>

               <h2>Important information</h2>

               <p class="emphasis">
               Although we maintain a safe environment, it is important for
               hikers to always be on guard for wildlife and erosion on the
               trails. Occasionally we close hiking trails when bears are spotted
               in the area.
               </p>

               <h2>Useful Resources</h2>
```

```
<a href="http://www.hiking-trails.com/">Hiking Trails</a> - A
searchable database of hiking trails around the world.<br/>
<a href="http://www.camping.com/">Camping Information</a> - For all
aspects of camping.<br/>
<a href="http://www.black-bears.org/">Black Bears</a>- Information
about all aspects of black bears, including habitat, diet, and
links to many more resources.

<p>
This page was updated on

<script type="text/javascript" language="javascript">
<!--
//      <![CDATA[
        document.write (document.lastModified);
//      ]]>
//-->
</script>

</p>

</body>
</html>
```

➤ Save the *campingplain.htm* file and view it in Internet Explorer.

➤ Move your mouse pointer over the image and pause for a second to see the pop-up from the alt attribute appear.

You should not see any noticeable changes to the document in the browser. The document is now XHTML compliant, however. So you've built in forward compatibility!

XHTML Validation

We can validate the document against XHTML standards, in case there's something we've missed. The W3C has a markup validation service available at `http://validator.w3.org/`

➤ Load the W3C markup validation page (`http://validator.w3.org/`) in the Web browser.

➤ Validate your page by file upload. To do this, follow the instructions on the page; click the browse button, select your file, click the *Open* button, and then click the *Check* button.

If your page contains errors, you will see each one listed. If your page is valid, conforming to XHTML standards, you will see results something like the message in Figure 7.9.

tip
∴ In order to view a Web page on a cell phone, PDA, or other small appliance, you also have to design for a small viewing area. Web developers will create sites specifically for these small screens. They will add some code to detect the browser, and then redirect to the Web site designed for the small screen.

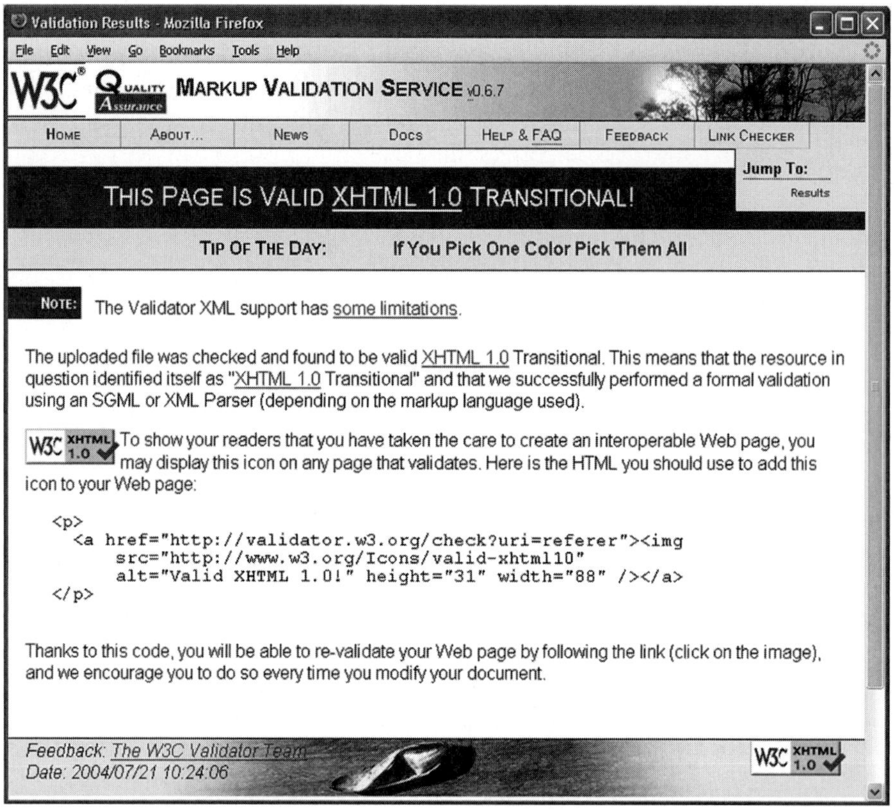

Figure 7.9   WC3 Markup Validation Results. Courtesy of W3C Validator Service http://validator.w3.org.

Occasionally, you may find that the W3C Markup Validator returns the following error message, "Sorry, I am unable to validate this document because its content type is text/plain, which is not currently supported by this service." This can happen if you are using Internet Explorer and it is configured to send the file as plain text. As Internet Explorer does not have options for the user to set the type of file sent, the best option is to use another Web browser, such as Netscape, Firefox, or Mozilla.

Database Driven Web Applications

As we've been touching on some of the main concepts in Web page design, your intuition is probably telling you that there is far more than meets the eye. You are exactly right. Although some Web sites comprise a few simple pages, you have probably noticed that Web sites that accommodate customer feedback and E-Commerce transactions are quite complicated.

A Web page is only one part of a more complex site. As an example, let's look at what might be going on when you make an online purchase. Let's say you'd like to purchase concert tickets through a Web site for this weekend in the nearest city. You would navigate through the Web site to find information about concerts this weekend in the nearest city and select a concert. Next, you would find information about ticket prices, select your tickets, and then find an order form. Once you've keyed in your personal ordering information, you would probably click some sort of "purchase" button. If you've missed some information, or keyed some information incorrectly, you may find the information displayed again, with directions to complete the missing or incorrect information and click "purchase" again. When your information has been accepted, a Web page is displayed indicating that your purchase has been successful and the tickets are on their way.

➤   Open a Web browser and open the Ticketmaster site at
    `http://www.ticketmaster.com`

➤   Search for a concert in the nearest city, and notice that the procedure is similar
    to the description in the paragraph above. You can even click to the order page,
    but you do not need to order tickets.

So what's happening in the background? Well, when you first look for your concert, you may choose to display all concerts in a particular city on a particular date. This information is most likely stored in a database, perhaps on the Web server. When your request for the city and date is sent, this information is used to search a database to find the records that match your request, and a Web page is automatically generated, displaying the results. The Web page does not physically reside on the Web server. The Web page containing the results is a **dynamic Web page**, which means that it has been created by a program on the Web server and generated on-the-fly. Otherwise, someone would have to create a Web page for every possible concert search, and there would have to be hundreds or thousands of Web pages residing on the Web server to cover all possible searches. A Web page that resides on a Web server and has content that does not change is called a **static Web page**. In this chapter, we have been creating static Web pages.

Once you send your customer information and your transaction purchase information, all this is likely stored in a database. There may also be a person checking the database for new purchases, generating the tickets, and putting them in the mail. So, in our example of purchasing concert tickets online, there is a Web site, perhaps containing some static pages such as the main home page, and there is a database containing information about concerts, customer information, and transaction information.

But how is the database searched? How are the dynamic Web pages generated? And how is your customer and transaction information transferred to the database? Well, there is a programming component that receives the order form data, sends search queries to the database, and generates the dynamic Web page using the database search results. This programming component is called **middleware**.

Middleware is software that glues together two other software components. In this case, the middleware bridges between the Web pages and the database and performs tasks such as sending and receiving information from the database, generating automatic emails, creating dynamic Web pages, and much more. Middleware is often written using languages such as Active Server Pages .NET (ASP.NET), PHP, and JSP. The language chosen will often depend on things such as the operating system on the Web server, but the same major tasks can be performed using any of these languages.

A database driven Web site, as described above, is composed of three layers or tiers. The first tier is the Web interface layer. A Web page is a human-computer **interface**. The term interface refers to something that connects two things. A Web page connects the human to some feature of the Internet; in our case, to our database driven Web site. The second tier is the middleware. In our example, the third tier is the database. This structure is called a **3-tier architecture** and it is the common structure for a **Web application**.

Our ticket-purchasing example is a good example of a Web application. A Web application is more than a collection of static Web pages. It is typically a three-tiered structure, comprising Web pages, middleware, and some type of service such as a database, email, or some other service that is used as a resource. Figure 7.10 is a diagram showing the three tiers. The Web pages are displayed on your computer. The middleware and database reside on the Web server. When you request a Web page that is part of a Web application, the Web page request goes to the Web server via the Internet (using all the concepts described in Chapter 2—DNS, TCP/IP, and so forth). Once the Web server receives the request, the middleware takes over to process the request, fetch information from the database if necessary, generate a dynamic Web page if necessary, and send it back to your computer.

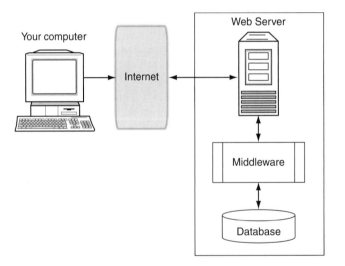

tip

∴ There are many turnkey Web applications available for purchase. These include packages for shopping carts, email feedback, and content management systems. Your Internet Service Provider may be able to offer suggestions and support if you need to install one of these packages.

Figure 7.10   Web application architecture.

A general understanding of how a Web application functions is really quite an advanced concept. However, hopefully it gives you some appreciation for the underlying technical complexity behind building an E-Commerce Web site.

SUMMARY

Now that you've read throught the chapter, you are prepared to:

- Author Web pages linking to style sheets, specifically adhering to: style rules, the use of multiple selectors, style classes, and deprecated tags.
- Add a small JavaScript snippet to your Web page.
- Prepare your Web pages for backwards and forward compatibility by holding fast to XHTML rules.
- Appreciate how database driven Web applications work.

Review Questions and Hands-on Exercises

Review Questions

1. What is the purpose of the `<link>` tag?

2. What is contained in a CSS file?

3. What is the purpose of the `<span>` tag?

4. What is a style class?

5. What is a deprecated tag? Provide three examples of deprecated tags.

6. What is JavaScript? Provide two examples of functionality that JavaScript can add to a Web page.

7. What is a Java Applet?

8. Define the terms *backwards compatibility* and *forward compatibility*.

9. What is XHTML?

10. Why should someone develop a Web site using XHTML instead of HTML?

11. Define the terms *static Web page* and *dynamic Web page*.

12. What are the three tiers of a Web application?

13. What is the purpose of middleware?

14. What is a Web interface?

Hands-on Exercises

1. Add the `<link>` tag to the *campinginfo.html* file to link the *styles.css* file.

2. Create a style sheet for the resume page that you created in the Hands-on Exercises in Chapter 6. The tasks are as follows:

    a. Save the style sheet as *resumestyles.css*.

    b. Link the *resumestyles.css* sheet to the *resume.htm* page.

    c. Remove all `<b>` and `<i>` tags from the *resume.htm* page.

    d. The *resumestyles.css* file should contain style rules to provide the following effects:

        i. Set the background color for the entire sheet to #ccffcc.

        ii. Set the text color for the entire sheet to #003300.

        iii. Remove underlining from all hyperlinks.

        iv. Set the link color for the entire sheet to #993333 with a white background when the mouse pointer hovers over it.

        v. Set the visited link color for the entire sheet to #339933.

        vi. Use center alignment for all heading tags.

        vii. Create a class called .jobtitle for the job titles. This class should use bold, italics, and color #336699. Make use of the `<span>` tag to apply this class to the job titles in the *resume.htm* page.

3. Review the *campinginfo.htm* file that you created in the Hands-on Exercises in Chapter 6 and edit it to ensure that it conforms to XHTML standards.

4. Review the resume file that was created in the Hands-on Exercises in Chapter 6 and edit it to ensure that it conforms to XHTML standards.

HTML Editors

Chapter Objectives

This chapter helps you understand

- what a text editor is.
- how to use a programming editor.
- what a WYSIWYG HTML editor is.
- how to use a WYSIWYG HTML editor.
- some of the different types of WYSIWYG HTML editors.

Text Editors

There are a variety of methods used in Web site development, and no single method has yet emerged as a *de facto* standard. In Chapters 6 and 7, we used Notepad as our development tool. Notepad is a text editor. Text editors are not word processing applications and do not format text or perform other tasks that we associate with word processing. The general procedure for simple Web page development is to edit the code using a text editor, then view the Web page in the Web browser, as we have done.

There are many free text editors available with more features than Notepad provides. We used Notepad because it was convenient, and we were able to get the job done with it. But as we saw, when working with multiple files, it quickly became cumbersome, as we required a new instance of Notepad for each file. Many of the other text editors allow you to use multiple documents simultaneously, add line numbers, use multiple undo/redo, block indenting, sort, and spell-check.

Text editors edit plain text and are suitable for writing code using markup languages, such as HTML and XML, and for scripting languages such as JavaScript, PHP, and ASP. Some good examples of text editors include TextPad (`http://www.textpad.com`), Notetab (`http://www.notetab.com`), and EditPad (`http://www.editpadpro.com`).

Programming Editors

If you're looking for a little more help than a text editor provides, the next level of editors are called programming editors. These editors are designed for writing code in specific languages, including HTML, XML, PHP, ASP, and Java. They often include color coded tags, support for a variety of programming languages, Web browser preview, ready made scripts for browser detection and other common tasks, wizards for creating tables and frames, detailed references for commands, and tags for an assortment of languages, unlimited undo/redo, and automatic tag closing.

There are a variety of good programming editors that are free, including jEdit (`http://www.jedit.org`), Bluefish (`http://bluefish.openoffice.nl/`), EditPlus (`http://www.editplus.com/`), and CoffeeCup HTML Editor (`http://www.coffeecup .com/`). Let's look at CoffeeCup HTML Editor as an example of a programming editor and continue our Wilderness Camping site design. CoffeeCup HTML Editor has a trial version. We'll look at some general techniques for developing Web pages using a programming editor, and using CoffeeCup HTML as an example. You will find that many of the features and techniques we will use are available in a variety of programming and other editors.

CoffeeCup HTML Editor

➢ Open a Web browser and load the CoffeeCup URL: `http://www.coffeecup.com/`.

➢ Download CoffeeCup HTML Editor and install.

➢ Use the commands *Start, Programs, CoffeeCup, CoffeeCup HTML Editor*, to load the CoffeeCup HTML Editor program. You should see the startup screen appear, as shown in Figure 8.1.

➢ Click the *Start the Editor* item.

The CoffeeCup HTML Editor application should look something like Figure 8.2.

Let's open the Wilderness Camping main page and look at some of the CoffeeCup HTML Editor features.

tip

∴ You can find many more programming and HTML editors by using your favorite search engine! Use the key words "HTML editor," "text editor," or "programming editor."

➢ Use the sidebar folder pane and double-click to open the *wildernesscamping* folder. You should see the listing of files appear in the file-listing window below the folder-listing window, as shown in Figure 8.2.

➢ Double-click the *campingplain.htm* file name to load this file.

Notice that the HTML tags are color-coded.

Figure 8.1   CoffeeCup HTML Editor startup screen.

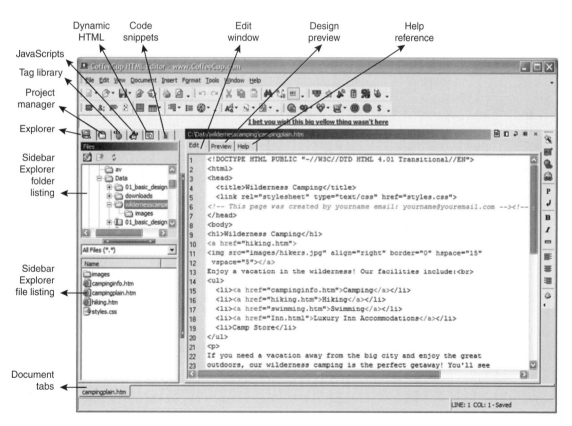

Figure 8.2   CoffeeCup HTML Editor with the *campingplain.htm* file displayed in the code window.

➤ Click the *Preview* tab to see the Web page in Preview mode.

Notice that the HTML page is rendered, with the styles interpreted as well, as shown in Figure 8.3.

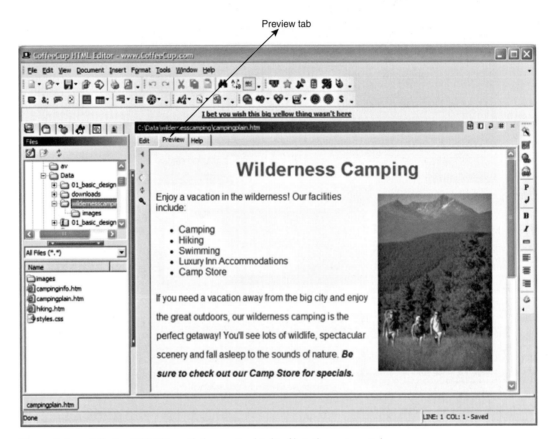

Figure 8.3 CoffeeCup HTML Editor with the *campingplain.htm* file in the preview window.

Adding a Hyperlink One of the fun and interesting shortcut features of programming with HTML editors is the ability to drag elements from one pane to another. Let's add a link from the *campingplain.htm* page to the *campinginfo.htm* page by dragging the *campinginfo.htm* filename from the file window to the edit window.

➤ Position the mouse pointer on the *campinginfo.htm* filename on the file window, drag the file name to the edit window, and drop it after the `<li>` tag for *camping* in the list of facilities, as shown in Figure 8.4.

➤ A dialog box will open, asking if you would like to insert the file as a link or open it for editing. Click the *Insert* button to insert the link.

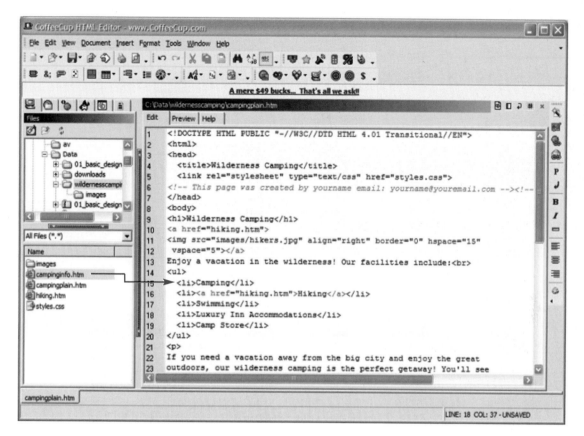

Figure 8.4   Dragging the *campinginfo.htm* file name to the Edit window in CoffeeCup HTML Editor.

You should notice that the `<a href="campinginfo.htm"></a>` tags have been inserted into the *campingplain.htm* page.

➤ Move the word *Camping* between the `<a href="campinginfo.htm"></a>` tags so that it reads `<a href="campinginfo.htm">Camping</a>`. You can do this by using drag and drop, as shown in Figure 8.5, or by using the commands *Edit, Cut and Edit, Paste*, as you would use in any other Windows application.

➤ Save the file using the *File, Save* menu commands. Your *wildernesscamping* folder is not inside the working folder created by CoffeeCup HTML Editor, so you will be prompted to save this file to your working folder. Click the *No* button to save this file in the *wildernesscamping* folder rather than the working folder.

CoffeeCup HTML Editor and most of the other HTML and programming editors provide fairly good code references within the application and online. You can look up information for any of the HTML tags, and get general help for building HTML pages.

➤ Click the *Help* tab. The reference information will be displayed in the editing window similar to that shown in Figure 8.6.

```
<img src="images/hikers.jpg" align="right" border="0" hspace="15"
 vspace="5"></a>
Enjoy a vacation in the wilderness! Our facilities include:<br>
<ul>
 <li><a href="camplinginfo.htm"></a>Camping</li>
 <li><a href="hiking.htm">Hiking</a></li>
 <li>Swimming</li>
```

Figure 8.5   Dragging text after the <a> tag has been inserted.

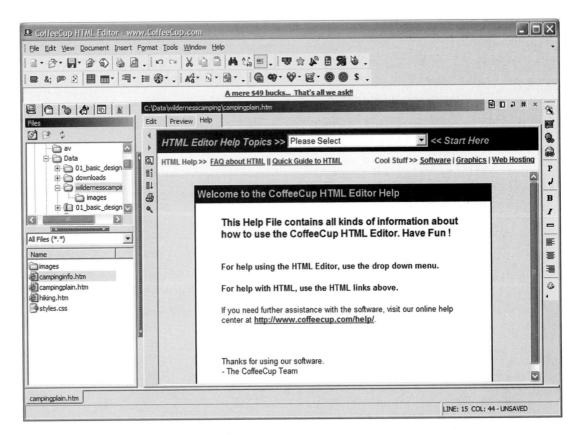

Figure 8.6   CoffeeCup HTML Editor *Tag Help* tab.

Basic Formatting Tags   Now that we've had a look at the CoffeeCup HTML Editor features, let's create the *Swimming* page from scratch. You can refer to Figure 8.2 for the parts of the HTML Coffee Cup window.

➤   Click the *Edit Window* tab.

➤   Click the menu commands *File, New Blank Page* to create a blank Web page.

➤   Working from the Edit window, edit the <title> </title> tag area and add the title *Swimming* so that it reads <title>Swimming</title>.

➤ Save the page as *swimming.htm* in the *wildernesscamping* folder.

➤ Click the *Tag Library* tab to display the list of HTML tags.

➤ Scroll down so that the <h1> tag is visible.

➤ Drag the <h1> tag to the Edit window, positioning it under the <body> tag, as shown in Figure 8.7.

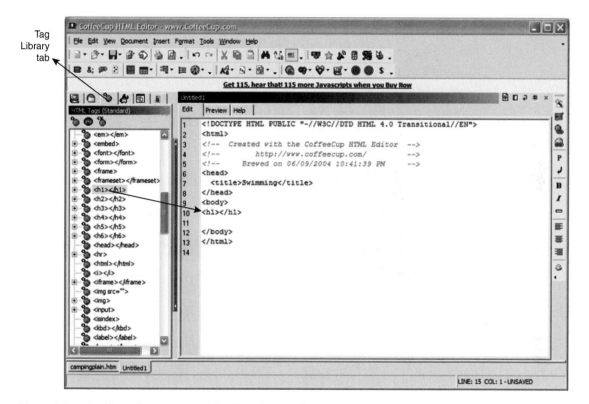

Figure 8.7 Tag library, dragging <h1> to the Edit window in CoffeeCup HTML Editor.

➤ Edit to add the heading *Swimming*, between the <h1> and </h1> tags so that it reads: <h1>Swimming</h1>.

➤ Remember to use the *File, Save* command to save the file periodically as you are working.

➤ Preview the file by clicking on the *Preview* tab. Notice that the page so far is very plain. Let's add the style sheet link.

➤ Return to the Edit window by clicking on the *Edit* tab.

➤ Add a blank line after the <title>Swimming</title> line. We will be adding the style sheet link in this blank line.

➤ Type the style sheet link tag as follows:

```
<link rel="STYLESHEET" href="styles.css" type="text/css">
```

The HTML code should look something like Figure 8.8.

```
<head>
 <title>Swimming</title>
<link rel="STYLESHEET" href="styles.css" type="text/css">
</head>
<body>
```

Figure 8.8 Enter the `<link>` tag for the *styles.css* file in the edit window in CoffeeCup HTML Editor.

➤ Save the page and preview it by clicking the *Preview* tab. Notice that the styles have now been applied and the heading is centered and colored green.

➤ Click the *Tag Library* tab to display the list of HTML tags.

➤ Scroll down so that the `<p>` tag is visible.

➤ Drag the `<p>` tag to the Edit window, positioning it under the `<h1>` heading, as shown in Figure 8.9.

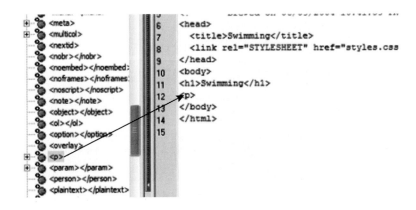

Figure 8.9 Dragging the `<p>` tag to the Edit window in CoffeeCup HTML Editor.

➤ Edit to add the following paragraph of text. You will have to add the closing `</p>` tag:

```
<p>Swim in our beautiful Waterfall Beach area. The Waterfall Beach
is a scenic location with a swimming pond naturally fed by fresh
water from the waterfall. You may see deer and other wildlife as
you enjoy an afternoon on the sandy beach. Lifeguards patrol
during public swimming times. </p>
```

This is a long paragraph of information, so you will have to press the *Enter* key at the end of each line in the paragraph, otherwise the paragraph will extend as one long line of text.

Let's add some formatting to the paragraph.

➤ Drag to highlight the phrase *swimming pond naturally fed by fresh water*.

➤ Click the menu commands *Format, Italic*. Notice when you select the menu items that there is a *Ctrl* shortcut combination listed beside many of the menu items. For instance you can use *Ctrl*+I for italic text.

➤ Feel free to click the *Preview* tab to view the document, and then click the *Edit* tab again to return to the Edit window.

Let's add some font enhancements.

➤ Drag to highlight the sentence *Lifeguards patrol during public swimming times*.

➤ Click the menu commands *Format, Fonts, Font Color*. The Font Color palette should be displayed as in Figure 8.10.

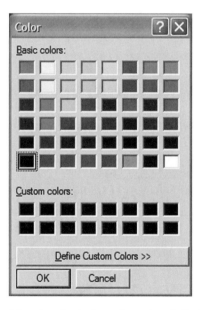

Figure 8.10   Color palette for the Font selection from CoffeeCup HTML Editor.

➤ Click the red color swatch.

➤ Click the *OK* button to select the red color.

➤ With the sentence and `<font>` tags still selected, click the *Format, Italics* menu item to add italic formatting to the sentence.

➤ With the sentence and HTML tags still selected, click the *Format, Underline* menu item to add underlining to the sentence.

The Edit window and code should look something like Figure 8.11.

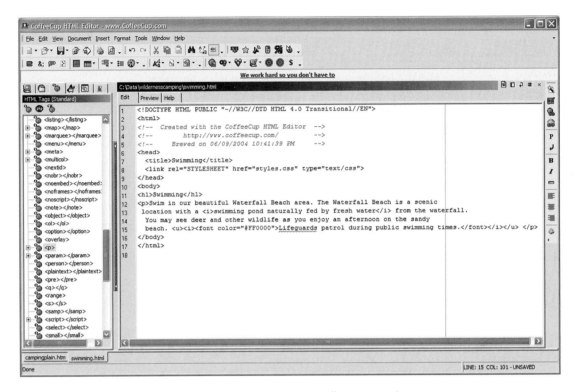

Figure 8.11 Edit window and code for the *swimming.htm* document in CoffeeCup HTML Editor.

Inserting an Image Let's add an image to our document.

➤ Position the flashing insertion point after the paragraph and before the **</body>** tag and press the *Enter* key a few times to add some vertical space. As the tags become cluttered, feel free to add space like this in the code to make it easier for you to see the tags. As you may recall, the Web browser will not render this space. It is for your convenience as the designer.

➤ Click the menu command *Insert, Image*.

➤ Click the drop-down button to explore folders, and find the *Images* folder inside the *wildernesscamping* folder, as shown in Figure 8.12.

Take a moment to explore the options in the Image dialog box. As you can see in Figure 8.12, there are input boxes for border, vspace, and hspace. There is also a drop-down box for alignment, which will allow you to select options such as left, right, middle, and top. CoffeeCup HTML Editor will also create a thumbnail version of the image, as indicated in the *Thumbnail* tab.

➤ Click the *Alt Text* box and add the text *Waterfall Beach*.

⚙ *tip*

∴ Remember to save your file often while you are editing, to prevent loss of data. If your computer freezes and you have not saved your work, you will lose any changes you have made.

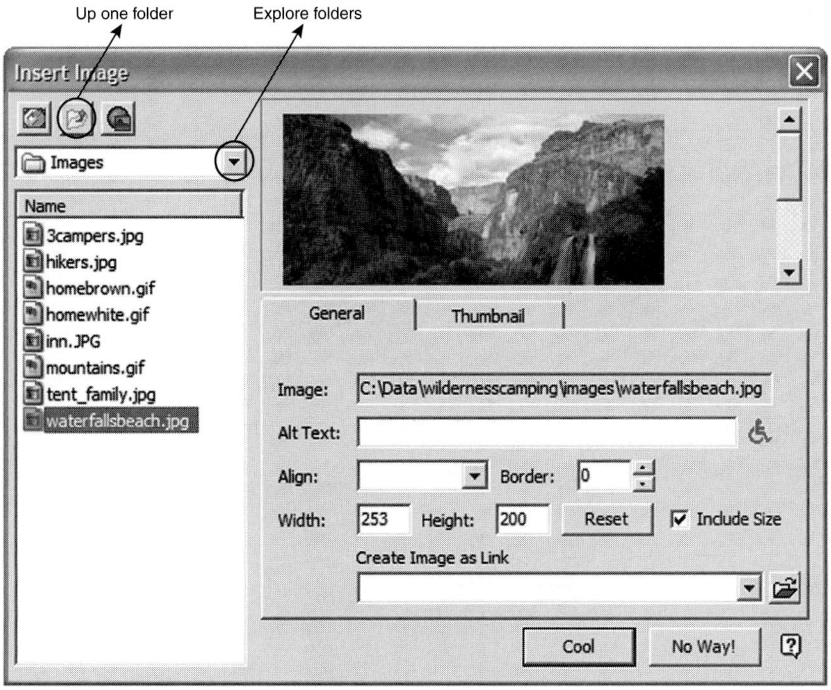

Up one folder   Explore folders

Figure 8.12 Image dialog box in CoffeeCup HTML Editor.

➤ Click the *Cool* button to select the image. The developers of CoffeeCup HTML Editor use "Cool" and "No Way" rather than "OK" and "Cancel" in their dialog boxes.

➤ Again, since we are not storing the site in the *Working* folder, you will be prompted to copy the file into the *Working* folder. Click the *No* button to continue to use the *wildernesscamping* folder and insert the image.

Let's center the image horizontally.

➤ Drag to highlight the <img> tag in the Edit window.

➤ Click the menu items *Format, Center.*

The tags should look something like the following:

```
<center><img src="images/waterfallsbeach.jpg" width="253"
height="200" border="0" alt="Waterfall Beach"><center>
```

➤ Click the *Preview* tab to view the document.

The document should look something like Figure 8.13.

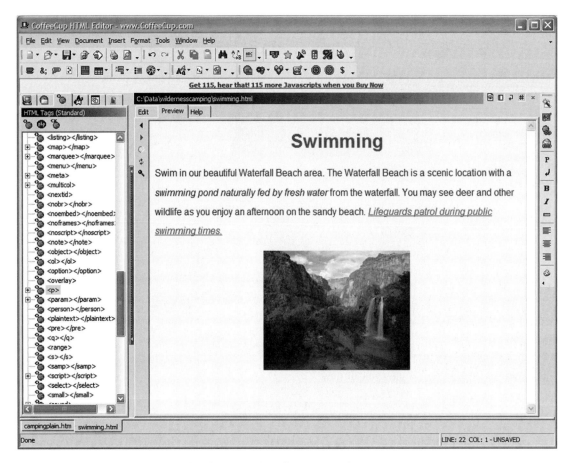

Figure 8.13 Preview of the *swimming.htm* document in the CoffeeCup HTML Editor.

Using Tables For placement of text, images, form items, and other elements, the layout tool used is a table. A table is a grid of rows and a column of cells, and each cell can contain text, an image, a form item, a hyperlink, or another HTML element.

➤ Click the *Edit* tab to return to the Edit window.

➤ Position the insertion point after the `<img>` tag. Press the *Enter* key twice to add a blank line and give yourself some vertical space.

➤ Drag the `<h2>` tag to this location in the Edit window, and edit to add the text *Public Swimming Hours.*

➤ The tag and text should look as follows:

```
<h2>Public Swimming Hours</h2>
```

➤ Position the insertion point after the `</h2>` tag and press the *Enter* key twice to add some vertical space.

Let's create a simple table for the public swimming hours for the Waterfall Beach.

➤ Position the insertion point after the `<img>` tag.
➤ Select the menu command *Insert, Table Designer*.

The Insert New Table dialog box should appear, as shown in Figure 8.14.

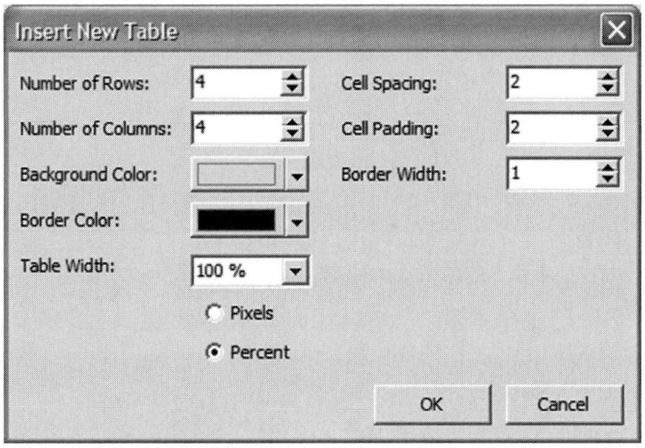

Figure 8.14   Insert New Table dialog box in CoffeeCup HTML Editor.

We'll create a table that has four columns and four rows. The table will also have a black border.

➤ Make sure the number of columns is four and the number of rows is also four, as shown in Figure 8.14.
➤ Click the drop-down arrow for the border color to select the color as black.
➤ Click the *OK* button to form the table grid.
➤ Click each cell in turn, and input the text, as shown in Figure 8.15.
➤ Click the *Cool* button to insert the table.
➤ Click the *Preview* tab to preview the document.

Your document should look something like Figure 8.16.

➤ Remember to save your file periodically as you are working on it, using the *File, Save* menu commands.

Figure 8.15 Table dialog box containing public swimming hours in CoffeeCup HTML Editor.

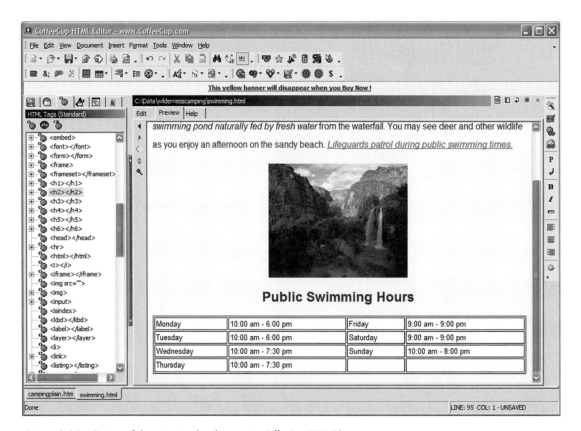

Figure 8.16 Preview of the *swimming.htm* document in CoffeeCup HTML Editor.

Adding a Remote Hyperlink Let's add a remote hyperlink. We will link to a page with information on swimming safety.

➤ Click the *Edit* tab to return to the Edit window. You can see the long list of tags required to build the table!

➤ Position the insertion point just before the </body> tag, and press the *Enter* key twice to give yourself some vertical space.

➤ Drag the <br> tag into the Edit window below the </table> tag twice, to place two <br> tags in the document. This will provide a blank line under the table.

➤ Type the following text: Remember that swimming safety is important!

➤ Drag to highlight the words *swimming safety*. We will link this to a remote page.

➤ Click the menu items *Insert, Link* to display the Insert Link dialog box.

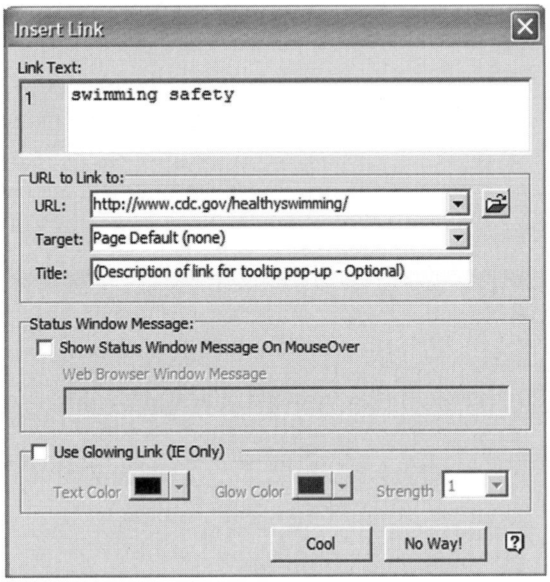

Figure 8.17 The Insert Link dialog box containing the swimming safety URL from CoffeeCup HTML Editor.

➤ In the URL text box, type the URL: http://www.cdc.gov/healthyswimming/ Feel free to find a swimming safety site of your own choosing, and enter the URL for that page instead. The dialog box should look something like Figure 8.17.

➤ Click the *Cool* button to place the hyperlink tag in the document.

The sentence, with the hyperlink, should read as follows:

```
Remember that <a href="http://www.cdc.gov/healthyswimming/">
swimming safety </a> is important!
```

Let's create a link back to the main page.

➤ Drag the `<br>` tag into the Edit window below the safety swimming sentence, twice, to place two `<br>` tags in the document. This will provide a blank line under the safety swimming sentence.

➤ Click the *Explorer* tab to display the file listing, and drag the *campingplain.htm* file name to the Edit window, below the `<br>` tags.

➤ In the dialog box that asks you whether to insert the link or edit the file, click the *Insert* button.

The tags `<a href="campingplain.htm"></a>` should be inserted at this point.

➤ Edit the hyperlink tag by adding the text: `Back to the main page` so that the tag reads as follows:

`<a href="campingplain.htm">Back to the main page</a>`

And finally, let's add a comment tag that identifies you as the author of this page.

➤ Position the insertion point before the `<head>` tag and press the *Enter* key twice to give yourself some vertical space. Leave the tags inserted by CoffeeCup as a courtesy to the company, particularly since you are using a trial version.

➤ Type: `<!-- This page was created by: Your Name, youremail@domain.com -->`

The code for the *swimming.htm* page should look something like this:

```
<!DOCTYPE HTML PUBLIC "-//W3C//DTD HTML 4.0 Transitional//EN">
<html>
<!--   Created with the CoffeeCup HTML Editor   -->
<!--           http://www.coffeecup.com/              -->
<!--        Brewed on 06/09/2004 10:41:39 PM          -->
<!-- This page was created by: Your Name, youremail@domain.com -->

<head>
    <title>Swimming</title>
    <link rel="STYLESHEET" href="styles.css" type="text/css">
</head>
<body>
<h1>Swimming</h1>
<p>Swim in our beautiful Waterfall Beach area. The Waterfall Beach is
a scenic location with a <i>swimming pond naturally fed by fresh
water</i> from the waterfall. You may see deer and other wildlife as
you enjoy an afternoon on the sandy beach. <u><i>
<font color="#FF0000">Lifeguards patrol during public swimming
times.</font></i></u> </p>
```

```
<center><img src="images/waterfallsbeach.jpg" width="253" height="200"
alt="Waterfall Beach" border="0" align=""></center>

<h2>Public Swimming Hours</h2>

<FONT size=2 color="#000000" face="Arial">
<DIV><TABLE width=100% bgcolor="#FFFFFF" border=1 cellpadding=2
bordercolor="#000000" cellspacing=2>
<TR valign=top>
<TD><FONT size=2 color="#000000" face="Arial">
<DIV>Monday</DIV>
</FONT>
</TD>
<TD><FONT size=2 color="#000000" face="Arial">
<DIV>10:00 am - 6:00 pm</DIV>
</FONT>
</TD>
<TD><FONT size=2 color="#000000" face="Arial">
<DIV>Friday</DIV>
</FONT>
</TD>
<TD><FONT size=2 color="#000000" face="Arial">
<DIV>9:00 am - 9:00 pm</DIV>
</FONT>
</TD>
</TR>
<TR valign=top>
<TD><FONT size=2 color="#000000" face="Arial">
<DIV>Tuesday</DIV>
</FONT>
</TD>
<TD><FONT size=2 color="#000000" face="Arial">
<DIV>10:00 am - 6:00 pm</DIV>
</FONT>
</TD>
<TD><FONT size=2 color="#000000" face="Arial">
<DIV>Saturday</DIV>
</FONT>
</TD>
<TD><FONT size=2 color="#000000" face="Arial">
<DIV>9:00 am - 9:00 pm</DIV>
</FONT>
</TD>
</TR>
<TR valign=top>
<TD><FONT size=2 color="#000000" face="Arial">
<DIV>Wednesday</DIV>
</FONT>
</TD>
```

```
<TD><FONT size=2 color="#000000" face="Arial">
<DIV>10:00 am - 7:30 pm</DIV>
</FONT>
</TD>
<TD><FONT size=2 color="#000000" face="Arial">
<DIV>Sunday</DIV>
</FONT>
</TD>
<TD><FONT size=2 color="#000000" face="Arial">
<DIV>10:00 am - 8:00 pm</DIV>
</FONT>
</TD>
</TR>
<TR valign=top>
<TD><FONT size=2 color="#000000" face="Arial">
<DIV>Thursday</DIV>
</FONT>
</TD>
<TD><FONT size=2 color="#000000" face="Arial">
<DIV>10:00 am - 7:30 pm</DIV>
</FONT>
</TD>
<TD> 
</TD>
<TD> 
</TD>
</TR>
</TABLE>
</DIV>
</FONT>

<br>
<br>

Remember that <a href="http://www.cdc.gov/healthyswimming/">swimming
safety</a> is important!
<br><br>
<a href="campingplain.htm">Back to the main page</a>

</body>
</html>
```

In order to complete this exercise, let's go back and add a link on the *camping-plain.htm* page to the *swimming.htm* page.

➤ Open the *campingplain.htm* page in CoffeeCup HTML Editor, if it is not already open.

➤ Activate the Edit window for the *campingplain.htm* page.

➤ Highlight the word *swimming* in the facilities list.

➤ Click the menu items *Insert, Link* and use the *Explore folders* button to find and select the *swimming.htm* file name, as shown in Figure 8.18.

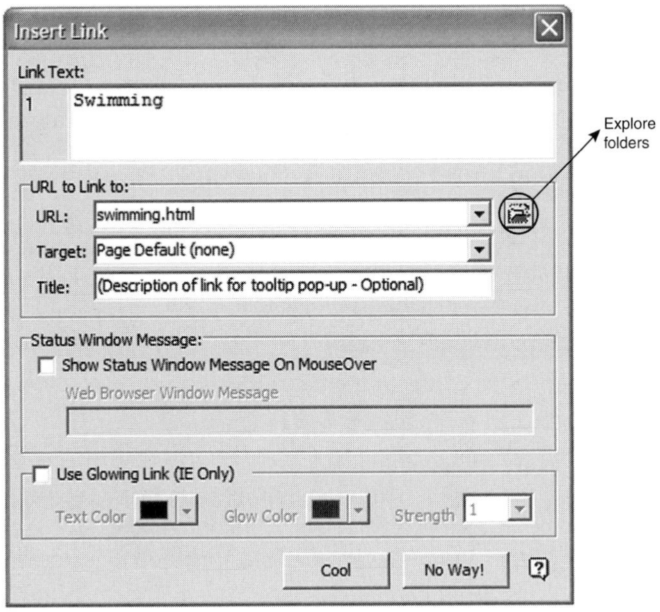

Figure 8.18   Insert Link dialog box with *swimming.htm* filename from CoffeeCup HTML Editor.

➤ Click the *Cool* button to add the link to the *campingplain.htm* page.

➤ Be sure to save the *campingplain.htm* file and the *swimming.htm* file using the *File, Save* menu command for each file.

➤ Close CoffeeCup HTML Editor when you have finished editing and looking at the code.

As you can see from our example of CoffeeCup HTML Editor, programming editors offer helpful features for creating HTML pages, including drag and drop for tags, and easy table creation. Some include dialog boxes for inserting elements such as hyperlinks, tables, and images. This is just a brief overview of some of the basic features of this particular programming editor, but hopefully it's enough to give you a good start, and you can explore more advanced features on your own!

WYSIWYG Editors

If you prefer a more visual environment, rather than spending most of your time looking at HTML code, then you will enjoy using a **WYSIWYG Editor**. The term WYSIWYG is an acronym for What You See Is What You Get, and has been used for years with respect to application packages such as word processing and spreadsheets. It means that you see the completed document, including formatting, as it will look when it is printed or displayed.

Word Processing Applications

Most word processing applications will allow the user to save a document as an HTML file. Typically, the application uses XML styles to replicate the look of the document and although they do the job, you will find that they generate a large amount of code.

Let's look at a brief example.

➤ Open Microsoft Word, or another word processing application package you may have.

➤ Type your name.

➤ Use the *File, Save As* menu command to save the file.

➤ In the Save As dialog box, choose an HTML file type such as "Web Page" or "HTML," and save this file as *testword.htm*.

➤ Close the word processing package.

➤ Open Notepad and open the *testword.htm* file.

➤ Close Notepad when you have finished looking at the code.

You will notice that there is a large amount of code that has been generated, just to display your name in the Web page. So, although a word processing application package will work in a pinch, it is a very inefficient method for creating a Web page.

Netscape Composer

A good example of a free WYSIWYG editor is Netscape Composer. This application is suitable for designing single pages and medium-sized Web sites.

➤ Open a Web browser and load the Netscape Home site at: http://home.netscape.com

➤ Download and install the current version of Netscape.

➤ Open Netscape and use the menu commands *Window, Composer* to launch the Composer window. It should look something like Figure 8.19.

Let's use Netscape Composer to create the Luxury Inn page for the Wilderness Camping Web site.

tip

∴ If you need to edit an HTML file that was created using a Word processing application such as Word, there is a way to clean up the bloated code. You can open the Web page in Dreamweaver and use the "Clean up Word HTML" or "Clean up XHTML" feature!

Basic Formatting

➤ Click the drop-down arrow on the *Paragraph Format* button and select *Heading 1*, as shown in Figure 8.20.

➤ Type: Luxury Inn Accommodations

➤ Press the *Enter* key to move the insertion point to the next line.

As you can see, this is very much like word processing. You can select the formatting first, and type the text, or you can type the text first, then highlight the text and select the formatting. Move your mouse pointer over the buttons and hover for a

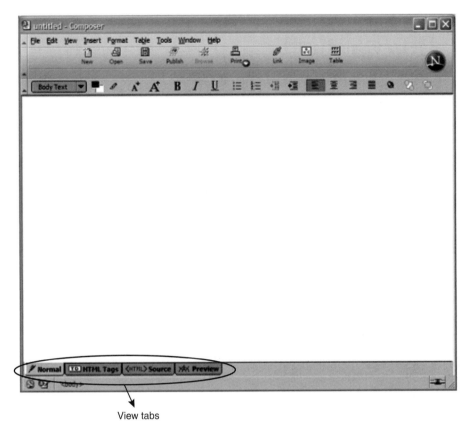

Figure 8.19   Netscape Composer 7.2 window.

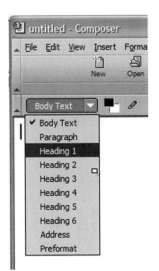

Figure 8.20   Selecting the heading text type in Netscape Composer 7.2.

moment over each button to see the name of the button. You can see buttons on the button bar indicating bold, italic, underline, centering options for align left, align center, align right, align justify, and list buttons as well. Let's look at the different views available.

➤ Click the *HTML Tags* tab. You should see icons for each of the HTML tags used in this document, as shown in Figure 8.21.

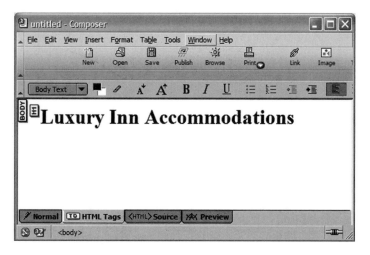

Figure 8.21   *HTML Tags* view in Netscape Composer 7.2.

➤ Click the *<HTML> Source* tab. You should see the HTML source code for this document, as shown in Figure 8.22.

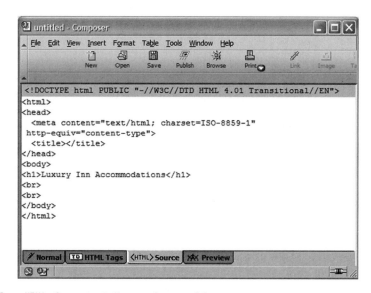

Figure 8.22   *<HTML> Source* view in Netscape Composer 7.2.

The *Preview* tab will display the Web page as it would look in the Web browser. At this point, the Preview view will display the same as the Normal view because we are using very simple features at the moment. We will look at the Preview view later.

➤ Click the *Normal* view tab.

➤ Click the menu commands *File, Save*.

➤ Netscape Composer will prompt you to add a title for this page. In the text box, type: `Luxury Inn`

➤ Click the *OK* button and save the file in the *wildernesscamping* folder as *inn.htm*.

We will be using the *styles.css* style sheet. To link the style sheet, we will use the `<link>` tag and enter it in the source code window.

➤ Click the *HTML Source* tab to reveal the Source window.

➤ Edit the code to add the `<link>` tag in the `<head>` area as follows:

```
<html>
<head>
        <meta content="text/html; charset=ISO-8859-1" http-equiv="content-type">
        <title>Luxury Inn</title>
        <link rel="stylesheet" type="text/css" href="styles.css">
</head>
<body>
        <h1>Luxury Inn Accommodations</h1>
        <br>
</body>
</html>
```

➤ Click the *Normal* view tab. You should see that the styles have been applied to the Web page.

Let's add a paragraph of information with some font formatting.

➤ Position the insertion point on a new line below the *Luxury Accommodations* heading.

➤ Click the drop-down arrow on the *Paragraph Format* button, and select the *paragraph* type, as shown in Figure 8.23.

➤ Type the following paragraph:

```
Enjoy all of our facilities, and sleep in comfort in our Luxury
Inn. Our rooms are available year round, and our staff is happy to
ensure that your stay is memorable.
```

➤ Drag through the words *available year round* to highlight them.

➤ Click the *I* button to apply italic formatting to the words.

➤ Click the menu items *Format, Text color* to reveal the color palette.

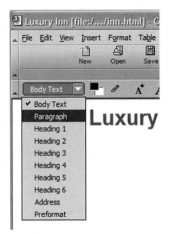

Figure 8.23   Selecting the paragraph text type from the paragraph menu in Netscape Composer 7.2.

▷   Click the red swatch to select the color for the text, as shown in Figure 8.24.

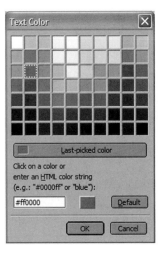

Figure 8.24   Text color dialog box in Netscape Composer 7.2.

As you can see, you can type text and format it afterwards. The *Format* menu reveals a variety of choices for formatting font, font size, text color, list, paragraph types, and page properties. We will be creating a simple page, so feel free to experiment later on your own with some of the formatting options.

The Web page should look similar to Figure 8.25.

Using a Table for Layout   The layout tool used for placing images, text, and other HTML elements is a table. We used a table for the public swimming hours in the *swim-*

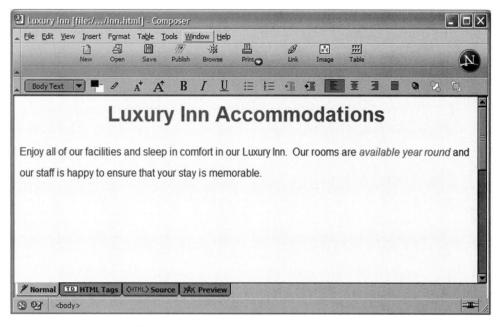

Figure 8.25 Luxury Inn Web page in Netscape Composer 7.2.

ming.htm page to align the days of the week and hours. Let's use a table to align an image with a list of items. We will use a table that contains one row with two cells. We will place an image in the cell on the left and a list in the cell on the right.

➤ Position the insertion point below the paragraph.
➤ Click the *Table* button, or use the menu commands *Table, Insert, Table*.
➤ Select the number of rows to be *1* and the number of columns to be *2*, as shown in Figure 8.26.

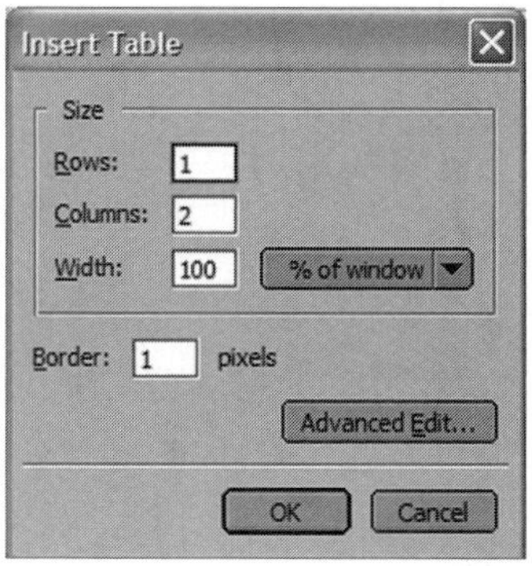

Figure 8.26 Table dialog box in Netscape Composer 7.2.

➤ Position the insertion point in the cell on the left. We will place an image in this cell.

➤   Click the *Image* button, or use the menu commands *Insert, Image*.

Let's insert the *inn.jpg* image into the table cell. We will also include some alternate text.

➤   Click the *Choose File* button and select the *inn.jpg* file from the *Images* folder.
➤   In the *Alternate Text* box, type: `Luxury Inn`

The Image dialog box should look similar to Figure 8.27.

➤   Click the *OK* button to place the image in the table cell.

Let's add a list of items to the other cell.

➤   Click the cell to the right to place the insertion point in the cell. Be sure that you have placed the insertion point in the second cell, rather than beside the image. The second cell may be a narrow cell on the right-hand side of the window.
➤   Click the drop-down arrow on the *Paragraph Format* button and select *Heading 2*.
➤   Type: `Facilities`
➤   Press the *Enter* key to position the insertion point below the heading.

You should notice that the cell width changes as you add text. The cell width will accommodate the widest text.

➤   Click the *Bulleted List* button, as shown in Figure 8.28, or use the menu commands *Format, List, Bulleted* to start a bulleted list.

Figure 8.27   Image dialog box from Netscape Composer 7.2.

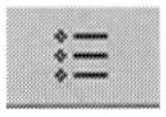

Figure 8.28   *Bulleted List* button from Netscape Composer 7.2.

➤ Enter the following list. At the end of each line, press the *Enter* key, just as you would if you were using a word processing package:

```
King and queen sized beds
Jacuzzi rooms available
Room service
Fine dining in our mountain view dining room
Continental breakfast
Dry cleaning
Indoor pool
Coffee maker and hair dryer in each room
Mini bar available
Spa services
Weekend getaway packages available. Book now!
```

The page should look something like Figure 8.29.

Figure 8.29   Luxury Inn Web page from Netscape Composer 7.2.

As you can see, the list is longer than the height of the image. Without a table, the list items would continue below the image. A table will keep elements together in a block, and can be flexible, as the size of the browser window changes.

Table and Cell Alignment   Let's adjust the alignment of the image in the cell. You can see that the image is in the upper right corner of the cell. Let's set the alignment of the cell contents so that the image is centered both vertically and horizontally.

➤   Click the image to select it.

➤   Use the menu commands *Table, Table Properties.* This will display the Table Properties dialog box.

➤   Click the *Cells* tab, as shown in Figure 8.30, so that we can adjust the cell alignment properties.

➤   Check the checkbox for content alignment, *Vertical* and click the alignment drop-down box and select *Middle*, as shown in Figure 8.30.

➤   Click the checkbox for the content alignment, *Horizontal* and click the alignment drop-down box and select *Center,* as shown in Figure 8.30.

Notice that there are many other cell formatting options, such as background color, size, and text wrap. While we have this dialog box open, let's also adjust the properties of the table itself.

➤   Click the *Table* tab to display the properties for the whole table.

➤   Change the *Border* pixels number to 0. This specifies the number of pixels for the border. When this is set to 0, the border disappears.

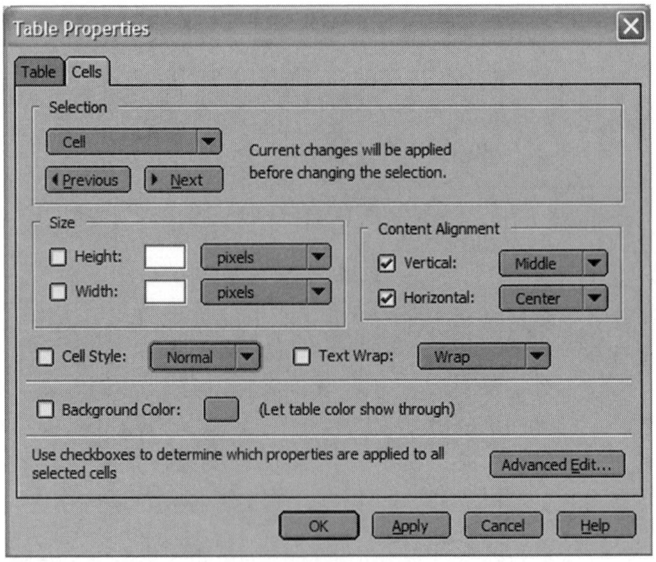

Figure 8.30   Table Properties dialog box in Netscape Composer 7.2.

➤ Delete the number *100* from the width option. By deleting this number, the table width will not be 100% of the window, but will simply accommodate the contents of the cells. When the table width is 100%, the widths of the columns adjust, and this will bring the list further from the picture. We'd like to keep the list close to the picture.

➤ Click the drop-down arrow for the table alignment button, and select *Center* as the alignment. This will center the table horizontally on the page.

➤ Click the *OK* button to apply the changes to the cell and table.

Notice the red border around the table cells. In Normal view, this is for your reference, so you can see the boundaries of the cells. Let's switch to Preview to see how the page will be displayed in a browser.

➤ Click the *Preview* tab to see the page as it would look in a Web browser.

The Web page should look something like Figure 8.31

Notice that the red border is not displayed. The table is used for layout purposes, and aligns the list with the image.

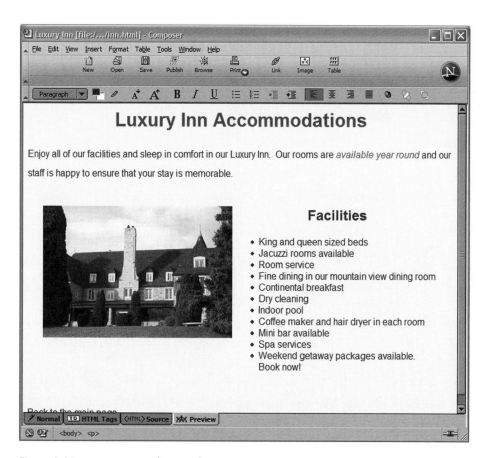

Figure 8.31 Luxury Accommodations Web page in Preview in Netscape Composer 7.2.

Hyperlinks Let's add a remote hyperlink and a local hyperlink to the Luxury Inn Web page. Let's start with adding a remote hyperlink pointing to the Travelocity site (http://www.travelocity.com/) so customers can book their trips to our Wilderness Camping resort.

➤ Click the *Normal* view tab to return to the Normal view.

➤ Drag to highlight the words *Book now!*

➤ Click the *Link* button or use the menu commands *Insert, Link* to reveal the Link Properties dialog box.

➤ In the link location box, type the URL: http://www.travelocity.com/

The dialog box should look something like Figure 8.32.

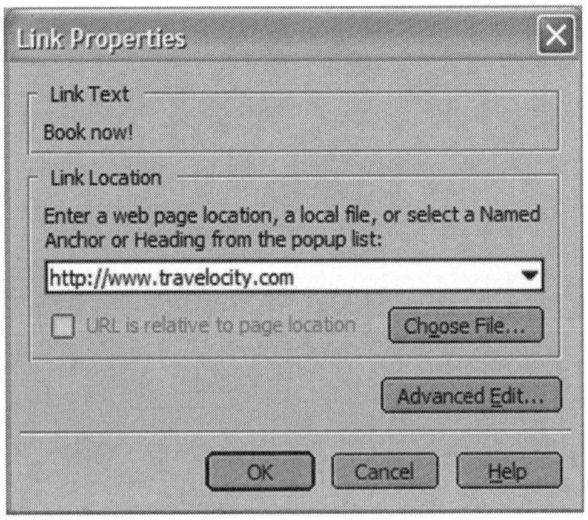

Figure 8.32   Link Properties dialog box in Netscape Composer 7.2 with the remote URL selected.

➤ Click the *OK* button to add the hyperlink around the words.

Let's add a local link back to the main page.

➤ Move the mouse pointer below the table and click to position the insertion point below the table.

➤ Type the following: Back to the main page

➤ Highlight the words: *Back to the main page.*

➤ Click the *Link* button, or use the menu commands *Insert, Link* to reveal the Link Properties dialog box.

➤ Click the *Choose File* button and select the *campingplain.htm* file from the listing.

➤ Click the *Open* button to select the *campingplain.htm* file. The dialog box should look something like Figure 8.33.

➤ Click the *OK* button to add the local link.

tip

∴ You do not require permission to link to another Web page. In fact, linking to another Web page will elevate that Web page's ranking in the search engines.

Figure 8.33   Link Properties dialog box in Netscape Composer 7.2 with the *campingplain.htm* file selected.

➤ Remember to use the *File, Save* commands or click the *Save* button to save the file.

The completed Web page should look something like Figure 8.34.

Figure 8.34   Luxury Accommodations Web page in Netscape Composer 7.2.

Let's open the *campingplain.htm* page and add a link to the *inn.htm* page.

➣ Click the *Open* button or use the menu commands *File, Open*. Select the *campingplain.htm* page and click the *Open* button to open the page in a new Netscape Composer window.

➣ Drag to highlight the words *Luxury Accommodations* in the features list.

➣ Click the *Link* button or use the menu commands *Insert, Link* to display the Link Properties dialog box.

➣ Click the *Choose File* button and select the *inn.htm* file from the listing. Click the *Open* button to select the file, and click the *OK* button in the Link Properties dialog box to create the link.

➣ Click the *Save* button or use the *File, Save* menu commands to save the file.

Macromedia Dreamweaver

The editors we've looked at thus far are good choices for building small Web sites, or editing existing pages. Once a Web site becomes a bit more complex, there are other techniques in site design that are useful. For instance, to maintain the same look and feel for each page, you might design a template and use it to build each individual page. A more robust design tool will track each page designed using a particular template, and when the template is changed, it will automatically update each page created from that template. Another useful tool is synchronization. Files that are stored on the Web server can be synchronized with files stored locally so that the most recently updated files are uploaded to the server, and the designer doesn't have to keep track of which files need to be uploaded.

To build truly robust Web sites, you will want to use a design tool that can handle template-based design and site management, store libraries of code snippets, draw a visual map of your site, and synchronize the files on the server with the files stored locally. A *de facto* standard for site design has not emerged, but there are two very popular tools used today; Macromedia's Dreamweaver and Microsoft's FrontPage. Macromedia releases 30-day free trials of its products, so let's take a look at designing a Web page using Dreamweaver MX 2004, and view some of the features available in this package.

Let's install and open Dreamweaver, and open the *campingplain.htm* file so we can take a look at the environment.

∴ Macromedia offers a suite of Web design products including Dreamweaver, Fireworks, and Flash. Many software companies such as Macromedia design their products to work well together. If you enjoy using one design tool, it's worth the time to investigate using other design tools from the same company.

➣ Open the Macromedia URL at `http://www.macromedia.com` and download the trial version of Dreamweaver.

➣ Install Dreamweaver, and start the program.

➣ When prompted for designer view or coder view, ensure that designer view is selected and click the *OK* button, as shown in Figure 8.35.

➣ Select the 30-day trial version option, and click the *Continue* button.

➣ Click the *Open* button and find the *campingplain.htm* file, and open it, as shown in Figure 8.36.

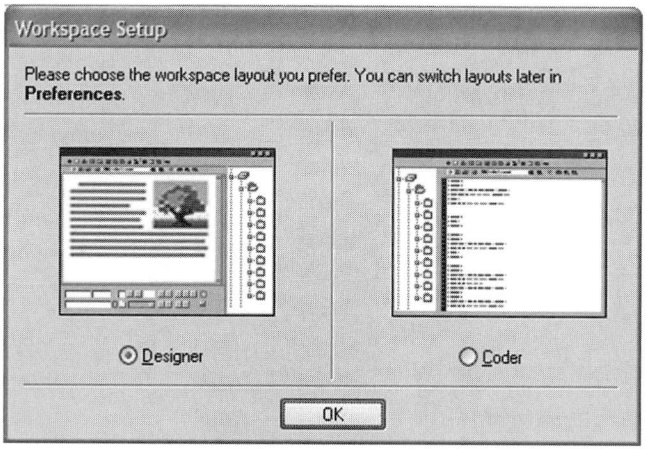

Figure 8.35   Designer view selected in Dreamweaver MX 2004.

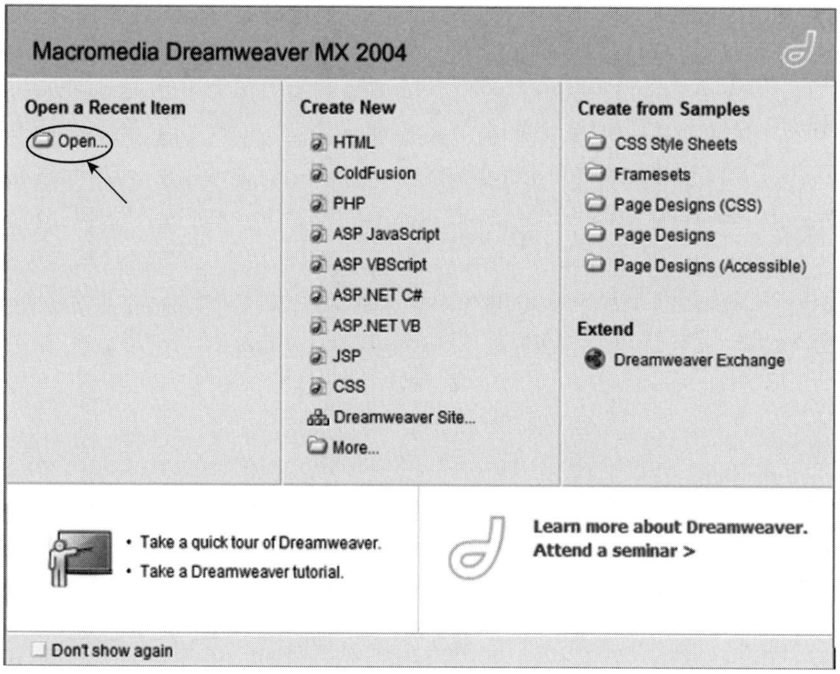

Figure 8.36   Open a file in Dreamweaver MX 2004.

If this dialog box does not display, use the *File, Open* menu commands to open the *campingplain.htm* file.

The Dreamweaver window should look something like Figure 8.37.

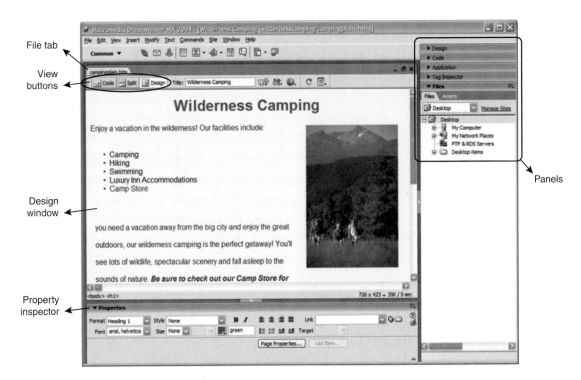

Figure 8.37 Dreamweaver MX 2004 window.

Basic Formatting The Property Inspector will display properties for the selected Web page element. The insertion point is at the top of the page, and the properties displayed are for the *Wilderness Camping* heading. Notice that properties include paragraph format, color, font, alignment, and others.

➢ Pause your mouse pointer over each button in the Property Inspector to view the description of the button.

➢ Click the image to select it.

Notice that the Property Inspector now contains properties for the image, including the name of the file (src), link, vspace, hspace, and alignment.

➢ Feel free to click other parts of the Web page, and notice that the Property Inspector contains properties for the selected elements.

The panels on the right include features such as the file and folder explorer, and the styles. There is a style sheet linked to the *campingplain.htm* file and this can be seen in the *Design* panel.

➢ Click the arrow on the *Design* panel to open the *Design* window, as shown in Figure 8.38. You can click this arrow again to collapse the *Design* panel as well.

Figure 8.38 Click on the arrow on the
Design panel in Dreamweaver MX 2004.

The *CSS Styles* tab should open, as shown in Figure 8.39.

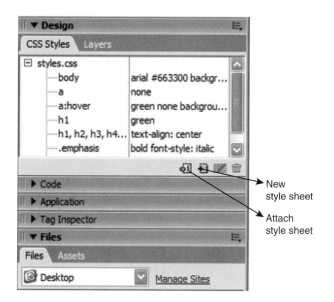

Figure 8.39 Style Sheet in the *Design* panel in Dreamweaver MX 2004.

We will be using this panel to add the style sheet when we design a new page. Let's create the Camp Store page.

➤ Click the menu commands *File, New*. The New Document dialog box will be displayed, as shown in Figure 8.40.

➤ Click the HTML option in the *Basic Page* panel, and click the checkbox for *Make document XHTML compliant*, as shown in Figure 8.40. We might as well think "forward compatible" since it's easy enough to do while we're here.

➤ Click the *Create* button to create the new page.

Let's design the page, and then attach the style sheet when we're done.

➤ In the Properties Inspector, click the drop-down arrow for *Format* and select *Heading 1*.

➤ Type: Camp Store

➤ Press the *Enter* key to move the insertion point down a line. Notice that the format in the Properties Inspector has returned to *paragraph*.

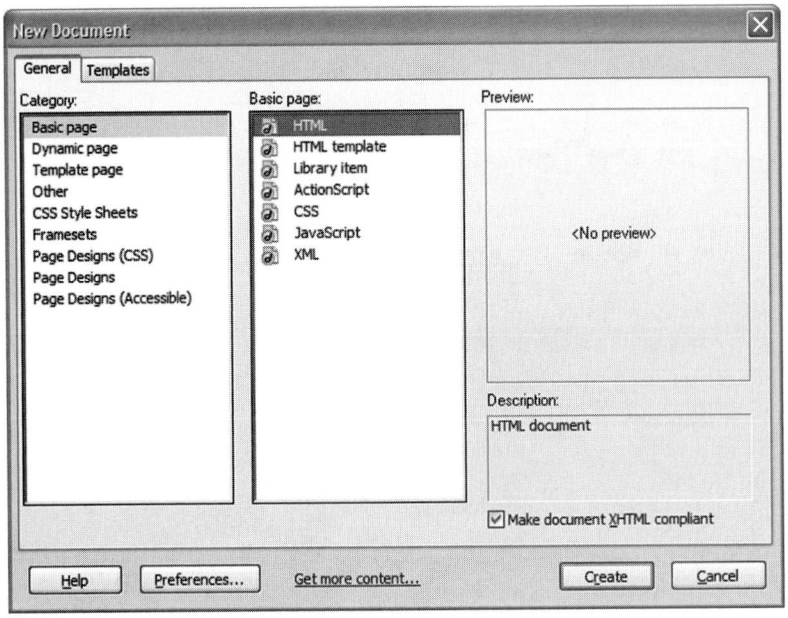

Figure 8.40   New Document dialog box in Dreamweaver MX 2004.

➤   Type the following paragraph:

Our camp store has a fabulous selection of all of your camping needs. You will find groceries, firewood, hiking gear, sleeping bags, and tents. You will also find a selection of clothing including bathing suits and rain gear. Seniors enjoy a 15% discount.

➤   Drag to highlight the sentence: *Seniors enjoy a 15% discount.*

Let's add some formatting to this sentence. We will apply italics and color the font red.

➤   In the Properties Inspector, click the drop-down arrow for the *font color* and select the *red* swatch, as shown in Figure 8.41.

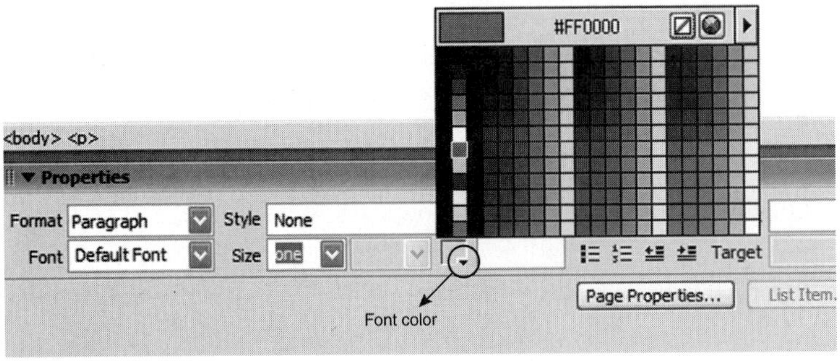

Figure 8.41   Properties Inspector, font color in Dreamweaver MX 2004.

▶ Click the *Italics* button to add italic formatting to the sentence.

▶ Press the *Enter* key to move the insertion point down one line.

Adding an Image   Let's add an image.

▶ In the *Files* panel, explore the folder listing to find the *wildernesscamping/images* folder. Click the *Images* folder to make sure that the list of images is visible.

▶ Drag the *3campers.jpg* image from the *Files* panel to the Design window, as shown in Figure 8.42.

▶ Click the image to select it.

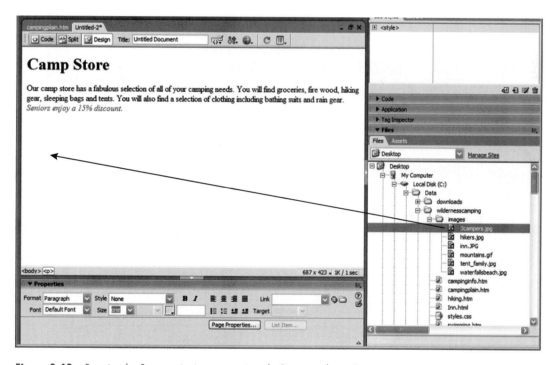

Figure 8.42   Dragging the *3campers.jpg* image name into the Design window in Dreamweaver MX 2004.

You should see the image appear in the Design window, and the Properties Inspector will contain properties for the image once you click it.

▶ Click the *Center Align* button to align the image in the center of the page, horizontally, as shown in Figure 8.43.

Center align

Figure 8.43   Properties Inspector for the image, with *Center Align* button selected in Dreamweaver MX 2004.

Adding a Table   Let's add a table for the store hours.

➤ Press the *Enter* key to move the insertion point down one line. Notice that the center alignment is still in effect.

➤ In the Property Inspector, click the drop-down arrow on the *Paragraph Format* button and select *Heading 2*.

➤ Type: Store Hours

➤ Press the *Enter* key to move the insertion point down one line.

➤ Click the *Table* button or use the menu commands *Insert, Table,* to display the Table dialog box, as shown in Figure 8.44.

➤ Edit the number of rows as 2 and the number of columns as 4, as shown in Figure 8.44.

➤ Edit the *Table width* to 100 *percent*. You will have to click the drop-down box to select *percent* rather than pixels, as shown in Figure 8.44.

➤ Click the *OK* button to add the table to the Web page.

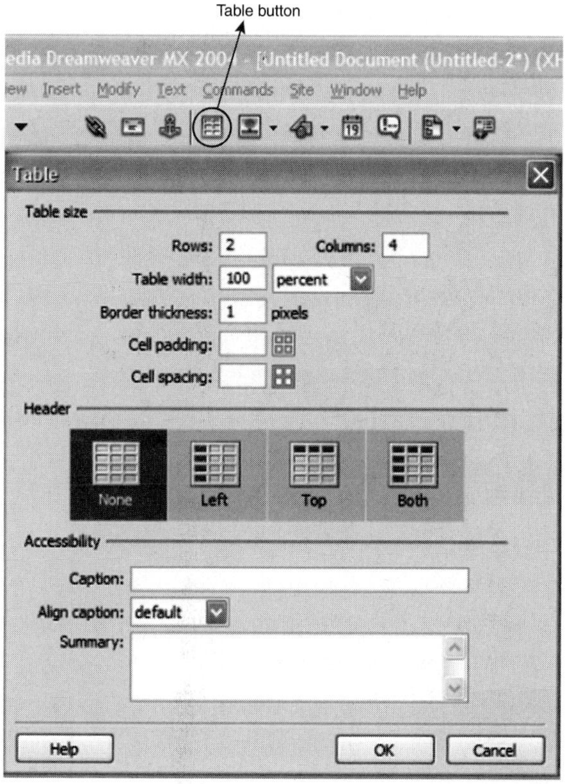

Table button

Figure 8.44 Table dialog box in Dreamweaver MX 2004.

▶ Click in each cell and add the hours information as follows:

Monday–Thursday	9:00 am–6:00 pm	Friday	9:00 am–10:00 pm
Saturday	11:00 am–8:00 pm	Sunday	10:00 am–5:00 pm

The table should look something like Figure 8.45.

Let's save the file.

▶ Click the menu commands *File, Save As,* and save the file as *campstore.htm* in the *wildernesscamping* folder.

Let's preview the file in a Web browser. One method you can use is to open a Web browser and then open the saved file. Dreamweaver also has a browser preview feature, and it will open a Web browser and automatically load the page.

▶ Click the menu commands *File, Preview in browser, iexplore.* If Internet Explorer is not your default browser, it may not appear in the browser preview list. If you do not have any browsers in the preview list, then open a Web browser and

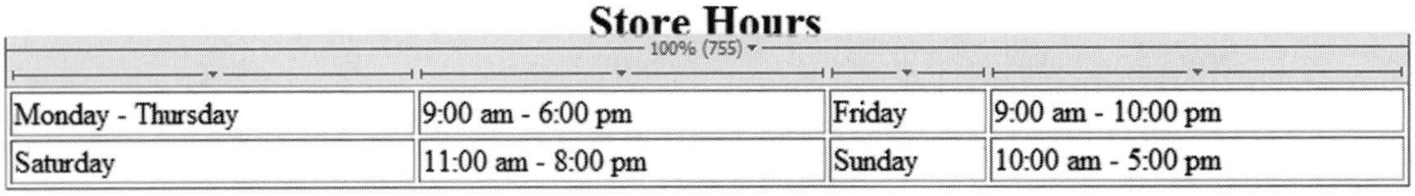

Store Hours
100% (755) ▾

| Monday - Thursday | 9:00 am - 6:00 pm | Friday | 9:00 am - 10:00 pm |
| Saturday | 11:00 am - 8:00 pm | Sunday | 10:00 am - 5:00 pm |

Figure 8.45   Store hours table in Dreamweaver MX 2004.

open the saved *campstore.htm* file. Dreamweaver will allow you to specify browsers, but in the interest of time, we will use this manual method.

Your Web page should look something like Figure 8.46.

Figure 8.46   *Campstore.htm* file in the Web browser.

Remote and Local Hyperlinks in Dreamweaver Let's add a remote hyperlink to our page.

➤ Click the area below the table in the Design window.
➤ Click the left-align button in the Properties Inspector to position the insertion point at the left margin, as shown in Figure 8.47.

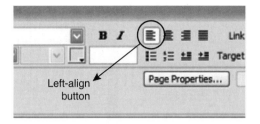

Figure 8.47   Properties Inspector, *Left-Align* button in Dreamweaver MX 2004.

➤ Type: Camping equipment information can be found at
   http://about.camping.com

➤ Drag to highlight the URL http://about.camping.com

➤ In the Link box in the Properties Inspector, type the URL:
   http://about.camping.com, as shown in Figure 8.48.

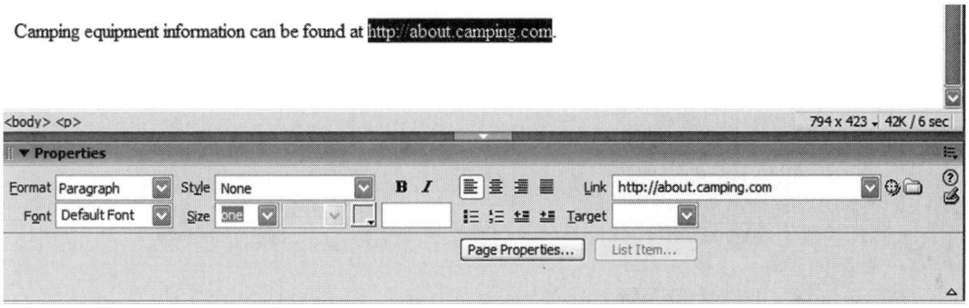

Figure 8.48   Properties Inspector, creating a link in Dreamweaver MX 2004.

Let's add a local link back to the main page.

➤ Click the area below the "camping equipment" sentence to position the insertion point at the end of the Web page.

➤ Type: Back to the main page

➤ Drag to highlight the words, *Back to the main page.*

We can use a dragging technique to point to a local file in our site.

➤ Drag the link target to the filename *campingplain.htm* in the file listing in the *File Panel*, as shown in Figure 8.49. You could also click the *Browse File* button and find the file as well, or type the name of the file in the *Link* box.

➤ Be sure to save the file using the *File, Save* menu commands.

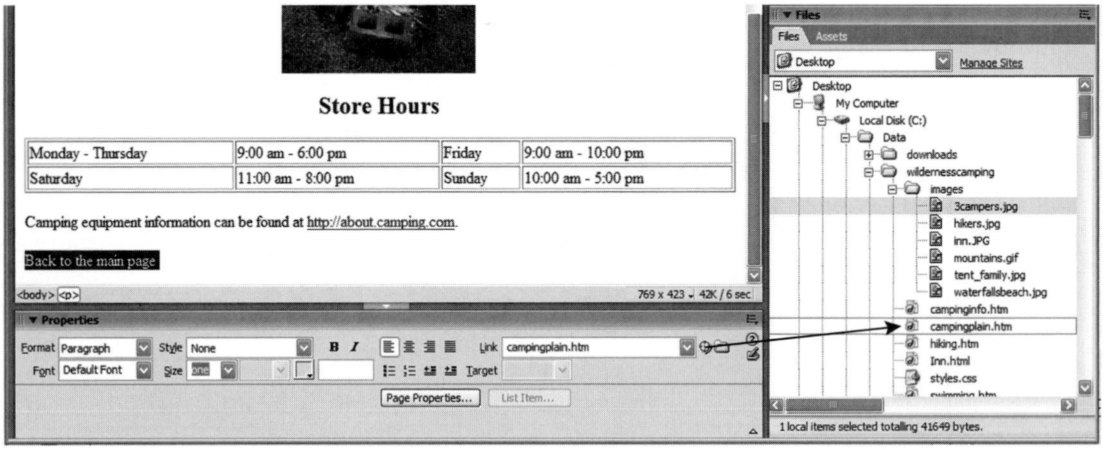

Figure 8.49 Drag the link target to the filename *campingplain.htm* in the *File* panel window to create the local link.

Let's add a title to our page.

➤ Click in the Title box and type: Camp Store, as shown in Figure 8.50.

Figure 8.50 Title box in Dreamweaver MX 2004.

Let's add a comment to our page identifying you as the page author.

➤ Click the top of the page to position the insertion point at the beginning of the page.
➤ Click the *Comment* button to add a comment at the insertion point location, as shown in Figure 8.51.
➤ In the Comment dialog box, type: This page was created by: *Your Name*, as shown in Figure 8.51.
➤ Click the *OK* button to insert the comment into your code.

You may see a dialog box explaining that your comment will not be visible unless visual aids options are selected. If this dialog box appears, click the *OK* button to continue.

➤ Click the *Code* view button to see the code. You should see your comment in the code after the <body> tag.

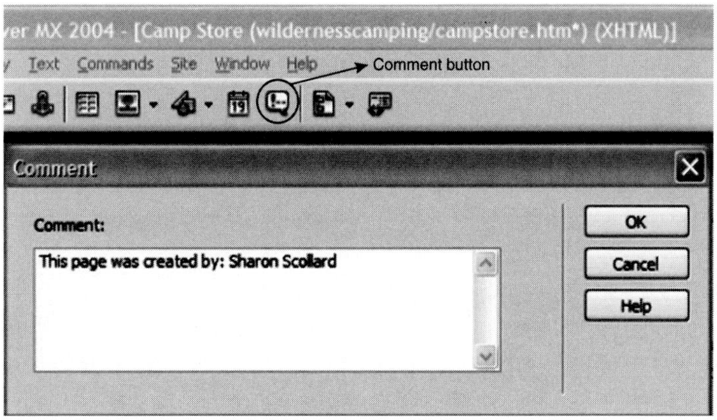

Figure 8.51   Comment dialog box in Dreamweaver MX 2004.

➤   Click the *Design* view button to return to Design view.

Finally, let's add the style sheet to this Web page and view the results.

➤   In the Design panel, click the *Attach Style Sheet* button, as shown in Figure 8.52.

The Attach External Style Sheet dialog box will appear, as shown in Figure 8.52.

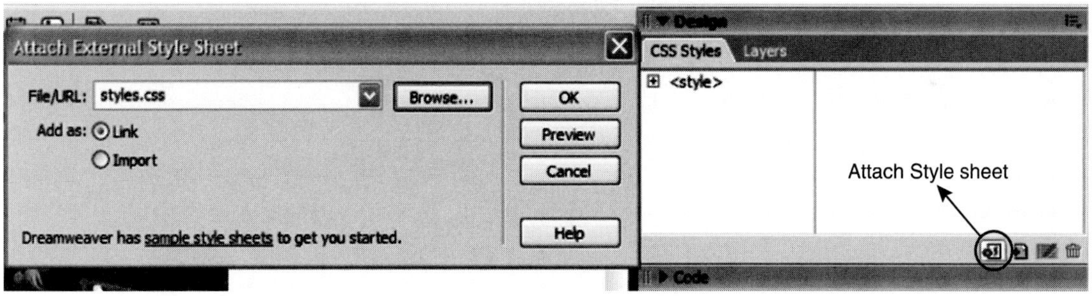

Figure 8.52   Add the style sheet in the Design panel in Dreamweaver MX 2004.

➤   In the Attach External Style Sheet dialog box, click the *Browse* button.

➤   Select the file *styles.css* from the *wildernesscamping* folder.

➤   Click the *OK* button to select the file.

➤   Click the *OK* button again to attach the style sheet.

Let's view the Web page in the browser to see how it looks!

➤   Click the menu commands *File, Preview in browser, iexplore*. Again, if you do not have a browser listed in the preview list, open a Web browser and open the *campstore.htm* file.

➤ Feel free to click the *Code* view button and have a peek at the code generated by Dreamweaver.

The completed file should look something like Figure 8.53.

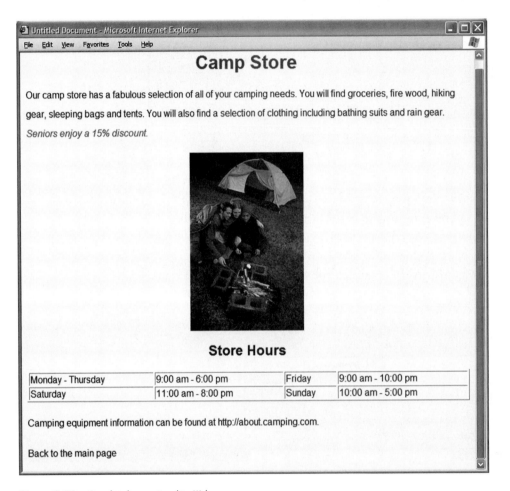

Figure 8.53   Completed *campstore.htm* Web page.

Microsoft FrontPage

FrontPage and Dreamweaver have similar features for larger Web site design. They will allow the designer to define a Web site, and will map out the hyperlinks, allowing the designer to add and remove links from the site map. Figure 8.54 shows a screenshot of FrontPage 2002 with the *campingplain.htm* file displayed.

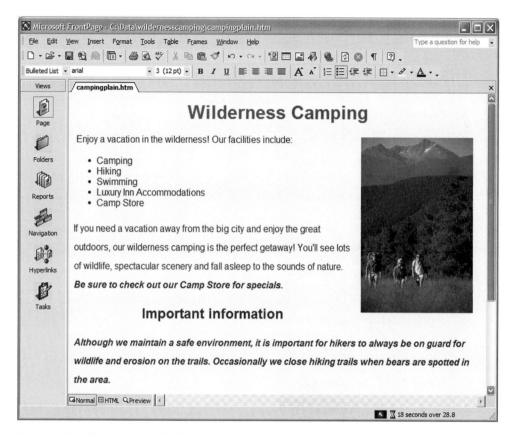

Figure 8.54 The *campingplain.htm* file in Microsoft FrontPage 2002.

As you can see, many of the editing tool buttons are familiar and common to the Microsoft Office products. The environment, as a WYSIWYG editor, is similar to Dreamweaver and CoffeeCup HTML Editor with tabs for preview, editing, and code views.

FrontPage and Dreamweaver include a site-mapping feature, indicating the links in a site using a hierarchical map. A portion of the site map for the *campingplain.htm* file as the top page of our site is shown in Figure 8.55.

These Web development applications also have site management tools and other advanced features so you can FTP your pages, synchronize the files on the Web server with the files you have saved locally, create templates, and save a collection of parts of Web pages in a library for use in other sites.

If you are going to be designing a large site, or a number of smaller sites, a product such as Dreamweaver or FrontPage would be suitable.

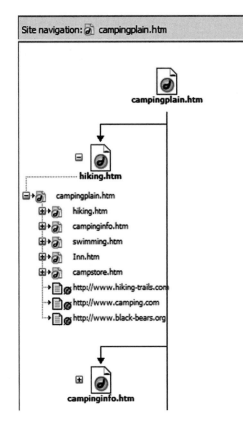

Figure 8.55   A portion of the site map for *campingplain.htm* in Dreamweaver MX 2004.

SUMMARY

Now that you've read through the chapter, you are prepared to:

- Use a text editor to build a Web page.
- Employ a programming text editor, like CoffeeCup HTML Editor to:
  - Add a hyperlink to your Web page.
  - Introduce basic formatting tags into your Web page.
  - Insert an image into your Web page.
  - Use tables as a guide for information and images.
  - Add a remote hyperlink.
- Employ a WYSIWYG HTML editor to build Web pages.
- Employ Netscape Composer for:
  - Basic page formatting.
  - Using tables as frames for layout.
  - Aligning tables and cells.
  - Adding hyperlinks.
- Employ Macromedia Dreamweaver for:
  - Basic page formatting.
  - Adding an image.
  - Adding a table.
  - Creating remote and local hyperlinks in Dreamweaver.
- Understand the difference between a text editor, a programming editor, and a WYSIWYG editor, and choose a suitable tool for your Web site design.

Review Questions and Hands-on Exercises

Review Questions

1. What is meant by the term *WYSIWYG*?

2. What's the difference between a text editor and a WYSIWYG editor?

3. What types of features can be found in a programming text editor?

4. Describe several advantages of using a WYSIWYG editor over a simple text editor.

5. What is the purpose for using a table in Web design? Use an example in your explanation.

6. If you needed to create one or two small Web pages, which Web page design tool would you use and why?

7. What sorts of advanced features are available in FrontPage and Dreamweaver that are generally not available in a programming text editor?

Hands-on Exercises

1.   Use CoffeeCup HTML Editor, or another programming text editor of your choice to create the following Web page, as shown in Figure 8.56.

   a. The title *Hiking Safety* uses *Heading 1* formatting, color #800080.

   b. The sentence *Hiking is a wonderful form of exercise!* is formatted italic.

   c. The second paragraph is colored red.

   d. The sentence *Here are some useful hiking safety links:* is underlined.

   e. Find a Web page for *First Aid,* and another for *Hiking Trails* and use the URLs to create remote links.

   f. The links and image are centered horizontally on the page.

   g. The image is *hikers.jpg.*

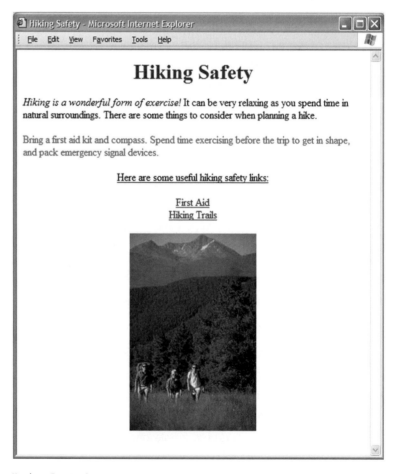

Figure 8.56   Hands-on Exercise 1.

2. Use Dreamweaver or FrontPage to create the following Web page, as shown in Figure 8.57.

    a. The title *Park Animals* is formatted as *Heading 1*, color CC6600.

    b. The sentence *Please do not feed the animals!* is formatted as bold and italic, colored red.

    c. The list and image are in a table that is 1 row and 2 columns.

    d. The list title *Animals in the park:* is formatted as *Heading 2.*

    e. The table is 100% width, border 1 pixel.

    f. The image is *waterfallsbeach.jpg.*

    g. The title *Useful Links* is formatted as *Heading 2.*

    h. For the unordered list of links, find a Web page for *Wildlife conservation* and another for *Moose* and use the URLs to create remote links.

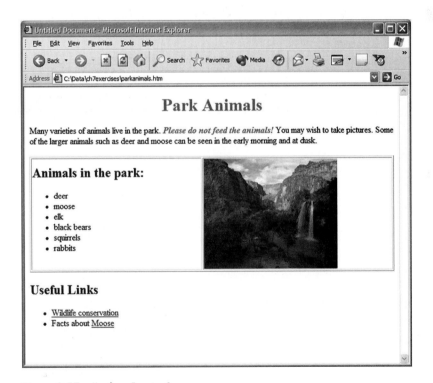

Figure 8.57 Hands-on Exercise 2.

3. Use any tool of your choice to create a Web site for your favorite hobby. This page must include the following features:

   a. At least one image, centered horizontally on the page.

   b. At least two headings, using any heading style.

   c. At least two paragraphs.

   d. An unordered list.

   e. At least two remote links.

   f. A table containing at least two cells.

4. Use any method you have learned to add a hyperlink on the *campingplain.htm* page, in the list of facilities, to the *campstore.htm* page.

Graphics and Multimedia on the World Wide Web

chapter

9

Chapter Objectives

This chapter helps you understand

☐ some basic design principles: contrast, repetition, alignment, and proximity.

☐ the most appropriate image file types for the Web.

☐ how to create rollover images using Macromedia Fireworks.

☐ the advantages of using a transparent image.

☐ several techniques for working with larger images.

☐ how to design animated images.

☐ the different types of audio and video you can employ in a Web page.

☐ what Webcasts are, and how to successfully run one.

☐ Web page usability and accessibility guidelines.

Now that you are familiar with the basic and advanced features of HTML, and are able to use an HTML editor, we need to examine the role that graphics and multimedia play in designing Web pages. One of the things you learned at the close of Chapter 8 was that graphics and multimedia can be included in a Web page. Indeed, the graphics and multimedia bring a site to life.

There's an old adage in the publishing community: "content is king and design is queen." It's important to look at some design principles, and get a glimpse of learning to effectively use visual media in Web design.

Basic Design Principles: CRAP

Becoming a skilled Web designer will take some time. Let's begin with an understanding of some of the basic principles of design. Robin Williams, a highly respected designer, the author of several graphic design textbooks, emphasizes four key principles: contrast, repetition, alignment, and proximity (Williams and Tollett, 1998).

Contrast

Contrast, at the most basic level, is the difference between graphic elements on a page. The primary purpose for contrast is to emphasize some elements and de-emphasize others. High contrast will create focal points that attract attention. So the key thing to remember with contrast is that if you want to make it different, make the contrast noticeable. Black contrasts with white, for example.

Repetition

When it comes to graphic design, repetition is used to pull a Web site together so that individual pages are clearly connected to one another. This means that every page on a Web site ought to share elements with other pages: the same colors, graphic images, fonts, and so forth. Many times, when new designers begin creating pages, their first impulse is to use a variety of fonts, colors, graphics, animation, and type styles. But instead of being visually stimulating (which is the intention of novice designers), these pages end up being visually frustrating. Instead of using multiple elements, you should repeat just a few to keep your page from becoming cluttered and over-designed.

Alignment

Alignment is how the text is lined up on the page. Text can be lined up on the left, the right, or down the center of the page. The best advice for alignment is to choose one and stick with it throughout the page. Most beginning Web designers center the title of their page, left-align most other things, and sometimes right-align special content. Although it might be fun to play with alignment, the fact is that many alignments on a page make it look messy. If everything is lined up the same way on the page, it creates an imaginary, but very strong, edge.

Centered alignment on a page is very balanced, calm, and formal, and it is appropriate when that look is your intent. It works well for opening splash screens and home pages. But left or right alignment, when it is done consistently on the whole page, unifies the content and makes it easier to read. Content in tables that is consistently aligned to the left margin makes it possible to remove the borders of the table, because the constant edge of the content creates its own invisible line. You also need to keep vertical alignment in mind. Tables allow you to align the content at the top, middle, or bottom of the cell. Aligning it at the top ensures that the **baselines** (the lines that text "sits" on) of the text are lined up. Using middle alignment means that text that spans two lines does not align with single lines of text.

Proximity

Proximity is the distance between two objects. The more closely related your content is, the closer together it should be. Placing content in close proximity on the page implies a connection, while putting space between items disconnects them from one another. When you glance at a Web page, the visual layout ought to group elements together.

Image File Types

Images or Graphics?

Technically a digital picture is a file, and people will tend to use the term *image* to refer to the picture file, and *graphics* to describe the format, broad category, or capability of displaying images. For example "in order to display the image, the software must support graphics." Some people use the terms *image* and *graphics* interchangeably to describe a picture file. The term *graphics* is often used to describe the image format. For example, "the image is stored using the GIF graphics format." And it is also used to describe the field of manipulating images, for example "a *graphics* technique used in Web design." Don't spend any time worrying about which term to use if you're talking about a picture file—for most people, the terminology is fairly loose.

Raster and Vector Graphics

There are two methods of storing digital images: using **raster graphics** or **vector graphics**. In the case of vector graphics, or geometric modeling, the image is described in terms of lines, curves, and shapes. For instance, a circle is described using a point and a radius. These types of images are scalable, meaning that with each of the elements described mathematically, it's easy to make the image larger or smaller, and not lose any detail. These types of graphics formats are used in 3D modeling applications, designing logos, and other graphics requiring scalability, and not used on the Web, *per se.*

Raster graphics are used extensively on the Web. In the case of raster graphics, the image is divided into tiny dots called **pixels**. Each pixel contains one color, and the picture is mapped out as a grid of pixels represented by bits defining the color, hence these images are called *bitmap images*. If you were to look closely at your television or a picture in a newspaper you would see the individual pixels. The color is represented by some number of bits. If the color were represented by only 1 bit, there would be only 2 colors available, black and white. More bits per pixel means there will be more colors available equal to 2^{bits}. For instance 4 bits allows $2^4 = 16$ colors, 8 bits allows $2^8 = 256$ colors, 16 bits allows $2^{16} = 65,536$ colors and 24 bits allows $2^{24} = 16,777,216$ colors. While the highest possible number of colors will produce the best picture, it also produces the largest picture in terms of storage; easily a megabyte per picture or more. One of our biggest considerations when creating Web pages is optimization, such that all file sizes are as small as possible so they download quickly. So the trade-off quickly becomes quality versus size.

One solution to this problem is a combination of compression and reduced color choices. Let's look at some of the most common graphics formats.

Graphics Formats

.bmp—BMP files, the original *bitmap* files, were created for use in the Windows operating system, and are a commonly used bitmapped format in graphic design. However, they are grossly inefficient for Web use because they are so large and cannot be adequately compressed for quick viewing.

⊹ tip

∴ When you come across a Web page you really like, notice how the principles of Contrast, Repetition, Alignment, and Proximity have been used. The professional looking Web sites will choose a theme and use it throughout the site.

.gif—The Graphics Interchange Format, or GIF (pronounced with either a hard or soft "g," depending on who you ask). GIF images use **lossless compression**, which means that the file size is reduced without reducing the quality of the picture. Essentially, when a GIF file is created, it scans the picture line by line, and turns a long block of one color into two numbers: one that tells what color the block is, and another that tells how long the block is. GIF images are bitmapped images, made up of many pixels that combine like a mosaic to form the picture. GIF images use a maximum of 8 bits per pixel to store the color information, thus 8 bits allows 2^8 = 256 colors. Because they are limited to 256 colors, and because of the method of compression, GIF images are best used for line drawings, bullets, icons, lines, and other images made up primarily of large blocks of color.

Two additions to the GIF format have made them even more popular on Web pages: animation and transparency. **Animated GIFs** are created using a series of GIF images. The images cycle from one to the next using a timer and the animated image is a single GIF file.

GIF images are always rectangular or square; however, **transparency** gives the graphic artist the ability to use a transparent background and simulate any imaginable shape. The transparent areas allow the background of the Web page to "show through."

.jpeg, .jpg—The Joint Photographic Experts Group, or JPEG (pronounced "jay-peg"), is also an efficient file format used in Web graphics. Like GIF images, JPEGs are bitmapped images, but JPEGs use 24 bits per pixel. Because of this, JPEGs can include more than 16 million colors (2^{24} = 16,777,216). To reduce the size of the graphic files, JPEG's use a **lossy** compression scheme. In lossy compression, some of the information in the image is lost, which reduces the quality of the image slightly. However, given the amount of data in a picture, the files can be greatly reduced in size without a noticeable loss in quality. Since JPEGs support 24-bit color, this format is often used for photographs, textures, smooth gradients, and other complex images.

.png—The PNG format (Portable Network Graphics) was developed as a possible replacement for the GIF format when Unisys, holder of the patent for the compression algorithm used in GIF files, announced in 1995 that it would begin to enforce the patents it held, and charge royalties to developers of GIF-supporting software. In 1996, the World Wide Web Consortium adopted the PNG format as a recommended image format. The PNG format is a bitmapped format supported by most Web browsers. It supports 48-bit color (2^{48} = 281,474,976,710,656) using a lossless compression, so no color data is lost. It supports full transparency and even partial transparency; many browsers do not render the partial transparency effect. PNG does not support animation. The PNG format is not widely used, as most of the patents for the GIF compression have since expired, and GIF image files are still widely used.

.tiff—The Tagged Image File Format (TIFF) is a de facto standard format used for scanning and used by graphic artists in image editing software packages such as Adobe Photoshop and Macromedia Fireworks. Typically a graphic artist will use an image-editing package, design the image, save it as a TIFF file for later editing, and export the image as a GIF or JPG for use in a Web page.

Let's use Microsoft Paint or your favorite image-editing tool to create an image and save it using different file types to see the difference in file size.

➤ Open Microsoft Paint. You may find it in *Start, All Programs, Accessories.* You can use your favorite image-editing tool for this exercise as well.

∴ If the Web browser does not support a file type that has been used for a Web page, it will display an image placeholder. If there is an alt attribute, the Web browser will display the alt value with the placeholder.

➤ Use the drawing tools to draw some random lines and shapes as shown in Figure 9.1. Drawing skills are not necessary. We simply want to save an image.

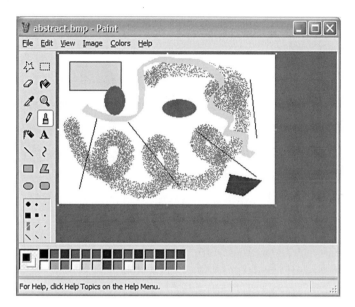

Figure 9.1   Simple abstract drawing in Microsoft Paint.

➤ Select the *File, Save As* menu commands, and select the file type *24-Bit bitmap* in the *Save As* drop-down menu.

➤ Choose an appropriate folder and use the file name *abstract*.

➤ Click the *OK* button to save the file.

Now let's save the same image as a JPG and as a GIF file.

➤ Select the *File, Save As* menu commands and select the file type *JPEG* and click the *OK* button to save the file.

➤ Select the *File, Save As* menu commands and select the file type *GIF*. If a dialog box appears warning you that there may be loss of color with this file type, click the *Yes* button to save the file.

➤ Close Paint, or your image-editing tool, after you have finished saving the files.

➤ Use *File Explorer* to view the folder containing the files on your hard drive.

You should notice a big difference in the file sizes between the .bmp and the .gif and .jpg files. As shown in Figure 9.2, the *abstract.bmp* file is 212 KB, and the .gif and .jpg files are 25 KB. You may notice that the .gif file has some color loss when you look at the file again.

Name ▲	Size	Type
abstract.bmp	212 KB	Bitmap Image
abstract.GIF	25 KB	GIF Image
abstract.JPG	25 KB	JPEG Image

Figure 9.2 File size comparison of .bmp, .gif, and .jpg.

Creating Rollover Images Using Macromedia Fireworks

Macromedia Fireworks is a robust image-editing and creation tool. It can create and edit bitmapped and vector graphics, and has optimization features for creating graphics for the Web. If you have an artistic flair, you may enjoy spending some time learning to use this tool. You will find a large selection of tutorials and tips at the Macromedia Web site (http://www.macromedia.com).

Creating Buttons

As a demonstration of creating images, let's create some simple buttons using Macromedia Fireworks. Although Fireworks provides other tools for creating buttons, we will create ours manually so that we can have a brief overview of creating an image. We will be able to use these buttons for a rollover effect, and learn a few basic things about image editing as well.

➤ Open a Web browser and open the Macromedia site at http://www.macromedia.com

➤ Download and install the current version of Macromedia Fireworks, 30-day trial version.

➤ Open Macromedia Fireworks.

➤ If a dialog box appears prompting you to purchase or try, select the try for 30 days option, and click the *OK* button.

➤ When Fireworks opens, click the option for *Create new Fireworks file*.

We'll create a *Home* button for the *Wilderness Camping* site pages. The button will be 80 pixels wide and 26 pixels tall.

➤ In the New Document dialog box, type the width as 80 and the height as 26 as shown in Figure 9.3.

➤ Click the *OK* button to create the new document.

The Fireworks window will open, as shown in Figure 9.4. As you can see, the Fireworks window is very similar to the Dreamweaver window, with the document window in the center of the application, the Property Inspector below, and the panels on the right. The left pane contains drawing and editing tools. The canvas is inside of the document window, and this is the area where we can draw and edit an image. We set the canvas size to be rather small because we are designing a button.

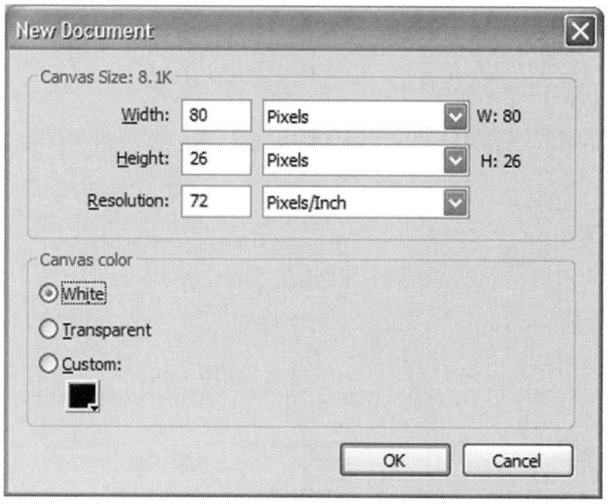

Figure 9.3 New Document dialog box in Fireworks MX 2004.

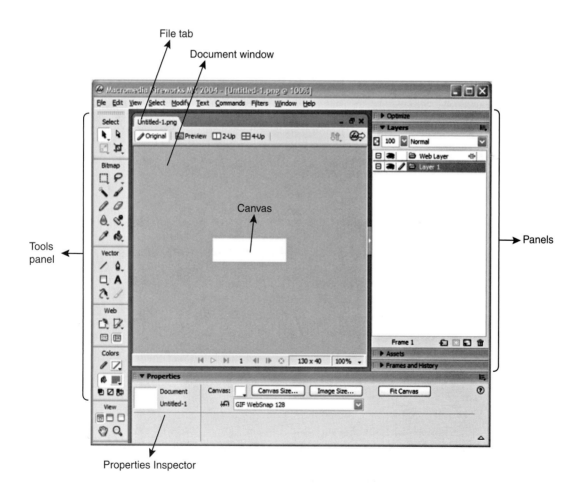

Figure 9.4 The Fireworks MX 2004 window.

Our button will be very simple, consisting of a background color and some text. We will create two versions of our button, changing only the text color, so that the buttons can be swapped for a rollover effect.

We will choose a canvas color, and then add text to the image. The text will simply be the word *Home*. We will be saving two versions of this image; one with the text colored light yellow, and one with the text colored brown.

➤ Click the menu commands *Modify, Canvas, Canvas color*.
➤ Click the color swatch for the *Custom* color, and choose one of the green colors, as shown in Figure 9.5.

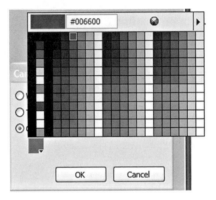

Figure 9.5   Choosing a canvas color in Fireworks MX 2004.

➤ Click the *OK* button.

The background color of the canvas should now be green.
Let's add some text to this button.

➤ Click the *Text Tool* button.
➤ Click in the middle of the canvas.

A blue outline will appear on the canvas as shown in Figure 9.6.

➤ Drag the corners of the blue outline so that it outlines the whole canvas as shown in Figure 9.6. This will allow us to center the text easily.
➤ You should see a flashing insertion point appear as well. Type the word: Home
➤ Drag to highlight the word *Home* and select the text size to be 16 point, as shown in Figure 9.6.
➤ Click the *Text Color* button and select the color #FFFFCC (very light yellow), as shown in Figure 9.6.
➤ Click the *Center Text* button to center the word in the text area, as shown in Figure 9.6.

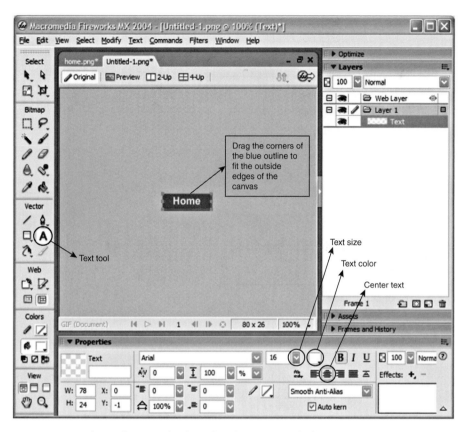

Figure 9.6   Selecting the *Text* tool and stretching the text area to fit the canvas.

We've created the image for the button, so let's save the file.

➤ Click the *File, Save* menu command.

➤ Use the *Save in* drop-down box and find the *images* folder in the *wilderness-camping* folder. Save the file as *home.png* and click the *Save* button to save the file.

Fireworks saves files in the .png format for editing later, but we would like to save this file as a .gif file to use in a Web page. To save this file as a .gif file, we will use the export feature. Fireworks has an Export Wizard feature, which will display the image using GIF and JPG formats so that you can compare and choose the format you prefer. Since our little image is not detailed and uses very few colors, we will save it as a GIF, although the JPG format would be fine as well.

➤ Click the *File, Export* menu command.

➤ Use the *Save in* drop-down to find the *images* folder in the *wildernesscamping* folder.

➤ Save this file as *homeyellow.gif*.

Now let's use the same *home.png* file to create a button image with brown instead of yellow letters.

➤ Drag to highlight the word *Home*.

➤ Click the *Text Color* box and choose the color #663300. This color will match the text in our Wilderness Camping site.

➤ Click the *File, Export* menu command.

➤ Use the *Save in* drop-down to find the *images* folder in the *wildernesscamping* folder.

➤ Save this file as *homebrown.gif*.

➤ Click the *File, Save* command to save this file as *home.png*.

Adding Rollover Images Using Dreamweaver

Now we have two images, each with different colored text. We will use these images in our Wilderness Camping site as rollover images.

➤ Open Macromedia Dreamweaver.

➤ Open the *campinginfo.htm* page.

We will add a rollover button to the bottom of the page, and this rollover button will link back to the *campingplain.htm* page.

➤ Highlight the words *Back to the main page*, and press the *Delete* key.

➤ Click the menu commands *Insert, Image Object, Rollover Image*.

We will now specify *homeyellow.gif* as the original image and *homebrown.gif* as the rollover image. We will link back to the main page.

➤ Click the *Browse* button for the Original image, and find the file *homeyellow.gif*. Select this file and click the *OK* button to select it, as shown in Figure 9.7.

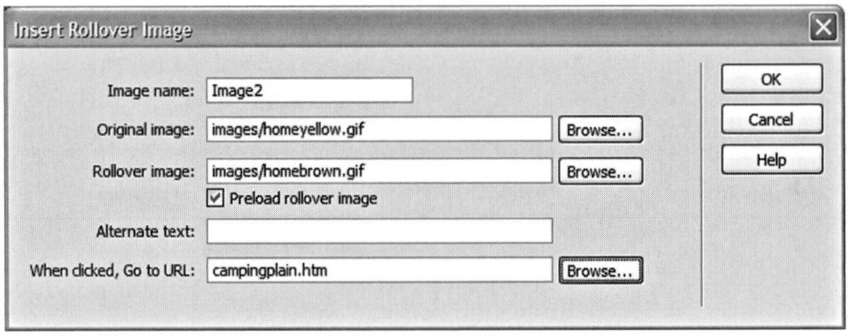

Figure 9.7   Insert Rollover Image dialog box in Dreamweaver MX 2004.

➤ Click the *Browse* button for the Rollover image and find the file *homebrown.gif*. Select this file and click the *OK* button to select it, as shown in Figure 9.7.

➤ Click the *Browse* button for the *When clicked, Go to URL* box and find the file *campingplain.htm*. Select this file and click the *OK* button to select it, as shown in Figure 9.7.

➤ Click the *OK* button in the Insert Rollover Image dialog box to complete the rollover image.

➤ Use the *File, Save* menu command to save the *campingplain.htm* file.

You will not be able to see the effect of rollover images within Dreamweaver. You will have to view the page in a Web browser.

➤ Open a Web browser and open the *campinginfo.htm* page.

➤ Position the mouse pointer over the *Home* button.

You should see the image rollover to display the brown letter image. When you move your mouse pointer away from the image, it should rollover back to the yellow letter image. Dreamweaver generates JavaScript code to create this rollover effect.

You can edit this button to change the word, and use the same technique to create two buttons with different colored text. You can add them to the Web page, side by side, or one below the other, and create a navigation bar using this method.

Creating a Transparent Image

In addition to creating buttons, Fireworks is a powerful image-editing tool. Let's get a small taste of it by creating a logo for the Wilderness Camping site. Let's create a transparent image, so that the background color shows through. We'll clip parts of other images to create our logo as well.

➤ Use the *File, Open* command and open the *3campers.jpg* file.

➤ Use the *File, Open* command and open the *waterfallsbeach.jpg* file.

➤ Use the *File, New* command and specify the new canvas as 200 pixels wide, 200 pixels high, and click the *Transparent* radio button to specify a transparent canvas.

➤ Click the *OK* button to create the new canvas.

The transparent background is represented by the checkerboard pattern. We will select the waterfalls from the *waterfallsbeach.jpg* file and the tent from the *3campers.jpg* file, and we'll add some text to create a logo. We will need to use the *Marquee* tool, the *Lasso* tool, and the *Pointer* tool, as shown in Figure 9.8.

We will use the *Marquee* and *Lasso* tools to define the areas of the images we wish to copy. We will use the *Pointer* tool to move selected images.

≈ *tip*

∴ When creating a rollover image, use the preload rollover image feature in Dreamweaver. Without the preload rollover image feature, the user will hover over an image, and there will be a pause while the Web browser requests the image from the Web server and it loads.

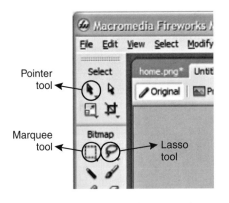

Figure 9.8   *Pointer, Marquee,* and *Lasso* tools in Fireworks MX 2004.

Copying Part of an Image

➤ Click the *waterfallsbeach.jpg* tab to select this picture.

➤ Click the *Marquee* tool to select it. We will select the waterfalls.

➤ Drag the mouse pointer, starting from a location above and to the left of the waterfalls, and drag diagonally down and to the right, so that the dotted marquee draws a rectangle containing the waterfalls, as shown in Figure 9.9.

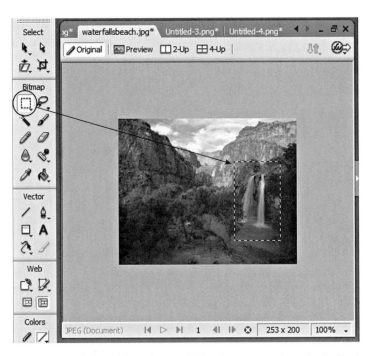

Figure 9.9   Marquee around the waterfalls in the *waterfallsbeach.jpg* image in Fireworks MX 2004.

If you are using the *Lasso* or *Marquee* tool and make a mistake drawing, you can press the *Esc* key to remove the lasso or marquee, and try again.

➤ Position the pointer inside the dotted rectangle, and right-click to reveal the shortcut menu.

➤ Select the menu items *Edit, Copy* from the shortcut menu.

➤ Click the tab containing the new untitled file to activate it.

➤ Position the mouse pointer on the canvas and right-click to reveal the shortcut menu.

➤ Select the menu items *Copy, Paste*. The image should appear off to the right-hand side of the canvas.

➤ Click the *Pointer* tool and move the mouse pointer on top of the waterfalls image. Drag the waterfalls image to the top left corner of the canvas, as shown in Figure 9.10.

Figure 9.10 Waterfalls in the new transparent image in Fireworks MX 2004.

The *Marquee* tool allows us to define an area that is a rectangle shape. If we wish to draw around an odd shape, we can use the *Lasso* tool. Let's demonstrate this by creating a copy of the tent in the *3campers.jpg* file.

➤ Click the tab for the *3campers.jpg* file to activate it.

➤ Click the *Lasso* tool.

➤ Position the mouse pointer somewhere on the edge of the tent and drag while you outline the tent, as shown in Figure 9.11. Again, if you are using the *Lasso* or *Marquee* tool and make a mistake drawing, then you can press the *Esc* key to remove the lasso or marquee, and try again. You don't have to do this perfectly. It's not as easy as it looks!

➤ Once you have the lasso outline around the tent, right-click to reveal the short-cut menu.

Figure 9.11 Lasso around the tent in the *3campers.jpg* image in Fireworks MX 2004.

➢ Select the menu commands *Edit, Copy* from the shortcut menu.

➢ Click the tab containing the new untitled file to activate it.

➢ Position the mouse pointer on the canvas and right-click to reveal the shortcut menu.

➢ Select the menu items *Copy, Paste*. The image should appear off to the right-hand side of the canvas.

➢ Click the *Pointer* tool and move the mouse pointer on top of the tent image. Drag the tent to the top right corner of the canvas, as shown in Figure 9.12.

Figure 9.12 Waterfalls and tent in the new untitled image in Fireworks MX 2004.

Let's add some text to our image.

 Click the *Text* tool and click in the middle of the canvas, below the waterfalls and tent images.

 The selections for dark green color, 16 point, and center from our previous text drawing should be active in the Properties Inspector. If these properties are not selected, select them.

 Type: `Wilderness Camping`

 Click the *Pointer* tool to move the text under the tent and waterfalls if necessary, as shown in Figure 9.13.

Figure 9.13 Wilderness Camping text under the tent and waterfalls images in Fireworks MX 2004.

You can see that the canvas is a bit large. We can easily trim it to fit the items it contains.

 Click the menu command *Modify, Canvas, Fit Canvas*. You should notice that the canvas has shrunk to accommodate the items it contains, as shown in Figure 9.14.

Figure 9.14 Canvas trimmed in Fireworks MX 2004.

➤ Click the menu commands *File, Save* and save this file as *wildernesslogo.png* in the *images* folder.

➤ Click the menu commands *File, Export* and save this file as *wildernesslogo.gif* in the *images* folder.

Let's use this image in the *campinginfo.htm* file.

➤ Activate Dreamweaver, and the *campinginfo.htm* page.

➤ Drag through the heading *Wilderness Camping* and delete it.

➤ Click the menu commands *Insert Image* and insert the new *wildernesslogo.gif* image.

The page should look something like Figure 9.15.

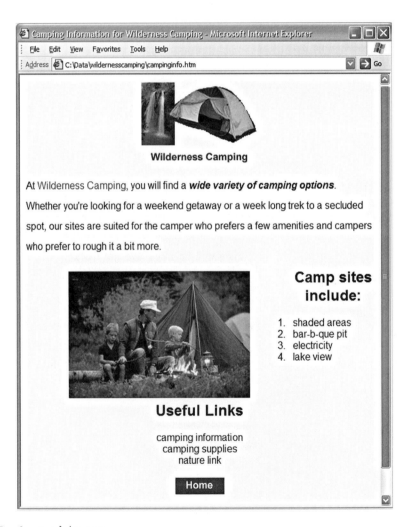

Figure 9.15 *Campinginfo.htm page.*

Notice that the effect of the transparent image is that the background of the Web page shows through.

Fireworks and other image-editing applications have features that include rotating and cropping images, drawing shapes, layering, blurring, creating gradients, and many other features.

Techniques for Working with Larger Images

Sometimes you need to display a larger image on your Web page, whether it's a logo or a picture with a lot of detail. Essentially, users will not wait for large images to download, so you need your page to load as quickly as possible. There are two techniques that can be used to achive this: **interlaced images** and **sliced images**.

Interlaced Images

When the Web browser renders the `<img>` tag, it requests the image from the Web server, and does not display the image until the entire image has been downloaded from the server. The GIF format supports interlaced images, a method used to display the image in multiple passes. The image is saved as an interlaced image in the image-editing package. When the Web browser downloads an interlaced image, the image is displayed progressively. At first, the image appears fuzzy, but with each pass the image becomes clearer. The trade-off is that the image size is slightly larger when the image is interlaced, however since it begins to appear as the page is loading, the user is much more inclined to wait.

Sliced Images

Another method that works quite well for dealing with larger images is to slice them, or cut them up into smaller images. Rather than downloading one large image, the Web browser will download several smaller images, and the image will appear in pieces like a jigsaw puzzle. Another advantage to slicing larger images is that a slice can also be used as individual JavaScript rollovers, or defined as an HTML text area. An image-editing application such as Fireworks will allow the designer to specify slicing guides, so that an image can be sliced into several smaller images. When Fireworks exports a sliced image, it generates the HTML table and individual slices. This can be imported into Dreamweaver, or copied manually into another Web page. Figure 9.16 shows the slicing guides applied to the *waterfallsbeach.jpg* image, which would slice the image into three images.

Animation

Animation is pervasive in Web design and is used for banner ads, eye-catching Web site introductions, product demonstrations, and entertainment. Animation is not the same as video, which will be discussed shortly.

There are a variety of methods used to create and add animation to a Web page, including animated GIF images, JavaScript, Java Applets, and Macromedia animation products: Flash and Shockwave.

tip

∴ Some Web page designers will design an entire Web page using an image-editing package. They will slice the image and include slices for text.

Figure 9.16   *Waterfallsbeach.jpg* slice guides in Fireworks MX 2004.

Animated GIFs

The GIF image file format supports animation. An image design tool is used to create several GIF images, and combine them with a timer element, into one GIF file. You will see examples of this in many Web pages as pictures of a smiley face smiling, an envelope opening and closing, a cute animal hopping, and so forth. You will find a large variety of animated GIFs at Gifworks (`http://www.gifworks.com`) and many other sites. Animated GIFs can be treated like any other image when using the `<img>` tag in that you specify the name of the single animated GIF file as the `src` value in the `<img>` tag as usual. If you'd like to try your hand at creating your own animated text, load the 3D Textmaker Web page at `http://www.3dtextmaker.com`.

JavaScript Animation

Another method used to animate images is JavaScript. In fact, we have already seen an example of this in the rollover button effect we created using Dreamweaver earlier in this chapter. The images swap because JavaScript code senses the mouse movement and swaps the images as the mouse moves over and away from the image. JavaScript can be used to swap images after a specified time to create a banner effect, and even to move images around the Web browser document window. This method is still widely used, but it's not as common as animated GIFs or Flash.

Java Applets

As mentioned in Chapter 7, Java Applets can be used to add interactivity to a Web page. Java Applets can also be used to create a simple animation, a banner, or animated logo. In order to run a Java Applet, the Java plug-in must be installed. If the purpose of a Java Applet is simple animation, it may be better achieved by using an animated GIF, as the user is not required to run a separate plug-in.

Flash and Shockwave Animation

Macromedia's Flash animation is tremendously popular for creating interactive animation in Web design. Shockwave animation is the older brother of Flash, and although it's no longer widely used, you will still find it from time to time. The user must have the Flash or Shockwave plug-in installed in order to view the animation, however, Flash plug-ins are generally preinstalled with current Web browsers.

Shockwave animation files are created using Macromedia Director; it's an older technology which was used to create highly interactive presentations on CDs. As such, Shockwave animation had features that were not supported by Web browsers. When the Web became popular, Shockwave animation authoring was modified for use on the Web and required a plug-in. Later, Macromedia developed Flash specifically for creating interactive animation for use on the Web.

Flash animations have gone well beyond simple animation, and even user-interactive games and applications. Flash animations can be designed to pull information from a database on a server, and can be used to build robust E-Commerce Web sites. These files require a lot of bandwidth as they tend to be large.

Audio and Video

Downloading

Whether the file is audio or video, it must be downloaded from the Web server to the user's computer, and played in order for the user to hear and/or see it. In most cases, the file will be downloaded entirely, and then begin to play. This can take quite a while if the file is large and the user's connection is slow. If your audio or video file is in one format and you'd like to convert it to another, there are file conversion programs that will facilitate this. Beware, though, that this is not always possible.

Streaming

Another option is streaming audio and video. In this case, the media file is sent as a steady stream of packets, and begins to play as soon as the first packets have been received. The rest of the packets play as they are received, hence the term **streaming media.** Some of the compressed media file formats are also suitable for streaming media. In order to use streaming media, the Web server must support the technology of serving the media stream, and a plug-in or **helper application**, such as RealPlayer, must be installed.

Audio

Audio is something you should use sparingly on your Web site, if at all. Some audio files can be quite large, thus increasing the download time. There are a variety of different audio file types used on the Web. In order to play audio, the Web browser will either require a separate plug-in or a helper application. A helper application may be Windows Media Player, Winamp, or some other application that can read a particular file type.

tip

∴ When downloading and saving an audio file, beware of copyright violation. You can listen to the audio file, but do not post it on your own Web page or otherwise publicly share it.

Here are some of the more common audio file types, some information about them, and the plug-in or helper application required to play them.

WAV (WAVEform): The WAVEform audio format is an uncompressed file format developed for audio files for the PC. You can record WAV files from a CD or microphone using your PC, and the sound quality tends to be very good, but because it is an uncompressed format, the file sizes tend to be quite large for small bites of sound.

AIF or AIFF (Audio Interchange File Format): The AIF file format provides a good sound quality and can be played in most Web browsers without a plug-in. However, like WAV files, the file sizes can be quite large.

MID or MIDI (Musical Instrument Digital Interface): The MIDI format is designed for instrumental music, and must be created using a synthesizer on a computer, an electronic keyboard, or some similar device. The sound quality can be very good, but this is dependent on the sound card on the user's computer. It is an efficient file format, and long sound clips can be stored in relatively small files.

MP3 (Motion Picture Experts Group Audio Layer 3 or MPEG Audio-Layer 3): The MP3 file format is a compressed format with a very good sound quality. Depending on the compression selections chosen, the MP3 file can rival CD quality, yet the file size can be as little as 10% of the equivalent WAV file. MP3 files require a helper application or plug-in to play, such as Windows Media Player, Winamp, QuickTime, or Realplayer. MP3 files can be downloaded or streamed.

RA, RPM, or RAM (RealAudio format): RealAudio files have a higher degree of compression than the MP3 files, and can be either downloaded whole or streamed from a Web server. The sound quality is a poorer quality than MP3 files, but this technology is constantly improving. In order to listen to RealAudio files, the RealPlayer helper application must be installed.

AU or SND (Sun or Java format): These file formats are similar to WAV and AIFF file formats. These file types are used for Java Applets.

Internet Radio

Internet radio began in the late 1990s and uses a streaming technology to simulcast radio transmissions. Internet radio stations transcend geography, as you can now listen to radio stations from all over the world. In addition, Internet radio stations can include images and other information on their broadcast Web pages. This allows the listener to have more of an interactive experience as the radio station Web sites can contain links to advertisers, documents referred to in radio shows, and video. Radio broadcast sites often include listener feedback forms, sometimes received by the broadcaster in real time. The cost of getting "on the air" is much less for Internet radio, and if the broadcast is strictly over the Internet, it has become possible for individuals to run their own radio stations. You will find radio stations from all over the world, using the Pandia Radio search engine (http://www.pandia.com/radio/).

tip

∵ If you wish to be up-to-date with local news in a far-away location, search for an Internet radio station in that location! You may be able to listen to news, local recording artists, or talk shows.

Video

Like audio, video should also be used sparingly on your Web site. Video files tend to be quite large because they combine audio with the video images. Whenever possible, provide a link for the user, with an indication of the file size, and then the user can initiate the download. Like audio, video files require a helper application or plug-in, typically Windows Media Player, QuickTime, or RealPlayer.

Here are some of the more common audio file types, some information about them, and the plug-in or helper application required to play them.

AVI (Audio/Video Interleave): This is the most common video file type for Windows computers. It can be played by a variety of different video applications including Windows Media Player.

ASF (Advanced Streaming Format), WMV (Windows Media Video), or WMA (Windows Media Audio): These Windows media files can also be viewed using Windows Media Player.

MOV (QuickTime): QuickTime files can be viewed using the QuickTime viewer or plug-in available from Apple Computing (`http://www.apple.com/quicktime`), and will play on both Windows and Apple operating systems. The QuickTime Pro version supports creating streaming QuickTime movies.

RM or RA (RealPlayer): These are streaming video files, which require RealPlayer in order to view them. They are generally not downloadable.

Adding Sound to a Web Page

Let's create a small Web page with a link to download a sound file, and also embed a sound in the page so that the user can play it in the browser. We'll start by creating a link to download a file.

➤ Create a folder on your hard drive called *testpages*.

➤ Inside the *testpages* folder, create a folder called *sounds*.

➤ Use the search feature on your computer to find a sound file. Choose a sound file that has the file extension .wav or .mid.

➤ Copy the sound file you have selected into the *testpages/sounds* folder.

➤ Open Notepad.

➤ Type the following, but use the name of your sound file instead of *sound1.wav*:

```
<html>
        <head>
           <title>music test</title>
        </head>
<body>

        Download a <a href="sounds/sound1.wav">sound file</a>

</body>
</html>
```

➤ Save this file as *sounds.htm* in the *testpages* folder.

Notice that there is nothing special about the `<a href>` tag. This is the same tag we have used previously for linking to a Web page. In this case, the link is pointing to a sound file. We could also use this method to point to a video file, or another type of document file.

➤ Open the *sounds.htm* file in a Web browser.

➤ Click the *sound file* link. A dialog box should appear prompting you to save the file. You can save the file if you wish.

Now, let's add a tag that will embed sound in the Web page. The tag we will use is the `<embed>` tag. This tag will embed a sound file or video file in the Web page so that when the file is opened, an instance of the media player software will appear in the browser window, including controls so the user will be able to play the file. The `<embed>` tag can be used to embed sound or video, and we can specify the dimensions of the player that is displayed. We need to specify the name and location of the sound or video file.

➤ Add the following to the *sounds.htm* file, again using the name of your sound file instead of *sound1.wav*:

```
Download a <a href="sounds/sound1.wav">sound file</a>

<br><br>

Play a sound<br>
<embed src="sounds/sound1.wav" autostart="false" width="144"
height="50" loop="1">

</body>
</html>
```

➤ Save the *sounds.htm* file and refresh in the Web browser window. The *sounds.htm* file should look something like Figure 9.17.

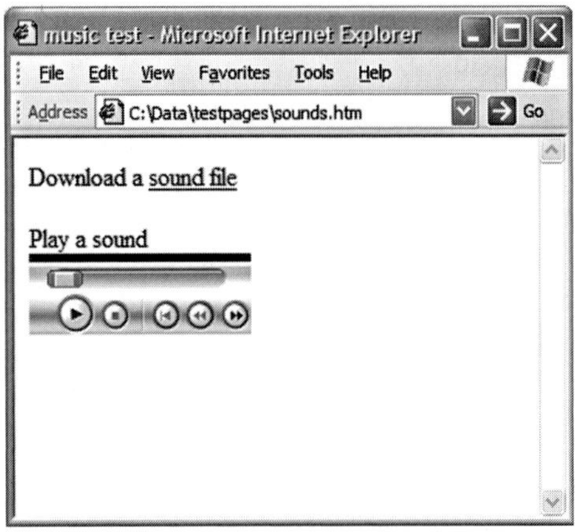

Figure 9.17   Sound embedded in a Web page in Internet Explorer.

The `<embed>` tag specifies autostart as false, which means that the sound file will not start playing until the user clicks the play button. If autostart were set as "true," the sound file would begin to play as soon as it had downloaded. The height and width are specified in pixels. When the loop attribute is set to 1 or true, the sound will loop until the user clicks the stop button. The loop attribute can be set to any number to loop through the sound the number of times specified.

➤ Feel free to click the *Play* button to play the sound file in the browser!

Webcasts

A Webcast is a stream of audio or video broadcast over the Internet. Typically it is a live broadcast, although it can also be a recording as well. Webcasts use a streaming technology, especially if the event is broadcast in real time. A Webcast could be a simple broadcast of an event, or it could also be an interactive online conference, where participants at various locations are also sending audio and video. A Webinar (Web Seminar) is another application of a Webcast, often requiring the audience to register and pay for the broadcast, and often allows for some interactive online communication with the audience.

If you wish to arrange for a Webcast of an event, there are many companies providing streaming media broadcast and Webinar services. A Webinar can be an important part of a business marketing plan.

How to Run a Successful Webinar

If you've decided that you'd like to run a Webinar to promote your company, product, or service, there are a few helpful tips to keep in mind.

1. Work with a reputable Webcasting company who will deal with the technical end of broadcasting. Some Webcasting companies will also deal with registration and other aspects of broadcasting as well.

2. Rather than creating an infomercial, choose a topic that will speak to the audience. Give them useful information and make it a learning experience, so that the Webinar is educational or addresses a problem your audience may have.

3. Choose the main presenter to be someone who is a recognized expert, an author, or someone who has had experience solving the problem you are addressing. If the main presenter is someone from outside of your organization, that can lend credence to the Webinar. You can also include others from your organization as well.

4. Time your Webinar so that it is not broadcast on a holiday or the days immediately before or after one. Also, do not plan it for a Monday or Friday, and try to choose a time that will work with the time zones your audience is likely to reside in. If your market is across the continental U.S. and Canada, a good time for a Webinar is 1 P.M., when most people would be at their desks. Also, make sure the date does not conflict with major trade shows in your subject area.

5. Start promoting your Webinar and taking registration approximately 30 days prior to the event. Consider a series of Webinars so that you are able to capture more of your audience.

∴ If a Web page contains a sound or audio file and the Web browser does not support the sound or audio file type, the controls may display but the play button will be disabled.

6. Promote your Webinar using your existing customer base and sales force, through normal promotions, or perhaps through some special promotion.

7. Make sure the registration process is simple and quick.

8. Once the participant registers, send a confirmation email, follow up with another one 10 days prior to the event, again the day before the event, and another one an hour before the event. Statistics show that without reminders, as much as 67% of registrants will not show up for the Webinar!

9. Record the Webinar as a Flash file, and provide a link to the attendees and to those who could not attend so they can view it later.

10. Immediately following the Webinar, ask your attendees to complete a quick online survey. Approximately 77% of attendees will complete the survey, so plan your questions carefully.

Other Media

In addition to images, audio, and video media, there are other types of files that can be displayed. These include word processing files, spreadsheet files, and other document files.

Word Processing and Spreadsheet Documents

Sometimes it is necessary to provide the user with a word processing document, such as a file created using Microsoft Word, or a spreadsheet document, such as a file created using Microsoft Excel. You can provide these files in the form of a hyperlink and the user can click the link to download the file. What happens next depends on the browser used. If the user clicks on a link that points to a Microsoft Word document, Internet Explorer will use Microsoft Word as a helper application and will run an instance of Microsoft Word in the browser window and display the file. Netscape, Mozilla, Safari, and other Web browsers will prompt the user to save the file, or open it using the registered application. Similarly, if the user clicks on a link that points to a Microsoft Excel spreadsheet file, Internet Explorer will load an instance of Microsoft Excel in the browser window and display the spreadsheet file. Again, Netscape, Mozilla, Safari, and other Web browsers will prompt the user to save the file, or open it using the registered application.

Portable Document Format (PDF) Files

The PDF file format was created by Adobe (http://www.adobe.com) to display and print a document identically on any computer or printer. This solves the problem of individual configuration differences. For instance, if you were to create a Word document, save it, and print it using two different printers, you will likely notice differences between the printed documents. Printer configurations vary, and the same font may be displayed or printed differently. The differences are often enough to affect where page breaks occur. This can mean that a table of contents or index may have to be regenerated when the document is printed using a different printer. When a file is downloaded from the Internet, it may be optimized for a particular computer system and your system may display or print the document differently from how the originator had intended. Furthermore, the document may not display at all if you do not have the software version required. The

tip

⁖ If you are interested in up-to-date information in your profession or area of interest, there are lots of free Webinars available. Many of the Webinars also archive broadcasts so that users may view them at a later time.

PDF file format solves all of these problems. The originator can use the Adobe Acrobat software to save any file as a PDF file. Adobe offers Acrobat Reader, a free plug-in that allows the user to view, but not change, a PDF document. The PDF file preserves all formatting and pagination, so that the file views and prints exactly the same on every printer, and in every Web browser. This is particularly important when providing files such as legal documents, or manuals, where pagination is important.

Other Document Formats

Essentially, when you click a link that points to any sort of document, the Web browser will render it if it is an HTML file, and if not, will look through its configuration for a plug-in or helper application. If it finds a plug-in, it loads the plug-in and loads the document into the plug-in to be displayed. If it does not find a plug-in or helper application, the Web browser will prompt you to save the file.

Web Page Usability and Accessibility

In a round-about way, the thrust of this chapter has also been about Web Page usability and accessibility. Usability refers to the ease with which the user can navigate through the Web site and find content. Accessibility refers to the ease with which a user with special needs or disabilities can navigate through the Web site and find content. A user with special needs may have limited vision or motor-skill abilities, for instance.

The World Wide Web Consortium established the Web Accessibility Initiative (WAI) found at `http://www.w3.org/WAI/`. WAI establishes guidelines for creating Web content that is accessible to people with disabilities. These guidelines include techniques such as using contrasting colors for foreground and background for high visibility, including alternate text for images, and many more tips. WAI works in conjunction with organizations around the world including the U.S. Department of Education's National Institute on Disability and Rehabilitation Research, the European Commission's Information Society Technologies Programme, Canada's Assistive Devices Industry Office, and an assortment of corporations in the private sector.

Section 508 and the Americans with Disabilities Act (ADA)

Some institutions and governments require official Web pages to conform to the WAI guidelines. For instance, in 1998 the U.S. Congress amended the Workforce Rehabilitation Act with Section 508 to require all federal agencies to ensure that their electronic and information technologies are accessible to people with disabilities. Section 508 includes specifications for Web content, among other technologies, based on the WAI guidelines. Furthermore, in 1990 the Americans with Disabilities Act became law. The ADA prohibits discrimination against people with disabilities and, in general, requires employers and places of public accommodation to ensure that people with disabilities are able to access those services. Some have argued that the Web is a place of public accommodation and Web sites should conform to WAI standards.

The U.S. Department of Health and Human Services has an excellent collection of usability guides, which also includes guidelines for accessibility, posted at `http://www.usability.gov/guides/index.html`

≈ *tip*

∴ To see if a Web page meets WAI or Section 508 guidelines, you can use a validation tool such as Bobby (`http://bobby .watchfire.com`). Try this tool on some of the Web pages you use often!

Here is a short list of some of the accessibility guidelines suggested by WAI.

- Provide text alternatives for all non-text content.
- In visual presentations, make sure that foreground text and images are distinguishable from the background.
- Make sure that the user can access all functionality using a keyboard.
- Allow users to avoid content that could cause photosensitive epileptic seizures.
- Help users to avoid mistakes and make it easy for them to correct mistakes.
- Organize content consistently from page to page and make interactive components behave in predictable ways.

The guidelines above are some of the broad guidelines and WAI provides specific details on how to achieve these. Here are a few, to give you an idea of some of the "little" things that can be done to make it easier for people with disabilities to use your Web pages.

- For multimedia content, provide a written script describing visual information.
- Sites larger than 50 pages are required to have a table of contents, site map, or similar navigation.
- Section headings and links should be understood when read as a group.
- Components that occur on multiple pages should be repeated in the same way, for one presentation format.

SUMMARY

Now that you've read through the chapter, you are prepared to:

- Design Web pages according to contrast, repetition, alignment, and proximity.
- Recognize and use different image file types, including:
    - .bmp
    - .gif
    - .jpeg
    - .png
    - .tiff
- Create rollover images using Macromedia Fireworks.
- Create Web page buttons using Macromedia Fireworks.
- Add rollover images to a Web page using Macromedia Dreamweaver.
- Create a transparent image for your Web page.
- Use some simple techniques, such as interlacing and slicing, for working with larger images.
- Understand the difference between animated .gif images, JavaScript animation, Java Applets and Flash and Shockwave animation.
- Work with downloadable and streaming audio, such as:
    - .wav
    - .aiff
    - .midi
    - .mp3
    - .ram
    - .au or .snd
- Use Internet radio stations.
- Work with downloadable and streaming video, such as:
    - .avi
    - .asf
    - .mov
    - .rm or .ra
- Add sound to a Web page.
- Run a successful Webinar.
- Use other media, such as:
    - Word Processing and spreadsheet documents.
    - Portable Document Format (PDF) files.
    - Other document formats.
- Work toward Web page usability and accessibility compliance.

Review Questions and Hands-on Exercises

1. In reference to designing a Web page, describe the considerations for contrast, repetition, alignment, and proximity.

2. What is a bitmap image?

3. Which image file types would be appropriate for use in Web pages?

4. What is a rollover image?

5. What is the difference between an animated GIF and a Flash file?

6. What is meant by the term "transparent image"?

7. What is streaming media?

8. Describe two different techniques for adding sound to a Web page.

9. What is a Webcast?

10. You've decided to set up a Webinar for your company.

    a. What time of day should you broadcast the Webinar?

    b. How could you advertise it?

    c. After your customers have registered, when should you email them to remind them about it?

11. You work for a leasing company who would like to make a lease document available on the Web. It's very important that when the document is printed, it looks exactly the same for every user. What advice would you give the company for saving the file and making it available?

12. You are designing your Web site, keeping in mind that some people who will access the site will have disabilities. What sorts of techniques can you use to make your site more accessible?

1. Open a Web browser and load a Web site for a major retail store. Feel free to use a search engine to choose one. As you surf through the Web site pages, answer the following questions.

    a. Which elements are repeated on every page?

    b. Which elements grab your attention?

    c. What is it about the design of the pages that causes these elements to grab your attention? For instance, are they larger, contrasting colors, different fonts?

     d. How many different fonts are on each page?

     e. Where is the company logo placed on each page?

2. Open a Web browser and load the 3D Textmaker page (`http://www.3dtextmaker.com`). Make an animated banner image, containing the text "Hiking." Save the file and add it to the top of the *hiking.htm* page, replacing the heading text.

3. Create rollover buttons for the Wilderness Camping site, one set for each of the links. The buttons should contain the names of the links. For instance, create two rollover buttons for the hiking link, two for the swimming link, and so forth. Place the buttons at the bottom of each page, one beside the other, to create a navigation bar effect.

4. Open a Web browser and load the Pandia Radio search engine (`http://www.pandia.com/radio/`) site.

     a. Are any of the radio stations from your city listed on the site?

     b. Choose any of the radio stations, and listen for a few minutes.

5. Open a Word processing package, and type your name and address in the document. Save the document and create a small Web page that contains a link to this document. Open the document in the Web browser and click the link to verify that the user will be prompted to save the file.

COMMUNICATION ON THE INTERNET

part **4**

Chapter

Mass Communication	10
Real-Time Communication	11
Entertainment and Education	12

Mass Communication Tools

chapter **10**

Chapter Objectives

This chapter helps you understand

- ☐ the various means of public communication on the Internet.
- ☐ what mailing lists are, and how newsletters and discussion lists differ.
- ☐ what newsgroups are, and how they function.
- ☐ what Web-based discussion boards are, and how they work.
- ☐ what blogs are, and their many uses.

Mass communication *is defined as one person or agency communicating to many people through technological means. Newspapers, magazines, radio, television, and movies are all* mass mediums. *We commonly refer to these mass mediums as our* mass media. *Clearly, the World Wide Web can serve as a mass medium. After all, if you build an interesting Web site, it has the potential to reach hundreds—if not hundreds of thousands—of audience members. Of course, many Web sites don't reach mass audiences; but they have the potential to do so.*

There is yet another side of the Internet and World Wide Web with which you may not be familiar: the world of mailing lists, newsgroups, Web boards, and blogs. These mass communication tools, which will be explained in this chapter, also have the potential of reaching large audiences. And if you really want to know how to utilize the Internet and World Wide Web to its fullest, you have to be fluent with these technologies.

Mailing Lists

A mailing list can be a list of email addresses of your friends and family, or work colleagues. You may use your list of email addresses to send a joke or friendly letter to all the email addresses you select. You would include all of the email addresses as To, Cc, or Bcc recipients and send the message. You may find that at work, there are group email addresses available to you so that you can send a message to an entire department. These are *ad hoc* methods of mass communication.

To contact groups of people with similar interests, or members of an organization to which you belong, there are thousands of structured mailing lists available. **Mailing lists** are email-based discussion groups where email messages are delivered to those who subscribe to the list. The mailing list is administered, and mail is distributed using mailing list software. Mailing lists are geared to particular topics, and are one of the oldest forms of communication still vibrant today on the Internet. There are mailing lists for professional organizations, genealogy mailing lists for individual families, lists for people in a certain geographic area, or those interested in particular hobbies, support group mailing lists for people with particular illnesses, and lists for pen pals; the variety is mind-boggling. Some mailing lists are true discussion lists, and others function as a distribution system for newsletters.

There are many types of mailing list programs available. One of the most popular of these programs is called LISTSERV. For this reason, mailing lists are sometimes called listservs. So, if you hear someone talking about belonging to a "listserv" they are really referring to a mailing list. As you search for mailing lists, you will also see other mailing list software names such as listproc and majordomo. Mailing lists come in many subscriber sizes, too. Some are small, with only a handful of members. And some are enormous, with thousands of subscribers.

How Do Mailing Lists Work?

Here's how mailing lists work: First, you have to subscribe, or be subscribed, to one. In some instances, you may have to send an email message to the subscription email address, and then send a confirmation. Replying to a confirmation minimizes the chances that someone has subscribed you to a list without your knowledge. You may have to follow the same procedure of sending an email to a specified email address in order to unsubscribe.

Once you've subscribed, your email address is added to a text file on the mailing list server. If the mailing list is a discussion list, you can send your email messages to the mailing list address, and the message will be forwarded to all the members of the mailing list.

Moderated or Unmoderated?

Sometimes mailing lists are **moderated**, meaning that there is a moderator who decides whether or not to post a message to the list. The moderator's job is to serve as a gate-keeper. He or she keeps erroneous posts off the list, and keeps the discussion on topic. It can be a huge responsibility to be a moderator because of the work involved. On the other hand, lists are sometimes **unmoderated**, meaning that messages can be freely posted to the mailing list without editorial restraint. These mailing lists can be very lively, but can also involve a lot of irrelevant postings, spam, and discussions that go on wild

ↄ *tip*

∴ A mailing list could be used as a newsletter distribution or as a discussion list. If the mailing list is a discussion list, you can send messages to the list to be distributed to all list members. You can reply to messages you receive from the list as well. If the list is a newsletter distribution, then you will receive a newsletter periodically, but you cannot send messages to the list.

tangents because there is no moderator restraint. Some might think that having a moderator is a form of censorship, and it is. But the Internet culture is pretty much "anything goes" and if you don't like the idea that a list is moderated, you are free to start your own unmoderated list and address your interests that way.

Restricted or Open?

In addition to being moderated or unmoderated, a list membership can also be restricted or open. A restricted membership is one in which the moderator or list administrator personally approves your subscription request. For instance, there are mailing lists that restrict membership to a particular professional association, geographic region, industry, or membership in a community group. If you try to subscribe to a restricted mailing list, the worst that will happen is that your request will be denied, so don't be shy about it. An open list membership is a list where anyone can join.

What is the Difference between a Mailing List and a Newsletter?

The difference is only in how the list is used. To put it simply, with mailing lists, you typically have the ability to contribute a message and the email posts take on the form of discussions. Newsletters, on the other hand, are ordinarily publications that are produced by an agency or organization, and you simply subscribe to receive them. If you are looking to be part of the communication flow, and contribute to an online conversation, you are likely looking to subscribe to a mailing list. If you desire to receive some type of information on a regular basis published by a source, you want a newsletter. To make matters a little confusing, you will find that sometimes a newsletter subscription is called a *mailing list*.

Finding a Listserv List

Listserv is a special case as far as mailing lists, in that there is a comprehensive global list of public listservs available and this list is searchable. This is one of the few Internet resources where a comprehensive list is maintained and updated regularly. Listserv is developed by L-Soft and the global list search site is called *CataList* (`http://www.lsoft.com/catalist.html`).

It is a function of the listserv software that allows a global list to be maintained. Other list administration software programs, such as majordomo and listproc, do not have an equivalent resource. Mailing lists using this software can be found using a variety of search engines, but like the Web, there is no comprehensive index of mailing lists that are not listserv based.

Let's start by searching for a listserv list and subscribing to it. There is a large variety of music newsletter lists hosted by hollywoodandvine.com. Let's search for the mailing lists hosted at hollywoodandvine.com and subscribe to one.

> Open a Web browser and load the CataList site at
> `http://www.lsoft.com/catalist.html`
> In the search box type: `hollywoodandvine`
> Ensure that the checkbox for search by host is checked, and the others for list name and list title are not checked, as shown in Figure 10.1.

tip

∴ Don't just hit reply! If you are on a mailing list, remember that if you reply to a message you are typically responding to the entire list. If you wish to reply to the individual who wrote the message, you can use the "from" address instead of the "reply to" address if it displays in the email header.

tip

∴ You can search for mailing lists using a search engine. Try search terms such as "mailing list," "discussion list," and "listserv," along with your topic of interest!

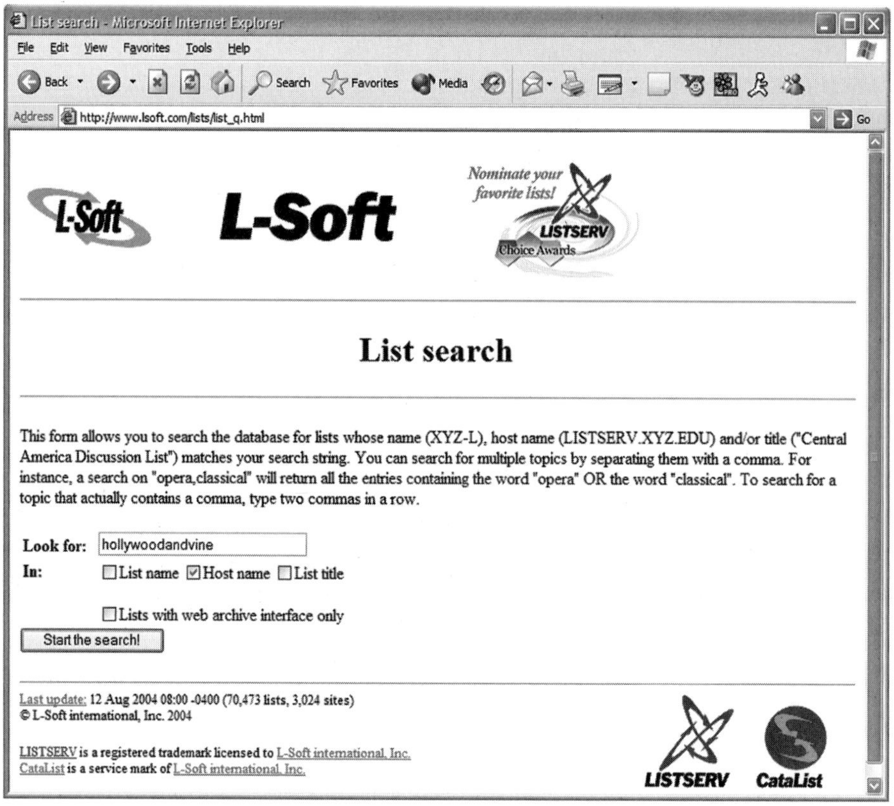

Figure 10.1   CataList site showing hollywoodandvine host search.

➢   Click the *Search* button to launch the search.

➢   Take a few minutes to browse through the available lists. You will find dozens of music lists.

➢   Click the link for a list you wish to subscribe to.

Subscribing to a Listserv Mailing List

We will use the Beatles list in this example, but you can tailor it to the list you've chosen. When you click the link for the desired list, you will see instructions for sending a subscription message to the listserv address. In the case of the Beatles list, you would send a message to `listserv@mail.hollywoodandvine.com` and the email will contain the subscribe message in the body, without any information in the subject line. In fact, you are sending a command to the listserv software program to subscribe you to the list. You should also add your name or "anonymous" to the subscription command, as most listserv programs require this as well.

➢   Open your email program and open a composition window.

➢   Enter the listserv address in the To: field and the subscription command in the body of the message, and send the message.

For example, to subscribe to the Beatles list, the following email message in Figure 10.2 would be sent.

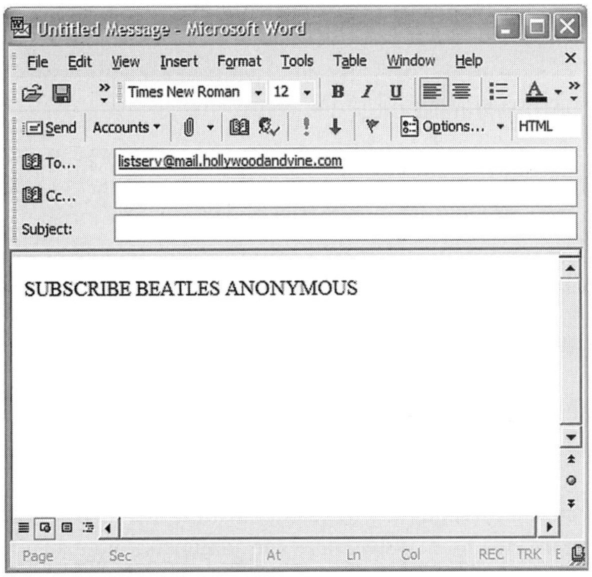

Figure 10.2   Email subscribing to the Beatles newsletter mailing list.

Once you've sent your message, you should receive a confirmation message within minutes. Since you are sending a command to the listserv software program, the program is also generating the return message as well. This confirmation message will contain information for unsubscribing from the list, so it's wise to keep this message for future reference. The confirmation message might look something like the following:

```
Your subscription to the ABC list has been accepted.
Please save this message for future reference. If you ever
need to unsubscribe from the list, you will find the necessary
instructions below.

To send a message to everyone currently subscribed to the list,
just send mail to ABC-LIST@SOMEDOMAIN.COM. This is called "sending
mail to the list," because you send mail to a single address and
LISTSERV copies everyone who has subscribed. You must never try to
send any command to that address, as it would be distributed to
everyone who has subscribed. All commands must be sent to the
"LISTSERV address," LISTSERV@SOMEDOMAIN.COM.

You may UNSUBSCRIBE from the list at any time by sending a "SIGNOFF
ABC-LIST" command to LISTSERV@SOMEDOMAIN.COM.

More information on LISTSERV commands can be found in the LISTSERV
reference card, which you can retrieve by sending an "INFO REFCARD"
command to LISTSERV@SOMEDOMAIN.COM.
```

```
You can also unsubscribe by visiting our Web interface at
http://www.somedomain.com and follow the instructions to unsubscribe.

Do NOT reply to the ABC newsletter or this message. If you do, you
will continue to receive mail from the list.
```

Subscribing to a Discussion Mailing List

Let's subscribe to the interneteffectively discussion list hosted by pearsontc.net and send a quick message. This discussion list is for people like you who are reading this book and would like to test out a list, and perhaps even make a new friend!

The procedure used to subscribe to a discussion mailing list is exactly the same as subscribing to a newsletter mailing list. The difference between these two lists is that there will be two email addresses associated with a discussion list. The two email addresses for the interneteffectively list are:

Administrator address: `majordomo@lists.pearsontc.net`
List address: `interneteffectively@lists.pearsontc.net`

As we saw when subscribing to a newsletter mailing list, the administrator address is used to send commands such as *subscribe*. The administrator email address may also be used to unsubscribe by sending a command such as *unsubscribe* or *signoff*, or there may be a Web site available to unsubscribe from the list. The unsubscribe instructions may be contained in the welcome email you receive when you subscribe to a list and the method can vary from one list to another.

Let's subscribe to the interneteffectively list at pearsontc.net.

➤ Open your email program and open a composition window.
➤ Enter the administrator address in the To: field (`majordomo@lists.pearsontc.net`) and the subscription command in the body of the message (`subscribe interneteffectively`). After the subscription command, type the command: `end`. Send the message. The email message should look as shown in Figure 10.3. The `end` command is required if you have a signature, or are using Web-based email. The `end` command ends the list of commands, and any further text is ignored. You do not need any information in the subject line when sending a command to a listserv.

Some lists require a reply to the confirmation message. If a reply is required, the confirmation message will be something like the following:

```
Someone (possibly you) has requested that your email address be added
to or deleted from the mailing list
"interneteffectively@lists.pearsontc.net".

If you really want this action to be taken, please send the following
commands (exactly as shown) back to "Majordomo@lists.pearsontc.net":

    auth 2ccfc276 subscribe interneteffectively
    sscollard@gmail.com
```

If you do not want this action to be taken, simply ignore this message
and the request will be disregarded.

If your mailer will not allow you to send the entire command as a
single line, you may split it using backslashes, like so:

auth 2ccfc276 subscribe interneteffectively \
sscollard@gmail.com

If you have any questions about the policy of the list owner, please
contact "interneteffectively-approval@lists.pearsontc.net".

Thanks!

Majordomo@lists.pearsontc.net

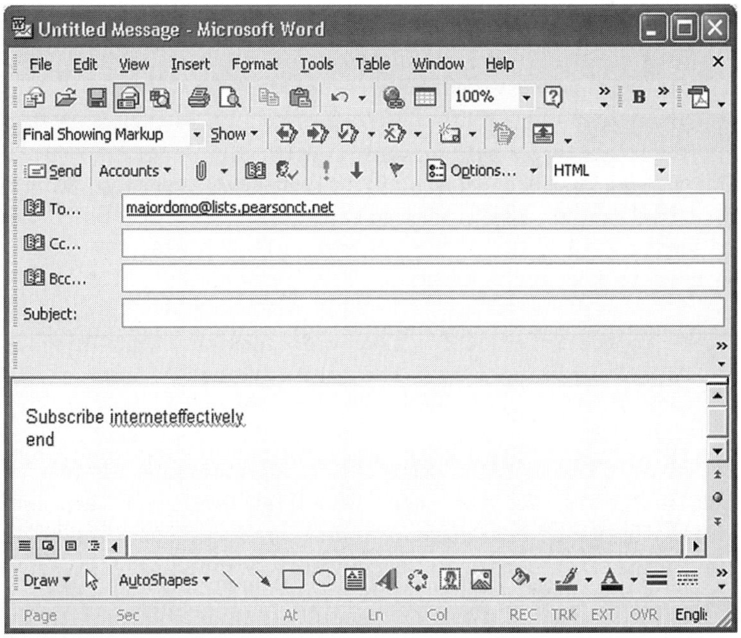

Figure 10.3 Subscription message to the interneteffectively list at pearsontc.net.

If the mailing list sent you a confirmation request such as the one above, you will
need to follow the confirmation directions. Some lists require you to confirm with only
"OK" in the body. This list requires the authorization information left in the message.

➤ Click the *reply* feature and delete everything except the authorization line.
➤ Send this confirmation email.

Sending a Message to a Mailing List

Once your subscription to the mailing list has been successful, you should receive a confirmation message and a welcome message like the one we saw for the newsletter mailing list. Again, keep this message, as it has information about unsubscribing from the list.

The welcome message should be something like the following:

```
Welcome to the interneteffectively mailing list!

Please save this message for future reference. Thank you.

If you ever want to remove yourself from this mailing list, you can
send mail to <Majordomo@lists.pearsontc.net> with the following
command in the body of your email message:

unsubscribe interneteffectively

or from another account, besides sscollard@gmail.com:

unsubscribe interneteffectively sscollard@gmail.com

If you ever need to get in contact with the owner of the list,
(if you have trouble unsubscribing, or have questions about the
list itself) send email to <owner-interneteffectively@lists.
pearsontc.net>. This is the general rule for most mailing lists when
you need to contact a human.

Welcome to the interneteffectively discussion list. This list has been
created for people who read the book Internet Effectively: A Guide to
the World Wide Web by Tyrone Adams and Sharon Scollard.

This is a moderated list. When you send a message to the list, it will
be delivered to the list owner. The list owner will approve the
message for distribution to the list members, but this may take some
time as the list owner checks for messages periodically during the
week.

To send a message to the list:
----------------

Compose a message as usual with a subject and message in the body.
Send the message to this address:
interneteffectively@lists.pearsontc.net

To unsubscribe from the list:
----------------
Send the message to: majordomo@lists.pearsontc.net
```

```
You do not need to add a subject.

In the body of the message type:

unsubscribe interneteffectively
end
```

Once you've received the confirmation message that your subscription was successful, send a friendly message to the list, using the list address in the To: field, a subject line as usual, and a friendly message in the body of the text.

Your message might look something like Figure 10.4.

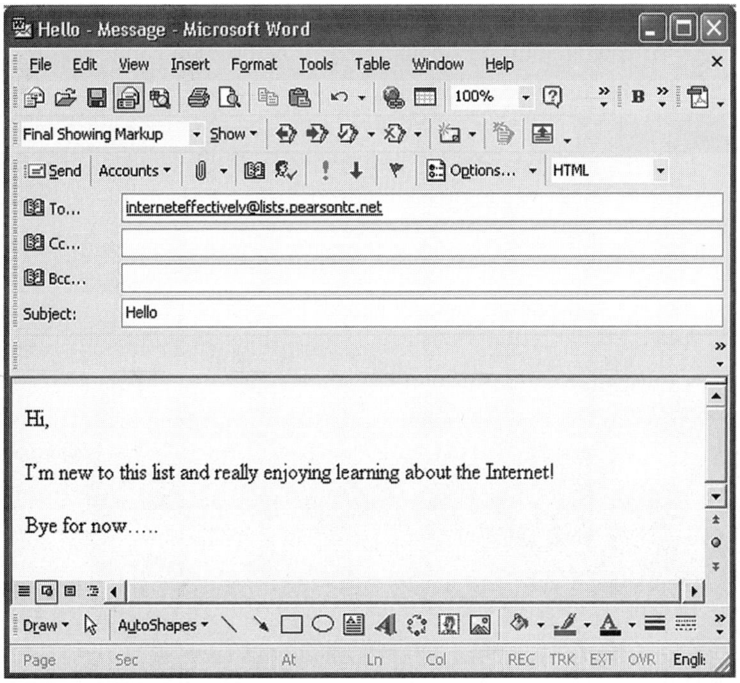

Figure 10.4 Sample email message to the interneteffectively mailing list.

➤ Send your message to the list.

If the list is moderated, you might receive a message confirming that your message has been received and will be posted after it has been approved. You may not receive any message at all, so don't panic if you don't see your message delivered for a while.

Once the moderator has approved your message, it will be posted for everyone on the list. If the list is not moderated, it will be posted right away and you should receive it in your inbox as well.

Mailing List Commands

There are often a variety of mailing list commands available. These commands allow you to do things like suspend your subscription while you are away, or send you only one message per day, grouping that day's messages in a digest form. The commands can also be sent to you in an email message, as a help message. The subscription message may indicate some of the commands that can be sent, and instructions on how to use them. You can often send a help command to the administrator address to receive a message containing commands that can be used.

Let's send a message to the interneteffectively administrator address to obtain the list of commands. Again, we send commands to the administrator address, and messages to the list address for distribution to the members of the list. The command used to receive the list of commands is *help*. We will receive the reference card of user commands.

➤ Open your email program and open a composition window.

➤ Enter the administrator address in the To: field (majordomo@lists.pearsontc.net) and the command in the body of the message, and send the message. The command is: Help

➤ On a separate line, add the command: end

➤ Send the message.

Your message should look something like Figure 10.5.

Within a few minutes, you should receive the email message containing instructions for using the various mailing list commands.

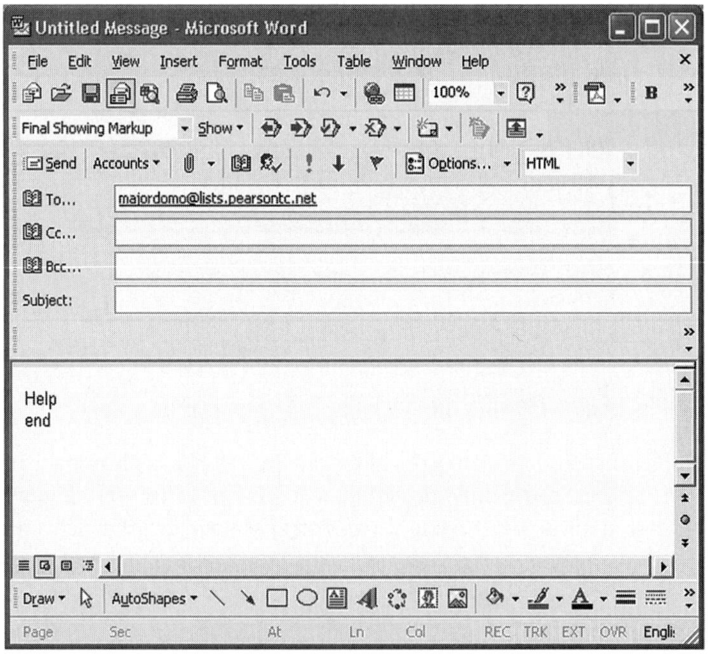

Figure 10.5 Message to pearsontc.net requesting the help information.

Digest Mode

Some lists are available in digest mode. When your list setting is in digest mode, you will receive only one email from the list per day, and this digest email will consolidate all the email messages sent to the list each day. This is particularly convenient when the list is a busy one, and you find yourself receiving many messages per day. Another alternative to managing a volume of posts from a mailing list is to use a filter in your email package and automatically route emails from the mailing list to a particular folder.

Unsubscribing from a Mailing List

When you're ready, you can unsubscribe or signoff the interneteffectively list. Again, this is an email message to the administrative address with an unsubscribe or signoff command as follows:

➤ Open your email program and open a composition window.
➤ Enter the mailing list administrator address in the To: field (majordomo@lists.pearsontc.net) and the command in the body of the message. The command is: `unsubscribe interneteffectively`
➤ On a separate line, add the command: `end`
➤ Send the message.

Your email message should look something like Figure 10.6.

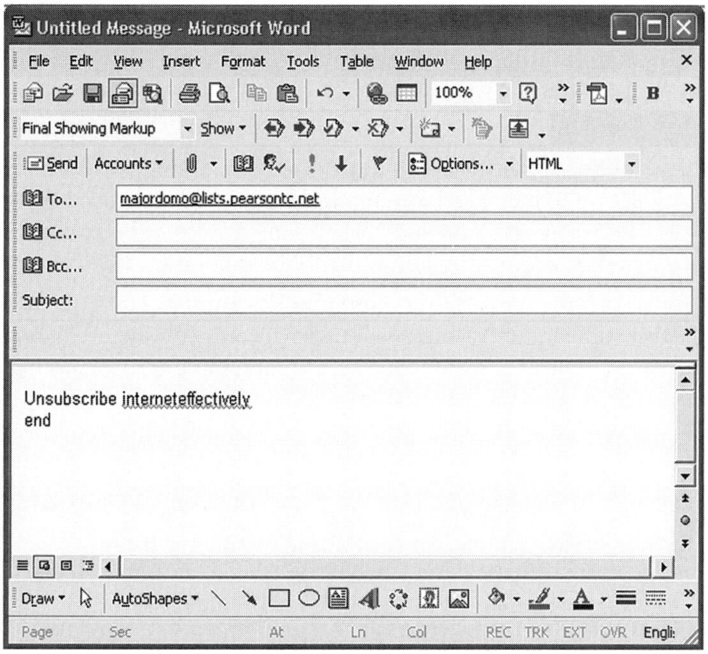

Figure 10.6   Email command to unsubscribe from the interneteffectively list.

∴ The digest mode is a good way to keep current with a list, and not have your inbox cluttered with each and every email sent to the list.

Listserv, Majordomo, Listproc, and Other Mailing List Software

You will find that mailing lists that have an administrator address and a list address will also have a variety of different methods for subscribing and unsubscribing. Typically, listserv, majordomo, and listproc require the user to send a subscription command similar to the subscription command we have been using. Again, signoff or unsubscribe procedures will be outlined in the subscription confirmation message. Some lists require a message to be sent to a specific "join" or "request" email address, without anything in the subject or body of the message. This blank message is used as a request to join and your email address is extracted from the header in your message.

Discussion Lists with Web Access

Yahoo! Groups are mailing lists, or discussion lists, which can be subscribed to; and incoming messages will be received via email just as on traditional mailing lists. Yahoo! group messages can also be viewed via the Yahoo! Groups site (`http://groups.yahoo.com`) without subscribing to the group. With a Yahoo! account, the user can also post messages to the group using the Yahoo! Groups site as well.

➢   Open a Web browser and load the Yahoo! Groups site
    `http://groups.yahoo.com`

➢   Browse through the categories available for groups, and select a group that interests you. View some of the messages posted. Some groups are private and will only allow group members to view messages, but most groups are public.

Notice when you are looking at the group page that there are several group email addresses indicated. The email addresses include addresses for posting messages, subscribing, unsubscribing, and sending a message to the list owner. In the case of Yahoo! Groups, you need only send a blank message to the subscribe email address in order to subscribe to the group. Do not send a message to the list owner unless you have a pressing question that cannot be answered by the group, or if you have difficulty unsubscribing.

If you have a Yahoo! account, you can join a group by clicking on the "Join Group" link on the individual group page. Once you have joined the group, you can post messages, view archives, and chat, if someone from the group is also signed in. You can also start your own group using Yahoo! Groups.

Topica (`http://www.topica.com`) also hosts mailing lists that can be joined via email subscription, and messages will be emailed to you like traditional mailing lists. Topica has a Web feature like Yahoo! Groups for joining groups, posting messages, and viewing archives. You can create a Topica account and join lists directly from the Topica site, or you can subscribe using the subscription email address indicated.

➢   Open a Web browser and load the Topica site `http://www.topica.com`

➢   Browse through the categories available for mailing lists.

Like Yahoo! Groups, once you have a Topica account, you can also set up a discussion list of your own.

Finding Mailing Lists

If you are searching for a particular mailing list topic, there are several ways to go about finding the list you need. First, we'd like to suggest that you use the search engine of your choice and enter the terms: `mailing list` and *your topic*. Browse through some of the publicly available mailing lists from these results. You might find exactly what you are looking for without having to go to a mailing list portal to find it. If you don't find anything that interests you, don't worry. Chances are good that somewhere on the Internet, someone has dedicated a mailing list to your topic.

Secondly, you should try to search some of the popular mailing list directories. We have discussed some of these already. Some companies provide free mailing lists for discussion as long as they can post tail advertisements to the emails going out to the list participants.

- Listserv search
  - CataList (`http://www.lsoft.com/catalist.html`)
- Discussion lists with Web access
  - Yahoo! Groups (`http://www.yahoo.groups`)
  - Topica (`http://lists.topica.com/`)
  - CoolList (`http://www.coollist.com/`)
- General mailing list search
  - Tile.net (`http://tile.net/lists/`)

Some Discussion List Etiquette and Tips You Need to Know

1. **Always keep a copy of your mailing list welcome letter.** Whenever you subscribe to a mailing list, the server automatically sends you a welcome letter. This message includes tips for sending mail to the list, and how to unsubscribe from the list. This may be a separate email in addition to the subscription confirmation email, or it may be the subscription confirmation email.

2. **Check your mailing list emails daily.** Depending upon the volume of messages carried by the mailing list you have subscribed to, you should make the commitment to stay on top of the conversation daily. If there are a lot of messages each day, you can either filter them to a folder as they are received, or set the digest mode feature. Some people also choose to get a free Web-based email account for subscribing to discussion mailing lists, in order to separate this email from work or personal email inboxes.

3. **Please participate.** Discussion mailing lists work because the people subscribed to them share vitally important information about the topic at hand. If someone on a list is seeking help, and you can provide it, either post a message to the list if it is relevant to the discussion, or email the person directly.

4. **Please identify your messages posted to the mailing list with a meaningful subject line.** You may not want to read all the discussions, and neither will the other people on the list. If you're replying to a discussion email, leave the subject intact so others can follow the discussion as well.

5. **Do not send an attachment to a mailing list.** Because of bandwidth issues and storage for archived lists, it is not a good idea to post attachments to a discussion mailing list.

6. **Unsubscribe from the group if you are going to be away.** If you know that you will not be checking your email for an extended period of time, you should unsubscribe from the mailing list, and subscribe again upon return. Some mailing list software, such as listserv, will allow you to suspend your subscription so that messages are not sent to you, but you are still subscribed.

7. **Look at the reply address when you are responding to a mailing list message.** Email that is generated from a mailing list generally has a "reply to" email address and a "from" address associated with it. Typically the "reply to" address is the address of the list itself and the "from" address is the address of the person who sent the email. Typically, when you select "reply" in your email package, the "reply to" address is used, so that the email will go to the mailing list itself—and NOT to the individual sender of the posted message. If you wish to reply privately to the person who sent a message to a mailing list, ensure that the person's email address, not the mailing list address, is in the To: field.

Newsgroups

In 1979, long before the Web, two Duke University graduate students, Tom Truscott and Jim Ellis, developed the idea of connecting computers in order to exchange information with the Unix community. Some information topics or **newsgroups** were formed and a newsreader client called 'A' News was developed by Steve Bellovin to read and post messages to the newsgroups. By 1980, there were 15 sites accessing these newsgroups. By 1981 there were 150 sites, and currently there are millions of such sites. This network of newsgroup communication was called Usenet. In 1979, email was the main method of online communication and the Usenet news system was based on sending email postings to the various newsgroups through software called a **newsreader**, and this system still exists today. News servers are not centralized and when a news posting is received by one news server, it is passed on to several others and gradually makes its way to all the other news servers on the Internet. In the early days, it could take days before all news servers received a posting, but technologies have improved and depending on the method selected, new postings can be viewed by all within minutes.

In the early days, newsgroups were used to post new research, disseminate information, ask advice, and carry discussions. Ideas were exchanged freely, and the culture that emerged was one of helpfulness. If you knew the answer to a question, you posted a response. To a great degree, this is still the case, and if you're looking for expertise and just can't find answers, Usenet newsgroups can be a tremendous resource. Newsgroup topics range from technical to hobbies and recreation, from scientific to support groups, from educational to adult content groups, from local community groups to global groups. The range is mind-boggling. Some people refer to Usenet newsgroups as the Internet Underground because this is a vast resource that is not particularly well-known.

There are a variety of methods that can be used to access newsgroup postings. We will look at accessing newsgroups via the Web, using a newsreader to access an ISP's news server, and some subscription services.

Understanding How Newsgroups Are Organized

There are more than 100,000 newsgroups available, and they are loosely organized into broad topics and sub topics. The eight mainstream Usenet groups are as follows:

comp.	computer hardware, software, and consumer info
humanities.	fine art, literature, and philosophy
misc.	employment, health, and miscellaneous
news.	info about Usenet news
rec.	games, hobbies, and sports
sci.	applied science and social science
soc.	social issues and culture
talk.	current issues and debates

You will see sub-groups organized in a hierarchy, such as comp.graphics.animation or misc.health.diabetes. In order to add a sub-group to one of these eight original groups, there is a formalized process, which includes posting a proposal for a new group to news.groups, and after some discussion, there is a vote by the Usenet Volunteer Vote-takers (UVV). More information can be found in the *How to Create a Usenet Newsgroup* document at: http://www.faqs.org/faqs/usenet/creating-newsgroups/part1/.

By far the most popular group is not a mainstream Usenet group; it is the alt. group. Some think that "alt" refers to "alternate" but in fact it stands for "Anarchists, Lunatics, and Terrorists." Technical jargon is fraught with edgy humor and this is one example. There is no vote required to add a topic to the alt. hierarchy of groups, so you will find that this section really is filled with "alternative" groups. You will often see reference to the groups as groupname.* where the * represents all sub-groups below. For instance, the alt.* groups refers to the alt hierarchy of groups.

In addition to the eight mainstream Usenet groups and the alt. hierarchy of groups, there are many other groups such as biz (business), corporate groups, community groups, and private groups for educational institutions and ISPs. One trend in distance education, for instance, is to use newsgroups as a form of communication for a distance education class.

Many of the posts to newsgroups are discussions, but there are also many groups where file attachments are regularly posted. These groups typically have **binaries** in the group name. The word binaries refers to the fact that a binary file type is attached. A binary file is a non-text file such as an image, video, or audio file.

Accessing Newsgroups Using the Web

Let's start by having a look at some of the groups and postings available. The most convenient way is by using Google's group site.

➤   Open a Web browser and load the Google Groups page at
`http://groups.google.com`.

You will notice the eight mainstream Usenet groups plus the alt.* group and perhaps a few others, including biz.

➤   Click the link for the *rec* group.

You should see a list of rec.* groups displayed, with a reference to the number of sub-groups in each group.

➤   Click the *rec.antiques* group.

You should see a listing of postings as well as a listing of more specific antiques groups available.

The postings are organized by date but also by **thread**. A thread is a discussion, and when the user posts a reply, the reply is grouped with the original message and any further replies. This method of grouping messages is called **threading**, and you may hear that in order to read newsgroups it is important to use a threaded newsreader. This means that the newsreader software will group the discussions into threads and it makes it much easier to follow a discussion. People will refer to following a discussion as "following a thread." Newsreaders these days handle threading, so this is not an issue as it was in the past. Email clients, however, are typically not threaded, so you will find that your email discussions are not as neatly organized as they are in a Usenet discussion group.

➤   Feel free to click one of the messages in the *rec.antiques* group to view the post.

Navigating the `groups.google.com` site is intuitive and you can feel free to spend some time browsing through the different groups and posts within them. If you'd like to post to one of the groups, you will need a google.com account, but you can freely read them without an account. You will find a link on the Web page for each group to post a new message, and a link on a message page to post a follow-up message. A form will be displayed, allowing you to add a comment and post to the group.

FAQs

Most of the groups have an associated Frequently Asked Questions (FAQ) posting that appears in the group once a month or so. The purpose of this posting is to provide some basic information about the subject at hand to prevent the same questions being asked repeatedly. You will see references in some of the postings to "reading the FAQ before you post." Rather than waiting until the FAQ file is posted, you can find it at the Internet FAQ Archive (`http://www.faqs.org`). Even if you aren't posting to a newsgroup, you will find this is a good resource for information about a wide variety of topics.

Like discussion mailing lists, you will find that some newsgroups are moderated, and some are private, where only approved members can view the posts. To add to the confusion, you will also find that some of the more popular listserv mailing lists are

tip

∴ Always read the Frequently Asked Question (FAQ) file before posting a message or question to a newsgroup. Each newsgroup has its own communication culture and norms for posting certain types of information and queries.

also available as Usenet newsgroups. Typically these groups are in the bit.listserv.* hierarchy and are identified by -L at the end of the newsgroup name, such as `BIT.LISTSERV.MUSEUM-L`.

Searching Usenet

There are very few resources for searching Usenet groups and posts. Google maintains an archive of postings and a list of many global groups and is searchable. Let's do a sample search to see what types of results we can expect.

➤ Load the Google Groups page at `http://groups.google.com`

➤ In the search box type: `bicycle`

➤ Click the *Search* button to perform the search.

You should notice that several group names appear at the top of the results page including *rec.bicycles.misc* and a variety of postings containing the keyword *bicycle*. You will also see references to the newsgroup in which each post was found, and a link to view the entire thread for each of the posts.

As you look through some of the messages in the newsgroups, you might notice that the language can get a little bit colorful (and sometimes hostile). That's because some people are engaging in a **flame war**, where disgruntled parties use abusive communication to try to convey their point. More often than not, however, the discussions are helpful and useful.

Using Your ISP Newsfeed

Although the Google groups site is an excellent resource for global and public groups, it does not list many local groups, or private groups. Local groups should be available through your ISP's newsfeed, and private groups will be available through the organization, corporation, or educational institution you may belong to.

If you subscribe to an ISP, you should also have access to the ISP's Usenet newsfeed. The newsfeed is available through the ISP's news server. You will have to check the ISP's technical support Web page, or support phone line, to determine the name of the news server. You can use a variety of newsreader software, but Microsoft Outlook or Outlook Express also has a newsreader feature available.

Let's set up Outlook to view Usenet newsgroups and post messages as well.

➤ Open Microsoft Outlook Express and select the commands *View, GoTo, News* to open the news window.

➤ Click the link *Setup a Newsgroup Account*. Be sure to have the name of your ISP's news server handy.

➤ Fill in your name when requested, and click the *Next* button.

➤ Fill in your email address when requested, and click the *Next* button.

➤ Fill in the name of your ISP's news server and click the *Next* button.

➤ Click the *Finish* button to complete the news server setup.

For first-time use, Outlook should automatically start downloading the names of the groups available on your news server. You should see a download box that looks something like Figure 10.7.

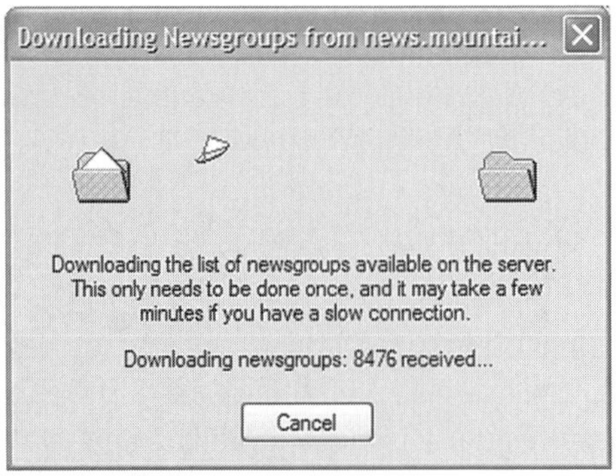

Figure 10.7 Downloading newsgroups.

If you have followed all these steps and Outlook does not seem to be downloading the groups, call your ISP's technical support line and ask a technician to walk you through the setup. Your ISP may also have directions on their Web site for setting up the connection to the news server as well.

It can take several minutes to download all the available newsgroups, as there could be 100,000 or more group names. Once the list has downloaded completely, you will be able to select newsgroups to view. The newsgroup subscription window will open and should look something like Figure 10.8.

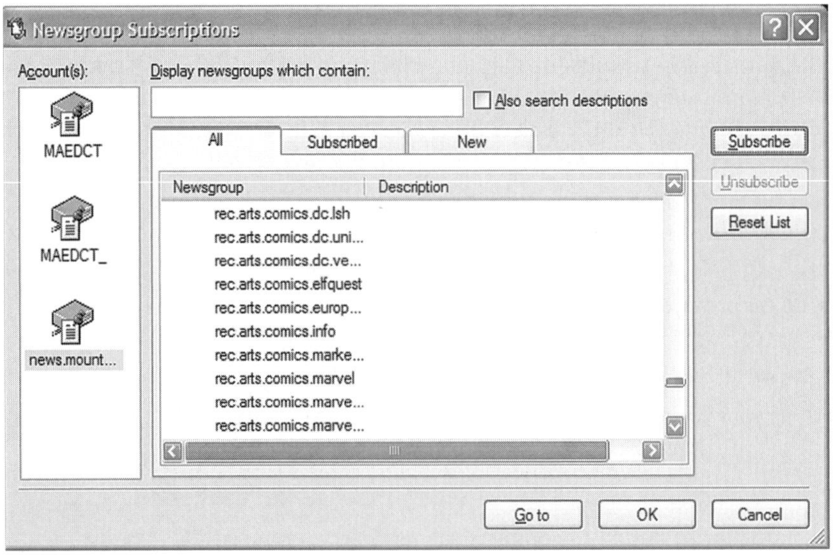

Figure 10.8 The Outlook newsgroup subscriptions window.

⤵ Scroll through the list of newsgroups to browse the available newsgroup names.

Selecting a newsgroup in a newsreader is called **subscribing to a newsgroup**. Unlike discussion mailing lists, you will not be sending any sort of subscription request. Subscribing to a newsgroup means that you are selecting the newsgroup name for your short list of newsgroups you would like to view.

Let's subscribe to a newsgroup. You can search for newsgroups in the listing. On the Web, we were looking at the *rec.antiques* newsgroup. Let's subscribe to the *rec.antiques* newsgroup using Outlook.

⤵ In the *Display newsgroups which contain* box, type: `rec.antiques`

The newsgroup subscription window should look something like Figure 10.9.

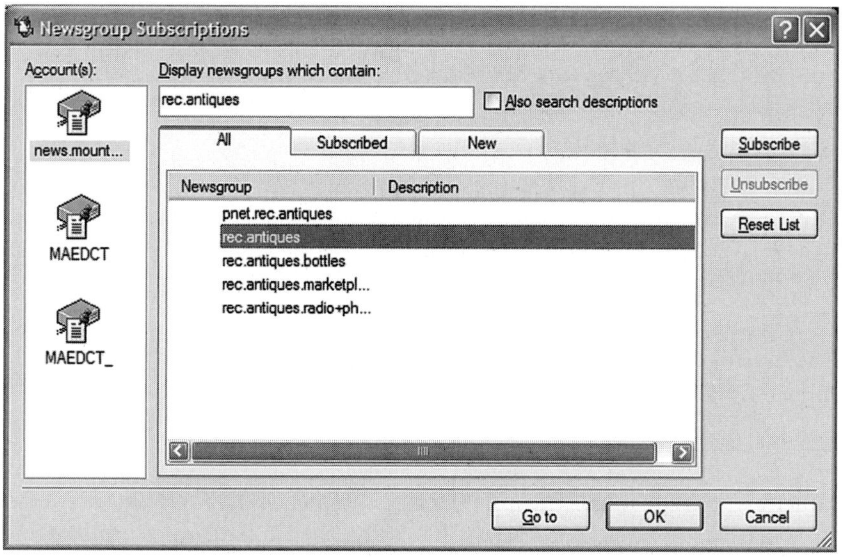

Figure 10.9   Selecting a newsgroup in Outlook.

⤵ Click the *rec.antiques* newsgroup, and click the *Subscribe* button to subscribe to this group.

⤵ Click the *Go To* button to view the messages in the *rec.antiques* group. It may take a few minutes for the messages to download.

The message window should open with the message headers in the top pane and the discussions threaded by subject. The message will display in the lower pane when you click a header in the upper pane. The window should look something like Figure 10.10.

You can usually tell right away if a group is unmoderated because there will be many posts which are clearly not on topic.

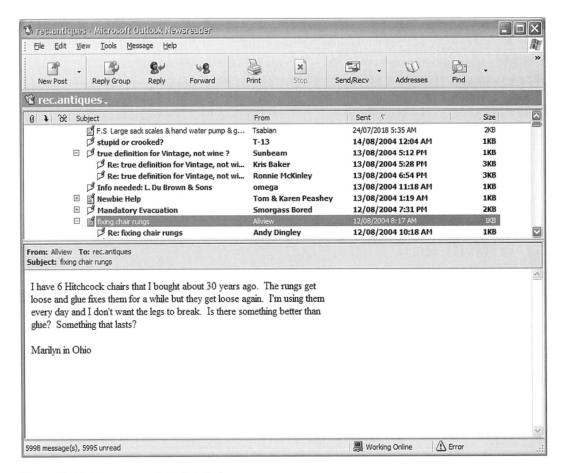

Figure 10.10 News message window in Outlook.

When you're ready to reply to a message, you can click the *Reply Group* button. You will notice that the name of the newsgroup is displayed in the *Newsgroup* input box (rather than the To: box). This is a mail composition window, and you can compose your message as you would any other email message. You can also Cc the message to yourself or someone else, and click the *Send* button when you're ready to send the message. You can also reply to the individual who sent the message post to the newsgroup by clicking on the *Reply* button.

➤ Select a message and click the *Reply Group* button. Notice that the name of the news server is in the header area, and the name of the group is also in the head area above the Cc: field.

➤ Close the message window to cancel sending the message.

➤ Click the *Reply* button. Notice that the email address of the sender of the post appears in the To: field. This message would be sent directly to that email address, and not posted to the group.

➤ Close the message window to cancel sending the message.

To post to a newsgroup, you can click the *New Post* button, compose your message, and click *Send*. Postings are not generally stored for more than a few weeks. The administrator of the news server for your ISP will set the length of time to keep messages, and it often depends on space available on the server. If you lose a posting that you wished to keep, you can also try to find it at the Google Groups site. Otherwise, you can also save the message in Outlook using the *File, Save As* feature.

Subscription-Based Newsfeeds

In addition to the free Web-based newsgroup sites and the newsfeed provided by your ISP, there are also subscription-based newsfeeds available. If you find that your ISP does not have a newsfeed or does not carry postings for a long time, you can choose to pay a subscription fee for a newsfeed. Some of the newsfeed services will include large download bandwidth and will archive messages for a month or longer. Below is a list of some of the subscription-based newsfeeds. Feel free to have a look at each one to see their available features. Some include a secure connection so that your traffic cannot be logged by your ISP, thumbnail newsreaders so that you can see thumbnail pictures of images attached to postings, and other features.

Web Newsgroup Service	URL
100 Proof News	`http://www.100proofnews.com/`
All the Newsgroups	`http://www.allthenewsgroups.com/`
Usenet.com	`http://www.usenet.com`
Usenet ROCKET	`http://www.usenetrocket.com/`

Some Newsgroup Etiquette You Need to Know

When you are sending postings to newsgroups, there are a few basic etiquette rules that you should keep in mind. Like anything else, you will find that there are folks who ignore these rules completely, but many people follow them, and become agitated when others don't.

1. **Lurk.** This means observe the postings in the newsgroup for a while before you decide to post. You'll get a feel for the culture of the group.
2. **Review the FAQ.** Many of the questions that people ordinarily ask of a newsgroup have already been asked. Be sure yours isn't one of them.
3. **Avoid flame wars and DON'T YELL.** Remember that at the other end of your message are people, who have feelings and opinions of their own. Typing in all caps is interpreted as yelling and is considered rude. Usenet newsgroups tend to be self-policing. When someone misbehaves, he or she may receive hundreds of angry emails in return.
4. **Do not leave a lengthy message and simply reply "yes."** Feel free to delete some or most of the message, and leave the parts that are relevant, including your reply.
5. **Keep it short and simple.** Whether you're responding, or posting for the first time, less is more. Most people do not want to read long messages, unless, of course, you're posting to a creative writing group.

6. **Be aware of copyright issues.** Before you post any content created by another copyright holder, make sure that you are contributing something of original value or have the expressed permission of the copyright owner to repost. Usenet is a public forum and copyright rules apply.

7. **Don't be ethnocentric.** Before you call someone "un-American" think about what you are saying for a moment. This is a global mass medium. You might be talking to someone from Zimbabwe, who isn't American.

8. **Do not post advertisements.** This is frowned upon in discussion groups. Some select groups are specifically for advertising products and services, but outside of these groups, advertising is spam.

9. **Ignore "trolls." Trolls** are statements made to incite people to respond in anger. For instance, posting a message in the *rec.antiques* group such as "antiques are really recycled junk and would make great firewood," is the type of statement that might incite a flame war. Ignore messages that are blatantly inflammatory.

Web-Based Discussion Boards

A **discussion board** is a Web-based discussion list, which is neither a mailing list nor a Usenet newsgroup. This could be a feedback page at a radio station Web site, a discussion forum at a Web developer resource Web site, a comment board on a personal journal Web site, or another similar site. These discussion boards work something like the corkboard message center in your home or office. An example of a Web-based discussion list is the Ultimate Wedding site shown in Figure 10.11. You can post messages for others to view on a Web page at a later date.

On the discussion board, you can easily navigate through messages that others have posted, and post messages yourself. Depending on the setup, you may need an account with the site in order to post messages, and messages may be threaded as well.

Start Your Own Discussion Board

As we have seen, there are a variety of methods of starting your own discussion group. You can create a group at Google, Yahoo!, or request an alt.* group. You can also create your own discussion group using a free site such as EZBoard (http://www.ezboard.com/). Once you've registered and created your own group, you'll notice that EZBoard also has some subscriber services available. You will be provided with a URL, which will allow you to see your new discussion board, and you can use the URL to promote it on your Web site or email it to friends and family. The title and keywords that you provide to identify your discussion board will also be searchable on the EZBoard site, so you may attract some visitors interested in the topic you proposed.

Blogs

Short for Web logs, blogs are personal Web diaries and journals that are frequently updated and designed for public viewing. Blogs typically mirror the individuality of the author of the blog, and allow the **blogger** the opportunity to rant philosophically on

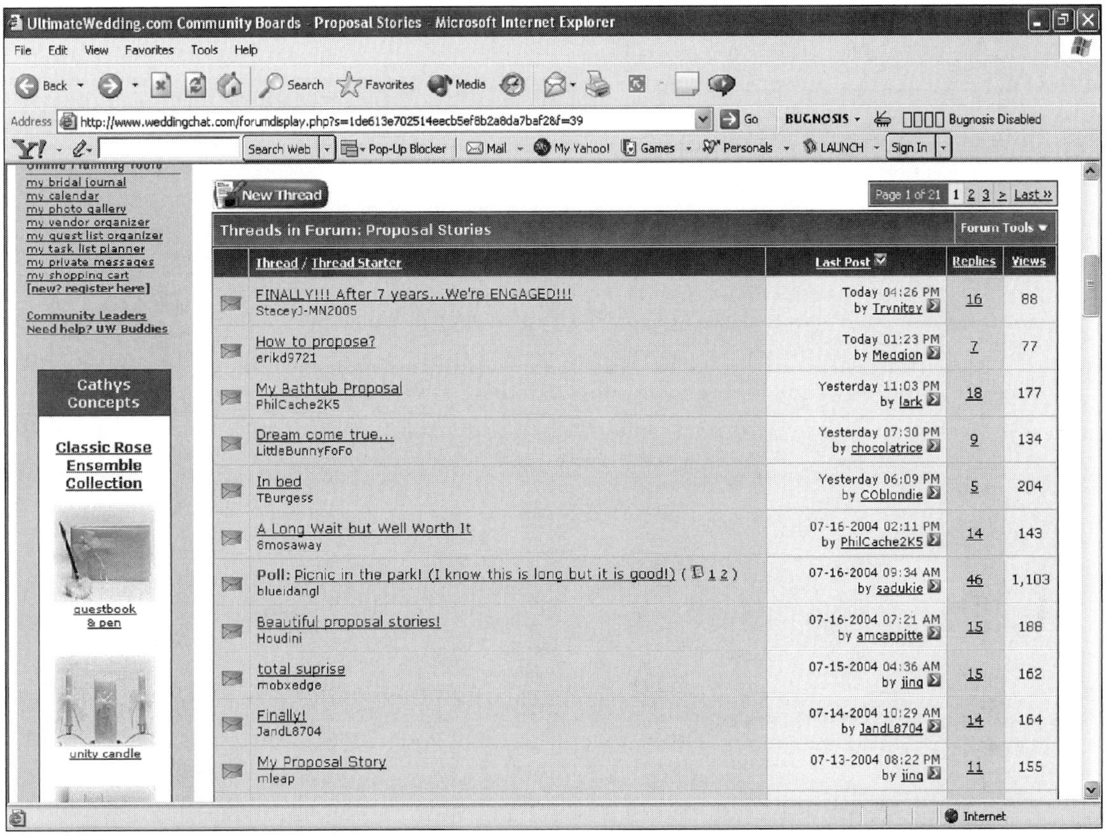

Figure 10.11 UltimateWedding.com's (http://www.ultimatewedding.com/) discussion board, featuring stories on engagements, party planners, and much more.

personal, social, or other topics of interest. However, there are collective blogs as well, which are usually moderated by the blog owner, and visitors are encouraged to comment to the ongoing blog. If the posts received by the blog owner are deemed acceptable, he or she posts them to the developing blog. Figure 10.12 shows an example of a blog.

One of the largest blog sites is Blogger (http://www.blogger.com). For a fee, you can even define part of the URL so that your blog is easy for others to find. For instance, your blog could be located at http://yourname.blogger.com. Other advanced blog features are available for a fee.

Interestingly, businesses are also using blogs for strategic advertising and marketing purposes. Companies seeking to have more direct relations with their customer base are starting blogs for their products in an effort to by-pass traditional media outlets with information. Karpinski writes: "There's no doubt that Weblogs have reached a critical mass. Google's recent acquisition of Weblog pioneer Blogger.com and waves of media coverage on the subject, plus adoption of the blog format at MSNBC, Slate, and elsewhere, have put the blog squarely at the center of the Web consciousness" (2003). It's a clever advertising technique, and may catch you off guard when you first come upon one of these "advertising" blogs.

Figure 10.12   An example of UL Lafayette Internet Communication instructor Lance Winder's personal blog, located
at http://www.silverwulf.com.

Searching for Blogs

If you have a friend who has a blog, the easiest way to find it is to ask your friend for
the URL. Blogs can be almost impossible to find. One search engine for blogs is Blogwise (http://www.blogwise.com/). Sven Latham, from southern England, created this
service in 2002. Once you've created your blog, you can submit it to Blogwise and they
will catalog your blog.

RSS (Rich Site Summary, Really Simple Syndication)

RSS, also known as Rich Site Summary or Really Simple Syndication is an XML-based
method of sending headlines or summaries of sites to your desktop. This is a subscrip-
tion-publication type of service, where you can subscribe to a particular RSS feed.
Netscape developed RSS in 1999. It was used to provide headline feeds that could be
customized by users for their "My Netscape" page. Users could select headlines and
other content, and the headlines would be provided by RSS feeds from the originator.
My Netscape benefited greatly from a large supply of RSS feeds, and originators of RSS
feeds benefited from the exposure of millions of users.

∴ Evaluate a blog for reliability just
as you would evaluate information
on a Web page. What is the purpose for the blog? What bias does
the author have?

In early 1999, with the immense popularity of RSS feeds in the My Netscape portal, came the growth of desktop-based headline viewers. These allowed the user to download hundreds of RSS feeds, and browse through the headlines at their leisure.

Some RSS feeds group together other RSS feeds and allow filtering of headlines. For instance, one RSS feed may consolidate all headlines of a particular subject over a particular time, from other RSS feeds it monitors. This type of feed is called an **aggregator**. Some people also use the term aggregator to refer to a desktop RSS reader client.

Searching for RSS Feeds

These days, there are millions of RSS feeds available. They originate from news sites, Weblogs (blogs), and a multitude of corporations and organizations who wish to make daily or even up-to-the-minute information available. The definitive collection of syndicated RSS feeds is maintained at Syndic8 (`http://www.syndic8.com`). You will also find RSS links on many news sites, blog sites, and other corporate or institution sites. This technology is still in its infancy, but becoming quite popular.

➤ Open a Web browser and load the Syndic8 URL `http://www.syndic8.com`

➤ Use the search feature and type the keyword `news` or another keyword of your choice.

➤ Click the *Search* button to find RSS feeds that satisfy your keyword search.

➤ Feel free to spend some time browsing through the master list of RSS feeds from the main page as well.

RSS Desktop Headline Viewer—FeedReader

As an example of an RSS desktop headline viewer, we will use FeedReader. Once installed, it is simply a matter of finding the URL for an RSS feed, and entering it as a new feed site in FeedReader. FeedReader is open source software with versions available for Windows and Mac users.

➤ Open a Web browser and load the FeedReader URL `http://www.feedreader.com/`

➤ Download and install the latest version. When you are looking for the appropriate file, choose *binaries* for your operating system.

➤ Once you have downloaded and installed FeedReader, open it.

The FeedReader window should look something like Figure 10.13.

We will add some RSS feeds, and be able to see the headlines in the upper right pane, and the contents of the selected headline in the lower right pane. Essentially, we need to find the URL for the RSS feed, and point to that URL in FeedReader to set up the RSS feed.

Let's add an RSS feed for a popular technical news site, Slashdot.

➤ In the Web browser, load the Slashdot URL `http://www.slashdot.com`

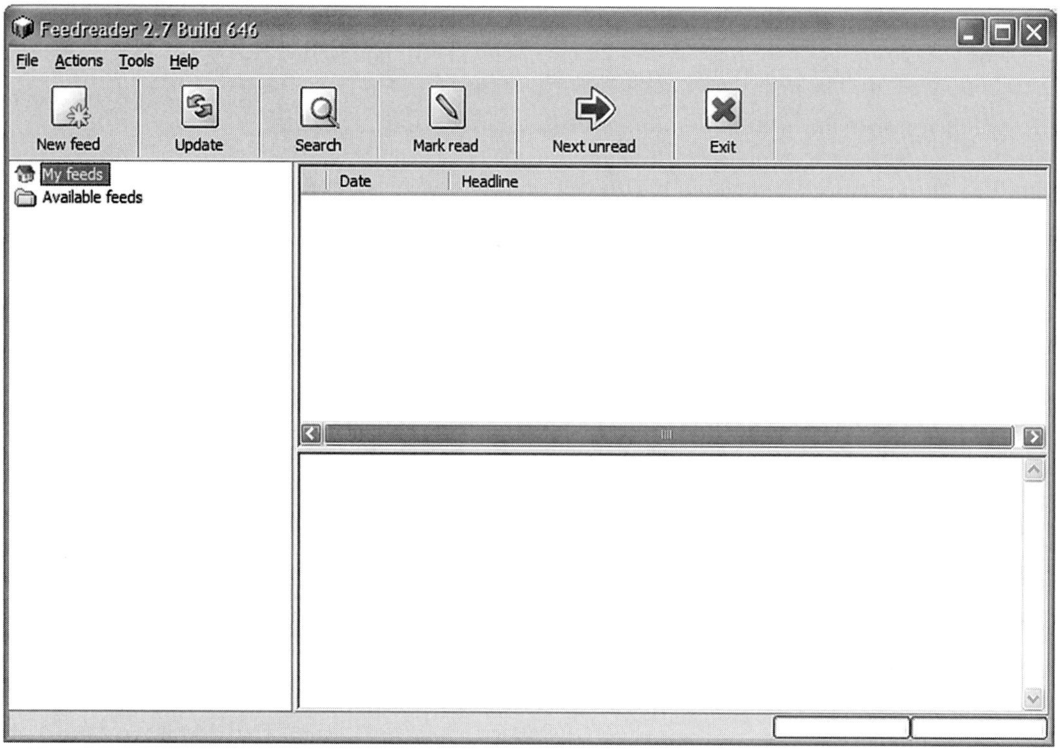

Figure 10.13   FeedReader RSS desktop headline viewing software.

> ➤ Click the RSS link in the Slashdot window. You may find it at the bottom of the window. If you are having difficulty finding it, use the browser's search feature to find it in the page.

> ➤ You should see the XML code appear in the browser window. We don't need the code, but we do need the URL for the RSS feed, which is in the address bar of the Web browser.

> ➤ Drag to highlight the URL in the Web browser, and right-click to reveal the shortcut menu.

> ➤ Click the *Copy* command from the shortcut menu.

> ➤ Activate the *FeedReader* window and click the *New Feed* button. The New feed wizard dialog box should appear.

> ➤ Click in the URL text box, and right-click to reveal the shortcut menu.

> ➤ Click the *Paste* command to paste the URL into the New feed wizard dialog box, as shown in Figure 10.14.

> ➤ Click the *Next* button.

> ➤ FeedReader will suggest the name of the feed as Slashdot. Click the *Finish* button to add the Slashdot feed.

> ➤ The Slashdot feed will appear in the pane on the left. Click the Slashdot feed to download the current headlines.

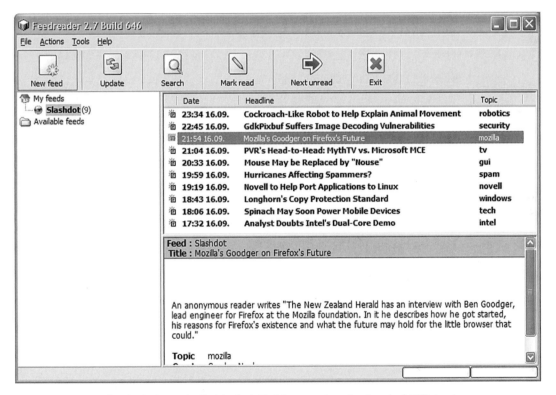

Figure 10.14 FeedReader *New feed wizard* dialog box.

➤ Click one of the headlines in the upper right pane to display the contents in the lower right pane, as shown in Figure 10.15.

Figure 10.15 FeedReader displaying the Slashdot feed. Slashdot is a registered trademark of OSTG, Inc. in the United States and other countries. Used with permission.

You can delete headlines after you read them, by selecting the headline and pressing the delete key. You can also refresh the headlines by clicking on the *Refresh* button. If you keep FeedReader open, but minimized, it will refresh the headlines periodically, and when new headlines are received, an alert box will pop up on your desktop.

➤   Feel free to add other RSS feeds using the same steps as above. View the following Web pages to find the link for the RSS feed. Some of these sites, such as the *New York Times*, have a variety of interesting RSS feeds available. Some RSS feeds are simply labeled on a site as "XML." Try these in your RSS feed reader, and they will likely work just fine. A few sites with RSS feeds include:

▫ National Hurricane Center (`http://www.nhc.noaa.gov/`)
▫ Yahoo! News (`http://news.yahoo.com/rss`)
▫ All Headline News (`http://www.allheadlinenews.com`)
▫ SmartMoney.com (`http://www.smartmoney.com`)
▫ *New York Times* (`http://www.nytimes.com`)

Atom

Although RSS is quite popular for conventional newsfeeds, a popular format for Weblog feeds is **Atom**. Atom was adopted by Google as a format for sending blog feeds. Many RSS feed readers will also read the Atom format.

Other RSS and Atom Feed Readers

There are alternatives to reading RSS feeds, other than using a desktop client such as FeedReader. If you'd like a client that runs inside of Internet Explorer, you can use a program such as Pluck (`http://www.pluck.com`). This application is an RSS feed reader, and will also consolidate Web searches, and track information on sites such as Amazon and eBay.

Another option for viewing RSS feeds in the browser is the Dogpile toolbar (`http://www.dogpile.com`). You will find the toolbar from a link on the main page for tools and tips. Dogpile is a search engine, and has developed a free toolbar to facilitate searches, block pop-ups, and also read RSS newsfeeds. The FireFox Web browser will also read RSS feeds.

As we have seen, Microsoft Outlook is an email client, and will also allow you to read newsgroup postings. If you'd like to be able to read RSS feeds through Microsoft Outlook, NewsGator (`http://www.newsgator.com/`) is a client available to read RSS feeds inside Microsoft Outlook.

SUMMARY

Now that you've read through the chapter, you are prepared to:

▫ Use the popular means of communicating in the public sphere.

▫ Exploit mailing lists, including newsletters and listservs.

▫ Employ listservs, knowing when one is required, and the basic command features used to manage them.

▫ Find a publicly accessible mailing list.

▫ Make use of newsgroups, while understanding the difference between a newsgroup and a listserv.

▫ Manage Web-based discussion boards, and even build your own message board.

▫ Start your own blog, while comprehending their varied communicative uses.

Review Questions and Hands-on Exercises

Review Questions

1. Why do some mailing lists have two or more addresses associated with them? Describe what these addresses might be used for.

2. You send a message to a mailing list address, but it doesn't seem to be posted for quite a while. Describe what might be happening to prevent your message from being posted immediately.

3. How can you tell if your mailing list subscription request was successful?

4. What is the definition of the term "listserv"?

5. You've joined a mailing list and find that there are many messages sent daily. What options might you have for making this situation a bit more manageable?

6. What's the difference between a mailing list and a Usenet newsgroup?

7. What are people referring to when they use the term *Underground Internet*?

8. What is a Usenet newsfeed?

9. Describe two different methods that can be used to view and post messages to Usenet newsgroups.

10. What is a thread?

11. What is meant by the term *lurking* in reference to newsgroups or mailing lists?

12. What is a flame war?

13. You decide that you'd like to start your own discussion forum for your favorite hobby. Describe at least two different Internet resources you can use to do this.

14. What is a blog?

15. What is an RSS feed?

16. How would you read an RSS feed?

Hands-on Exercises

1. Search the CataList (`http://www.lsoft.com/catalist.html`) site for a mailing list related to your profession.

   a. Follow the instructions to subscribe to the mailing list.

   b. What is the administrator address?

   c. What is the list address?

   d. When the subscription confirmation email arrives, store it in a separate folder in your email package.

   e. Is this group moderated or unmoderated?

   f. Is digest mode available for this list?

   g. Send the command LISTSERV REFCARD to the list administrator address to receive the reference information email.

   h. Keep your subscription for a few days to see some of the postings.

   i. Send the SIGNOFF command to unsubscribe from the list.

2. Search the bit.listerv list of newsgroups and find the name of a list that interests you. Search the CataList site (`http://www.lsoft.com/catalist.html`) and find the subscription information for the same list.

3. Browse through the Yahoo! Groups site (`http://groups.yahoo.com`) and find two groups that you might be interested in joining.

   a. How many postings are there for each group on an average day?

   b. Are these groups public or private?

   c. Are these groups moderated or unmoderated?

4. Browse or search the Google Groups site (`http://groups.google.com`) and find two newsgroups that interest you.

   a. Do these newsgroups have a FAQ? Search the Internet FAQ Archive (`http://www.faqs.org`) to find out.

   b. Are these lists open or restricted?

   c. Are these lists moderated or unmoderated?

5. Search the Syndic8 site (`http://www.syndic8.com`) for an RSS feed of your interest. Add the RSS feed to FeedReader.

6. Find the Web site for the local television or newspaper in your area.

   a. Does it have an RSS feed available? If so, add it to the feeds in FeedReader.

   b. Search a major television or newspaper site for one of the largest cities in your country. Does this site have an RSS feed? If so, add it to the feeds in FeedReader.

Real-Time Communication

chapter *11*

Chapter Objectives

This chapter helps you understand

- ☐ what instant messaging is.
- ☐ what some of the key features of instant messaging are.
- ☐ what Voice over Internet Protocol (VoIP) is.
- ☐ how to engage in effective instant messaging etiquette.
- ☐ some of the common abbreviations used in instant messaging.
- ☐ how to hold an effective videoconferencing session over the Internet.
- ☐ how instant messaging is transforming the workplace.

Are you ready to get real? Real time, that is. In Chapters 4 and 10, we discussed email, newsgroups, and other forms of communication that work in flex-time. In flex-time, or asynchronous communication, you email, post a message to a discussion mailing list, or add a blog entry, and then you wait for a period of time until someone responds. This communication is asynchronous because it is happening at different times. Communication that happens at the same time is synchronous communication. Asynchronous communication is beneficial because it doesn't require the recipient to be sitting at his or her computer waiting to respond. These methods are particularly good for communication when people are in different time zones, or simply not able to respond at that moment.

But, asynchronous communication also has its drawbacks. For instance, what if both parties are online at the same time and want a more immediate response? What if the parties want to hear, or even see, one another? This chapter is about going live in real time. It is about using your computer and Internet connection to reach out to another party and make more direct contact. It's about synchronous communication.

Instant Messaging

When email just doesn't seem fast enough, there are a number of programs that will let you use your keyboard to chat in real time with someone who is online anywhere in the world. **Instant messenger (IM)** programs, also called **chat** programs, allow you to insert text and send it instantly to someone else who is using the same IM program. In return, that person will be able to see your message and respond to it immediately. Many people will refer to messages as IMs in context, such as *Send me an IM* or *Someone is IMing me*. They will also refer to an online conversation as a chat session.

We'll focus mainly on the very popular America Online Instant Messenger (AIM), and then talk about how some of the other IM clients differ. You will find that all the chat programs have the same essential features, including managing contacts (sometimes called buddies or friends) on a list, blocking so others cannot see your online status and send messages, and audio and video capabilities.

America Online Instant Messenger (AIM)

Available for download at `http://www.aim.com/`, AIM is adware. Subscribers to AOL already have a version of AIM built into their user-interface but nonsubscribers can download the chat client and begin using it right away. You'll need to create a nickname and password for yourself in order to download the software. Once you've downloaded and installed this program on your system, it should look something like Figure 11.1.

There are a variety of things you can do to acquire contacts or *buddies* for your list of people you would like to chat with. You can ask friends and family what their AIM nickname is, and you can search by email address. If you would like to add someone who uses AOL, you can extract his or her *buddy name* from his or her email address, and enter it into your *buddy list*. If you need an AIM buddy to start you off, you can use `tyroneadams@aol.com` or just tyroneadams for short.

➤ Open the AIM chat client.

➤ Click the *Setup* button, as shown in Figure 11.2. If you don't have a *Setup* button, you can also use the menu options, *People, Find a Buddy, By Email Address*.

➤ You'll see another window open on your desktop. At the bottom of this window, you'll see three preset folders, titled *Buddies, Family*, and *Co-workers*. Double-click the Buddies folder to open it.

➤ Click the *Add Buddy* button, as shown in Figure 11.3.

➤ Type `tyroneadams@aol.com` in the *Open Buddy Name* box, and press *Enter* on your keyboard.

You have just added Tyrone L. Adams, one of the authors of this book, to your buddy list. If he is online, go ahead and send him an IM.

➤ If he is online, his name will be boldfaced and appear in the *online* category of your AIM chat client screen. Double-click his buddy name, and the chat client screen will open. If he is not online, his nickname will appear in the *offline* category. If you leave your chat client open, it will notify you when he comes online.

tip

∴ Leave your instant messenger open when you want to engage in chat sessions. Your online "buddies" will be able to see that you are online, and may IM you. If you are busy or are going to be away from your computer for a while, change your status to "away" or "busy" so that others will know why you're not responding right away.

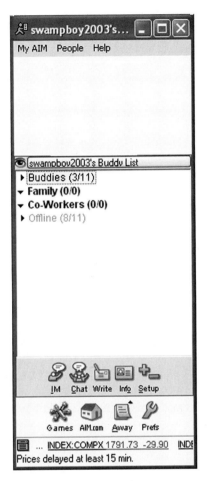

Figure 11.1   The AOL Instant Messenger Client (AIM) is an easy-to-use interface
that allows you to have control over several IM options.

Figure 11.2   The *Setup* button located on the
bottom-right corner of the AIM client.

Figure 11.3   The *Add Buddy* button lets you
add buddies to your watch list.

➤   Double-click on his name, type a message and press the *Enter* key. Some chat programs require you to click a *Send* button rather than pressing the *Enter* key. Send
him a message. It's that easy! When he replies, you will see his reply in the upper
pane after your message. The message window looks similar to Figure 11.4.

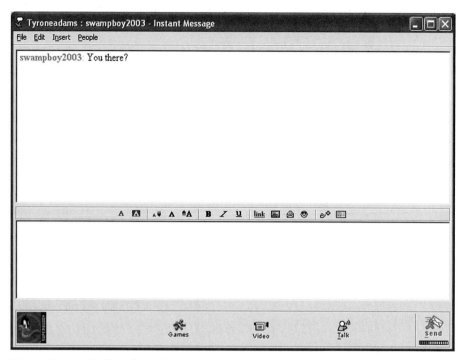

Figure 11.4   The IM window will open for you to begin conversation with a buddy who is online. All you have to do is double-click the buddy's name.

AIM Features

Blocking   The blocking feature allows you to **block** IMs from a contact or buddy you are blocking. It also prevents other users from seeing when you are online, and you will always appear offline in their lists. So, you'll have to watch your online etiquette a bit when engaging in chat sessions. This is how you can block a buddy or contact using AIM.

➤ Open your AIM chat client.

➤ There are a variety of methods you can use to block a contact. If your buddy IMs you, you can click the *Block* button to block this contact, as shown in Figure 11.5. You can also right-click the buddy name on your list to reveal the shortcut menu and select the *Block Buddy* menu option. Similarly you can unblock a buddy by right-clicking on the buddy name and selecting the menu item: *Unblock Buddy*.

Figure 11.5   The *Block* button allows you to block incoming IMs from someone you would like to suppress.

Private Chat Rooms Another feature that AIM boasts is the ability to host private chat rooms for more than two parties. These **chat rooms** are places where small groups of people can meet and discuss issues in real time. So, if you have a need for more than two people at a time to chat, and these users share AIM in common, you can create a multiple party chat room where the conversation can *really* unfold.

➤ Open your AIM chat client.

➤ Select *People* from the down-menu on your AIM Client.

➤ Select *Send Chat Invitation* to your buddy. At this time, you will have to wait for your buddy to *accept* the invitation to your private chat room.

➤ Repeat as necessary on your buddy list until all your contacts are in the private chat room. Once they are all in the chat room, begin communicating.

Sending Files Another feature of IM sessions is the ability to send a file to someone on your buddy list. For example, let's say that you are working on a team project for school, which requires a lot of group effort. And, let's also suppose that your team members cannot meet together physically to get their work accomplished. That's when IMs come in handy. Your group could meet in a chat room on AIM, and distribute graphics, spreadsheets, or just about any type of document necessary to accomplish its task. Sending files has become a versatile means of accomplishing many small-group, team-oriented tasks lately. Here's how you do it:

➤ Open your AIM chat client.

➤ Begin a chat session with one of your online buddies.

➤ Select *People* from the drop-down menu in your IM.

➤ Select *Send File* from the drop-down menu.

➤ A new window will open on your monitor, as shown in Figure 11.6.

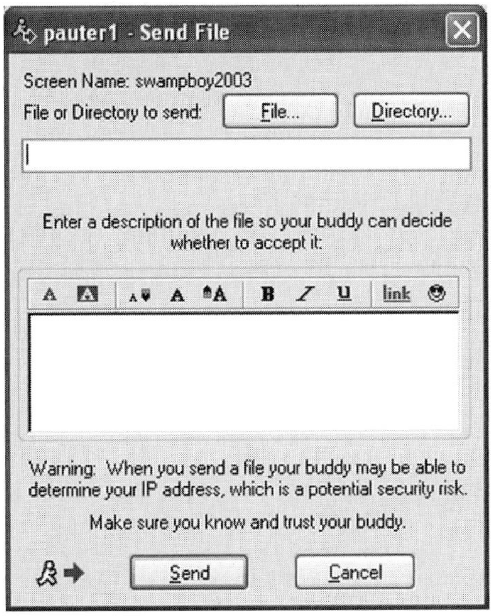

Figure 11.6   Looking to transfer a file to your buddy online? The *Send File* feature under the people drop-down menu will allow you to, while carrying on your IM session.

➤ Select *File* if you wish to send a simple file, **or**

➤ Select *Folder* if you wish to send an entire folder.

➤ Once you have the file or folder selected, click the *Send* button. It will initiate your transmission.

Your buddy will have the opportunity to *Accept* or *Decline* the file or folder you are trying to send. If your buddy chooses to accept, the file will be transmitted. If your buddy chooses to decline, you will receive a decline message.

Security and Sending Files

Be very cautious about receiving files through a chat client. These files can contain viruses. Use your anti-virus software to scan any files you choose to receive, particularly if the files are executable programs.

Some people are unable to receive files through a chat client because they are behind a **firewall**. Firewalls are typically configured to disallow attachments through chat clients. In order to transmit files, the chat client establishes a direct computer-to-computer connection between the two contacts, something like a peer-to-peer connection. Firewalls will block direct computer-to-computer connections because of the security risk that these connections pose.

Audio Chat

An added feature built into AIM and other chat clients is the audio chat feature. AIM uses **Voice over Internet Protocol (VoIP)** to send and receive audio. VoIP is a direct competitor of telephone communication, using the Internet as a carrier. With AIM, you can use your computer system just as you would a telephone, with bidirectional sound capabilities.

In order to use audio chat, your computer will require a microphone, speakers, and a full-duplex sound card. In computing, the terms **half-duplex** and **full-duplex** describe data transfer, and in the case of audio chat, the data is sound. Half-duplex means that data can travel only one way at a time. A walkie-talkie is a good example of half-duplex communication. One person talks, stops, and the next person talks, but both people cannot be talking and listening at the same time. In full-duplex communication, data is transferred in both directions simultaneously.

The telephone is a good example of full-duplex communication. In the case of the telephone, both parties can talk and listen at the same time. In the early stages of audio communication over the Internet, communication was half-duplex only. In order to receive full audio communication, your computer's sound card must support full-duplex sound. Recent computers have this technology, but you should be aware that if you are communicating with someone who has older technology, they might not be able to use audio chat because of this.

To initiate an audio chat, all you need to do is:

➤ Open your AIM chat client.

➤ Right-click a buddy name to reveal the shortcut menu, and click the *Send an Instant Message* menu item. This will open an IM window.

➤ Click the *Talk* button in your IM window, as shown in Figure 11.7. You may also have to click the *OK* button to initiate the audio chat.

∴ Be sure to scan any file you receive for viruses. Even if you know the person who sent you the file, check it for viruses. The person sending the file may not know it contains a virus!

∴ Make sure your microphone is not too close to your speakers. When the microphone is too close, it will pick up the voices of the other people and the feedback will be a terrible echo effect. Another option is to reduce the sensitivity of the microphone through the audio wizard if you cannot physically move your microphone.

Microphones, Speakers, Headsets, and Web Cams

- **Microphones:** In order to be able to use audio or teleconferencing chat, you will need a microphone. You do not need an expensive microphone for audio chat, so if you are purchasing a microphone for this purpose only, the least expensive one will do. Some computers come equipped with a built-in microphone. Place your microphone away from your speakers. If the microphone is close enough to the speakers, it picks up the speaker output, creating a feedback loop, which results in an echo effect. One effective way to reduce this is to use a headset with a microphone.

- **Speakers:** Most computers also come with speakers, but again, for audio conferencing, the least expensive speakers will do. The speakers should plug into your sound card. Some speakers require an AC outlet or batteries to power the amplifier, but speakers without an amplifier do not require power at all. You can also use headphones instead of speakers if you wish. If you are going to be using the speakers for music or other sound that requires high quality output, then it's worth investing in better speakers.

- **Headsets:** A headset is a combination of headphones and microphone. It may have a speaker for only one ear, or both, and an adjustable microphone you can position near your mouth. This may be an economical alternative to purchasing a microphone and speakers separately.

- **Web Cams:** If you plan to do audio and video conferencing on the Internet, you'll likely want to buy a **Web cam** (also known as a **cam**). Some Web cams have a microphone built in. These typically plug into a USB port. Videoconferencing really requires a broadband connection, as the combination of audio and video data requires significant bandwidth to transfer. The Web cam will come with installation software that must be run before you will be able to use your cam online. Individual chat programs may also require you to use the audio/video setup wizard in order to install the microphone and cam for online videoconferencing.

Figure 11.7   The *Talk* button allows you to use your microphone on your computer to engage in real-time voice conversations with your online contacts.

➤ Wait for the connection to be *Accepted* by the other party, and for the server to connect you. This may take some time, so be patient.

➤ Once a connection has been established, begin talking into your microphone. You should be connected and able to send and receive audio signals.

Videoconferencing

Many chat programs also have a videoconferencing feature. A videoconference is communication with audio and video. If you have never before held a videoconference, you are in for a treat. Many businesses, organizations, and individuals have Web cams installed on their systems so that people can communicate through videoconferencing.

You can initiate a videoconference by following these steps:

➤ Open your AIM chat client.

➤ Right-click a buddy name to reveal the shortcut menu and click the *Send an Instant Message* menu item. This will open an IM window.

➤ Click the *Video* button on the IM window, as shown in Figure 11.8. If this button does not appear *active*, it is because your buddy does not have a video connection available. This could be because your contact does not have a Web cam or is using an older version of AIM, which does not support videoconferencing.

Figure 11.8   The *Video* button will start a videoconference between you and your buddy, provided he or she has a Web cam, too.

A video display screen will open in a new window. It should look something like Figure 11.9.

It can take a few minutes to establish a connection. Once the connection is established, you should be able to hear your contact, and see his or her picture in the IM window. The screen refresh rate varies from one chat program to another and from one connection to another. With some programs and fast connections, the video should look fluid, almost as fast as a movie. Others are slower, and refresh the screen once every few seconds, more like stop motion.

Chat programs often include features such as sending a buddy list to another buddy, saving conversations, and leaving *away from computer* messages. You can also change your IM message window's font and background color.

➤ Click the *My AIM* menu option.

You should see menu options including *Away Message, Load Buddy List,* and *Edit Options.* The *Away Message* option will allow you to create an away message. When your online status is *Away,* the away message will be displayed on your contacts' buddy

tip

∴ Be patient when participating in videoconference sessions. Depending upon the speed of your connectivity, the program you are using, and the other videoconference participants' equipment, your success may vary. Try many different videoconference programs to make sure that you are using the right one for you.

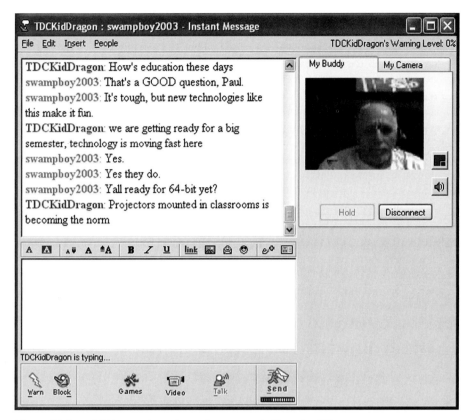

Figure 11.9   A Web cam videoconference between two buddies using AIM.

lists as your contacts hover the cursor over your contact name. The *Save Buddy List* and *Load Buddy List* options will allow you to save your contact list as a file and load it again later. You can also send someone your buddy list if you wish.

Let's have a look at some of the other options available.

➤   Click the menu items *My AIM, Edit Options, Edit Preferences.*

➤   Explore the options available by clicking on an option in the list on the left, and experimenting with the options that are displayed. You should see options for setting sounds as someone comes online or logs out, options for changing the background color and font in the IM window, file sharing, privacy, and so forth.

AIM will allow you to send a text message to a user who is offline, and will deliver the message the next time the user is online. It also includes features such as a stock ticker (15 minute delay), news from around the world, weather updates, and direct news alerts.

There are many other popular chat clients available, and you may find that you have some friends who use one program and other friends who use another. It's worth exploring some of the other chat programs to see the differences in features.

MSN Messenger

MSN Messenger (http://messenger.msn.com), like AIM, is adware, so you will see advertisements on the bottom of the window while using it. An example of the MSN window is shown in Figure 11.10. MSN Messenger's features include: sending messages to a mobile device such as cell phone or pager, **application sharing**, and a **whiteboard** feature. Application sharing allows you and another online user to share an application such as a spreadsheet program. Only one of you can control the application at a time, and you must pass control to the online contact in order for him or her to control your application. This feature is useful for online collaboration. The whiteboard feature allows you to post text to, or draw items on, a whiteboard shared by multiple users, also useful for collaboration.

You will find an *Add Contact* button in the main window, which allows you to add a contact to your list, and you can search for contacts by email address. You can use the advanced search feature to search by geographic region or interest. You can right-click on a contact name to find options in the shortcut menu for contacts, including *Send an Instant Message*, which opens an IM window, or *block* to block the user from seeing your online status or sending you messages. You will find configuration options including privacy options and sound options in the *Tools, Options* menu options. MSN Instant Messenger will not allow you to send a message to contacts who are offline.

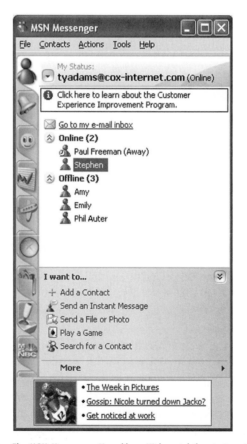

Figure 11.10   The MSN Messenger. More like a Web portal than just an IM client.

Yahoo! Messenger

AIM calls them *buddies,* MSN Messenger calls them *contacts,* and Yahoo! Messenger calls them *friends.* Yahoo! Messenger (`http://messenger.yahoo.com/`), shown in Figure 11.11, has the same basic functionality as the other chat programs including IM text chat, Web cam, and privacy settings. You will find some of the advanced features, including stock quotes, news from around the world, weather updates, and direct news alerts. One of the interesting features that Yahoo! Messenger has that the other chat clients lack is a built-in Web calendar with programmable reminders. You can set your computer to be your own digital secretary, and remind you of important appointments or meetings you have scheduled. You can also send a message to an offline friend. Yahoo! Messenger also has easy access to a large number of chat rooms in the *chat* feature. You will find a large assortment of Yahoo! rooms and the ability to create user rooms as you wish. When you join a chat room, you will find that the conversation can fly by if there are many people chatting in the room. There are chat rooms for subjects including hobbies, technical, professional, and social subjects. If a chat room doesn't exist for a topic you'd like to chat about, you can create your own user room. Your room will be displayed in the list of user rooms.

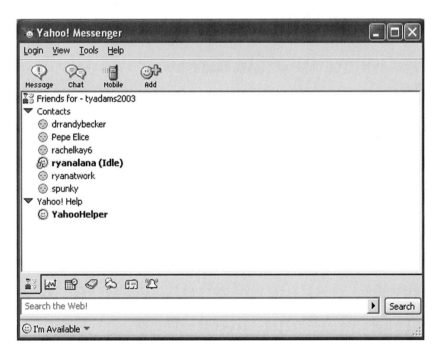

Figure 11.11   Yahoo! Messenger.

ICQ

ICQ (I seek you), as shown in Figure 11.12, is available at `http://www.icq.com/` and also has the basic features of text chat, contact list management, and video conferencing, using a plug-in for Microsoft's NetMeeting. The interface is a bit different from the other chat clients and the menu is accessed by clicking the *Main* button at the bottom of the

Figure 11.12   The ICQ Network is another popular chat client.
It offers many features that the other chat clients do not.

window. The menu items *Main, Preferences* will open a window containing preferences for sounds, colors, chat history, and other configuration options. You will have to enable chat history in order to save past chats. ICQ also allows you to float an individual contact name to your desktop, and rename contacts. You can change your online status to *invisible* so that your contacts see your status as offline, but you can still chat while your status is set to invisible. You can also send a message to a user who is offline.

ICQ offers some interesting features that other chat programs do not, including *ICQ chat.* The chat feature allows the recipient to see each character typed as the sender types it, and requires a plug-in. ICQ also attempts to make a *community* around its chat client, by offering services that the other chat clients do not. For instance, if you are just looking to find a random person who is also online, you can use the *Chat with a Friend* feature to locate someone. You will find that clicking the *Online Status* button reveals a menu that includes *Chat with a Friend*, and you can select *Find a Chat Partner* or *Available to Chat with a Friend*, to make yourself available for random chat. You can also search by geographic area or interests. So, if you are bored, or simply want to learn more about people who are available to chat, this is an intriguing way to meet new and, perhaps, interesting people.

Trillian

Each chat client (AIM, MSN, Yahoo!, and ICQ) accesses a different network. Thus, if your friend is online using AIM and you are using MSN, you won't see each other. There are several unified messengers that access your accounts on the main chat networks and consolidate your contact lists. The advantage is that you would only have to open one messenger program in order to use text chat with all the contacts on each of your chat clients. Trillian (`http://www.trillian.cc`), a popular unified messenger, is shown in Figure 11.13. You will need your userids and passwords from each of the chat clients you use, and Trillian will connect to each of these networks and download your contact lists. Trillian supports AIM, MSN Messenger, Yahoo! Messenger, and ICQ. Trillian will also allow you to use the news and stock quote features of the other chat clients.

Figure 11.13 Trillian basic is a free unified messenger client that helps you manage all of your chat clients in one simple interface.

The chat clients make use of Voice over IP (VoIP) in their audio streaming, but VoIP is a standalone technology that is becoming increasingly popular as an alternative to traditional ground line telephone connections. It requires a broadband Internet connection.

Effective Chatting

A Brief History of Text Chat

No one is certain who invented **Talk**, but it was heavily used between the lines connecting MIT, BBN Consulting in Massachusetts, RAND in Santa Monica, and UCLA in the late 1960s. Talk was a simple program that allowed users on networked computers to type messages to one another in real time. As more computers were connected to ARPANET during the 1970s, Talk became a means of communicating with anyone linked to ARPANET. This valuable tool, however, began to affect the productivity of government and corporate employees. Mandates were issued not to use Talk unless it was truly important. But throughout the 1970s and 1980s, users continued to hold chat sessions. Not only was the exchange of information useful, but also communicating with others in this fashion was enjoyable and personable.

::: **tip**

Unified messengers such as Trillian may not offer all the features of every IM program, but it's great if you primarily use basic IM features!

In 1988, a Finnish programmer named Jarkko Oikarinen wrote a program called Internet Relay Chat daemon (IRC-d) to allow for multi-user real-time communication. Oikarinen and his friends were **bulletin board service (BBS)** participants. BBSs allowed participants to post text messages to a virtual bulletin board for public reading. After his BBS became uselessly cluttered with brief personal messages, Oikarinen announced on the BBS that everyone should download his new software application, IRC, and connect to his server for real-time chat. From that moment on, his server was flooded with a flow of participants. IRC was truly revolutionary because it allowed up to 100 participants to engage in synchronous chat sessions, and shifted dialogues across the world into real time. Hundreds of variations upon the original IRC model are still being used today, but the basic model remains the same.

Chat Etiquette and Culture

Whether you're using a chat room or one-on-one chat window, there are a few trends related to etiquette and chat culture that have emerged. For the most part, you will find that there really doesn't seem to be any etiquette, in terms of social rules of politeness, as people feel free to say whatever they want, in whatever manner they feel is appropriate. And you may not feel that their approach is appropriate for you, in which case you can put the user on your block or ignore list.

- **Do not use all caps.** This is considered to be yelling, whether the communication is text chat or email.
- **Use emoticons and abbreviations to express emotions when communicating to friends.** But when using these interfaces for business communication, it is best to avoid the use of emoticons.
- **People can and do adopt any persona they wish when chatting.** Be streetwise. Although a great many people are exactly who they say they are, a great many more are not.
- **Chat rooms are fraught with adult chat.** If you are a parent, or supervising a child online, be very aware of the child's online activity.
- **People come and go quickly.** A chat can end abruptly because the user decided to close the window and finish the chat, or because there was an Internet connection disruption and technology prevented the user from continuing the chat. You have no way of knowing which situation occurred.

Effective Videoconferencing

A Brief History of Videoconferencing

Even though videoconferencing seems relatively new, it has actually been around since the 1960s. AT&T introduced its *Picturephone* at the 1964 World's Fair. For a number of reasons, including a lack of bandwidth, a lack of desire by executives to use the technology, and high cost—the product did not catch on. For this reason, most of the effort during the 1970s and 1980s went into developing high-end, expensive conferencing systems that were sold to corporations for use in executive board rooms.

It wasn't until the 1990s that personal videoconferencing became possible for the average user. In the early 1990s, AT&T introduced five product lines, including the

Voice over Internet Protocol (VoIP)

Voice over Internet Protocol (VoIP) Defined

VoIP turns the analog signals of voice and sound into a digital signal that can be transmitted over a network, such as the Internet. This technology has allowed many people to communicate using voice through their chat clients, and also make phone calls—using services like Dialpad.com (http://www.dialpad.com/) and Net2-Phone (http://www.net2phone.com/)—to ordinary telephones throughout the world. VoIP providers offer a viable alternative to the traditional telephone service. You will find a list of VoIP providers at
http://www.voipproviderslist.com/

What Equipment Is Required?

You will need a microphone, a broadband connection, and a VoIP service provider. VoIP service providers provide a wide-range of inexpensive domestic and international calling plans, so you should definitely shop around before choosing a service. Outside the U.S. and Canada, there has been a rise in the number of *telephony cafés* where people can go in and pay a reduced rate to place their call over the Internet using VoIP enhanced computers.

If you have a broadband connection already installed in your home, but do not have a computer, another way that you can use VoIP is to purchase a VoIP telephone adapter. The VoIP telephone adapter will connect to your broadband connection, and allow you to plug any ordinary telephone into the adapter.

Advantages versus Disadvantages of VoIP

Advantages of VoIP: VoIP is digital data and in some cases it will be clearer than a traditional phone line. VoIP typically offers services that aren't available on a traditional phone, such as voicemail and multiparty calling, and a permanent phone number regardless of where you move. It is an economical alternative to traditional telephone service, as long distance is not an issue over the Internet. And in the case of VoIP through a chat client, there is no cost at all.

Disadvantages of VoIP: While the disadvantages are few, two main issues arise in using VoIP. First, determining the location of a 911 call over VoIP is difficult because the call is coming from the Internet. Secondly, if the power goes out, so too does your computer and your VoIP telephony adapter. Traditional phone lines are exclusively powered, so you don't have to worry about power supply issues unless something happens to the lines.

VideoPhone 2500 for home use. But, according to most experts, it was Intel's involvement that caused Internet conferencing to come to life. Intel's CEO Andy Grove, in late 1990, pushed the company to add richer multimedia capabilities to PCs, which required greater processing power. By 1993, Intel had created a conferencing program called ProShare to take advantage of (and help sell) its more powerful chips.

In the next few years, several companies jumped into this breakthrough market. PictureTel worked with Microsoft, eventually creating a conferencing program called NetMeeting in 1995. Apple released QuickTime Conferencing in 1995, and Intel introduced their Video Phone in 1996. These programs could all run on a home computer over **plain old telephone service (POTS)**. CU-SeeMe, another company that sprang to life in the 1990s, introduced the first Internet conferencing system that let multiple people participate simultaneously in a conference over POTS. The other desktop programs were limited to the use of two people at a time.

In order for net conferencing to be practical and affordable, many technological developments had to occur, in addition to the increased processing power of PCs:

- **Compression standards:** In order for various Internet-connected computers to exchange video signals, they have to use the same compression standards. Compression condenses the video signal without losing quality. The development and widespread use of the H.32* compression standard has made this possible. Even though many conferencing software manufacturers have their own compression standards, nearly all also include H.32*.
- **Inexpensive video cameras:** Obviously, to get a video signal you need a video camera. The development of cheaper **CCD** (charged coupled device) chips, which are used to capture images, brought the cost of a PC video camera to an affordable level.
- **Digital signal processors (DSPs):** To convert the video and audio signals into digital information for transmission over the Internet, and convert the received signals to sound and pictures, you need a digital signal processor. This technology is included in your computer hardware.

Videoconferencing Etiquette

Videoconferencing requires a little extra consideration in order to be able to send clear video. There are also a few things to keep in mind if you are using videoconferencing for business.

Optimizing the Setting

Appearance: Remember, people can see you in a videoconference. Since videoconferencing is typically used for peer collaboration, casual attire is usually appropriate. However, if you're using Internet conferencing to conduct an important meeting, you'll probably need to dress more formally. Regardless, avoid white or light colored shirts; they are so bright they will wash out the picture. You also want to avoid shirts with narrow stripes, since the stripes often appear to wiggle on video. Red outfits tend to bleed, busy prints are distracting, and shiny jewelry reflects a lot of light. Your best bet is to wear a solid blue shirt, or a dark shirt with a subtle pattern.

Lighting: Lighting can make or break a video image. Don't rely on just the overhead fluorescent light that you find in most offices: the top of your head will be bright, while the lower half will be in shadow. Don't shine a light directly on your face either, since this will wash out your face. Too much light behind you will cause your face to

Common Abbreviations

AFAIK	as far as I know		IMO	in my opinion
AFK	away from keyboard		IOW	in other words
ASAP	as soon as possible		IRL	in real life
A/S/L	age/sex/location		JAM	just a minute
B4N	bye for now		JK	just kidding
BAK	back at keyboard		K	ok
BBL	be back later		LOL	laughing out loud
BBS	be back soon		LTNS	long time no see
BF	boyfriend		L8R	later
BFN	bye for now		MOTD	message of the day
BRB	be right back		MYOB	mind your own business
BTW	by the way		NP	no problem
CYA	see ya		OIC	oh, I see
FAAK	falling asleep at the keyboard		OOTB	out of the box
F2F	face to face		OTOH	on the other hand
FAQ	frequently asked question		PDA	public display of affection
FWIW	for what it's worth		POTS	plain old telephone service
FWD	forward		PPL	people
FYI	for your information		ROTF	rolling on the floor
G2G	got to go		ROTFL	rolling on the floor laughing
GF	girlfriend		RSN	real soon now
GL	good luck		TTFN	tah-tah for now
GR8	great		TTYL	talk to you later
IE	Internet Explorer by Microsoft		WB	welcome back
IMHO	in my humble opinion		YAOTM	yet another off-topic message

be very dark. Your best bet is to use a variety of indirect light sources. To make sure that you are looking your best, click the *Play* button of your net conferencing program to preview your image. This will give you a good idea of what you look like on screen to the other person.

Background: You need to pay attention to what is behind the subject of the picture, otherwise, it can appear as if trees are growing out of people's heads. A neutral-to-dark, plain background is best. Movement in the background will detract from the overall video quality, and should definitely be avoided.

Optimizing the Conversation

The lights are on and you're looking good—so, now what? For most people, talking into a camera is not a natural skill. Here are a few tips that may make the conversation look at bit more natural to the person receiving it.

Eye contact: We all know how important eye contact is in face-to-face conversations. The same is true with videoconferencing: good eye contact communicates interest in the other person and that you are paying attention. With videoconferencing, unfortunately, when you look at the other person's image on your screen you are not making eye contact. To make good eye contact, you have to look directly at the camera. Of course, then you can't see the other person. The best compromise is to mount your camera to your computer monitor, and then move the videoconferencing window so that it is as close as possible to the camera. So, for example, if you have your camera mounted to the top of your monitor, move the program window to the top of the screen directly below the camera.

Distance: The distance that you stand from another person communicates a great deal as well. The closer you stand, the more intimate the conversation is; the further away that you stand, the more formal. While you can't move closer to the other person in a videoconference, you can simulate social distance by how close you get to the camera. Adjust your position so that your head and shoulders fill most of the video frame. You should have no more than three people crammed into the video window at one location.

Audio over video: Most of the research that has been done on videoconferencing suggests that even though video is pretty cool, audio is more important for effective communication. If you have to choose between a videoconference with delayed and broken audio, or an audio-only conference, choose the audio. By shutting off the video, you can reduce or even eliminate the delay between when you speak and the other person hears you. This can make the conversation flow much more smoothly. In fact, in some instances you might decide to use the telephone for the audio side of the conference and use your computers for just the video signal. However, you need to be aware if you do this that the video signal on your computer will be slightly delayed and out of sync with the audio signal from the telephone.

Audio quality: You will end up with the best audio quality, and the least frustrating experience, if both people use headsets, or if you place the speakers far enough away from the microphone to avoid the echo sound feedback.

Video over audio: Even though responsive audio is more important than video, there are some times when video is extremely valuable. We know from interpersonal and nonverbal research that most of the emotional and relational dimensions of messages are communicated nonverbally. Use the video signal to determine the other person's attitudes and feelings when you can't infer them from the sound of their voice.

tip

∴ Try to set up your camera so that your head and shoulders are in view, so that others can read your facial expressions. People need to see how you react to information, as well as how you present it.

Obviously, the video signal is also crucial when you need to demonstrate actions—show them, don't tell them.

Etiquette: When you meet face-to-face, you typically shake hands. The equivalent greeting in a videoconference is to smile and wave. We are still working out many of the etiquette issues for videoconferencing. For example, if the phone rings while you are in a videoconference, do you answer the phone? When you are on the telephone, you can work on other tasks at the same time; can you write a memo while the other person is watching you? The best answer we can give you at this time is that it depends on your relationship to the other person. If it is someone you know fairly well, you can get away with not devoting your full attention to the videoconference. However, if it is a superior, or someone you need to impress, you ought to devote your full attention to the conference. It is probably best if your first contact with a person whom you never met is over the telephone instead of a videoconference, since the addition of the video signal makes it far more intrusive. Finally, if there are people in the room outside the camera's eye, you ought to introduce them to the other person.

IM in the Workplace

It may seem as if online chat is a purely social application, but it is a communication tool used widely at the workplace for business communication. In 2004, there were 65 million people worldwide using IM at work for business, and it is estimated that by 2005 there will be 330 million people worldwide using IM at work. Employees are using IM to communicate with coworkers, but also to communicate with clients, and offer more immediate support.

Major IM clients have an enterprise or business version, or have developed their primary version to meet business needs. Use of IM at the workplace has been shown to improve productivity as employees multi-task and hold several conversations simultaneously, but the biggest benefit is presence awareness. Employees can see who else is online, thus saving them the time wasted by telephone tag with someone who is unavailable.

IM clients can pose huge security risks in the workplace, which must be addressed. The IM equivalent of spam is called **spim**. These unwanted IMs could also contain viruses that can infect the network. A much larger security risk, however, is in the conversations themselves. Chat is transmitted in clear text, unencrypted, in most chat clients. So an employee can be having a legitimate, confidential chat conversation with someone outside the workplace, but if the conversation is not encrypted, it could be sniffed during transmission. Furthermore, employees could be using chat programs to divulge corporate confidential information inappropriately.

With IM increasing in popularity as a form of business communication, IT departments are also implementing solutions to address these security concerns. Some corporations install an enterprise version of IM software that is used strictly internally. In addition, they may also install IM management software, which searches for keywords in chats and prevents inappropriate chat transmissions. In addition to corporate confidential information, inappropriate chat could also include harassment, inappropriate humor, or illegal material. IM management software can also archive IM chats. This may seem like surveillance, however, in many places around the world all business correspondence including email, handwritten notes, and voice mail must be archived for some period of time, and is legally actionable. The American Management Society's

tip

∴ Don't say anything in an IM at work that you wouldn't say face to face. IMs can be logged, and it's too easy to type in the wrong window!

2004 study shows that only 11% of businesses were using IM management software, and yet, the same survey showed that 60% of businesses were using email monitoring software. Businesses are slowly coming to grips with IM as a business tool and starting to put policies and security measures in place to handle it as such. Just as you should be cautioned not to use your work email for personal use, you should also be cautioned not to use your work IM for personal communication. As you should know, any email sent or received from your work address is the property of the company, and as more and more businesses implement an IM management strategy, including archiving of IMs, these too, are the property of the company.

SUMMARY

Now that you've read through the chapter, you are prepared to:

- Block buddies, move to private chat rooms, transfer files using a chat client, and engage in chat client videoconferencing.
- Understand the revolutionary implication of Voice over Internet Protocol (VoIP).
- Employ effective instant messaging etiquette by understanding the history and culture that has evolved around the chat client.
- Hold successful videoconferencing sessions by adhering to videoconferencing etiquette, optimizing your environment, and optimizing the conversation.
- Appreciate how instant messaging is transforming the workplace, and use the chat client to suit your professional needs.

Review Questions and Hands-on Exercises

Review Questions

1. What is the difference between synchronous communication and asynchronous communication?

2. What is an IM?

3. You were online chatting last night and heard that one of your friends was also online chatting at the same time, but your friend did not appear online in your contact list. How could this be explained?

4. You try to send a file to a friend you are chatting with, but the connection does not seem to be working. What might be causing this?

5. What is VoIP?

6. You find yourself using three different chat clients because your friends use different chat clients. What can you do to chat with your friends, without having to install all three clients?

7. What is POTS?

8. Give an example of appropriate clothing, background, and lighting that could be used for someone who is going to be using videoconferencing.

9. You are using audio conferencing and you hear an echo of the person's voice as he or she is speaking. What is the likely cause and possible solution?

10. The corporate lawyer asks you for copies of your communication with a fellow employee. What type of communication should you provide?

11. Describe two security risks that IM poses in the workplace.

12. You are in the middle of a text chat with someone, when suddenly the conversation stops. Is this person being rude, or is there some other cause?

Hands-on Exercises

1. Open the AIM chat client and explore the options available in the menu *My Aim, Edit Options, Edit Preferences*. Perform the following tasks:

   a. Change the font for the buddy list *Entering Buddy, Online Buddy,* and *Departing Buddy*.

   b. In the *Away Message* feature create a new away message labeled *gone to lunch* and write some suitable text in the text window for this new message. Click the *I'm Away* button to set your status to *away*.

   c. In the *IM/Buddy Chat* option, set the color and font for the chat window.

   d. In the *IM/Buddy Chat* option, click the *Sounds* button to set sounds for each of the message events. Click the *OK* button when you are finished setting sounds.

2. Download and install MSN Instant Messenger (http://messenger.msn.com).

   a. If you have a Web cam and microphone, select the commands *Tools, Audio/Video Tuning Wizard* to configure your microphone and cam.

   b. Use the commands *Tools, Options* and select the *Personal* tab. Click the *Share my webcam capabilities with others* checkbox and type a nickname in the *Type your name as you want others to see it* box. Click the *OK* button to set these options.

   c. If you know someone else who uses MSN Instant Messenger, add that person to your contact list.

3. Download and install Yahoo! Messenger (http://messenger.yahoo.com). You may have to get a Yahoo! account if you do not already have one.

   a. Use the commands *Login, Preferences* and select the *General* category. Make sure the checkbox *Automatically start Yahoo! Messenger* is unchecked. That will ensure that Yahoo! Messenger does not start each time you turn on your computer.

   b. In the *Preferences* window, select the *Appearance* category. Change the text color and font for the main messenger window.

   c. In the *Preferences* window, select the *Alerts and Sounds* category. Select each of the alerts, such as *A friend comes online*, one at a time and feel free to choose appropriate alert methods at the bottom of the window.

   d. Click the *OK* button when you have finished setting preferences.

   e. Use the commands *Tools, Chat, Join Room* to display the listing of available chat rooms. Feel free to click the assorted category folders and on the *Yahoo! Rooms* tab and *User Rooms* tab. Many of the chat rooms are adult rooms, and you may find some of the names of the rooms offensive. You may join a room by selecting the room, and clicking the *Go to Room* button. If you are not interested in any of the chat rooms, click the *Cancel* button to close the chat room window.

   f. If you know someone who has a Yahoo! account, add that person as a contact to your contact list.

4. Download and install ICQ (http://www.icq.com). You will have to go through the steps to create an ICQ account.

   a. Click the *Online* button and select the options *Chat with a Friend*, and *Find a Chat Partner*. Click the *Find an Online Chat Friend* button in the *Chat with a Friend* window. Do this repeatedly until you come across someone you think you might like to chat with. When you find someone, click the *Send Message* button and send a friendly *hello* message to this person.

   b. Click the *Main* button and select the menu option *Preferences*. Click the *Status Mode* option and change the *Away* status to 15 minutes.

   c. In the *Preferences* window, select the *History, Alerts and Sounds* option. Click the *Sounds* tab. Feel free to select each event and choose a new sound for each.

   d. Click the *OK* button when you have finished editing preferences.

   e. If you know someone who uses ICQ, add him or her as a contact to your list. You can use the menu options *Main, Add/Invite Users, Find Users -> Add to List*, in order to find your friend.

5. Download and install Trillian basic (http://www.trillian.cc). You will need your userids and passwords for AIM, ICQ, and MSN. Configure Trillian to use each of these chat accounts.

6. Which chat package do you prefer, and why?

7. Find a VoIP provider in your area using the list of VoIP providers at http://www.voipproviderslist.com/. What does the VoIP provider charge for services?

8. If you have a Web cam and microphone and know someone else who does, try to arrange a videoconference using any of the chat tools discussed in this chapter. If you have time, try each one. You will notice big differences between the quality of video and audio for each of the chat packages. Which one do you prefer?

9. If you use IM at your workplace, find out if your workplace has a policy on monitoring or archiving IM messages, and what your responsibility as an employee is toward saving IM chat sessions.

Entertainment and Education

Chapter Objectives

This chapter helps you understand

- ☐ the rise of video and computer gaming.
- ☐ the use of the Internet in online gambling.
- ☐ the application of the Internet concerning distance education.
- ☐ how the Internet is being used for telemedicine and remote surgery.

Do you like to play video games? Maybe you like to make a little wager every now and then. Perhaps you have taken an online course at your university. Maybe you've even thought about getting an online degree or professional certification. Or, have you witnessed some of the advancements being made in online surgery? The Internet and World Wide Web are becoming versatile and promising tools for gaming, gambling, distance education, and the medical sciences.

As our computer graphics, network bandwidth, and programming capabilities advance, so too does the **virtual reality** of our computerized environments. Virtual reality allows users to feel like they are in an environment without actually being there. Environments that were traditionally only face-to-face (F2F) are now simulated to a lesser or greater degree on the Internet. This chapter examines some of these virtual environments, and shows you how the Internet is altering our concepts of entertainment, education, and medical practice.

Gaming

Interestingly, video gaming and computer gaming really have two parallel, but separate, historical timelines, that are converging now in the modern era of gaming. Video games developed as standalone game units, arcade games, and television consoles. Many of the television consoles and hand-held consoles will now support Internet broadband connections and include features such as surfing the Web and downloading data, in addition to multi-player game playing. Computer gaming began as text-only gaming using either email or early chat applications, and has evolved into **Massive Multiplayer Online Role-Playing Games (MMORPG)**. To put Internet gaming in perspective, it's useful to know a bit about the history of the development of video gaming and computer gaming as well.

History of Video Gaming

The first electronic video game was developed in 1958 by physicist Willy Higginbotham. It was a table tennis type game displayed on an oscilloscope. In 1961, Steve Russell developed the first interactive computer game. The game was *Spacewar* and it was played on a Digital PDP-11 computer, displaying line-drawn graphics on a green CRT monitor. In 1967, Ralph Baer, working for defense contractor Sanders Associates, developed some interactive games that could be played on a television set. These included a chase game and a table tennis game, and Magnavox later licensed them. The first arcade version of the computer game *Spacewar* was developed in 1971, but it was not entirely successful, as the public found it too difficult to play. In 1972, though, a breakthrough game, *Pong*, was born. *Pong* is a table tennis type game and the sound the ball makes when it hits a paddle is *pong*. Nolan Bushnell and Al Alcorn developed Pong, and Bushnell marketed the game himself, starting his own company, Atari. In 1976, Bushnell sold Atari to Warner Communications for $28 million. In 1972 Magnavox began distribution of its video console *Odyssey*, selling over 100,000 units. In 1977 Atari introduced the *Atari 2600*, a programmable game console, which was cartridge-based. In 1978 Atari introduced *Football* and *Space Invaders* as arcade games. *Football* was tremendously popular during football season, but *Space Invaders* proved to continue in popularity. The game of *Football* introduced a new pointing device, the trackball.

From 1980 onward, the pace of development in video and arcade games accelerated tremendously. In 1980, development included a home version of *Space Invaders* for the *Atari 2600* system, the development of Mattel's *Intellivision* console, Namco's release of the arcade game *Pac Man* (the most popular arcade game of all time), the first 3D game, *Battlezone*, which the U.S. army eventually used as a military training tool, and the release of the first virtual world game, *Defender*, by Williams, a Chicago based pinball manufacturer.

In 1981, Nintendo released *Donkey Kong*, U.S. arcades reached $5 billion in revenues, and the first video game magazine, *Electronic Games* was published. In 1983 Commodore introduced the *Commodore 64*, an inexpensive computer system, which could out perform any video game console, and in the mid 1980s the video game industry suffered as home computer games emerged. In 1986, game console development was fast and furious with the introduction of Nintendo's *Entertainment System* (*NES*) and its *Super Mario Brothers* game, the *Sega Master System* (*SMS*) and the *Atari 7800* game console. Throughout the 1980s and 1990s, video game console development continued and the home market expanded, particularly from 1989–1992 as game

tip

∴ Current game software will require upgraded video cards and more memory than other programs. Be sure to check the hardware requirements for the game you are purchasing and compare it to your available resources.

consoles became affordable entertainment units and video game rentals were available. In 1988, Nintendo released the *Game Boy*, a hand-held video game console.

The modern era of console gaming was ushered in with the release of the *Sega Dreamcast* system in 1998, which accessed the Internet for multi-player gaming. In 2000, Sony's *PlayStation 2*, which could also play DVDs, was released, and in 2001 Microsoft's long awaited *Xbox*, which contained a Pentium III chip was released. Nintendo's *Game Boy Advance* could connect to cellular phones for Internet access, including multi-player gaming, email access, and data download. A broadband adapter was released for the *Sega Dreamcast*, and Sega also released the first online role-playing game, *Phantasy Star Online*. A role-playing game is a game where the player assumes a character and travels through some sort of adventure, perhaps solving puzzles, fighting enemies, and interacting with other gamers who have assumed other characters, and working with them as a team, perhaps against other teams of characters.

History of Computer Gaming

The history of computer gaming also began in 1961 with Steve Russell's PDP-11 computer game, *Spacewar*. With the development of email, it also became possible for snail mail games to migrate to email. Snail mail games included playing chess, for instance, as the players mailed the next move to each other. In 1973, the first PDP-11 adventure game was developed by Will Crowther, suitably named *Adventure*. Although *Adventure* was a single-player game, it was widely played on ARPANET, and several years later a version for Radio Shack's TRS-80 and the Apple II computer was developed. In 1978, the first **MUD (Multi-User Dungeon)** was developed by Roy Trubshaw.

To backtrack, just a bit, in 1974 Gary Gygax and Dave Arneson turned their love for *Lord of the Rings* type fantasy games into the first role-playing adventure game called *Dungeons and Dragons (D&D)*. This game was played with dice, each player adopting a character, and the game leader, the Dungeon Master, who had a handbook, would describe the fantasy environment to the game players as they threw their dice and made decisions for the next step in their adventure. Through the 1980s, this and other role-playing games became enormously popular, particularly among teenagers and college students, and these types of pen, paper and dice-based role-playing games are still played today. The term MUD (Multi-User Dungeon) refers to the *Dungeons and Dragons* game for its terminology, where a dungeon is a fantasy room.

With the development of *MUDs*, fantasy role-playing games became electronic multi-user games, played in real time. In 1988, **Internet Relay Chat (IRC)** was developed and role-playing games were also played in IRC chat rooms.

In 1981, with the development of home computers and the 5¼ inch floppy drive, games were developed by young game software companies such as Epyx, Broderbund, and Sierra On-Line, and distributed on floppy disk. Games included arcade style games, card games, sports, and action and adventure games. In 1983, *Electronic Arts (EA)*, one of the largest game software companies today, began publishing games. By 1986, the software gaming industry was thriving and developing games in multiple platforms. Popular games had versions for Apple, Commodore-64, Amiga, and IBM personal computers. In 1987, adventure and role-playing games topped the charts for most popular games.

The year 1989 was a pivotal year for computer game technology development. Sound cards, 256-VGA graphics cards, and CD-ROM drives emerged, and the first games that could be played over a modem were developed.

꙾*tip*

∴ To experience a MUD, simply search on your favorite search engine for MUD. Or, you can go to one of the online libraries of MUDs, such as: http://www .mudconnect.com/

368 Chapter 12   Entertainment and Education

In 1993 the game *Wolfenstein 3D*, by ID Software, introduced the concept of first-person shooter games. Although it isn't 3D by today's standards, it changed the perspective of the player in the game to feeling like a character in the game rather than manipulating the characters. This paved the way for *Doom* in 1994, which was a runaway success. The first truly 3D graphical game was *Quake*, developed by ID Software, released in 1996. A free add-on program called *QuakeWorld* allowed users to play *Quake* over the Internet. Also in 1996, the first massive multiplayer Internet game, *Meridian 59* was released. Massive multiplayer refers to the fact that dozens or hundreds of players can play the game simultaneously, as opposed to multiplayer referring to a very small number of players. In 1999, Sony released *Everquest,* the first fully 3D Massive Multiplayer Online Role-Playing Game (MMORPG).

Computer games developed in the 1980s, such as card games, board games, racing and flying games, and adventure games, were also developed for video game consoles and vice versa. Today, many of these games can be played over the Internet at sites such as Microsoft Game Zone (`http://www.zone.com`), Yahoo! Games (`http://games.yahoo.com`), and Electronic Arts' Pogo (`http://www.pogo.com`).

Gaming Today

The convergence of video game development and computer game development is continuing right now. Games that were traditionally available only for game consoles are available in formats for computer play and vice versa. Multiplayer games that were available only on game consoles or single PCs became available for play across networks. As their popularity increased and technology advanced, they were played across a LAN, and eventually used game servers across the Internet for massive amounts of players simultaneously. **Massive Multiplayer Online Games (MMOG)** can be played over the Internet from game consoles and personal computers, through game servers on the Internet. Whether the gamer is using a game console, or installed game software on a personal computer, an Internet subscription to a game server can be purchased, which enables the gamer to play with other gamers. Typically there is a subscription fee charged to connect to these servers.

In 2003, the worldwide revenue from MMOG was estimated at slightly over $1 billion and it is estimated to be $9.8 billion by 2009. And that represents only 25% of overall forecasted gaming revenue for 2009. This is big business. The growth in the popularity of broadband connections is driving the online gaming usage. Console game units such as *Xbox* and its *Xbox Live* service connect players via a broadband connection to play with other *Xbox* gamers.

Although MMOGs receive a lot of attention, they are not the only games played over the Internet. Board and card games available at sites such as Game Zone, Yahoo! Games, and Pogo routinely each accommodate 150,000 or 200,000 players simultaneously as users play and chat.

Types of Games

As you know, there are many types of computer games. Games essentially fall into one of the following groups. Some games fall into more than one category.

tip

Make sure to use a headset and microphone for the Massive Multiplayer Online Games (MMOGs). If the software is equipped, you'll be able to talk with your teammates in real time, while strategizing play.

- **Sports:** Games for individual sports; some emphasize strategy and some emphasize playing. Almost any sport imaginable has an associated computer or online game.

- **Simulation:** May be a mixture of a game of chance, strategy, and skill; one that simulates something like a civilization. Examples include *Civilization* and *SimCity*.

- **Action/Adventure:** The characters in the game generally go through some kind of adventure while the player manipulates them to shoot objects, solve puzzles, and gather items. Some consider these to be simple role-playing games (RPG). Examples include *Zelda* and *Doom*.

- **Racing and Flying:** The player races or flies a vehicle. The game is usually based on skill.

- **Turn-Based Strategy:** Each player takes a turn, used in board games, for instance.

- **Real-Time Strategy:** The game progresses in a continuum or real time not based on turns, where more technologies or funds are available based on the passage of time. Examples include *SimCity* and *Dune 2*.

- **First-Person Shooters:** The player sees the environment as if standing in it, and uses weapons to shoot. These are graphics intensive games. Examples include *Doom*, *Half-Life*, and *Quake*.

- **Role-Playing Games (RPG):** The player assumes the role of a character, where the character gains abilities, makes decisions, and moves through environments in an adventure. Examples include *Diablo*, *Everquest*, and *Warcraft*.

- **Massive Multiplayer Online Role-Playing Games (MMORPG):** A role-playing game where the player assumes the role of a character, which is represented graphically by an **avatar**. Many players play in the same environment simultaneously and players see the avatars of other players and can interact with them. Examples include online versions of *Everquest*, *Asheron's Call*, and *Lineage*.

- **Massive Multiplayer Online Sports Game (MMOSG):** Players assume the role of one of the players and play with a team against another team. This is an emerging technology. An example is *Ultimate Baseball Online*.

How Games Are Played on the Internet

Today there are really four main methods used to play games over the Internet: (1) games played via email, (2) games played directly in a browser window by visiting a Web site, (3) text based games played via IRC, telnet, chat forum, or a MUD, and (4) highly graphical games for which the user is required to purchase standalone software, or play through a game console.

Games Played via Email Games played via snail mail date back to the 1960s and include games such as *Diplomacy*, and other board games including chess. Game players would mail in orders to a moderator or opponent once a week and the results or next move would be mailed back. These days, this type of game playing is still popular but has taken on an electronic form using email. Games played via email include board games, war games, fantasy role-playing games, and strategy adventure games. A good resource for more information about playing games by mail is the *Play by Mail* site at `http://www.pbm.com/~lindahl/pbm.html`.

Games Played in a Web Browser Window Games played in a Web browser include board games such as checkers, chess, backgammon, and card games. Players can play other players, or play the computer, and chat with other players while they play. Some sites, such as MSN Games (http://www.zone.com) provide tournament play for the more serious players, and rooms for casual play. Figure 12.1 shows an example of an online card game.

Figure 12.1   An example of an online card game.

Text-Based Games Played via IRC, Chat Forum, or MUD These games are typically played in real time in a *Dungeons and Dragons* style role-playing atmosphere where the moderator, or Dungeon Master, keeps the game on track, and players acquire skills and items as the adventure unfolds. Players will be able to use text commands such as *look*, *move east*, *drop object*, and *say*.

Graphical Games Where the User Purchases Software "Down! Set! Hut, hut!" Sports games are a popular online genre because many people enjoy the vicarious experience of playing as particular sports figures or teams. The season never ends with the multitude of sports games.

Massive Multiplayer Online Role-playing Games (MMORPG) fall into this category as well. Players connect to the game server via their computer game or game console. As a player, you assume a role, represented by an avatar, and your avatar encounters other avatars that are controlled by other players.

There are also first-person shooter games played online. These games are something to marvel at from an artistic standpoint alone.

There are also online simulations that are multi-user. A simulation recreates a realistic environment. The U.S. Army spent millions of dollars developing the shooter game *America's Army* in an effort to bring realism to virtual battle. They even went as far as to distribute the game free to potential recruits. In *America's Army* (http://www.americasarmy.com/), you choose whether you are on the assault or defense team. You are given a specific mission: capture or defend a base. Then, you engage in a very convincing series of maneuvers against the opposing force with handguns, rifles, machine guns, and grenades to achieve your mission, as shown in Figure 12.2.

Figure 12.2   Here, a U.S. Special Forces M-60 gunner gets pinned down by sniper fire behind a station wagon. *America's Army* has become one of the more popular shooter simulation games online.

Computer simulation games can be based on learning how to fly a Jumbo 747 or drive in the Indianapolis 500. Online computer simulation games have come of age. Today, computer simulation games are more sophisticated with their settings, and many are taking on a more realistic tone. Consider the case of the game *Virtual U* where you are appointed the president of a comprehensive university with designs on expansion. Your job, should you choose to accept it, is to manage the university through hiring and firing employees, while overseeing the general budget. You report to a Board of Directors that oversees the university's well being, and you receive an annual evaluation.

Gambling

Casinos worldwide are big business. Gamblers know when they enter the house that the odds are not in their favor. Still, perhaps for entertainment value, the thrill, or the chance to make some quick money—casinos thrive upon financial risk takers. In 2003, U.S. brick-and-mortar casinos took in roughly $22 billion. What's interesting to note, however, is that online casinos (which have largely been an international affair) took in an estimated $6.3 billion. Datamonitor, a market information research company estimates that by 2015, online gambling will reach $125 billion in worldwide revenue.

In many countries, brick-and-mortar casinos are regulated by a combination of federal and state or provincial laws. But, when you are gambling over the Internet, does geography really matter? Not according to the 2004 World Trade Organization (WTO) report that oversees trade disputes between countries. Sometimes, the local laws strongly conflict with the global nature of the Internet with respect to the issue of online gambling. U.S. legislative attempts to ban online casinos are being met with strong diplomatic opposition overseas and by the WTO, and disputes are pending.

In 2001, Britain became the first world power to specifically legalize betting over the Internet. On the other end of the spectrum, many individual states in the U.S. have laws prohibiting online betting completely, or with the exclusion of currently licensed casinos and lotteries. If the laws are not clear on the legalities and enforceability, it may become more difficult for someone to gamble online as corporations fear crossing the line. In the U.S., credit card companies such as Visa and Mastercard began prohibiting their members from using their cards to transfer funds to gambling Web sites in 2003. In June 2003, the online pay service, PayPal, agreed to pay the U.S. government $10 million as a settlement for knowingly transferring funds to offshore gambling sites and, needless-to-say, will not be doing business with offshore gambling sites until it is clearly legalized.

Although online betting may be illegal in some jurisdictions, typically the intent of the law is to target the online operation rather than the $5 bettor. But the challenge of the global nature of the Internet occurs when the online operation is outside of the country whose laws prohibit unlicensed gambling operations. Does this mean that every online gambling operation needs to be licensed in every country in the world? Many people speculate that eventually online gambling will be legal worldwide; they compare the gambling issue to alcohol and prohibition in the 1920s.

Some gambling sites are government run. Canada's first government run site was established by the Atlantic Lottery Corporation, which began selling lottery tickets online in July 2004. The corporation expects to attract a new market, and not compete against their retail sales. The Atlantic Lottery Corporation places a limit on the amount of money that any one person can spend on tickets per day, and requires verification that the player is at least 18 years of age.

Mobile gambling over a wireless connection from a hand-held device is the next hottest trend in online gambling, and it is expected that revenues from mobile gambling will reach $6 billion by 2006 and $16 billion by 2008. Gamblers will be able to bet on sports events in real time while the game is in play using their mobile phone.

And who is gambling? Demographically, according to the media consultancy firm, Screen Digest, 64% of casual gamblers are women between the ages of 35 and 54, and

60% of those are married. These casual gamblers prefer card games such as solitaire where the best player wins a prize, bingo, pub quizzes, and casino games such as one-armed bandits, roulette, and poker. Many casual gambling sites offer a chance to play for free to learn the rules. Men dominate the group of hardcore gamblers who bet high stakes regularly.

Casinos

The number of online casinos is literally astounding. In fact, a simple Web search for *online casino* is really all you need to do to find one. You will find useful information including casino reviews at Online Casino Reports (`http://www.onlinecasinoreports.com/`). Unless you are running a pop-up blocker, however, beware of the advertisements. You'll be inundated with ads promising you everything from a 10% to 100% first-time deposit bonus. Most online casinos ask that you download software onto your computer so that you can play through their specially designed interfaces.

Some online casinos will actually allow you to practice for free, without risking any money at all. It's a good idea to do this, since you can see what the casino games look like without investing any money whatsoever. Plus, if you like to play casino games, but hate to put money down on the table, this is also a good way to just have fun. Most of the playing environments are aesthetically convincing, and some are absolutely fantastic, as shown in Figure 12.3.

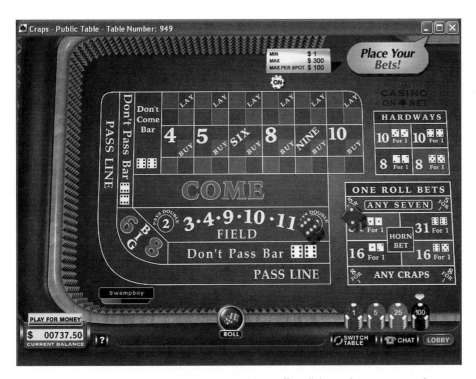

Figure 12.3   Casino on Net (`http://www.casino.net`) offers all the usual casino games with a very attractive graphical interface. Pictured here is their craps table.

Sports Betting

NFL, NBA, NHL, MLB, NCAA football, NCAA basketball, MLS, international soccer, golf, boxing, tennis, auto racing, horse racing—pick your insider persuasion. If casinos don't fit your bill, then online sports betting just might. Online sports betting sites insist that betting on sports is more a matter of skill than luck. Your challenge is to "gather and analyze as much information as you can about a game, weigh the probabilities of each team winning, and subsequently compare your opinion to the oddsmaker's" (Sportsbetting.com, 2004). Of course, lady luck must be factored into these analyses, too. Use your discretion whenever gambling online, and remember that these sites exist to make money.

Casual Gambling

For the casual gambler, there are a variety of online games that do not carry the high stakes of casino games and sports betting. These include card games, slots, bingo, and lotteries. You will find card games and slots at casino sites. Card games, board games, and pub quizzes can also be found at an assortment of gambling sites, including casino sites. You will find bingo game portals such as Bingo (`http://www.bingo.com`), where you can play free bingo games. Sites that charge for games may range from $.25 to $1.00 per game or more. Lotteries can be found through individual state and province run lottery sites, and through portals such as The Big Lotto (`http://www.thebiglotto.com/`).

Tips for Choosing an Online Gambling Site

According to survey research by Harrods-Casino.com people choose specific online gambling sites based on six major factors.

1. Confidence and trust in a casino they have previously used
2. Quick cash-outs
3. Favorable odds of winning
4. Good customer service
5. Ease, speed, and quality of play
6. Sign-up and other bonuses

If you've researched your local laws, and decided to gamble online, you shouldn't start your experience betting on whether an online gambling site is reputable. Here are some tips that may help you to choose a site confidently.

1. Know your local laws and abide by them.
2. Watch for reputable domain names. Avoid names that you know to be free Web sites such as geocities. This may indicate that the site is illegal or fly-by-night.
3. Look for accreditation such as the Interactive Gaming Council (`http://www.igcouncil.org/`) as approval. This body has established a voluntary code of conduct for online gaming, to which the more reputable sites will adhere.

4. Does the site operate a toll free number and customer service via email? If so, try them out to make sure they work.

5. Ensure that the site keeps transaction logs and watch your logs. This is a running report of every wager you make at the site.

6. Always take a screen capture of winnings.

Gambling As an Addiction

Just a final word on gambling, online and otherwise; compulsive gambling is an illness, which is progressive. Some casino sites watch for signs of overdoing it and offer online counselors and support. There is some suggestion that people who use the Internet to gamble may be more likely to develop more serious problems than those who use slot machines or lotteries. A University of Connecticut Health Center survey found that the majority of the study's participants with Internet gambling experience had more serious levels of gambling behaviors than those who used other gambling methods.

Distance Education

Distance Education Defined

As the need for education in our ever-changing economies becomes more evident, teaching institutions throughout the world are adapting to cope with the need to serve a populace of students that cannot meet, regularly, in a traditional classroom setting. **Distance education** occurs when, ". . . a teacher and student(s) are separated by physical distance, and technology (i.e., voice, video, data, and print), often in concert with face-to-face communication, is used to bridge the instructional gap" (Willis, 2004). Distance education itself is not a new thing. In 1883 correspondence courses were first recognized by Chautauqua College of Liberal Arts, authorized by the state of New York to grant degrees to students who included correspondence courses in their studies. Since then, the debate over whether distance education delivery would replace traditional face-to-face delivery has raged. The difference is that in 1883 the delivery method was the postal system and today the educational technology is electronic, including the resources of the Internet.

Distance education students tend to be students in a traditional educational setting, adults who are challenged by the schedules of their careers and other commitments, people who are disadvantaged by geography, or even those with a physical disability who wish to pursue formalized instruction.

Distance Education Delivery Tools

According to Willis (2004) there are four basic distance education delivery tools: (1) voice, (2) video, (3) data, and (4) print. We will cover each below:

Voice Voice is usually delivered via telephone or audioconferencing systems. These tools are called "active voice" media because they allow for feedback (two-way communication). Passive audio technologies are those that allow no feedback, such as audiotapes and CDs.

tip

If you suspect that compulsive gambling may be a problem in your life or you're just interested in more information, visit the Gamblers Anonymous site at http://www.gamblersanonymous.org/, or the Center for Online and Internet Addiction at http://www.netaddiction.com/.

Video Educational video technologies can be as simple as still photographs, slideshows, and prerecorded videotapes. New communication technologies have done much with these older technologies to transfer them to the Internet and World Wide Web. It is not uncommon for students taking online instruction to encounter still images, slideshows, or video feeds from their instructor. With the advent of videoconferencing software, students now also have the ability to cross-communicate with their classmates or even their instructors.

Data Obviously, any information transmitted across the Internet is technically considered data. But the type of data we are talking about here is data files. These include emails, mailing lists such as listservs, file attachments, FTP files, newsgroups, discussion boards, real-time computer conferencing, and the World Wide Web.

Print The basis of any good education, of course, is printed material. These tools, which are the same as in a traditional classroom, are syllabi, textbooks, books, articles, workbooks, study guides, and case studies.

Popular Web Courseware Tools

There are many software companies that have developed distance course management systems for the Web to facilitate distance education delivery. These turnkey suites, which include all of the major tools necessary to run a basic distance education course, are used throughout the world. They are not used exclusively for distance education, however. These tools and others like them are also used for traditional face-to-face course delivery to facilitate group work, assignment submissions, and instructor feedback. Three popular Web courseware tools include Blackboard, FirstClass, WebCT, and eCollege. We'll also look at some alternatives. Although these course management tools are popular for distance education delivery, they are also used in traditional face-to-face delivery as well.

The major Web course management tools will contain most or all of the following features: discussion forums, file exchanges (left in the course material for the student to pick up and upload to the course drop-box area), email which may be internal or Internet email, real-time chat, video streaming, whiteboard, calendar for due dates, group work folders, and self-assessment tools (multiple-choice questions, for instance). They will also provide course management and administration tools including Web site management, restricting access to specific accounts and features, and course templates.

Blackboard Blackboard Inc. (`http://www.blackboard.com`) produces a suite of educational tools, including the Blackboard Learning System. This system includes course management tools for teachers such as a grade book to calculate grades, timed release course material, course templates, chat forums, internal email, calendar and appointment scheduler, and question pools and test management tools for multiple choice, true/false, and essay questions.

Some interesting features include a Whiteboard area that supports group Web browsing for synchronous Web collaboration and Web page slide shows, student home pages, and support for video streaming.

FirstClass FirstClass, developed by Open Text Corporation (`http://www.education`
`.softarc.com/`) includes the basic features of class and group forum discussion areas, chat forums, and calendar scheduling. Whiteboard, testing, and videoconferenc-

ing features are not included. One interesting feature is internal email that also receives and sends Internet email.

A FirstClass course area might look something like Figure 12.4.

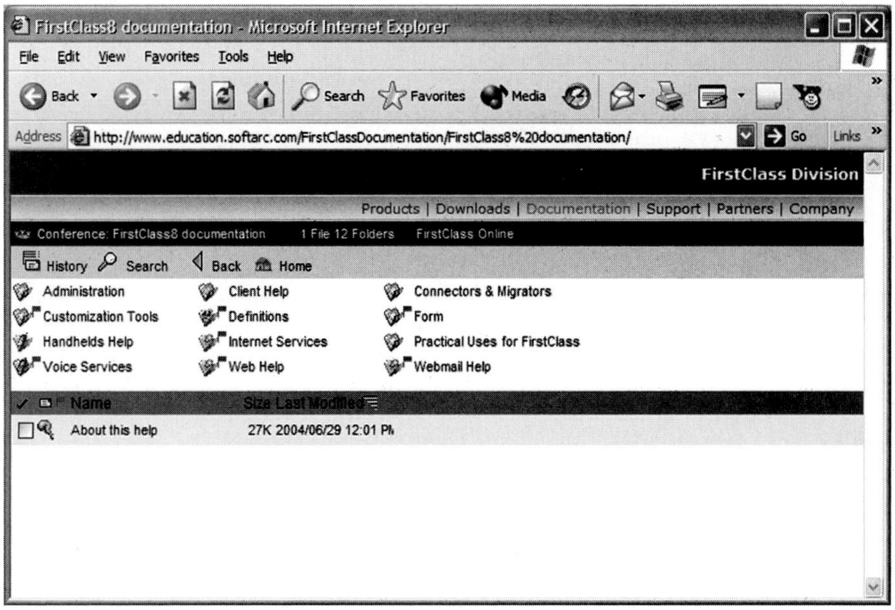

Figure 12.4   FirstClass view of documents in a course conference area.

WebCT WebCT Inc. (http://www.webct.com) produces the WebCT Vista course management tool, which includes the basic features of class and group chat forums, calendar scheduling, Whiteboard, and course area. This could include HTML files so that teachers can create course sites rather than a folder of documents. Videoconferencing is not included.

Some interesting features include course drop-box areas for assignment submissions, anonymous postings for chat forums, private folders for students to store files, and student home pages.

eCollege eCollege AU+ Course Management System (http://www.ecollege.com) includes the basic features of class and group forum discussion areas, chat forums, and course scheduler. It also includes tools for real-time collaboration.

A WebCT teacher view of a student discussion group might look something like Figure 12.5.

Newsgroups and Email Distance education does not require the use of a formal software tool such as Blackboard, FirstClass, WebCT, or eCollege. Some successful institutions are making use of simple email and newsgroups. Newsgroups can be managed using a Microsoft Exchange Server. We made reference to Exchange Servers in Chapter 4, Email, as a special case of connection to email. In Chapter 10, Mass Communication, we looked at using Microsoft Outlook to connect to an ISP Usenet newsfeed. Similarly,

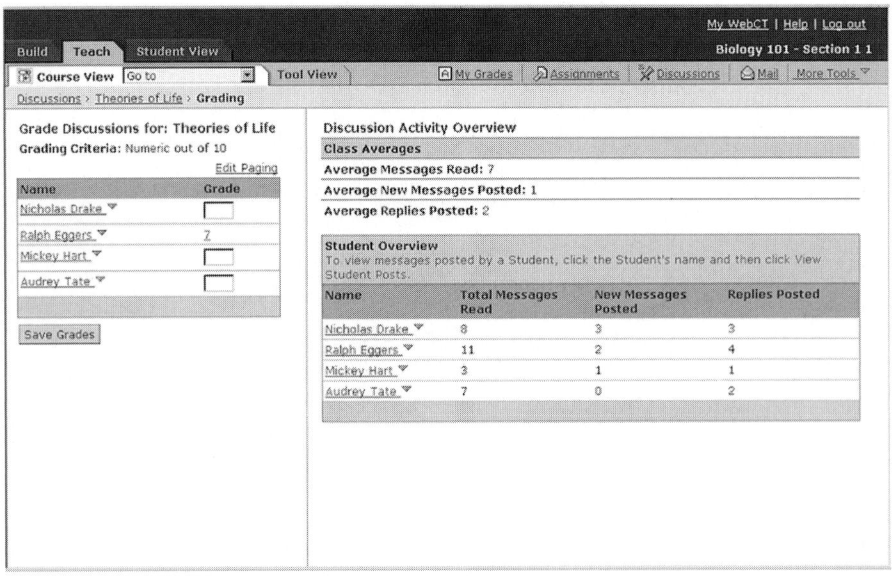

Figure 12.5 WebCT teacher view of student discussion board.

you can use Outlook to connect to an Exchange server that is hosting newsgroups for distance education. For instance, the University of Phoenix Online campus (`http://www.phoenix.edu`) uses this method extensively for course delivery. Students post messages in course newsgroups, submit assignments to newsgroups, and work on group work in newsgroups assigned to each group of students. Research facilities are available through the online library, and include bibliographic databases and subscription-based resources.

An online delivery of a course using newsgroups might look something like Figure 12.6.

Comparing Web Courseware Tools A particularly helpful site for comparing a wide variety of course management tools is the Maricopa Center for Learning and Instruction courseware comparison site at `http://www.mcli.dist.maricopa.edu/ocotillo/ courseware/compare.html`. You will find this invaluable if you are interested in researching the Web courseware tools that are available, or involved in education and trying to decide which route to take for course delivery. Each tool, of course, has its pros and cons, and before deciding which tool to choose, you should assess your course delivery needs, decide which features you require for your specific course delivery, and determine which resources are available to you.

Compressed Interactive Video Networks

Something that deserves an honorable mention here regarding distance education is the expansion of **interactive video networks (IVN)**, which use dedicated video equipment and bundled telecommunication lines to conduct multiple-setting interactive video and audio sessions between sites. Although these networks may make use of the Internet, typically they use a dedicated WAN (wide-area network), across an entire state or region. To date, compressed interactive video is the closest thing that we have to simulating the actual classroom environment.

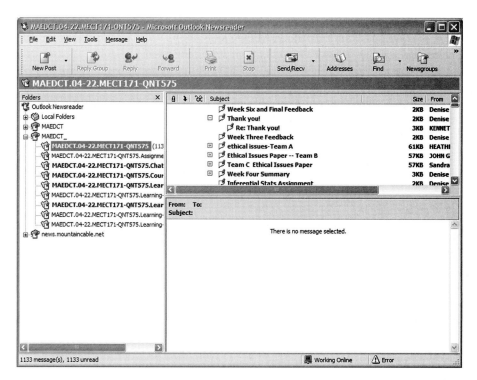

Figure 12.6   Microsoft Outlook displaying newsgroups for an online course.

Since these systems require dedicated equipment to function, participants must be at a local site which is connected to the dedicated network, but IVN can also make use of Webcasting to broadcast video over the Internet. The digital signal provided over the IVN can be of far better quality than anything provided over the Internet. And since the network is digital, and uses the same protocol structure of the Internet itself, all the traditional technology tools that can be used in a normal classroom—such as slide presentations, overhead transparencies, and videotape—can be used without any compromise in signal quality. The University of Louisiana at Lafayette's compressed interactive video parlor is shown in Figure 12.7.

Figure 12.7   The University of Lafayette's IVN facility.

Telemedicine and Remote Surgery

Telemedicine is not a separate medical specialty, but refers to practicing medicine remotely. It basically includes anything that uses electronic communication to improve a patient's health care. It is part of the broader practice of telehealth, which encompasses remote diagnosis, including nursing call centers, transmitting still images for diagnostics, patient Web portals, and education.

Like IVNs, telemedicine makes use of dedicated networks; it also makes use of the Internet nonsurgical techniques such as diagnostics and communications. In 2004 there were approximately 200 telemedicine networks in the United States involving approximately 2000 medical institutions. Uses also include home-to-monitor center connections where patients can be monitored in their own homes.

One aspect of telemedicine that is particularly exciting is the use of robots online through dedicated WANs (wide-area networks) to perform surgery. Here's how it works: A surgeon, miles away from the patient he is going to treat, engages a virtual workstation where he or she can perform complex procedures using a fiber-optic connected robot on the other end of the line. The robot actually helps doctors by controlling hand-tremor and making cuts more precise. Figure 12.8 is a picture of a doctor performing a telerobotic procedure.

The Current Science and Technology Center reports that, "On September 7, 2001 a doctor in New York removed the diseased gallbladder of a 68-year-old patient in Strasbourg, France. The surgeon used a computer with a high-speed network connection to move robotic tools in the French operating room" (2004). This was the first recorded surgical operation, using a telemedical device.

∴ If you live in a rural or suburban area of a major city, see if your neighboring university does instruction via compressed interactive video networks. While they aren't as seamless as a traditional face-to-face environment, they do provide an engaging atmosphere.

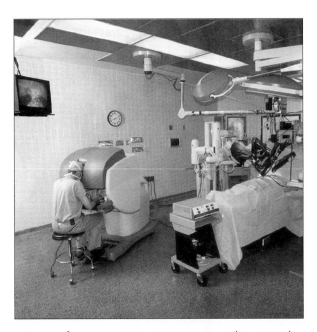

Figure 12.8   A surgeon performs an operation on a patient using a robot connected to a workstation. These procedures can be performed miles away, using a dedicated WAN. Figure courtesy of Intuitive Surgical.

Certainly the benefits of telemedicine in rural and remote areas are obvious. But in addition, telemedical research is underway to develop techniques for health care and medical emergencies at the International Space Station. It doesn't get much more remote than that! The NASA Extreme Environment Mission Operations (NEEMO) project uses the National Oceanic and Atmospheric Administration's (NOAA) Aquarius Underwater Laboratory, located 62 feet below the surface of the water off the coast of Key Largo, Florida. This underwater habitat houses aquanauts and a mock patient. Research involves surgery performed by a doctor in Hamilton, Ontario, Canada, using a two-way telecommunication link guiding the aquanauts.

SUMMARY

Now that you've read through the chapter, you are prepared to:

- Engage in various forms of video and online gaming.
- Understand some of the legal issues surrounding gambling online.
- Define and recognize several distance education environments.
- Appreciate how surgeons are now using cutting edge technology to enhance their surgical practices using technology enhanced networks.

Review Questions and Hands-on Exercises

Review Questions

1. What is the difference between a video game and a computer game?
2. What is a role-playing game?
3. What is meant by the term *Massive Multiplayer Online Role-Playing Game*?
4. How can email be used to play a game?
5. Describe how video games can be played over the Internet.
6. Describe, in general, the legal challenges that online gambling has posed.
7. What types of gambling sites are available online?
8. What types of things should someone consider when they're looking for an online gambling site?
9. What is distance education?
10. Describe how a Web courseware tool can be used to deliver distance education courses.
11. Describe another online distance education option other than a Web courseware tool.
12. What is IVN and how can it be used in education?
13. What is telemedicine?
14. Describe how the Internet can be used for telemedicine.

Hands-on Exercises

1. Open a Web browser and load the Play by Mail site (`http://www.pbm.com/~lindahl/pbm.html`) for email games. Browse through the list of PBEM games and find three games from different types of games that might interest you. Briefly describe each, and how you would find out more information.

2. Load the Yahoo! Games site (`http://games.yahoo.com`). List five different games that are available, in addition to card games.

3. Search the Web to try to determine if there is a government run lottery site in your area. What payment methods does the site accept?

4. Find the Web site for your local college or university. Does this institution offer distance education courses? If so, can you determine what kind of online course tools are required?

5. Load the American Telemedicine site (`http://www.atmeda.org`) and find the news section. Describe one of the most recent news stories.

THE IMPACT OF THE INTERNET

part 5

	Chapter
The Internet's Impact on Traditional Media	13
The Internet and the Law	14
Keeping Pace with Innovations	15

The Internet's Impact on Traditional Media

chapter 13

Chapter Objectives

This chapter helps you understand

- [ ] trends occurring in new media.
- [ ] how traditional media are interacting with the Internet.
- [ ] how peer-to-peer (P2P) networks function.

Now that you know how to design Web sites and use the various communication tools available, it is time to consider the impact that the Internet has had on traditional media. Throughout this book, we've treated the Internet as a new communications medium. As a new medium, older, preexisting media influences its characteristics, and it is forcing older media to adapt. We'll be examining that complex relationship in this chapter, first by looking at the trends that new media typically follow when they are introduced, and second at how the Internet and the older media affect each other. Finally, we'll discuss the rise of peer-to-peer networks that have challenged traditional media outlets.

Trends in New Media

Once upon a time, there was an inventor of a new communications medium. The inventor demonstrated his invention to a chief executive officer. The inventor was very excited by his creation, but the CEO was skeptical. The CEO argued that this new medium would weaken peoples' minds and their ability to remember things. Creativity could be destroyed, because people would rely on external images instead of the workings of their own minds. He was also afraid that it would give people all sorts of information, and make them "think" they were knowledgeable. But in fact, they would only have the illusion of wisdom: information without understanding. Now, try to guess what the invention was.

If you said television, you would be off by a few thousand years. The invention was writing, the inventor was the Egyptian god Theuth, and the CEO was the pharaoh Ammon (you can find this story in Plato's Phaedrus). The point of this brief trip into history is to illustrate that when a new medium is introduced, many people are not enthusiastic about it. Each time a new medium is introduced, the stages of growth and adoption are quite similar. This is because humans generally understand and apply new things in the same way that they understand and apply the old. Three very common trends follow the introduction of a new medium, particularly in Western societies, and most particularly in North America: (1) depiction of the medium as Satan or Savior, (2) commercialization, and (3) concentration.

Depiction as Satan or Savior

As was the case with writing, the introduction of any new medium creates polarized reactions (Cristin, 2002). On one hand, critics of the medium see it as the destroyer of civilization. Communications media make it possible for us to communicate with people far away and, for some critics, this ability causes more problems than it solves. All mass media make it possible to participate without getting involved or committed (Scannell, 1996). This means that when you talk with someone in a far-off place, it is easy to step away and keep your distance from the other person's problems. For some people, the chance of developing a new superficial relationship with someone far away is more appealing than putting in the work necessary to develop existing relationships. The only things critics see people really committing to when new media arrive are the new forms of entertainment.

On the other hand, supporters believe the new medium will save society from impending doom. A long-standing tradition in America is to continually proclaim every new medium to be the new savior of participatory democracy. Assuming that new communication must mean better communication, many in the U.S. have celebrated each new advance, from photography to communications satellites (Zynda, 1984). Local media such as radio and community newspapers have always been hailed by some as the best means to make it possible for everyone to have their opinions heard by everyone else. Or perhaps a new medium can save society by revolutionizing education. Radio, television, and now the Internet have all been pitched as promising educational tools. Perhaps you had *Cable in the Classroom* at your elementary school; certainly you have heard of *Sesame Street!*

The shining promises and gloomy predictions about the Internet are not new ones. In fact, the claims made about this new medium are much like those made about previous media. In the end, the influence of the Internet will not save democracy or mean the collapse of society. The future of the medium lies somewhere in between, down a path shaped by two other trends: commercialization and concentration.

Commercialization

You might expect that the earliest samples of writing that we have are great sagas, or poems, but actually, they are records of grain harvests. The earliest radio stations were owned by local furniture stores and other merchants (Hilliard and Keith, 2001). When communication media are introduced, enterprising people quickly find ways to use the

tip

∴ All new media go through a cycle of being first introduced to the elites, then becoming popularized, and then becoming specialized in their focus. We call this the EPS cycle and will discuss this further in Chapter 14.

increased communication to increase their profits. And even though the Internet began as a joint project between the military and educational institutions, it has quickly become a commercial enterprise. Sites ending in .com vastly outnumber those ending in .edu; and .mil is almost nonexistent these days.

We can see the increase in commercialization in two arenas: E-Commerce and advertising. As discussed in Chapter 5 in more depth, E-Commerce is growing at a truly phenomenal rate. In 2003, an estimated $56 billion was spent online ($17.5 billion of it during the holiday season alone) according to the U.S. Department of Commerce. This accounts for 2% of all sales. With so much money being spent online, it's not surprising that advertisers are flocking to the Web as well. The growth in online advertising represents a significant aspect of the trend toward commercialization in Western media. You don't have to pay to receive traditional radio or television broadcasts if you use an antenna, other than buying the set—at least, not in the U.S. and Canada. Although we may think of receiving radio and television broadcasts as a free service, this is somewhat misleading. In the U.S. and Canada, and some other countries, advertising revenues support these broadcasts. We ultimately pay for these services when we purchase products and services (Wells, Burnett and Moriarty, 2002).

This is not the case all over the world. In many countries, government funding supports broadcast media. While many people might be upset at the thought of government control over the media, they don't think twice about paying extra for a product that costs more in order to pay for the advertisements. The cycle goes like this: companies pay broadcasters to air an ad, you watch the "free" programming, but you pay a higher price for the product. Two interesting things are happening: first, you are paying companies to persuade you to buy their product because the advertising dollars are included in the price of the product you purchase. Second, one of the primary purposes of broadcast media (television and radio stations) becomes attracting a large audience, which, in turn, is attractive to advertisers. The key point is this: the recent trend of "free" Internet services that are actually paid for by advertising is not a recent phenomenon at all. It is the model Western media have been following for quite some time.

The critique of the advertising-driven media is not a new phenomenon either. There are advantages to this model: free (at least on the surface) services and content. But many critics argue that the commercialization of our existence has a net negative effect. It is becoming increasingly impossible to make any choices that aren't somehow related to products (Luria, 1996). On the Web, even searching for information will subject you to corporate sponsorship. Most search engines are sponsored by advertising, and when you search, you will find that the sponsor sites displayed are context sensitive. If you are searching using the keyword "photography," for example, you will find that among the results there are links to sponsor sites selling cameras and camera equipment. In a consumer culture, shopping can quickly turn from the second most popular form of entertainment (behind television) into a compulsive illness (Sedgwick, 1994). As an informed Internet user, you need to ask yourself, "how closely do I want what I have to see, tied to what I need (or want) to buy?"

Concentration

You've probably learned that capitalism thrives on, and perhaps even depends upon, open competition in a free market. It encourages and even forces companies to compete with one another, producing better and better products at lower and lower prices. All this presumably benefits the consumer. But how many of you remember Betamax? Or,

🌀*tip*

∴ Some people wonder if the Internet will replace the traditional brick-and-mortar university institution. However, as other media have shown, the university grows to rely upon the new media as an additional educational tool.

🌀*tip*

∴ If you are taking a course at a college or university, you may have free access to the Internet on campus. Many universities offer dial-up accounts to students as well. There may also be a Free-Net in your community, and the local library may also offer Internet access for a nominal fee.

to pick something more recent, the streaming audio format called Crescendo? On the other hand, you probably do remember the anti-trust lawsuit against Microsoft. What ties these three things together? One word: concentration. And it occurs in two ways: through standardization and mergers.

We need standards. Imagine what your life would be like without standards. Let's say you wanted to listen to a CD. If every CD manufacturer used their own **proprietary** (or unique, special) format, then you would either have to have a different adaptor to play each type of CD, or worse, yet an entirely different player. As far-fetched as this may sound, this is actually what happens over and over when new technologies are introduced. When something like digital videotape is invented, several different companies often develop it simultaneously, and each company might have a slightly different format. These companies realize that unless they can come to an agreement about the format, no one will buy their products. After all, would you buy six different CD players? So the major players get together and agree to follow a set of standards. We saw this in the past with digital videotape, as VHS tapes eventually took over the market, pushing Sony's (in many ways superior) Betamax format into oblivion. More recently, digital television broadcasting standards have solidified, and **HDTV** (high-definition television) has emerged.

There are benefits and drawbacks with standardization. For consumers, one benefit is that they do not have to worry that the video or audio format that they purchase is going to disappear next week. Digital audio tape (DAT) is a good example of an early technology that was released before standardization, and disappeared as CD recording technology emerged. Standards also make competition possible. All CDs are using the same format, so there is competition within the CD manufacturing industry for recordable CDs. One drawback is that standardization also stops innovation to a certain extent, and sometimes it stops it in the wrong place. Many times the agreed-upon format is not the best, but simply the format with the most powerful backers, or backers with the most political clout. This was the case with the battle between VHS and Betamax. Sony's Betamax had many advantages over VHS, including sharper colors, higher resolution, and a larger head drum, which resulted in a better signal-to-noise ratio, fewer problems with tracking, and less tape wear (since fewer heads were needed than with VHS to achieve the same effects). But in the end, Betamax lost to the more powerfully backed VHS (Buckingham and Coffman, 1999, p. 124). As a result, consumers lost as well, as they were left with the inferior format.

Standards are not the only pressure toward concentration. In recent years, we have seen a rapid increase in media mergers. ABC and Disney, Time and Warner, and Viacom and CBS have paired up over the past decade to become massive media conglomerates, buying up other media companies. By the end of 2000, the three largest media companies had a combined total revenue of $75 billion, owning companies in every medium, including television and radio stations, film and record companies, and newspaper and book publishers (not to mention theme parks!). Online, we have seen companies such as Microsoft, Amazon.com, and AOL/Netscape do the same thing; buying up smaller content providers and technology companies as quickly as their stocks would allow. Competition declines as the concentration forces of standardization and mergers enable strong companies to grow stronger, buy out smaller companies, and grow stronger yet again.

As the Internet matures, you can expect to see these three trends that follow the introduction of a new medium shape its development. Opponents and proponents will continue to overestimate its impact, either negatively or positively. The Web's growth will be tied to the growth of E-Commerce and advertising as sources of revenue (Kuegler, 2000). And finally, standards and mergers will increase the concentration of media ownership, as more and more, the giants of the Internet will swallow up smaller online companies. And whether you believe the Internet is Satan or Savior, you can't deny its commercial nature and resulting societal impact.

Media Interaction

People in Western cultures often have a tendency to see cause and effect relationships where none exist (*post hoc ergo propter hoc*, after this therefore because of this). A black cat crosses your path, and later in that day you stub your toe. When a black cat crosses your path, it means you will have bad luck. Stubbing your toe is bad luck. Therefore, you stubbed your toe because the black cat crossed your path, right? Did the black cat crossing your path cause you to stub your toe? If the black cat had not crossed your path would you have stubbed your toe? Although this is an example of superstition, the fact remains that people often take two phenomena that occur together, and label the first one as the cause and the second as the effect. While it might be tempting to conclude that the introduction of the Internet is causing many changes in older media, it would be more accurate to conclude that the Internet and older media are simultaneously undergoing mutual dramatic change. In this section, we'll examine the interactions of the Internet with books, newspapers and magazines, the radio and recording industries, film, and television.

Books

Online Sales   Probably the most obvious connection between the Internet and books is the rapid growth of online booksellers. Amazon.com (`http://www.amazon.com`), which now sells a wide variety of products, began as an online book retailer. Online book selling is a very profitable business. In fact, according to Forrester Research, "online book sales will grow from $2.8 billion in 2003 to $5.5 billion in 2008." Book sales in general are decreasing, accounting for 14% of all retail sales in 2000 but only 3% in 2003. So, while online book sales are surging, the market for books is predicted to get rather tight (bookweb.org, 2004). This trend indicates a shrinking online book market, as book sales in general shrink.

Even though traditional *brick-and-mortar* bookstores still sell the majority of books, many of them are also setting up Web sites, turning themselves into *click-and-mortar* businesses. In 2004, BarnesandNoble.com (`http://www.bn.com`) was the second largest online book retailer, after Amazon.com.

One reason Amazon.com and other online book retailers have been so successful is that they have taken advantage of the interactivity possible on the Web. Web sites can keep track of your earlier purchases and make recommendations about what other books you might like to buy, either by recommending books in the same category, or books purchased by other people who bought that same book. What they provide, in effect, is a digital version of a knowledgeable and attentive sales clerk, who knows your personal tastes and lets you know when new books that you might find interesting arrive. They also allow you to rate the book, write a review about the book, or read reviews that others have written. Finally, you can also interact with other information, following links provided by the Web site to learn more about the author or content of the book.

tip

∴ When different types of media collapse into one interactive format, this is called "convergence." For example, traditional news media such as newspapers and television news shows also have companion Web sites.

Electronic Books A recent innovation in book publishing is the electronic book, which you can purchase online and download directly to your computer or your PDA (Personal Digital Assistant, such as Palm Pilot) if you wish. Usually, these **eBooks** are less expensive than the actual text and allow for immediate viewing, as opposed to having to wait for delivery. There are drawbacks to this method. For one, the book publishers realize that an unsecured copy of an electronic book could be widely distributed, crippling their sales. So, the file is encrypted and secured for use on one machine. Additionally, most publishers will not allow you to print the material, forcing you to read it on your screen in a *reader program* like Adobe Acrobat (`http:// www.adobe.com/`) or Microsoft's Reader (`http://www.microsoft.com/reader/`), as shown in Figure 13.1. Still, if you want the book right away, the electronic book is an excellent option to a traditional paper text.

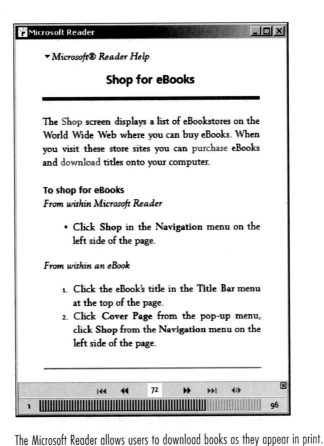

Figure 13.1   The Microsoft Reader allows users to download books as they appear in print.

∴ Create a separate folder on your computer for all your eBooks. That way, you can build a library and maintain it over time. You will also find many classics, available for free at the Gutenberg Project (`http://promo.net/pg/`).

Death of the Book? Does this mean that traditional paper books are doomed to extinction? Not in the foreseeable future. People who are enthusiastic about new technology will adopt eBooks. However, avid book readers and buyers enjoy experiencing books:

leafing through them in the bookstore, getting hardcover versions autographed by the author, and building up a library that they can see on their shelves. Additionally, eBooks are viewed by many as an inappropriate use of technology. Traditional paper books have been around for centuries, and are a good example of just enough technology.

Newspapers and Magazines

Supplementing or Circumventing Online newspapers and magazines fall into one of two categories. Many are set up by already existing, traditional paper publications. Newspapers from the *Financial Times*, as shown in Figure 13.2, to the *Grand Forks Herald*, as shown in Figure 13.3, have created digital versions of themselves, as have many magazines. Sometimes available free of charge, and sometimes by subscription, these sites typically duplicate the print version while including some additional features. The supplemental features include late-breaking news stories, links to other online content, the ability to personalize the content of the Web page, and searchable archives of previous editions.

Figure 13.2 FT.com is a good example of an international scope newspaper that can be found on the Internet.

Figure 13.3 The *Grand Forks Herald* is a publication that is more local in scope, but enjoys the global reach of the Internet.

However, some publishers are bypassing print completely, and producing online magazines that are never published on paper. Salon.com (http://www.salon.com) is one example of a completely online publication. This is an electronic publication as it is published on the Web. Salon.com calls itself a daily destination. Many online magazines call themselves **ezines** (electronic magazine)—also referred to as eZine and e-zine. Instead of sections, ezines have sites for such topic areas as arts and entertainment, books, and technology. And unlike traditional newspapers and magazines, ezines are not limited by time deadlines. A quick glance at any of Salon.com's current pages reveals that the articles were written any time during the previous week. Instead of being locked into final form and printed by a specific date, the content at ezines can be continually refreshed. New articles can be written and posted to the appropriate site at any time, while older articles can be removed from the site and stored in an archive (from which they can be retrieved). The articles can also be organized in many different ways. Salon.com gives readers links organized by topic area, columnist, or date, and allows readers to search by keyword. Figure 13.4 shows an example of an e-zine.

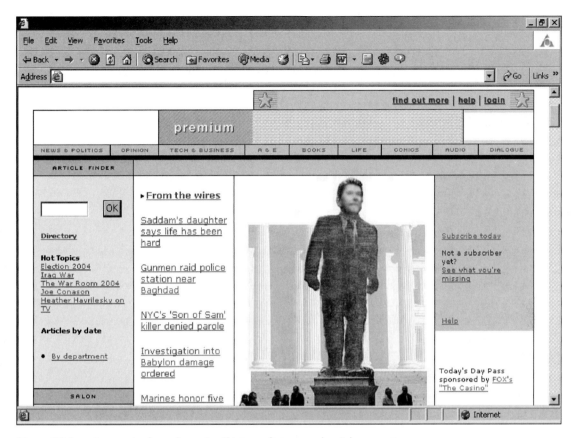

Figure 13.4   An example of an online e-zine. This image first appeared on Salon.com, at `http://www.salon.com`. Reprinted with permission.

Extending the Local   Traditionally, newspapers have been highly local media. Most of the content in the paper and readers of the paper have come from a specific region. Residents living in the northern Red River Valley around the city of Grand Forks, for example, primarily read the *Grand Forks Herald*. In the past, if you moved from a city and wanted to keep up with the news from that region, you would probably have to purchase a subscription to the paper and have it mailed to your home. With more and more papers online, it is becoming much easier (and cheaper) to keep up with local news from your hometown via the Web. In a society that is increasingly mobile, the Internet might help some people feel a greater sense of connectedness by increasing the reach of local newspapers.

Targeting Interests   If newspapers are in part defined by their targeting of a specific region, magazines are in part defined by their targeting of specific interests. *Car and Driver*, *Fitness*, and *Field and Stream* have obvious target markets. If enough people are interested in the subject, an agency will print a magazine devoted to it. The Internet is changing this by redefining what we mean by the word *enough*. It does not cost

⁂ **tip**

∴ If you want to keep up with your hometown newspaper online, look at `http://www. onlinenewspapers.com`— a repository of links to newspapers around the world.

any more to produce an online magazine for an audience of five than it does to produce it for an audience of 500,000. Since there are no printing or distribution costs, highly specialized special-interest ezines can be set up on the Web. Of course, whether or not these sites can be economically viable is a different issue that we will discuss shortly.

Radio, Video, and Recordings

Streaming Media As bandwidth has increased, it has become possible for richer media to be transmitted over the Web. One of the more significant advances has been the development of streaming audio and video. With streaming audio and video, files can begin playing while they are being downloaded into your computer. Prior to this, you had to wait for the entire file to be sent to your computer before you could begin playing it. For a long audio file or even a short video file, this downloading process could take several minutes. But with streaming audio and video, the file can start playing as soon as it is stored for a few seconds into your computer's memory (a process called buffering, shown in progress in Figure 13.5). This has made it possible for people to virtually broadcast over the Internet. With a streaming audio server such as RealAudio's RealServer, anyone can send out a continual stream of music, talk shows, and any other audio content over the Web. And anyone else can listen to this content by simply installing on their computer a streaming audio player such as RealAudio's RealPlayer and then clicking on a link to an audio stream.

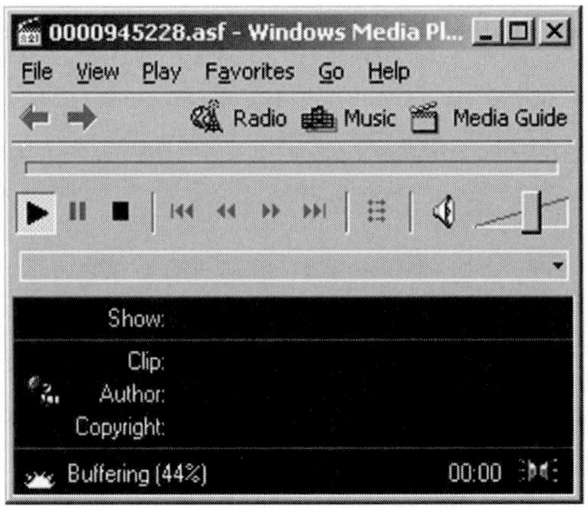

Figure 13.5   The Windows Media Player, buffering an audio file.

∴ News from Arbitron can be found at http://www. arbitron.com. However, specific market indices are a paid subscription service. Arbitron is the standard bearer for data on radio listening.

The Internet has also made it possible for radio stations to reach audiences far beyond the range of their broadcasting towers (Priestman, 2001, p. 4). You can now listen to radio stations from all over the world broadcasting every imaginable format live over the Internet. And these stations are not necessarily tied to a specific physical location. Some of them are tied to a time-period, some are tied to a theme, and some are tied to a music movement. In fact, even ezines like Salon.com have their own radio program, which they send out through streaming audio. In a sense, we're returning to the early days of radio, when stations were owned by furniture stores and car dealerships, and were used to announce sales.

What hasn't been figured out yet is the economics of Internet radio. Local radio stations rely on local advertising to pay for their broadcasts. If a local radio station makes its broadcast available over the Internet, it can be heard by an audience around the world. For instance, if an Internet listener in California is listening to a RealAudio stream from a radio station located in New York, chances are slim that he or she will patronize any of the local (as in New York) businesses that advertise on the radio station. In fact, many local radio stations are concerned that Internet broadcasts will cut down on the number of local listeners, thus decreasing the rates they can charge for advertising. Arbitron is a company that compiles data on radio listening. Radio stations use the data from Arbitron to set their advertising rates, and Arbitron also tracks Web audio listening.

Custom CDs and MP3s Like books, CDs and tapes can now be purchased over the Internet, at many of the same Web sites. Music clubs, such as Columbia House and BMG, now offer their services online as well. But one of the revolutionary changes that the Internet brings to the marketing of music is customization. At sites like Rhapsody.com (`http://www.rhapsody.com`) and Walmart.com (`http://www.walmart.com`), you can pick and choose what songs you want, legally download (for a small fee), and burn them onto a custom CD. Now you can build your own *greatest hits* CD with songs from multiple artists, or a personalized Valentine's CD for that special someone.

The greatest change that the Internet brings to the recording industry is the completely digital distribution of CD-quality sound via MP3 files. MP3 is a format for digitally encoding sound. CD audio files (.wav format) can be easily converted to MP3 files, uploaded to a server on the Internet, then downloaded and played on a computer, or converted into CD audio files, which can be recorded onto a CD. Sites such as MP3.com (`http://www.mp3.com`) allow aspiring artists to upload their songs, which can then be downloaded either for free or for a small fee by Web users. There is software available that will extract the song files from CDs. This is referred to as **ripping** a file. Once the music file has been ripped from the CD, it can be converted to .mp3, or recorded onto another CD. This process is a matter of some debate in the recording industry, as it raises issues such as sharing music files without paying royalties, and bootlegging. We will discuss the ways that copyright law is being adapted to the changes brought about by the Internet in Chapter 14.

Film

Microcinema If MP3 files on the Internet are revolutionizing the recording industry, so too is the film industry being shaken up by the combination of digital video cameras, editing suites that run on personal computers, and distribution over the Internet. For around $10,000, independent filmmakers can purchase a professional-quality digital camera, computer, and editing software suite that will allow him or her to

tip

∴ Feedroom.com (`http://www.feedroom.com`), launches TV broadcasting feeds into an easy-to-use themed portal for free. You can easily track what's going on in the world with news, entertainment, movies, fashion, technology, and more.

produce an infinite number of films. When you add in the possibility of distributing these films through streaming video over the Internet, you have a unique situation: the average person can shoot, edit, and distribute their own film without having to go through a studio.

The **Microcinema Movement**, a term coined in 1991, is a community of independent filmmakers who produce everything from animated shorts to feature-length movies at a fraction of the cost of the major studios. With digital equipment, these films are now rivaling the quality of multi-million dollar productions. And now, with the Web as a distribution medium, the microcinema community is rapidly growing. Sites such as AtomFilms.com feature new shows each week, providing a direct connection between independent filmmakers and audiences. If you are wondering if there is any profit in the microcinema world, the answer is *yes*. *The Blair Witch Project* was shot on Hi8 video and 16mm film cameras by the actors and produced for $40,000, and grossed over $150 million at the box office.

Higher Hype   Part of the success of *The Blair Witch Project* was due to another connection between the Internet and film: online marketing campaigns. Thanks to a clever and suspenseful Web site, and private individuals spreading the word about the film through email, this film managed to create a high level of hype despite a minuscule budget. Nearly every film produced today has a Web site. Quite often, the Web site is online long before the film is actually shown in theaters. Film Web sites help promote movies by providing access to downloadable trailers, behind the scenes information about production, stars, plot lines, and (of course) movie-related merchandise. But beyond increasing the hype level, the Internet is not affecting the Hollywood film industry very much—yet. In part, this is because the two media are very different: films are designed to be viewed on massive screens in dark theaters; the Internet is accessed from a personal computer. But as films make increasing use of digital technologies, such as computer-generated graphics, you should expect to see more connections between these two media.

Television

Blurring the Lines   As many newspapers now have Web sites that serve to supplement their print publication, so too do the major television networks. Major television networks and specialty television networks all have Web sites that offer show trailers, programming schedules, late-breaking news, in-depth stories, and even games. And just as we are seeing completely online magazines, so too will we soon see more and more completely online television stations.

This is only a hint of things to come. Many people see the convergence of technologies and predict that soon you won't be able to distinguish between your PC, your television, and the Internet. There have been some interesting innovations in the attempt to converge these technologies into one easy-to-use interface that will make interactive television a viable, popular medium. Bill Gates frequently refers to this forthcoming device as an **information appliance**. Microsoft's purchase of WebTV, a product that allows you to surf the Web from a television set, is one of the innovations. Microsoft has also introduced a hand-held entertainment PC called the Portable Media Center and a Media Center version of the Windows operating system, as shown in Figure 13.6.

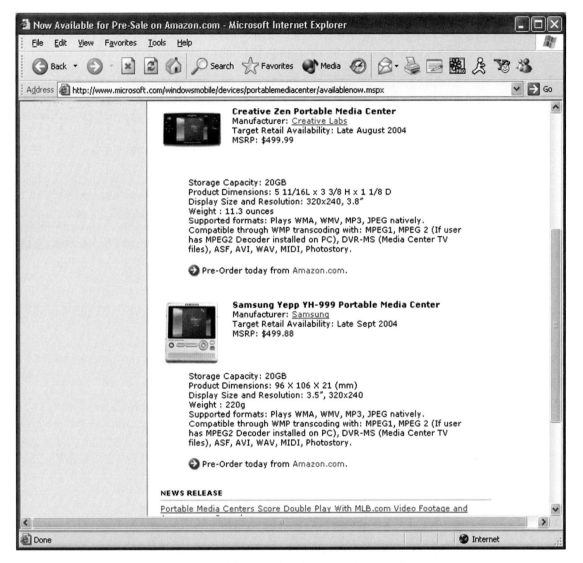

Figure 13.6   Portable Media Center devices and the Microsoft Windows XP Media Center Edition are designed to converge your PC and TV set into one platform.

Lazy Interactivity   Most experts foresee that people will not be using their interactive televisions to access information. They will use it to purchase products. As we have discussed, Western media are particularly driven by the advertising and consumption of consumer goods. Many experts imagine the following scenario: you sit down to watch your favorite television show. As the theme song plays, a link appears on the side of your screen that urges you to *buy the soundtrack CD now!* You use the button on your remote to move the mouse over to that link, click on it, and your PC/TV instantly transmits your credit card information and mailing address over the Internet to the company selling the soundtrack. Two days later, the CD arrives at your door. This simple, easy-to-use, basic level of interactivity is what marketing people dream of, but what many critics fear. The combination of these technologies could launch impulse purchasing to new heights, which, in turn, could increase consumer debt to unheard of levels.

Faster News, or Bigger Rumors? Traditionally, television and radio broadcasters have had one major advantage over newspaper and magazine publishers when it comes to the news: speed. While newspapers and magazines are published periodically, television and radio stations broadcast around the clock. Thus, when there is breaking news, television and radio stations can announce it between programs at the top of the hour or even interrupt programs when the news is particularly important, while newspapers and magazines have to wait until the next day, or week, or even month. But the development of the Internet has leveled the playing field, and now publishers can publish news as quickly as their Webmasters can code a new page. However, many critics are concerned that the push for ever-faster news may cause media outlets to publish unverified information in their attempt to be the first with the story. This happened in 1999 during the Clinton/Lewinski scandal, when several news Web sites published a rumor about a Secret Service agent who supposedly had witnessed the two together. When this turned out to be untrue, the pages were removed from the Web sites, but the damage had already been done. In this age, when mass media are pushing the envelope of speed, it becomes even more important to verify information.

Peer-to-Peer Networking (P2P)

What is Peer-to-Peer Networking?

Peer-to-peer (P2P) networking has revolutionized the way that media files are distributed—architecturally and legally (Oram, 2001). This section deals with the architectural issues inherent to P2P networking; the legal issues are detailed in Chapter 14. A **peer-to-peer network** does not have a central server. Each computer on the network can share resources with another computer by connecting to it directly. A simple example of a peer-to-peer network is a small home network with two computers and a printer. The computers are connected to a router or hub using network cable. The hub is just a switching device to allow the computers to communicate with each other. The computers can share their hard drives and printer, as shown in Figure 13.7.

How Does a P2P File Sharing Network Work?

In order to connect to a P2P file sharing network, you need to install and run a P2P software client such as Kazaa or WinMX. When the P2P client is open, it connects to the P2P network. The first time you connect, you will have to set up an account and specify which folder on your computer contains files that can be shared. Other users will not be able to search your entire hard drive, unless you specify that the top level of your hard drive is available. Once your computer connects to a P2P network, you can search for files on other computers, and users can search your specified sharing folder for files. When a search request is made, gradually each computer on the P2P file-sharing network will be probed for the list of files it has available. If your computer has a file that someone else on the network wants, a connection will be

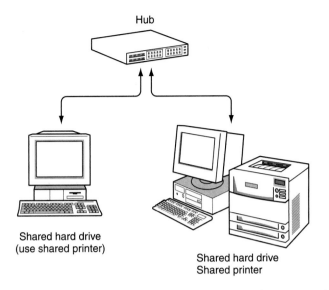

Hub

Shared hard drive
(use shared printer)

Shared hard drive
Shared printer

Figure 13.7 Diagram of a Peer-to-Peer network—two computers connected to a router, and a printer connected to one of the computers.

established between your computer and the computer making the search request and a copy of the file will be transferred. Some of the P2P clients will allow you to disable the file-sharing feature in which case your computer will be requesting and downloading, but not sharing.

There are some interesting aspects of the P2P file sharing networks. The P2P network facilitates real-time transmission of data or messages between peers. Each peer's connection to the network can restrict the transfer speeds. For instance, a peer connected via dial-up will transfer files much more slowly than a peer connected through a broadband ISP.

The peer machines provide the primary content of the network. This means that the file you wanted yesterday, and was readily available from dozens of peers, may not be available at all today because different peers are connected. The files available today depend entirely on who is connected and what they have available. It also means that you could be in the middle of downloading a file from another peer when that peer suddenly disconnects. You can also stop other users from downloading from you by disconnecting them from your computer individually. If you choose to use one of these file-sharing networks, please realize that in the U.S. and most parts of the world, it is illegal to download and share copyrighted data over these networks.

Social Issues with P2P Networking

Obviously, a medium like this, which provides direct, unimpeded connectivity between computers, has the recording industry and others who manufacture content very concerned. Illegal file-sharing through P2P networks has proliferated to such an extent that the Recording Industry Artist's Association has reacted, and is filing suits

⚛ *tip*

∴ P2P clients have been notorious for installing spyware along with the client. Some P2P clients will not run if you are using a spyware blocker. Be sure to look for P2P software that specifies it does not contain spyware.

against those who upload and download files online in the U.S. Copyrighted books, full CD albums, pictures, and music videos—all this and more can be found on a P2P network.

On the other hand, this technology has opened the floodgates to sharing information—whether legal or illegal—among the public. One of the benefits is the possible wide distribution for creative people such as recording artists. Recording artists who are unable to acquire a distribution contract from a large recording company have a new distribution mechanism in P2P networks for their music files.

SUMMARY

Now that you've read through the chapter, you are prepared to:

- Recognize trends in new media, such as:
  - The depiction of a medium as Satan or Savior.
  - Commercialization and concentration.
- Appreciate how the Internet and traditional media interact. As is the case with:
  - Books
  - Newspapers and magazines
  - Radio, video, and recordings
  - Film
  - Television
- Understand issues surrounding P2P networks.

Review Questions and Hands-on Exercises

Review Questions

1. Describe how the Internet influences traditional media, and how traditional media influences the Internet.

2. What are the three trends that commonly follow the introduction of a new medium?

3. Describe an advantage and a disadvantage of standardization.

4. Describe the relationship between concentration and competition. How is competition affected, as more companies are concentrated into larger ones?

5. Do you think electronic books will replace printed books one day? Why or why not?

6. What are some of the advantages of newspapers publishing an online version of their paper on the Web?

7. What is an ezine?

8. What is streaming media?

9. Some friends tell you that you should use a P2P file-sharing program because there are free music and video files available. How would you reply to them?

10. You have made a movie and wish to distribute it, but do not have a contract with a movie company. How can you distribute it yourself?

Hands-on Exercises:

1. Open a Web browser and load the eZINESearch site (`http://www.ezinesearch .com/`). This is a search directory for ezines. Find an ezine in each of the following categories. State whether the ezine requires a subscription, or is free.

   a. Jokes and funny stories

   b. Organic gardening

   c. General sports

   d. Fashion trends

   e. Travel tips

2. There are a variety of different eBook readers available. These are software packages that will display eBooks on computers or PDAs. Search About.com (`http://portables.about.com/cs/ebookreaders/`), or one of your favorite search engines and find two eBook readers. Answer the following questions about each.

   a. What features do the eBook readers support?

   b. What types of documents will they read?

   c. Do they have versions for different devices including PC and PDAs?

3. Use a search engine to find the Web site for your local newspaper. If your town or city does not have a newspaper site on the Web, use the closest large city to you. Answer the following questions.

   a. Notice the posted date/time of the articles. How current are the most recent articles posted?

   b. Do any of the articles also include video clips?

   c. What traditional newspaper sections are available on the Web site?

   d. Is an online subscription available?

   e. Is there a searchable archive of past articles? If so, how many weeks, months, or years of articles can you search?

   f. Did any of the available features surprise you? If so, which ones?

4. Use a search engine to find the Web site of one of your local radio stations. Answer the following questions.

   a. What sorts of features are available on the Web site?

   b. Is there a comment board for listeners' comments?

   c. Is there programming information and information about radio personalities?

    d. Are there community events listed, and other information about your community?

    e. Does this radio station have a streaming broadcast available so that you can hear it over the Internet?

    f. Did any of the available features surprise you? If so, which ones?

5. Use a search engine to find the Web site of one of your local television stations. Answer the following questions.

    a. What sorts of features are available on this Web site?

    b. Is there programming information available and information about individual shows available?

    c. Is the site a local television station, an affiliate of a larger network, or a specialty channel?

    d. Does the television station offer any streaming video?

    e. Is there a bulletin board or feedback area available for viewers' comments?

    f. Did any of the available features surprise you? If so, which ones?

6. How do the available Web site features differ from newspaper, radio station, and television station Web sites?

7. Search the How Stuff Works site (http://www.howstuffworks.com) and find the section explaining P2P file sharing (http://computer.howstuffworks.com/file-sharing.htm). What is the major difference between Napster's architecture and Gnutella's architecture? Which one do you think would return search results faster, and why?

The Internet and the Law

chapter **14**

Chapter Objectives

This chapter helps you understand

- ☐ the basics of intellectual property law (copyrights, trademarks, and patents) and how it applies to the Internet.
- ☐ the intersecting issues related to free speech and the Internet.
- ☐ the matter of tort liability, and how the Internet complicates current law.

For many attorneys, communications law has become one of the most complex areas in which to practice. This is not because the theories behind communications law are any more complex than those governing, say, criminal or corporate law. Rather, it is because in many cases, we do not yet have fully developed precedents. Throughout the course of history, every mass medium has temporarily befuddled the governments of the world and their judicial systems.

Of course, this is to be expected. Governments and legal institutions always incur something of a system shock whenever encountering unorthodox issues, and it takes a while for the laws to catch up to the issues that new technologies bring. In this chapter, we will look at the three major areas of communications law affected by the Internet: (1) intellectual property law, (2) freedom of speech issues, and (3) civil or tort liability.

Intellectual Property Law

Ideas are not tangible like physical objects, but they are protected by intellectual property law, which provides penalties for abusing another party's famous marks, copy, or inventions (Schechter and Thomas, 2003). There are three main areas to intellectual property law: copyright law, trademark law, and patent law. Each of these areas is guided by its own set of federal statutes.

One of the interesting facets of the Internet is the global nature of the medium. Each country has its own laws governing intellectual property in varying degrees. Internationally, the **World Intellectual Property Organization** (WIPO—http://www.wipo.int) promotes the protection of intellectual property rights around the world, and may arbitrate disputes as well. WIPO is responsible for the global rules, such as the Berne Convention, which is a treaty protecting literary and artistic works, respected by many countries. In the U.S., the intellectual property laws are federal statutes called the U.S. Code (or Federal Code). Every year, Congress passes acts or amendments to update the U.S. Code. Once Congress and the President have passed laws, courts may rule upon the constitutionality of these laws.

Copyright Law

What Is Copyright Law? Copyright law, recorded in Title 17 of the U.S. Code, is principally constituted by the sweeping changes made in the Copyright Act of 1976. The Digital Millennium Copyright Act of 1998 (DMCA), and the TEACH Act of 2001, focus exclusively upon online communication.

Set forth in Title 17, copyright law is designed to protect the expression of ideas. Once an idea is fixed in a tangible form, it is eligible for protection under copyright law. According to Title 17, section 102, *works of authorship include the following categories: (1) literary works; (2) musical works, including any accompanying words; (3) dramatic works, including any accompanying music; (4) pantomimes and choreographic works; (5) pictorial, graphic, and sculptural works; (6) motion pictures and other audiovisual works; (7) sound recordings; and (8) architectural works.* This means that graphic images, sound files, text, email messages, and Java programs on the Web can all be protected by copyright. Some computer programs, though, are more likely to be granted a patent than a copyright, depending upon the amount of original content being used.

The crucial terms to copyright law are "expressed" and "fixed." This means that intangible things, such as an *idea, procedure, process, system, method of operation, concept, principle, or discovery* (Title 17 Sec. 102) cannot be protected; only the tangible expression of an intangible thing can be. So if you have an idea for a really great logo, but you never actually create it, you can't claim to own that idea. Some other things that cannot be protected are facts (such as 2 + 2 = 4, or *the Earth is round*), titles, names, or short phrases.

So, what do you have to do to register a copyright? Nothing, really. The second you express your ideas in a fixed form, the work becomes your copyright. To demonstrate that you wish to have your copyright respected, you may use the © symbol to declare your copyright. Typically, this symbol is used in conjunction with the name of the owner of the work and the first year of copy publication. To officially register your copyright, a $30 application can be filed with the U.S. Copyright Office. Whether you go through the U.S. Copyright Office formally or declare a statutory copyright, the copyright is good for the life of the author plus 70 years (to protect inheritance rights). As well, if the copy is made as *work for hire,* then the copyright extends to the holder for 95 years from publication or 120 years from creation (Stim, 1999).

∴ To keep up on the latest concerning intellectual property law in the U.S., see the U.S. Patent and Trademark Office online: http://www.uspto.gov/

∴ To copyright something, all that you really need to do is publish your idea in a fixed tangible form. It is not necessary to officially copyright something, unless that something is going to be a significant source of income.

But what exactly does it mean to say that copyright law protects something? If you break apart the word, you will see that it means that only the author of the work (or owner of the copyright) has the *right* to *copy* it (or in some cases, perform, display, or even synchronize the property with other media). The assumption behind copyright law is that copying should not occur unless the copyright owner grants permission. Sometimes that permission comes at a price: for example, the recordings you hear on the radio are copyrighted, and each radio station must pay a "play fee" each time they air a song. This, of course, brings us back to the topic of peer-to-peer (P2P) file-sharing discussed in the previous chapter.

Generally speaking, you can use copyrighted materials without seeking permission as long as your use constitutes fair use. Fair use is a slippery concept, determined by four factors listed in Section 107 of Title 17.

- **Purpose and character of use:** Fair use purposes include criticism, comment, news reporting, teaching, scholarship, or research. This test also considers whether or not the use is for a nonprofit educational purpose, or for profit. Obviously if you're going to profit from using something, it is less likely to be considered fair use.

- **Nature of the work:** This test essentially asks: Is the original work worthy of copyright protection?

- **Relevant amount:** The most slippery test of all, this factor asks if a reasonable amount of the work was copied. Generally, 10% is considered fair use.

- **Effect on the market:** Finally, the courts look at the potential harm that your copying of the work may have on the sales of the original work. However, every fair use issue must be weighed on the merits of its own case.

Complications of the Internet Copyright law establishes that once the expression of an idea is fixed, it becomes intellectual property. Technically, you are not supposed to copy an entire work without permission. The interesting thing about the Web is that it violates this premise everyday. When you visit a Web page, the server sends that page to your computer. At this point, a copy of that page now resides in the memory of your computer, and usually on the hard drive in your browser's cache. Is this a copyright violation? Most reasonable people would say no. The point is that on the Internet, copying must take place on a regular basis, although its use is private and not publicly displayed. It is the nature of the technology.

Copying images or text from a Web site without referencing them is illegal. If you copy a significant amount of a Web page, you must seek copyright permission.

The hyperlink nature of the Web makes it quite easy to build a composite Web page that pulls elements of many Web pages together from different Web servers. For instance, the `<img>` tag requires an `src` attribute that specifies the name of the image file. It could also specify a URL pointing to an image on another Web server such as `<img src="http://www.somewhere.com/image.jpg">` in which case the actual image isn't on your server, thus not infringing copyright, but appears in your Web page. So your Web site could contain background images, pictures, and sound files that you never actually copied to your server. Is this copyright infringement? The law is not clear on this point.

Another interesting facet of copyright and the Web is that an individual frame in a Web page can contain a page from a remote Web site. You can basically recreate

tip

∴ If you use the computer workstation at your place of employment to create a document, your employer likely owns the document, even if the document was created for your own personal use. It's wise to check your employer's policy on using company resources and ownership of materials!

tip

∴ It is always best to use original images wherever possible on a Web page. If you are going to use images from another site, by all means, ask for permission.

Peer-to-Peer File-Sharing of Copyrighted Materials and U.S. Law

As you probably know, P2P file-sharing of copyrighted music is illegal in the U.S. and in most countries respecting WIPO. Copyright law extends to every medium in which copyrighted information can be fixed. The law reserves the copy *right* of the intellectual property to the copyright holder. This right includes public performances, recordings, and rebroadcasts of those performances—whether live or captured. If you upload or download music or movies to a P2P network, you are a direct infringer of the copyright holder's exclusive rights to the intellectual property. But, there are also secondary (contributory and vicarious) infringers to copyright law. At one point P2P software systems were under legal attack because they were doing nothing to police their network for copyright infringement (thus, Napster's initial demise—http://www.napster.com). The Recording Industry Association of America (RIAA —http://www.riaa.com) actively pursues litigation against individuals suspected of distributing and downloading music files over P2P networks, rather than going after the P2P networks.

The law is unresolved on contributory and vicarious copyright infringement, where P2P networks are concerned because of the *Betamax defense*. The Betamax video recorder came under attack in the *Universal City Studios* v. *Sony*, 464 U.S. 417 (1984) case, when it was argued that the device permitted the unlawful taping of movies for time-shifting purposes. The defense was that many legitimate uses of the device were also

being made, and that it would be impossible for the device to be monitored. In contrast to Sony's victory with the Betamax defense, in *A&M Records* v. *Napster*, 239 F.3d 1004 (9th Cir. 2001) the court ruled that Napster held contributory liability, as did Aimster in Aimster Copyright Litigation, 334 F.3d 643 (7th Cir. 2003). On the other hand, in *MGM* v. *Grokster*, 259 F.Supp.2d 1029 (C.D. Cal. 2003) the court ruled that the *Betamax defense* insulated the makers of Grokster and Morpheus from any liability because they could not reasonably police such a vast network. So, the law is currently divided over the issue. In short, the issue of copyright liability, right now, seems to be primarily aimed at the end-user.

However, it is important to note that not all countries subscribe to the same U.S. law or WIPO conventions. Canada, for instance, has deemed downloading of copyrighted music legal and uploading illegal. To quote Cnet.com (http://www.cnet.com): "the Copyright Board of Canada imposed a government fee of as much as $25 on iPod-like MP3 players, putting the devices in the same category as audio tapes and blank CDs. The money collected from levies on 'recording mediums' goes into a fund to pay musicians and songwriters for revenues lost from consumers' personal copying. Manufacturers are responsible for paying the fees and often pass the cost on to consumers" (2004). So, the interpretation and enforceability of any given nation's law depends, in large measure, on where you are.

another Web site by creating your own frames page that loads individual pages in the frames from another site. Federal courts have ruled that it is legal to link to another Web site or Web page, however it is a copyright infringement to knowingly use another party's work to create the impression that it is, in fact, your work. If you use frames, make sure that you note explicitly when a link is—or is not—your original content. It might also be good manners to email the owner and ask for permission, just to be safe.

In the U.S., the Digital Millennium Copyright Act (DMCA) was passed on October 12, 1998. This legislation addressed some of the issues raised by electronic works. Unfortunately, the DMCA did not address many of the fundamental issues inherent to how the Internet operates. It did limit copyright infringement liability for ISPs and higher education institutions, however. For example, if you create a page that includes copyrighted images and store it on your university's server, the university (under most circumstances) would not be held liable for your copyright infringement. The DMCA also required the Register of Copyrights to make recommendations to Congress on how to balance the rights of copyright owners and the needs of users in our new digital age. Those recommendations have not yet been formalized.

Interestingly, the DMCA does not completely free ISPs from the responsibility of content on their servers with respect to copyright. If, for instance, someone were to file a copyright infringement complaint with an ISP about one of the sites it hosts, and the ISP did not shut the site down, the ISP could also be held liable for copyright infringement damages. In such a case, the owner of the site-in-question has little recourse. The site-in-question, according to the DMCA, should be shut down by the ISP (unless the ISP decides to risk incurring liability). While the owner of the site-in-question can defend his or her actions as either mistake or coincidence, the site must remain inoperable until the dispute is settled.

Copyright versus Copy-Respect The DMCA specifically included language to protect the fair use defense. What if you come across a graphic image on someone's page that you really want to use? Technically, if it is less than 10% of the Web page, you can use it and cite it, however in this case, we would encourage you to think about copy-respect instead of copyright. The culture of the Internet evolved as a research network where sharing of information was encouraged. This culture was based on the simple principle of respect: if you wanted to use something that someone else had created, you just had to ask. This free spirit has been eroded somewhat by the commercialization of the Internet. Still, if you ask someone if you can link to a graphic image they created, or even copy it and save it on your own Web server, they will likely say yes. The assumption here is that if the situation is reversed, you will also say yes.

The TEACH Act of 2001 Another important piece of legislation in the U.S., signed into law on November 2, 2002 is the 21st Century Department of Justice Appropriations Authorization Act (H.R. 2215), which includes the Technology, Education, and Copyright Harmonization (TEACH) Act of 2001 with technical amendments to the 1976 Copyright Act (Diotalevi, 2004). This Act extends certain privileges to online *distance* educators, regarding the copyright act. In essence, the Act allows for distance educators to use copyrighted works, in a limited fashion, on servers to help foster the dynamic environment presented by extended education. Diotalevi writes:

> The TEACH Act calls for safeguards against retention or distribution of copies other than as needed to teach and against interference with technological measures used by the copyright owner as well as permitting institutions to upload a copy-

righted work onto a server under specific instances as defined by the Act and set out below. This will afford opportunities to allow certain schools to show audio-visual works via Internet and other related means. Let us examine how this is to be achieved. The Act extends Section 110 as to the expansion of uses allowed to include the performance and display of more works in the distance educational realm, by analog as well as digital means. The TEACH Act amends Sec. 110(2) to broaden permitted uses to include the performance of any work by "reasonable and limited" portions. It also gets rids of the need for a physical classroom, a sort of neutral application regarding medium of information transmission so to speak. The Act clears up instructional activities exempted in Sec. 110(2) as applicable to analog and digital transmissions, allowing in a limited fashion the reproduction and distribution of copies created as part of the automated process of digital trans-missions. It also applies technological measures for unauthorized using and access thereto and permits safeguards for copyright owners by requiring institutions using the exemption to promote compliance with copyright law. (2004)

While this only applies to online distance education programs, it is an important development in the course of history for copyright law. The TEACH Act still has many courtroom hurdles to face, however.

Trademark Law

What Is Trademark Law? Title 15, Chap. 22 of the U.S. Code encompasses trademark law. The key legislation guiding Title 15 today is the Trademark Act of 1946, popularly known as the *Lanham Act*. The Lanham Act remains intact—a testimony to its effectiveness as intellectual property law. But, in order to address some of the challenges posed by the Internet, in 1995, Congress passed the Federal Trademark Dilution Act (FTDA), and in 1999 passed the Intellectual Property and Communications Reform Act (IPCRA), which contained a piece of rider legislation known as the Anticybersquatting Consumer Protection Act (ACPA). We'll discuss the FTDA and the ACPA after we've covered the basics of trademark law.

A **trademark** can be a logo, acronym, word, color scheme, combination of sounds, or any other symbolic device used to distinguish a product or service as unique. For instance, Domino's Pizza® has developed the slogan, *Get the door, it's Domino's!*™ through much expense and effort. Domino's is quite serious about their financial investment in that phrase, as is the case with Coca-Cola®, Dodge®, Nike®, or any other major company that advertises heavily. It should go without saying then, that companies would protect this consumer recognition whenever it is threatened.

As you know, copyright does not extend to the names that a company calls itself or its products. This is where trademark law evolves as a means to solve issues of identity conflict. Trademarks protect company logos and names, product brand-names, slogans, jingles, and the like. This legal protection can be exercised when one company believes that another company has encroached upon the distinguishing elements of a certain trademark. Unlike copyrights or patents, which have a preset expiration date, trademarks can endure forever. Some trademarks in the U.S. are more than 100 years old. And, as long as the company keeps using the famous marks, trademark law can provide indefinite legal protection through trademark renewal.

For a trademark to have standing in the eyes of the court, three criteria must be met: (1) the trademark must be in active use by the company for a specified product

∴ If you're publishing material in Canada, you can register with the copyright licensing agency, Access (http://www.accesscopyright.ca/).

or service, (2) the trademark cannot be ambiguous or ordinary, such as calling a new broom you have developed *The Broom*™, and (3) the trademark cannot be misleadingly comparable to preexisting trademarks in the marketplace. This last point needs some explanation. Often, products will be called the same thing, but not be made by the same company or even be in the same product line. For example, Mean Green™ the all-purpose cleaner, is not the same thing as Mean Green™ the weed-eater. Here, the courts assume that the reasonable consumer will recognize the limits of language, and not confuse such divergent consumer categories. As well, you have probably seen Wal-Mart's® generic version of Mountain Dew™ called Mountain Lightning™—close, but no violation of trademark law. If any of these three above criteria are not met, then the court can render the trademark null and void.

Complications of the Internet　The Internet complicates trademark law in a variety of ways. We will examine the issues of pre-existing trademark claims, global trademark disputes, trademark dilution, domain name disputes, and the resulting introduction of the U.S. Anticybersquatting Consumer Protection Act of 1999.

Preexisting trademark claims can cause problems when people declare statutory trademarks on intellectual properties without having searched for potentially conflicting claims. Inexperienced executives will sometimes declare a statutory trademark without having explored whether or not the property is truly unique in the marketplace. Corning Fiberglass once won a lawsuit against a competitor because they held the trademark to *pink* fiberglass. That's why generic brands of fiberglass are either yellow or white.

Many trademark infringement cases are emerging in courts due to the oversight of not investigating the uniqueness of a potential trademark and therefore using a trademark that already exists, is ambiguous, or misleading. The instant communication of the Internet makes it easy for entities to immediately and publicly declare statutory trademarks, making subsequent similar requests a violation of trademark law. Since the Internet is one of the most effective tools for conducting exact searches, the ability to easily find potential infringements has caused a sharp increase in legal disputes. The moral to this story, of course, is that you should invest in research assistance before committing to a slogan, logo, or other distinct trademark attribute. This should become even more apparent when you recognize that in the U.S., each state has its own statutes in operation, some of which do not report to the national register. Even if the research is not wholly accurate, doing some homework will reduce your liability if, indeed, a similar trademark does exist in the universe.

Global trademark disputes are becoming more and more common in this global communication context. Before the Internet, the parameters of trademark law were somewhat negotiable. The World Intellectual Property Organization (WIPO) has, historically, served as the principal arbitration agency between disputing international parties. Could companies in Canada with similar trademarks as those operating in the U.S. file complaints because of an infringement, for example? Or, vice versa? That's where WIPO steps in to help resolve matters.

Trademark dilution is another important issue in trademark law, dealing with the diminishment of a trademark's value. For instance, McDonald's® cannot take the widely recognized Burger King® logo and negatively position it in their advertisements without consent. The Internet provides a simple and effective way to diminish the value of a trademark to the corporation because of the ease with which someone can distribute negative advertising quickly via the Web and mailing lists. The Trademark Dilution Act of 1995 protects companies by making such attacks on their trademarks illegal.

Disputes over domain names often crop up, because during the early years of domain name registration, those who could see the development of the Web as a device for commerce began securing both humorous and profitable URL addresses. This practice, called cybersquatting, mirrors the settlement of the Wild West during the 1800s—except in this case, the squatters used computers instead of pistols. Once E-Commerce became popular, many brick-and-mortar companies tried to use the name of their business as part of their URL, only to discover that another pseudo-organization or individual had already purchased that domain name. Most of these issues settled themselves naturally, of course. The company would offer a purchase price to the cybersquatter, and negotiations would ensue until a settlement could be reached. However, sometimes, a mutual price could not be reached between the two parties. That's when the expense of legal action became necessary, and the government was prompted to intervene with legislation.

On November 29, 1999 the Anticybersquatting Consumer Protection Act (ACPA) became law and updated Title 15, Chap. 22. It allows companies to legally act against those who would, in bad faith, profit by their famous marks. It is a violation of trade-

Classic Domain Name Disputes

- Adam Curry, once a video-jockey for Music Television, was an early adopter of Internet technologies. He secured MTV.com (http://www.mtv.com) to promote the network via the Internet in 1993. When he was released as a VJ, Curry continued to promote the domain name and Web site until MTV filed suit against Curry. The issue was eventually settled out of court.

- The People for Eating Tasty Animals (PETA) purchased domain name rights to PETA.org (http://www.peta.org) in 1995, lampooning the People for the Ethical Treatment of Animals (PETA). The issue was eventually settled in arbitration.

- Hasbro® Industries, makers of the classic child game *Candyland*, won their case against the Internet Entertainment Group, Inc. in 1996, who purchased Candyland.com (http://www.candyland.com) for an adult entertainment site. In part, the Hasbro ruling was based on the premise that Hasbro held trademark rights to such a distinctive entertainment moniker. But, in larger measure, the spirit of the ruling also held that the domain name could be confusing for children venturing into cyberspace (as you can no doubt vividly imagine).

mark law if: (1) a party uses a mark that is "identical or confusingly similar to a mark that was distinctive when the domain name was registered," (2) a party uses a mark that is "dilutive of a mark that was famous when the domain name was registered," or (3) a party infringes upon "marks and names protected by statute such as the Olympic symbol or Red Cross" (Deutsch, 2000). The ACPA legislation is retroactive, meaning that the Act applies to domain names registered on or before the passage of the legislation on November 29, 1999. And while most of the usual .com domain names have already been selected, there are many other top level domain names registered and this will continue to expand. Within the new domains, companies will be able to start fresh, aware of the E-Commerce context (this time) and armed with the provisions provided by the ACPA.

Patent Law

What Is Patent Law? Title 35 of the U.S. Code details how U.S. patent law is to be applied. Many people confuse patent law with trademark and copyright law. Patent law is specific to "any new and useful process, machine, manufacture, or composition of matter, or any new and useful improvement thereof." For instance, Kentucky Fried Chicken® has a patent on their batter recipe. What is most important to understand is that the Patent and Trademark Office is bound to two important patent-granting criteria: (1) the product must serve some *useful* purpose to individuals or society, and (2) the product must be explicitly detailed. Abstract ideas cannot be patented. Inventions must be explicit, certain, and clearly demonstrate their impact. A patent provides the inventor with the right to prevent foreigners or domestics from "making, using, offering for sale, or selling" (U.S. Code, Title 35, Part 3, Chap. 8) the invention in the U.S. for 20 years after the patent was initially filed (assuming it is granted). Patent law protects the discovery from being capitalized upon by another.

Complications of the Internet The Internet doesn't exactly affect patent law directly, but its ability to communicate new ideas so seamlessly causes some concern (Reindl, 1998). Because email, the Web, and attached data files are used so much in business communication today, patent development secrets face increasing risks (Hodkowski, 1997). This is a serious concern both for major corporations and start-up firms alike looking to secure a patent. At any stage along the development of a particular idea, from the abstract to the concrete, a party on the inside can communicate critically important information to a party on the outside. This communication could seem innocent enough—a moment of glee sent to a close friend from college in an email: "We found it! We found the missing Q28X gene! Man, we're gonna be rich!" Or, it could be more subversive, using anonymous email accounts to reveal the full-specifications of company secrets.

First Amendment Issues

More than at any other time in the history of humankind perhaps, free speech philosophy is being widely and popularly advocated. Practically speaking, we can now send and receive all types of information with the click of a mouse, anywhere in the world. But exactly how far do these individual freedoms run before they violate law? Just how free are you, really, to communicate with the world as you might choose?

tip

∴ It might be a good idea to check to see whether someone has registered your name as a URL. If not, you may want to reserve it for future Web site use. See Network Solutions: http://www.networksolutions.com to look up domain names.

Free Speech Law

The First Amendment to the U.S. Constitution reads: *Congress shall make no law respecting an establishment of religion, or prohibiting the free exercise thereof; or abridging the freedom of speech, or of the press; or the right of the people peaceably to assemble, and to petition the government for a redress of grievances.* The popular interpretation of the First Amendment is that freedom of speech is unrestricted. While Congress *shall make no law* abridging these freedoms, on occasion it has. And in some cases, the Supreme Court has even upheld these laws due to *compelling state interests.* Why is this? Basically, this is because the U.S. Supreme Court has historically subscribed to a centrist interpretation of the First Amendment. This means that a majority of the Justices, during the history of U.S. rulings, decided that the words of the First Amendment needed to be softened to ensure the functioning of society. Since none of the authors of the Constitution remain with us today, what they intended becomes a matter of interpretation. And, when interpretation is involved, these are matters upon which reasonable Justices will disagree. The first thing that you must recognize about free speech law is that certain types of speech are treated differently by the courts. For example, the Supreme Court would be more inclined to uphold a citizen's right to publicly debate the merits of socialism than another citizen's decision to loudly proclaim controversial opinions that are distasteful, hateful, or incite illegal or immoral activities as deemed by society. Individual rights, under certain circumstances, can be forfeited if you go against the prevailing wishes of society (Salbu, 1998). Most people do not recognize this and, to their own detriment, interpret the First Amendment literally. While many free speech scholars and attorneys might applaud it, idealism and the law are treated differently in court.

Where the Internet and free speech are concerned, almost all the contemporary cases revolve around one of three dynamics. The first concerns whether or not the First Amendment should be extended to protect unpopular, controversial, and even offensive communications. The second deals with issues of online indecency and obscenity. The final dynamic deals with the use of screening or filtering devices, both in the home and at public institutions.

Unpopular, Controversial, and Offensive Communications

We have all encountered unpopular, controversial, or offensive communications, and the definition of what is controversial or offensive can vary greatly from one region or country to another. The main issue here concerns whether or not content conveyed over the Internet that is unpopular, controversial, or offensive should enjoy First Amendment protection. In the following section, we look at cyberstalking, the use of spam, and hate speech to help us understand how free speech law functions online.

Cyberstalking Suppose someone sends you 20–30 uninvited emails a day. Imagine what your life might be like if these emails became threatening or harassing in nature? Would you want to open your email account? The Interstate Stalking Act of 1996 provides federal protection against those who physically cross state lines to *stalk* another party. Title 18 875(c) of the federal code makes it a federal crime *to transmit any communication in interstate or foreign commerce containing a threat to injure the person of another.* Even so, many lawyers argue that the statute is not specific enough. In an attempt to make such legislation tailored to Internet communication, the Department of Justice released a report in 1999 titled: *Cyberstalking: A New Challenge for Law Enforcement and Industry.* The report argues that federal law must be changed to *prohibit the transmission of any communication in interstate or foreign commerce with intent to threaten or harass*

tip

∴ To help prevent cyberstalking, maintain a separate user account for close personal friends and family only. Make sure that this user-id is not posted anywhere publicly, and you do not use it to subscribe to mailing lists, because users can search for you online.

another person, where such communication places another person in fear of death or bodily injury to themselves or another person.

Spam The basic question here is: does spam enjoy First Amendment protection? Currently, there are no federal laws preventing marketers from doing bulk email distributions over the Internet, but some state laws do exist. Several unsuccessful attempts by the U.S. Congress to stymie the flow of spam have presented themselves, in the form of the Unsolicited Commercial Electronic Mail Act of 2001 (H.R. 718) and the Unsolicited Electronic Mail Act of 1998 (H.R. 3888). So, spamming is legal. However, your ISP may have you agree not to do bulk emailing.

Hate Speech and Hate Literature Some of the most violent communication is very difficult to regulate, because extremist political speech enjoys sweeping First Amendment protection. Even if the statements and opinions offered by some people violate the sensibilities of the reasonable person, the U.S. courts have protected the open expression of political content above all other forms of speech. The Internet has brought new challenges to those who wish to stop hate literature. If one country has strict laws against hate literature, how can those laws be enforced around the world? For example, if someone has a Web site containing hate propaganda and then stores these viewpoints on a server in The Netherlands—how could U.S. law affect them? The enforcing arm of U.S. law could only control the downloading of such information within its borders (O'Rourke, 1998).

Private entities enjoy private rules over their own equipment. If the agency is a private corporation or university, the proprietor of the equipment should govern what can or cannot be communicated on their machines (Hash and Ibrahim 1996; Gantt 1995). This is not a violation of First Amendment law, since the government has not made any provision against the free exercise of speech. Ordinarily, extremist expressions will not be tolerated by these monitored services because of liability concerns. As well, ISPs enjoy the right to terminate a user's service contract whenever provisions of that contract are broken. Almost all ISP contracts incorporate statements in their End User License Agreements (EULA) that consider harassing, threatening, and extremist speech cause for termination. Of course, there are always exceptions to the rule, especially on a global medium like the Internet. Recent legislation in the wake of the 9/11 tragedies, however, is giving the government more leverage to combat information that has the *potential* of inciting violence. An interesting initiative in the U.S. is the 2001 Uniting and Strengthening America by Providing Appropriate Tools Required to Intercept and Obstruct Terrorism Act, also known as the **2001 Patriot Act.**

Extremist speech loses its First Amendment protection when it becomes directly threatening to or harassing of any specific person or group. Communications of this genre fall under tort liability, which will be covered in greater detail later in this chapter.

"Indecent" and "Obscene" Communications

Every new communication medium has had to balance the issues of human sexuality and free speech. Some of the first materials ever produced on the printing press were Gutenberg Bibles and off-color limericks. When photography emerged as a popular medium, the art of nude portrait (of both the male and female forms) became an underground phenomenon. Likewise, as film, television, cable, and portable video debuted, each medium had to survive its own round of public criticism and scrutiny in order to define its appropriate place within the community. Likewise, this has emerged on the Internet in the form of *cyberporn* or *Internet pornography*.

The U.S. Patriot Act Debate

Following the events of 9/11, there has been significant legal reaction in the U.S. Congress and courts concerning the effectiveness of counterterrorism intelligence. One of the principal tools used to increase the U.S. Government's ability to deal with terrorism and conspiracy is the Patriot Act. Let's examine both sides of the debate concerning the U.S. Patriot Act:

For the U.S. Patriot Act

per "Preserving Life and Liberty"— http://www.lifeandliberty.gov

(Uniting and Strengthening America by Providing Appropriate Tools Required to Intercept and Obstruct Terrorism)

Congress enacted the Patriot Act by overwhelming, bipartisan margins, arming law enforcement with new tools to detect and prevent terrorism. The USA Patriot Act was passed nearly unanimously by the Senate 98-1, and 357–66 in the House, with the support of members from across the political spectrum.

The Act Improves Our Counter-Terrorism Efforts in Several Significant Ways:

1. **The Patriot Act allows investigators to use the tools that were already available to investigate organized crime and drug trafficking.** Many of the tools the Act provides to law enforcement to fight terrorism have been used for decades to fight organized crime and drug dealers, and have been reviewed and approved by the courts. As Sen. Joe Biden (D-DE) explained during the floor debate about the Act, "the FBI could get a wiretap to investigate the Mafia, but they could not get one to investigate terrorists. To put it bluntly, that was crazy! What's good for the mob should be good for terrorists." (Cong. Rec., 10/25/01)

   ▫ **Allows law enforcement to use surveillance against more crimes of terror.** Before the Patriot Act, courts could permit law enforcement to conduct electronic surveillance to investigate many ordinary, non-terrorism crimes, such as drug crimes, mail fraud, and passport fraud. Agents could also obtain wiretaps to investigate some, but not all, of the crimes that terrorists often commit. The Act enabled investigators to gather information when looking into the full range of terrorism-related crimes, including: chemical-weapons offenses, the use of weapons of mass destruction, killing Americans abroad, and terrorism financing.

   ▫ **Allows federal agents to follow sophisticated terrorists trained to evade detection.** For years, law enforcement has been able to use "roving wiretaps" to investigate ordinary crimes, including drug offenses and racketeering. A roving wiretap can be authorized by a federal judge to apply to a particular suspect, rather than a particular phone or communications device. Because international terrorists are sophisticated and trained to thwart surveillance by rapidly changing locations and communication devices such as cell phones, the Act authorized agents to seek court permission to use the same techniques in national security investigations to track terrorists.

◻ **Allows law enforcement to conduct investigations without tipping off terrorists.** In some cases if criminals are tipped off too early to an investigation, they might flee, destroy evidence, intimidate or kill witnesses, cut off contact with associates, or take other action to evade arrest. Therefore, federal courts in narrow circumstances long have allowed law enforcement to delay for a limited time when the subject is told that a judicially-approved search warrant has been executed. Notice is always provided, but the reasonable delay gives law enforcement time to identify the criminal's associates, eliminate immediate threats to our communities, and coordinate the arrests of multiple individuals without tipping them off beforehand. These delayed notification search warrants have been used for decades, have proven crucial in drug and organized crime cases, and have been upheld by courts as fully constitutional.

◻ **Allows federal agents to ask a court for an order to obtain business records in national security terrorism cases.** Examining business records often provides the key that investigators are seeking to solve a wide range of crimes. Investigators might seek select records from hardware stores or chemical plants, for example, to find out who bought materials to make a bomb, or bank records to see who's sending money to terrorists. Law enforcement authorities have always been able to obtain business records in criminal cases through grand jury subpoenas, and continue to do so in national security cases where appropriate. These records were sought in criminal cases such as the investigation of the Zodiac gunman, where police suspected the gunman was inspired by a Scottish occult poet, and wanted to learn who had checked the poet's books out of the library. In national security cases where use of the grand jury process was not appropriate, investigators previously had limited tools at their disposal to obtain certain business records. Under the Patriot Act, the government can now ask a federal court (the Foreign Intelligence Surveillance Court), if needed to aid an investigation, to order production of the same type of records available through grand jury subpoenas. This federal court, however, can issue these orders only after the government demonstrates the records concerned are sought for an authorized investigation to obtain foreign intelligence information not concerning a U.S. person, or to protect against international terrorism or clandestine intelligence activities, provided that such investigation of a U.S. person is not conducted solely on the basis of activities protected by the First Amendment.

2. **The Patriot Act facilitated information sharing and cooperation among government agencies so that they can better "connect the dots."** The Act removed the major legal barriers that prevented the law enforcement, intelligence, and national defense communities from talking and coordinating their work to protect the Ameri-

can people and our national security. Boxes on an organizational chart should not restrict the government's prevention efforts. Now police officers, FBI agents, federal prosecutors and intelligence officials can protect our communities by "connecting the dots" to uncover terrorist plots before they are completed. As Sen. John Edwards (D-N.C.) said about the Patriot Act, "we simply cannot prevail in the battle against terrorism if the right hand of our government has no idea what the left hand is doing." (Press release, 10/26/01)

- Prosecutors can now share evidence obtained through grand juries with intelligence officials—and intelligence information can now be shared more easily with federal prosecutors. Such sharing of information leads to concrete results. For example, a federal grand jury recently indicted an individual in Florida, Sami al-Arian, for allegedly being the U.S. leader of the Palestinian Islamic Jihad, one of the world's most violent terrorist outfits. Palestinian Islamic Jihad is responsible for murdering more than 100 innocent people, including a young American named Alisa Flatow who was killed in a tragic bus bombing in Gaza. The Patriot Act assisted us in obtaining the indictment by enabling the full sharing of information and advice about the case among prosecutors and investigators. Alisa's father, Steven Flatow, has said, "When you know the resources of your government are committed to right the wrongs committed against your daughter, that instills you with a sense of awe. As a father, you can't ask for anything more."

3. **The Patriot Act updated the law to reflect new technologies and new threats.** The Act brought the law up to date with current technology, so we no longer have to fight a digital-age battle with antique weapons—legal authorities left over from the era of rotary telephones. When investigating the murder of *Wall Street Journal* reporter Daniel Pearl, for example, law enforcement used one of the Act's new authorities to use high-tech means to identify and locate some of the killers.

- **Allows law enforcement officials to obtain a search warrant anywhere a terrorist-related activity occurred.** Before the Patriot Act, law enforcement personnel were required to obtain a search warrant in the district where they intended to conduct a search. However, modern terrorism investigations often span a number of districts, and officers therefore had to obtain multiple warrants in multiple jurisdictions, creating unnecessary delays. The Act provides that warrants can be obtained in any district in which terrorism-related activities occurred, regardless of where they will be executed. This provision does not change the standards governing the availability of a search warrant, but streamlines the search-warrant process.

- **Allows victims of computer hacking to request law enforcement assistance in monitoring the "trespassers" on their computers.** This change made the law technology-neutral; it placed electronic trespassers on the same footing as physical trespassers. Now, hacking victims can seek law enforcement assistance to combat hackers, just as burglary victims have been able to invite officers into their homes to catch burglars.

4. **The Patriot Act increased the penalties for those who commit terrorist crimes.** Americans are threatened as much by the terrorist who pays for a bomb as by the one who pushes the button. That's why the Patriot Act imposed tough new penalties on those who commit and support terrorist operations, both at home and abroad. In particular, the Act:

- **Prohibits the harboring of terrorists.** The Act created a new offense that prohibits knowingly harboring persons who have committed or are about to commit a variety of terrorist offenses, such as: destruction of aircraft; use of nuclear, chemical, or biological weapons; use of weapons of mass destruction; bombing of government property; sabotage of nuclear facilities; and aircraft piracy.

- **Enhanced the inadequate maximum penalties for various crimes likely to be committed by terrorists,** including arson, destruction of energy facilities, material support to terrorists and terrorist organizations, and destruction of national-defense materials.

- **Enhanced a number of conspiracy penalties,** including for arson, killings in federal facilities, attacking communications systems, material support to terrorists, sabotage of nuclear facilities, and interference with flight crew members. Under previous law, many terrorism statutes did not specifically prohibit engaging in conspiracies to commit the underlying offenses. In such cases, the government could only bring prosecutions under the general federal conspiracy provision, which carries a maximum penalty of only five years in prison.

- **Punishes terrorist attacks on mass transit systems.**

- **Punishes bioterrorists.**

- **Eliminates the statutes of limitations for certain terrorism crimes and lengthens them for other terrorist crimes.**

The government's success in preventing another catastrophic attack on the American homeland since September 11, 2001, would have been much more difficult, if not impossible, without the USA Patriot Act. The authorities Congress provided have substantially enhanced our ability to prevent, investigate, and prosecute acts of terror.

Against the U.S. Patriot Act
per the Electronic Frontier Foundation—http://www.eff.org

What is PATRIOT?

The USA PATRIOT Act (officially the Uniting and Strengthening America by Providing Appropriate Tools Required to Intercept and Obstruct Terrorism Act) was quickly developed as anti-terrorism legislation in response to the September 11, 2001 attacks on the World Trade Center and Pentagon. The large and complex law received little Congressional oversight and debate, and was signed into law by President Bush on October 26, 2001.

PATRIOT gives sweeping anti-privacy powers to domestic law enforcement and international intelligence agencies and eliminates checks and balances that previously gave courts the opportunity to ensure that those powers were not abused. PATRIOT and follow-up legislation now in development threaten the basic rights of millions of Americans.

Why should I care?

Under PATRIOT, civil liberties, especially privacy rights, have taken a severe blow:

- The law dramatically expands the ability of states and the Federal Government to conduct surveillance of American citizens. The Government can monitor an individual's Web surfing records, use roving wiretaps to monitor phone calls made by individuals "proximate" to the primary person being tapped, access Internet Service Provider records, and monitor the private records of people involved in legitimate protests.

- PATRIOT is not limited to terrorism. The Government can add samples to DNA databases for individuals convicted of "any crime of violence." Government spying on suspected computer trespassers (not just terrorist suspects) requires no court order. Wiretaps are now allowed for any suspected violation of the Computer Fraud and Abuse Act, offering possibilities for Government spying on any computer user.

- Foreign and domestic intelligence agencies can more easily spy on Americans. Powers under the existing Foreign Intelligence Surveillance Act (FISA) have been broadened to allow for increased surveillance opportunities. FISA standards are lower than the constitutional standard applied by the courts in regular investigations. PATRIOT partially repeals legislation enacted in the 1970s that prohibited pervasive surveillance of Americans.

- PATRIOT eliminates Government accountability. While PATRIOT freely eliminates privacy rights for individual Americans, it creates more secrecy for Government activities, making it extremely difficult to know about actions the Government is taking.

- PATRIOT authorizes the use of "sneak and peek" search warrants in connection with any federal crime, including misdemeanors. A "sneak and peek" warrant authorizes law enforcement officers to enter private premises without the occupant's permission or knowledge, and without informing the occupant that such a search was conducted.

The Department of Justice, with little input from Congress and the American people, is developing follow-on legislation—the Domestic Security Enhancement Act (nicknamed Patriot II)—which would greatly expand PATRIOT's already sweeping powers.

See: http://www.eff.org/Privacy/Surveillance/Terrorism/PATRIOT/

Some Federal Court Reactions to the U.S. Patriot Act

On September 29, 2004, according to the *Washington Post*:

A federal judge in New York ruled that a key component of the USA Patriot Act is unconstitutional because it allows the FBI to demand information from Internet service providers without judicial oversight or public review. The ruling is one of several judicial blows to the Bush administration's anti-terrorism policies in recent months. In a sharply worded 120-page ruling, U.S. District Judge Victor Marrero found in favor of the American Civil Liberties Union, which filed a lawsuit on behalf of an unidentified Internet service provider challenging the FBI's use of a type of administrative subpoena known as a national security letter. Such letters do not require court approval and prohibit targeted companies from revealing that the demands were ever made. Marrero, whose court is in the Southern District of New York, ruled that the provision in the Patriot Act allowing such letters "effectively bars or substantially deters any judicial challenge" and violates free-speech rights by imposing permanent silence on targeted companies. Writing that "democracy abhors undue secrecy," Marrero ruled, "an unlimited government warrant to conceal...has no place in our open society."

On January 26, 2004, according to the *Associated Press*:

LOS ANGELES, California (AP)—A federal judge has declared unconstitutional a portion of the USA Patriot Act that bars giving expert advice or assistance to groups designated international terrorist organizations. The ruling marks the first court decision to declare a part of the post-September 11, 2001 anti-terrorism statute unconstitutional, said David Cole, a Georgetown University law professor who argued the case on behalf of the Humanitarian Law Project. In a ruling handed down late Friday and made available Monday, U.S. District Judge Audrey Collins said the ban on providing "expert advice or assistance" is impermissibly vague, in violation of the First and Fifth Amendments.

On July 3, 1995, *Time* magazine ran a cover story by Philip Elmer-Dewitt with the title: "On a Screen Near You: Cyberporn." Citing the preliminary research of U.S. Senator Jim Exon (D-NE), the article concludes that this new form of interactive pornography might best be left at the corner video store. The result was a public awareness, which bordered on hysteria, about the availability of endless categories of point-and-click risqué material. In order to discuss the legalities of this material, we must first discuss the legal definition of obscene.

The CDA　In the U.S., the Communications Decency Act of 1996 (CDA) was a subsection (Title V) of the larger Telecommunications Reform Act of 1996. Introduced by Senators Jim Exon (D-NE) and Dan Coats (R-IN), the CDA sought to amend Title 47 of the

So What Is Obscene, Really?

To grasp the significance of laws about online pornography, you need to understand what is meant legally by the word *obscene*. The *Miller* v. *California*, 413 U.S. 15 (1973) case produced the *Miller obscenity test*, which is used to determine what materials are obscene. In *Miller* and subsequent decisions, the courts determined that a work is legally obscene if to the average adult person or its intended or probable recipient group:

1. the work, taken as a whole, appears to have arousing or sexual material or is advertised as if it has arousing or sexual material; and,

2. the work depicts or describes, in an offensive way, sexual conduct specifically defined by applicable state law, or which the judge or member of the jury believes was intended to be included in the definition even though no exhaustive list is supplied; and

3. if to the *reasonable person* the work, taken as a whole, lacks serious literary, artistic, or political value. (Tedford 1997, 146).

U.S. Code. The CDA tried to achieve several content-specific restrictions: (1) to ensure that the existing federal communications laws barring *obscene* material also applied to the Internet, (2) to criminalize the display or transmission of *indecent* (e.g., non-obscene) material on the Internet where children might encounter the material, and (3) to prohibit the availability of information referring to abortion services. The bulk of the change proposed by the CDA would have been applied to Section 223:

> *Whoever in interstate or foreign communications knowingly uses an interactive computer service to send to a specific person or persons under 18 years of age, or uses any interactive computer service to display in a manner available to a person under 18 years of age, any comment, request, suggestion, proposal, image, or other communication that, in context, depicts or describes, in terms patently offensive as measured by contemporary community standards, sexual or excretory activities or organs, regardless of whether the user of such service placed the call or initiated the communication; or knowingly permits any telecommunications facility under such person's control to be used for an activity prohibited by paragraph with the intent that it be used for such activity, shall be fined under Title 18, U.S. Code, or imprisoned not more than two years, or both.*

In the election year of 1996, Congress quickly approved the act, passing it on to President Clinton, who signed it into law. Clinton noted that the CDA would help parents by keeping their children from ...*being exposed to objectionable material transmitted though computer networks.*

Reno v. ACLU   The American Civil Liberties Union (ACLU) and American Library Association (ALA) wasted no time in filing a joint lawsuit against the Department of Justice. Strategically, the ACLU decided not to oppose the legislation bearing upon obscenity, since obscene content (e.g., bestiality, child pornography, snuff films, etc.) was already illegal. The ACLU focused its efforts instead upon reversing the *indecency* and *abortion* aspects of the CDA. Estimating that the abortion legislation was likely unconstitutional, the Department of Justice focused its efforts upon defending the CDA's indecency statutes. What was truly at issue here was whether legally indecent material should be protected under the First Amendment. Indecent material is offensive, but not obscene. Should legally indecent content be allowed to freely reside online? The government claimed that all other communications mediums had socially mandated age-verification procedures. On the other hand, the ACLU claimed that the Internet was unlike any of these other mediums, citing the fact that the network would circumvent any unconstitutional regulations upon online speech in any case.

In June of 1996, the U.S. District Court for the Eastern District of Pennsylvania overturned the indecency sections of the CDA, noting their unmistakable breach upon the First Amendment and overturned the abortion section as well. As well, it upheld the federal obscenity legislation aspects, extending these laws to include the Internet. The indecency legislation was found unconstitutional because: (1) the laws were geared toward ordinary citizens and not merely pornographers, (2) the means of securing an age-verification system on the network was both unavailable and likely a financial burden upon the average citizen, (3) the law would be an unnecessary burden upon the adult citizen's right to discuss or exchange adult content, (4) any age-verification system proposed could not possibly be foolproof, (5) the terms *indecent* and *patently offensive* were unfair absent an existing legal measurable standard, (6) such a law would only allow for scant enforcement, causing an imbalance in due process, and (7) the law would create an unnecessary chilling effect upon kindred forms of speech, thus diminishing expressive diversity. In short, the Court ruled that free speech would be needlessly burdened by the CDA.

The Department of Justice pursued the matter further by appealing the lower court's decision (*Reno v. ACLU*, 521 U.S. 844, 117 S. Ct. 2329). In June of 1997, the Supreme Court unanimously upheld the District Court's decision, overturning major sections of the CDA as violations of the First Amendment. Writing for the majority, Justice John Paul Stevens said, "As a matter of constitutional tradition, in the absence of evidence to the contrary, we presume that governmental regulation of the content of speech is more likely to interfere with the free exchange of ideas than to encourage it." In the end, what will be recorded by law is that it is not illegal to display or transmit indecent material online.

COPA   In October of 1998, Congress drafted and President Clinton signed into law a revised version of the CDA named the Child Online Protection Act of 1998. This act sought to remedy the apparent constitutional flaws of the CDA by using the Supreme Court's opinions as a gauge for what might be considered constitutional limitations to the Internet. This time, the legislation targeted Title 47, Section 231 of the U.S. Code, seeking penalties for the "commercial" circulation of any material that could be considered "harmful to minors."

Nicknamed the *Son of CDA*, *CDA II*, and now *Reno v. ACLU II* for its similarity to the CDA, COPA was challenged by the ACLU as unconstitutional. Backed by the Electronic Frontier Foundation (`http://www.eff.org`) and the Electronic Privacy Information Center (http://www.epic.org) as co-plaintiffs, their first line of attack was to amass a list of plaintiffs who, alongside their counsel, would testify that the law injured their right to free speech.

The ACLU then filed for a restraining and injunction order against the law in light of its predecessor's unconstitutionality. On November 19, 1998, Federal Justice Lowell A. Reed granted the restraining order, but not the injunction order, making the law temporarily unenforceable until he could rule upon the necessity for an injunction. On February 1, 1999, Justice Reed ruled for a temporary injunction against the COPA. As well, Justice Reed acknowledged that the ACLU's arguments were likely to succeed if the matter were left in his court. On April 2, 1999 the Department of Justice appealed Justice Reed's injunction, requiring yet another hearing on the matter. However, the fate of COPA would be similar to the original failed CDA: *In August 1999, A federal District Court issued a preliminary injunction against enforcement of the law, on the grounds that it is unconstitutional. On June 22, 2000, the Third Circuit Court of Appeals upheld the injunction* (EFF.org, 2004).

Controversies over Filtering Devices

One of the popular solutions to protecting children from objectionable online material is the use of Internet filters such as Cybersitter™, NetNanny™, and CyberPatrol™, as shown in Figure 14.1. These products filter questionable material so that Web pages containing it are not displayed in the Web browser. Levels of filtering can be customized. For instance, you could select the *no full nudity* checkbox or the *no offensive language* checkbox to customize the type of filtering (Wagner, 1999). The filtering software then works in two ways when a remote Internet connection is made: (1) it retrieves the software company's blocked list of domains from a downloadable online directory, ensuring that the remote browser remains current, and (2) it previews all incoming pages by scanning them against an objectionable keyword list. When the filter detects an objectionable Web site, the browser displays a Web page telling the user that the site has been blocked.

Filtering Device Problems Of course, nothing is foolproof. Web sites are added daily and the list of blocked sites is never completely accurate. Sometimes perfectly acceptable sites are filtered because they contain a keyword on the blocked list. Medical sites, for instance often contain keywords on the blocked list, in their proper and acceptable context. It becomes a trade-off between filtering most of the sites containing objectionable material and filtering some sites that do not contain objectionable material. Many public institutions, such as libraries and elementary schools, err on the side of caution and use filtering programs.

The Children's Internet Protection Act of 1999 (HR 896 & S97) Introduced by Rep. Bob Franks (R-NJ) as part of the Juvenile Justice Bill of 1999, this bill proposed that all public schools (K–12) must install an FCC-approved filtering device on their Internet applications. Focusing on Title 47 of the U.S. Code, this legislation amended Section 254 of the Communications Act of 1934.

tip

∴ If you are considering using filtering software, find out if your ISP already includes it in your service. Some ISPs run filtering software on their servers.

> *To be eligible to receive universal service assistance...an elementary or secondary school shall certify to the Commission that it has (A) selected a technology for computers with Internet access to filter or block (i) child pornographic materials...(ii) obscene materials...and (iii) during use by minors, materials deemed to be*

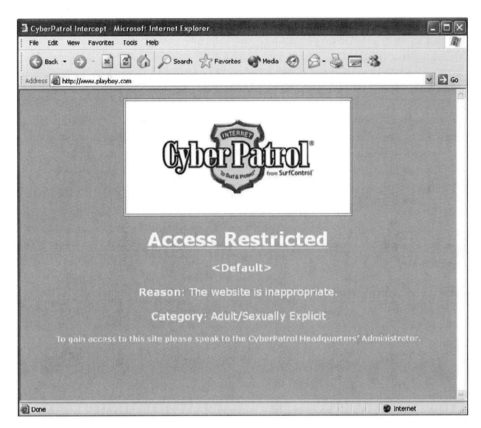

Figure 14.1 CyberPatrol's (`http://www.cyberpatrol.com/`) Access Restricted page. The software can deem that a Web site is inappropriate for a number of reasons. In this case, the page deals with adult/sexually explicit content.

harmful to minors...and (B) installed, or will install, and uses or will use, as soon as it obtains computers with Internet access, a technology to filter or block such material.

Although this bill met resistance by the American Library Association, on June 23, 2003, the U.S. Supreme Court upheld it, declaring it constitutional for filtering software to be installed in public libraries receiving federal funds or discounts. This was a reversal of a lower court decision by the Eastern District of Pennsylvania, who deemed the act an unconstitutional restraint on free speech. The U.S. Supreme Court's rationale was that the need to protect minors from such information prevailed over an adult's right to obtain such information. So, CIPA stands as law.

Tort Liability

What Is Tort Law?

Tort law is an extremely broad area of law dealing with civil wrongs caused to a party for which another party is liable and involves monetary damages. Civil wrongs are matters in which the state does not get involved. The state will only get involved if criminal infractions have occurred. For the most part, torts are "physical world" issues involving things such as car accidents, or property damage. In communications law, rarely, if ever, is tort liability a physical issue. Unless parties are dealing with property rights—e.g., signal frequencies, cable-line ownership, tax surcharge rights—communications law generally focuses upon four areas of non-physical tort: (1) the invasion of privacy, (2) the intentional infliction of mental distress, and defamation, including (3) libel, and (4) slander. These four areas focus on the harm caused to someone's personal privacy, psychological state, or personal or professional reputation. Before we explicitly cover these four areas, however, it is imperative that you understand how malice and a lighter burden of proof are important in tort liability.

The Importance of Malice   Malice is the desire or intent to harm others or see others suffer. Establishing malice is not a requirement in tort cases, because tort deals with civil matters and the civil court must determine who possesses liability and how much, and then attempt to make the damaged party whole again. Even if the tort were caused by accident, the wrongdoer is still liable for compensatory damages to some extent. Thus, malice is clearly not necessary for securing actual damages. When malice can be proven, however, this does increase the possibility of securing punitive damages. Punitive damages are the court's method of punishing the unreasonable behavior by compensating the injured party.

A Lighter Burden of Proof for Civil Action   Civil and criminal law are practiced with different rules, using different burdens of proof. For example, in civil matters, the burden of proof for the plaintiff is *a preponderance of the evidence*. This means that when you compare the evidence on both sides, the side that outweighs the other has the preponderance of the evidence. In criminal issues, the burden of proof is *beyond a reasonable doubt*. A preponderance of the evidence is much easier to prove than beyond a reasonable doubt.

Privacy Law

A theorized right to privacy was first proposed by two Boston attorneys, Louis Brandeis and Samuel Warren, in what has become an historic *Harvard Law Review* article (1890). In that article, they assert that people should have the right to be left alone to perform their daily life duties. This article comes from the fact that the two attorneys were being hounded by the media in both their private and public places. In 1903, New York adopted a formal right to privacy using many of the ideas generated by Brandeis and Warren. Eventually, every state in the U.S. adopted a privacy policy. Privacy laws vary greatly from one country to another.

The Four Privacy Torts   Today in the U.S., the right to privacy has been interpreted to mean that people have a right to be left alone, to be portrayed correctly in the news, and not to be commercially exploited. Let's look at four major parts of privacy policies and the issues raised by Internet technology. Again, the laws in each country vary greatly, but in general there are some interesting issues raised when applying traditional definitions and enforcing privacy laws. Let's look at it in the context of the U.S. laws.

1. **Public disclosure of embarrassing private facts:** Defined as the publication and dissemination of non-newsworthy private facts about a person's life that

would be considered highly offensive to the reasonable person. Some examples include information about someone's sexual activity, health, or economic position. Private facts are true, therefore not defamatory, but disclosure to the public via online communications incurs liability. This includes information published on Web pages, sent via email, file attachments, and mailing lists.

2. **Intrusion:** Defined as an intentional intrusion into an individual's private space, seclusion, or solitude, caused by an electronic, mechanical, or physical means. This tort involves trespassing, but is usually hinged to some technological means of invasion. Third-party wiretapping, paparazzi photography, and hidden videotaping are excellent examples of privacy intrusion. Many of the Internet broadcasting technologies can be included here. Any techniques that unlawfully intrude into an individual's privacy present certain liability issues.

3. **False Light:** Occurs when someone knowingly disseminates highly offensive erroneous publicity with reckless disregard for its lack of merit or truth. Publishing stories that contain incorrect facts about a person's life on a mailing list or Web site would fall into this category. Even if the names of the persons involved are fictionalized in a false light narrative, the story can be considered a thin disguise depending upon how the tort is interpreted.

4. **Commercial Appropriation:** Occurs when a profiting agency uses a person's name, likeness, or symbolic identity for commercial purposes without obtaining prior consent. News agencies are free of this concern, if they are reporting newsworthy information to the public. Pictures taken in the public sphere are considered safe for publication, excepting those that have a clear commercial interest at stake. Of course, you should also remember copyright law, which declares the commercial appropriation of an image to be a violation of copyright. So, in order to protect yourself from liability, make certain that whenever you use someone's name or likeness online you obtain explicit, signed prior consent. The same should be respected for other people's intellectual property.

The Electronic Communications Privacy Act of 1986 Another interesting law regarding online communication in the U.S. is the Electronic Communications Privacy Act (ECPA) that makes it illegal for the government or a third party to intercept email. The ECPA provides certain exclusions to this act, many of which are geared toward assisting System Operators (SysOps) in their duties. The ECPA provides a legal basis for these SysOps to intercept emails given any combination of the following scenarios: (1) if the message appears to pertain to the commission of a crime, then the message can be disclosed to legal officials, (2) if either the sender or one of the recipients deems it permissible, and (3) if the message incurs transmission difficulties and must be opened to route it to one of its addressed recipients. Of course, these rules apply to private email accounts only. If you use a company-owned email account, your email messages are the company's property. As company property, email can be monitored without much opportunity for recourse. Interestingly, many people obtain private ISP accounts to free themselves of potential censorship and invasion of privacy issues. Typically ISPs include the right to intercept email message in the End User Licensing Agreement (EULA). ISPs also have the right to back up all messages sent and received as a means of insulating the company from incurring any liability for a user's activity (Lawson, 1999).

EFF's Top 12 Ways to Protect Your Online Privacy

by Stanton McCandlish,
EFF Technology Director Vers. 2.0—Apr. 10, 2002

1. **Do not reveal personal information inadvertently.**

   Do not provide your email address or other personal information unless you know that the site is using secure transmission and you are clear how the information will be used. Most sites have a privacy policy outlining the usage for personal information.

2. **Turn on cookie notices in your Web browser.**

   Many E-Commerce sites require cookies turned on in order to use secure protocols for transactions, so turning cookies off completely is not a good idea. Cookie notification allows you to be prompted when cookies are set. Some sites use cookies to record values of text boxes on forms or other preferences you may set for a site. If you'd prefer that sites are not able to remember you, delete cookies from your hard drive periodically. You can delete cookies from Internet Explorer from the menu options Tools, Internet Options, General, Delete Cookies.

3. **Keep a *clean* email address.**

   When mailing to unknown parties, posting to newsgroups, mailing lists, chat rooms and other public spaces on the Net, or publishing a Web page that mentions your email address, you may want to consider getting a free Web-based email account. Making your email available on Web pages, and other Internet resources leaves you vulnerable to more spam, as savvy online marketers use programs that will scan Web pages and other Internet resources for email addresses.

4. **Don't reveal personal details to strangers or new friends.**

   This is basic street-proofing. The more information you reveal to people you do not know personally, the more likely it is that the information will be misused.

5. **Realize you may be monitored at work, avoid sending highly personal email to mailing lists, and keep sensitive files on your home computer.**

   In fact, assume that your company monitors all your online activity. Remember that the company owns your email; so do not use it for personal use. Some employers also use keystroke recorders, which will record all keystrokes and send them to a log file, so if you are using your work computer for chats and such, that activity may be monitored as well, without your knowledge.

6. **Beware of sites that offer some sort of reward or prize in exchange for your contact information or other personal details.**

   There's a very high probability that they are gathering this information for direct marketing purposes. Keep a free Web-based email account handy for this purpose.

7. **Do not reply to spammers, for any reason.**

   As soon as you reply to a spam message, the spammer has confirmation that your email address is legitimate. You will not be able to cut down on the amount of spam you receive by replying to the spammer and asking to be removed from the list. Instead, use spam blocking software or subscribe to an ISP that uses spam blocking software on their mail server.

8. **Be conscious of Web security.**

   Do not provide your personal information unless it is clear that the server is using a secure connection and you understand the privacy policy of the site. There should be an indication in your browser status bar of a lock icon or other indication that the site is secure. Never send confidential information, such as a credit card number via email, unless you are using an encryption product such as Pretty Good Privacy (PGP).

9. **Be conscious of home computer security.**

   If you have a broadband connection, invest in a firewall to prevent intrusion. There are freeware and shareware firewall products available, such as Zone Alarm (`http://www.zonealarm.com`), which can be configured to keep out most intruders.

10. **Examine privacy policies.**

    If you're not sure if you should provide your personal information to a particular Web site, look for the privacy policy and read it. If there is no privacy policy, consider not providing your information, or provide a Web-based email address and minimal information.

11. **Remember that YOU decide what information about yourself to reveal, when, why, and to whom.**

    Except in rare circumstances, like a government census, when someone asks you for information you can choose not to provide it. You can provide a new Web-based email address and include minimal information or obviously fake information like, *Jane Doe, 123 No Street Name St.* and so forth.

12. **Use encryption!**

    Last but certainly not least, there are other privacy threats besides abusive marketers, nosy bosses, spammers, and scammers. Some of the threats include industrial espionage, government surveillance, identity theft, disgruntled former associates, and system crackers. Use an email encryption program such as Pretty Good Privacy (PGP) (`http://www.pgpi.org/`).

You should also know that ISPs and universities often maintain network logs to monitor the browsing behavior that occurs on any given PC. Additionally, marketing firms like Doubleclick have become experts in the use of cookies, and Web bugs enable them to track user activity to a certain extent. Given this ambiguous context, what are the things you should do to protect your privacy online? For some excellent advice, check out the box on pages 430 and 431 detailing the Electronic Frontier Foundation's Top 12 ways to protect your privacy when online.

Libel, Slander, and Defamation

Libel and Slander **Libel** deals with written untruths about an entity published to third parties, and **slander** deals with spoken untruths about an entity to third parties. Determining what constitutes actual libelous or slanderous communications can sometimes be difficult. The statement cannot simply be perceived as false by the person (or entity) being discussed. The court must also find the statement false. To determine this, the court requires a thorough investigation into all the legal elements constituting defamation. This research can be costly, tedious, and potentially embarrassing.

Defamation **Defamation**, closely related to both libel and slander, occurs when someone communicates untrue information that lowers a person's status or subjects a person to public disdain, embarrassment, or humiliation. Specifically, defamation must demonstrate the following legal elements: (1) a false statement of fact about an entity, not an opinion, (2) an unprivileged publication of that false statement to a third party, (3) fault or wrongdoing with malice, and (4) a documented level of harm or damage. In the U.S., defamation is not a criminal matter, but it is a civil matter.

As you might have guessed, free speech law and defamation law often intersect on a number of levels. Defamation law is a means of stopping people from defaming others, while free speech law seeks to allow for the free expression of ideas—be they factual, political, or critical.

There are a number of defenses that one can use against defamation suits. If the statement is true, it does not meet the definition of defamation, but it may be a breech of privacy. Opinions are also protected under the law because they do not constitute facts. The court must determine whether statements were made on the basis of fact or opinion. There are, of course, a number of other qualified privileges that can be used in a defamation defense, including the accurate reporting of material that is in the public record, including court records, statements made at government proceedings, etc.

New York Times v. Sullivan In the landmark case of *New York Times v. Sullivan* (1964), the Supreme Court ruled that before a public official could receive damages for defamatory statements, he or she must first prove that the statement was made with *actual malice*. This determination federally trumped all lower state statutes providing for the recovery of accidental (negligent) defamation. In a later decision, the court expanded the ruling to include public figures, meaning people who involve themselves in public controversies. What this essentially did was to require that all parties involved in the public sphere interested in bringing defamation suits to trial have proof of actual malice to receive any compensation for injury.

So, what does this mean for your online communications? Obviously the Internet makes the dissemination of information much easier today than ever before. One email posted to a mailing list of 15 individuals could be delivered to two or three associates who, in turn, send it to 30 or 40 more recipients—and on and on and on. When making potentially critical comments about people on the Internet, assume that the person you're criticizing will read it and ask yourself if you really want to put that in writing.

Intellectual Property	What is Protected	Term of Protection
Utility Patents	any new and useful process, machine, manufacture, or composition of matter, or any new and useful improvement (chemical, mechanical, or electrical)	20 years from the date of filing (subject to payment of maintenance fees)
Design Patents	a new, original, and ornamental design for an article of manufacture (the appearance of a functional product)	14 years from date of grant
Plant Patents	any distinct and new variety of plant invented or discovered and asexually reproduced	20 years from the date of filing
Trade Secrets	a formula, pattern, process, or device that a company keeps secret to give it an advantage over the competition	as long as the owners are able to keep it secret
Trademarks	a word, name, symbol, or device that is used in trade to indicate the source of goods and to distinguish them from the goods of others	as long as it is still in use and renewal fees are paid
Copyright	original works of creative expression fixed in any tangible medium	**Works created 1/1/1978 or after:** Life of author + 70 years **Works created before 1/1/1978 but published between 1/1/1978 and 12/31/2002:** Life + 70 years or 12/31/2047 whichever is greater **Unpublished works created before 1/1/1978:** Life + 70 years or 12/31/2002 whichever is greater **Works published between 1964–1977:** 28 years + automatic extension of 67 years

(continues)

(continued)

Copyright	**Works published between 1923–1963:** 28 years + possible renewal of 47 years, extended 20 years by Sonny Bono Term Extension Act for a total protection of 95 years
	Works published before 1923: in the public domain
	Works published by the U.S. Federal government: in the public domain, unless authored by a private contractor

Created by Statewide Information Services, Wyoming State Library

See: `http://www-wsl.state.wy.us/sis/ptdl/IPchart.html`

SUMMARY

Now that you've read through the chapter, you are prepared to:

- Respect and understand intellectual property law, including:
  - Copyright law
  - Trademark law
  - Patent law
- Discuss how intellectual property law is complicated by the Internet.
- Appreciate the complexities of *free speech* and the U.S. First Amendment, especially where unpopular, controversial, and offensive communications come into play.
- Define tort law, explain how liability is assessed, and note the importance of malice.
- Explain privacy law, with particular attention to the four privacy torts.
- Take steps to protect your privacy when online.
- Recognize defamation, libel, and slander.

Review Questions and Hands-on Exercises

Review Questions

1. What is WIPO and what role does it play in policing intellectual property disputes?

2. What should you do to make sure your Web page is protected by copyright?

3. What is fair use, with respect to copyright?

4. If an ISP receives a copyright infringement complaint, what action, if any, should be taken by the ISP?

5. How long is a trademark protected in the U.S.?

6. What is cybersquatting?

7. How are global trademark disputes resolved?

8. What's the difference between a patent and a trademark?

9. The global nature of the Internet presents a challenge for regional laws such as free speech and hate literature. Describe, with an example, the challenge of enforcing regional laws.

10. Describe the advantages and disadvantages of using filtering software such as NetNanny.

11. If someone publishes a true, but embarrassing fact about you on a Web page, in the U.S., which aspect of the law would this fall under?

12. Why might it be a good idea to keep a Web-based email address in addition to your personal email address?

13. What is the EFF?

14. What is PGP and under what circumstances would you want to use it?

1. Open the WIPO site at `http://www.wipo.int` in a Web browser and search the site to answer the following questions.

   a. What is the WIPO copyright treaty?

   b. Is computer software protected by copyright?

   c. Can you find out about rules related to copyright in countries around the world? Describe the WIPO resources available to research rules and legislation in other countries.

2. Use your favorite search engine to find one of the filtering software sites. Describe at least three options or level of filtering available for the software you have selected.

3. Open the EFF site (`http://www.eff.org`) in your Web browser and search the site to answer the following questions.

   a. What are the top three hot topics today?

   b. The EFF has an archive of recent and past cases involving intellectual property. Choose one aspect of intellectual property and find a recent case. Describe the issue and the outcome of the case.

4. Open the main Web site for your ISP and find the privacy policy or EULA and answer the following questions.

   a. What is your ISP's policy on private information?

   b. Do they reserve the right to disconnect your account for certain activities? If so, which activities does your ISP disallow?

Keeping Pace
with Innovations

Chapter Objectives

This chapter helps you understand

☐ the societal phases that each new medium goes through when diffusing into popular culture.

☐ the role of change agents in the diffusion of innovations.

☐ how the Internet is decentralizing our world and the institutions that govern it.

☐ which resources are available to you in order to keep abreast with the rapid changes occurring with the Internet.

When Gutenberg invented the printing press in 1450, the church was unprepared for a machine that could automate the work of a hundred monks in a fraction of the time. When Marconi debuted his wireless telegraph in 1890, the state was equally unprepared for a medium more difficult to govern than mass-produced print. History offers countless such examples, where media innovations are introduced and adopted, and societies must adapt to the new method of communication (Jonash, 1999). Similarly, when the Internet was introduced, it caught almost everyone unprepared—changing how radio, film, television, telephony, print publication, and even interpersonal correspondence are practiced (Owen, 1999).

Even more intriguing, though, is the rate at which the Internet has spread. When you consider that a publicly accessible Internet has been available for just over a decade, its pervasiveness as a medium among governments, companies, organizations, cultures, and individuals is nothing short of astounding (Canton, 1999). How has the Internet been accepted by society so rapidly? How have our concepts of community and self been altered? What in the world could possibly be coming next? How do we keep pace with a medium that is constantly reinventing itself?

Adopting a Medium

Mass communication theories help us explain how media mature over time. As an evolving mass communication medium, the adoption of the Internet in society follows the patterns of its predecessors. One of the leading theories of mass media adoption is the **Elite-Popularization-Specialization (EPS) cycle,** formulated in 1971 by Merrill and Lowenstein. The EPS cycle suggests that all mass communication media are first introduced to (or by) elites, then get dispersed among the popular masses, and finally expand in availability so that content can become specialized, as shown in Figure 15.1.

Phase One: Elites

In general, a new medium is expensive when it is first introduced. It will likely offer

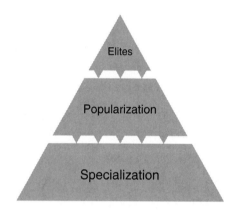

Figure 15.1   The Elite-Popularization-Specialization cycle.

communicative (and thus strategic) advantages over pre-existing media, but the new medium inevitably requires different, and initially expensive, equipment. Consequently, our traditional power structures—being government, military, higher education, and research and development organizations—usually gain access to such equipment first.

Once an innovation has been experimented with by the primary elites and has been deemed socially acceptable, it is then introduced to the public. If it is deemed unacceptable, policies and enforcement attempt to restrict or ban its use. A clear example of this in the U.S. was in 1996 when the U.S. Bureau of Export Administration issued a usage and export ban against certain encryption programs. The encryption programs scrambled data to protect both the sender and recipient from a third-party interception. These encryption tools, federal authorities argued, could be easily employed by terrorists to evade monitoring. In the U.S., communication methods are regulated by the **Federal Communications Commission** (http://www.fcc.org/). The FCC, established by the Communications Act of 1934, is responsible to Congress and charged with regulating both national and international communication in the U.S.

If you will recall, the Internet in the U.S. was initially developed (Chapter 2), as a government defense project. As time progressed, the government slowly began

tip

∴ You probably know some people who are elites. These are the people who are the first on the block to have any new gadget or technology!

pulling itself away from the project, dedicating large segments of the physical network to public use. Eventually, in the early 1990s, the popularity of the Internet exploded, and there was an infusion of millions of new users (Shenk, 1998). When this happened, the EPS cycle moved into the next phase, popularization.

Phase Two: Popularization

As more individuals discover the benefits of a new innovation, they will begin to use it in their daily lives. Information about the new innovation is then passed on from person to person in something of a grass-roots campaign. Ask yourself, for example, how many times one of your friends has mentioned the Internet to you. Companies using commercialized advertising and strategic public relations efforts also promote this appreciation. Web site addresses and email addresses appear on billboards, television commercials, and other traditional advertising media. However they heard about it, suddenly everyone is discussing the new medium. It occurred this way with print, radio, television, citizens' band radio (CB), cable television, VCRs, radar detectors, compact discs (CD), and now the Internet. The new medium becomes a part of the culture in coffee-shop discussions, radio and television programming, and formalized classroom instruction.

Once the public becomes aware of the emerging medium, an informal self-literacy movement usually commences. This is where members of society begin to experiment with the medium and educate themselves, alerting the government (usually through universities and colleges) to the need for popular instruction. For example, following the popular emergence of radio, colleges and universities eventually believed it important enough to offer curriculum in radio broadcasting (and later television broadcasting), where citizens could be properly trained in the theories and applications of the medium. The same EPS cycle pattern is occurring with the Internet.

Social adoption depends upon a great number of *economic forces*, too. For instance, the device required to start up your own low-power television station costs about $600,000, so the chances of a popular, widespread adoption of this technology is rather low. On the other hand, as the *power* of PC technology continues to increase, while the *costs* of PC technology continue to decrease, we are seeing in increase in home computer ownership (Gleick, 1999).

The trend suggests that PC and Internet usage will escalate worldwide. In short, if the medium warrants it, popularization happens. It happens when you begin spending hours instead of minutes online every week. It happens when our news magazines and newspapers begin covering the Internet as front-page stories. And it happens when your friends, family, and coworkers are talking about some aspect of the Internet every day.

Phase Three: Specialization

Once the popularization phase of the EPS cycle is underway, mass media have the tendency to *demassify*. **Demassification** occurs when mass media saturate the market, and then shift perspective to capture niche audiences. To explain how demassification works, let's consider the examples of cable television and direct satellite broadcast feeds. During the late-1970s, when cable television lines were being installed in our neighborhoods and communities, most television owners could not understand why. After all, their television sets already received the major television networks through local affiliates, ABC, CBS, and NBC. Cable certainly improved the television reception, but more

❧ *tip*

∴ Try to have conversations about the Internet with your friends often. You'll likely find that they are aware of things that you aren't and that can save you time and energy. Likewise, share your knowledge about the Internet with them.

importantly, cable television also introduced us to specialty programming stations—such as CNN, ESPN, MTV, the Weather Channel, and TBS. Cable made it possible for stations to target a more specialized audience, since it was drawn from a larger pool of viewers.

Better technology allows for more demassification, and therefore, more media and audience specialization. As cable service providers began to reach the maximum number of stations that they could carry over cable lines, direct satellite broadcast systems evolved to allow for further medium specialization. CNN became CNNfn (financial news) and CNNsi (Sports Illustrated), and music lovers were targeted more narrowly as Video Hits 1 (VH1), Black Entertainment Television (BET), and Country Music Television (CMT) joined MTV.

Of course, no one is really certain what our preoccupation with a fragmented media landscape might be doing to us, either as a community or as individuals. New technologies like the Internet are making it possible to target audiences with increasing sophistication and precision. Critics are concerned that highly specialized sites might assume more importance in our lives than the local, federal, or global news.

Because the Internet allows for both the consumption as well as the production of content, specialization has occurred even more quickly than usual. Once popularization of the Internet began, the average user could become a producer as well as a consumer. Web sites are about as diverse as humanity and imagination allow. Sites exist with information about every religion and culture, health issues, government services, song lyrics, celebrity fan clubs, recipes for chocolate chip cookies, even pictures of your cousin at the Grand Canyon National Park—the public and the personal—everything conveniently hyperlinked for our browsing pleasure (Negroponte, 1996). Fascinating times are ahead, whether you are an advocate or critic of this popularized medium.

The Role of Change Agents in the Diffusion of Innovations

While the EPS cycle explains the larger social processes involved in adopting new technologies, diffusion of innovations theory offers more subtle insights about the interpersonal nature of change. Proposed by Rogers in the late-1950s, the theory suggests that interpersonal networks (and the power-brokers governing these networks) sometimes have more to do with the adoption of new ideas than the ideas themselves. To explain how social systems work, Rogers (1995) identified five adoption profiles that he argues exist in all organizations and cultures: (1) innovators, (2) early adopters, (3) members of the early majority, (4) members of the late majority, and (5) laggards. Of course, some of us are, by nature, extremely open to change. Likewise, some of us are highly resistant to change. As would normally be expected, most people fall somewhere in one of the two majorities (listed below):

- **Innovators (2.5% of the average sample):** adventurous, cosmopolitan, networked with fellow innovators and early adopters, have access to financial resources, have high exposure to mass mediated content, understand complex technical knowledge, and are able to cope with high degrees of uncertainty.

- **Early adopters (13.5%):** respected, innovative, networked with other early adopters and innovators, prefer a local geography more than the innovator, have access to financial resources, have high exposure to mass mediated content, provide strong opinion leadership with the organization or culture, can deal with uncertainty but prefer certainty.

- **Early majority (34%):** prefer a local geography, interact frequently with their peers for data, have access to relatively modest financial resources, have medium exposure to mass mediated content, seldom hold positions of opinion leadership, are rarely innovative, prefer certainty.

- **Late majority (34%):** skeptical, cautious, prefer a local geography, interact infrequently with peers for data, have access to relatively modest financial resources, have medium exposure to mass mediated content, rarely hold positions of opinion leadership, are seldom innovative, prefer certainty, innovation adoption might result from economic/social necessity due to the diffusion effect.

- **Laggards (16%):** suspicious, doubtful, are mostly localites, point of reference is the past, wary of change agents and innovations, generally have meager resources, may never adopt the innovation.

If you placed yourself within one of the first two adoption categories listed above, there is a distinct possibility that you could be a change agent in waiting. Rogers defines a **change agent** as "an individual who influences clients' innovation-decisions in a direction deemed desirable by a change agency" (p. 355). In most organizations and cultures, it is the change agents who encourage others to adopt the technology of the Internet. These people are the first to set up their own Web page, use Dialpad.com (`http://www.dialpad.com/`) for their long distance communication, and videoconference with people on the other side of the globe. But most importantly, they tell others in their organization about how wonderful it all is.

By doing so, they speed up the EPS cycle as they help popularize the new medium. Of course, since innovation and change are often political issues in organizations and cultures—which are ordinarily more concerned with holding on to power than innovating—change agents sometimes encounter resistance to their ideas, even if their ideas are valid. But without these innovators and early adopters of technology, and their interpersonally persuasive contacts with those who are slower to change, the Internet would never have moved out of research circles and into your home.

Decentralizing Our World

Before the Internet, you had to go to the post office to get things like postage stamps and tax forms. Before the Internet, you had to word-process a letter, print it out on paper, and physically mail it in an envelope to the recipient(s). Before the Internet, you had to go to a department store, possibly even use actual money to purchase your goods. Today, we have online services like Stamps.com (`http://www.stamps.com`) and electronic tax filing. We use email to communicate with our friends and colleagues throughout the world. And, we use E-Commerce to buy almost anything we could ever possibly want without leaving our homes.

As we have discussed, the Internet is a distributed data model as opposed to routing through a central server. So, the points of data communication are decentralized and spread out to millions of computers, rather than centralized within a brick-and-mortar location (open between 9:00 A.M. and 5:00 P.M.). All you need is (1) access to an Internet-ready PC and (2) some of the basic Internet literacy skills that we have covered in this book. Figure 15.2 is a simple diagram of how a traditional centralized communication structure differs from an online decentralized communication

tip

∴ TechTV (`http://www.g4techtv.com/`), which can be seen on many cable and satellite networks, provides some cutting-edge information about the Internet and computer technology, in general. Take a peek and see what's new today!

environment. Instead of one central source producing messages that are then dispersed to audiences, in a decentralized system the production and consumption of information is spread throughout society. As a result, we are faced with two important questions: how does decentralized communication alter the way we interact with and perceive our traditional societal institutions (including government, education, the economy, and community), and how does it change ourselves?

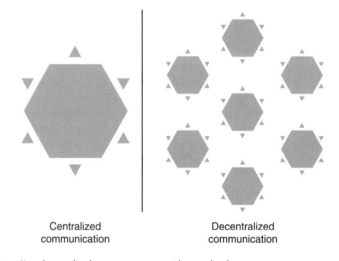

Centralized
communication

Decentralized
communication

Figure 15.2   How decentralized systems compare with centralized systems.

Decentralizing Government

On an international, federal, state, and local level, the decentralized networks provided by the Internet have allowed governments to disseminate an enormous amount of data online (Garson, 1999). And, while almost every nation in the world maintains a Web presence, not every nation boasts the architecture necessary (e.g., computers, phone lines, networking systems, and strength of satellite connectivity) to reach its citizenry.

Finding Government Information Online The U.S., Canada, and other more technologically developed nations, each have a strong government online presence. The White House (http://www.whitehouse.gov/), U.S. Senate (http://www.senate.gov/), and the U.S. House of Representatives (http://www.house.gov/) each have Web sites dedicated to public data. And, all you need to do to find your respective state government online is to go to http://www.state.ny.us/, substituting the abbreviation of your state for the *ny* in the address. Canada also has a strong government presence with the federal government site (http://www.canada.gc.ca/), provincial sites such as Ontario (http://www.gov.on.ca), and municipal sites. A convention for municipal site domain names is emerging using a format such as *www.city.on.ca* where *city* is the name of the city you are looking for. In general, city and county government directories may require some searching to find, but naming conventions are slowly emerging. A good place to start is always with the official state government site. Most of these sites list links to major cities and communities.

Gate-Keeping   What is more intriguing to us than the data-delivery aspects of government Web sites is their data-receiving potential. Before the Internet was adopted by the masses, elected officials normally heard from their constituents in one of three manners: (1) a direct letter or telegram, (2) a phone call, or (3) an office visit. Due to the volume of contact, the public official's staff functioned as a gate-keeping mechanism filtering and consolidating information and feedback. The same dynamic occurs to some extent with email. For instance, the President will not read email sent to president@whitehouse.gov, without its first having progressed through the proper gate-keeping channels.

On the other hand, within various levels of government, mid-level officials can be directly located and contacted without much, if any, gate-keeping. That is the beauty of decentralized communication systems. Here, the citizen could shop the bureaucracy, and pinpoint exactly whom they should consult about their issue with very little running around. This has the potential to increase participation in government, if public servants engage in an active online dialogue with their constituents. This dialogue, in theory, should provide for a wider spectrum of ideas, beliefs, and values upon which to draw when making important community decisions.

Bypassing the Traditional Media   Most political candidates today recognize the important outreach function that online technology offers and, therefore, directly incorporate it into their campaign. This is usually done via email lists and Web sites. Campaign Web sites have come to function as a base for fund-raising efforts, strategic public relations, and direct constituency contact. For many politicians, though, the most exciting part of their Web site is its ability to bypass the traditional media entirely. Since free presses were first conceived, politicians have been leery of a broadcast media prone to sound-bite journalism and editorialization. Creating their own Web pages allows politicians to publish unedited and comprehensive public relations messages.

What will become of online government is still unclear. Will we someday hold our political elections online? Will we even have a need for these political elections? Is it possible that we could move democracy to a new form of government by direct public referendum? The answers to these questions are obviously more about the distribution of power, than the ready capabilities of our new media technologies. How a medium as slippery and elusive as the Internet will, once firmly rooted in an educated public, restructure these notions of centralized authority is yet to be seen. Moreover, how centralized institutions like government will have to rethink the very ways in which they have traditionally *represented* the masses, who can now arguably represent themselves, is probably a much more unknown dynamic.

Decentralizing Education

Self-Instruction   The most important contribution that the Internet has provided to education comes in its ability to allow the user to teach himself (Palloff and Pratt, 1999). Let's say, for example, that you happen to reside in the deep recesses of the Amazon jungle, where no formal education exists. Here, the Internet might evolve as a *de facto* community library. Think about all the social programs and agricultural bounties that could be gained through a simple laptop and wireless connection in that isolated region of the world. Likewise, even in more developed nations, when a student goes online to discover how oil and gas teams pinpoint hydrocarbons deep within the Earth, it constitutes a form of education. In this way, the Internet works to empower the individual and the community.

tip

Bookmark your municipal, state/provincial and federal government Web sites. They will come in handy when you're looking for information on regulations, taxes, or the hours for the local library.

Decentralizing the Institution and the Classroom   The most obvious change occurring in our academic institutions is the amount of computer equipment being used. Computer labs, open access computer areas, cybraries (cyber libraries) and wireless hotspots have changed the technology landscape at educational institutions. Regardless of whether you are studying computer science, mathematics, or music, computers have evolved as the chief means by which we now study. A major reason why institutions are installing this equipment is to get their students online. Both educators and administrators recognize the value of promoting decentralized communication portals via the Internet. Doing so can alleviate the tedium of question-and-answer stress on faculty and staff, while also reducing the informational complexity that students often face in bureaucratic institutions.

And given that students can afford their own Internet-ready computer and obtain connectivity through either their university dial-up lines or a private ISP, the traditional centralized educational model has, in effect, decentralized away from campus. Students register for a class online, choose their class schedule, and are assigned an email address. They are given the URL for the institution's portal, access to newsgroups, campus announcements, and access to course material sites. Students can download the PowerPoint presentation from the lecture that afternoon, send their instructor an email attachment containing the spreadsheet they are working on, and get direct feedback. Students can hold virtual meetings with classmates and instructors online, using a chat program, and submit their assignments online.

The Rise of the Virtual University   **Distance learning** is the term used for courses delivered to students who are not physically on campus, and this began long before the Internet became so popular. Throughout the 1970s and 1980s, in fact, most distant learning courses were correspondence courses offered via the postal service. During the late-1980s and early-1990s, cable television helped institutions further promote the concept of *tele-education* within their local communities, and videotaped lectures were mailed to students as well. When the Internet roared into our schools and homes during the 1990s, many distant learning programs shifted to the new online, or virtual, delivery systems, at the very least providing students with email contact for instructors.

The emergence of online courses offered by traditional brick-and-mortar institutions and by virtual universities, which exist entirely online, has made it possible to obtain almost any form of education via the Internet. Many people are concerned that someday all education will be delivered via the virtual model. However, this fear has existed since distance education first appeared, and experience shows that most students prefer face-to-face learning in the classroom. Critics argue that the campus will always hold a certain face-to-face aesthetic that the online environment will never be able to simulate. Either way, the concept of virtual education has emerged as a realistic model. Now is the time when the institution and the student begin the social negotiation process to determine the feasibility of such a model.

Decentralizing the Children   In the U.S., one of the major initiatives undertaken during the 1990s by the Clinton administration was the promise to provide *Internet access in every school and in every classroom, throughout the nation*. In a 2000 report, the National Center for Education Statistics (NCES) indicates that this goal is near completion, with 95% of schools and 63% of classrooms now connected. There's a difference, however, between infusing computers in classrooms, and using the technology in curriculum. Inconsistent computer facilities abound, as some schools have computer labs, some have a class set of laptops, and some have one or two computers in each classroom.

tip

∴ If you need to do bibliographic research, an interesting tool to use is Endnote by Researchsoft Corporation. This tool allows you to search publicly accessible libraries via the Internet and download bibliographic reference by desired style guide format. See:
http://www.
endnote.com.

There are infrastructure inequities, in that some school districts have centralized comprehensive technical support and others have a single over-worked technician, and teachers are expected to troubleshoot their own computer systems. If you are interested in an individual school district's vision for computer and Internet usage in the classroom, ask to see the technology plan. Some districts have comprehensive plans including budgets and long-term vision. Others do not have a plan at all. In addition to infrastructure issues, some teachers have done a much better job of using computers in curriculum than others. It will be years before computer technology in schools is deployed equally, and the effects fully realized.

Decentralizing the Economy

Even if you don't follow the stock market closely, chances are good that you have heard about the enormous wealth that was generated (or in some cases lost) in the information technology sector during the *dot com* era. Until 1995, conventional industrial, energy, agricultural, and service-related markets had typically led the U.S. economy. Between 1995 and 2000, however, the U.S. economy was driven by a raging-bull market in the information technology sector; the Dow Jones Industrial Average rose nearly 188% (point 1 to point 2 on Figure 15.3), while the technology-rich NASDAQ went up an astounding 466% (point 1 to point 2 on Figure 15.4). Still, with that said, you should probably know that what goes up often goes down. And, in the case of the Internet and the stock market, the "bubble" of momentum trading popped, leaving a lot of Internet start-ups bankrupt, thus dragging the entire market down with it (points 2 to points 3 in both charts).

Led by industry giants such as Intel, Motorola, Microsoft, Cisco Systems, and AOL, the need to connect to the Internet ushered in a new economy, which is still active today. The decentralized communication systems of the Internet touch nearly every aspect of commerce, from the raw materials broker, to the manufacturer, to the distributor, to the retailer. Little by little, the intermediaries who once weighted down economist Adam Smith's vision of *friction-free capitalism* (where the buyer and seller could identify one another's best price without brokers) are now being replaced by highly reliable automated information systems.

The Virtual Office   One interesting aspect of Internet use is the virtual office. The virtual office is a concept. Using the Internet, you may be able to work anywhere, anytime. You can use email and you may be able to connect to your workstation and use it as if you were there, teleconference with colleagues, and do almost everything you would be able to do if you were physically in your office.

Once early innovators understood the Internet in business and industry, they began to apply its functionality into their office and plant operations. Email became commonplace and expected, a way of using flex-time to communicate across vast geography. Naturally, the Web emerged as a means of publicly distributing data, and even a method of practicing corporate public relations. As the virtualization of the office continued throughout the late-1990s, the demand for computer equipment also soared, creating a pattern of self-perpetuation of technology. Companies purchased faster computers, other companies created new uses for those computers, which in turn required faster computers, which computer manufactures were more than happy to sell.

Now, with a laptop and a cellular modem, business users can access their email, company databases, their organization's **intranet**, and critical information from anywhere

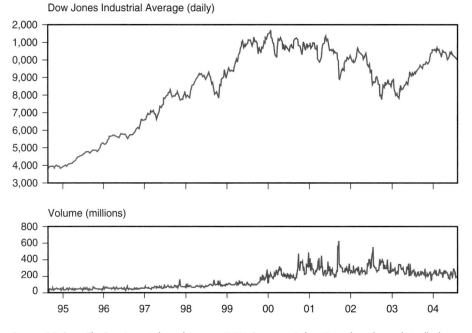

Figure 15.3   The Dow Jones Industrial Average (DJIA) Composite Index. Notice how the market rallied between 1995 and 2001. Then, notice how the market has readjusted to the proverbial dot com bubble between 2001 and the present.

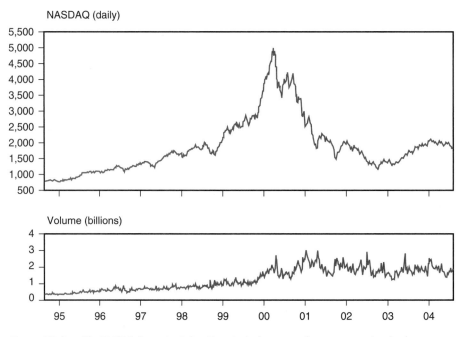

Figure 15.4   The NASDAQ Composite Index. Here, in the bottom graph, you can see that the dot com bubble burst soon into the year 2000. Recall that the NASDAQ market is especially fond of new technology companies, so its downturn is more indicative of how the Internet played a role in reshaping the economy.

in the world. Collaborative applications far beyond basic videoconferencing programs make it possible for people distributed around the world to work together as a team. The team can share a whiteboard, surf the Web, and share files as they collaborate.

Decentralizing the Community

In the past, people met in town halls and schools to discuss issues as communities. While these assemblies still occur, a great deal of our community discussions have shifted to the electronic. Beginning in the mid-1970s, some saw computer networks as a way to serve local community needs. Since that time, the use of computer networks as a community communication medium has taken many forms, and been called by many names: community networks, local bulletin boards, civic networking, telecottages, community information systems, community computing, community telecomputing, Free-Nets, and more.

Whatever form or name community networks take, they share four goals: (1) connecting all members of their community to the Internet for no cost or a minimal fee; (2) advancing local issues; (3) providing an electronic space for local news, announcements, and information; and (4) preaching the gospel of political empowerment to local residents (Shuler, 1996). Some communities still support Free-Nets, run substantially by volunteers, as discussed in Chapter 1. However as the price of subscribing to an ISP has become more competitive, some of the Free-Nets have disappeared.

The concept of community is traditionally tied to a physical location. We tend to think of community as people who live in the same neighborhood or town. The Internet challenges that concept, as the global communication possibilities redefine the concept of community. In the online environment, we define communities by topic. Perhaps this topic community might be events and issues in a particular neighborhood, town, or region, but an online community might also be a group of people with a similar hobby or interest. These virtual communities can have their own town hall meetings via mailing lists, Web pages, and teleconferencing.

Virtual communities can be highly developed and specialized, because they build upon themselves over time. As they grow in membership and in data, they evolve a certain community personality. This is why many virtual communities have a FAQ file listed prominently on their Web page or group discussion list. The FAQ ensures that new users will engage the community on a more evolved level of interaction rather than asking repeated . . . *does anyone know how?* questions. There is a topic community dedicated to just about any possible topic that is broad enough for general interest. At Yahoo! Groups (`http://groups.yahoo.com/`) you will find *hundreds of thousands* of topic communities. Some groups are moderated, some have restricted memberships, and others are completely public.

This is not to say that our actual communities have been substituted for virtual communities. But it is to say that we are spending a great deal more of our time in communities that are not tied to any concrete location. Instead, people search for and interact with people around the world who share a common *interest* (Rheingold, 1993). This occurred before the Internet, of course, but the Internet has brought interest communities to a whole new level. Prior to the Internet, virtual communities were formed via snail mail, or through traditional media, such as radio and television. Where television is mostly passive, these Web sites, groups, and mailing lists are interactive. They invite our feedback and draw us into the dialogue. With the ease of joining a

tip

∴ If you are searching for information you just can't find, join one of the virtual communities and ask your questions there. You may even meet a new friend who shares your interests!

virtual community, the traditional community has been decentralized so that it is no longer restricted by geography or time. While there are still traditional communities, virtual communities are also thriving. People can access information from around the globe, engage in correspondence with people on different continents, or get involved in issues that matter to them personally. Critics of virtual communities fear that as people become increasingly decentralized from their physical communities, they may become increasingly oblivious to the problems in their town, seeking out the fulfillment of their own interests.

Decentralizing the Individual

Most of our current academic research focuses on how the Internet affects us as a society, leaving us to deduce how these answers bear upon the individual. We do know some things about how people are using the Internet. As we saw in Chapter 1, the most frequent Internet activity is email, followed by doing research for work or school.

Logical Diversity and Desensitization   But what happens to individuals as they use the Internet? With billions of available Web pages, and such a variety of information available, it becomes difficult to know exactly how the Internet affects the individual. The diversity of information available on the Internet is astounding. Critical audiences will carefully evaluate information, but is that enough? Some critics contend that our interaction with potentially false data subtly desensitizes us. In other words, as we continually encounter bad data, our proverbial moral and ethical sensors no longer go off. So, from this perspective, we intellectually consume everything with a lack of consideration for the self (Shenk, 1999; Shenk, 1998). The equally valid counterpoint to this argument is that desensitization is really just another form of sensitization. By experiencing the new and unique, we are actually learning about each another—the good, the bad, and the ugly. In other words, the more we encounter data, the better off our knowledge (Shapiro, 1999; Davidson, 1997).

A third perspective is that both these processes are continually at work. Every day, a user on the Internet can learn something new and also be exposed to something completely untrue. This new information can either confirm or deny his or her previously held assumptions. Either way, each new argument encountered forces the individual to reconsider previously held assumptions; this will happen even if the new argument is not accepted. So, in a sense, we are logically decentralizing ourselves: not dogmatically rejecting bad data, or uncritically accepting everything, but continually adjusting the boundaries of our understanding. The critical factor in growing as individuals, from the information we see on the Internet, is to continually question whether the information we see is reliable and accurate.

Social Isolation   If you are a curious person, the Internet can be both a blessing and a curse. It can be a blessing because you enjoy the process of learning a great deal. Yet, if you find yourself staying up until 3:00 A.M. to browse the Web, you also realize how the Internet can be a curse (Rawlins, 1998). There are statistics that indicate that the longer we have had Internet access, the more time we spend online. This would ordinarily make sense, of course, since the more you use the Internet, the more you discover all the neat things you can do. The potentially disturbing issue lying dormant in these statistics, however, is that the more time we spend with our computers generally means the less time we have to engage in other life activities. Researchers are concerned that some Internet users tend to live a virtual life online, rather than engaging in face-to-face contact and life's activities.

Lifestyle Impacts Statistics on Internet usage also demonstrate that some heavy Internet users are increasingly spending: (1) less time talking with friends and family over the phone, (2) less time with friends and family, and (3) less time at actual events away from the home. Although heavy Internet users seem to communicate less in face-to-face dynamics than nonusers, this does not mean that they are necessarily communicating less. In fact, they could be using technology to communicate *more* than nonusers. In fact, Internet users are clearly engaging the world in a much different way than nonusers ordinarily engage it (Negroponte, 1996). Of course, it is important to realize that there aren't just users and nonusers, but different levels of use. The key thing to examine in your own life, as you spend more time using the Internet, is where that time is coming from. Any activity requires sacrificing some other activity.

Resources: Keeping Pace with the Internet

So, how do you keep abreast of all the dramatic changes occurring with the Internet, given that the medium is constantly becoming something new every day? Well, the answer is simple. As is the case when keeping up with any fast-paced technology, you need to become an active self-learner. You need to focus upon all the avenues of information available to you, and immerse yourself in new information *daily*. While this book does a lot to help you along your way to becoming a more literate Internet user, your education should not stop here. Mailing lists, news alerts, new Web sites, magazines, and books should *all* be a part of your new educational calculus.

Mailing Lists, Discussion Groups, and Online Journals

As you no doubt have figured out, the Internet is a large topic to try and canvas. We've done our best in this book to get you acquainted with the overall picture. But, by now you are likely developing particular interests in some of the subjects we've addressed within this text, and will want to know more about each. You can search for mailing lists and discussion groups for the topics of your particular interest. And, as you know from previous chapters, one of the good things about belonging to a mailing list is that the information is delivered to you. One of the most popular comprehensive mailing lists available for Internet reports is the Internet Scout Report.

Internet Scout Report Since 1994, the Internet Scout Project has focused on research and development projects that provide better tools and services for finding, filtering, and delivering online information and metadata. You can find the main Web site for the Scout Report at `http://scout.wisc.edu`, where you can view the report online, search the archive for previous report topics, and subscribe. This is, by far, one of the best ways of staying current with new developments and information being offered on the Internet. Don't forget to access Yahoo! Groups (`http://groups.yahoo.com`) to find your specialized topic in the *Computers & Internet* subdirectory, as well. Yahoo! has done an excellent job of preparing their groups for quick perusal. Google has also done an outstanding job of managing its group site at `http://groups.google.com` and you can search archives as well. If that fails, you can always do a search using the keyword *listserv* (which is a term for the mailing list program used to distribute mailing list messages) or *mailing list* and your desired target term. Chances are good that someone somewhere has developed a mailing list or group that encompasses your needs.

There are many journals available online about Internet technology. If you are interested in education, for instance, you will find a repository of online journal links

tip

∴ Try to find some time away from the computer. Balance is important. If you find that most of your existence is "screen life" lately, take a break and take in the beauty of nature!

at the University of Glasgow's Education Center (`http://www.scre.ac.uk/is/webjournals.html`). You will find information on using technology in teaching. Often you will find information about the Internet and technology in journals related to specific noncomputer fields, including business, education, medicine, and so forth.

News Alerts

No matter what type of method you are using to get your news—be it a workstation, laptop, cell phone, or handheld device—there are Internet services that will stream news, in real time, as it happens. This is a great way to keep current with the Internet and current events. Google.com (`http://www.google.com`) has a powerful news alert system located on their news page (`http://www.google.com/newsalerts`). You can enter whatever word you desire, and set the news robot to work for you. Desktop chat programs such as AOL have stock ticker and newsfeeds, which will scroll stock quotes or news on your desktop. Of course, if you are looking for something more technologically savvy, insiders prefer ZDNet's News Page, and their industry-specific news alert service (`http://www.zdnet.com`).

Bookmark Web Sites

Another important thing to do is to bookmark your favorite Web sites as you browse the Internet. It's annoying not being able to find a Web site you have already visited. As you encounter something that piques your interest, make sure to bookmark it for later use. If you forget to bookmark a site, you can also look in the history list for the most recently viewed sites.

Magazines

Magazines are a great resource, and provide a depth of coverage that you won't always find on the Internet. The newsstand is full of computer magazines. There are many magazines that we can recommend: *BEA Weblogic Developer's Journal*, *Business 2.0*, *Cold Fusion Developer's Journal*, *Communications Convergence*, *Computer Gaming World*, *Computerworld*, *Database Trends and Applications*, *Digital Photographer*, *Electronic Publishing*, *eWEEK*, *GamePRO*, *Government Computer News*, *Information Systems Management*, *InfoWORLD*, *Java Developer's Journal*, *MacAddict*, *Mac World*, *Mobile PC*, *Network Magazine*, *Network World*, *PC Magazine*, *PC World*, *Sys Admin*, *Web Services Journal*, *WebSphere Developer's Journal*, *Windows and .NET Magazine*, and *Wired*. Most magazines also have a comprehensive Web site with popular articles, downloads, tips, and so forth. You'll probably find others out there that suit your tastes and interests.

tip

∴ Bookmark your favorite online journals so you can find them quickly when you have a few spare moments to catch up. Consider setting your Web browser home page as one of your favorite news sites as well.

Books

Books are, without a doubt, different from magazines in that they take *months* or even *years* to publish. You are likely to find a greater depth of insight and analysis in books than in magazines and on the Web. So, if you really want to get to know a topic well, your best bet is to buy a book on your particular subject. Hopefully this book has served you well as an introduction to the Internet and the social, legal, and technical issues surrounding it.

SUMMARY

Now that you've read through the chapter, you are prepared to:

- Explain how new media get adopted by society, using the EPS cycle:
  - Phase One: Elites
  - Phase Two: Popularization
  - Phase Three: Specialization
- Recognize who a *change agent* is, and be able to discuss their role in the diffusion of innovations.
- Conceptualize what *decentralizing* is, and explain how the theoretical concept is impacting:
  - The government
  - Education
  - The economy
  - The community
  - The individual
- Keep yourself educated and up-to-date with many of the new ideas and technologies bearing upon the Internet through:
  - Mailing lists, discussion groups, and online journals
  - Internet Scout Report
  - News alerts
  - Bookmarking Web sites
  - Magazines
  - Books

Review Questions and Hands-on Exercises

Review Questions

1. Describe the Elite-Popularization-Specialization (EPS) cycle of mass media adoption, with respect to the adoption of the Internet.

2. With respect to the EPS cycle, who are the elites in today's society?

3. What is a *change agent* and how does a change agent influence the adoption of a new communications medium?

4. Which of the five adoption profiles suits you best, and why?

5. We all know someone who is an innovator or early adopter, whether this is with technology or some other aspect of life. With that person in mind, answer the following questions.

    a. What new things has this person adopted in the last couple of years?

    b. How does this person research new technologies and other things?

    c. Does this person try to convince you and others to try new things?

6. What does the term *decentralizing* mean?

7. How has contacting your government representatives changed because of the popularity of the Internet?

8. What is meant by the term *virtual office*?

9. Describe how the concept of *community* is evolving, due to the Internet.

10. Some say that the vast amount of information available on the Internet is both desensitizing and sensitizing at the same time. Describe what this statement means.

Hands-on Exercises

1. Find your local city's Web site. You may need to use a search engine to find it. Answer the following questions.

    a. What are the email addresses for the mayor and your local representative?

    b. Is there information available for local parks and recreation facilities?

    c. Is there information available for community events?

    d. Is there information available for city services such as garbage collection, animal licensing, and other services?

    e. Is there information available about the local libraries?

    f. Is there a feedback form available for you to be able to ask a question about city services?

2. Find the Web site for your local college or university. Does this college or university offer distance education courses? If so, what computer technology or Internet access do they require the students to have?

3. Load your favorite search engine and find information about the following mailing lists. Include in your information a general description of the mailing list and instructions on how to subscribe and unsubscribe.

    a. World Almanac E-Newsletter

    b. Research Buzz newsletter

    c. Internet Resources newsletter

    d. Edupage from Educase

    e. Cool Tricks and Trinkets newsletter

4. For each of the following technology magazines, find the URL for the online version. List the top three stories, top three downloads available (if any), and describe three other features available on the magazine site.

    a. PC Magazine

    b. Wired Magazine

    c. eWeek

    d. Web Developer's Journal

5. The following sites are online news sites. For each one, list the top three stories, and three other features available on the site.

    a. Slashdot (`http://www.slashdot.org`)

    b. Internet World (`http://www.internetworld.com`)

    c. Geek.com (`http://www.geek.com`)

    d. Internet Week (`http://www.internetweek.com`)

GLOSSARY

A

3-tier Architecture: A software development term referring to an application that includes a user interface, middleware, and database. In Web development, the user interface is the Web site; middleware is written using a language such as ASP.NET, PHP, or J2EE and the database could be mySQL, Oracle, or Microsoft SQL.

Abilene Network (U.S.): Also known as Internet2, Abilene is a high-speed backbone networking system that interconnects network collection points. It is a venture of the University Corporation for Advanced Internet Development (UCAID).

Acceptable Use Policy (AUP): A legal document, written to protect ISPs, corporations, and educational institutions from unlawful use of its service, and in doing so, outlines prohibited and acceptable uses of the service, and possible consequences of misuse.

ADSL: ADSL (Asymmetrical Digital Subscriber Line) technology makes use of the fact that the telephone line will carry a larger number of frequencies than those limited few necessary for human voice transmission. ADSL uses the frequencies not used for voice, and transmits data over them. The transmission speed ranges between dial-up and cable services.

Advanced Research Projects Agency (U.S.): A government agency established in 1957 by the Department of Defense, charged with considering strategic issues made possible by new scientific discoveries, and seeking out countermeasures to pre-existing technological problems.

Advocacy Marketing (Viral Marketing): Electronic word-of-mouth marketing wherein consumers promote a product or service by telling other consumers about it.

Adware: Advertising; might be in the form of rolling banners, or in a pop-up or pop-under window. Adware is also advertising supported software likely to be necessary for generating revenue in order for that software to remain freely available.

Affiliate Marketing: An arrangement between two businesses, where each places a banner ad or logo of the other on their Web site, and pays a commission for sales completed as a result of the online referral.

Aggregator: A type of newsfeed that consolidates all headlines of a particular subject over a particular time.

AIF or AIFF (Audio Interchange File Format): The AIF file format provides a good sound quality, and can be played in most Web browsers without a plug-in. However, like the WAV file, the file sizes can be quite large.

Alignment: How text and images are lined up on a page. Text can be lined up on the left, to the right, or centered down the middle of the page.

Animated GIF: A series of GIFs; the images cycle from one to the next using a timer and producing a single GIF animated image.

Anti-Spam Software (Spam Blockers): Software that automatically routes unwanted email into a separate folder or directly into the trash.

Application Sharing: Allows you and another online user to share an application, such as a spreadsheet program.

ARPANET (U.S.): The forerunner to the Internet. Advanced in the late-1960s and early-1970s by ARPA (Advanced Research Projects Agency) as a wide-area-network to link computers that were each running independent systems.

ASCII Text (American Standard Code for Information Interchange): Unformatted text.

ASF (Advanced Streaming Format), WMV (Windows Media Video), or WMA (Windows Media Audio): Windows media files that can be viewed using Windows Media Player.

Asynchronous Communication: Often referred to as "flex-time" communication; users communicate at different times, waiting for a response before replying. Email is a form of asynchronous communication, as correspondents can delay their reading and writing of messages via a computer.

Atom: Adopted by Google as a format for sending blog feeds.

Attributes: The variety of options available for text size, color, and font face.

AU or SND (Sun or Java format): These file formats are similar to WAV and AIFF file formats, and are used for Java Applets.

Avatar: Graphical representation of a character in a role-playing game.

AVI (Audio/Video Interleave): A very popular video compression type. It can be played by a variety of different video applications, including Windows Media Player.

B

Backbone (U.S.): A high-speed data line that forms the main conduit within an overall communication system. (This is a varying definition, because the Internet has several backbones, and smaller networks also have their own backbones.)

Backwards Compatibility: Refers to ensuring that a new product, application, or program will work with the predecessor technology.

Bandwidth: The data transmission rate over a network or the Internet.

Baseline: In text, the line that the words sit on.

Bibliographic Databases: Reference collections used to research materials such as journals and books.

Binary or Binaries: A non-text file such as a spreadsheet, word processing document, image, video, or audio file.

Bit: A unit of measurement of information.

BITNET: An acronym that stands for "Because It's Time NETwork," and was a vast wide-area network (WAN) that maintained its own set of operating protocols apart from TCP/IP.

Block: Term used in IM to disallow buddies access.

Blogger: The author of a blog.

Blogs (Web Logs): Personal Web diaries and journals that are frequently updated and designed for public viewing. A blog typically mirrors the individuality of its author, and allows the blogger the opportunity to rant philosophically on personal, social, or other topics of interest.

BMP: A BMP file, the original bitmap file, was created for use in the Windows operating system, and is a commonly used bit-mapped format in graphic design.

Boolean Operators: Terms such as "and", "or", and "not" used to manage the logical operations of the search engine. As search engines are not standardized, they write their own rules when it comes to which advanced features they support.

Browser Hijacker: A browser hijacker is a program designed to change the settings on your Web browser. A home page hijacker changes the home page in order for you to see advertising or increase the hit count for their page.

Browser-Safe Colors: The 216 colors that display essentially the same in any browser.

Bulletin Board Service (BBS): BBSs used for game-playing or distributing information. Participants using a Bulletin Board Service can post text messages to a virtual bulletin board for public reading.

Business-to-Business (B2B) Commerce: These transactions include bulk purchases between businesses. They constitute the majority of online business transactions today.

Business-to-Business-to-Consumer (B2B2C) Commerce: Essentially this model is manufacturer-to-retailer-to-customer where, for instance, a manufacturer of saws sells saws to the hardware store, which in turn, sells them to the consumer. This is simple supply chain management, as the product is supplied from the manufacturer to the retailer to the consumer.

Business-to-Consumer (B2C) Commerce (or e-tailing): These include retail transactions on the Internet, and are often what people think of when they hear the term E-Commerce.

C

Cache: Temporary files stored on the hard drive.

CA*Net (Canada): The offspring network following NetNorth. In 1990, as Canadian network traffic increased due to the adoption of standardized TCP/IP protocols, bandwidth became insufficient. CA*Net was launched using primarily 56 Kbps lines.

CA*Net II (Canada): The success of CA*Net was so great that, in 1997, the Canadian government launched CA*Net II, using a core fiber-optic network.

CA*Net 3 (Canada): More fully implementing CA*Net II. In 1998, CA*Net 3 became the first full-scale national optical Internet.

CA*Net 4 (Canada): Canada is currently in the deployment stage of CA*Net 4, which will yield four to eight times the information capacity of CA*Net 3.

Cascading Style Sheet: In a document, a style sheet containing all of the style notes which describe the formatting.

Change Agent: An individual who influences clients' innovation decisions in a direction deemed desirable by a change agency. For instance, a change agent may be a person who initiates change in an organization.

Chat: Communication in real time with someone who is online anywhere in the world.

Chat Room: A place on the Internet where small groups of people can meet to discuss issues in real time.

Clear Text Transmission: An unencrypted message that can be read by someone who intercepts it using packet-sniffing software.

Commercial Software: Software that is purchased, either online or from a retail outlet.

Consumer-to-Business (C2B): One example of C2B includes an individual consumer selling to a business or organization, but C2B also includes an individual consumer who seeks sellers to bid on products or services.

Consumer-to-Consumer (C2C): This type of transaction entails consumers selling or buying directly between each other, and includes online classified ads or individual Web sites.

Contrast: At the most basic level, the difference between graphic elements on a page. The primary purpose for contrast is to emphasize some elements, and de-emphasize others.

Cookies: A small amount of text stored on a user's computer to be read later by the Web site that stored it.

COSINE Project (Cooperation for Open Systems Interconnection in Europe): A program sponsored by the European Commission, aimed at tying together European research networks.

Crossed Signals: The job of a satellite transponder is to receive a radio signal (in this case, data transmission) on one radio frequency, and to amplify it with power (generated from solar panels and rechargeable batteries) back to Earth on another radio frequency. That way signals don't get crossed.

D

DANTE Project: A company established by the national research networks in Europe to provide international network services.

Data Files: Files such as spreadsheets, word processing documents, videos, and others you might deal with on a daily basis.

Day Trading: Traders buy and sell stocks through the course of the day, ending the day with all stocks closed and no open positions.

Defamation: Closely related to both libel and slander, defamation occurs when someone communicates untrue information that lowers a person's status, or subjects a person to public disdain, embarrassment, or humiliation.

Demassification: Occurs when mass media saturate a given market and then shift perspective to capture niche audiences.

Desktop Client Software: Software that is stored and executed from the client's hard drive on a client-server system.

Direct Access Trading: A method of trading stocks that allows traders to directly access positions without waiting for a brokerage to execute the position.

Directory Outline: An enormous list of Internet resources containing a list of topics that can be browsed and searched, ranging from a series of general-to-specific lists of subtopics and Web sites.

Discussion Board: A Web-based discussion list that is neither a mailing list nor a Usenet newsgroup. This can be a feedback page at a radio station site, a discussion forum at a Web developer resource site, a comment board on a personal journal site, or another similar site.

Distance Education: Occurs when a teacher and student(s) are separated by physical distance and technology (e.g., voice, video, data, and print), often in concert with face-to-face communication; is used to bridge the instructional gap.

Distance Learning: Term used for courses delivered to students who are not physically on campus.

Dithering: The technique of mixing colors.

Domain Name: The name assigned to an IP address, which makes it easier to find a World Wide Web site online. For example, `http://www.cnn.com` is the domain name for CNN.

Downloading: Data transmission from another computer over the Internet received by your computer.

DSL (Digital Subscriber Line): A high-speed telephone Internet connection.

Dynamic Web Page: A Web page that has been created on-the-fly by a program on the Web server.

E

E-Books (Electronic Books): A recent innovation in book publishing where a user can purchase a book online and download it directly to a computer or PDA (Personal Digital Assistant, such as Palm Pilot).

E-Business or Electronic Business: Includes transactions between business partners, but also includes transactions within the organization, servicing customers, and collaboration with business partners. This implies buying and selling of goods and services in addition to customer relations management, communication with business partners, inventory control, purchasing, and many other business functions.

E-Commerce or Electronic Commerce: Entails the transactions between business partners. This implies buying and selling of goods and services.

Electromagnetic Pulse (EMP): Can surge from a nuclear explosion, rendering much electronic equipment inoperative.

Electronic Data Interchange (EDI): A method of transmitting data in a standardized format from one computer system to another either within an organization, or, more importantly, from one organization's computer system to another.

Electronic Tendering: Organizations make purchases through a tendering system where the buyer places an item for tender on a request for quote (RFQ) system. Suppliers bid on the job or product. This is also called a reverse auction.

Elite-Popularization-Specialization (EPS) Cycle: Suggests that all mass communication media are first introduced to (or by) elites, get dispersed among the popular masses, and finally are expanded in availability so that content can become specialized.

Email Client: A computer program designed to send, receive, and manage email. Examples of email clients include Microsoft's Outlook Express, Netscape Communicator's Mail, and Eudora.

Email (Electronic Mail): A message sent from one person to another, which can be retrieved at a later time. Email is sent and received using an email client such as Microsoft Outlook or Eudora, or through the use of a Webmail service such as Gmail, Yahoo!, or Hotmail. Your Internet Service Provider may also provide a Webmail service for email.

Email Trackers: These email add-ins trace the path of a user's email as it is received and forwarded from one person to the next.

E-Mexico Initiative (Mexico): A $400 million project designed to provide Internet access to Mexico's entire population.

E-tailing: Business-to-consumer commerce; retail transactions on the Internet.

Ethernet: A method of networking computers using copper cabling.

Ezine (Electronic Magazine): A magazine published on the World Wide Web.

EuropaNet (Europe): A result of Cambridge University's DANTE Project (between 1993 and 1997), EuropaNet connected 18 nations running 2 Mbps data lines. The most important switch during this time was that EuropaNet implemented TCP/IP, allowing it to interconnect with other computers using the communications suite.

Expert Inquiries: Direct requests for data from a recognized expert, or body of experts.

Explorer I (U.S.): Launched January 31, 1958; the first U.S. satellite to orbit the Earth.

F

Face-to-Face (FTF): In person communication as opposed to email or telephone.

Federal Communications Commission (FCC): Established by the Communications Act of 1934; is responsible to Congress and charged with regulating both national and international communication in the U.S.

File Transfer Protocol (FTP): The data instruction set used for downloading and uploading files to a server.

Firewall: A combination of software and hardware that filters traffic between the user and the Internet, or acts as a gateway to a network, protecting the network from unwanted traffic from other networks or the Internet.

Flame War: An email conversation wherein disgruntled parties use abusive communication to attempt to convey their point.

Flex-Time: Asynchronous communication; users communicate at different times, waiting for a response before replying. Email is a form of flex-time communication.

Forward Compatibility: Refers to developing products, applications, and programs that will be compatible with devices and programs developed in the future.

Freeware: Software that is completely free and may be freely distributed. Often, it has been created by a Good Samaritan, with an assumption that credit will be given to the programmer, and that the program will not be altered in any way.

Frequently Asked Questions (FAQ) Pages: Compilations of the most frequently asked questions (and their answers), pertaining to a given topic, usually assembled on a single Web page. FAQ documents are usually very thorough and well organized, evolving over time as a result of much online dialogue in special interest groups.

Full-Duplex: In audio chat, sound data that is transferred in both directions simultaneously, e.g., a telephone.

G

Gateway: A special-purpose computer used by ISPs, which connects to a powerful leased Internet line, such as a T3 or OC48.

Gbps (Gigabits per Second): One-billion bits per second, or roughly 12,500 characters per second.

GÉANT (Europe): Network that connects 32 countries across Europe at speeds between 2.5 Gbps and 10 Gbps. The GÉANT network is one of the world's most advanced telecommunications structures designed for distributed networking.

General References: Are similar to what you would find if you were looking at a traditional almanac, dictionary, encyclopedia, or other resource. Online versions are searchable, hyperlinked, and more easily retrievable via the Web.

Geosynchronous Orbit: When satellites hover over a particular geography with the assistance of rocket power. They are in sync with the Earth's axis rotation.

GIF: GIFs are bitmapped images, made up of many pixels that combine like a mosaic to form a picture. GIFs use a maximum of 8 bits per pixel to store the color information, thus 8 bits allows $2^8 = 256$ colors. Because they are limited to 256 colors, and because of the method of compression, GIFs are best used for line drawings, bullets, icons, lines, and other images made up primarily of large blocks of color.

Gopher: A simple system of text menus; users had to "dig" their way through to get information.

H

Half-Duplex: In audio chat, sound data that can travel only one way at a time, e.g., a walkie-talkie.

Helper Application: A Web browser points to a program as a helper application to be used for specific data files. For instance, Windows Media Player may be defined as the helper application to use for audio files.

High-Definition Television (HDTV): A type of television display that doubles the 525 lines of resolution to 1050, and changes the screen ratio from 12:9 to 16:9.

Host: The main computer connected directly to a network. But, it can accommodate many workstations connected to it, which can be used to access the resources of the network.

Hotspots: A location where a wireless signal is detected by the wireless network card. This signal is sent from a wireless access point, which is connected to a computer, and typically a network as well.

HyperText Documents: Documents constructed using the HyperText Markup Language. These are the most common type of document on the Web, and can include text, hypertext links, graphics, movie files, Java Applets, and more.

HyperText Link: In hypertext markup language, the code used to define a series of text or images as clickable. Ordinarily, this involves going to another Web site, moving to a target anchor on a Web page, or executing the download of some type of file.

HyperText Markup Language (HTML): The markup language used to construct Web pages.

HyperText Transfer Protocol (HTTP): The protocol governing the exchange of files on the Web.

HyperText Transfer Protocol Secure (HTTPS): A specific protocol set employed when a page of a Web site must be encrypted for secure transfer, such as where a credit card number will be transmitted.

I

IMAP (Instant Message Access Protocol): IMAP connections access email messages directly on the server and do not download them locally to the user's hard drive. Mailboxes can be managed directly on the server, and outgoing messages are sent from there, not your ISP's outgoing mail, as well.

Information Appliance: Term coined by Microsoft as a forthcoming device that will merge technologies into one interface.

Instant Messenger (IM): Programs that allow you to type text and send it instantly to someone else who is using an IM program. In return, that person will be able to see your message and respond to it immediately.

Interactive Video Networks: IVNs use dedicated video equipment and bundled telecommunication lines to conduct multiple-setting interactive video and audio sessions between sites.

Interface: A connection between two dissimilar devices.

Interlaced Image: When the Web browser downloads an interlaced image, the image is displayed progressively. At first the image appears fuzzy, and with each pass the image becomes clearer.

Internet: The worldwide network of computer networks, and all its supporting structure.

Internet Explorer: Microsoft's Web browser.

Internet Protocol (IP) Address: A numeric identifier for a computer or peripheral device connected to a network. For example, 127.324.0.89 could represent your computer on the Internet.

Internet Service Provider (ISP): A company that provides a home or business access to the Internet.

Internetwork: A collection of computer networks joined so that a computer on one network can send messages to a computer on another network.

Intranet: An internal Internet for employees to access information about a company; not meant for public consumption.

IRC (Internet Relay Chat): An application that allows a number of individual users to exchange text messages simultaneously, in real time, over the Internet.

J

JPEG: A popular image compression format suitable for photographs and other images requiring a rich selection of colors.

K

Kbps (Kilobits per Second): One-thousand bits per second, or roughly 125 characters per second.

Keywords Meta-Tag: An HTML tag used to identify the potential contents of a page for search engines.

Knowbots: Computer programs used by search engines and designed to crawl from one Web page to another through the links on each Web page, gathering keywords or whole pages as they go. They may also be referred to as "robots," "bots," "spiders," or "crawlers."

L

Libel: Deals with written untruths about an entity published to third parties.

Local Area Network (LAN): A collection of computers and resources, such as printers and shared network drives, spread out over a localized area.

Lossless Compression: Reducing the file size of a graphics file without reducing the quality of the picture.

Lossy Compression: When some of the information in an image is lost, slightly reducing the quality of the image.

Lurk: When someone observes the postings on a newsgroup or mailing list for a while to get a feel for its nature.

M

Mailing Lists: Email-based discussion groups where email messages are delivered to those who subscribe to the list.

Mailto: Used in HTML, it allows users to click on an email address and automatically send a message using the default email client.

Markup Language: A type of computer language that defines the layout of text and images on a page.

Mass Communication: One person or agency communicating to many people through some technological means.

Mass Media: Newspapers, magazines, radio, television, and movies.

Mbps (Megabits per Second): One million bits per second or roughly 1250 characters per second.

M-Commerce: Mobile Commerce transactions completed in a wireless environment that may involve using a cell phone, or other hand-held device capable of sending and receiving data over a wireless connection.

Media File: A specialized data file that contains audio or video data.

Metasearch Engines (Meta-Engines): Search engines that submit a key term to several search engines, consolidating the results.

Microcinema Movement: A term coined in 1991; a community of independent filmmakers who produce everything from animated shorts to feature-length movies at a fraction of the cost of the major studios. With digital equipment, these films now rival the quality of multi-million dollar productions.

MID or MIDI (Musical Instrument Digital Interface): The MIDI file format is designed for instrumental music, and must be created using a synthesizer on a computer, electronic keyboard, or similar device.

Middleware: Software that glues together two other software components.

MIME (Multipurpose Internet Mail Extension): A system for recognizing the type of data within a file based upon its suffix extension. MIME is a resident protocol in many Web browsers and email clients; it allows the user to freely send and receive binary files (documents, graphics, photographs, audio, and video).

Mini Distributed Denial of Service Attacks (mDDoS): A distributed denial of service (DDoS) attack occurs when a group of compromised computer systems simultaneously send messages to the computer system under attack. Effectively, that system is overwhelmed and cannot accept messages from other systems while the attack is happening. Service to any computers that require it legitimately is denied while it is under attack. A mini distributed denial of service attack (mDDoS) occurs on a smaller scale, such as a small collection of PCs sending messages to another PC.

MMOG (Massive Multiplayer Online Games): Computer games played on the Internet from game consoles and PCs through game servers.

MMORPG (Massive Multiplayer Online Role-Playing Game): A genre of computer games that brings people from all over the world into a dynamic environment where they can interact with each other and experience a rich new virtual world.

Modem (Modulator/Demodulator): A device connecting a computer to a communications network by translating a signal such that it is suitable for the channel through which it must pass. For example, telephone lines are analog-based channels. Telephone modems, accordingly, translate the computer's digital signal into the telephone line's required analog signal, and back again.

Moderated List/Group: A mailing list or discussion group that has a person who manages the list serving as a message gatekeeper.

MOV (QuickTime): Files that can be viewed using the QuickTime viewer or plug-in available from Apple Computing (http://www.apple.com/quicktime), and will play on both Windows and Apple operating systems.

MP3 (Motion Picture Experts Group Audio Layer 3 or MPEG Audio-Layer 3): The MP3 file format is a compressed audio format with a very good sound quality. Depending on the compression selections chosen, the MP3 file can rival CD quality, yet the file size can be as little as 10% of the equivalent WAV file.

MUD (Multi-User Dungeon): Early computer game that derived its name from *Dungeons and Dragons*.

N

National Control Protocol: In the late-1960s, ARPA requested that software engineers develop a more stable protocol than NPL. This redeveloped software was released as the National Control Protocol (NCP) in 1970, and stabilized most of the data exchanges between early ARPANET members. The release of NCP allowed ARPANET to begin its first expansion phase in the U.S.

NCSA Mosaic: A Web browser developed in 1993 by the National Center for Supercomputing Applications, led by Marc Andreessen. Mosaic's main contribution to the Web was that it allowed for the downloading of images, along with text.

Netiquette: The general rules, both written and unwritten, of expected online etiquette.

NetNorth (Canada): Between 1984 and 1985, NetNorth was a successful governmental initiative to interconnect all Canadian universities within one year. In 1988, Canada connected to NSFNET and began the switch to TCP/IP. However, in 1990, as Canadian network traffic increased, bandwidth became insufficient, and CA*Net was launched.

Network Access Server (NAS): Connects software between the user and a VPN.

Newsgroups: An online discussion group. There are thousands of newsgroups available, covering almost every imaginable attraction.

Newsreader: Software that sends email postings to the various newsgroups.

Notepad: A text-editing program included in the Windows operating system.

NPL Network (U.K.): At the National Physical Laboratory in 1967, Donald W. Davies developed the NPL Network using the first packets to transfer data.

NSFNET (U.S.): The National Science Foundation Network is a high-speed backbone network of all the major networks in the U.S. NSFNET has connections running to Canada, Europe, Mexico, and the Pacific Rim.

O

Online Auctions: Allow consumers to bid on products and services. The highest bidder wins the purchase for the item, and the seller ships it.

Online Trading: Refers to buying and selling stocks and mutual funds through an online brokerage, as opposed to using the telephone and a full-service brokerage.

Open Source: The source code, or original program, is made available and others are invited to help with the development and submit improvements, becoming part of the group who is developing it. Open Source can also mean that the software use requires a paid license, and the source code is available.

P

2001 Patriot Act: Legislation passed in the wake of the 9/11 tragedies giving the U.S. government more leverage to fight terrorism.

Packet Header: Each packet is tagged with a header including details about its journey. The header identifies: (1) originating IP address and information, (2) when it was issued according to the sending server clock, (3) destination IP address and information, (4) the subject of the data, or data-type, and (5) transmission error information.

Packets: A file or message may be broken into several packets, each packet taking a different route over a network to reach its destination.

Packet-Switching: The process by which email messages, chat-sessions, and Web pages are segmented into numerous packets as they are transported from one computer to another via the Internet.

Payload: The malicious code contained in a virus or worm.

Peer-to-Peer Network: A networking term referring to a network where there are no central servers, and each computer on the network can share resources.

Pixel: A word invented from "picture element." A pixel is the basic unit of a programmable color on a computer image.

Plagiarism: Presenting someone else's words or ideas as your own.

Plug-in Components: Small programs that provide an environment in your browser to run a specialized software program, such as a Java Applet, or for viewing a specialized file, such as a video or animation. There are hundreds of plug-ins available (usually free), which have been written for a variety of applications.

PNG: An image compression proposed by the World Wide Web Consortium as an alternative to the GIF format.

POP (Post Office Protocol): A means of email access where the email client downloads email from the server to your local computer, then disconnects.

Portals: Customizable Web pages consolidating features such as: email, news, calendar, weather, and in the case of business portals, specialized search.

POTS (Plain Old Telephone Service): Network over which a home computer could connect to an Internet conferencing system.

Privacy Policy: Document that outlines an Internet Service Provider's policy for protecting your personal information.

Proprietary: Privately developed, owned, and held technology.

Protocol: A system of communicating data from one location to another.

Proximity: The distance between two objects.

R

RA, RPM, or RAM (RealAudio Format): RealAudio files have a higher degree of compression than MP3 files, and can be either downloaded whole or streamed from a Web server.

Random Access Memory (RAM): Fast computer memory that provides temporary storage required for programs to run.

RARE (Europe): The first pan-European attempt to interlink independent networks began with the founding of RARE (Réseaux Associés pour la Recherche Européenne/European Association of Research Networks) in 1986.

Raster Graphics: These files are bitmapped graphics files. The picture is mapped into a grid of pixels and the color of each pixel is stored to create the picture.

Real Time: Live time.

Repetition: In graphic design, repetition is used to pull a site together so that individual pages are clearly connected to one another. This means that every page on a site should share visual elements with other pages: the same colors, graphic images, fonts, and so forth.

Reverse Auction: In B2B E-Commerce, suppliers bid on a job or product.

Ripping: Copying music from a commercial CD to individual files.

RM or RA (RealPlayer): Streaming video files, which require RealPlayer to view them. They are generally not downloadable.

S

Satellite: A communication station orbiting, or in a geosynchronous position above Earth.

Search Engine: A Web-based program that allows users to submit key-term requests to an online database.

Shareware: Software that may be freely distributed and is essentially on a "try before you buy" basis. Most shareware is limited, either as partially functional, time-limited such as a 30-day trial, or perhaps includes a logo in a user's final product.

Site Map: Outline of a Web site's layout that can be used as a navigational guide.

Site Notification: A method of submitting your Web site or Web page to a search engine so that it will be recorded in its database.

Site-Specific Search Engines: Search engines that search only the data on a particular Web site.

Slander: Deals with spoken untruths about an entity to third parties.

Sliced Image: A cut up image used to expedite downloading a large image to a Web page.

Sniping: Using specialized software to monitor online auctions and bid at a preset maximum price to win an auction.

Software Review Sites: Sites where software shoppers can get expert evaluations on software titles available.

SPAM: Unsolicited email or newsgroup postings.

SPAM Blockers (Anti-SPAM Software): Software that automatically routes unwanted email into a separate folder or directly to the trash.

SPIM: Unwanted instant messages, usually from companies promoting their products.

Sputnik I (U.S.S.R.): Launched into orbit on October 7, 1957; Earth's first artificial satellite.

Spyware: Often associated with adware; any computer program that takes advantage of your Internet connection and reports the list of Web sites you have visited, or tracks your Internet usage in some other way.

Stack: A group of layered programs, each of which communicates with the others in the stack.

Static Web Page: A Web page that resides on a Web server and has content that does not change.

Streaming Media: The rapid transmission of audio and video in packets over the Internet.

Subject-Specific Search Engines (Directory Outlines): Engines that seek out the data stored on many different Web sites about a particular topic or theme.

Subscribe to a Newsgroup: Selecting a newsgroup in a newsreader.

Supply Chain Management (SCM): The collection and integration of business processes involved in the provision of products and services from the supplier or originator, to the customer or end user. These activities include purchasing, materials handling, production, warehousing, inventory control, distribution, and delivery. SCM involves coordinating all these activities.

Surf the Web: A figure of speech used to describe the activity of browsing the Web.

Synchronous Communication: Communication that happens at the same time.

T

Tag Attributes: In HTML, attributes that specify values for alignment, color, size, and other elements.

Talk: A simple program that allowed users on networked computers to type messages to one another in real time.

Telepresence: Using telecommunications to simulate "being there."

Temporary Files: Term used by Internet Explorer to describe the files in the cache.

TEN-34 (Europe): Stage 2 development of EuropaNet's 18-country pan-European network, running at 34 Mbps.

TEN-155 (Europe): Stage 3 development of EuropaNet's 19-country pan-European network, running between 155 Mbps and 622 Mbps.

Thread or Threading: An online discussion; when the user posts a reply, the reply is grouped with the original message and any further replies.

TIFF (Tagged Image File Format): A *de facto* standard format used for scanning and by graphic artists in image-editing software packages such as Adobe Photoshop and Macromedia Fireworks.

Topic Ring: A Web site in a series of sites with a common theme (also called a WebRing). Web sites in the topic ring contain links to the next and previous Web sites in the series.

Top Level Domains (TLDs): The last part of a URL that helps to categorize the type of organization. You may have encountered many of the original six TLDs, such as .com (commerce), .edu (education), .org (organization—for non-profit organizations), .net (network), .gov (government), and .mil (military).

Trademark: A logo, acronym, word, color scheme, combination of sounds, or any other symbolic device used to distinguish a product or service as unique.

Transmission Control Protocol (TCP): Having evolved considerably since it debuted in 1975, the TCP suite is responsible for connection-oriented, transport-level communications. It was initially tested during the first satellite link-up of ARPANET between Hawaii and Great Britain.

Transmission Control Protocol/Internet Protocol (TCP/IP): Developed in the 1970s, TCP/IP is a suite of computer-to-computer communications protocols that deals with packet transportation, session communications, email, and file transfer.

Transparency: An addition to the GIF format; gives the graphic artist the ability to use a transparent background and simulate any imaginable shape.

Transponder: A device inside a satellite used to recast a signal on a different frequency so that signals do not get crossed. Satellites typically have thousands of transponders in them to manage communications traffic flow.

Trojan Horse: A Trojan Horse is a small program designed to gather information, such as userids and passwords, and send those to the person who wrote the program.

Tunneling: Employing a protocol to connect to a virtual private network (VPN).

U

Uniform Resource Locator (URL) or Universal Resource Locator (URL): Each Web page on the Internet has a distinct address, just as each dwelling has a distinct address. A Web page can be requested by entering the address in the Web browser, or by selecting a link from another Web page. A Web page address is called the URL.

Unmoderated List/Group: Mailing lists or discussion groups where messages can be freely posted without editorial restraint.

Uploading: Sending data transmissions from your computer to another computer on the Internet.

Userid: The login identification used for logging into a Webmail, network, or ISP service.

V

Vector Graphics: These files use math equations to calculate the lines required to draw the shapes for an image. The advantage of vector graphics over bitmapped graphics is that they are easily scalable.

Vertical Marketplace: A special type of e-marketplace, called a vertical marketplace (or vertical portal, or vortal); services only one industry.

Viral Marketing: Electronic word-of-mouth marketing wherein consumers promote a product or service by telling other consumers about it.

Virtual Private Dial-up Network (VPDN): A private telephone modem connection to a private network.

Virtual Private Network (VPN): A LAN or series of LANS that are secured behind a firewall or gateway, and have restrictions for user connections.

Virtual Reality: Allows users to feel like they are in an environment without actually being there.

Virus: A small computer program; the level of destruction it can cause ranges from simple annoyance and use of computer processing time, to erasing files on your hard drive and rendering your computer inoperable.

Voice over Internet Protocol (VoIP): VoIP turns the analog signals of voice and sound into a digital signal that can be transmitted over a network, such as the Internet. This technology has allowed people to communicate using voice through their chat clients, and also make phone calls.

W

Wardriving: The technique of driving around a city in a vehicle, with a notebook computer and an antenna, detecting open WLANs (Wireless Local Area Network), often with exploitation in mind.

WAV (WAVEform): The WAVEform audio format is an uncompressed file format developed for audio files for the PC. You can record WAV files from a CD or microphone using your PC, and the sound quality tends to be very good, but because it is an uncompressed format, the file sizes tend to be quite large.

Web Application: A software program that uses HTTP for its core communication protocol and delivers Web-based information to the user in the HTML language. Also called a Web-based application.

Web Browser: The software you use to download and view Web pages.

Web Bug: A small, invisible image on a Web page designed to track the Web pages you view as you surf to other pages, which also contain Web bugs.

Webmail Interface: A Web page provided by your ISP that allows you to log in and see your email messages via the Web.

Web Pages: HTML documents that can be viewed with a Web browser.

WebRing: A Web site in a series of sites with a common theme (also called a Topic Ring). Web sites in the Webring contain links to the next and previous Web site in the series.

Whiteboard: A feature that allows you to post text to, or draw items on, a whiteboard shared by multiple users. It is especially useful for collaboration in teleconferencing.

Whois: An Internet program that allows users to investigate information about Internet domain names, hosting networks, and contact information.

Wide Area Network (WAN): A collection of computers and resources, such as printers and shared network drives to store files, spread out over a wide area. Typically, WANs cover several buildings or are integrated through several cities.

Wildcard Characters: Variables used in a Boolean search.

Wired Equivalent Privacy (WEP): A wireless access point encryption system used to block unwanted wireless systems from accessing your network.

Wireless Fidelity (WiFi): Refers to a high-frequency wireless local area network (WLAN). You may also see this term written as Wi-Fi. A computer is said to be WiFi enabled if it has a wireless network card installed.

Wireless Local Area Network (WLAN): A network using wireless connections facilitated by wireless access points, rather than physical wiring. Often a wireless network connects computers to a wired network that has access to the Internet and other network resources.

World Intellectual Property Organization (WIPO): (http://www.wipo.int) Promotes the protection of intellectual property rights around the world, and may arbitrate disputes as well. WIPO is responsible for global conventions such as the Berne Convention, a treaty protecting literary and artistic works, respected by many countries.

World Wide Web: An immense collection of hyperlinked documents that allows you to easily access vast amounts of information.

World Wide Web Consortium: A not-for-profit research organization (`http://www.w3c.org/`) geared toward promoting standards and innovations in Web-based communication, including HTML.

WORM: A program designed to copy itself and send itself to other computers on the network.

WYSIWYG Editor: Acronym for What You See Is What You Get; used for years with respect to application packages such as word processing and spreadsheet packages. It means that you see the completed document, including formatting, as it would look when it is printed or displayed.

X

XHTML: A markup language used for building Web pages that conform to XML standards.

XML (eXtensible Markup Language): Describes the data using standards agreed upon by the two parties who are communicating. You can think of XML as a customizable HTML tagging system.

References and Readings

508 law. (n.d.). *Section 508*, (2004). Retrieved September 17, 2004, from http://www.section508.gov/index.cfm? FuseAction=Content&ID=3.

2004 workplace email and instant messaging survey summary, (2004). Retrieved August 17, 2004, from http://www.amanet.org/research/pdfs/IM_2004_Summary.pdf.

Ackerman, E. and Hartman, K. (1998). *The information specialist's guide to searching and researching on the Internet*. Wilsonville, OR: Franklin, Beedle & Associates.

Adams, R. (2003). *www.advertising*. New York: Watson-Guptill Publications, Inc.

Anderson, D., B. Benjamin and B. Paredes-Holt. (1998). *Connections: A guide to online writing*. Boston: Allyn and Bacon.

Andriot, L. (1998). *Internet blue pages*. Medford, NJ: CyberAge Books.

Banks, M. A. (2000). *The modem reference: The complete guide to PC communications* (4th ed.). Toronto: Cyberage Books.

Baron, N. (2000). *Alphabet to email: How written language evolved and where it's heading*. New York: Routledge Press.

Baron, N. S. (1998). "Letters by phone or speech by other means: The linguistics of email," *Language and Communication*, 18(2), 133–170.

Basch, R. (1998). *Cybersearch: Research techniques in the electronic age*. New York: Penguin Reference.

Baughman, M. (1999). "Recent legislation: Regulating the Internet," *Harvard Journal on Legislation* 36:230.

Bauman, L. (1997). "Personal jurisdiction and Internet advertising," *The Computer Lawyer*, 1:14.

Benkler, Y. (1999). "Free as the air to common use: First Amendment constraints on enclosure of the public domain," *New York University Law Review*, 74(2), 354–446.

Benne, K. and Sheats, P. (1948). "Functional roles of group members," *Journal of Social Issues*, 4, 41–49.

Berinstein, P. and Bkorner, S. (1998). *Finding statistics online*. Medford, NJ: Information Today.

Berlind, David, (2004). *Protecting yourself against mini-DDoS attacks*. Retrieved July 25, 2004, from http://www.zdnet.com.au/news/security/0,2000061744,39143572,00.htm.

Berners-Lee, T. and Fischetti, M. (1999). *Weaving the web*. San Francisco: HarperSanFrancisco.

Berry, M. and Browne, M. (1999). *Understanding search engines: Mathematical modeling and text retrieval*. Philadelphia: Society for Industrial and Applied Mathematics.

Boone, L. A. (1993). "Electronic mail and the right to privacy: Organizational communication issues," *News Computing Journal*, 8(4), 19–36.

Borgmann, A. (1999). *Holding on to reality: The nature of information at the turn of the millennium.* Chicago: University of Chicago Press.

Brennen, B. and Primeaux, D. (1997). "Public or private? E-mail and the ethics of privacy," *Convergence,* 3(3), 22–26.

Buckingham, M. and Coffman, C. (1999). *First, break all the rules: What the world's greatest managers do differently.* New York: Simon & Schuster.

Burwell, H. Ernst, C. and Sankey, M. (1999). *Online competitive intelligence.* Tempe, AZ: Facts on Demand Press.

Calishain, T. and Nystrom, J. A. (1998). *Official Netscape guide to Internet research.* Albany, NY: Coriolis Group Books.

Campbell, K. (1994). *A net.conspiracy so immense...Chatting with Martha Siegel of the Internet's infamous Canter & Siegel,* Retrieved July 29, 2004, from http://www.eff.org/Legal/Cases/ Canter_Siegel/ cands_summary.article.

Canton, J. (1999). *Technofutures: How leading-edge technology will transform business in the 21st century.* Carlsbad, CA: Hay House Press.

Carlson, B. (1997). "Balancing the digital scales of copyright law," *Southern Methodist University Law Review* 50:825.

Carmichael, J. (1996). "In support of the white paper: Why online service providers should not receive immunity from traditional notions of vicarious and contributory liability for copyright infringement," *Loyola Los Angeles Entertainment Law Journal* 16:759.

Carter, P. I. (1999). "Health information privacy: Can Congress protect confidential medical information in the information age?" *William Mitchell Law Review* 25:223.

Carter, R. and Frith, C. (1999). *Mapping the mind.* Berkeley, CA: University of California Press.

Castells, M. (2003). *The Internet galaxy: Reflections on the Internet, business, and society.* Oxford: Oxford University Press.

Castells, M. (2000). *The rise of the network society.* Oxford: Blackwells.

Christin, A. M. (2002). *A history of writing: from hieroglyph to multimedia.* New York: Flammarion-Pere Castor.

Cochrane, P. (1999). *Tips for time travelers: Visionary insights into a new technology, life and the future on the edge of technology.* New York: McGraw-Hill.

Copyright in an electronic environment (Guidelines from consortium of college and univeristy media centers) (n.d.), (2004). Retrieved July 27, 2004, from North Carolina Department of Instruction Web site: http://www.dpi.state.nc.us/copyright1.html.

D'Agostino, D. (2004). *Instant messaging: IM here to stay, eWeek.* Retrieved August 17, 2004, from http://www.eweek.com/article2/0,1759,1571642,00.asp.

Davidson, J. D. (1997). *The sovereign individual: How to survive and thrive during the collapse of the welfare state.* New York: Simon & Schuster.

Davis, R. (1999). *The web of politics: The Internet's impact on the American political system.* Oxford: Oxford University Press.

Davison, T. (2004). *How to host a successful webinar,* In *MarketingProfs.com.* Retrieved September 17, 2004, from http://www.marketingprofs.com/4/davison1.asp.

De Kare-Silver, M. (1999). *E-shock: The electronic shopping revolution: Strategies for retailers and manufacturers.* New York: American Manufacturing Association.

Denning, D. (1998). *Information warfare and security.* New York: Addison-Wesley.

Deulloa, J. (1999). *The step-by-step guide to successfully promoting a website.* Escondido, CA: PromoteOne.

Deutsch, S. (2000). *Anticybersquatting Consumer Protection Act*, International Trademarking Association Web site. New York: International Trademarking Association. Retrieved May 21, 2000, from http://www.inta.org/cyberpiracy.htm.

Dikel, M. R. (2004). *Guide to Internet job searching 20042005.* New York: McGraw-Hill.

Dimmick, J., Kline, S. and Stafford, L. (2000). "The gratification niches of personal e-mail and the telephone: Competition, displacement, and complementarity," *Communication Research,* 27(2), 227–248.

Diotalevi, R. N. (2003). *The teach act: Teaching old dogs new clicks,* Retrieved July 27, 2004, from http://www.ipfw.edu/as/tohe/2003/papers/Diotalevi.htm.

Divine, R. (1993). *The sputnik challenge.* Oxford: Oxford University Press.

Doyle, A. (1999). "A practitioner's guide to snaring the Net," *Educational Leadership,* 56, 12–16.

Dueker, K. S. (1996). "Trademark law lost in Cyberspace: Trademark protection for Internet addresses," *Harvard Journal of Law & Technology* 9:483.

Eklundh, K. (1996). "A dialogue perspective on electronic mail: Implications for interface design," *Advances in Discourse Processes,* 58, 121–136.

Electronic data interchange, (2004). In *Wikipedia: The free encyclopedia,* Retrieved July 27, 2004, from http://en.wikipedia.org/wiki/Electronic_Data_Interchange.

eMarketer tallies the number of e-mail messages sent in 1998, (1999). Retrieved July 21, 1999, from http://www.emarketer.com/estats/020199_e-mail.html.

Engholm, C. and Grimes, S. (1997). *The Prentice Hall directory of online business information.* Paramus, NJ: Prentice Hall.

Exhibits. (2004). *Networks,* (timeline) Retrieved July 29, 2004, from Computer History Museum Web site: http://www.computerhistory.org/timeline/timeline.php?timeline_category=net.

Falk, J. (1998). "The meaning of the web," *Information Society,* 14, 285.

Forno, R. and Baklarz, R. (1999). "The art of information warfare: Insight into the knowledge warrior philosophy," Upublish.com.

Fraser, S. (1998). "The conflict between the First Amendment and copyright law and its impact on the Internet," *Cardozo Arts & Entertainment Law Journal* 16:1.

French, J. R. P., Jr. and Raven, B. (1968). "The bases of social power," In *Group dynamics: Research and theory,* 3rd ed. Edited by D. Cartwright and A. Zander, 256–269. New York: Harper & Row.

Gantt, L. O. (1995). "An affront to human dignity: Electronic mail monitoring in the private sector," *Harvard Journal of Law and Technology* 8:345.

Garson, G. D. (1999). *Information technology and computer applications in public administration: Issues and trends.* Harrisburg, PA: Idea Group Publishing.

Garton, L. and Wellman, B. (1995). "Social impacts of electronic mail in organizations: A review of the research literature," *Communication Yearbook,* 18, 434–453.

Gershenfeld, N. A. (1999). *When things start to think.* New York: Henry Holt and Company.

Gleick, J. (1999). *Faster: The acceleration of just about everything.* New York: Pantheon Books.

Glossbrenner, G. and Glossbrenner, E. (1998). *Search engines: For the World Wide Web.* Berkeley, CA: Peachpit Press.

Glymore, C. and Cooper, G.F. (1999). *Computation, causation, and discovery.* Boston: Massachusetts Institute of Technology Press.

Good, A. B. (1998). "Trade secrets and the new realities of the Internet age," *Marquette Intellectual Properties Law Review* 2:51.

Greenspan, R. (2004). *Q1'04 U.S. E Com Sales=$15.5B*, Retrieved July 28, 2004, from Clickz Networks Web site: http://www.clickz.com/stats/markets/retailing/article.php/3361411.

Grimes, B. (2003). *Instant messaging, PC Magazine*. Retrieved August 17, 2004, from http://www.pcmag.com/article2/0,1759,844024,00.asp.

Hacker, D. (2002). *A writer's reference*. New York, NY: Bedford Books.

Hacker, K. L., Goss, B., Townley, C. and Horton, V. J. (1998). "Employee attitudes regarding electronic mail policies: A case study," *Management Communication Quarterly,* 11(3), 422–452.

Hafner, K and Lyon, M. (1998). *Where wizards stay up late: the origins of the Internet.* Carmichael, CA: Touchstone Books.

Harte, L. and Kellogg, S. (1998). *The comprehensive guide to wireless technologies.* New York: APDG Technologies.

Hash, P. E. and Ibrahim, C. M. (1996). "E-mail, electronic monitoring, and employee privacy," *Texas Law Review* 37:893.

Hayles, N. K. (1999). *How we become post-human: Virtual bodies in cybernetics, literature, and informatics.* Chicago: University of Chicago Press.

Heim, M. (1997). *Virtual realism.* Oxford: Oxford University Press.

Hilliard, R. L. and Keith, M. C. (2001). *The broadcast century and beyond: A biography of American broadcasting* (3rd ed.). New York: Focal Press.

Hodkowski, W. A. (1997). "The future of Internet security: How new technologies will shape the Internet and affect the law," *Santa Clara Computer and High Technology Law Journal* 217:13.

Hogan, M. (1996). *Hiroshima in history and memory.* Cambridge, MA: Cambridge University Press.

Holmes, M. E. (1995). "Don't blink or you'll miss it: Issues in electronic mail research," *Communication Yearbook,* 18, 454–463.

How satellites work (n.d.), (2004). Retrieved July 27, 2004, from How Stuff Works Web site: http://science.howstuffworks.com/satellite.htm.

Hunter, J. and Allen, M. (1992). "Adaption to electronic mail," *Journal of Applied Communication Research,* 20(3), 254–274.

Jaison, B. A. (2002). *Converting HTML documents to XHTML*, Retrieved August 1, 2004, from beeandnee.com Web site: http://www22.brinkster.com/beeandnee/techzone/articles/htmltoxhtml.asp.

Johnson, K. (1999). *Internet e-mail protocols: A developer's guide.* Reading, MA: Addison-Wesley.

Johnson, S. (1997). *Interface culture: How new technology transforms the way we create and communicate.* San Francisco: HarperSanFrancisco.

Jonash, R. S. (1999). *The innovation premium.* New York: Perseus Books.

Jones, G. (1997). *Cyberschools: An education renaissance.* Englewood, CO: Jones Digital Century.

Kahaner, L. (1998). *Competitive intelligence.* New York: Simon & Schuster.

Kamarck, E. C. (1999). *Democracy.Com: Governance in a networked world.* Hollis, NH: Hollis Publishing Company.

Kennedy, S. (1997). *Best bet Internet.* Chicago: American Library Association.

Komsky, Susan H. (1994). "Electronic mail and democratization of organizational communication," *Organization Communication: Emerging Perspectives,* 4, 175–212.

Komsky, Susan H. (1991). "A profile of users of electronic mail in a university: Frequent versus occasional users," *Management Communication Quarterly,* 4(3), 310–340.

Kushilevitz, K. and Nisan, N. (1997). *Communication complexity.* Cambridge, MA: Cambridge University Press.

Landau, M. B. (1997). "Problems arising out of the use of 'www. trademark.com': The application of principles of trademark law to Internet domain disputes," *Georgia State University Law Review* 13:455.

Lane, C. and Burwell, H. (1996). *Naked in cyberspace: How to find personal information online.* Wilton, CT: Pemberton Press.

Lappin, S. (1997). *The handbook of contemporary semantic theory.* Oxford: Blackwell Publishing.

Lawson, J. (1999). *The complete Internet handbook for lawyers.* Chicago: American Bar Association.

Leary, T. (1994). *Chaos and cyberculture.* Berkeley, CA: Ronin Publishing.

Lee, L. W. (1999). "Child pornography prevention act of 1996: Confronting the challenges of virtual reality," *Southern California Interdisciplinary Law Journal* 8:639.

Lessig, L. (1996). "Reading the Constitution in Cyberspace," *Emory Law Journal* 869:45.

Lemley, M. and Volokh, E. (1998). "Freedom of speech and injunctions in intellectual property cases," *Duke Law Journal* 48:147.

Loperfido, Allison M. (1993). "Electronic mail as a media choice for managers," *Electronic Journal of Communication,* 3(2).

Lyman, P. (1998). "The Article 2B debate and the sociology of the information age," *Berkeley Technology Law Journal,* 13(3),1023–1063.

Mabrito, M. (1991). "Electronic mail as a vehicle for peer response: Conversations of high- and low-apprehensive writers," *Written Communication,* 8(4), 509–532.

Macromedia Dreamweaver support center, (n.d.). *Macromedia.* Retrieved September 17, 2004, from http://www.macromedia.com/support/dreamweaver/insert_media/addingsandv/addingsandv03.html.

Mairs, J. L. (2001). *VPNs: A beginner's guide.* Emeryville, CA: McGraw-Hill Osborne Media.

Mann, J. (1998). *Tomorrow's global community: How the information deluge is transforming business and government.* Philadelphia: Trans-Atlantic Publications.

Marcus, J. (1998). "Commercial speech on the Internet: Spam and the First Amendment," *Cardozo Arts & Entertainment Law Journal* 16:245.

McDonald, T. (2000). *Microsoft's monopoly on security flaws, ECommerce Times.* Retrieved July 29, 2004, from http://www.ecommercetimes.com/perl/story/4059.html.

McGonagle, J. and Vella, C. (1999). *The Internet age of competitive intelligence.* Westport, CT: Quorum Books.

McLaughlin, M., Osborne, K. and Smith, C. (1995). "Standards of conduct on Usenet," In *Cybersociety: Computer-mediated communication,* edited by S. Jones, 90–111. London: Sage.

Mead, H. and Clark, A. (1997). *The online research handbook.* New York: Berkeley Books.

Metcalfe, R. M., Walden, D. and Salus, P. (1996). *Packet Communication.* New York: International Thomson Computer Publishing.

Michael, A. and Salter, B. (2003). *Marketing through search optimization.* New York: Butterworth-Heinemann.

Miller, H. S. (1997). "The little locksmith: A cautionary tale for the electronic age," *Journal of Academic Librarianship,* 23, 100–108.

Miller, M. (2000). *The complete idiot's guide to Yahoo!* Indianapolis: Que Publishing.

Minoli, D. (2002). *Hotspot networks: Wifi for public access locations.* New York: McGraw-Hill Companies.

Minsky, B. D. and Marin, D. B. (1999). "Why faculty members use e-mail: The role of individual differences in channel choice," *Journal of Business Communication,* 36(2), 194–217.

Mizel, D., Behringer, R. and Klinker, G. (1998). *Augmented reality: Proceedings of IWAR 1998.* Wellesley, MA: A. K. Peters Ltd.

Morris, D. (1999). *Vote.com: How big-money lobbyists and the media are losing their influence, and the Internet is giving power back to the people.* Los Angeles: Renaissance Books.

Morris Worm. (2004). In *FreeDictionary.com.* Retrieved July 29, 2004, from http://encyclopedia.thefreedictionary.com/Morris%20worm.

Moschovitz, C., Poole, H., Shuyler, T. and Senft, T. (1999). *History of the Internet: A chronology, 1843 to the present.* Santa Barbara, CA: ABO-CLIO.

Negroponte, N. (1995). *Being digital.* New York: Knopf.

Newhagen, J. E., Cordes, J. W. and Levy, M. R. (1995). "Nightly@nbc.com: Audience scope and the perception of interactivity in viewer mail on the Internet," *Journal of Communication,* 45(3), 164–175.

Newhagne, J. E. and Rafaeli, S. (1996). "Why communication researchers should study the Internet: A dialogue," *Journal of Communication,* 45, 4–13.

Notess, G. (1998). *Government information on the Internet.* Lanham, MD: Bernan Press.

Obie, D. (2004). *Determine the goals of your small business web site,* Retrieved July 27, 2004, from SCORE Web site: http://www.score.org/eb_6.html.

O'Donnell, J. J. (1998). *Avatars of the word: From papyrus to Cyberspace.* Cambridge, MA: Harvard University Press.

Ohm, P. K. (1999). "Comment: On regulating the Internet: Usenet, a case study," *UCLA Law Review* 46:1941.

O'Neill, D. (1995). *The Firecracker Boys.* New York: St. Martin's Press.

Online banking report: Strategies for financial institutions (Report No. 103, p. 2), (2004). Retrieved July 27, 2004, from http://onlinebankingreport.com/free_sample/OBR_103_ex.pdf.

Online book sales to double over the next five years, report predicts, (2003). Retrieved August 1, 2004, from American Booksellers Association Web site: http://news.bookweb.org/news/ 1708.html.

Oram, A. (2001). *Peer-to-peer: Harnessing the power of disruptive technologies.* O'Reilly & Associates.

O'Rourke, M. (1998). "Fencing Cyberspace: Drawing borders in a virtual world," *Minnesota Law Review* 82:609.

Palloff, R. M. and Pratt, K. (1999). *Building learning communities in Cyberspace: Effective strategies for the online classroom.* San Francisco: Jossey-Bass Publishers.

Palme, J. (1995). *Electronic mail.* Norwood, MA: Artech House.

Panettieri, J. C. (2001). *Who let the worms out? eWeek.* Retrieved July 29, 2004, from http://eweek.com/article2/0,1759,1245602,00.asp.

Parks, M. (1996). "Making friends in cyberspace," *Journal of Communication,* 46(1), 80–97.

Phan, D. T. (1998). "Will fair use function on the Internet?" *Columbia Law Review* 98:169.

Pinch, T. J. and Collins, H. (1998). *The golem at large: What you should know about technology.* Cambridge, MA: Cambridge University Press.

Phillips, S. R. and Eisenberg, E. (1993). "Strategic uses of electronic mail in organizations," *Electronic Journal of Communication,* 3(2).

PNG, (2004). In *Wikipedia.* Retrieved September 17, 2004, from http://en.wikipedia.org/ wiki/Png.

PNG image format: The larger the GIG the bigger the saving with PNG (n.d.), (2004). *Web colors.* Retrieved September 17, 2004, from http://www.webcolors.freeserve.co.uk/png/.

Porter, D. (1997). *Internet culture.* New York: Routledge Press.

Priestman, C. (2001). *Web Radio: Radio production for Internet streaming.* New York: Focal Press.

Pusey, N. (1963). *The age of the scholar.* Cambridge, MA: Belknap Press.

Radu, C. (2002). *Implementing electronic card payment systems.* Norwood, MA: Artech House.

Raggett, D., Lam, J., Alexander, I. and Kmiec, M. (1998). *A history of HTML,* In *Raggett on HTML 4* (chap. 2). England: Addison Wesley Longman. Retrieved July 28, 2004, from http://www.w3.org/People/Raggett/book4/ch02.html.

Raven, B., Centers, C. and Rodrigues, A. (1975). "The bases of conjugal power," In *Power in families,* edited by R. E. Cromwell and D. H. Olson, 217–234. New York: Halsted Press.

Rayport, J. F., Jaworski, B. J., "Breakaway Solutions Inc., Breakaway Solutions Inc. Staff," (2003). In *Introduction to e-commerce,* (2nd ed.). New York: McGraw-Hill.

Rawlins, G. J. E. (1998). *Slaves of the Machine: The Quickening of Computer Technology.* Cambridge, MA: MIT Press.

Reed, B.S. (1997). "What kind of lever? How scholars use the Internet in their work," *American Journalism,* 14, 217–218.

Reidenberg, J. R. (1998). "Lex informatica: The formulation of information policy rules through technology," *Texas Law Review,* 76(3), 553–594.

Reindl, A. P. (1998). "Choosing law in Cyberspace: Copyright conflicts on global networks," *Michigan Journal of International Law* 19:729.

Renfro, C. G. (1997). "Economic database systems: Further reflections," *Journal of Economic and Social Measurement,* 23, 43–86.

RFC 2795. (2004). *The Infinite Monkey Protocol Suite (IMPS),* Retrieved on May 9, 2004, from http://www.faqs.org/rfcs/rfc2795.html.

Rheingold, H. (1993). *The virtual community: Homesteading on the electronic frontier.* Reading, MA: Addison-Wesley.

Rice, R. P. (1997). "An analysis of stylistic variables in electronic mail," *Journal of Business and Technical Communication,* 11(1), 5–23.

Robbins, C. (1997). *Exploring the Web: Using Internet hypermedia.* Berkeley, CA: NetQuest Publishing.

Rogers, E. M. (1995). *Diffusion of Innovations.* New York: Free Press.

Rose, L., Rogers, S. and Cuthbertson, J. (1995). *Netlaw: Your rights in an online world.* Emeryville, CA: Osborne Publishing.

Rosenberg, D. K. (2000). *Open source: The unauthorized white papers.* New York: Wiley & Sons.

Rowland, L. M. (1994). "Libraries and librarians on the Internet," *Communication Education,* 43, 143–150.

Salbu, S. R. (1998). "Who should govern the Internet? Monitoring and supporting a new frontier," *Harvard Journal of Law & Technology* 429:11.

Samoriski, Jan H., Huffman, John L. and Trauth, Denise M. (1996). "Electronic mail, privacy, and the Electronic Communications Privacy Act of 1986: Technology in search of law," *Journal of Broadcasting and Electronic Media,* 40(1), 60–76.

Schecter, R. E. and Thomas, J. R. (2003). *Intellectual property: The law of copyrights, patents, and trademarks (Hornbook series student edition).* Emeryville, CA: West Publishing Company.

Schiller, D. (1999). *Digital capitalism: Networking the global market system.* Cambridge, MA: MIT Press.

Schlein, A. and Kisaichi, S. (1999). *Find it online: The complete guide to online research.* Tempe, AZ: Facts on Demand Press.

Schmitz, J. and Fulk, J. (1991). "Organizational colleagues, media richness, and electronic mail: A test of the social influence model of technology use," *Communication Research,* 18(4), 487–523.

Schneider, F., Fredricksen, E. and Blachman, N. (2003). *How to do everything with google.* New York: McGraw-Hill Companies.

Schuler, D. (1996). *New community networks: Wired for change.* New York: ACM Press.

Schultz, T. (2000). "Mass media and the concept of interactivity: An exploratory study of online forums and reader email," *Media, Culture and Society,* 22(2), 205–221.

Schwartau, W. (1996). *Information warfare: Chaos on the electronic superhighway.* New York: Thunder's Mouth Press.

Shapiro, A. L. (1999). *The control revolution: How the Internet is putting individuals in charge and changing the world we know.* New York: The Century Foundation.

Shapiro, Y. and Lehoczky, E. (n.d.). (2004). *Keywords: Titles, meta tags and more,* In *Using your HTML title effectively* (html title). Retrieved July 31, 2004, from searchengines.com Web site: http://www.searchengines.com/HTMLtitle.html.

Sherblom, J. (1988). "Direction, function, and signature in electronic mail," *Journal of Business Communication,* 25(4), 39–54.

Shenk, D. (1998). *Data smog: Surviving the information glut.* San Francisco: HarperSanFrancisco.

Shenk, D. (1999). *The end of patience: Cautionary notes on the information revolution.* Bloomington, IN: Indiana University Press.

Siddiqi, A. (2003). *Sputnik and the Soviet space challenge.* Gainesville, FL: University Press of Florida.

Simmons, C. (2004). *How to do everything with your Blackberry.* Emeryville, CA: Osborne/McGraw-Hill.

Sklar, B. (2001). *Digital communications* (2nd ed.). Upper Saddle River, NJ: Prentice Hall Technical Reference.

Slevin, J. (2000). *The Internet and society.* Cambridge, MA: Polity Press.

Smith, R. (2003). *Wi-fi home networking.* New York: McGraw-Hill Companies/TAB Electronics.

Snyder, H. and Rosenbaum, H. (1998). "How public is the Web? Robots, access, and Scholarly communication," *Proceedings of the ASIS annual meeting, 35,* 453–462.

Sonnereich, W. and MacInta, T. (1998). *WebDeveloper.com's guide to search engines.* New York: Wiley & Sons.

Spam celebrates silver jubilee, (2003). Retrieved July 29, 2004, from BBC Web site: http://news.bbc.co.uk/1/hi/technology/2996319.stm.

Stefik, M. (1996). *Internet dreams: Archetypes, myths, and metaphors.* Boston: MIT Press.

Stefik, M. (1999). *The Internet edge: Social, technical, and legal challenges for a networked world.* Cambridge, MA: MIT Press.

Stepka, D. T. (1997). "Obscenity On-line: A transactional approach to computer transfers of potentially obscene material," *Cornell Law Review* 905:82.

Stewart, W. (2000). *The living Internet: How email was invented,* Retrieved May 6, 2000, from http://www.livingInternet.com/.

Stim, R. W. (1999). *Copyright law.* New York: Delmar Learning.

Sullivan, C. B. (1995). "Preferences for electronic mail in organizational communication tasks," *Journal of Business Communication,* 32(1), 49–65.

Summary of section 508 standards (n.d.), *Section 508,* (2004). Retrieved September 17, 2004, from http://www.section508.gov/index.cfm?FuseAction=Content&ID=11.

Swisher, K. (1999). *Aol.com: How Steve Case beat Bill Gates, nailed the netheads, and made millions in the war for the Web.* New York: Times Books.

Tapscott, D. (1997). *Growing up digital: The rise of the net generation.* New York: McGraw-Hill.

Taylor, H. (2004). *Online activity grows as more people use Internet for more purposes,* Retrieved July 25, 2004, from http://www.harrisinteractive.com/harris_poll/index.asp?PID=433.

Tedford, T. (1997). *Freedom of speech in the United States.* State College, PA: Strata.

Teicher, J. (1999). "An action plan for smart Internet use," *Educational Leadership,* 56, 70–75.

The world fact book, (2004). Retrieved July 27, 2004, from http://www.cia.gov/cia/publications/ factbook/.

Thomasson, J., William, F. and Press, L. (2002). *The diffusion of the Internet in Mexico,* Latin America Network Information Center, University of Texas at Austin. Retrieved May 6, 2004, from http://lanic.utexas.edu/project/etext/mexico/thomasson/thomasson.pdf.

Trevino, L. K. and Webster, J. (1992). "Flow in computer-mediated communication: Electronic mail and voice mail evaluation and impacts," *Communication Research,* 19(5), 539–573.

Turban, E. and King, D. (2003). *Introduction to ecommerce.* New Jersey: Prentice Hall.

Turban, E., King, D., Lee, J., Warkentin, M. and Chung, H. M. (2002). *Electronic commerce 2002: A managerial perspective.* Upper Saddle River, NJ: Prentice Hall.

Underdahl, B., Underdahl, K. and Priesach, J. (2000). *Internet bible* (2nd ed.). Hoboken, NJ: Wiley & Sons.

Usenet, (2003). Retrieved August 15, 2004, from http://www.usenet.com/articles/ history_of_usenet.htm.

Video Streaming. (n.d.), (2004). *Academic technology web support services,* Retrieved September 17, 2004, from Virginia Commonwealth University Web site: http://www.vcu.edu/web/publish/design/converting.html.

Virus info. (n.d.). *F-Secure virus descriptions: Loveletter (virus descriptions),* Retrieved July 29, 2004, from FSecure Web site: http://www.fsecure.com/vdescs/love.shtml.

Wagner, R. P. (1999). "Filters and the First Amendment," *Minnesota Law Review* 83:755.

Walker, P. (2003). *Truman's dilemma: Invasion or the bomb.* Gretna, Los Angeles: Pelican Publishing Company.

Want, R. (1999). *How to search the Web: A quick reference guide to finding things on the World Wide Web.* New York: Want Publishing.

Web accessibility initiative (WAI), (2004). W3C. Retrieved September 17, 2004, from http://www.w3.org/WAI/.

Web content accessibility guidelines 2.0 (n.d.), (2004). W3C. Retrieved September 17, 2004, from http://www.w3.org/TR/2004/WDWCAG2020040730/.

Werst, B. M. (1997). "Legal doctrine and its inapplicability to Internet regulation: A guide for protecting children from Internet indecency after *Reno v. ACLU,*" *Gonzaga Law Review* 207:33.

Whitesitt, J. E. (1995). *Boolean algebra and its applications.* Dover: Dover Publications.

Williams, V. (1995). *Wireless computing primer.* Chicago: IDG Books.

Wiring the world, (1998). Retrieved July 27, 2004, from PBS Web site: http://www.pbs.org/opb/nerds2.0.1/wiring_world/business.html.

XHTML 1.0 the extensible hypertext markup language. (2002). Retrieved August 1, 2004, from http://www.w3.org/TR/xhtml1/.

Yassini, R., Schley, S., Ellis, L. and Brown, R. (2003). *Planet broadband.* New York: Pearson Education.

Zakon, R. (2004). *Hobbes Internet timeline v4.2,* Retrieved May 4, 2004, from http://www.isoc.org/zakon/Internet/History/HIT.html.

INDEX

3D Textmaker, 305
3-tier architecture, 224

A

abbreviations, 357
Abilene network, 38, 42
Acceptable Use Policy (AUP), 11
accessibility, 301
accessiblility guide, 301
ACLU, 425–426
active link, 179
ADA. *See* Americans with Disabilities Act
Adobe Acrobat, 54, 301
ADSL, 7
Advanced Research Projects Agency (ARPA), 32, 39
advocay marketing. *See* marketing, advocacy
adware, 22, 342
affiliate marketing. *See* marketing, affiliate
aggregator, 333
AIM. *See* America Online, Instant Messenger
Alcorn, Al, 366
alignment, design, 278
America Online (AOL), 45, 86, 161, 342
   Instant Messenger (AIM), 342–346, 350, 352–353
American Standard Code for Information Interchange. *See* ASCII
Americans with Disabilities Act (ADA), 301
Andreessen, Marc, 161
animated GIF, 280, 293–294
animation, 293, 295. *See also* animated GIF, Flash, Shockwave
animation, JavaScript, 294
Anti-Phishing Working Group, 132
anti-spam software. *See* spam blocker

anti-virus
   signature, 130
   software, 23–24, 130–131
application sharing, 350
Arneson, Dave, 367
ARPANET, 33, 35–36, 38–39, 86, 126, 353, 367
ASCII text, 96
ASP.NET, 223
asynchronous communication, 341
Atkinson, Bill, 161
Atom, 336
auction, B2B, 145
auction. *See* online auction
audio, 295
   download, 295
   streaming, 295, 299, 396
AUP, 11
avatar, 369, 371

B

B2B (Business-to-Business), 138, 141, 143–144, 146
B2B2C (Business-to-Business-to-Consumer), 139, 141
B2C (Business-to-Consumer), 139, 141–144
B2G (Business-to-Government), 143
backbone, 38, 45
backwards compatibility, 216
Baer, Ralph, 366
BANANARD, 86
bandwidth, 6
banking, online, 152
banner ad, 143, 294
baseline, 278
BBS (Bulletin Board Service), 354
Bellovin, Steve, 322

Berners-Lee, Tim, 40, 44–45, 161
bibliographic database, 61
binaries, 323
binary file, 96
bit, 279
bitmap image, 279–280, 282
Bitnet, 40
Blackboard, 376
blog, 143, 145, 332–333, 336
blogger, 330
Blogwise, 332
books, 391
Boolean operator, 59, 73
  and, 73–74
  near, 74
  not, 74
  or, 74
Boucher, Frederick, 137
Brandeis, Louis, 428
broadband, 7, 25–26, 88, 347, 353, 355, 366, 368, 431
browser
  helper object (BHO), 23
  hijacker, 23
  plug-in, 53–54, 295–296, 301
  safe color, 171–172
Brunning, John, 130
bulletted list, 188, 190
Bushnell, Nolan, 366
Businesss-to-Business. *See* B2B
Business-to-Business-to-Consumer. *See* B2B2C
Business-to-Consumer. *See* B2C
Business-to-Government. *See* B2G
byte, 38

C

C2B (Consumer-to-Business), 140–141
C2C (Consumer-to-Consumer), 140–141, 143
CA*Net, 40
cache, 15
cache, clearing, 15
Canada, Internet development, 40
Canter and Seigel, 126
Cascading Style Sheet. *See* CSS
Case, Steve, 86
case-sensitive, 213, 217
casinos, 373
CataList, 311
CCD (Charged Coupled Device), 356

CD quality, 296
CDA (Communications Decency Act), 423–425
centralized network, 30
CERT (Computer Emergency Response Team), 130
chain letter, 130–131
change agent, 440–441
chat, 342–354
  audio, 346
  etiquette, 354
  room, 345
  virus, 346
citing Internet resources, 78–79
Clark, Jim, 161
clear text, 132
click-through, 22
CoffeeCup HTML Editor, 228–245
commercial software. *See* software, commercial
commercialization, 388–389
compression. *See* file compression
  standards, video, 356
Compuserve, 45, 86
Computer Emergency Response Team. *See* CERT
computer game, 366
  history, 367
Consumer-to-Business. *See* C2B
Consumer-to-Consumer. *See* C2C
contrast, design, 278
convergence, 391, 398
cookie, 128, 151, 430, 432
COPA (Child Online Protection Act), 425
copyright, 330, 408–412, 415, 429, 433
COSINE Project, 42–43
CPYNET, 86
crawler, 59
credit card information, 24
Crocker, Steve, 86
Crowther, Will, 367
CSS, 201–212, 217
  alignment, 207
  background-color, 202, 204
  color, 202, 204
  font-family, 209
  heading style, 207
  line-height, 210
  multiple selectors, 207
  style classes, 207–208
  text-decoration, 202
cybersquatting, 414
cyberstalking, 416
cybrary, 444

D

DANTE Project, 43
data file, 55
database, 223–224
database driven Web application, 222–224
day trading, 152
defamation, 432
demassification, 439–440
Depew, Richard, 126
deprecated tag, 208, 216
dial-up service, 6, 149
diffusion of innovations, 440
Digital Signal Processor (DSP), 356
direct access trading (DAT), 152
direct marketing, 141
directory outline, 60–61, 64
discussion board, 330, 449
    start your own, 330
discussion list, 310, 320
    etiquette. *See* netiquette
distance education, 375, 411–412, 444
distributed network, 30
dithering, 171
DMCA (Digital Millenium Copyright Act), 411
DNS. *See* Domain Name System (DNS)
domain name, 43, 45, 147–148
    dispute, 414
Domain Name System (DNS), 26, 37, 224
download, 6, 194, 293
Dreamweaver, 194, 258–270, 282, 286–287, 292
    comment, 268–269
DSL, 7, 10
dynamic Web page, 223–224

E

eBook, 392
EBSCOhost, 61
E-Business, 137–138
eCollege, 377
E-Commerce, 137–156, 222, 224, 414–415, 430, 441
EDI (Electronic Data Interchange), 138, 141, 146–147
EDIFACT (Electronic Data Interchange for Administration, Commerce and Transportation), 146
electromagnetic pulse (EMP), 32, 39
electronic book, 392. *See also* eBook

Electronic Data Interchange (EDI). *See* EDI
electronic exchange, 144–145
Electronic Frontier Foundation, 421, 425, 430
Electronic Funds Transfer (ETF), 138
electronic marketplace (E-Marketplace), 144
electronic tendering, 143
Elite-Popularization-Specialization (EPS) cycle, 438–441
Ellis, Jim, 322
email, 22, 24, 33–35, 85–136
    address, 87, 104, 149
    address book, 105
    Bcc (Blind Carbon Copy), 93–94, 104, 107, 110, 120, 310
    bounced, 114
    Cc (Carbon Copy), 93–94, 104, 107–108, 110, 120, 310
    client, 22, 86–125
    deleting, 120
    encryption, 132
    file attachment, 87, 96–98, 120, 129–130, 144
    filter, 125, 319
    forward, 120
    header, 94, 102, 114–117, 119
    history, 85
    HTML format, 98
    importance indicator, 103–104
    managing in folders, 110, 121–125
    multiple email accounts, 126
    multiple recipients, 92, 94–95, 130
    offline usage, 89
    plain text, 98
    printing, 126
    receiving, 110–117
    redirect, 120
    reply, 117–120
    reply all, 120
    return receipt, 102–104
    security, 129
    sending, 91–111, 120
    signature, 125
    sorting, 125
    spam. *See* spam
    spoof, 131
    tracker, 127
    trash, 120–121
    undisclosed recipients, 96
    unsolicited. *See* spam
E-Marketplace. *See* electronic marketplace
e-Mexico, 42

emoticon, 100
encryption, 24, 150, 431
End User License Agreement (EULA), 417, 429
Englebart, Douglas, 160
EPS cycle, 388. *See also* Elite-Popularization-Specialist cycle
ERIC, 62
e-tailing, 139
Ethernet, 10
etiquette, 101
Eudora, 86, 91–125
EuropaNET, 43
Europe, Internet development, 42
exchange. *See* electronic exchange
Exchange Server. *See* Microsoft Exchange Server
executable file, 79
expert inquiry, 68, 72
eXtensibe HyperText Markup Language. *See* XHTML
eZine, 394, 397

F

face-to-face (FTF), 128–129, 365
FAQ. *See* Frequently Asked Questions
Federal Communications Commission (FCC), 438
FeedReader, 333–336
file
  compression, 80, 296
  conversion, 295
file type, 279–280
  .aif, 296
  .asf, 297
  .au, 296
  .avi, 297
  .bmp, 279
  .gif, 280–281, 285, 293
  .jpg (.jpeg), 280–281, 285
  .mid, 296–297
  .mov, 54, 297
  .mp3, 296, 397
  .pdf, 54, 300–301
  .png, 280, 285
  .ra, 296
  .rm, 297
  .rpm, 296
  .snd, 296
  .tiff, 280
  .wav, 296–297, 397

  .wma, 297
  .wmv, 297
filtering software, 426
firewall, 24, 346, 431
Fireworks, 282
First Amendment, 415, 425
FirstClass, 376
flame, 102
flame war, 325, 329–330
Flash, 54, 293–295, 300
flex time, 341
font
  monospaced, 172–173
  sans-serif, 172–173
  serif, 172–173
forward compatibility, 216, 261
Free-Net, 7, 447
freeware, 78
Frequently Asked Questions, 67–68, 72, 149, 324, 329, 447
FrontPage, 194, 258, 270–271
FTP (File Transfer Protocol), 66, 194–195, 271
full-duplex, 346

G

gambling, 372–377
  addiction, 375
game server, 368
gaming, 366
gateway, 10
gbps, 6
GEANT, 43
general reference, 68, 72
Google groups, 323–324, 449
Gopher, 45
graphics, 277, 279
group purchasing, 144
Grove, Andy, 356
Gygax, Gary, 367

H

half-duplex, 346
helper application, 295–296, 300–301
Higginbotham, Willy, 366
hoax, 130–131, 144
home page, 12, 19
host, 26, 33, 36, 43, 45
Hotmail, 87

HTML, 13, 45, 159–200, 201–212, 217, 261, 293

HTML
  comment tag, 191, 193, 268–269
  font color. *See* tag attribute, color
  font face, 172
  font size. *See* tag attribute, size
  formatting tags, 167
  heading tags, 166
  list, 188
  page properties, 179

HTML tag
  `<!--`, 191
  `<a>`, 175, 188, 202
  `<b>`, 167, 217
  `<br>`, 165
  `<center>`, 181–187
  `<embed>`, 298
  `<font>`, 167, 169, 173, 208, 217
  `<h1>`, 165–166, 207
  `<html>`, 165
  `<i>`, 167
  `<img>`, 181–188, 293–294, 409
  `<li>`, 188–191
  `<link>`, 203, 210, 249
  `<meta>`, 192–193
  `<ol>`, 188–190
  `<p>`, 167, 210
  `<script>`, 213
  `<span>`, 208
  `<u>`, 168
  `<ul>`, 190

HTML tag attribute, 169, 173, 175
  `align`, 174, 181
  `alink`, 179
  `bgcolor`, 179
  `color`, 170
  `href`, 175, 203, 297
  `hspace`, 187
  `link`, 179
  `size`, 170
  `text`, 179
  `vlink`, 179
  `vspace`, 187

HTTP (HyperText Transfer Protocol), 13, 45, 161, 175, 192
HTTPS (HyperText Transfer Protocol Secure), 13
Hypercard, 161
hyperlink. *See* hypertext, link
hypertext document, 45, 54, 160

hypertext link, 13, 45, 55, 159, 175–179, 202, 210, 230, 256, 300, 409
  local, 178, 188, 256, 266–268
  remote, 177–178, 241, 256, 266–268
HyperText Markup Language. *See* HTML
HyperText Transfer Protocol. *See* HTTP

I

ICANN, 44, 46–47
ICQ, 351–353
IM. *See* instant message
image alignment, 181–187, 254
  bottom, 181–187
  left, 181–187
  middle, 181–187
  right, 181–187
  top, 181–187
image as a link, 188
images, 180–187, 236, 263, 279, 282–287, 294
IMAP (Internet Message Access Protocol), 88–89
inbox, 87, 110–111, 115, 117, 122–123
information appliance, 398
instant message, 342–353
  block, 344
  sending files, 345
  virus, 346
  workplace, 359
intellectual property law, 407
Interactive Video Network (IVN), 378
interface, 223
interlaced image, 293
Internet
  growth, 35, 45
  history timeline, 38
  radio, 296, 396
Internet Architecture Board (IAB), 47
Internet Assigned Numbers Authority (IANA), 47
Internet Corporation for Assigned Numbers and Names. *See* ICANN
Internet Engineering Task Force (IETF), 46–47
Internet Explorer, 12–20, 152, 222, 336
Internet Message Access Protocol. *See* IMAP
Internet Relay Chat. *See* IRC
Internet Scout Report, 449
Internet Service Provider. *See* ISP
Internet Society (ISOC), 46–47
Internet Underground, 322
Internet2, 38, 42
internetwork, 33, 36

intranet, 10, 445
IP address, 25–26, 43, 102, 117, 127–128, 131
   static, 26
IRC (Internet Relay Chat), 354, 367, 370
ISP, 5, 10–11, 25–26, 40, 43, 45, 86–89, 92, 117,
   126–127, 130, 148–150, 192, 322, 325,
   343, 411, 417, 429, 432
IVN. *See* Interactive Video Network

J

Java Applet, 215, 293–294
JavaScript, 212–215, 287, 293
   `lastModified`, 214
JSP, 223

K

kbps, 6
keyword, 57–59, 73, 192
keyword density, 193
keyword proximity, 193
knowbot, 59, 61, 64

L

LAN, 5, 11, 368
Latham, Sven, 332
libel, 432
link popularity, 194
Linux, 80
listproc, 310–311, 320
Listserv, 68, 310–311, 320, 324
   subscribe, 312–313
   unsubscribe, 313
Local Area Network (LAN), 5, 10
lossless compression, 280
lossy compression, 280
lurk, 329

M

Macromedia Dreamweaver. *See* Dreamweaver
Macromedia Fireworks. *See* Fireworks
Macromedia Flash. *See* Flash
Macromedia Shockwave. *See* Shockwave
mail server
   incoming, 89, 92
   outgoing, 89, 92
mailing list, 68, 310–322, 449
   administered, 310
   administrator address, 314, 320

commands, 318
confirmation, 314–315
digest, 318–319, 321
interneteffectively, 314–319
list address, 314, 320
moderated, 310–311, 317, 324
open, 311
restricted, 311
searching, 321
sending a message, 316–317
subscribe, 310, 314
unmoderated, 310, 314
unsubscribe, 319
`mailto`, 13
   majordomo, 310–311, 320
marketing
   advocacy, 143
   affiliate, 143–144, 150
   viral, 143
markup language, 160
mass communication, 309
mass media, 309, 330
mass medium. *See* mass media
mbps, 6, 38
MCI, 45, 86
M-Commerce (Mobile Commerce), 141
media file, 55
meta-engine. *See* metasearch engine
metasearch engine, 65–66, 72
Mexico, Internet development, 41
Mexico, National Technology Network (NTN),
   41–42
microcinema, 397
Microsoft Exchange Server, 89, 377
Microsoft FrontPage. *See* FrontPage
Microsoft Outlook Express, 86, 89–125, 130
   contacts, 105
Microsoft Word, 246
middleware, 223–224
MILNET, 38
MIME (Multi-Purpose Internet Mail Extension), 96
mini distributed denial of service attack
   (mDDoS), 23–24
MMOG (Massive Multiplayer Online Game),
   368–369
MMORPG (Massive Multiplayer Online Role
   Playing Game), 366, 368, 371
MMOSG (Massive Multiplayer Online Sports
   Game), 369
modem, 5–6, 26

Monty Python's Flying Circus, 126
Morris, Robert T., 130
Mosaic, 40,45, 161
Mozilla, 20–21
MSG, 86
MSN Messenger, 350, 352–353
MUD (Multi-User Dungeon), 367, 370
multimedia, 277
Multi-Purpose Internet Mail Extension. *See* MIME

N

Napster, 410
NASA, 32, 39, 43
National Control Protocol (NCP), 33, 35, 39
National Science Foundation (NSF), 38, 40,
    44, 137
National Science Foundation Act, 137
navigation bar, 287
NCSA Mosaic. *See* Mosaic
netiquette, 101, 321
NetNorth, 40
Netscape, 20–21, 45, 86, 332
    Communications, 161
    Composer, 246–258
Network Access Server (NAS), 11
network interface card (NIC), 7–8
network operations center (NOC), 8
Network Solutions Inc., 40, 44
news server, 322, 325
newsfeed, 325
    subscription-based, 329
newsgroup. *See* Usenet newsgroup
newsletter, 310–311
newsreader, 322
NPL Network, 34, 39
NRD, 86
NSF. *See* National Science Foundation
NSFNET, 38, 40
NSI. *See* Network Solutions Inc.
NTN, 41–42
nuclear attack, 30, 32, 39
numbered list, 188

O

Oikarinen, Jarkko, 354
online auction, 140–142, 144, 150
online banking. *See* banking, online
online journal. *See* blog
online trading, 152–153

open source. *See* software, open source
ordered list, 188
Outlook Express. *See* Microsoft Outlook Express

P

P2P (Peer-to-Peer), 400–402, 409–410
packet, 33–34, 295
packet-sniffing, 132
password, 88, 194
patent, 408
    law, 415, 433
Patriot Act, 417–423
payload, 129
Pegasus, 86
PGP (Pretty Good Privacy), 132, 431
phishing, 131–132
PHP, 223
pixel, 279
plagiarism, 78
plug-in. *See* browser plug-in
Pong, 366
POP (Post Office Protocol), 86, 88–89, 91, 126
pop-under, 22, 127
pop-up, 22–23, 127
portal, 59, 137, 139, 151, 333
Post Office Protocol. *See* POP
POTS (Plain Old Telephone Service), 356
privacy law, 428
privacy policy, 12
programming editor, 228
proprietary, 390
protocol, 10, 13, 33–34
proximity, design, 278

Q

QuickTime, 54, 297

R

RAND, 30, 34, 39
RARE, 42
raster graphics, 279
RD, 86
READMAIL, 86
real-time communication, 341, 354
RealPlayer, 54
repetition, design, 278
Request for Quote (RFQ), 140, 143
reverse auction, 143

RFC (Request for Comments), 36
RGB, 172, 179
ripping, 397
Robert, Lawrence, 86
rollover image, 23, 282–287
router, 9, 24, 37, 117
RPG (Role Playing Game), 369
RSS, 332–333
   headline reader, 333–336
Russell, Steve, 366–367

S

Safari, 12
satellite Internet access, 7–8
scalable, 279
SCM. *See* supply chain management
search engine, 56–60, 63–64, 73, 149, 194
   optimization, 192–194
   site-specific, 63–64, 70, 72–73
   subject-specific, 64–65, 72–73
searching
   for jobs, 70
   for mailing lists. *See* mailing lists, searching
   for people, 70
   strategies, 72
Section 508, 301
shareware, 79
Shoch, John, 130
Shockwave, 293, 295
Shockwave Rider, 130
Simple Mail Transfer Protocol. *See* SMTP
site notification, 59
site map, 63
slander, 432
sliced image, 293
smiley, 100
SMTP (Simple Mail Transfer Protocol), 89, 126
SNDMSG, 86
sniping, 151
software
   commercial, 25, 80
   downloading, 24–25
   finding, 78
   freeware, 25
   open source, 25, 79–80
   shareware, 25
source code, 79, 160, 191
Spacewar, 366–367

spam, 6, 126, 128, 310, 330, 417, 431
   blocking software, 23, 127
spider, 59
spim, 359
sports betting, 374
spreadsheet document, 300, 350
spyware, 23–24
standardization, 390
static Web page, 223–224
stock trading, 152
storefront, 150–151
streaming media, 295, 299, 396
style rule (CSS), 201–212
supercomputer, 30
supply chain management (SCM), 145–146
synchronize, Web pages, 258, 271
synchronous communication, 341, 354

T

tables, 238–240, 250–255, 264–266, 278
Talk, 353
TCP/IP, 35–36, 39–40, 42–43, 161, 224
TCP/IP stack, 37
telehealth, 380
telemedicine, 380–381
television, 398
template, 258
template-based design, 258
temporary files, 15
TEN-34, 43
tendering. *See* electronic tendering
text editor, 227–228
thread, 324
Tomlinson, Ray, 85–86
Top Level Domain (TLD), 43, 46
topic ring. *See* WebRing
Topica, 320
tort law, 427–428
Torvalds, Linus, 80
trade secret, 433
trademark law, 412–415, 433
Transmission Control Protocol (TCP), 34, 37, 39
transparency, image, 280, 287–293
transponder, 8
Trillian, 352–353
trolls, 330
Trubshaw, Roy, 367
Truscott, Tom, 322
tunnel, 11

U

undisclosed recipients. *See* email, undisclosed
    recipients
unified messenger, 352–353
unordered list, 190–191
upload, 6, 194, 258
URL, 13, 17, 43, 45, 59, 75, 98, 131, 149, 159,
    175, 194, 214, 409, 414
usability, 301
    guide, 301
USB, 7
Usenet newsgroup, 66, 126, 322–330, 377
    etiquette, 329
    posting a message, 329
    reply, 328
    subscribing, 327
    Web access, 323–324
Usenet Volunteer Votetakers (UVV), 323
userid, 87–88, 194

V

VBScript, 213
vector graphics, 279, 282
vertical
    market, 144
    portal, 144–145
video, 295–296
    download, 295
    streaming, 54, 295–296, 299, 396
    game, 366
    game history, 366–367
videoconference, 347–350, 354–359
videoconferencing etiquette, 356
viral marketing. *See* marketing, viral
virtual office, 445
virtual private network (VPN), 11
virtual reality, 365
virus, 22, 24, 129, 151, 346
    fake, 131
    love bug, 130
    Morris worm, 130
    payload. *See* payload
    trojan horse, 22, 24
    worm, 22, 24, 129–130
Vittal, John, 86
Voice over Internet Protocol. *See* VoIP
VoIP (Voice over Internet Protocol), 346, 353,
    355

VoIP Service Provider, 355
vortal. *See* vertical portal
VPN Dial-up Network (VPDN), 11

W

W3C. *See* World Wide Web Consortium
W3C Markup Validator, 221–222
WAI (Web Accessibility Initiative), 301
WAN, 5, 378, 380
wardriving, 9
Warren, Samuel, 428
Web application, 224
Web browser, 12–13, 15, 22, 86, 96, 151,
    159–160, 179, 192, 216, 265, 293, 426
    bookmark, 16–17
    favorites, 16–17
    history, 16–18
Web
    bug, 23, 127–128, 432
    cam, 347, 351
    courseware tools, 376–378
    hosting, 148
    interface, mail. *See* Webmail
    log. *See* blog
    page, error, 16
    server, 194, 215, 223, 258, 295–296
    site management, 258, 271
Web-based discussion board. *See* discussion board
Webcast, 299, 379
WebCT, 377
Webinar, 299–300
Webmail, 86–87, 94, 96, 102, 104, 112
WebRing, 66–67, 72
WEP, 9
    key, 9
white space, 186
whiteboard, 350
whois, 50, 147
Wide Area Network (WAN), 5, 40
Wi-Fi, 8–9
wildcard character, 73
Williams, Robin, 278
WIPO. *See* World Intellectual Property
    Organization
Wired Equivalent Privacy (WEP), 9
wireless
    access point, 9
    fidelity, 8–9

Wireless Local Area Network (WLAN), 9
word processing
  application, 246
  document, 300
Workforce Rehabilitation Act, 301
  Section 508. *See* Section 508
World Intellectual Property Organization (WIPO),
  408, 410, 413
World Trade Organization (WTO), 372
World Wide Web, development, 44–45
World Wide Web Consortium (W3C), 161, 192,
  216, 218, 280, 301
worm. *See* virus, worm
WYSIWYG, 245
  Editor, 245, 271

X

XHTML (eXtensible HyperText Markup
  Language), 162, 192, 201–202, 208,
  215–222, 261
XHTML validator, 219, 221–222
XML, 146–147, 162, 215–216, 246, 332, 334,
  336

Y

Yahoo!
  Groups, 320, 449
  Messenger, 351–352
Yonke, Marty, 86